The Long Southern Strategy

The Long Southern Strategy

How Chasing White Voters in the
South Changed American Politics

ANGIE MAXWELL

TODD SHIELDS

OXFORD
UNIVERSITY PRESS

OXFORD
UNIVERSITY PRESS

Oxford University Press is a department of the University of Oxford. It furthers
the University's objective of excellence in research, scholarship, and education
by publishing worldwide. Oxford is a registered trade mark of Oxford University
Press in the UK and certain other countries.

Published in the United States of America by Oxford University Press
198 Madison Avenue, New York, NY 10016, United States of America.

© Oxford University Press 2019

CIP data is on file at the Library of Congress
ISBN 978–0–19–026596–0

3 5 7 9 8 6 4

Printed by Sheridan Books, Inc., United States of America

For Sidney, who is always there when it rains,
and for Elizabeth, my sunshine.
A. M.

In memory of Diane D. Blair.
Her success in teaching, research, service,
and activism continues to motivate and inspire.
I couldn't have asked for a better role model and mentor.
T. S.

Contents

Figures and Tables

Figures

Tables

Acknowledgments

FOR EVERY IDEA presented in the book, there is a list of people to thank—people who have written books that shaped my thoughts, people who have listened to my thoughts and shared their own, and people who have encouraged me as the thoughts quietly churned in my mind. No matter how old I get, I will always thank my teachers Elspeth Rostow, Roderick Hart, and Walter Dean Burnham. I am indebted to Siva Vaidhyanathan, Charles Bullock, Wayne Parent, Jim Cobb, Ted Ownby, Susan MacManus, Julia Mickenberg, Susan Carroll, Shirley Thompson, Rebecca Onion, Janet Davis, Keith Gaddie, Susan Ferber, Steve Hoelscher, Joe Aistrup, and my editor, David McBride, for their own work and for our conversations over the years. Marjorie Spruill has been a gracious mentor, and without her books I could not write mine. The feedback, red ink, and friendship from Allison Wright, Matt Hedstrom, and Joel Dinerstein have been priceless. On a practical note, the time and support necessary to write would not be possible without the support of Jim and Nancy Blair, the Diane D. Blair Center of Southern Politics and Society, and the J. William Fulbright College of Arts and Sciences at the University of Arkansas.

On a personal note, I am grateful for my village at work; Pearl Ford Dowe, Xavier Medina Vidal, Lisa Corrigan, Lisa Hinrichsen, Elliot West, and Jeannie Whayne have been both kind and encouraging in ways great and small. My village at home includes the most remarkable collection of neighbors with open doors and open hearts. The Gundermans, the Gills, the Farnets, the Rawns, the Bartons, and the Devlins may never know how important they are to my family. Nicole Clowney and Boriana Andrews showed up when I needed them, and still do. They know the life-saving nature of meaningful work, and they give the work meaning for me. My coauthor and friend Todd Shields never let me doubt my ability to pursue this idea even when my office walls were covered completely in sticky notes. He embraces uphill battles, even when climbing the mountain seems impossible. His kind of positivity is rare, and this book would not be here without it. My family has sacrificed countless long hours and late nights so I could write this book. My husband Sidney Burris has never once asked me to explain myself, and that is a gift that grows more precious as the years pass. I hope that my beloved daughter Elizabeth forgets the times that I was not there and one day understands why. I'm grateful to her for always bringing the joy.

—Angie Maxwell

THIS RESEARCH WOULD not be possible without the financial support of the Diane D. Blair Center of Southern Politics and Society. National post-election surveys are expensive, particularly when they include oversamples of underrepresented populations. Many of the findings in this manuscript would not have been possible without the generous financial support of the Blair Center and its partners, including the Winthrop Rockefeller Institute, the William J. Clinton School of Public Service, and the Department of Political Science at the University of Arkansas. Further, this manuscript became a reality because my colleague, Angie Maxwell, took the lead on the entire project, shouldered the heavy lifting, and introduced me to several new areas of scholarship. She deserves the credit for the ideas and findings throughout this entire manuscript. I also want to express my sincere appreciation to my colleagues in the J. William Fulbright College of Arts and Sciences Dean's office who regularly accommodated my unconventional insistence on combining fundraising, alumni visits, and scholarly conference presentations. I would be remiss if I did not thank the mentors and the scholars whose work continues to inspire me, including Mark Peffley, Ellen Riggle, Don Gross, Bruce Williams, Earl and Merle Black, Alan Abramowitz, Sunshine Hillygus, Susan MacManus, Joe Aistrup, Keith Gaddie, Kirby Goidel, Chi Huang, Pearl Ford Dowe, Xavier Medina-Vidal, and all of the scholars who have participated in the Blair Legacy Series. Finally, I would like to thank my family. I am very grateful for my wife Karen, my daughter Savvy, and my son Dane. You have always been my greatest source of encouragement and have always supported me and my career.

—Todd Shields

Notes on Data and Appendices

2010, 2012, and 2016 Blair Center Polls

The Diane D. Blair Center of Southern Politics and Society at the University of Arkansas (https://blaircenter.uark.edu) conducted national surveys following the 2010 midterm elections as well as the 2012 and 2016 presidential elections. These surveys are the primary data sets used throughout the analysis. The 2010 Blair Center Poll was administered by Knowledge Networks (www.knowledgenetworks.com), while the 2012 and 2016 surveys were conducted by GfK (www.gfk.com), a market research firm that acquired Knowledge Networks in 2011. The GfK proprietary database includes a representative sample of adults living in the United States, including the growing number of individuals living in cell phone–only households. Participants in this database are recruited through address-based sampling. GfK's probability-based recruiting methodology improves the degree to which samples accurately represent the US population and increases the participation of otherwise difficult-to-reach groups, such as individuals living in rural areas, the elderly, or minority groups. Importantly, participants who do not have access to the Internet are provided with a web-enabled device and free Internet service in exchange for participation in the online panel.

The 2010 Blair Center Poll included a total sample of 3,406 individuals aged 18 years or older including 932 Latinos(as), 825 African Americans, and 1,649 non-Hispanic white respondents. Similarly, the 2012 Blair Center Poll included a total sample of 3,606 participants including 1,110 Latinos(as), 843 African Americans, and 1,653 non-Hispanic white respondents. Finally, the 2016 Blair Center Poll included a total of 3,668 participants including 1,021 Latinos(as), 915 African Americans, and 1,732 non-Hispanic white respondents. Each survey included representative samples of respondents living in the geographic South, defined as the 11 states of the former Confederacy. The 2010 Blair Center Poll included 1,717 respondents from the Non-South and 1,689 respondents living in the South. The 2012 Blair Center Poll included 1,814 respondents living in the Non-South and 1,792 respondents living in the South. The 2016 Blair Center Poll included 1,840 participants living in the Non-South and 1,828 respondents living in the South. The margin of error for each survey is approximately +/−2.4. Throughout the analyses that follow, the data were weighted to reflect national demographics and improve the representativeness of the sample.

2007 and 2010 Baylor Religion Surveys

The Institute for Studies of Religion and the Department of Sociology at Baylor University conducted national surveys exploring religious attitudes, behaviors, and experiences. The 2007 Baylor Religion Survey was a 16-page self-administered mail questionnaire. Partnering with the Gallup Organization, researchers employed a mixed-mode sampling design, using both telephone and self-administered mailed surveys. Initially, the Gallup Organization conducted 1,000 random telephone interviews with a representative sample of adults living in the continental United States. Respondents were informed that the Gallup Organization was conducting an important study about Americans' values and beliefs and were offered a $5.00 incentive to complete a self-administered questionnaire. In addition to the telephone calls, the Gallup Organization mailed 1,836 questionnaires to preselected individuals in Gallup's national database. A total of 2,460 questionnaires were mailed to adults agreeing to participate in the survey. Ultimately, 1,648 respondents completed and returned the questionnaire. Similarly, the 2010 Baylor Religion Survey was conducted in collaboration with the Gallup Organization and was a self-administered 16-page questionnaire. As before, the Gallup Organization used a mixed-mode sampling design using both telephone calls and self-administered mailed surveys to recruit participants. Ultimately, 1,714 individuals completed and returned the questionnaire. For both the 2007 and the 2010 survey, weights are provided to improve the representativeness of the samples. Additional information about the data collection for the Baylor Religion Surveys may be found at https://www.baylor.edu/BaylorReligionSurvey.

1992 and 1994 Southern Focus Polls

The Southern Focus Polls were conducted by the Odum Institute for Research in Social Science at the University of North Carolina, Chapel Hill. These telephone surveys were conducted from 1992 through 2001. The target population for each survey included adults living in households with telephones across the

United States. The surveys also oversampled residents living in the 11 states of the former Confederacy. The Fall 1992 South survey included 795 respondents, the Fall 1994 South survey included 938 respondents, and the 1999 combined South and Non-South survey included 1,365 respondents. The data sets for the South and Non-South samples are generally saved separately and weights are provided to improve the representativeness of the samples. Additional information about the data collection for the Southern Focus Polls may be found at http://www.thearda.com/Archive/Sfocus.asp.

American National Election Studies

The American National Election Studies (ANES) are national surveys conducted immediately following each presidential and midterm election since 1948. The "ANES 1964 Time Series Study," the "ANES Time Series Cumulative Data File (1948–2012)," and the "ANES 2016 Time Series Study" are utilized in this book. Additional information about the ANES surveys can be found at http://www.electionstudies.org/index.html.

Appendices

Appendix A presents the questions and responses for each of the variables used throughout the book. Appendix A also presents the coding of response categories, how scales were created, and the corresponding alpha levels of those scales. Appendix B presents the sample sizes for each figure and table, and appendix C presents the significance tests for each figure and table in the study. Throughout the analyses, unless explicitly stated otherwise, the data and findings are weighted to improve the representativeness of the survey samples. Throughout the analyses, difference of means tests were conducted when the dependent variable contained five or more response categories, chi-square tests were conducted when the dependent variable contained three or four response categories, and logistic regressions were conducted when the dependent variable contained two response categories. Since the direction of the relationships between the independent and dependent variables are predicted, the significance levels reported in appendix C, as well as in the models presented in Tables 3.2A, 3.2B, 4.2, 5.1, 6.1, and C.2, are based on one-tailed tests. Sources for each figure and table are included in both appendix B and appendix C.

Introduction

THE LONG SOUTHERN STRATEGY EXPLAINED

[T]he South did not become Republican so much as the
Republican Party became southern.

—GLENN FELDMAN[1]

THERE IS, INDEED, an art of the deal. Sometimes only a prescient few can describe it. Such was the case in the wake of the 1948 southern white revolt from a Democratic Party that was beginning to question Jim Crow. This time, southern secession took the form of a third-party, segregationist bid for the White House, by which these aptly named Dixiecrats intended to prove just how indispensable they were to a Democratic Party victory. The rebellion would bring Democrats to their knees begging for reconciliation with their southern base, thus halting the party's march toward racial equality in its tracks—or so the Dixiecrats hoped. However, the Democratic presidential nominee, incumbent Harry Truman, won without them. The Dixiecrats had gambled and lost. In the election postmortem that followed, two seemingly unrelated books appeared, both of which exposed that wager for what it was: a modern expression of an old tribal arrangement. Neither the prescient authors nor their disciplines could have been more different, and yet both books, each as relevant now as then, dissected an ailing South, stripping the region to its political bones and laying bare the mechanisms by which this Democratic stronghold would turn Republican red.

In her part memoir, part polemic *Killers of the Dream*, Lillian Smith, a southern, white, privileged intellectual, describes—as only a former insider-turned-outsider can—the politics of fear that was paralyzing the region at mid-century. At the base of that fear was what Smith calls the "grand bargain" of white supremacy, buttressed by paternalism and evangelicalism, whereby the southern white masses relinquished political power to the few in exchange for maintaining their social status as better than the black man. It was a bargain that required no paperwork or signatures. This deal was silent, embedded so deeply in southern white culture that it functioned as a political institution in and of itself, checking and balancing the forces of change. "No white southerners, rich or poor," says Smith, "ever sat down and wrote out this bargain as a creed to believe and to live by, or ever said aloud or whispered in their own minds all of it at one time, or even faced in their hearts its full implications for people who claim to be Christian and democratic; for it grew on them, little by little," she explains. "It was absorbed by them from their newspapers, from their friends' talk, in smoking compartments of trains, in wispy little odds and ends of jokes and rumor," Smith noted, and "from politicians' speeches and promises."[2]

That same year V. O. Key Jr., a University of Chicago–trained political scientist, published *Southern Politics in State and Nation*, a detailed audit of the aberrant political behavior of the eleven states of the former Confederacy. Whereas Smith employed memory, Key offered data and maps, which also affirmed the formidable command of southern white elites who "succeeded in imposing their will on their states" to become the "backbone of southern political unity."[3] Such unity allowed southern whites at the top of the ladder to maintain control internally despite being outnumbered by poor southern whites and African Americans. The grand bargain was the source of that success, and so it was avowed time and time again, via spectacle, violence, pageantry, statutes, heritage, or all of the above. Repetition maintained that unity, which, in turn, protected the critical one-party political system. After all, any political division would permit a competition of ideas and policies that could nullify the deal. One-party politics provided another advantage as well. It made for a robust voting block nationally, thereby insulating southern white control from federal forces above, just as it corralled the masses below. Ever the dealmakers, these southern white elites bent their culture to their political will, trading democracy for power. When that power was threatened by the civil rights revolutions, they struck another grand bargain—this time with the Grand Old Party—the terms of which have yet to expire.

This is not a book about the 2016 or 2018 elections. It was conceived of long before "nasty women," "bad hombres," and "me too" became part of the political vernacular. Yet so many of the ideas offered here seem confirmed not only by recent election results, but also by the tone and temper, the rhetoric and rage, that have characterized the races. This book is not about any single election, for that matter, nor is it a history of realignment or a longitudinal quantitative study. Rather, it is a panned-out, backward glance at the long-term implications of the Republican Party's decision to court southern white voters. Initially, the GOP acted on the advice of Senator Barry Goldwater of Arizona who, in a speech following Richard Nixon's loss to Democratic candidate John F. Kennedy in 1960, told fellow Republican leaders, "We're not going to get the Negro vote as a bloc in 1964 and 1968, so we ought to go hunting where the ducks are."[4] To do so, the GOP decided to capitalize on white racial angst, which was not in short supply in the South. However—and this is critical—that decision was but one in a *se-ries of decisions* the party made not just on race, but on feminism and religion as well, in what is called here the "Long Southern Strategy." Outlining this broader arc is possible now because of the ground forged by the tireless work of political scientists, historians, sociologists, psychologists, literary critics, cultural critics, journalists, and by the sheer passage of time. Only with all of the pieces uncovered and with the distance of a half-century can one begin to assess why and how the Long Southern Strategy worked and what the cost of the deal has been for the region and the country.

WHEN SENATOR STROM Thurmond of South Carolina ran at the top of the segregationist Dixiecrat ticket in 1948, his intention was to flex that muscle of southern unity in order to show how necessary his fellow white southerners were to keeping the national Democratic Party upright and on the winning side of the Electoral College map. However, with limited time and facing the complex rules governing each individual state election, the Dixiecrats only won four states (and one rogue elector in Tennessee). They had made trouble for the Democrats, but they did not have the leverage to quell the progressive spirit catalyzed by the New Deal. Over the next two decades, as the tectonic plates began shifting underneath Jim Crow and the Solid South conceded some electors to Republican candidate Dwight D. Eisenhower, southern white voters like Thurmond lingered in a partisan purgatory of sorts. They felt increasingly abandoned by the Democratic Party's swelling support for racial equality, climaxing in Lyndon B. Johnson's successful passage of the 1964 Civil Rights Act (CRA). That feeling of impending betrayal proved so intense that in 1960, one-third of Mississippi voters cast their ballots for "unpledged electors" when the choice stood between a Republican and the pro–civil rights Kennedy.[5] Four years later, when the GOP nominated Goldwater, who had voted against the CRA, Thurmond promptly changed his party affiliation from Democrat to Republican[6] and signed on to stump for the GOP.

Political scientist Walter Dean Burnham, noted for his scholarship on critical realigning elections, published a study of the 1962 Alabama Senate election that same November when Goldwater faced off against Johnson in the presidential contest of 1964. Burnham, who studied under V. O. Key Jr., mapped the cracks in the solidly Democratic South based on his analysis of the Alabama race, which featured a twenty-four-year Democratic incumbent, Lister Hill, and a Republican challenger, James D. Martin. Hill would eventually be declared the winner, albeit by the slimmest of margins. Martin took home 49 percent of the vote, a shocking accomplishment for a Republican in the South in 1962. However, Martin wasn't just any Republican; rather he was an early convert to the GOP who, during his acceptance speech for the Republican nomination, proclaimed to the Birmingham audience, "we will not again be forced to take up rifle and bayonet to preserve these principles. . . . Make no mistake, my friends, this will be a fight. The bugle call is loud and clear! The South has risen."[7] Martin, as journalist Ralph McGill prophetically noted, sounded more Dixiecrat than Republican. In his analysis of the race, Burnham summarizes what he saw as the conditions that would give rise to a southern realignment, including the organization of interest groups based on "perceived deprivation or the threat of deprivation"; the spreading of negative attitudes toward outgroups; and a zero-sum outlook that caused "politics to be regarded by many as virtually total in character." Such conditions had appeared in Alabama and were cropping up across the South, by which Burnham concluded: "a point of no return might be reached if the Republican Party should nominate a candidate whose particularist, states'-rights and economically conservative views, like Martin's in 1962, could appeal to a racially-aroused Southern electorate as the lesser evil. With such a nomination the Southern tinderbox might be ignited at last."[8] Burnham was right, and it was Goldwater who struck the match.

Despite a fairly progressive record on black equality, Goldwater voted against the CRA because he did not believe federal enforcement was possible and state and local enforcement was preferable. He insisted that "the more the Federal government has attempted to legislate morality, the more it actually has incited hatred and violence."[9] Goldwater's campaign strategists convinced the candidate to highlight that vote and that sentiment in his final swing through the South, called "Operation Dixie." With Thurmond as his champion, Goldwater received a warm welcome in states like Alabama, where he was actually endorsed by the Grand Dragon of the state chapter of the Ku Klux Klan.[10] Come election day, Goldwater managed to flip five Deep South states red. Among those five states, only Louisiana had voted Republican since Reconstruction, which it did when voters supported Eisenhower in 1956 after the Democrats chose Estes Kefauver over Kennedy, the Catholic, for the vice-presidential spot on the ticket. Goldwater's greatest margins of victory came from counties with the highest population of African American residents, where any change to the racial pecking order proved the most alarming.[11] In Mississippi alone, Goldwater received 87 percent of the vote, causing the journalist Hodding Carter III, who lamented Mississippi's decision, to warn that white southerners had to stop "walk[ing] down dead-end streets, waving our tattered banners in defiance. No one is going to walk with us anymore."[12]

The hardcore Jim Crow rhetoric may have turned away as many moderates as it won extremists. Or at least that was how it must have looked in the moment because, other than his native Arizona, these were the only states Goldwater won. He even deeded back to the Democrats Eisenhower's peripheral South gains. Goldwater's landslide loss nationally seemed to spell the end of the GOP's Operation Dixie. However, elections have consequences, particularly losing elections. Johnson's victory made the passage of the 1965 Voting Rights Act (VRA) the following year possible. The VRA, of course, heightened the angst of these southern dealmakers, many of whom relied on the disenfranchisement of African Americans to maintain their power. In response, over the decades that followed, many conservatives both championed legal challenges to invalidate the VRA and, simultaneously, used the VRA to splinter Democratic coalition districts, all while fanning the ever-burning flame of racial polarization.[13] That is how powerful that angst was—and how deep its roots stretched. Though several generations removed, the memory of Confederate disenfranchisement during postwar military occupation, and the resulting election of hundreds of former slaves and freedmen to local, state, and even national office, made the threat to white power anything but abstract. Through the lens of Reconstruction, the consequences for southern whites, if the law were enforced, seemed real, even predictable. Therefore, in the first post-VRA election cycle, Thurmond made a devil's pact with the GOP that over time altered American politics well beyond the Mason-Dixon line, the scope of which is just now coming into focus.

The tale of the deal itself is well known, but the arc of the story stretches much further and wider than has been remembered. When George Wallace, the reactionary, segregationist governor of Alabama, launched his third-party presidential campaign in 1968 (previously he sought the Democratic Party nomination in 1964 and would again in 1972 and 1976), Thurmond knew that Wallace would win the hardliners. However, like Goldwater, Wallace could win the Deep South but lose the country. The only hope of defeating the Democratic nominee, sitting vice president Hubert Humphrey, was to channel southern white moderates toward the GOP. It had been Humphrey, after all, who had led the charge at the 1948 Democratic National Convention to strengthen the party's commitment to civil rights. He successfully advocated for the addition of a "minority plank" to the Democratic Party platform. In turn, southern Democrats splintered, and the Dixiecrats formed in retaliation. Now, twenty years later, faced with a reactionary, third-party southern governor who could not win and a pro-civil rights, liberal vice president who might, Thurmond went for the middle.

He sat down with GOP hopeful Richard Nixon in an Atlanta motel where many believe Thurmond traded his endorsement and campaign support for Nixon's "benign neglect" of civil rights enforcement,[14] while others claim the two primarily discussed national security issues.[15] Nixon, who once shared a friendship with Martin Luther King Jr.[16] and who received praise from NAACP leader Roy Wilkins[17] during his unsuccessful 1960 presidential bid, did pivot away from his pro–civil rights stances of the past. So, if neither the Dixiecrats, nor Goldwater, nor Wallace could win nationally—if the tide could not be turned back—then perhaps this new Nixon could, at least, prevent any additional erosion of the southern white way of life. That June, Thurmond publicly professed his support for Nixon, and he whipped up delegate votes on his behalf at the Republican National Convention in Miami when a late campaign by Ronald Reagan left Nixon's fate hanging in the balance. Thurmond gathered these early white southern Democrats-turned-Republicans and pleaded, "I know you want to vote for Reagan, the true conservative, but if Nixon becomes president, he has promised that he won't enforce either the Civil Rights or the Voting Rights Acts. Stick with him."[18] They stuck, giving Nixon the nomination with a first-ballot majority.

In terms of appealing to white southern voters still bent on preserving the segregated South, Nixon took a more subtle approach than Goldwater's direct opposition to the CRA (particularly his stance as portrayed by his southern surrogates). Nixon had to find a way to reach alienated southern whites who wanted to maintain their facade of moral patriotism to the nation at large while protecting the racial hierarchy at home. To allow many to save face, particularly in light of the intense media criticism of the region that became part of the civil rights beat of most newspapers, Nixon's team adopted a racial code. Calls for the restoration of "law and order," most famously, translated into an end to protests and picketing and boycotts, and even a return to the racial status quo, while Nixon's "War on Drugs" drove the incarceration rates of black Americans to historic highs.[19] Support for law and order was hardly controversial or even partisan, yet it gave white southerners hope for the outcome they wanted without having to articulate it. Pivoting helped Nixon hit the sweet spot—mostly white, suburban, professionals in the outer South[20]—between Wallace and the Democrats.

It was political pragmatism at its finest, though Nixon and Thurmond were not the first to cut such a southern deal. Ninety-six years earlier in another hotel meeting, this time at Wormley House in Washington, DC, southern Democratic leaders brokered a trade with friends of Republican presidential candidate Rutherford B. Hayes. They would yield the contested electors in Florida, South Carolina, and Louisiana, giving Hayes the 1876 Electoral College win in exchange for the new president's withdrawal of federal military troops still stationed in the reconstructing South.[21] Deliberately swinging the election to the party of Lincoln would have been inconceivable to white southerners unless it meant protecting their "way of life." In the aftermath, left to their own devices, reactionary southern white elites turned the clock back in as many ways as they could, reasserting their control and supremacy.

Beyond the well-chronicled horrors of lynchings, Ku Klux Klan rallies, the convict lease system, sharecropping, poll taxes, literacy tests, and race riots that ended in African Americans being run out of town or worse, post-compromise, white southerners also doubled down on partisan loyalty. In 1890, several southern congressmen penned *Why the Solid South?*, in which they describe the vengeful treatment of the region by Congress. The Radical Republicans elected after Robert E. Lee surrendered at Appomattox "claimed full power of the late insurrectionary states, on the ground that it was for Congress to decide when the war had ceased; *and*" the authors complained, "*they decided it was not yet over.*"[22] White southerners could only protect themselves from such punishment and overreach, they reasoned, by uncompromised, unified political action. In an often overlooked chapter in *The Ethnic Southerners*, historian George Tindall describes the way in which "Democratic propaganda dominated political discourse" in the post-Reconstruction era by stoking anger toward scalawags, carpetbaggers, and "outrage mills" (fake news reports of southern atrocities) and fear of "Negro domination."[23] The "us vs. them" mentality of actual war remained the organizing cosmology in its aftermath. Such rhetoric served as scripture in a civil religion hell-bent on saving the power of those at the top by reinforcing regional loyalty, which is exactly how white southern elites had enough national clout to broker the end of military occupation. Less than a century later, however, they didn't even have the leverage within the Democratic Party itself to stem the tide toward integration. Rather, as Goldwater's Operation Dixie and Nixon's Southern Strategy revealed, for white southerners intent on protecting their way of life, it was the Republican Party that was open to negotiation.

Those negotiations have been successful but protracted, which is exactly what Nixon himself had imagined. As Reg Murphy and Hal Gulliver proclaim in the first book (published only three years after the election) to chronicle the tactic, "The Nixon Southern Strategy did not end with his narrow victory in the 1968 presidential election." Rather, they contend, "it became apparent, not just that he [Nixon] wanted to keep his promises to Strom Thurmond and others, but that this was a long-range strategy." Nixon, they insist, "hoped to woo Southern support so ardently that there might once again develop a solid political South—but this time committed as firmly to the Republican party as it once had been to the Democratic party."[24] And that takes time. Yet too often the Southern Strategy is remembered as a fixed, short course, relegated to a few election cycles and singularly focused on exploiting racial animus. This characterization of the Southern Strategy is not unlike the way in which the Civil Rights Movement was, for many years, framed as a 1950s and 1960s phenomenon. That changed in 2005 when the historian Jacqueline Dowd Hall challenged Americans to abandon the popular timeline of the movement. Hall argues that centering the movement on Martin

Luther King Jr.'s more public campaigns obscures decades of legal challenges, protests, organizing, and political participation by African American activists and their compatriots. Hall points to the NAACP leader E. D. Nixon, for example, who "was a veteran of the Brotherhood of Sleeping Car Porters, the black-led union that was central to the movement in the 1940s,"[25] and who also was the man who actually recruited King to join the Montgomery Bus Boycott. Failing to see the prequel to the more public phase of the movement stripped these activists of their agency—their choices and discipline and groundwork. This limited view renders the successes of the Civil Rights Movement as accidental or the result of an idea whose time has come. To the contrary, generations of human beings made change happen in what Hall called the Long Civil Rights Movement.

Likewise, generations of people have directed the sequel, a backlash or counter-punch to the progressive victories of the Long Civil Rights Movement, not just for African Americans, but also in the fight for women's rights, gay rights, Chicano rights, and civil rights writ large. The Long Southern Strategy targeted white southerners who felt alienated from, angry at, and resentful of the policies that granted equality and sought to level the playing field for all of these groups. And it did not just target the diehard fringe; the GOP courted white southern moderates who might accept an abstract notion of equality but often objected to any kind of tangible federal efforts to achieve it. That is why the CRA and the VRA met such massive resistance, and why racial equality, specifically, became the pilot issue. Neither Nixon nor Goldwater would have stood in a doorway and blocked an African American child from attending public school, but they also did not think that whites should have to bus their children across town to force integration. Nevertheless, the results are the same. Those who did not live under Jim Crow could not see that southern whiteness was a gravitational force holding everything in its place. Neighborhoods were segregated by custom and covenants, which meant school districts were as well. To change that, to change any of it, required propulsion and enforcement, and when state governments would not comply, federal action became the only option. Thus, when Nixon espoused his theoretical opposition to government overreach, he might as well have been waving a Confederate flag.

This southern white way of life, however, is not based solely on white superiority. Rather, it is best viewed as a triptych with religious fundamentalism and patriarchy standing as separate hinged panels that can be folded inward—bent to cover or reinforce white supremacy throughout much of the region's history. The stereotype of southern white womanhood, for example, by which delicate, sacred white women of privilege need constant protection from black males, was constructed and maintained to justify everything from slavery, to lynchings, to segregation. It was a red herring from its inception, promoted to cast white supremacy as chivalry while relegating southern white women to a distant pedestal where they could be seen and not heard. This two-for-one deal criminalized black men while silencing white women and kept southern white male power unchallenged. Any threat to such authority by African Americans could be met with swift violence. Southern white women, on the other hand, needed cultural reinforcement of their "special" status as the fairer of the sexes, or so they were taught from childhood via countless Sunday sermons where patriarchy came wrapped in scripture. As a result, the cult of southern white womanhood requires women to participate in misogyny—or at least in the way that philosopher Kate Manne describes in her 2018 book, *Down Girl*, where misogyny is defined as the constant practice of correcting and policing women's behavior to maintain male power.[26] For many southern white women, at a subconscious level, submissiveness became their duty. Their oppression became their privilege. Tradition became their cause, and faith became their defense, just as it had been for much of the Confederacy.

The politicization of these southern white conservative and, more often than not, religious women in opposition to Second-Wave Feminism resuscitated and kept the GOP strategy alive. The cult of southern white womanhood had primed this audience for generations; thus, the anti-feminism rallying cry became as successful as the well-known dog whistles of race and religion. It is, in fact, a bridge between the two. White resentment toward a more level racial playing field was easily transferred to, or simply intensified by, the goal of a level gender playing field, and the promotion of "family values" by anti-feminists in their attacks against feminists paved the way for the Christian Right. Moreover, the Southern Baptist Convention (SBC), the largest governing religious body in the South, and one to which many of these women belonged, shifted its focus from racial politics to reinstating doctrinal dictates regarding traditional gender roles. This reactionary response was spearheaded by the fundamentalist wing of the SBC, which staged a takeover of the convention during the national battle over the Equal Rights Amendment (ERA). The successful SBC fundamentalists purged moderate Baptists from their ranks, aligned their spiritual and political missions, fostered interdenominational unity with other fundamentalists and evangelicals, and did so under the GOP label, which proved to be the ultimate nail in the coffin of the blue South. To that end, what Earl and Merle Black called "The Great White Switch"[27] was actually "The Great White, Anti-Feminist, Christian Switch." Absent an understanding of the role of southern white sexism in this realignment, racism and religiosity read as two chapters of separate books. They were and are an ensemble cast in the same story, better known as "The Long Southern Strategy."

THE SOUTHERN POLITICAL landscape is red now, but it did not turn red with one brushstroke. White racial angst during the dismantling of segregation drove some southern white Democrats into the arms of the GOP temporarily. It was not enough voters to be the sole cause of sustained realignment. Even though Nixon's plan had held Wallace to only 50 percent of the vote in the South in 1968, white southerners returned to the Democratic Party by a margin of two to one in 1970, a "snapback" reflecting the region's partisan default, particularly in a midterm election year.[28] By 1976, only 30 percent of conservatives in the South considered themselves Republicans[29]—a major accomplishment for the GOP, but by no means a solid majority. As Murphy and Gulliver concluded in 1971, "The two great political parties in America may splinter someday, but it probably will not happen over the South; after all, the nation held together after the war of the brothers a century ago, and one cannot imagine a threat that serious now."[30] Thus, the southern white psychological attachment to the Democratic Party[31] proved persistently stubborn.

Post-Watergate, Republicans worried that those inroads would be permanently washed away. Southern Democrats had an opportunity,[32] which they seized via the candidacy and victory of an insider: the white, southern, born-again peanut farmer Jimmy Carter recaptured the southern states lost to Nixon, patching up the solidly Democrat South, at least on the surface. Though the GOP had taken a sharp right turn on civil rights enforcement in order to attract white southerners, Carter was authentically one of them. And for white southerners, identity, when absent an impending threat, trumped everything. Additionally, Goldwater and Nixon had both benefited from a sense of urgency about impending racial changes that made racial appeals highly salient to this coveted political bloc of white southerners. As Lillian Smith described, "it is a strange thing, this umbilical cord uncut. In times of ease, we do not feel its pull, but when we are threatened with change, suddenly it draws the whole white South together in a collective fear and fury."[33] Yet after the immediate shock of the Supreme Court rulings and congressional actions that struck at the heart of Jim Crow wore off, many southern whites found ways to recreate their all-white spaces, often in the suburbs or in private schools, particularly in a still-growing economy. Without constant reinvention, crises and outrage grow stale. To incite more white southerners to break rank and vote for them—or in some cases to re-defect—Republicans not only needed to restore the race relations state of emergency, but they also needed to manufacture and broadcast new threats. Only by striking at the heart of southern white identity could they hope to overcome the allegiance that Carter, as the first true southern president since secession, would surely rebuild. They did both.

Reconstituting the racial threat is made easier by the pliancy of whiteness. Whiteness, is, after all, merely a vantage point, and white superiority exists only in the comparative. Without the legal designation of slave and slave owner, southern whiteness required legal, codified segregation to protect white superiority. And after this de jure segregation was struck down, only a cultural promotion of whiteness or a demonization of non-whiteness could maintain that gap. White flight neighborhoods, for example, and private white academies not only served as an escape hatch from integrated public spaces, but also continued to glorify a white America. Such is "The Not-So-New Southern Racism" (chapter 1) in a region unable to shake its past. And as overt racism became more socially unacceptable, it had to be laundered via other channels. The GOP took its cue from a future Democratic senator from New York, Daniel Patrick Moynihan, whose infamous Moynihan Report and subsequent writings blamed the dynamics of the African American family for racial inequity. Black families were "dominated by women, never acquiring any stable relationship to male authority," he claimed, and as a result, "that community asks for and gets chaos."[34] The message, which Lawrence Bobo called "laissez-faire racism," whereby blacks are blamed for their standing in society,[35] was repackaged in the Long Southern Strategy so that federal support for programs aimed at racial uplift became fiscally irresponsible. White Citizens Councils throughout the South even distributed Moynihan's report in their communities. In the South, emphasizing the undeserving status of blacks and their responsibility for their own poverty acquitted and applauded white southern culture while further distancing poor white southerners from African Americans. Attacking poor whites as "welfare queens" would, after all, tarnish the whiteness brand and also break the grand bargain upon which southern white power depended.

Railing against entitlements did more than just inflate whiteness by contrasting it to an underserving blackness; it also pulled at the southern white purse strings to which racism has always been tied. More than just an admission ticket to the "right side" of the tracks, whiteness was and is, as David Roediger called it, a wage. Protecting whiteness was tantamount to protecting an investment. Jobs, promotions, loans—all were easier for southern whites to get, free of competition from an entire oppressed portion of the population who had been denied equal access to education, indeed to everything. So perilous was the idea of a level playing field—and increasingly so as the country entered the economic downturn of the 1970s[36]—that "Southern White Privilege" (chapter 2) became the new lost cause for which many were willing to go down fighting. Any policy or government expenditure deemed as providing a leg up for African Americans was understood only as an attack on whites in this zero-sum game. Over the course of the Long Southern Strategy, the coded racial mantras shifted from whites being better suited at governing, to whites having the right to protect whites-only private spaces, to whites being victims of reverse discrimination. But equality feels like an attack when privilege is all one knows. Together, the coded language provided deniability and the urgent threat of potential peril consolidated resistance. Politically malleable, whiteness has proven to be the GOP's blank check that always clears.

Playing a different hand of race cards may have won back some of the GOP's lost chips, but it did not solidify their lead alone. Another "tell" for southern white voters—one that very few noticed—was a long-standing objection to any assertion of women's rights. As far back as the ratification of the Nineteenth Amendment, for example, 9 of 11 southern states voted against women's suffrage. Few noticed because, in terms of politics, the research on southern white women is meager,[37] receiving little mention even in V. O. Key's *Southern Politics*. Some of that inattention reflects equally meager participation by southern white women in politics. To this day, there have been only 51 white women from southern states who have served in the US House of Representatives, 19 of whom succeeded their husbands (often after their deaths) or were the daughters of such famous politicians as William Jennings Bryan. Fourteen white women have served in the US Senate representing a southern state, half of whom were first either appointed to their husbands' seats when their husbands died, appointed to temporarily hold the seat by their own husband who was serving as governor at the time, or appointed by their governor as a symbolic gesture. The last category was the case for Rebecca Felton of Georgia, who served for 24 hours. No woman has ever served in the US Senate from Virginia or South Carolina—not even as a placeholder—and Mississippi has yet to elect any women to the US House of Representatives. There has been substantial progress in state legislatures, but not to the degree that has happened in states outside of the South.[38] In southern white culture, the formal political arena has overwhelmingly been the purview of men. Thus, when Second-Wave Feminism moved onto the public stage in the 1970s, many southern whites undoubtedly felt that "umbilical tug," giving the GOP another opportunity to "go hunting where the ducks are."

The feminist movement, supported by women of both parties, peaked at the National Women's Conference in Houston in 1977, the only national women's convention ever held.[39] Passage of the ERA served as the driving force behind the gathering, though countless efforts for justice and equal treatment by the courts in terms of divorce proceedings, property ownership, educational access, and protection from sexual harassment in general also prompted women's organizing. Moreover, just as the Democratic and Republican platforms proved virtually indistinguishable on civil rights in the 1950s, both President Gerald Ford and challenger Jimmy Carter supported the ERA while still professing to be personally pro-life. Both candidates actively courted women with Ford's team issuing his "76 Fact Book" detailing his record on and commitment to women's rights,[40] while Carter opted to deliver his preeminent speech on the subject to one of the leading feminist organizations,[41] the Women's Action Alliance. Houston, how-ever, presented a new fork in the road.

When pro-ERA forces gathered at the National Women's Conference in 1977, they were countered by a "Pro-Family Rally" organized by Phyllis Schlafly that attracted an audience of 20,000.[42] Schlafly, a movement in her own right, had found a way to coerce southern white women off their pedestals, so that they might march and protest and organize to protect their own subordinate status. Schlafly's group, STOP ERA, founded in 1972, stood for Stop Taking Our Privileges. They presented an ideological defense of anti-feminism that resonated, not just with men primed to protect their own advantages, but with women too. The anti-feminists attended state women's commission meetings and demanded equal time on the airwaves and equal representation on government boards. In doing so, they established their movement as a false equivalency to femi-nism. Charged by the new slogan "family values," these anti-feminists, many of whom, at that time, were southern white Democrats unturned yet by the GOP,[43] worked to kill the ERA in enough states to prohibit national ratification. They also spearheaded campaigns against "liberal" textbooks and for parental influ-ence over school teachings. Nevertheless, just like the United Daughters of the Confederacy, who shaped southern curricula about the Civil War throughout the early twentieth century, these southern anti-feminists limited their activism to their gendered sphere of influence.[44]

The cult of southern white womanhood was anti-feminist before the label existed, and so it is no surprise that Schlafly's marketing would attract so many southern white customers. The ERA would force women to put their newborns in government-run daycare, or serve on the front lines of combat, or embrace lesbianism, or work, for that matter—all accusations that threatened the promise of protection made to southern white women. That promise, though only ful-filled for elites, was both physical and financial, but more important, emotional. In such a culture of anti-feminism or "family values," as its supporters proclaimed, women remained shielded from the harder decisions of life and were allowed to be morally passive in times of public crisis. Equality thus meant more than just a fair wage. It meant choice, which is, of course, what feminism was supposed to champion. But southern white culture depended on political monopolies, hier-archy, and social control. Choice was kryptonite.

In the "Grand Bargain" of southern white womanhood, oppression is coded as privilege, whether experienced or aspirational. Southern white women are often still portrayed as polite and beautiful and charming, and they are defined in opposition to feminists, who are denounced as overly ambitious, greedy, manip-ulative, and untrustworthy. That sacred goodness associated with southern white womanhood renders southern white women ill-suited for the rough terrain of political life, or so the story goes, narrated time and again by men and women justifying and promoting "The Not-So-New Southern Sexism" (chapter 4). Yet southern white women who embrace this ideology can rally for "family values" because those values are patriarchal or traditional or biblical and because those values are all southern. The Republican establishment took notice of this energy and slogan quickly, politicizing abortion and gay rights, both of which they associated with feminism, and recycling the anti–big government rhetoric aimed at halting the federal enforcement of African American rights and applying it to the federal enforcement clauses included in the ERA.[45] "As the new racism (mostly) replaced the old in politics," historian Kiera V. Williams has noted, "sexism ascended."[46] By the 1978 midterm elections, which saw victories for a new cohort of southern, white, male Republicans such as Thad Cochran in Mississippi and Newt Gingrich in Georgia,[47] the Long Southern Strategy seemed to be making a comeback. Two years later, after forty years of supporting some version of the ERA, the GOP dropped it from their 1980 platform. At the fork in the road, they turned right again.

Second-Wave Feminism was made to seem as destructive and anxiety-inducing as integration. In some ways, for many southern whites, women's liberation was even more personal because it touched the core of every heterosexual family. Every married woman who chose to work—if she had any choice at all—altered the dynamics of her household. Once again defined in opposition to an "other," southern white femininity, shaped to justify white supremacy, necessitated a distinct southern white masculinity that remains fixed, as if cemented atop the social order—so expected as to go unquestioned. The "Southern White Patriarchy" (chapter 5) requires, at least among enough of its constituents, an aggressive, rugged, defiant masculinity that is dominant sometimes to the point of violence,[48] segregated by race and gender, and performed relentlessly, particularly in times of perceived vulnerability. Feminism exacerbated that sense of vulnerability in and of itself, but in tandem with the progressive victories for racial equality, it seemed catastrophic to many. The idea for the National Organization for Women (NOW), as Republican feminist Tanya Melich notes in her memoir, surfaced during a 1966 meeting regarding the lack of protection for the sex discrimination clauses in the 1964 CRA,[49] and much of the gender-neutral language that feminists encouraged was aimed at exposing explicitly sexist policies, just as civil rights activists had appealed to a common humanity to overthrow Jim Crow.[50] In the South, as Marjorie Spruill reveals, members of the John Birch Society and the Ku Klux Klan joined the fight to defeat the ERA, recognizing, as the Mississippi KKK leader told the media, that "women's rights and civil rights go hand in hand."[51]

Beyond just the ERA battle, Men's Rights Associations organized against feminism in general, co-opting much of their language in accusations of reverse discrimination against men this time. In the 1980s, these groups pushed an agenda "that re-entrenches privilege," while staking claim "as the 'true' defenders of reason, choice, equality, liberty, the individual, the family, the social order, citizenship, God, and nation."[52] The double-threat of race and gender transformed "the masculinity of politics to masculinity as politics."[53] Southern white men, especially politicians, embodied it; many southern white women extolled it. Despite being a major component of the Long Southern Strategy, however, too often "gender has been relatively neglected by people explaining power and authority in the recent South."[54] Reagan's hyper-masculine, cowboy, Marlboro man image (whether real or staged),[55] his traditional marriage (despite being divorced), the photographs of him working at Rancho del Cielo (his other White House),[56] and his hawkish patriotism brought Second-Wave Feminism to a screeching halt. Republican strategists manufactured the storm, issued dire warnings—many in coded language[57]—and offered their party as the shelter. Once the GOP was seen as the protector of the southern sacraments of white privilege and patriarchy, many southern white voters flocked to it, turning the South solidly red in 1984 for the first time in history.

That same year, Congressman Trent Lott of Mississippi confirmed the major shift, telling the Sons of the Confederate Veterans, "the spirit of Jefferson Davis lives in the 1984 Republican Platform." In an interview with Richard T. Hines for *Southern Partisan* magazine, Lott reiterated his claim, but he also hinted at the need to solidify this newly red South, which actually remained blue at the state level. Splitting from Democrats on civil rights enforcement and women's liberation had done much to delineate the national GOP in the hearts and minds of white southerners—Republicans offered "a choice, not an echo," as Schlafly's 1964 conservative polemic by the same name explained.[58] Taking their cues from the party elites, many white southerners sorted themselves accordingly.[59] By 1996, 70 percent of US senators from the South called themselves Republicans, up from 0 percent in 1960.[60] However, the rebranding of the party had to extend beyond national election campaigns. In order for Republican Party allegiance to trickle down, the Long Southern Strategy needed to politicize not just the hearts and minds or even pocketbooks of white southerners, but also their souls. "Look," Lott explained to Hines, "if the religious people don't get involved in politics, it's going to be run by others."[61]

The southern "way of religion" is part culture and part identity, embedded with rituals, symbols, and gestures,[62] and distinct from the rest of the country by the sheer number of adherents. With such high levels of religiosity and church membership, religion in the South infects daily life in ways that render it inseparable not only from culture and identity, but also from politics. This particular white southern strain of religiosity, in some ways, reflected the unique history of the region. For example, since many of the initial white settlers in the South were running toward land ownership, as opposed to fleeing religious persecution, their "errand into the wilderness" was fundamentally economic. Consequently, the southern version of the Great Awakening was delayed. Moreover, due to the often-isolating conditions of the region, when it did arrive, it fulfilled not only a spiritual need, but also a social one as a rare source of entertainment. Sermons were delivered at circus-like tent revivals with large crowds and high drama. Over time, individual relationships with God, the conversion of neighbors near and far, the inerrancy of the Bible, and moral dictates governing personal behavior became the brew served hot to the hungry masses. The certainty provided by "The Not-So-New Southern Religion" (chapter 7) reinforced the pillars of white supremacy and misogyny that steeled southern white culture from opposition, while serving as a code in and of itself. If patriarchy was God's will, then it was not sexist. If traditional gender roles were biblically sanctioned, then women's submissiveness is but a testament of faith, another "Grand Bargain" for the promise of salvation.

The sheer number or religious believers creates a "sacred canopy" of like-mindedness that shields communities from diversity of faith, thought, and policy. Such cultural reinforcement of one perspective can, in turn, create a distinct and acceptable—but often false—reality.[63] Without pluralism or even an awareness of pluralism, too often the default is righteousness and intolerance.[64] So powerful is the reach and breadth of some southern churches, that even nonbelievers in proximity receive their social cues indirectly.[65] That only fortifies this insulated worldview. Thus, radical political changes—the bubbling up of social movements into the public consciousness or Supreme Court decisions, for example—seem to violate this reality. And shock can be a powerful catalyst. So Second-Wave Feminism and integration and all the tangential issues and events that preceded or followed in their wake exposed just how different much of the rest of America had become. In turn, in the decades that followed, evangelicals, the bulk of whom were white southerners, mobilized with an unprecedented intensity.[66] Many white southern women, who only allowed themselves to enter the public arena as moral crusaders, honed their political skills on issues that were related in some manner to this southern white womanhood they wanted to protect. They participated in campaigns to keep prayer in public schools and to fund parochial schools, for example. Such issues naturally galvanized evangelicals in general—men and women—to engage in the worldly concerns that theology had long discouraged as a distraction from spiritual progress. Religious issues had become political, so religious people had to engage in politics. But it was the fundamentalist takeover of the SBC, beginning in 1979, that took that engagement to another level and provided the GOP the opportunity to close the deal with white southern voters.

Prior to the fundamentalist takeover, moderation among Southern Baptists, the largest denomination in the region, toward issues regarding race and gender relations had crept in slowly. The convention, which only truly exists when electors from member congregations convene annually, functioned primarily as a faith gathering and a forum for theological discussions. Fundamentalist members, however, felt their anxiety regarding such moderation was consistently ignored, and, in turn, they successfully executed a decades-long plan to seize control of the meeting and reshape the SBC to reflect their extremist views. They won the elected offices, appointed fundamentalist majorities to the governing committees, exiled moderates from the denomination almost entirely, re-codified the inferior status of women in the church,[67] and replaced their Washington, DC, lobbying firm with one charged not to protect freedom of exercise, but to advocate for Christianity. Inerrancy triumphed over interpretation, absolutism over compromise, and political power became a false idol worshipped by many. Over the next ten years, mainstream church membership declined as evangelical and fundamentalist churches boomed. Their new converts are not opposed to worldly engagement.[68] Rather, political engagement is part of the spiritual pilgrimage that leads to salvation.

Republicans, on the other hand, had been straddling the church-and-state line since Eisenhower's participation in the American Legion's "Back to God" program[69] and Nixon's decision to hold church services in the East Room of the White House.[70] The rise of televangelism and megachurches made many ministers as politically powerful as CEOs of major corporations, and the large weekly audiences and authoritarian structure made them ripe for the political picking. By the 1960s, scholars noticed that conservative Protestants were starting to bend toward the GOP.[71] Carter's status as a born-again Southern Baptist, followed by Bill Clinton's as well, may have stemmed the tide in the white South. At the least, it made observers assume that Democrats had the faith advantage. However, it was the GOP that embraced moralistic, evangelical, "Southern White Fundamentalism" (chapter 8)—and all that came with it—as part of a Long Southern Strategy. In order to court southern evangelical voters, the Republican Party took hardline stances on social conservative issues like gay marriage and abortion. Such issues could be folded under the banner of family values, cribbed from anti-feminism, which had been propping up white supremacy in the house, so to speak, that the white South built. As a result, over the course of the 1970s and 1980s, the partisanship of evangelicals went from being statistically, significantly correlated with one policy issue—school prayer—to being statistically, significantly correlated to, according to Ted Jelen, "sexual morality," "homosexuality," "public feminism," "abortion," "tolerance," and "pornography"—and those are only the issues he tested.[72]

Under the umbrella of the Christian Right, these faith-based activists rose in opposition to what they perceived to be widespread social upheaval, claiming with conviction that "there is no arena of human activity, including law and politics, which is outside of God's lordship." And it was indeed a strategy by which religious clergy and secular, conservative players—specifically, the leaders of the Conservative Caucus, the National Conservative Political Action Committee, as well as major Republican fundraisers—forged a partnership.[73] Thus, just as the SBC began its purge of so-called moderates, the Christian Right provided a new outlet for their conservative fervor. In his analysis of the advantages of zealotry in the Christian Right, Steve Bruce contends that conservative Protestants make strong political activists because they already buy into "a system of beliefs that encourages enthusiastic support. It supposes a simple world of good and evil; it asserts certainty and castigates doubts; it divides people into believers and apostates." There is an edge that is gained by zealotry, Bruce proclaims, "hence when such people can be persuaded to become politically active they form a powerful resource."[74]

As political scientists such as Sidney Verba have shown, the skills acquired from an active church life translated well in the political arena; in fact, such sacred volunteerism produced an "activist corps."[75] Moreover, used to tithing to the church, southern white fundamentalists and evangelicals also willingly gave of their own financial resources to political campaigns, which Republican strategists knew early on could help them make inroads in the South.[76] A southern state like Virginia, after all, was home to televangelist Jerry Falwell's Moral Majority Political Action Committee—a precursor to the Christian Right—which defined itself as "pro-life, pro-family, pro-moral, and pro-America" and sought to unify the "170 million 'moral' Americans," equal parts "idealistic moralists," "religious moralists," and "born-again Christians."[77] Virginia was also home to Pat Robertson's Christian Coalition, which would prove to be a major player in the Christian Right in the 1980s. Similar sub-organizations in South Carolina, Texas, and Florida gave the whole movement a "southern stronghold."[78]

On the one hand, this is due to the fact that the Bible Belt of the South had the country's largest concentration of religious conservatives. However, for white southerners specifically, the cultural changes against which the Christian Right rallied may have felt more threatening or more radical in light of the seemingly unbreakable forces of white supremacy and patriarchy. In addition, such changes may have felt more threatening because that was exactly how the Long Southern Strategy made them feel. Invited by the GOP, southern fundamentalism, still enmeshed with these key tenets of southern white identity, was making a last stand, forming an intense "cultural defense movement"[79] that was both decidedly political and very southern. Alongside civic skills, money, and membership numbers, such intensity among the southern white faithful proved to be an invaluable resource, particularly on Election Day. It is the kind of thing, when strategically triggered time and time again, that causes an electoral map to change colors.

This relentless fishing for southern white voters with racial and gendered and religious bait resulted in the GOP's lines becoming permanently entangled. As Numan V. Bartley described, Reagan's 1980 platform alone "disavowed busing and abortion, ignored the ERA, demanded prayer be allowed in public schools, and advocated family values,"[80] all while the candidate himself promised southern whites, "I know what it's like to pull that Republican lever for the first time because I used to be a Democrat myself. But I can tell you—it only hurts for a minute."[81] Casting often and with a variety of bait yielded a big catch, but it also muddied the water so completely that it is impossible to know exactly who was caught by what. There were those who bit primarily because of racial angst, and those who bit primarily because of gender-role angst, and those who bit primarily because of evangelical angst, which is why criticism that accuses a white southerner of sexism, when religion lured him or her to the GOP, is met with such hostility and defensiveness. For while there were some who would have taken any of the three types of bait, faced with only two major party choices, white southerners need not to have agreed on all of the right turns the GOP took during its southern courtship. They only needed to feel one issue so intensely as to eclipse any other objections. The GOP thus had to find the issues that would set enough southern hearts and minds aflame and ignite as many of them as possible, as often as possible, so that a majority, in sum, would flip from blue to red, no matter at which point or for which reason.

Majorities may be made in that murk, but so too are myths—myths that, in turn, obstruct the long view of the past, misinform the present, and mis-forecast the future. "The Myth of the Social Conservative" (chapter 9), for example, is based on the claims that religious Americans over the past several decades began voting for candidates based on their moral conscience instead of their economic well-being and that these social conservatives represented a new strain of conservatism within the Republican Party. But, in many ways, social conservatives were the product of a deliberate Long Southern Strategy. After the fundamentalist takeover of the SBC and the rise of the Christian Right, the GOP gave the faithful a prime seat at the political table. Once evangelicals and fundamentalists were at the table, however, their support was sought not only when it came to traditional moral issues, but also for a host of what many would see as "secular" policy initiatives. However, "religious" and "secular" are constructed categories that are fluid. After all, the environment and the economy, for example, are just as much "religious" issues as are questions of gender roles, sexuality, or whatever else is thought of as "religious" issues if powerful voices declare them to be.

Therefore, as a result of the Long Southern Strategy, "social conservatism" is not limited to faith-based social preferences like support for abstinence education or opposition to reproductive rights, gay adoptions, and transgender bathrooms; this partisan merger of church and state now colors attitudes toward climate change, healthcare, terrorism, and foreign policy, to name a few. Moreover, having been disappointed by the lack of moral progress made by the born-again Carter and feeling somewhat duped by Reagan—who preached more than he practiced—many of these white social conservatives now operate as seasoned politicos. Consequently, to outsiders, their motives often seem more political than religious. This is also why authentic religious beliefs or credentials are no longer required if a candidate wants to win their support. Candidates who promise to deliver the desired outcome or even simply validate these voters' desire for that outcome is all that is needed. Even if social conservatives split their support in the GOP primary, as they did in 2016 among highly religious candidates Ted Cruz and John Kasich and a less religious Trump, they were as unified in their support of the party's nominee as any other Republican faction. That unity is also the product of the Long Southern Strategy—most notably via the GOP's use of the "family values" slogan that it commandeered from the anti-feminists.[82]

What started as a defense of traditional gender roles morphed into an offensive drive for Christian nationalism, in part sparked by southern, white, primarily Christian women who demonstrated against their own liberation. They too wanted to conserve their pedestal and the status quo. Yet their ascendance as political conservatives is ignored, an omission that perpetuates "The Myth of the Gender Gap" (chapter 6). The gender gap was a term coined in the 1980s to describe the percentage of women voting for Democratic Party candidates compared to the percentage of men voting for those same Democratic Party candidates. Feminists touted this positive gender gap as evidence that the Democratic Party's embrace of feminism had won the party women voters. They also used the gender gap to ensure the party paid attention to women's policy concerns and to persuade the party to nominate female candidates for elected office. In the years that followed, many scholars continued to assert that the gender gap did indeed result from the Democratic Party's alliance with feminism. Others argued that the gender gap was actually a consequence of men's increasing tendency to vote Republican. Southern white men, of course, comprised a great deal of that shift as they followed Strom Thurmond's lead to the GOP. Southern white women, however, were seldom mentioned—much less differentiated from non-southern white women—when it came to assessing the gender gap. In one rare case, southern white women were briefly lauded for maintaining their assumed allegiance to the newly pro-feminist Democratic Party.[83] It turns out, however, they were on their way out because southern white women are almost as conservative as southern white men. On certain issues, they perch further to the right, despite expectations that they won't or shouldn't. Removing southern white women from a national sample of white women actually drives the gender gap higher, though such regional distinctions are hardly ever made. Southern white women are often overlooked to the point that their level of support for Trump over Hillary Clinton in 2016 and their support for Brian Kemp over Stacey Abrams in the 2018 Georgia gubernatorial election is met with shock. But many were never—and still are not—feminists, and they won't vote for a woman who is one. Some even deny the ongoing existence of sex discrimination in general.

The denial mimics many whites' attitudes toward structural racism, a belief that took hold as Nixon's benign neglect of civil rights enforcement became Reagan's invitation of colorblindness. That belief underscores "The Myth of a Post-Racial America" (chapter 3), where the federal government no longer needs to ensure equal access to housing or education. Affirmative action is no longer needed in a post-racial and post-sexist America, and its continuance becomes reverse discrimination against whites and males. Feminists and people of color see through these denials, which, over the course of the Long Southern Strategy, alienated them almost completely from the GOP. Still such denials persist, at least until election season when white privilege and patriarchy are repeatedly framed as in dire threat of slipping away, which is exactly how they remain intact. They are protected by both old and new "structural mechanisms of exclusion,"[84] of which denial is one.

All are mirages. And all are products of the Long Southern Strategy to turn the South red—a strategy that continues to impact national politics. In a post-racial America, there would not be a surge in overt racism and white nationalism in reaction to the first black president. A more complex understanding of southern white women and the lack of a gender gap that results from their conservatism would have quelled the hope that a female presidential candidate would pull southern white female voters even across party lines. Few would have expected that an established history of authentic Christian fundamentalist belief would no longer be a litmus test for whether southern white evangelicals would support the Republican nominee. Such mirages appear to those for whom the white South's historically aberrant political behavior is simply too foreign or too painful. "Even yet, in the South," Lillian Smith waxes in a timely reflection from 1949, "the old signs are still over the minds of men. Custom and conscience still divide our children and southern tradition is a ghost that everyone still believes in."[85]

WHETHER OR NOT GOP leaders admitted or even recognized fully that their campaign tactics extended such loaded invitations does not matter anymore. What matters now is understanding why the long view of the Southern Strategy is important, considering why that view has been obstructed, and assessing the consequences of both its existence and its invisibility. The Long Southern Strategy did, indeed, work, but there has been a heavy cost to the deal. Beyond the myths to which it has given rise, the broad arc of the Long Southern Strategy is vital for a host of reasons, not the least of which is the way it necessitates a re-examination of some of the fundamental tenets of the fields of American political behavior and public opinion. Scholarly research investigating the voting behavior of the American electorate took a major leap forward with the advances in survey research and the resulting sophistication with which scholars were then able to assess the electorate, as seen in the 1960 publication of *The American Voter* by Angus Campbell, Philip Converse, Warren Miller, and Donald Stokes.[86] Using quantitative survey data, the authors deemed American voters surprisingly una-ware and uncomplicated, casting ballots primarily based on party identification that they simply inherited from their parents. That identification functions more as an emotional attachment, not a reasoned political decision. Once the emo-tional attachment was made, voters sought out information that confirmed what their parents and they now believed, with their party affiliation functioning as a "perceptual screen" through which they listened to voices only from their own party. All contrary evidence was discounted. Even though the authors chastised citizens for this weak justification, they nevertheless concluded that to under-stand American politics, one must study party identification because it drives everything. Writing four years before the launch of the Southern Strategy, they contended that in addition to being meaningful, party identification was self-reinforcing and thus largely stable.

In the more volatile years that followed, critics argued that the electorate was discerning, pointing to cases of upended incumbents, and highlighting critical realignments in American history. There was a need for many to believe that the progressive changes of the 1960s had forever raised the collective human con-science. And in the moment of the purple South, Norman Nie, Sidney Verba, and John Petrocik contended in *The Changing American Voter*[87] that issue positions had become important to the electorate in the two decades since Campbell, Converse, Miller, and Stokes staked their claims. Edward Carmines and James Stimson elaborated, explaining that data showed that when an issue mattered to voters, they proved knowledgeable about that particular issue,[88] and when the parties diverged on that issue, it could influence their behavior and it could spark a realignment—but all of this primarily occurred in the South.[89] Morris Fiorina offered additional nuance, arguing that voters kept a "running tally" of the things they liked and disliked among the political parties.[90] So they could appear to be irrational at times, because they may still identify with one party while voting for the candidate from the other party. Changing their party affiliation, he claimed, only occurs when the score reaches a certain level, which is why there was something critical at stake in every election over the course of decades in terms of realignment. Despite the fact that they seem to counter one another, there is truth in all these perspectives, and all are pieces to the puzzle of the red South. Party identification is the primary predictor of vote choice. It is emotional. It is inherited. It is stable until the voter encounters a dramatic threat, whether real, orchestrated, or perceived. And whichever policy issue represents that threat will be understood fully, at least through the partisan screen. If it is dangerous enough, that single issue may flip the voter, or over time it could be the sum of a Long Southern Strategy.

Yet, this picture of the Long Southern Strategy, despite connecting the dots between the work of so many important minds in the field, has proven hard to see. It is, of course, clear now that the states of the old Confederacy are awash in a sea of crimson, not just in national elections, but at the state and local levels as well. There are exceptions—Louisiana's Democratic governor, John Bel Edwards, for one. Barack Obama did pick up three southern states in 2008 (Florida, North Carolina, and Virginia) and held on to two of them in 2012, ceding North Carolina to Mitt Romney. And in 2016, Virginia proved the only southern state to give its electors to Hillary Clinton. There are signs this could change in the near future, but not because the GOP is changing; rather, it seems to be doubling down on these key elements of the Long Southern Strategy. That boldness, however, has triggered counter-movements, a "resistance," as evidenced by the nationwide Women's Marches and student protests for gun reforms. In 2018 the SBC elected its first non-fundamentalist president in nearly forty years with the help of young members.[91] There was a surge in Democratic candidate filings in southern states in the 2018 midterms, particularly by women, and as a result there were significant congressional victories. In the South, Democrats picked up nine seats in the House of Representatives—one in Georgia, one in South Carolina, two in Texas, two in Florida, and three in Virginia. Women account for seven of those nine victories. Outside of the South, however, the blue wave was much bigger.

The long view of GOP "duck hunting" and its consequences has been obstructed by, in many cases, conditions beyond anyone's control. Too often the realignment of the South with the Republican Party was considered through a snapshot of a single election. For example, in its moment, the Southern Strategy was believed by some to be an anomaly, while others denied its existence altogether. On the other hand, those scholars writing somewhere in the middle of the transformation, correctly, but often optimistically, described a purple South, which those tired of demagoguery and obstructionism hoped would signal true two-party competition in the region. Snapshot views of single elections have also prematurely announced on multiple occasions that the GOP had failed to secure its southern base. Indeed, gains made by Goldwater and Nixon were washed away by native-son Carter, and gains made by Reagan were temporarily lost to Bill Clinton, until George W. Bush, a southern white Republican, entered the arena. That ebb and flow has caused some to point to Reagan as the culmination of the Southern Strategy,[92] while others note the significance of the 1994 Republican takeover of Congress via the "Contract with America,"[93] or George W. Bush's 2000 sweep of the South,[94] the first since Reagan's rout.[95] In truth, the movement from blue to red has been a game of two steps forward and one step back, and to see the continuity of the shift requires distance and a wide-angle lens.

Without a sense of a Long Southern Strategy, more recent assessments have downplayed the distinctiveness of the South almost entirely—*The End of Southern Exceptionalism*, as Shafer and Johnson proclaim.[96] Others point to an equally red Midwest—*What's the Matter with Kansas?*, Thomas Frank asks[97]— and a newly red Rust Belt, where *The Politics of Resentment*, Katherine Cramer shows, are driving Wisconsin voters.[98] Yet, in the 2018 midterm elections, Kansas elected a female Democrat, Laura Kelly, as governor, and Wisconsin voters ousted Republican incumbent governor Scott Walker in favor of a Democratic ticket that included an African American lieutenant governor, Mandela Barnes. However, Democratic gubernatorial candidates in the South, Stacey Abrams in Georgia and Andrew Gillum in Florida—both African American—lost, al- beit by the slimmest of margins and after extensive complaints about voter suppression. Perhaps the "southernization of America," as John Egerton, Peter Applebome, Darren Duchok, and Jonathan Cowden all describe,[99] is prima- rily a southernization of the GOP, aspects of which do appeal to many in the Midwest and Wisconsin, but with limits.[100] That complexity, however, is hard to recognize, particularly when single variables are considered independently or are credited exclusively for the South's realignment with the Republican Party, including post–World War II economic growth, generational changes in the elec- torate, in-migration,[101] rising class consciousness, the development of suburbs,[102] etc. To the degree that they can be separated, each of those landmark shifts did mark a new base camp on this path to Republican ascendancy in the South, and each is a part of the story. But sometimes the whole—the multidimensional Long Southern Strategy—gets lost among the pieces.

The American National Election Studies (ANES) conducted by the University of Michigan since 1948 and considered the gold standard in academic research for understanding national voting behavior provides an opportunity to

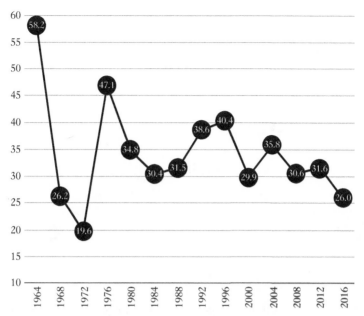

FIGURE I.1 Percent Vote for Democratic Candidate in Presidential General Election, Among Whites Who Live in the South, 1964–2012

Data are from the American National Election Study Time Series Cumulative Data File (1948–2016) available at https://electionstudies.org/.

take in that whole picture. Using the ANES cumulative file, Figure I.1 shows the percent Democratic vote in each presidential election since 1964 among white Americans who reside in one of the eleven former Confederate states. Mapping the percentage of the Democratic vote is important because in many elections there were substantive third-party candidates that often split the Republican vote. Thus, when the Republican vote is examined, it can, at times, be misleading. It dips not necessarily because of true competition between Democrats and Republicans, but because of competition on the right.

Rather than a linear shift away from voting for Democratic presidential candidates, Figure I.1 illustrates this "two steps forward, one step back" pattern: again, Nixon's support is eroded by Carter, re-established by Reagan, eroded by Clinton, and re-established by George W. Bush. Each setback came when Democrats ran a southern candidate. In fact, no Republican presidential candidate has ever won when facing a white, male, southern Democrat, except for Reagan in 1980 and George W. Bush in 2000, but of course, in that case Bush and Gore were both southerners. However, despite this incremental back-and-forth voting pattern, white southern identification with the Democratic Party is a much smoother line charting downward over the past half-century, as shown in

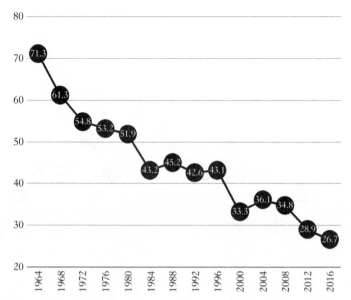

FIGURE I.2 Percent Party Identification as Democrat, Among Whites Who Live in the South, 1964–2016

Data are from the American National Election Study Time Series Cumulative Data File (1948–2016) available at https://electionstudies.org/.

Figure I.2. Whites in the South wavered on which candidate they would support, which is why the Southern Strategy had to turn into the Long Southern Strategy, taking southern white stances on race and gender and religion. As they did, the white South's seemingly unbreakable Democratic Party allegiance followed a steady path of decline.

The continuous data provided by the ANES is one of the only options to chart such a broad picture, but it too has its limits in terms of studying the transformation of southern politics. The available data, particularly in the early years of the series, may have inadvertently distorted the view. For example, the limited data may have led to underestimations of Goldwater's appeal to white southerners, which, in turn, gave credence to the Southern Strategy deniers. A closer look reveals that when the data are weighted, the 1964 ANES includes 861 whites who live in the South, but the actual number of southern whites who were surveyed was 287 (129 men and 158 women). Of those 287 southern whites, 92 men and 86 women claim to have voted in that election. The overwhelming majority (88 percent) of these southern white voters did not live in the Deep South, meaning only 21 white voters total were surveyed from the five states that went red that year. Only two white voters from Mississippi were surveyed, where, again, Goldwater won 87 percent of the vote. Over 20 percent of the sample of southern white voters were actually Texas residents in 1964, the southern state that had native-son candidate Lyndon Johnson in the race. If Deep South voters were so resentful or fearful of civil rights changes or so disillusioned with or angry at the Democrat Party that they voted for a Republican, but they are not captured in the sample, then the true strength of that angst is unknown. Moreover, that angst did not solely affect presidential vote choice; it surely clouded political attitudes in general. Tracking realignment, particularly in just one region of the country, was not the primary mission of the ANES. It was and is a first-rate national survey, and including large samples of states that may or may not be going through a major political transition (if that could even be forecast), is exceptionally costly and beyond the scope of the project. Still, despite being able to sketch a broad outline, it was hard to see how the South was changing when the starting point is fuzzy. It is made harder when the voices remain that limited. Overall, between 1952 and 2016, the average number of actual southern white voters in the ANES is 277, roughly 46 percent male, and 54 percent female, and yet these data have been the backbone of realignment scholarship.[103]

Where there are countless analyses of the what, when, and why of southern realignment, one "who" remains largely ignored.[104] Southern white women have not received much scholarly attention from political scientists—though they have fared better among sociologists, literary critics, and historians—and that too has obscured the long view. Often variables that are not significant in statistical models in quantitative political science research go overlooked. Null findings are rarely published, particularly in top journals. When analyzing the political behavior or policy positions of southern whites, gender is often one of those non-significant variables. However, it is the fact that gender is not a significant predictor of political behavior among whites in the South that makes this non-significant variable so important. It means that southern white women are often just as conservative as southern white men, which means they deserve to be part of the discussion.

White women in the South have also been overshadowed by white women in the Non-South or by men in their own backyard. The gender gap phenomenon that arose in the 1980s, for example, portrayed all white women as moving toward the Democratic Party. Or, white men in the South, such as Strom Thurmond, seemed to flip so dramatically and so quickly to the Republican Party that they captured more headlines and more scholarly attention than women. For example, as Warren Miller and J. Merrill Shank chart in *The New American Voter*, when the Southern Strategy commenced in 1964, among voters in the South, Democrats benefited from a 43-point party identification advantage among white men and a 48-point advantage among white women. By 1992, they show that Democrats still held an 11-point gender advantage among women, whereas Republicans held a 1-point advantage among men. The fact that white men had crossed the partisan line, a 44-point shift, and now favored the GOP seemed the important point. However, as their own chart indicates, white women had moved 37 points as well—a massive shift in its own right.[105]

Those numbers have a deeper problem too. Despite the fact that whites in the South, slowly and over time, threw off their Democratic Party label does not mean they embraced the Republican label wholeheartedly. Voting for Republican candidates was one thing, but the Democratic label was so intertwined with southern white identity that when they defected, many whites in the South just called themselves independents. Miller and Shank's chart looks only at party identification at the two ends of the spectrum, but there were so many in the white South who were caught in the middle of a changing political landscape. Reorienting themselves as Republicans has taken a Long Southern Strategy. Figures I.3A and I.3B report the mean party identification of white men and white women in the South from 1964 to 2016 using ANES, despite the relatively small southern samples. The scale of party identification ranges from 1, strong Democrat, to 7 strong Republican, with 4 reserved for pure independents. Once the average is above a 3.5, the group as a whole has moved into an independent range. Once it moves above 4.5, the group—white men or women in the South, in these cases—are in the GOP camp.

White men in the South, as shown in Figure I.3A, enter that independent zone in 1972, dip back slightly in 1976, and then remain there until 2000, when the average score leans Republican. White women in the South, as shown in Figure I.3B, shift into the independent range in 1984, where they remain until 2004, dipping back slightly in 2008, and then into the Republican range again in 2012. The movement of white women in the South, a full two points on average across the scale, is exactly the same as white men in the South, and thus they are an equally critical piece of the puzzle.

There is still another crucial obstruction that is difficult to describe, and it relates back to the white South's historically aberrant political behavior. The squashing of the populist impulse in the South—and later of labor unions—where the ground was ripe for an alliance of workers and agrarians, demonstrated the unrivaled power of southern identity. Interracial political and economic alliances were unsustainable, if not unimaginable, particularly under the grand bargain of whiteness. Moreover, many early union organizers were deemed Yankees or carpetbaggers and met with mistrust as outside agitators, and they did not seem to understand the paternal culture and reverence to hierarchy long embedded in southernness. Those two failures demonstrate that most white southerners have never been rational-choice economic voters, and continuing to measure them by that yardstick further distorts the view. They can desperately need access to

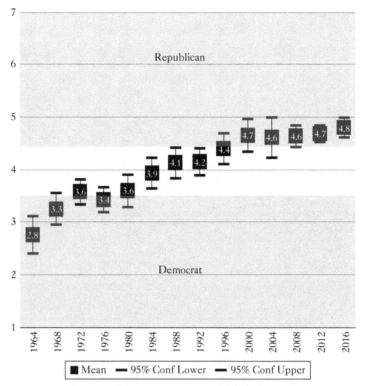

FIGURE I.3A Mean Party Identification, Among White Men Who Live in the South, 1964–2016

Data are from the American National Election Study Time Series Cumulative Data File (1948–2016) available at https://electionstudies.org/.

healthcare and yet still vote for a candidate who will repeal it. They have been rational-choice identity voters long before the phrase "identity politics" entered the scholarly or punditry vernacular. They vote for someone they perceive to be like them (or who they want to be) because the election of one of their own is their best protection for their way of life. This is why Carter's candidacy and Clinton's candidacy paused realignment. This is why the Confederacy—once synonymous with the Democratic Party—elicits empathy from many inside the Republican Party, so much so that in 2017, President Donald Trump, in trying to sway the Virginia governor's race toward GOP contender Ed Gillespie, defended maintaining Confederate memorials in public spaces as to not wipe away "heritage."[106] Even to crowds outside of the South, like one gathered in Lebanon, Ohio in 2018, Trump praised Confederate general Robert E. Lee.[107]

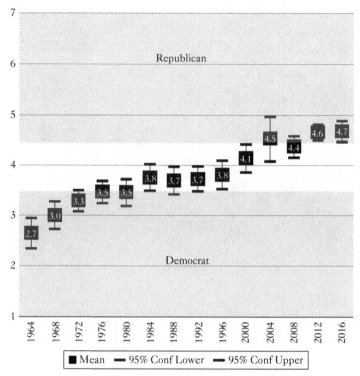

FIGURE 1.3B Mean Party Identification, Among White Women Who Live in the South, 1964-2016

Data are from the American National Election Study Time Series Cumulative Data File (1948–2016) available at https://electionstudies.org/.

Reflective of another way in which southern identity was misunderstood was the complexity ascribed to white southern voters throughout the realignment metamorphosis. Outside observers pointed to the gap between actual white southern votes for a GOP presidential contender compared to registered Republicans in the region, with the latter lagging. That too suggested some kind of nuanced thought or indecision. Others noted the tendency of white southerners to be split-ticket voters, casting ballots for a Republican presidential candidate but for Democrats in down-ticket races, or voting GOP in one election and against the GOP four years later. That inconsistency generated rigorous debate about, for example, how southerners must perceive the executive branch and the legislative branch of government differently. Joseph Aistrup has shown clearly how Republican realignment in the South has been a top-down phenomenon, with voters in the white South choosing GOP candidates for national office first, then eventually doing so at the state and local levels.[108] There are structural reasons; it takes a long time to build a Republican organization in what amounted to a one-party political region.[109] Yet, here again, southern identity can help explain this trickle-down reddening. At the national level, white voters in the South often had to choose between two non-southern candidates. When GOP nominees seemed more "southern" than their opposition, they captured more white southern votes. However, in state and local races, both candidates were southern—unless a newcomer dared to run—which meant that in order for the Republican southerner to beat the Democratic southerner, the meaning of the party labels themselves had to change. Over the course of the Long Southern Strategy, that is exactly what happened. Throughout realignment, the power of southern identity was rarely taken into consideration, and consequently, both the GOP pull in the South was often underestimated and southern white partisanship was made out to be overly complicated. In truth, for whites who proclaim themselves to be southern, *that* has been the only party that really mattered.

IT IS ESSENTIAL to note that none of these efforts to woo white southerners can be neatly divided chronologically. They ebbed and flowed and overlapped. Nor were they part of a singular, master scheme. The motivation was always the same; the techniques recycled. However, beyond Kevin Phillips's laying out the plans for the original Southern Strategy in his book *The Emerging Republican Majority* in 1969, no single architect drafted the full rendering. In that sense the word "strategy" fits only in its broadest meaning as part of this backward glance. But it was also not a naturally occurring backswing of the pendulum[110] or even an unavoidable reciprocal chain reaction.[111] It is more than "backlash politics."[112] It is *orchestrated* backlash politics. Campaigns made choices, set fires, and even poured on the gasoline if accelerant was needed, which is why the passage of time has not, in fact, extinguished such prejudice. It is kept aflame as long as it is stoked.

Perhaps most important, none of these operations captured white southern voters exclusively—another point that Phillips made and a lesson that Nixon learned watching Wallace draw crowds as far away as Wisconsin.[113] The coded campaign rhetoric attracted Americans well outside of the South, sometimes because they did not understand the code and sometimes even when they did. Privilege and patriarchy and fundamentalism, of course, have no geographical limitations. And sometimes what is heard on the surface resonates irrespective of the lack of context, particularly if it strikes an emotional chord. Fear and rage and resentment, the bread and butter of the Long Southern Strategy, often drive more people to the polls than optimism or likability or hope, no matter where they live.

To fill in some of these gaps and to sharpen the image of the current southern and national political landscapes, the contemporary data throughout are drawn primarily from the Blair Center Polls—national, post-election surveys conducted by Knowledge Networks in 2010, 2012, and 2016. The polls include an oversampling of the historically under-sampled population—particularly in rural areas—living in the geographic South, defined here as the eleven states of the former Confederacy. When weighted, these data offer a more accurate image of the region with all of its variation, as well as a comprehensive look at the country at large as a basis for comparison. Moreover, where there is limited variation, such as between southern white women and southern white men, rather than being ignored, that sameness is shown to be of critical importance, particularly within the context of what has been written about southern white women beyond the walls of political science.

For insight regarding religious attitudes, data from the Blair Center Polls are supplemented by the Baylor Religion Surveys conducted in 2007 and 2010 by the Baylor Institute for Studies of Religion in partnership with the Gallup Organization. The geographic divisions in the Baylor Religion Surveys are based on the US Census Bureau, meaning that their South includes five states (Oklahoma, West Virginia, Delaware, Kentucky, Oklahoma, as well as the District of Columbia) beyond the former states of the Confederacy. Though Baylor's "South" region is broader than the measure in the Blair Center Poll, the Baylor Religion Surveys are such an extensive probing of American religious beliefs that the insight they offer far exceeds any cost of this inconsistency. Finally, because they too provide such rich information, the Southern Focus Polls, conducted by the University of North Carolina's Odum Institute for Research in Social Science, also supplement the Blair Center Poll data. Starting in 1991, Larry Griffin fielded the Southern Focus Polls twice a year from 1991 to 2001 (19 polls in total), asking demographic and public opinion questions geared toward understanding southern culture and history. The topics covered in each poll varied greatly, and, as a whole, they are not primarily focused on political or public policy attitudes. The Southern Focus Polls do define the geographic South as the eleven former Confederate states, and they also consistently include another extremely important variable—southern identity.

Measuring region by identity may be fairly common for sociologists unpacking sociocultural constructs, but it is somewhat of a radical notion in terms of analyzing American political behavior. After all, folks vote where they live, and electoral maps are exactly that—maps. But the Long Southern Strategy was both geographical and psychological. Thus, the Blair Center Polls measure the "South" as a place and "southern" as a personal identity. According to the 2016 Blair Center Poll, of all white Americans who identify as southern, 77.5 percent currently reside in the geographic South and 22.5 percent reside beyond its borders. Narrowing to within those borders exclusively, the percentage of whites who identify as southern and who live in the South stands at 44.6 percent. And here is but one example of why that matters: among whites who reside in one of the eleven states of the former Confederacy, 55.3 percent identify as Republican, 20 percent are Independents, and 24.7 percent report being Democrats. However, among whites who reside in the South and who also identify as southern, the partisan breakdown shifts to 69.6 percent Republican, 14.3 percent Independent, and 16.1 percent Democrat. The same reddening happens for whites who identify as southern but live outside of the South.

It turns out that asking respondents how strongly they identify as a "southerner" and comparing whites who do with those who do not, presents a pretty striking picture of two Americas, in much the same way that partisanship and ideology do. It is important to note also that southern identity is not exclusive to whites. However, the label means something very different to people of color[114] because southern identity has been politicized among whites by the Long Southern Strategy. For that reason, in terms of political behavior and public opinion, its influence among whites must be considered independently. Southern white identity remains more than a regional affiliation, as Glen Feldman insisted; rather, "it is an ethos, a milieu, a mentalité, a worldview,"[115] and it transcends the Mason-Dixon line. Sociologists, anthropologists, historians, and even some cultural geographers as well, including George Tindall, Lewis Killian, Carl Degler, John Shelton Reed, James Cobb, Charles Reagan Wilson, Wilbur Zelinsky, and countless others, have made that point for more than four decades. Carole Hill, who characterized the "solid South" as a "mental construct," speculated in 1977 that "the distinctiveness of the South may lie not in its empirical differences from other regions, but in its unique belief system."[116]

THEREIN LIES THE key to calculating the true cost of the Long Southern Strategy, and this is why: to win those voters, the GOP had to do more than take the right policy stance. They had to infiltrate that system, endorse those truths, attack those foes, and promise to preserve the way things should be—the southern white edition. By definition, white southern identity is rooted in opposition to something or someone else. Whiteness is meaningless without blackness. Confederate is meaningless without Yankee. George Wallace, who pounded his fists on this substructure of the southern white psyche, described a very clear "them" to which his audiences did not want to belong—a technique called "positive polarization."[117] Hippie agitators, pinhead intellectuals, and liberal socialists all became emblematic of who he was not. Whether they liked Wallace did not matter; he became their "us" in an "us vs. them" dichotomy deeply familiar to white southerners. That rhetorical style and its intensity was not lost on GOP strategists, as it became their pitch in the battles between feminists and anti-feminists, makers and takers, believers and heretics, patriots and traitors. The more that is believed to be at stake, the more unified the "us" and the more demonized the "them," and the more the threat is repeated, the more it is believed. Advantages for the other side equaled disadvantages for the home team in the zero-sum game that has always been the essence of southern white identity.

As team allegiance—to whiteness, patriarchy, or fundamentalist Christianity— grows stronger through rivalry, so too does the demand for total loyalty. Any changes to the rules, so to speak, whether by court or Congress, were met by many southern whites with creative noncompliance, or massive resistance, or both until directly enforced. Compromise, after all, was a slippery slope, and absolutism the only anchor. And yet there were moderates, a majority of whom were silent, who did not want to seem resistant to progress or to be judged by others or even by themselves. To remain loyal, those folks often needed deniability, a "Great Alibi,"[118] as Robert Penn Warren called it. Coded rhetoric provided political cues without provoking rebuke or even one's own conscience. Just as it had done during the southern atrocities of lynchings and slavery,[119] noted anthropologist John Dollard, who studied the South in the 1930s, this moral passivity or non-engagement enabled extremism. There were only a handful of people in any given community who could, Dollard claimed, actually bring themselves to do the lynching. But there were multitudes who were content to watch. If they were not content, they were, at the least, not outraged enough or too fearful of the social consequences to protest. Yet by their silence, sadism became their spokesman, while the rest of the country—and the world, for that matter— observed such strange fruit in disbelief. That kind of extremism, even when only rhetorical, further entrenches absolutism, which then silences moderation, which then amplifies zealotry, a repeating cycle through which southern whites have too often staved off progress in the region. So choosing to chase southern white electors means racing to the polar end and dragging the party there too, until the middle cannot hold. Because of those historic decisions, GOP candidates are "An Echo, Not a Choice" (Conclusion), and voters have to pick sides—"you're either for it, or you're against it," as Wallace said[120]—in the latest battle of what has been an ongoing cultural civil war.[121]

Such absolutism was also reflected in the way that white southerners maintained their power via top-down control without compromise. Those most likely to challenge that hierarchy internally were made to feel like they were connected to those at the top. They had the same culture, or the same enemy, or the same skin color. They were both gentlemen or rebels or agrarians or they attended the same church. They might all be natives to the county or their parents had been. They were all superior to the black man and, of course, they were the king of their castle, no matter how humble it may be. Whatever the common ground, if promoted enough, it created an illusion of common opportunities, even if only aspirational, whereby threats to those opportunities became threats to them all. So powerful was the illusion that it trumped class alliances, even though fidelity often meant voting against one's economic self-interest,[122] sometimes in ignorance, sometimes by choice, depending on how deeply the voter needed to believe in that common "us." So just as folks who did not own slaves or profit financially from slavery took up the collective cause of the Confederacy, so too did many southern whites vote for wealthy, "maker" candidates who wanted to cut the federal programs on which so many rely—from Social Security to welfare to food stamps to healthcare subsidies—rather than self-identifying as a "taker." And if that program was portrayed as leveling the playing field between whites and blacks or even men and women, or if it was the signature accomplishment of an African American leader or advocated for by a feminist, then opposing it— as irrational as it may seem—becomes part of a larger campaign to defend the southern white way of life, even as it pragmatically makes daily life that much harder. Poor southern whites have long been conditioned to forfeit a personal battle in the service of winning an imagined war from which they do not benefit.

Thus, the GOP's success is not solely the result of the policy positions that the party took on civil rights enforcement or the ERA or on the separation of church and state. It was also the way they did it, selling those positions with a southern accent, so to speak. The Long Southern Strategy had to have both substance and a not-so-new style. To that end, Republican candidates didn't just campaign down South, they blended into the southern landscape so completely as to seem as if they had always been there. So much so that in an August 2017 national poll conducted by the Economist and YouGov, the majority of all Americans surveyed (54 percent) now report believing that Confederate monuments are symbols of "southern pride," not "symbols of racism" (26 percent). The rest claim they don't know. The fact that a majority of whites do not know or do not acknowledge the racist history of many of these monuments proves a critical point made by Rebecca Solnit in her article "The American Civil War Didn't End. And Trump Is a Confederate President." Solnit writes: "We never cleaned up after the Civil War, never made it an anathema, as the Germans have since the second world war, to support the losing side."[123] She's right; for those very reasons, southern white identity has been both politicized and nationalized. Among Republicans, specifically, the "southern pride" believers swell to 84 percent.[124] They may not all identify as southern, but Republicans in general are sympathetic to the lost cause. The duck hunt turned out to be a massacre. The Long Southern Strategy not only tapped into racial and gender-role and evangelical angst,[125] it perpetuated it, sometimes even constructing it whole cloth. Over time, that made the party southern, not in terms of place, but in its vision, in its demands, in its rhetoric, and in its spirit. And that has changed American politics.

PART I

The Grand Bargain

*What is the Southern Strategy? It is this. It says to the
South: Let the poor stay poor, let your economy trail the nation, forget about decent homes and medical care for all your
people, choose officials who will oppose every effort to benefit
the many at the expense of the few—and in return, we will try
to overlook the rights of the black man...*

—GEORGE MCGOVERN[1]

The racial legacy of the Long Southern Strategy extends beyond the use of coded
language, beyond the dog whistles of states' rights and local control, and beyond
the issues of busing and affirmative action. The practice of trading on southern
white racial hostility for votes was not limited to Barry Goldwater in 1964 or
Richard Nixon in 1968 and 1972, or even to Ronald Reagan in 1980 and 1984.
Rather, the decision to chase white southern voters in order to build a new
Republican coalition was not only intentional, strategic, and effective, but it
was also unabating. Over time, this repeated choice turned the Republican Party
into a safe space for white racial anger, resentment, anxiety, and denial, much of
which it promoted or even manufactured. In doing so, it allowed those feelings
to persist, spread, and unite many white southerners and Americans alike in their
common whiteness. This partisan race-baiting has taken different forms with
varying degrees of intensity, prioritized by some GOP presidential candidates
much higher than others. What began as Goldwater's depiction of federal enforcement of racial equality as government overreach morphed into Nixon's benign neglect of integration policies, was translated by Reagan into proclamations
of colorblindness, and now survives in the denouncement of entitlements or
immigrants or Muslims or any group deemed racially or ethnically "other."

Despite the abstruse language, "the words and deed of the Southern Strategy
have hidden meanings to adherents."[2] Those words and deeds, no matter how
much deniability any coded language may have provided, were still crystal-clear

to many southern whites. Nevertheless, the real meaning was never lost on African Americans, three-fourths of whom would call Reagan a racist by the end of his terms.[3] Now, in the aftermath of the two-term administration of the first African American president, such coded language seems to have fallen by the wayside. That is, in part, because the vast majority of the South is currently dominated by the GOP at the national and state level; therefore, the game is no longer about making inroads, but rather about keeping the base fired up so as to not cede any ground. It is important to note that there have been many Republicans in recent years who have advocated for a return to the pro–civil rights campaign strategy of Nelson Rockefeller, who Richard Nixon defeated for the GOP presidential nomination in 1968 and who was appointed vice president by Gerald Ford after Nixon's resignation. These Republicans have promoted greater minority outreach, believing that doing so is tantamount to the party's survival in a rapidly diversifying population.[4] However, *Real Clear Politics* analyst Sean Trende, in his analysis of the 2012 election, contended that the GOP had lost some white voters and that the party could be more competitive if those voters were brought back into the fold.[5] According to Jonathan Chait of *New York Magazine*, "a handful interpreted Trende's analysis as a blueprint, even salvation." Specifically, Chait notes that Senator Jeff Sessions, his aide, Stephen Miller, and Steve Bannon met and decided that "the path to Republican dominance lay not in tamping down racial polarization but in ramping it up."[6] In 2016, their vessel for that message was Donald Trump. During both Trump's campaign and his administration, the appeals to white racial angst have exploded in terms of frequency and intensity, including renewed calls for "law and order"[7]—most notably against the "threats" of Black Lives Matter[8] and Mexican "rapists,"[9] among others. What was coded into fundamental tenets of GOP ideology is unmasked in efforts to delegitimize everything from Barack Obama's health care legislation to his birth certificate, all while building walls to protect Americans from "bad hombres."[10] The road to this point has been long, but it has also been consistently trod.

All of these appeals function as examples of strategic racism, which Ian Haney López defines as "purposeful efforts to use racial animus as leverage to gain material wealth, political power, or heightened social standing."[11] Such strategic racism is the foundation of white southern culture, politics, and life, not only during Antebellum slavery, but also via the convict lease system, Jim Crow, the ongoing mass incarceration of African Americans, and the renewed fights against disenfranchisement. The desire to maintain the "grand bargain"[12] of white power is most critical in the Deep South, where the African American population is the largest and, thus, most threatening to the white racial hierarchy. These were the states who cast electors for the Dixiecrats in 1948 after President Harry Truman decided to desegregate the military by executive order and chose to speak to the NAACP. So it is no surprise that Goldwater's first use of strategic racism won him five of those Deep South states where the stakes of civil rights seemed the highest.[13] A half century may have passed, yet in 2012, while 96 percent of African Americans voters in Mississippi cast ballots for Obama, 90 percent of white voters in Mississippi did not.[14] That kind of power—not just to flip a state, but to keep it, even dominate it—does not arise from one policy position, nor is it the doing of one candidate. It grows when tended to vigilantly over the long haul from seeds planted deep in the soil.

The key to winning the geographic South permanently was to understand southern whiteness and to cater to its fundamental elements—everything from supremacy to inferiority to alienation. In his famous, or perhaps infamous, assessment, *The Emerging Republican Majority*, Kevin Phillips argued that the 1968 candidacy of George Wallace shed light on the path forward for the GOP. "Most of the poor whites whom Wallace broke loose from the Democrats," he concluded, "have lined up against newly enfranchised Negroes just as they did in the somewhat comparable Reconstruction Era of a century ago." That threat to southern white identity, demonstrated by the "alienation of white Wallace voters," he projected, "is likely to persist."[15] That alienation was not just from the Democratic Party, but from the media who they believed "looked down" on them, particularly as it covered the Civil Rights Movement. Underneath "The Not-So-New Southern Racism" (chapter 1) lurked a familiar "mood of being hell-hacked and needing to forget, of being the only Americans to know (until 1970) what it was like to lose a war."[16] Thus, when Nixon's administration—which the Southern Regional Council assessed as having reversed progress on civil rights[17]—and the nation along with him, "lost its commitment to the priority of desegregation, the white southerners felt their position was being justified."[18] Many believed their white supremacy was being protected and that their way of life was being endorsed. Recent research even shows that southern counties with high participation rates in the Ku Klux Klan fled to the GOP in greater numbers during those first years of the Long Southern Strategy.[19]

However, holding on to these new converts and recruiting more required that the threat to white supremacy be constantly reasserted, particularly after the initial shock waves of the Civil Rights Movement had subsided. The threat to one's way of life, as life changed, had to morph into a threat not only to whiteness itself, but also to the specific advantages it provided. Southern historian George Tindall did not believe that the GOP would be successful at breaking white southern allegiance to the party of "their daddies, their granddaddies, and assuredly their great-granddaddies,"[20] suggesting that the "tug between voting one's prejudices and voting one's pocketbook" would show that

"Democratic loyalties die hard."[21] However, whiteness itself is a wage,[22] and the Long Southern Strategy successfully married the two. Federal expenditures on social programs were packaged as a zero-sum game, whereby African Americans, deemed as undeserving, threatened white advantages. Political strategist Lee Atwater highlighted this dynamic in his recovered interview with political scientist Alexander Lamis when he asserted that "non-producers"[23] would help to grow the conservative base.

Though Reagan is often credited with officiating the marriage of white racial and economic anxiety, it continued long after his administration. In the wake of the 1994 GOP congressional midterm landslides, new Speaker of the House Newt Gingrich of Georgia often contrasted the rising white southern suburbs against the urban centers of the region. He did not base his claims on standard demographic markers. "The pristine work ethic of Cobb," his home county, was set in opposition to "the 'welfare state' values of Atlanta, a pitch," notes Earl and Merle Black, "as old as the South."[24] Federal expenditures were personalized as funded by the tax dollars of the "producers," a sentiment still promoted on conservative cable news programs. Bill O'Reilly, former host at Fox News, for example, told his audience, "I don't believe that my money and everybody's money who's worked for a living should be going to people who are on crack. . . . Yet it continues and continues into trillions of entitlement money that goes right down the rat hole."[25] So powerful was this threat to white privilege at the hands of government programs, that by 1999, Martin Gilens finds that "the perception of blacks as lazy is consistently the most powerful predictor of white Americans' opposition to welfare."[26] So relentless was the framing of this black and, eventually, Latino threat against "Southern White Privilege" (chapter 2) that new claims of discrimination targeting whites popped up in countless courtrooms and on websites and in chatrooms.[27] Such claims of unfair treatment had long been part of southern white identity. The punishing Yankee has been replaced by the politically correct mass media, by liberals, or by big government. White southerners were victims in a narrative of oppression many knew intimately—just from the other side of the oppression. The language associated with what is often referred to by whites as "reverse racism" was even co-opted from civil rights battles.

In addition to efforts to galvanize southern white voters by appealing to their anger or fear, or to reframe whiteness as the subject of oppression as opposed to the subjugator, the Long Southern Strategy mimicked the southern white proclivity toward denial, which became more important as Jim Crow receded into the background of American memory. Promotion of colorblindness ignored racism altogether while sounding wholly egalitarian. Convincing voters that racism was no longer a problem was welcomed among white southerners who were eager to move past race. When scholars, specifically, started measuring what is called "Symbolic

Racism" or "Racial Resentment" among respondents, what they really found was a widespread belief in "The Myth of a Post-Racial America" (chapter 3). So prevalent was the belief and so fundamentally tied to the GOP, that after 1994, it is predictive of partisanship in the region. If you subscribe to the notion that African Americans have "gotten enough," as one of the questions asks, then you are likely a Republican.[28] The colorblindness phase of the Long Southern Strategy, much like Nixon's benign neglect, halts progress not because programs and regulations are unfair, but because they are unnecessary. In the wake of Barack Obama's election, such rhetoric intensified dramatically, with any efforts toward leveling the playing field between racial and ethnic groups or any allusions to structural racism routinely dismissed while a reactionary backlash was encouraged. Rather, after Obama took office, over half of Americans reported that race relations between blacks and whites had actually worsened,[29] debunking the myth of post-racialism.

The politics of denial were not limited to assessments of ongoing racial disparities. Republican leaders, with few exceptions, have repeatedly denied that a Southern Strategy ever existed or continues to exist. Former senate majority leader Trent Lott, for example, once met with the revamped White Citizens' Council and denied knowing its racist past.[30] Republican consultant Pat Buchanan wrote a memo to Nixon in 1971 proposing that bumper stickers promoting African American Democratic presidential and vice-presidential contenders should be "spread out in the ghettoes of the country"[31] to drive white voters to the GOP. Michael Steele, former Republican National Committee chairman and an African American, would only say that the GOP had not reached out to black voters.[32] Donald Trump insisted that "the African Americans love me."[33] Even Nixon claimed that his "administration has no Southern Strategy, but rather a national strategy which, for the first time in modern times includes the South rather than excludes the South from full and equal participation in national affairs,"[34] which is, in and of itself, a southern strategy that harkens back to the notion of a mistreated South.

Goldwater sketched the possibilities of a then unnamed Long Southern Strategy in his journal in 1953 when he wrote about the potential partnership between the midwestern and western Republicans and southern white Democrats. "I sense here a realignment," he noted. For the New Deal Democrats, he observed, "the dictates of the stronger minority groups are felt in almost every decision they make, in almost every debate they enter." That, he knew, would destroy the Democratic coalition. "I think," he concluded, "it is going to develop as one of the major issues in the future and that will be the federal government against the states and individuals, and it should be an interesting one to pursue."[35] Only in 2005, after the region was solidly red but before Obama loomed on the horizon, Ken Mehlman, another former RNC chairman, apologized publicly for the Southern

Strategy, but only for the 1960s version.[36] Yet it is the longer version that matters, not because it is interesting to pursue, but because its legacy of racialized anger-baiting, fear-baiting, denial, and the protection of white supremacy and privilege, all in the service of a favorable Republican electoral map, is much more damaging than that for which Mehlman apologized.

I

The Not-So-New Southern Racism

Writ large, the Southern strategy sought to drum up white resentment toward the "other" in American society, i.e., minorities, and present the Republican Party as the institution that was on the side of the resentful.

—IAN REIFOWITZ[1]

IN THE SPRING of 1988, Republican strategist Lee Atwater assembled focus groups at the mall in Paramus, New Jersey, hoping to find a way out of the 17-point deficit plaguing his candidate, then vice president George H. W. Bush, in the presidential contest against Democratic nominee Michael Dukakis. Atwater's idea, which he was there to test, was sparked by a debate comment made by Dukakis's Democratic challenger, Senator Al Gore, in the days leading up to the New York primary. Gore criticized Governor Dukakis for permitting "weekend passes for convicted criminals," a furlough program aimed at rehabilitation that Dukakis conceded had been terminated. According to Sidney Blumenthal, at that time a *Washington Post* journalist covering the election, the remark went largely unnoticed except to the Bush campaign's research director, Jim Pinkerton. "I thought to myself," noted Pinkerton, "This is incredible . . . it totally fell into our lap."[2] Atwater, an expert in southern politics, along with Bush campaign media director Roger Ailes,[3] knew exactly how to keep the GOP's Southern Strategy going. Take a black prisoner, in this case Willie Horton, accused of committing a violent crime while on furlough and use fear of "the very scary looking, disheveled, wild-eyed black man"[4] to portray Dukakis as soft on crime. The focus groups told Atwater what he wanted to hear: "Tell Dukakis voters about Willie Horton and they stop being Dukakis voters," and if it worked in New Jersey, then the white South would prove putty in Atwater's hands.

White southern identity was constructed on the backs of such Willie Horton imagery, with white power necessary to control some manifestation of black threat for centuries. There was, however, a moment of hope in the years following the victories of the Civil Rights Movement. A reconstructed white South seemed possible, perhaps primarily because federal legislation ending Jim Crow

had seemed so impossible. If segregation could fall, then maybe the consciousness of southern segregationists could rise at the very least to mirror the rest of
the country. The sociology journals first noticed the shift in research published
in the 1970s and 1980s. Studies such as those conducted by Glen Firebaugh and
Kenneth Davis, Harold Schuman and Lawrence Bobo, and Steven Tuch,[5] among
others, did not suggest that southern white racist attitudes had vanished, but that
they were no worse—not distinct—from non-southern white racist attitudes.
Moreover, based primarily on cohort analysis, research began to suggest that
among younger white southerners, the racist tide had turned. Leading southern
sociologist John Shelton Reed concluded in his 1993 book *Surveying the South*
that "the differences in racial attitudes between white southerners and other
white Americans are now differences only of degree, and of relatively small degree at that."[6] Even as late as 2001, Byron D'andra Orey claimed in the *American
Review of Politics* that "to be sure, the South no longer serves as the haven for
racist demagogues and the home of Jim Crow laws. Similar to the rest of the
country, overt racism is no longer tolerated in this region."[7]

The waning of overt or what political scientists have called "Old-Fashioned
Racism" to levels consistent outside of the South seemed to many a radical step
forward for a region built upon and devoted to white supremacy. Even as social
scientists developed new theories of indirect racism, including Racial Resentment,
racial threat, Ethnocentrism, status threat, authoritarianism, neo-conservatism,
and social desirability, to name a few,[8] the notion that racism functioned differently now carried a note of optimism. Yet, masking these attitudes does not
make them less egregious or any less dangerous. To be fair, scholars, for the most
part, intended only to deconstruct the way in which "new racism" worked and its
impact on a post–Jim Crow country. James Glaser even spliced "Racio-political
attitudes" from traditional measures of prejudice, separating individual beliefs
from political preferences;[9] others, however, question the notion that they can
be separated in the first place. So this dissection, as necessary as it may have been,
obscured the forest for the trees. Because it turns out that white Americans, and
even white southerners, may have been less willing to cop to beliefs in racial
stereotypes or overt racism, but white superiority once planted has proven to be
perennial.

In their new book, *Deeply Divided: Racial Politics and Social Movements
in Post-War America*, Doug McAdams and Karino Kloos point to the current
blooms. They dismiss the Tea Party, cable news networks, and even Obama's 2008
victory as catalysts of contemporary American partisan polarization—"our present morass," they call it. Harkening back to the groundbreaking work on the
political evolution of race by Edward Carmines and James Stimson,[10] McAdams
and Kloos argue that the civil rights victories of the 1960s actually "spawned a

powerful national 'white resistance' countermovement."[11] And they were writing long before Donald Trump announced his candidacy for the 2016 election. While this countermovement surely blanketed the country as a whole, white southerners were primed by history and needled by the GOP's Long Southern Strategy not just in the 1960s when Barry Goldwater and Richard Nixon went "hunting where the ducks are," but in every decade since. These racial "dog whistles" functioned at a psychological level, using coded language as an end-around of public displays of overt prejudice, tapping and even breathing life into the "new racism" in all of its varied explanations. Moreover, it worked particularly well in the South because despite the shifts in public rhetoric, white superiority remained the foundation upon which the entire southern house was built. The racial arm of the Long Southern Strategy tugged at not just one aspect of personal identity but two: whiteness and southernness—two cosmologies that share a common structure.

Neither whiteness nor southernness has a definable essence. Both remain not only socially constructed, but also, exist only in opposition to an "other"—an "other" that shifts and moves over time.[12] Of all of the scholarship on whiteness, Ruth Frankenberg's 1993 definition remains the clearest. Drawing on the feminist scholarship of Nancy Hartsock, Frankenberg frames whiteness as a "standpoint," a location "from which white people look at ourselves, at others, and at society."[13] Therefore, whiteness can morph constantly depending on where one stands and in which direction one is looking. Ever elusive, both whiteness and southernness are so pliant that they can be molded by politicians. Over time, southern whiteness, in addition to being constructed in opposition to blackness, has stood against a pantheon of shifting others, including northern troops, the teaching of evolution, industrialization, union organizers, and the intervention of the federal government in general. The list, ever expanding, created a collective sense of persecution and a perception of victimhood.[14] Civil rights legislation, a foe to both southernness and whiteness, entrenched the two mutually reinforcing vantage points, making the labels almost indistinguishable and bonding those who wore them in a common defense.

The production of a common enemy, from war to segregation to politics, is how southern white supremacy is manipulated and politicized over and over again, and it is one of the key ways in which the Long Southern Strategy effectively launched a realignment, the impact of which remains as powerful as ever. The coded racial rhetoric—the "dog whistles"—both subtle and unsubtle polarized the parties, not just in the 1960s but exponentially during the campaigns and administrations of Ronald Reagan and George W. Bush, and even under the leadership of Donald Trump. Now, well into the twenty-first century, five of the top six issues on which Republicans and Democrats are most polarized—as indicated in the Pew Research Center's 1987–2012 "Trends in American Values" study— are rooted in maintaining white racial dominance. They include opposition to the social safety net, labor unions, federal equal opportunity programs, and immigration, as well as disagreement on the size and scope of government.[15] Four years after this study and only months prior to the 2016 election, Reuters found that Trump's supporters, specifically, were more likely to hold negative views of African Americans.[16]

However, "dog whistles" are not just heard; they are felt. And coded language, and stories about black criminals on furlough, do not speak to a physical place, but to—as Benedict Anderson proposed—an imagined one as well.[17] The "new racism" and realignment research has centered almost exclusively on the geographic South, as was and still is common practice. Nevertheless, emotions shape identity. And identity persists, at times irrationally, beyond economic concerns, an expression of unspoken fear and unmanageable anger. As recently as 2011, Pew released a report investigating southern identity and—perhaps the greatest of all race-based campaigns—the American Civil War. Whites who identify as southern are still significantly more likely to cite states' rights as the source of Confederate motivation, to respond positively to the Confederate flag, and to deem contemporary politicians praising Confederate leaders as appropriate.[18] One hundred and fifty years later, southern white identity still burns red hot, fueled by partisan messaging intended to stoke the fire. Different party label. The not-so-new southern racism.

THE SOUTHERN STRATEGY and the "new racism" scholarship had one thing in common. Both reflected an understanding that the nature of white racism had changed in the aftermath of the Civil Rights Movement. Republican strategists had to reframe racial issues in order to let white southerners "vote their conscience on defensible grounds while retaining the antiquated and indefensible traditions,"[19] and "new racism" studies attempted to understand how this dynamic worked. The operating assumption, however, was that the tempering of public, unmasked prejudice reflected a positive and major change in American, and more specifically, southern politics. Indirect racism seemed not as bad as direct racism. Emerging scholarship in the late 1990s even began probing for implicit, subconscious racism. Project Implicit, founded by researchers at Harvard, the University of Virginia, and the University of Washington, created an online test that prompts participants to match words with faces. Both the content (which positive and negative words the respondent matches to white and black faces), as well as the speed at which the associations are made, comprise an implicit bias score and direction.[20] Similar techniques, including the Implicit

Association Test, the theory of evaluative priming, and the Affect Misattribution procedure, are all aimed at unearthing buried prejudices.[21]

Yet the notion of implicit bias has more significant political repercussions. Political correctness, rather than being the first step toward an egalitarian society, may have just covered up racial animus, which burrowed privately and safely in the subconscious mind, providing deniability while resentment grew. Thus, it was no longer necessary to mention that Willie Horton was black, rather only to show his image repeatedly, recount his crimes, and call for law and order. In fact, Lee Atwater "denied that the menacing image for Horton was an appeal to racial animus, especially in the South," claiming, as did other Republicans, that they'd have been "just as happy if their villain were white."[22]

This buried racism, misleading on the surface, can be reinforced by political messaging. It remains capable of responding to dog whistles, even silent ones that can only be heard at a psychological frequency. If threatened, it is still poised to reemerge at any given moment. Thus, it should come as no surprise that in 2013, political scientist Michael Tesler, writing in the *Journal of Politics*, marked the resurgence of Old-Fashioned Racism in the wake of the Obama presidency.[23] Gauged most often by a scale of three questions, Old-Fashioned Racism— sometimes called "Jim Crow racism" due to the historical time when racial stereotypes dominated the public landscape—asks respondents to indicate how hard-working, intelligent, and trustworthy they think various racial groups are. Tesler finds an increase in white Americans who are willing to confirm these previously declining racial stereotypes of blacks as lazy, unintelligent, and untrustworthy, and that Old-Fashioned Racism significantly predicted opposition to Obama in 2008. Moreover, Tesler demonstrates that statistically Old-Fashioned Racism is related to party identification (as Republican), was a strong determinant of 2010 midterm voting preferences, and helps to explain white respondents' change in party identification from Independent or Democrat to Republican from 2006 to 2011.

Maybe Old-Fashioned Racism, built on the fundamental notion of white supremacy, has been resurrected, catalyzed by the election of the first African American president. White supremacy groups are, indeed, surging throughout the country. Stormfront.org, the leading website for white supremacist activity, has seen its membership jump from 5,000 in 2002 to 286,000 one decade later. The Southern Poverty Law Center now counts 160 active Ku Klux Klan chapters.[24] That being said, critical race theorist Frances Lee Ansley is quick to define supremacy broadly, as not to limit the association only to extremist groups: "I refer instead to a political, economic, and cultural system in which whites overwhelmingly control power and material resources." This dynamic, Ansley finds, is "daily reenacted across a broad array of institutions and social settings."[25] In

"Rethinking White Supremacy," David Gillborn reaches a similar conclusion after analyzing two case studies—that "racism can operate through the accepted and mundane processes."[26] That is why it can so easily be hidden in politics.

Or maybe white supremacist attitudes have been there all along, masked by calls for candidates who were tough on crime, so that whites could be protected from the Willie Hortons of the world (whom an anonymous George H. W. Bush campaign staffer called "a big black rapist"[27]) or disguised by language attacking welfare dependency as rewarding laziness among African Americans. "We have reaped from these programs," announced Nixon in his acceptance speech for the 1968 Republican nomination, "an ugly harvest of frustrations, violence and failure across the land."[28] White superiority, after all, is a tough expectation to cast aside, particularly for many white southerners, or so it seems. Scholars like Josh Adams and Vincent J. Roscigno argue that the Internet has actually facilitated the rise of supremacist groups by linking social threats and creating a "collective identity"[29] for many white supremacy advocates. Moreover, Michael Kimmel, author of *Angry White Men*, highlights the increasingly rural nature of these "far-right groups."[30] Of course, both collective identity and rural isolation are characteristic of the South. Yet others, such as Desmond S. King and Stephen G. N. Tuck, contend that the white supremacist order that was reestablished in the post-Reconstruction South was not confined to regional borders, but rather characterized the country at-large. By "de-centering the South" as the hub of white supremacy, King and Tuck seek to explain the racial violence that breaks out in the North during the Red Summer of 1919 and during the late-1960s riots over housing and busing accommodations.[31]

It is a fair point. White supremacy has never been exclusive to white southerners. Perhaps they have just had unapologetic spokesmen. Antebellum southern writer and US Ambassador to Italy Thomas Nelson Page, for example, could and did champion racial hierarchy publicly, professing to "the absolute and unchangeable superiority of the white race—a superiority not due to any mere adventitious circumstances, such as superior education and other advantages during some centuries, but an inherent and essential superiority, based on superior intellect, virtue, and constancy."[32] Supremacy to Page was innate, primal, and, thus, unquestioned. The absolute, almost divinity of southern white superiority caused it to be ingrained fully in every public institution and rigidly protected in private life in a comprehensive manner that was lived and performed every day. Therefore, it was not just talk (which might have been easier to shake). Moreover, although Jim Crow existed beyond the confines of the Mason-Dixon Line, in no other region was the superiority of whiteness so systematically codified into modern law. From black codes to state constitutions, legalized white supremacy underscored the disenfranchisement, segregation, and oppression of African

Americans in the South. The effort remains ongoing, most notably in the passage of contemporary voter identification laws. "If you know the history," claims the North Carolina NAACP president, Rev. William Barber, "you understand why every North Carolinian ought to be sick to their stomach."[33]

Beyond the institution of slavery, it is this codification—the de jure racism—to which scholars point as the source of southern distinctiveness. However, there is another southern experience, more recent and yet too often overlooked, that contributes to the steadfast, seemingly immutable, belief in white superiority. For when the legal trusses of southern whiteness were dismantled by fresh Supreme Court interpretations of centuries-old Constitutional amendments and by federal civil rights legislative initiatives, the GOP propped it up. In no other region did Republican politicians consistently appeal to racial anxiety and fears for decades in order to realign white southern voters with their party. Mimicking homegrown third-party presidential candidate and governor of Alabama George Wallace, the Long Southern Strategy framed inequity as the result of minority weakness, which, in turn, championed white superiority without saying a word.

Just as Jim Crow translated the white supremacy of slavery into the language of the twentieth century, so too did the Long Southern Strategy carry it to modern audiences, protecting a belief system that should have long been abandoned. And so it makes sense that the political change that Obama represented would activate bolder expressions of white supremacy, as Tesler noted, particularly in the South where it has never been allowed to die. Illustrations of this resurrected brazen prejudice are not limited to scholarly articles. From Mississippi judges using the "N-word,"[34] to Texas students flashing white power signs at football games,[35] to elementary teachers in Georgia using references to slavery in math word problems ("if Frederick got two beatings per day, how many beatings would he get in one week?"[36]), to more collective expressions such as Ku Klux Klan flyers circulating in Selma, Alabama, on the same day as the 2015 anniversary march[37]—all are examples of public, unmasked racism that still mark, sometimes literally, southern life. In December 2013, media outlets reported on two banners that were hung on interstate 640 in Knoxville, Tennessee, that read, "Diversity is a code word for White Genocide."[38] In Harrison, Arkansas, a billboard sponsored by the Ku Klux Klan that proclaimed, "It is not racist to love your people," was finally taken down in September 2017.[39] Funding for the billboard came from donations solicited on Klan website *www.whiteprideradio.com* with the tagline "the voice of white resistance!"[40] Additionally, Floating Sheep, a group of geocoding academic experts, mapped the racist tweets—comments such as "I really want to meet Obama someday just so I can call him a n****er"—that appeared following the 2012 election with the gold, silver, and bronze medals going to Alabama, Mississippi, and Georgia, in that order.[41]

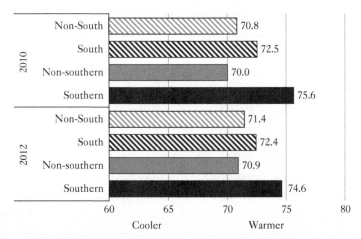

FIGURE 1.1A Mean Feeling Thermometer Evaluation of Whites, Among Whites, 2010–2012

Data are from the 2010 and 2012 Blair Center Polls.

Beyond mapping tweets, to measure the legacy of white supremacy in contemporary political culture and to assess whether these attitudes are distinctively southern requires an examination of both general and specific questions regarding whites' views about themselves. Using "feeling thermometers" ranging from zero indicating "very cold" and 100 indicating "very warm," respondents in the Blair Center Polls took their own temperature, so to speak. Figure 1.1A reveals whites' feeling thermometer evaluations of their fellow whites across a range of subgroups. Overall, in 2010 and 2012, the scores for whites, by whites, are well above the 50-midpoint mark, meaning they have a general positive view of their racial group, but these feelings are even more positive among whites who happen to live in the geographic South (72.5 degrees in 2010 and 72.4 degrees in 2012). More important, the highest praise for whites was reported by whites who identify as southern (75.6 degrees in 2010 and 74.6 degrees in 2012), temperatures that are significantly higher than those reported by non-southern whites.

Defining what constitutes that superiority, however, is more difficult than locating it. The results of digging deeper into specific characteristics that might account for this positive view are shown in Figure 1.1B. In 2012, white respondents were asked to evaluate the Old-Fashioned Racism questions regarding the work ethic, intelligence, and trustworthiness of a racial group—but this time their own—using a 7-point scale, with 1 indicating, for example, that the respondent thinks that whites are hard-working and 7 indicating they are lazy.

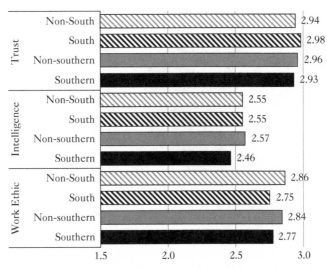

FIGURE 1.1B Mean Racial Stereotype Scores Toward Whites, Among Whites, 2012
Data are from the 2012 Blair Center Poll.

Despite the general positive view of whites, the specific evaluation of their work ethic was moderately positive, with average scores of 2.8, with 4 being the midpoint of the scale. Scores evaluating trustworthiness and intelligence hovered at 3 and 2.5 respectively for all whites. The largest gaps between whites who live in the South and those who do not were in their evaluations of work ethic, and between whites who claim a southern identity and whites who do not, the greatest gap was on their evaluations of intelligence. In both cases whites in the South or white southerners give their fellow whites slightly (0.11 points) better marks.

The fact that southern identity remains linked to a "warmer" evaluation of whites, though no specific characteristic such as intelligence, trustworthiness, or work ethic stands out as substantively distinct, points to how empty this notion of white supremacy is within the construct of southern identity. Yet that belief, brazen or masked, persists. And more so among white southerners who, as can be seen in Figures 1.2A and 1.2B, lay claim to their whiteness at dramatically and significantly higher rates than non-southern whites. According to the 2012 Blair Center Poll, close to three-fourths of whites who do not identify as southern still claim their whiteness strongly or very strongly. That number jumps to 90 percent among whites who do claim a southern identity, with 70 percent of that group disclosing that the attachment to whiteness was "very strong," compared to 51 percent of non-southern whites. No other subgroup of whites, geographically or in terms of identification, comes anywhere close to those kinds

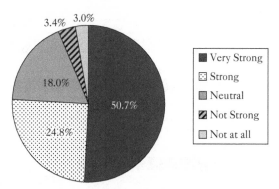

FIGURE 1.2A Percent Responses to: "How Strongly Do You Think of Yourself as White?" Among Non-southern Whites, 2012

Data are from the 2012 Blair Center Poll.

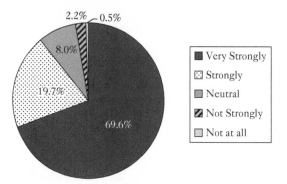

FIGURE 1.2B Percent Responses to: "How Strongly Do You Think of Yourself as White?" Among Southern Whites, 2012

Data are from the 2012 Blair Center Poll.

of numbers. So the whiteness part of southern identity is embraced and elevated, yet hollow.

THE REASON THE Long Southern Strategy is so important to understanding southern whiteness, in addition to its historically unique regional experience, is that identity constructs are not inherently political. Therefore, how they become politicized and stay politicized is a key piece of the current political puzzle. Cohesion and, more important, political action, as noted by Leonie Huddy, David Sears, and Jack Levy in the *Oxford Handbook of Political Psychology*, have three fundamental requirements: group strength (via saliency and positive feelings toward the group), clear political meaning (the group will be affected by certain policies), and the presence of group threats (real or imagined).[42] Southern whites clearly have positive feelings about their whiteness, despite the elusive justification for those feelings. Nevertheless, they lack clear political meaning. The hollowness of southernness and whiteness makes both politically malleable. Each exists only in opposition to something else, allowing for their continual transformation.[43] Without blackness, for example, whiteness had no meaning; over time, each defines the other. Journalist W. J. Cash recognized this dynamic in southern whites in his 1941 book *The Mind of the South*. "Negro entered into white man," he wrote, "as profoundly as white man entered into Negro—subtly influencing every gesture, every word, every emotion and idea, every attitude."[44] However, the relationship was not merely relative; it was hierarchal. Whiteness was both defined not only in opposition to blackness, but also as superior to it. Southernness is so similar in its structure and function that historian George Tindall attempted to define it as an ethnicity. Really, Tindall was making a case for southern distinctiveness and registering his rejection of the "consensus" notion of American identity "extolling homogeneity" that was popular at mid-century. Ironically, Tindall's primary evidence for the distinctiveness of white southerners was their preoccupation with race. Quoting James Weldon Johnson's 1912 observation, with which Tindall firmly agreed, "no group of southern white men could get together and talk for sixty minutes without bringing up the 'race question.'"[45] That preoccupation is a symptom of the emptiness of the racial and regional construct.

Maintaining that hierarchy of southern whiteness required fluidity. Any loss of white power (which nicked away at white supremacy) increased suppression of the black community in equal measure. The most radical retaliations accompanied threats to white political or economic dominance. Sociologists E. M. Beck and Stewart Tolnay presented the most tangible example in their 1990 study of lynchings. Using time-series analysis between emancipation and the Great Depression, Beck and Tolnay found that the frequency of southern lynchings (3,959 African Americans were lynched between 1877 and 1950, the majority of whom were taken from prisons)[46] corresponded to decreases in cotton prices. They concluded that "mob violence against southern blacks responded to economic conditions affecting the financial fortunes of southern whites—especially marginal white farmers."[47] Too often, poor whites were encouraged or manipulated by southern elites who even sanctioned violence to avoid an interracial, class-based coalition from forming. Southern writer Lillian Smith describes this dynamic in a fictional conversation that appears in her groundbreaking 1949 book, *Killers of the Dream*, in which "Mr. Rich White" tells "Mr. Poor White" that if you ever get restless when you don't have a job or your roof leaks, or the children look puny and shoulder blades stick out more than natural, all you need to do is remember you're a slight better off than the black man.... But if you get nervous sometimes anyway ... and you think it'll make you feel a little better to lynch a nigger occasionally, that's OK by me too.[48]

More often, white supremacy was used to create a political distraction. In 1960 future president Lyndon Johnson waxed candidly about this exact sentiment to then staffer Bill Moyers in a late-night, private conversation. Johnson and Moyers saw racist signs in the crowd, and the senator could not shake the images. "I'll tell you what's at the bottom of it," he started; "If you can convince the lowest white man he's better than the best colored man, he won't notice you're picking his pocket."[49] Identity-based hierarchies can, indeed, serve political ends if superiority is watered or even if its planted.

Politicians can serve that function to their own benefit. Smith's fictional conversation elucidates this point as well when "Mr. Rich White" tells "Mr. Poor White" that

if folks are fool enough to forget they're white men, if they forget that, I'm willing to put out plenty of money to keep the politicians talking, and I don't mind supporting a real first-class demagogue or two to say what you want him to say—just so he does what I want about my business. And I promise you this: Long as you keep the Negro out of your unions, we'll keep him out of our mills.[50]

Most important, politicians can provide the group threat needed to politicize an identity construct—in this case southern whiteness. The Long Southern Strategy is flush with cases of southern whites being made to feel threatened by minorities, and the GOP offering to defuse that threat. For example, the fact that Ronald Reagan as governor of California oversaw a similar prison furlough program to the one that released Willie Horton did not stop the GOP from manufacturing a black criminal threat in order to activate white solidarity for their candidate. Even when two men who were granted leave (of approximately 20,000 passes) committed a murder, and a defensive Reagan noted, "obviously you can't be perfect,"[51] the GOP ignored the hypocrisy and vigilantly attacked Dukakis anyway. Nearly 200 articles in a single Massachusetts newspaper detailed every aspect of the Dukakis furlough program; Georgia representative Newt Gingrich "read each installment aloud on the House floor."[52] Bush, himself, mentioned Willie Horton every single day on the campaign trail,[53] the constant buildup of a menacing "other" against which southern whites and the GOP could coalesce.

Moreover, it is no coincidence that the effectiveness of the Willie Horton ad corresponded to the rise of black leadership in the Democratic Party. Though his father had served on a South Carolina chain gang,[54] Willie Horton is portrayed by the GOP as protected by Democrats, implying that Horton's rights—despite his impoverished upbringing—trumped the safety of law-abiding Americans. Horton is so loved by Democrats, chided Atwater to southern Republicans, that he might be chosen as Dukakis's running mate. Atwater also described to his audience a rumored meeting between Jesse Jackson and Dukakis,[55] painting Democrats as the champions of black advancement and thus a threat to white supremacy. The "us vs. them" mentality consequently reaffirms the GOP as the protector of white power.

At its core, southern white identity when politicized "weaves a White worldview that attributes positive qualities to Whites and negative traits to People of Color."[56] Whether or not contemporary appeals to those beliefs are false threats, cloaked in politically correct language, or denied altogether, they are visible from a distance, a continuous pattern stretching back in time. Even anthropologist John Dollard, who published his groundbreaking fieldwork in the South in 1937, recounted a significant conversation with a man he called "a naïve Negro." "He was aware, of course," Dollard commented, "that southern white people say they do not hate Negroes and sometimes even assert that they love them. His view seemed to be that maybe once they did love the Negroes when they were all comfortably in their places and seemed likely to stay there permanently."[57] Maybe Dollard's subject was not so naïve after all. The violence and spectacle of lynchings and the politics of fear plagued the South then and perhaps always will. But it is the "us vs. them" impulse, in defense of southern white superiority, that proves so critical to understanding the not-so-new southern racism and its relationship to the Long Southern Strategy.

That impulse dovetails with one of the most popular emerging research topics in contemporary race relations. The measure of Ethnocentrism has been reinvigorated by the work of Donald Kinder and Cindy Kam in their 2009 book, aptly named *Us against Them: Ethnocentric Foundations of American Opinion.* The argument, as Kinder and Kam note, can be traced back to William Graham Sumner, who concluded that Ethnocentrism was the "technical name for this view of things in which one's own group is the center of everything."[58] At a theoretical level, Ethnocentrism is the tendency of individuals to see people like them as part of a community and to view others who are different as belonging to another group. According to Kinder and Kam,

> ethnocentrism is a predisposition to divide human society into in-groups and out-groups. People vary from one another in their readiness to look

upon the social world in this way: that is, they are more or less ethno-centric. To those given to ethnocentrism, in-groups are communities of virtue, trust, and cooperation, safe and superior havens. Out-groups, on the other hand, are not. To the ethnocentrist, out-group members and their customs seem strange, discomforting, perhaps even dangerous.[59]

Measuring how respondents feel toward their in-group *compared* to various out-groups has proven popular among scholars assessing the power of "otherness" in shaping views on racial inequities[60] and immigration.[61] Kinder and Kam spe-cifically find Ethnocentrism predictive of American support for "providing for the national defense, dealing harshly with enemies abroad, withholding assis-tance to foreign lands in need, stemming the tide of immigration, pushing back against gay rights, cutting welfare, and putting an end to affirmative action."[62] International scholarship even points to extreme ethnocentric attitudes as the source of modern genocides.[63] The explanatory power is, indeed, powerful.

Considering how it is measured, it should be, and for two critical reasons. First, Ethnocentrism, unlike the indirect and even implicit theories of prejudice, is relative. Whiteness, in this measure, functions as a vantage point. Rather than just examining how whites view themselves, the Ethnocentrism score indicates the size of the gap between how whites view themselves and how they view others. Political psychologists have confirmed that Ethnocentrism is "conceptu-ally and empirically distinguished from . . . outgroup negativity and mere ingroup positivity."[64] Rather than solely measuring differences, the formula accounts for superiority, making it a perfect match for assessing southern whiteness. Second, because of that relativity, Ethnocentrism is less likely to overlook persistent white supremacy because even though white respondents may report less racist assessments of blacks than they did fifty years ago, if they still report much higher evaluations of themselves as whites, then the gap remains wide open. And it is the gap that really matters.

Kinder and Kam actually offer two ways in which white-to-black Ethnocentrism can be measured. The first more general measure of Ethnocentrism utilizes feeling thermometers. The Ethnocentrism score results from subtracting the average of whites' "warmth" for blacks or other minority groups from their "warmth" toward their own ethnic group. Figure 1.3 shows the average feeling thermometer evaluation of whites toward African Americans and Latinos, presented alongside their evaluation of their fellow whites. In 2010 and 2012, both whites who live in the South and outside of the South, and among whites who claim a southern identity and those who do not, the average temperature to-ward African Americans hovers in the moderate-to-warm upper 50s.

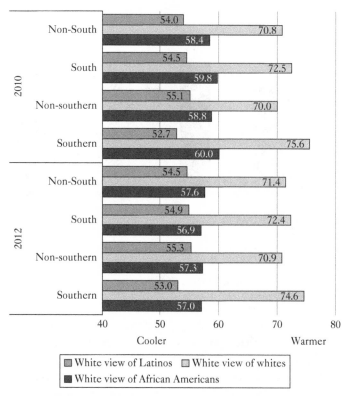

FIGURE 1.3 Mean Feeling Thermometer Evaluations of Whites, African Americans, and Latinos, Among Whites, 2010–2012

Data are from the 2010 and 2012 Blair Center Polls.

This slightly positive evaluation, considered in isolation, can be misleading. For example, Byron Shafer and Richard Johnston, in their book *The End of Southern Exceptionalism*, used feeling thermometers to show that by the 1990s whites' racial feelings toward blacks, when considered alongside whites' views on social welfare, did little to influence votes for Republican candidates.[65] However, white "warmth" toward African Americans has little meaning without knowing how whites feel about themselves—which is substantially warmer. In 2012, the average white southerner's feeling thermometer rating of African Americans was 57 degrees while the average white southerner's feeling thermometer rating of other whites was 74.6 degrees—a difference of 17.6 degrees.

The gaps are even greater when whites' view toward their own in-group is compared to their "warmth" toward Latinos. Among all whites, southern and non-southern, living in the South or outside of the South, "warmth" toward Latinos averaged around 54 degrees, compared to 72 degrees on average toward

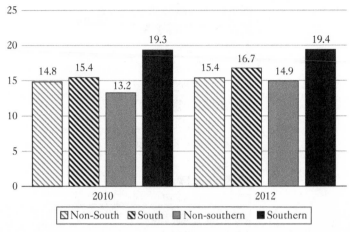

FIGURE 1.4A Mean Ethnocentrism Scores (Feeling Thermometer Measure), Among Whites, 2010–2012

Data are from the 2010 and 2012 Blair Center Polls.

themselves as whites. Once again, the gap is greatest among self-identified white southerners. The size of these gaps, which is one way to measure Ethnocentrism, is presented in Figure 1.4A. In both 2010 and 2012, the regional difference by geography is minimal. However, claiming a southern identity widens the gap, with white southerners well into the twenty-first century still reporting a nearly 20-point difference between how they see themselves compared to other racial groups.

The second measure of Ethnocentrism—and perhaps more important for evaluating this notion of not-so-new-southern racism—utilizes the direct Old-Fashioned Racism scale evaluating stereotypes. It is calculated by subtracting the average of whites' attitudes toward how hard-working, intelligent, and trustworthy they believe blacks and other minority groups to be from their corresponding assessments of whites. It is important to note that if a respondent, for example, has a positive stereotype of whites (positive answers receive a low score) and a negative stereotype of African Americans and Latinos (negative answers receive a high score), then the difference between white stereotypes of whites and the white stereotypes of African Americans and Latinos will be a negative number. The greater the negative numbers, the greater degree of distance and superiority indicated by the white respondent, as shown in Figure 1.4B.

The clear and consistent pattern in both 2010 and 2012 is that white southerners report the greatest distance regarding work ethic, intelligence, and trustworthiness between themselves and African Americans and Latinos, an example of the resurgent direct racism highlighted by Tesler. Their mean Ethnocentrism score

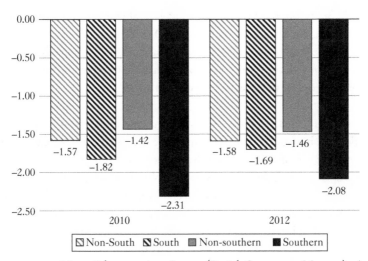

FIGURE 1.4B Mean Ethnocentrism Scores (Racial Stereotype Measure), Among Whites, 2010–2012

Data are from the 2010 and 2012 Blair Center Polls.

is followed in size by those who live in South, then those who live outside the South, then those who do not claim a southern identity respectively. These gaps may seem small numerically, but on a scale of 1–7 (as opposed to the Feeling Thermometer 100-point scale), they are substantial. Most notably, the gap reported by those who claim a southern identity is significantly larger than whites who do not call themselves southern, both in 2010 and in 2012.

Moreover, this measure of Ethnocentrism is particularly meaningful because it taps into such derogatory stereotypes—stereotypes that persist both in the South and beyond its borders. For example, in February 2015, seven workers at Matheson Trucking and Matheson Flight Extenders, Inc. based in California were awarded $15 million by a federal jury in a racial discrimination lawsuit. Their bosses were accused of calling them "lazy, stupid Africans." In an interview with the *Denver Post*, one of the plaintiffs, Ernie Duke, summarized his feelings toward the name-calling: "I thought I was back in the South again with the same old racist attitudes."[66] To those who have declared the end of southern exceptionalism, the finding may prove frustrating, but it is hardly shocking to others, particularly the accusations regarding work ethic. On average, whites see themselves as better than African Americans and Latinos in general, but whites who call themselves southern position themselves at a greater distance from racial minorities, even five decades beyond the dismantling of "separate but equal." Partisanship might have actually helped to perpetuate these attitudes, particularly as it relates to southern identity. Over ten years ago, Nicholas Valentino and David Sears found a link between ideological conservatism and racial antagonism stretching back twenty-five years. Over time, it has strengthened and now extends beyond ideology to partisan identification.[67] It may just be a long-term consequence of the GOP's decision to chase southern white voters via old-fashioned stereotypes that are made new again.

THESE IDENTITY-BASED GAPS are more than just numbers on a chart. Rather, they reflect the historical—and, for many, the current—lived experience of racial separation that has infiltrated the southern psyche at depths that sometimes seem bottomless. "I can't feel the same way about a Negro as a white person," confessed a white woman interviewed in Robert Penn Warren's 1956 study on the "inner conflict" of segregation; "it's born in me," she admits.[68] Performed daily, in a thousand ways, both subtle and aggressive, segregation underscored nearly every aspect of white southern culture. For much of its history, the South functioned as "a theater of racial difference, a minstrel show writ large upon the land," argued Grace Hale in her 1998 book *Making Whiteness: The Culture of Segregation in the South 1890–1940*. The "ritualistic enactment of racial difference was vital," she contends, "and southern whites commanded this performance of segregation for both a local and national audience, to maintain both white privilege at home and a sense of southern distinctiveness within the nation."[69] Performing segregation became inseparable from performing southern white supremacy, and despite increasing diversity in the region, despite greater levels of educational attainment, and despite personal relationships, such a link is not easily broken.

In fact, intimacy too often serves as the basis of self-assessment; cue the token "but I have black friends" comment. Yet, scholarship on contact theory by Mary Jackman and Marie Crane points to this fine distinction, concluding that "intimacy is less important than a variety of contacts."[70] The 2010 publication of Melvin Patrick Ely's award-winning work of Antebellum history, *Israel on the Appomattox: A Southern Experiment in Black Freedom from the 1790s through the Civil War*, pinpoints this exact paradox. Ely's study of the day-to-day interactions between a free community of blacks in Prince Edward County, Virginia, and white slave owners, reveals the "callousness and closeness"[71] of the black-white dynamic, and the resulting—perhaps counterintuitive—result. "The very friendliness that could arise between members of the dominant group and the oppressed," he writes in his postscript, "may have postponed change by encouraging white people to see their social system as less abusive than it was in fact."[72] Polite behavior and politically correct speech may have provided conscious or subconscious deniability to southern whites, many of whom would insist that they are not racist. Nevertheless, befriending an "other" or growing up with an "other" does not mean one recognizes the "other" need not be "other" at all. The opposite, in fact, may be true, particularly if one's identity—rather than geography—is built on the existence of the "other."

Thus, the greatest threat to the gap remains the dissolution of the "other" altogether. The purest indication might be attitudes toward interracial marriage, which was, perhaps, the greatest taboo in southern history. Only after *Brown v. Board* declared public school segregation unconstitutional, and only after the 1964 Civil Rights Act and the 1965 Voting Rights Act, did the Supreme Court overturn anti-miscegenation laws via the 1967 landmark case *Loving v. Virginia*. Many states, of course, had already repealed similar laws, some as early as 1780 (Pennsylvania), but when the verdict came down in *Loving v. Virginia*, similar laws remained in effect in sixteen states, including all eleven states of the former Confederacy.[73] Thirty years later, when John Shelton Reed and Larry Griffith conducted their 1999 Southern Focus Poll survey—one of the few polls that contain the southern identity variable—southerners remained distinct on the issue. The survey, which included 953 white participants, posed questions regarding experience with and approval of interracial relationships. Over 60 percent of self-identified southerners indicated that they had no family members who had dated someone from another race, and 77.3 percent admitted having no family members previously or currently in interracial marriages, compared to 42 percent and 69.7 percent of non-southerners reporting no family interracial dating or marriage respectively. Probing deeper into the respondents' individual experiences, 82.5 percent of white, self-identified southerners revealed that their own parents would have objected if they, themselves, had dated someone with a different racial background. In this case, the gap between southerners and non-southerners was a distinct 19 points. The participants professed their personal views, as well, which followed the exact pattern. Close to one-third of those who self-identify as southern admitted that they personally objected to interracial dating (32 percent) and marriage (29 percent) compared to 12 percent of non-southerners on both questions. Moreover, when southern and non-southern responses are compared across all five questions, southern identity proves significant every time.

This ultimate defense of the "otherness" of racial minorities persists in southern culture and continues to shape public opinion. In 2009, the documentary *Prom Night in Mississippi*, which chronicled Morgan Freeman's effort to finance an integrated prom in 2008 in Charleston, Mississippi, premiered on HBO.[74] In 2013, the *New York Times* covered a similar challenge in Abbeville, Georgia, where students were petitioning for the end of segregated school dances. In 2011, churches in both Tennessee and Kentucky banned members for their interracial marriages.[75] In addition, when Public Policy Polling surveyed 400 likely Republican primary voters in Mississippi in 2011, 46 percent said that interracial marriage should be illegal.[76] In polls conducted the next year by the same firm of both Republicans in Mississippi and Alabama, support for anti-miscegenation laws—forty-five years after *Loving v. Virginia*—remained at 29 percent and 21 percent respectively, with another 17 percent and 12 percent indicating they were undecided.[77] Such gaps provide opportunities for politicians. For example, when George W. Bush trailed John McCain in the 2000 primary race for the Republican presidential nomination, rumors that McCain's daughter of Bangladesh descent was actually an "illegitimate black child" reversed Bush's fortunes.[78] McCain, in turn, played the not-so-new southern racial card too by expressing his belief that the Confederate flag was a symbol of heritage not hate.[79] Politicizing key components of southern whiteness—a primary tenet of the Long Southern Strategy—seems to have become a rite of passage for GOP contenders.

Maintaining these racial gaps won over many southern voters come Election Day, but preserving these gaps hovers just below the surface of other policy initiatives, past and present, many of which have been repackaged in coded rhetoric. The mass incarceration of African Americans, a continuous cycle since the Reconstruction-era convict lease system rebuilt the South with prison labor, has been called the new Jim Crow by scholars such as Michelle Alexander,[80] not only because the population is imprisoned and separated from society, but also because of the disenfranchisement of prisoners and parolees both during and after incarceration. From Richard Nixon's calls for "law and order" to George H. W. Bush's demand for "more jails, more prisons, more courts, and more prosecutors,"[81] each stance reaffirmed southern whiteness and its segregated reality. The Willie Horton ad and accusations that Democrats were soft on crime indicated they were not committed to white supremacy, whether white southerners could articulate that or not. Democrats learned the lesson that on crime "they had to be more Catholic than the Pope, tougher than tough."[82] That overcorrection would result eventually in the 1994 Violent Crime Control and Law Enforcement Act (the "Crime Bill") now heavily criticized for exploding the African American prison population for the past two decades.

The impact is not limited to the criminal justice system. Even fair employment practices in the South stalled due to efforts to maintain the gaps between blacks and whites. "Appeals to preserve segregation," argued Michelle Brittain in *The Politics of Whiteness: Race, Workers, and Culture in the Modern South*, "which commanded extraordinary power as a cultural norm among southern whites, frequently served as the final justification for protecting traditional employment practices." However, as bold pronouncements, such as "God advocate[d] segregation" as proclaimed by 1940s Georgia Governor Herman Talmadge in his opposition to the Fair Employment Practices Commission, gave way to masked racial appeals, the GOP found ways to activate the same segregationist energy. Senator Goldwater, specifically, championed "qualifications" as a way of building a labor force on the implied racial superiority of whiteness and its advantages. Qualifications such as work ethic and trustworthiness and intelligence seem innocuous, but being deemed "qualified," notes Brattain "incorporated much of the ideological and emotional baggage" of southern white supremacy and segregation.[83]

The bait-and-switch rhetorical model applies to the use of the word "private" as well, specifically in terms of education. In addition to noncompulsory attendance laws and the advent of homeschooling, which anticipated and/or followed the desegregation of public schools in the South, hundreds of "private" academies allowed white students to continue to prop up Jim Crow. Using data from the National Center for Education Statistics, the Hechinger Report, which assesses inequality in American public education, counted thirty-five such white-flight schools still operating in Mississippi, all established between 1964 and 1972.[84] Profiled in *The Atlantic*, one such school in Indianola, Mississippi—a town where less than 20 percent of the population is white—enrolled 434 white students and 2 black students in the 2009–2010 school year. Many times advocacy for vouchers and charter schools in the South are attempts to support such schools financially. Neither are public schools immune to the power of the gap. The Harvard Civil Rights Project assessed that as of 2003, public school integration had declined to its lowest rate in three decades.[85] As of 2014, of the twenty most segregated state public education systems in the country, seven are in the South.[86] In 2016, sixty-two years after the *Brown v. Board* decision, a federal judge again had to order a school district in Mississippi to desegregate.[87] These schools, these employment practices, even segregated social functions, are not just about staying in one's own group. The negative ethnocentric score requires a hierarchical perspective, with the in-group on top, and the out-groups kept at an inferior distance.

Increasingly that "other" includes Latinos. Whereas protecting southern white superiority has been tied to criminal justice, employment, and education policies, it has been politicized effectively most recently in terms of immigration reform. Here again, despite coded language that characterized the debate as economic, scholars have shown that Old-Fashioned Racism, measures of indirect racism, and Ethnocentrism all influence white attitudes toward immigration.[88] In a working paper for the Kinder Institute for Urban Research at Rice University, Jessica Brown finds links between the GOP's Southern Strategy and the "racially divisive appeals (RDAs)" employed by Republicans in the last two election cycles. This "Southwestern Strategy," Brown argues, relies on a nativist, oppositional appeal and casts undocumented immigrants as "welfare abusers," "criminals," and "terrorists."[89] It invokes the "law and order" dog whistle via advocacy for a "stop and frisk" policy to crack down on illegal immigration.[90] Masked by appeals to qualifications and fairness, GOP candidates like Ron Paul once framed the narrative this way: "There is something said in economics that, if you subsidize something, you get more of it. This is what we do, we encourage it by giving free medical care, free education, and the promise of amnesty. No wonder more will come."[91] Native citizens (often presumed as white) are hard-working, and immigrants are looking for what GOP presidential candidate Mitt Romney deemed, repeatedly throughout his campaign, "a handout."[92]

In terms of the policy implications of this spirit, when asked whether they favor or oppose "tougher immigration laws like Arizona," whites who claim a southern identity remain significantly distinct from those who do not, as can be seen in Figure 1.5. Support among southern whites stands at 79.1 percent and 76.4 percent in 2010 and 2012 respectively, compared to 63.4 percent in 2010 and 59.4 percent in 2012 among non-southern whites. Moreover, fewer white southerners are on the fence or opposed than their non-southern counterparts. So powerful is the culture of separation that southern whites cannot be neutral on policies that they perceive as protective of southern white identity and its superiority.

THAT SENSE OF protection has only intensified since Obama's victory. Pundits and scholars wonder aloud how the country became so polarized, and many were shocked by Donald Trump's victory over nearly two dozen GOP primary challengers to emerge as the party's nominee. The shock stemmed from Trump's

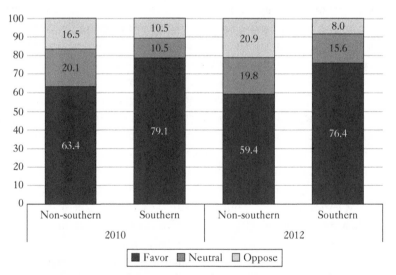

FIGURE 1.5 Percent Attitudes Toward "Tougher Immigration Laws Like in Arizona," Among Whites, 2010–2012

Data are from the 2010 and 2012 Blair Center Polls.

overt racial appeals, prompting questions as to how he could uncode the rhetoric and still remain competitive. Much of it has to do with how the primary system is structured, giving states in the South hefty influence. Yet, these southern white attitudes, albeit still significantly distinct, both caused and were caused by the GOP's right turn on race. Many party loyalists—whether living inside the South or not—have let the current take them right along. The "us vs. them" tactic, however, was often abstract. The election of an African American president makes it very real in ways that some whites could not even process until it happened. The ascension of a black man to the height of national power has been met with both a defensive elevation and assertion of whiteness. Trump's reactionary MAGA became the mantra, with "making American great again," perhaps meaning "before the possibility of an Obama," as outlined in Ta-Nehisi Coates's October 2017 essay in *The Atlantic*.[93]

Trump's desire to wipe Obama's presidency from the record books[94] underscored his "birtherism" movement, which sought to prove Obama was not a natural-born citizen. Doing so would invalidate Obama's election or, at the least, delegitimize his presidency by casting doubt on his Americanism. Trump's campaign promises and many of his early actions as president focus on rolling back Obama's major initiatives, including the Affordable Care Act and his executive order on Deferred Action for Childhood Arrivals (DACA).[95] Many of these efforts, thus, are clarion calls in support of whiteness, even if they are packaged as "fiscal conservatism" or support for "law and order." And those are calls that many whites who identify as southern will still answer—perhaps even more so now, as indicated in the 2016 Blair Center Poll conducted in the weeks after the presidential election. As shown in Figure 1.6, southern whites' evaluations of their own whiteness has increased since 2010 and 2012.

In 2016, when asked on a feeling thermometer scale of 1–100 how warmly whites feel toward whiteness, southern whites report an average temperature of 78.5 degrees, up almost 3 degrees in four years, and still significantly higher than non-southern whites whose scores have stayed relatively the same at 70.4 degrees. Whiteness isn't just getting "hotter," so to speak, as Figure 1.6 also shows, it is becoming slightly more popular. Among southern whites, it is borderline unanimous with 91.4 percent indicating that they "strongly" or "very strongly" identify as white, up from 2012 by over 2 points. This remains significantly distinct from non-southern whites, among whom white identity has dropped almost 9 points to 67.7 percent. Moreover, under half (44.6 percent) of non-southern whites fall into the "very strongly" identify as white category, but among southern whites, top-level intensity has held steady at close to 70 percent. This assertion of whiteness is one of the reasons why Trump's racial dog whistles drew massive white

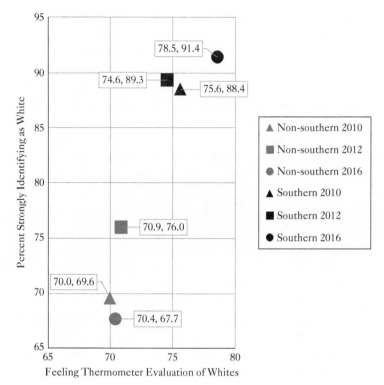

FIGURE 1.6 Mean Feeling Thermometer Evaluation of Whites and Percent "Strongly" or "Very Strongly" Claiming White Identity, Among Whites, 2010–2016
Data are from the 2010, 2012, and 2016 Blair Center Polls.

crowds across the country and massive margins of victories, particularly in ten of the eleven states of the former Confederacy.

Still, Trump didn't just blow dog whistles of whiteness; rather, he blew whistles that everyone could hear, making overt statements and campaign promises and tweets that attacked racial minorities. The Black Lives Matter movement, according to Trump, was actually instigating the killing of police offices, for which his administration might have to investigate the organization.[96] Pitting Black Lives Matter against the police further demonized black protests as violent and threatening to whites. His words resonated among white audiences, particularly those who claim a southern identity. On a feeling thermometer scale, as shown in Figure 1.7, these whites on average report their "warmth" toward Black Lives Matter at a freezing 28.5 degrees, a solid and significant 10 degrees lower than whites who do not claim a southern identity, and much lower than their general evaluation of African Americans. Police,

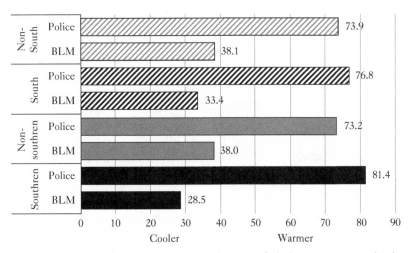

FIGURE 1.7 Mean Feeling Thermometer Evaluations of Black Lives Matter and Police, Among Whites, 2016

Data are from the 2016 Blair Center Poll.

however, receive an 81.4-degree evaluation from southern whites, roughly 8 degrees warmer than non-southern whites.

Trump's rhetoric also targeted Latino Americans with equal hostility. Mexican "rapists" and illegal aliens became the new Willie Horton. US District Judge Gonzalo Curiel, who ruled against Trump in a civil case, was denounced as incapable of fairness because of his Mexican ancestry.[97] Whiteness is sanctified by this demonized "other," and protecting its sacred supremacy requires separation, both by removing or deporting this "other" and by building a wall between "us" and "them." These seeds of fear had been planted for years, and the soil of southern identity proved rich, as can be seen in Figure 1.8. In 2016, almost half of whites who claim a southern identity (46.9 percent) "agreed" or "strongly agreed" with Trump's pledge to build a wall on the Mexican-American border, even though only one southern state—Texas—is impacted directly. That approval is a significant 15 points higher than whites who do not claim a southern identity. Walls, whether literal or figurative, have long been a part of southern whiteness, which is, in and of itself, a fortress, made to seem, yet again, as if it is under siege.

IT WAS GERALD Ford who first noticed that his party had become associated with white supremacy when he said, "most blacks wouldn't vote for me no matter what I did."[98] So effective was the Long Southern Strategy at politicizing southern white identity and tapping into that "us vs. them" dynamic that even

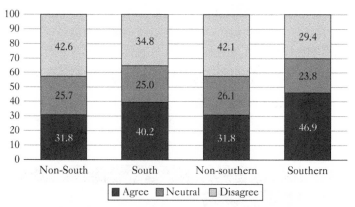

FIGURE 1.8 Percent Responses to: "A Wall Should Be Built Along the Entire Border with Mexico," Among Whites, 2016

Data are from the 2016 Blair Center Poll.

Bob Dole's efforts to expand its stark white base and to attract more African Americans to the GOP were doomed, with black Republicans characterized as "the loneliest people in the world."[99] The branding was so complete—the hunting so successful—that non-white conservatives, some have noted, who have ambitions in the Republican Party deny their heritage and adopt "a white mental outlook," which "renders it [racial animus] inoperable."[100] Looking specifically at the careers of former Louisiana governor Bobby Jindal, conservative writer Dinesh D'Souza, and then South Carolina governor Nikki Haley, Jeet Heer argues in the *New Republic* that "racial minorities can advance in the GOP by erasing their ethnic identity and/or attacking other minorities."[101] One must be a hunter.

Pointing to the election of Barack Obama or "hiding behind a minority"[102] candidate, Republican leaders continue to portray Jim Crow racism as something from America's past. But they are just as wrong as the "new racism" scholars were premature in announcing Old-Fashioned Racism's demise. Even a nonprofit organization called the Marshall Project warns that "Willie Horton–style ads have been making a comeback."[103] Perhaps that is because now the GOP must solidify loyalty and secure high turnout among whites in the South, and because whiteness itself relies on such political cues for its meaning. Even when issue framing is coded—"soft porn racism" as Dan Carter calls it[104]—it still works, triggering an emotional and habitual defense. This is most often and easily accomplished by contrasting whiteness to what it is not—by promoting the gap between white and other. When whites could no longer denigrate minorities publicly, the gap was maintained by an elevation of and clinging to whiteness. That elevation and unity is often achieved in reaction to a common enemy perceived as increasingly threatening, which, in turn, triggers a protection of separate, even walled-off, white spaces, as can be seen in white flight schools or support for strict immigration control or the mass incarceration and disenfranchisement of African Americans.

Geographical distinctions between the South and the non-South remain significant, but identity carries a heavier weight. In 2013, political scientists at the University of Rochester announced their discovery of the "slavery effect" (distinctly negative racial attitudes in areas where slavery was most prominent), which they argue "accounts for up to a 15-percentage point difference in party affiliation today."[105] The provocative finding, which connects the southern past to the southern present, is possible over such a long period and despite such substantial changes in society, but only if these attitudes are connected to some kind of persistent personal identification. Then the fire of racial animus must be stoked regularly and strategically over the long haul so that whiteness and southernness and superiority and partisanship become mutually reinforcing. It is a remarkable game plan that is anything but new.

2

Southern White Privilege

Operationally, white privilege is simply the flipside of discrim-
ination against people of color. The concept is rooted in the
common-sense observation that there can be no down without
an up, so that if people of color are the targets of discrimina-
tion, in housing, employment, the justice system, or elsewhere,
then whites, by definition, are being elevated above those per-
sons of color. Whites are receiving a benefit, vis-a-vis those per-
sons of color: more opportunity because those persons of color
are receiving less. Although I believe all persons are harmed in
the long run by racism and racial inequity—and thus, white
privilege comes at an immense social cost—it still exists as a
daily reality throughout the social, political and economic
structure of the United States.

—TIM WISE[1]

ON OCTOBER 31, 1964, Senator Barry Goldwater, the Republican presidential nominee, made one last pitch to the white southerners he hoped would
carry him to victory. After being welcomed by a large and vocal crowd of nearly
50,000 at the airport in Columbus, South Carolina, Goldwater and his motor-
cade encountered yet another group of nearly 1,000 supporters (some costumed)
along his route to the city auditorium.[2] Using a bullhorn from his convert-
ible, Goldwater thanked the enthusiastic crowd including the "ghosts, goblins,
monsters and other spooks out for Halloween trick or treating." Reporters covering the appearance noted that there were no visible Johnson signs, and at the
auditorium there were as many Confederate as American flags waving. Joined
by Senator Strom Thurmond, a recent Republican convert, and Governor James
F. Byrnes, Goldwater was greeted by the singing of "Dixie" and praised by his
colleagues for his "superb courage" in voting against the 1964 Civil Rights Act
(CRA), which the governor called his "finest hour."[3] The event was broadcast via
television on 85 channels[4] to all eleven states of the former Confederacy and three
more, an audience that represented 152 electoral votes.[5]

As a senator, Goldwater had often couched his opposition to civil rights enforcement as an ideological stance against federal overreach, and that, in and of itself, played well in the South. The only other Republican president who was in Congress during the debate on the 1964 CRA was a young George H. W. Bush, who also voted against it, arguing the bill was "unconstitutional and threatened more rights than it protected"[6]—which may have seemed true from the vantage point of a white congressman. Moreover, Goldwater's broader vision of what the federal government should and should not do proved so influential that even three decades later, GOP presidential nominee Bob Dole would feature Goldwater in his campaign.[7] Goldwater's war on big government would become a GOP war against government spending and the "welfare state," which promoted "the idea that the have-nots can take from the haves."[8] Leveling the playing field morphed into an attack on whites. Thus, Goldwater, who first managed to bundle "civil rights, juvenile delinquency, welfare cheating, crime and violence generally, and unnecessary government spending"[9] and sell it as a package deal, became their first champion on the issue, followed by many of his GOP successors. The mood at Goldwater's southern rallies, noted Richard Rovere, a reporter for the *New Yorker* who accompanied the candidate, was "a kind of joyful defiance, or defiant joy."[10] The coded packaging was palatable to the senator, attractive to white southerners, effective for Republicans, and influential, even now.

For example, the May 2014 issue of the *New Yorker* included an interview with Peggy McIntosh, a seventy-nine-year-old professor at Wellesley, whose 1988 book *The Invisible Knapsack* redefined the notion of white privilege for a new generation of scholars. In it, McIntosh set forth forty-six examples of white privilege by consciously asking herself "on a daily basis, what do I have that I didn't earn?"[11] Journalist Joshua Rothman conducted the interview because of the resurgence of the privilege debate, particularly across social media platforms. Tumblr sites such as "This . . . is white privilege" includes the tagline, "white privilege is hard (for white people) to see, so consider this a compilation album of White Privilege's Greatest Hits."[12] Buzzfeed's quiz "How Privileged Are You?," created by Rega Jha and Tommy Wesely and posted in April 2014, has had over two million views.[13] The quiz's subtitle references a popular slogan that encourages white audiences to "check their privilege." The phrase, common on college campuses, made national headlines with the publication of Princeton student Tal Fortgang's essay, "Checking My Privilege: Character as the Basis of Privilege," which appeared in the conservative journal *The Princeton Tory*.[14] Fortgang claims that the notion of white privilege diminishes "everything I have personally accomplished, all the hard work I have done in my life, and for ascribing all the fruit I reap not to the seeds I sow but to some invisible patron saint of white maleness who places it out for me before I even arrive." Ironically, Fortgang's argument reinforces McIntosh's original premise, which she revisits nearly three decades later in her conversation with Rothman. "In order to understand the way privilege works, you have to be able to see patterns and systems in social life," McIntosh surmises. Moreover, as she specifically addresses the Fortgang piece, you have to see that your own individual experience "is set within a framework . . . that is much bigger"—meaning that white privilege is easily missed when individual experiences, regardless of intention, are not considered within a larger, collective context.[15]

Exposing this framework is the mission of organizations such as the national White Privilege Conference, an annual event founded in 2000 and sponsored by the Matrix Center for the Advancement of Social Equity and Inclusion at the University of Colorado, Colorado Springs. Heidi Beirich of the Southern Poverty Law Center was one of the keynote speakers at the 2014 conference that was held in Madison, Wisconsin. Her talk, "The Rising Tide of Hate in America," focused on the 66 percent increase in hate groups since 2000, as well as the accompanying increase in "attendant violence."[16] Clearly the conference organizers see the link between the rise in racially based domestic terrorism and the spike in conversations regarding the invisible knapsack of white privilege. These surges follow the election of Barack Obama as the first African American president, and they have company. Pundits and scholars alike have questioned the motivation of the similarly timed rise of the Tea Party, with Obama himself at the movement's "subterranean agenda."[17] The American Values Survey, conducted biennially by the independent nonprofit Public Religion Research Institute, profiled Tea Party members in their September 2010 poll, examining their ideology, partisanship, religious affiliation, and views regarding the role of government.[18] In her assessment of the findings presented at the Brookings Institution, Susan Brooks Thistlewait, a senior fellow at the Center for American Progress, pointed to a comprehensive angst shared by self-reported Tea Party members regarding the changing American racial landscape. She claimed that "those attracted to the tea party are more comfortable with white privilege as a value and believe that leveling the playing field for minorities is not the business of government."[19]

The emergence of the Tea Party, however, is not the only way in which white privilege has been politicized in recent years. Senator James Webb, a Democrat from Virginia, penned an op-ed for the *Wall Street Journal* in July 2010 entitled "Diversity and the Myth of White Privilege" that called for the end of all affirmative action programs. Toward the end of his statement, Webb repositions white Americans as victims of unfair government treatment. Specifically, Webb notes the extremely low rate of college degrees obtained over the past three decades by white Baptists and Irish Protestants who he claims were "the principle ethnic group that settled the South." He disparages policy makers who have "ignored such disparities within America's white cultures when, in advancing minority

diversity programs, they treated whites as a fungible monolith."[20] Webb's po-
lemical proclamation set up a flurry of equally impassioned defenses, many of
which offered rich data to support the notion that white privilege is alive and
well in America. Larry Yates, a grassroots activist and member of the Virginia
Organizing Project (VOP), highlights the research of the Institute on Assets and
Social Policy, which concluded that as of 2010, "the dollar savings gap between
whites and African-Americans had increased from $20,000 in 1984 to $95,000
in 2007."[21] The gaps are indisputable, but Webb's defensive stance—though a sincere cry for help for his struggling constituents—demonstrates how exposure of
white privilege marshals a sense of white persecution. Yates makes this connection as well, invoking the poignant work of University of Maryland sociologist
Fred Pincus. Pincus tackles the notion of reverse discrimination by examining
white perceptions. His 2002 findings contend that "while half or more of all
white males believe that their group experiences discrimination, only 2–3 percent report personally experiencing it."[22] Moreover, he notes that the 1994 Equal
Opportunity Employment Commission classified only 1 percent of the reverse
discrimination cases as credible.

Fueling this notion of white persecution effectively politicizes racial competition to the Republican advantage. Since whiteness functions as a wage, a
commodity that has and continues to trade high,[23] the GOP's coded language—
suggesting that federal entitlements would result inversely in the economic oppression of southern whites—has consistently struck a powerful note. For example,
during his 1980 presidential bid, Ronald Reagan—echoing Goldwater—invoked
the image of the "welfare queen," a minority woman who supposedly lived high-
on-the-hog at the expense of hardworking taxpayers.[24] Reagan described her as
having "eighty names, thirty addresses, [and] twelve Social Security cards [who]
is collecting veteran's benefits on four non-existing deceased husbands. She's got
Medicaid, getting food stamps, and she is collecting welfare under each of her
names. Her tax free cash income," Reagan proclaimed, "is over $150,000."[25] The
economic argument barely masks the racial argument. Thus, the techniques of the
Long Southern Strategy are more complex than just creating white solidarity or
elevating whiteness to maintain the racial hierarchy in a politically correct, post–
civil rights era; the Long Southern Strategy actually turned the entire political
arena into a zero-sum economic game, in which only one group could prosper.

Powerful characterizations of the haves and have-nots, of the taxpayer
and the tax recipient,[26] of the makers and the takers, promoted the belief that
some Americans deserved privileges but others did not. "Reagan's rhetoric,"
noted Joseph Aistrup, "agrees with many whites who feel that black people are
impoverished because of personal reasons rather than because they have a true
need or that the past sins of discrimination are to blame for their lower social

standing." Since poverty was the result of poor personal choices, then welfare recipients were undeserving—an attitude, Aistrup contends, that is "especially prevalent in the Deep South."[27] Whiteness is portrayed as a meritocracy, despite being inaccessible to non-whites and based on nothing. Moreover, this fiscal disguise provided deniability for so long that many have forgotten the racial roots of these debates altogether. Even scholars studying the realignment of the South with the Republican Party, for example, have pointed to the rise of the southern suburban class, reflected in the growth of white neighborhoods, as evidence of an economic-based transformation.[28] Yet white flight can also be seen as an effort to recreate a reactionary world of white privilege that is shielded from social change—a physical manifestation of the invisible knapsack. Therefore, even though other studies have shown that race trumps class in terms of influencing partisanship,[29] the truth is that, particularly in the South, race and class are almost impossible to separate. The Long Southern Strategy intentionally muddied that water. Even now, minority advancement is tantamount to white persecution and opposition to federal entitlements somehow safeguards white privilege, both of which make southern whites vulnerable to identity politics and subject to vote against their economic self-interest.

SCHOLARLY INTEREST IN the concept of white privilege has increased substantially since McIntosh's 1988 study. The *Journal of Social Issues* even published a special issue entitled "Systems of Prejudice: Intersections, Awareness, and Applications" in March 2012, presenting new research on white privilege. In general, scholars in the field of psychology have experimented with the way privilege functions, while education researchers have focused on its impact. Their findings, echoed popularly by cultural critics such as Tim Wise, author of *White Like Me: Reflections on Race from a Privileged Son*, and Tobin Miller Shearer, who penned *Enter the River: Healing Steps from White Privilege to Racial Reconciliation*, are consistent.[30] Simply put, white privilege is defined as the unearned advantages and benefits "afforded to powerful social groups within systems of oppression."[31] Janie Pinterits, Paul Poteat, and Lisa Spanierman have developed a White Privilege Attitudes Scale (WPAS) that examines the behavioral, affective, and cognitive aspects of white privilege. Basing their scale on tangential work on "conferred dominance"[32] and on "an invisible corollary to racism,"[33] Pinterits, Poteat, and Spanierman present at twenty-eight-item scale with four primary factors: (a) Willingness to Confront White Privilege; (b) Anticipated Cost of Addressing White Privilege; (c) White Privilege Awareness; and (d) White Privilege Remorse.[34] Overall, the study exposes white resistance to acknowledging privilege, which they indicate is based on fear—"acknowledgement might lead to rejection by the minority population (eliminating said privilege)"[35]—as well as the guilt, shame, and anger that can accompany the recognition of privilege.

In her 1993 article "Was Blind, but Now I See," Barbara Flagg poignantly observed that unlike racial out-groups, "white people have an option, every day, not to think of themselves in racial terms."[36] This renders their unearned advantages—the "special provisions, assurances, tools, maps, guides, codebooks, visas, clothes, compass, emergency gear, and blank checks"[37] that are part of the McIntosh knapsack—invisible to themselves. Such blindness invites criticism. George W. Bush, for instance, faced accusations that racial bias influenced his actions during the aftermath of Hurricane Katrina, most notably when Kanye West proclaimed live on a televised fundraising relief effort that "George Bush doesn't care about black people."[38] Scholars such as Mychal Denzel Smith wrote in the *Nation* that West's outburst was the "first relatable expression of black rage on a national stage."[39] It was also an effort to bear witness to the consequences of unacknowledged white privilege by pointing to the inequity between how white and black victims of natural disasters have been treated. Bush claimed the moment was the "all-time low" of his tenure. For Bush, perhaps the criticism caused the pain of self-reflection about which many privilege scholars have written.

According to recent findings, however, this recognition can be framed so that whites will be more sympathetic to the institutional racism endured by African Americans. Adam Powell, Nyla Branscombe, and Michael Schmitt find that language describing inequality as "outgroup disadvantage" allows whites to render the backpack at least somewhat invisible. They can feel empathy without feeling bad about themselves. However, inequality framed as white privilege catalyzed collective guilt and mitigated racial animus. In other words, the rhetoric of disparity can mask white privilege, thereby perpetuating the denial of it, or it can implicate whites as "beneficiaries of the inequitable distribution of social resources,"[40] which triggers white defensiveness. That being said, research has shown that even negative reactions to consciousness-raising about white privilege can be transformed into "prejudice reduction" if awareness is paired with opportunities for social activism.[41] The perception of potential efficacy alone, as opposed to helplessness, allowed whites who were educated about privilege to alter their attitudes toward out-groups in a positive direction. Brian Lowery, Eric Knowles, and Miguel Unzueta conducted a series of similar framing experiments and found that white self-image impacted not only whether the white participants acknowledged the existence of white privilege, but also their attitudes toward "redistributive social programs."[42]

Framing matters and criticism, in particular, of unearned white advantages only heightens this sense of white persecution and triggers self-defense. That defense most commonly requires whites to shift the responsibility for inequity from their own shoulders to the backs of minorities whom they deem not meritworthy. "It becomes common," surmise Carole Lund and Scipio Collin in their editors' introduction to *New Directions for Adult and Continuing Education*, "for whites to believe falsely that their privilege was earned by hard work and intellectual superiority; it becomes the center of their worldview."[43] Goldwater attacked Medicare and other entitlement programs for exactly this reason—they were dangerous to the moral fabric of the country because they empowered the un-deserving. He called in his 1964 campaign brochure for a "halt to the relentless drift to the welfare state," which gives "special privilege favors at the expense of the general public taxpayer."[44] The programs of the New Deal and the Fair Deal and the Great Society on the horizon were leveling the playing field in decidedly tangible ways, perhaps none as vital as equal access to medical care. Goldwater's philosophy stood in direct contrast to civil rights leaders like Martin Luther King Jr., who in 1966 told the National Convention of the Medical Committee for Human Rights gathered in Chicago, "Of all the forms of inequality, injustice in health care is the most shocking and inhumane."[45]

Forty years later, GOP presidential nominee Mitt Romney spoke plainly to a group of Republican donors about the uphill battle he was facing against President Obama in the 2012 election. The speech, which was captured on video, was leaked and went viral. "There are 47 percent who are with him [Obama]," claimed Romney, "who are dependent upon government, who believe that they are victims, who believe the government has a responsibility to care for them, who believe that they are entitled to health care, to food, to housing, to you-name-it—that, that's an entitlement."[46] The comment came during a time in which white privilege and healthcare reform collided once again as Democrats worked to pass the Affordable Care Act, or Obamacare, as detractors called it. Many speculated that President Obama's background had racialized the debate, which had been ongoing through several election cycles. Obama himself denied the correlation in an appearance on *Meet the Press* in September 2009. However, Michael Tesler published a comprehensive study in the *American Journal of Political Science* that tracked healthcare attitudes for two decades, finding that "the racial divide in healthcare opinions was 20 percentage points greater in 2009–2010 than it was over President Clinton's plan back in 1993–1994."[47]

The media coverage of Obamacare invoked race often and without subtlety. Paul Krugman, writing in the *New York Times*, deemed "racial anxiety" as the source for healthcare opposition, for example. Antoine Banks's findings con-firm both Tesler's and Krugman's points: racial attitudes in white Americans do predict opposition to Obamacare. Moreover, the response is emotional, Banks noted, as "anger uniquely pushes racial conservatives to be more opposing of health care reform."[48] In fact, in previous research Banks and Nicholas Valentino found that anger was "uniquely powerful at boosting opposition to racially re-distributive policies among white racial conservatives,"[49] and Banks, along with Heather Hicks, found fear to trigger white support for new voter identification initiatives.[50] So somehow, via anger and fear and anxiety, healthcare under Obama fell into that category of "racially redistributive policies," which may help explain why GOP leadership in Congress attempted to repeal "Obamacare" repeatedly. Many members of Congress, along with President Trump, had campaigned on this repeal. Yet a February 2017 poll, as reported in the *New York Times*, found that roughly one-third of the American electorate did not know that the Affordable Care Act and Obamacare were one and the same.[51] Much of the repeal fervor was emotional rather than grounded. In the first year of Trump's administration, the GOP eliminated the individual mandate upon which the policy is built as part of a tax overhaul.

The source of this anger merits attention in a time in which whiteness proves unifying, particularly among southerners. Flagg's 1993 critical legal studies analysis of white privilege lists adequate healthcare as a major tenet of inequity, including "more frequent and more severe medical problems," "higher mortality rates," and "less comprehensive health care" for African Americans.[52] The Institute of Medicine of the National Academy of Sciences issued a report for Congress in 2003 entitled "Unequal Treatment: Confronting Racial and Ethnic Disparities in Healthcare" that exposed the fact that blacks and other ethnic minorities received worse care even when controlling for income and insurance status. They contributed this to "stereotyping, biases, and uncertainty on the part of healthcare providers."[53] The problem is real and deadly. The anger, Banks finds, still surges based on the rhetoric of the opposition. "When an issue is framed," he argues, "as an undeserved handout by the federal government, people's opinions may become colored with racial considerations."[54] This focus on who is deserving—and that "some people who are the beneficiaries of preferences are more deserving than others"—underscores the whole notion of white privilege, contends Fred Pincus, who cites it as a fundamental belief of whites who claim reverse discrimination.[55]

In the South, specifically, implementation of the Affordable Care Act's insurance exchanges has suffered, with several states forgoing millions of dollars in support for Medicaid expansion. The pattern of maintaining white privilege by obstructing policies that might benefit African Americans remains unbroken, even if doing so means that poor whites are harmed in the process. "Then as now," writes journalist Ryan Cooper, comparing the contemporary southern political landscape to post–Civil War Reconstruction, "the conservative power structure in the South prioritizes denying benefits to its most vulnerable citizens above everything else—and uses small government conservative ideology to do so."[56]

Perhaps more authoritative than any other source, Sarah Varney's investigative report "Mississippi, Burned: How the Poorest, Sickest State Got Left Behind by Obamacare" uncovers in vivid detail how the state's GOP and Tea Party leaders under Governor Phil Bryant killed the program. It was framed, Varney writes, "as an invasion from the North" and "it fractured along racial lines, stoking long-held grievances against the federal government."[57]

In 2010, the Blair Center Poll found that these attitudes remain steeped in the mind and identity of many white southerners. Table 2.1 presents the percentage of white Americans who both live in the South and outside the South, and those who claim a southern identity and those who do not, who expressed being "concerned or very concerned" that healthcare reform would lead to a host of dire consequences. White southerners report significantly more anxiety than do non-southern whites on every potential consequence, including accusations that healthcare reform would cause rationing, delays, a drop in quality, and increased taxes, as well as on the more radical notions that reform would lead to socialism and euthanasia of the elderly. Whites who live in the geographic South are a close second. Moreover, white, self-described southerners are the most concerned group when it comes to the idea that Obamacare will benefit people who do not work hard enough to deserve it. White superiority,

Table 2.1 Percent "Concerned" or "Very Concerned" That Proposed Health Care Reforms May Lead to the Following Consequences, Among Whites, 2010

	Non-South	South	Non-southern	Southern
Health care rationing	60.3	64.3	58.1	72.3
Long delays in getting needed medical treatment	63.8	69.3	61.8	77.9
Substantial drop in quality health care	64.9	69.0	62.4	78.1
Taxes being raised for average Americans	71.6	73.9	68.6	82.7
These reforms will lead to Socialism	46.9	55.1	46.5	61.6
Euthanasia ("mercy killing") of elderly patients	40.7	49.1	39.5	57.2
Benefits to people that do not work hard enough to deserve it	51.4	56.9	49.8	64.5

Data are from the 2010 Blair Center Poll.

justified by blaming minorities for their own oppression, is so fundamental to southern white identity that any challenge or perceived challenge to it was met with a vigorous defense, often to political ends. Those ends were GOP victories, secured at the expense of the same white southerners—many of whom overwhelmingly benefit from healthcare reform and other entitlements—who provided them.

WHEN IT COMES to activating this defense of white privilege, racial threats can be real, imagined, or manufactured, and the more directly they seem to affect white pocketbooks, the more ominous they seem. The potential spread of Populism in the early twentieth century, the emergence of labor strikes, and even the implementation of some New Deal programs met resistance from white southerners willing to sacrifice their own benefits to assuage their fears of black economic uplift—sometimes knowingly, sometimes unknowingly. Politicians who knew how to exploit these fears found easy targets.[58] Political scientist V. O. Key Jr., in his 1949 study of southern politics, observed this historic phenomenon in the region: "The specter of Reconstruction, of Negro government, can still be used to quell incipient rebellion by discontented whites."[59] That image of black leadership and power signaled southern white political and economic defeat, and though temporary, the rage and anxiety resulting from this fall from dominance shaped southern white identity for generations. In their presidential campaigns, both a defiant George Wallace and Donald Trump, four decades later, railed not only against African American progress, but also against the liberal elitists[60] and hippie agitators who championed it. Their supporters cheered. Though less blatant, southerners responded to the more coded and indirect pronouncement that America could turn back from the New Deal,[61] not simply halting implementation of programs designed to uplift the disadvantaged, but reversing course entirely. "We must begin to withdraw from a whole series of programs," demanded Goldwater in his book *Conscience of a Conservative.*[62] The Long Southern Strategy, in general, promised pessimistic southern whites that their candidates could restore their eroded privileges and halt or reverse white economic losses. Tea Party Republicans tapped into that ongoing pessimism stemming from a belief that the Obama administration would use hard-working American taxpayer dollars to expand entitlement programs, which many feared would chip away at the white power that Obama's election, itself, directly defied.

In the 2010 exit polls, white pessimism reached quantifiable levels, with 87 percent of American voters (78 percent of whom were white) expressing anxiety about the economy and 38 percent, more specifically, believing that the next generation would not be as financially successful.[63] Only a few months later, the *Washington Post* released polling results that disaggregated this angst by racial ethnicity. While a clear majority of African Americans (59 percent) expressed belief that Obama's fiscal policies were improving the economy, only 18 percent of whites agreed, with 36 percent of Hispanic respondents signaling the same optimism.[64] The trend was replicated repeatedly by various nonpartisan polling and research institutes, particularly in light of 2010 US Census findings that revealed that "all American workers slid backward."[65] The Pew Research Center described the changes as "a lost decade for the middle class" with median middle-class incomes falling from $72,956 to $69,487 in constant 2011 dollars.[66] In a poignant article that appeared in *The Atlantic* in October 2011 entitled "Why Whites Are More Pessimistic about Their Futures Than Minorities," Jim Tankersly, Ron Fournier, and Nancy Cococt highlight the recession's dramatic racial disparities. While African American and Latino incomes fell by 10 percent and 7.2 percent respectively, white households lost only 5.4 percent. This discrepancy broadened the gap between whites and non-whites, and in 2010, it reached 30–40 percent. Citing the Pew Research Center's Social and Demographic Trends project, Tankersly, Fournier, and Cook surmised that between 2005 and 2009, Latinos lost two-thirds of their net wealth; African Americans saw theirs cut in half, while whites lost less than one-fifth of their wealth overall.[67]

Yet, levels of pessimism are reported inversely. This "optimism gap," as they call it, reflects a sense of rising in status, of possibility. Thus, outlook mirrors trajectory. The same month, Demos, a progressive advocacy group, reported their similar findings that 55 percent of young whites (between the ages of 18 and 34) think they will be worse off than their parents are, with only 12 percent expecting to surpass their parents financially.[68] Among African Americans, 31 percent of young people believe they will improve upon their family standings, as well as 36 percent of Hispanics. The Associated Press–NORC Center for Public Affairs Research provided the most comprehensive assessment in their 2013 report "The Public Mood: White Malaise but Optimism among Blacks, Hispanics." Employing forty years of data from the General Social Survey, as well as other public polls, authors Trevor Tompson and Jennifer Benz reveal the dramatic and historic change. Looking specifically at the question, "The way things are in America, people like me and my family have a good chance of improving our standard of living—do you agree or disagree?," the report indicates a nearly 30-point decline in agreement by whites from 1987 to 2012.[69]

Tompson and Benz, among others, do point to the "symbolic importance of electing the first African American to the presidency" as an explanation for the increase in minority optimism despite continued and worsening economic hardship. On the other hand, for many white Americans, Obama symbolized a threat to white privilege, which may explain the timing of the surge in white pessimism. However, the net economic downturn for many whites is real, and that "fear of falling" in combination with the symbolic power of the Obama administration exacerbates this defense of white privileges that may be slipping away. Moreover, in regions like the South, where Republicans successfully connected the recession to Obama's policies—whether through messaging about the debt ceiling, the cost of Obamacare, or the alleged abuse of entitlement programs—protecting whiteness, even if it means voting against one's own economic self-interest, becomes personal and crucial. And for white southerners who have experienced the political posturing and rhetoric that has reinforced the invisible knapsack for decades, the threat is powerful in its familiarity and may prove significantly distinctive in its residual strength.

In order to understand how white Americans evaluate their own futures and how they perceive the well-being of others in the future, respondents to the Blair Center Polls were asked the following: "When you think of the following people and groups, do you think things will get much better or much worse in the future?" As seen in Figure 2.1, in 2010 almost half of white respondents across the board had a negative view of the future of the country, including the majority (53 percent) of southern whites. Overall, southern whites have significantly more negative outlooks than do non-southern whites, with 43.4 percent anticipating

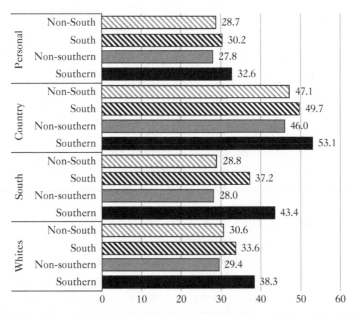

FIGURE 2.1 Percent Reporting That the Future Will Be "Somewhat" or "Much Worse," for the Following, Among Whites, 2010

Data are from the 2010 Blair Center Poll.

that the future of the South, as a region, was bleak, and over one-third (38.3 percent) believing that whites, as a racial group, would face similar hardships.

However, when asked about their own personal trajectory, a smaller percentage of whites in every subgroup expressed such pessimism compared to the number who anticipated a decline for the country, or for the South, or for whites. The largest gap for every group is between their personal future and the future of the country, which suggests there is a disconnect between this national angst and projections of one's own personal future success. The angst might be an expression of something else—something more abstract, something coded, or something racialized.

RACISM AND STATUS, particularly economic status, are anything but mutually exclusive. They were portrayed intentionally as conjoined twins to white southern audiences before and throughout the Long Southern Strategy. It did not take long for the latter to eclipse the former. Richard Weaver, conservative intellectual and author of *Ideas Have Consequences*, argued in 1957 against "racial collectivism," the communist-inspired reallocation of wealth that he believed was inseparable from the Civil Rights Movement. "'Integration' and 'Communization' are, after all," he wrote, "pretty closely synonymous."[70] Young Americans for Freedom (YAF), the most prominent GOP youth training organization in the 1960s, with members who went on to leadership positions in the Reagan and George H. W. Bush administrations, even obscured the mission of Martin Luther King Jr., by denouncing his followers as "conditioned to handouts." The YAF editorial issued in the wake of King's assassination summarized his core philosophy as "society owes the Negro," "income should be redistributed," and "private property need not be respected." They further framed King's alleged fight for a "guaranteed annual income" as "the best way to colonize, not liberate, the American Negro. It gives him security," they pronounced, "*not* opportunity."[71]

Even contemporary right-to-work laws, first passed in 1944, sprang forth from a desire to maintain Jim Crow at all costs. In the South, where the battle commenced, "equating union growth with race-mixing" was politically effective.[72] Thus, the 1964 kickoff of the Long Southern Strategy included a party platform specifically denouncing handouts as creating "perpetual dependency"[73] in the recipients. Goldwater himself even suggested that the welfare state would threaten law and order—two dog whistles blown at once. "If it is entirely proper for government to take from some to give to others," questioned Goldwater, "then won't some be led to believe that they can rightfully take from anyone who has more than them?"[74] Depicting federal entitlements as a slippery slope resulting in amoral behavior and criminal activity, Goldwater played on the fears of many southern whites for whom the zero tolerance attitude toward segregation had invoked the same catastrophic vision.

If southern whites felt their social power was threatened by integration, then government programs intended not only to provide equal opportunities to blacks, but also to close many of the economic gaps between the races, would only intensify these feelings. This shift is exactly what happened. The "post-1964 focus on broader goals emphasizing equal outcomes or result for blacks," argued Thomas and Mary Edsall, triggered heightened opposition from the right, particularly because these efforts were seen as a redistribution of resources. The resources included, of course, housing, education, and jobs, but also extended to "valuable intangibles such as cultural authority, prestige, and social space."[75] Many of those "intangibles" could not be discussed publicly in the post–civil rights era, when overt racism and overt superiority invited criticism or even legal complaints. The often-coded language of fiscal conservatism provided an ample coverage and just in time. Laura Kalman, in her book *Right Star Rising: A New Politics 1974–1980*, argues that "the question of who should get ahead came at a difficult moment in American history."[76] Whereas the civil rights initiatives of the 1960s were supported by a robust American economy, the financial crises of the 1970s solidified the zero-sum game perspective of the battle for equal access. African Americans climbing the economic and political ladder became commensurate with whites being pulled down from their positions of privilege—or so many white Americans feared. That fear underscores both white pessimism about their own futures and their suspicion of increased racial competition.

The racial threat dog whistle was so common and ingrained in the southern white mind that anthropologists identified it decades before Goldwater or Nixon or Reagan made it part of the Long Southern Strategy. "White aggression against Negroes and the social patterns which permit it are forms of social control; they are instrumentalities for keeping the Negro in his place and maintaining the supraordinate position of the white caste," concluded John Dollard in his anthropological analysis of the South. He continued: "we know from our study that the whites do not fight for social superiority just for fun; on the contrary, they are attempting to minimize or eliminate Negro competition in the spheres of economics, sex, and prestige."[77] Consequently, whiteness has ballooned and deflated over time when deemed advantageous. For example, Irish and Italian immigrants, once discriminated against, have been brought under this umbrella of whiteness usually for political advantage, as chronicled in Noel Ignatiev's *How the Irish Became White*. This "investment in whiteness" requires a shift in self-conception and group consciousness, which is rewarded by the privileges that are granted.[78] Some have even speculated that in order to compensate for shifting demographics, Republicans will have to let Asian Americans or even some Latinos into

"The Club of Privilege," doling out "honorary white privilege"[79] in an effort to break up growing minority coalitions.

The Long Southern Strategy, however, has rarely followed that path, particularly in the Trump era. Instead, when attempting to attract white southern voters, these candidates have relied on what scholars have called the "Racial Threat" thesis—the notion that a rise in the non-white population will trigger a white community to feel threatened and vote for more racially conservative candidates[80] who they believe will block entitlement programs or any initiative characterized as redistributing wealth. Stressing the racial contest becomes part of the coded campaign messaging. John McCain's use of "Joe the Plumber" in his 2008 campaign as a stand-in for white Americans under attack illustrates this dynamic.[81] Four years later, GOP-presidential nominee Mitt Romney accused President Obama of plotting to cut work requirements for welfare, which was characterized by Romney's director of policy as a "kick in the gut to the millions of hard-working middle-class taxpayers struggling in today's economy."[82] This threat to white privilege may be symbolic, as in the election of a non-white president, or it can be general such as the US Census projection that whites will be a racial minority by 2044,[83] or it can be emotional such as the "fear of falling" that accompanies an economic downturn, which is often cited by Tea Party activists. All of these messages have blanketed the southern political landscape, giving old anxieties new life again and again.

Such anxiety has been growing and it has tremendous political significance—even prior to the 2016 election when it was on full display.[84] As political scientist Ashley Jardina argues, "When the dominant status of whites relative to racial and ethnic minorities is secure and unchallenged, white identity likely remains dormant. When whites perceive their group's dominant status is threatened or their group is unfairly disadvantaged, however, their racial identity may become salient and politically relevant."[85] The threat of racial competition resonates among white southerners even now—or perhaps especially now. On a five-point scale ranging from "no competition" to "a lot of competition," the 2012 Blair Center Poll, as seen in Figure 2.2, indicates that a majority of whites report "some" or "a lot" of competition with African Americans and Latinos. Further, there are significant differences across both southern identity and geography.

Almost 70 percent of white respondents who call themselves southern and/or live in the South perceive competition with African Americans, compared to 64.8 percent of non-southern respondents and 62.4 percent of those who live outside of the South. The same pattern holds true for perceptions of competition with Latinos, though at slightly lower numbers. So much of white southern identity has been shaped in opposition to blackness and now "brownness" that

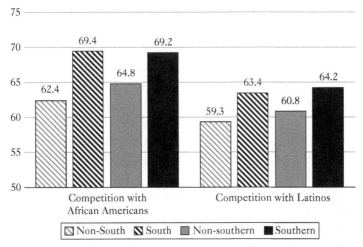

FIGURE 2.2 Percent Reporting "Some" or "A Lot" of Competition with African Americans and Latinos, Among Whites, 2012

Data are from the 2012 Blair Center Poll.

racial equality remains the greatest threat, often underscoring debates about government spending or fiscal conservatism.

Consequently, realignment scholars have devoured the race-versus-money debate in their quest to explain the metamorphosis of the South from blue to red. For example, Byron Shafer and Richard Johnston marry the defection of southern white Democrats to the GOP to the burgeoning economies of the southern rim states, while Matthew Lassiter, as previously noted, points to the exodus of southern whites to the suburbs, and a resulting middle class entitlement, as catalyzing realignment.[86] It was nearly twenty years ago that Alan Abramowitz challenged Edward Carmines and James Stimson's 1989 major work, *Issue Evolution: Race and the Transformation of American Politics*, arguing that the Democratic Party's position on social welfare, rather than civil rights, drove white southerners into the arms of the GOP.[87] More recently, Seth Ackerman, tracing the roots of the Tea Party, contended that affluence, and the narrowing gap between the North and the South, slowly cracked the once solidly Democratic region.[88]

Yet in the aftermath of Obama's election, and the hardening of GOP attitudes toward him, blaming economic changes for the realignment of the South with the Republican Party seemed a partial explanation at best. For example, in the first weeks of October 2013, an "internal Civil War" within the Republican Party erupted as the federal government butted heads against a debt ceiling, leaning over what was deemed a "fiscal cliff."[89] The consequential shutdown exposed a regional rift in America's Grand Old Party, with 80 percent of white southern Republicans, compared to 50 percent of non-southern, white Republicans, blocking appropriations for 2014, dangling the gutting of the Affordable Care Act as a bargaining chip.[90] The regional split fueled speculation that southern white distinctiveness hinges not just on conservative, but reactionary attitudes toward the economy, with the intensity and irrationality of those attitudes resulting from southern racial abuses and their ensuing structural legacy. Journalist Zack Beauchamp, in his attempt to explain the rift, points to this conflation of money and race. "Racial conservatism," he argues, "pulled Southern whites toward economic conservatism"; thus, "the same underlying structural trends in Southern public opinion produced both the Dixiecrats and hard-right Southern Republicans."[91] For many, fiscal conservatism was a smoke screen. Protecting white privilege was the common intention and the seeds of fear regarding its imminent erosion were planted, cultivated, and watered regularly by a Long Southern Strategy.[92]

THAT FEAR IS politically motivating only if people believe both that through government services others will have a seat at the table, so to speak, and that the seats at that table are limited. Whites are rendered victims or, as Chris Boeskool entitled his blog post for the *Huffington Post*, "When You Are Accustomed to Privilege, Equality Feels like Oppression."[93] For many, the privilege is invisible and the feelings are real. For example, racially motivated crimes on university campuses have increased, argues Jack Levin, because "the proto-typical college student: white, male and Protestant" has to "share with people who are different—Black, Latino and Asian students—and they don't like losing their advantage and privilege."[94] This notion of victimization is, of course, the natural result of viewing racial progress as a zero-sum game. CNN journalist John Blake summarized this national trend in his 2011 article "Are Whites Racially Oppressed?" He notes the rise in whiteness studies classes at universities and the advent of scholarship associations like the Texas-based "Former Majority Association for Equality." Blake interviewed sociologist Charles Gallagher, who contends that whites "went from being a privileged group to all of a sudden becoming whites, the new victims."[95] That same year, in *Perspectives on Psychological Science*, Michael Norton and Samuel Summers found that as whites perceived bias against blacks to be decreasing, they simultaneous perceived bias against whites to be increasing—a pattern limited only to white respondents. Moreover, on a ten-point scale, 11 percent of white respondents gave discrimination of whites the maximum score.[96] In research specifically examining perceptions of reverse racial discrimination in the South, the Winthrop University Poll found that 46 percent of whites in the South believe that they "are under attack in America."[97]

Claims of reverse discrimination, similar to dog whistles regarding racial threats, can unify whites politically, particularly when whites believe they have been hurt by certain public policies.[98] However, the label itself—"reverse racism"—disregards the power dynamic inherent in white racism toward people of color by suggesting that any group, irrespective of its historical dominance, can be the victim of racism. On the other hand, in an ironic way, these claims of reverse racism also render whiteness visible, though it is seen as a target of persecution. And they are not new either. Goldwater's 1964 campaign and its comprehensive defense of white privilege included in the party platform a direct statement opposing "federally sponsored inverse discrimination whether by the shifting of jobs, or the abandonment of neighborhood schools, for reasons of race."[99] Even the Trump administration, under then attorney general Jeff Sessions of Alabama—who has his own deep history with racial oppression as noted in a letter by the late Coretta Scott King[100]—threatened to both investigate and sue universities for reverse discrimination against whites in their admissions processes.[101] This feeling of being "under siege" is embedded in white southern culture, conditioned by the Civil War and Reconstruction and a host of other reinforcing experiences. Southern historian George Tindall coined the phrase "the benighted South" to describe how southern whites have historically been ridiculed and ostracized, a region perpetually at odds with American national identity.[102] The Long Southern Strategy made that work to the GOP's favor.[103]

The Southern Nationalist Network, founded in 2010, tracks discrimination and mockery of white southerners specifically (even in popular culture) and fuels this perception of white victimhood, utilizing the term "ethnic replacement."[104] White southern culture is being eliminated, or so goes the claim. Historian Clyde Wilson even authored a legal brief arguing for the protected ethnic status of white southerners in a South Carolina discrimination case against a student who wore a Confederate flag T-shirt. The range of his claim is extensive, stretching back to settlement patterns, regional climate, and cultural traits.[105] He even highlights the work of sociologist John Shelton Reed whose public opinion data, most notably in the Southern Focus Polls conducted in the 1990s at the University of North Carolina, show measurable distinctions regarding attitudes toward spirituality, family, and the separation of public and private spheres.[106] So southern white distinctiveness, shaped directly and indirectly by the institution of slavery and the codification of white supremacy, now becomes a justification for reverse racism claims in the post–civil rights era.

These feelings of disaffection are not always articulated in legal claims. Sometimes they just fester. Such was the driving sentiment behind the "silent majority," the label Richard Nixon would use to describe a community that George Wallace's campaign had brought to light. These "victimized people in the middle saw themselves as the mainstream and the upholders of traditional values which were under attack," notes Michael Perlman. "Wallace offered himself as their protector and spokesman," he continues, because "he understood them, and he invited and incited them to lash out and give vent to their anger and rage." Some GOP leaders have even tried to placate this white southern angst, such as Gerald Ford who signed a congressional bill in 1975 to restore citizenship to Confederate General Robert E. Lee. In his accompanying speech, Ford proclaimed that "General Lee's character has been an example to succeeding generations, making the restoration of his citizenship an event in which every American can take pride."[107] When rhetorical "pardons" of Confederate heroes did not work—or when the effect did not last—this resurgent resentment still found a partisan home. In a 2013 report out of Stanford University, Max McClure concludes that "southern evangelical churches and the GOP are acting as regional communities for racially disaffected whites."[108] Both have long been functioning as safe spaces for white victimhood. To that end, in 2013, sociologists Aliya Saperstein and Damon Mayrl found that of whites who claim reverse racism, most are religious southern Republicans.[109]

In Figure 2.3, respondents to the 2012 Blair Center Poll were asked the extent to which they believed the following things happen to them because of their "ethnic or racial background": (1) How often do you experience discrimination? (2) How often are you are treated with less respect than other people? (3) How often do you receive poorer service than other people at restaurants or stores? (4) How often are you are called names or insulted? (5) How often are you have been unfairly stopped by police? Overall, a substantial percentage—though by no means a majority—of white respondents report experiencing what they perceive as reverse discrimination, with over one-third of whites indicating the frequency of these encounters as "very often," "fairly often," or "once in a while." Among whites who live in the South, that number rises to 44 percent, and among whites who identify as southern it reaches 46.8 percent, a significant 10 points higher than non-southern whites. In every category, white southerners are the most likely to report experiencing discrimination. Moreover, the gaps between white southerners and white non-southerners are significantly distinct across the board—though on certain categories, such as discrimination by police, the numbers are very small overall. The gap is the largest on the question regarding general discrimination, and no specific category, from being disrespected to being called names to receiving discriminatory treatment in various service industries, reaches that level. In some ways, this too seems like an abstract perception with minimal concrete footing, though it has long been a part of southern white culture.[110] Perhaps simply the result of having "a tender skin to criticism,"[111] this perception feeds the larger belief in a war on whites. The

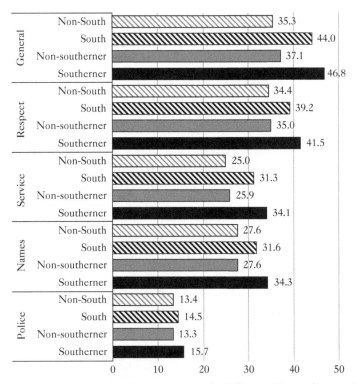

FIGURE 2.3 Percent Reporting Experience with the Following Types of Reverse Racial Discrimination, Among Whites, 2012

Data are from the 2012 Blair Center Poll.

southern front in that war seems to grow in strength when provoked, whether the provocation is real or contrived, and that has played a major role in turning and keeping the South red.

VICTORY IN THIS imagined "war on whites" is what will make America great again, or at least that is what Trump's candidacy means to a lot of his supporters. That is, in part, why his message resonated. Immediately after this election, the percentage of southern whites who report experiencing discrimination because of their whiteness dropped slightly in almost every category, though it remains significantly distinct from levels reported by non-southern whites in every category. In terms of general day-to-day experiences of reverse discrimination, the number fell slightly from 46.8 percent to 45.3 percent, for example. White southerners report higher levels in only two categories; reports of being disrespected because of their whiteness jumped 8 points, while reports of receiving lesser services increased 3.7 points. Trump's success, however, seems to have had a more consistent impact on perceptions toward the economy, due, in no small part, to the fact that the Long Southern Strategy made economic attitudes and racial animus hard to separate. Thus, many point to personal economic pessimism—as well as pessimism about the country and the South expressed by whites during Obama's tenure—as the source of Trump's popularity, conflating his voters with a surging working-class populist movement of sorts. However, critics of this conflation point to the fact that Trump's own record on labor is questionable, including accusations and lawsuits regarding unpaid workers and the hiring of illegal immigrants by his companies.[112] By his history, Trump was an unlikely champion of the working class, nor did his economic status make him someone with whom labor would naturally identify.

Figure 2.4 from the 2016 Blair Center Poll shines new light on this debate. Within weeks of the Trump's victory, personal economic dread among whites was fleeting throughout the country. In 2010 and 2012, whites who claim a southern identity were more pessimistic than non-southern whites when asked specifically about the fate of their personal finances, with 29 percent and 37.4 percent, respectively, believing that worse times were ahead of them. In 2016, however, immediately after Trump's victory, such economic anxiety fell to 10.8 percent among whites who identify as southern, slightly lower but still significantly distinct from non-southern whites at 13.8 percent. The timing of this drop in economic anxiety, which occurred immediately after Trump's election and absent a corresponding economic boom,[113] is perhaps just as telling as the timing of the Tea Party movement, which sparked

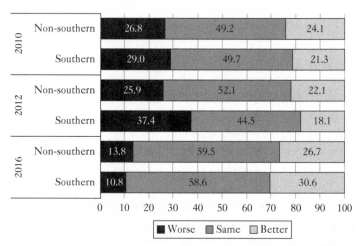

FIGURE 2.4 Percent Prospective Views of Respondents' Personal Economic Situation, Among Whites, 2010–2016

Data are from the 2010, 2012, and 2016 Blair Center Polls.

within days of Obama's inauguration.[114] The economic masks the racial, so much so that many do not even see it.

The same goes for whites' perception of competition with African Americans and Latinos. Trump's election has somehow diminished that fire too. Figure 2.5 reveals that among whites who call themselves southern, the percentage reporting they perceive competition from African Americans fell from 69.2 percent in 2012 to 55 percent in late November 2016. Among non-southern whites, the percentage fell from 64.8 to 52.5 percent. In terms of competition with Latinos, the number dropped from 64.2 to 49.8 percent among whites who claim a southern identity, and among those who do not, it fell from 60.8 percent in 2012 to 50.4 percent in 2016. These differences between non-southern whites and southern whites remain significantly distinct in 2016, but they are both shifting in the same direction. Perhaps the replacement of the Obama administration with the Trump administration, particularly in the South, makes them feel less threatened by minority competition and more optimistic about their prospective fortunes. This is not rational economic voting, it is rational identity voting. It is rational only in the sense that southern whiteness was constructed as a wage—and a valuable one

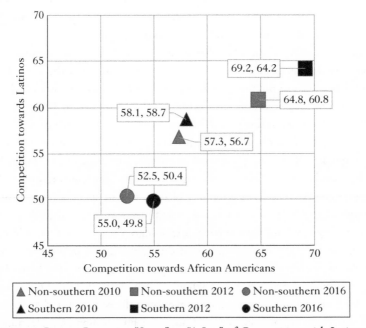

FIGURE 2.5 Percent Reporting "Some" or "A Lot" of Competition with Latinos and African Americans, Among Whites, 2010–2016

Data are from the 2010, 2012, and 2016 Blair Center Polls.

at that. Losing it meant losing everything. And so the scales always tip in favor of its protection.

IN THE 1998 anthology *White Reign: Deploying Whiteness in America*, leading education and cultural critics pointed to the new white victimization claims emerging in the aftermath of the Civil Rights Movement. "Whites are the 'new losers,'" notes Michael Apple, "in a playing field that they believe has been leveled now that the United States is a supposedly basically egalitarian, color-blind society."[115] However, the playing field has not been leveled and pressure to halt any progress to do so maintains the privilege and advantages inherent in American whiteness. That sentiment—the perception of an impending loss of white status via economic and political competition—was the lifeblood of the Long Southern Strategy. Even southern Democrats attempting to stem the bleeding toward the Goldwater campaign recognized the feeling. "The so-called backlash . . . does actually exist," wrote Tennessee Governor Buford Ellington. "People holding down jobs with industry are afraid they are going to be forced out of jobs to make room for people who are not qualified . . . that white people will be discriminated against. . . . There is a feeling that law violators are not being apprehended and convicted while they continue to destroy life and property," he elaborated.[116] The welfare state, threats to law and order, and claims of reverse discrimination were all part of the Goldwater deal, which he framed in a separate speech[117] only given to "hypersensitive"[118] southern audiences who bought it cheaply.

The threats, tangible or intangible, orchestrated or observed, galvanize white support perhaps more effectively than any other political tactic. The fear of falling from privilege was so powerful for white southerners, most of whom had voted for Democrats for generations, that GOP politicians, including Trump most recently, who stoked those fires of racial threat, "ripped those traditions to shreds."[119] Considering that it has been invisible for so long, white privilege ascends to the surface quickly when it is questioned or criticized or challenged. The political landscape of the twenty-first century is no exception. Economic pessimism, demographic changes, and the election of a black president are believed by many as endangering the dominant racial caste system. In addition, in these impending times of danger, whites have become increasingly vocal about their whiteness, arguing that they are the new victims of their old crime of oppression and discrimination, with the federal government as the perpetrator. The blueprint of the Long Southern Strategy was to tell white Americans this in a hundred ways in coded, and now not-so-coded, language about the economy and government spending. The proclamations sounded not once, but election after election over the long haul from blue South to red, with southern white privilege always in tow.

3

The Myth of Post-Racial America

The research is clear that colorblindness does not help us overcome racism; on the contrary, colorblindness as a strategy (rather than as a goal) forms part of the problem. Attempting to ignore what one has inevitably already noticed only makes it more difficult to recognize and thus control internalized racial stereotypes.

—IAN HANEY LÓPEZ[1]

ON AUGUST 3, 1980, Ronald Reagan gave the first southern speech of his presidential campaign since becoming the official nominee of the Republican Party. At the urging of Paul Manafort,[2] his southern campaign chairman, Reagan took the stage at the Neshoba County Fair, a popular spot for politicking less than ten miles from Philadelphia, Mississippi. The GOP nominee was accompanied by former governor John Bell Williams, a southern Democrat-turned-Goldwater supporter, and Trent Lott, Mississippi State party chairman and future US Senate majority leader.[3] Despite the fact that the location was well-trod political ground, one key statement in Reagan's thirty-three-paragraph speech hinted at a symbolic gesture inherent in the choice. "I believe in state's rights," proclaimed Reagan to a cheering crowd of ten thousand supporters. The bulk of the speech centered on welfare reform and economics,[4] which is, perhaps, one of the reasons that the dog whistle rang so inconspicuously. Merely sixteen years prior, Philadelphia, Mississippi, had provided the backdrop for one of the nation's most notorious Ku Klux Klan lynchings. Three civil rights workers—James Chaney, Andrew Goodman, and Michael Schwerner—lost their lives and captured the "national imagination" regarding how deep racial violence saturated white southern life.[5] By ignoring the infamous lynching and instead championing states' rights, Reagan's appearance simultaneously suggested that the country needed to move on from its racist past, while still harkening back to an unregulated, pre–civil rights South. This reactionary sentiment was reiterated in his 1984 endorsement of the "neo-Confederate slogan 'the South shall rise again.'"[6] Those choices suggest that Reagan's appeal to "colorblindness," so emblematic of his administration, was also coded. The "colorblind" message gave white Americans and, particularly, white southerners "a safe route through the minefield of race relations"[7] while rendering the need for federal programs to counteract institutional racism null and void. Race-baiting becomes race-burying in the arc of the Long Southern Strategy.

In many ways, Reagan's colorblindness catalyzed a political muteness on race that endures.[8] For example, nearly three decades later, during his 2008 bid for the Democratic nomination for the presidency, then senator Barack Obama delivered his now famous speech, "A More Perfect Union," at the National Constitution Center in Philadelphia, responding to videos of his former pastor, Rev. Jeremiah Wright, making fiery denunciations of the epidemic of white racism. Obama championed America's past racial progress, but he also condemned characterizations of his candidacy as "an exercise in affirmative action . . . based solely on the desire of wide-eyed liberals to purchase racial reconciliation on the cheap." He argued for the need for reviving the conversation about race in all of its complexity in an effort to break the "racial stalemate we've been stuck in for years."[9] Condemnation from the right was swift and extreme. Pat Buchanan, former active member of President Richard Nixon's Southern Strategy team and presidential-hopeful-turned-political pundit, published his response, entitled "A Brief for Whitey" on his website. Chronicling the discrimination of whites and special privileges granted to African Americans, Buchanan portrays Obama's call for a national conversation about race as "the same old con, the same old shakedown." "Some of us have heard it all before," Buchanan concludes, "about 40 years and 40 trillion tax dollars ago."[10]

Buchanan's insistence that it is time for America to move on, so to speak, echoes Reagan's colorblindness, and piggybacks on the need to protect white privilege in an increasingly politically correct climate. The notion of colorblindness appears wholly anti-racist, for if one cannot see color, then, logically, one cannot be prejudiced. Yet, despite how positive colorblindness may seem theoretically, in practice it dismisses the ongoing repercussions and active instances of racial oppression. This "color denial" is a "power denial," notes educational psychologist Derald Wing Sue[11] that reinforces—under a seemingly innocuous label—the old framework that impugns minorities for the inequity they experience due to structural racism. And at the same time colorblindness—just like fiscal conservatism—continues to mask the "dirty secret kept hidden by White Americans: much of what they have attained is unearned."[12] Obscuring this point was, in effect, exactly *the* point. The Long Southern Strategy tried to convince white southerners that the time for affirmative action and other federal initiatives to dismantle the effects of Jim Crow had ended. Additional efforts were cast as unfair.

The GOP avowal that the great American civil rights project was complete spread quickly. The Associated Press and Media General conducted a survey in 1988 that first located a partisan gap on this issue. Probing attitudes toward the colorblindness of the justice system, 13 percent more white Republicans believed in the fairness of the system as compared to white Democrats; by 2007, that gap had grown to 36 points.[13] Such attitudes have only become more entrenched in the wake of Obama's victory. In his book, *Ghosts of Jim Crow: Ending Racism in Post-Racial America*, Michael Higginbotham summarizes that "a majority of whites believe that racial discrimination is largely a thing of the past." That belief is particularly strong now since "whites tend to focus," he continues, "on individual black success stories, such as Super-Bowl-winning football coach Tony Dungy or political phenomenon President Barack Obama."[14] This premature declaration of post-racial America, while appearing optimistic, halts racial progress. As media pundit and author Touré argued on the opinion page of the *New York Times*: "Post-racial' is a mythical idea ... it's an intellectual Loch Ness monster. It is indeed a monster because it's dangerous."[15] It is dangerous because it renders the race conversation obsolete. Those who remain left behind are thereby "undeserving" of help and persistent inequities are attributed to a lack of work ethic—racial stereotypes, white privilege, and colorblindness all working in tandem.

The myth is also dangerous because it misconstrues not only the level but also the nature of racial animus still present in the hearts and minds of white Americans and white southerners, in particular. Colorblindness and post-racialism permit individuals to disassociate from the larger community. In other words, if someone believes they are not racist or if they claim they have not witnessed racist incidents personally, then they deny the existence of ongoing institutional racism. Their individual experience serves as their single source of evidence, a practice the Long Southern Strategy encouraged. From the very beginning, Republican presidential contender Barry Goldwater often advocated for the "individual" as the lens through which to view policy, and with lasting effect.[16] This disassociation or psychological splitting contributes to what political scientists have termed the "principle-policy" gap, wherein approval of equality as a general concept and disapproval of policies designed to eradicate these inequalities can coexist in the same person.[17] And that makes racism hard to measure.

Yet one set of questions called the Symbolic Racism scale (also referred to as the Racial Resentment scale) has provided great explanatory power on a host of policy attitudes for the past 40 years.[18] Developed in the post–civil rights era, the scale was originally designed to capture "a blend of anti-black affect and the kind of traditional American moral values embodied in the Protestant Ethic."[19]

Therefore, it was measuring overt racism as it morphed into something more palatable, a process catalyzed by the Long Southern Strategy. With hindsight, however, Racial Resentment, gauged by asking if respondents agree or disagree with statements such as "generations of slavery and discrimination have created conditions that make it difficult for blacks to work their way out of the lower class," could just as easily be called post-racial racism. Personal refutations of racism, denial of ongoing institutional racism, and conscious or subconscious protections of white privilege are all captured in the scale. Resentment factors in when assertions of racism persist, bursting the colorblind bubble. Even racially sensitive or inclusive language becomes mere "political correctness." Most recently, in the 2016 presidential campaign, Donald Trump frequently pitted "political correctness" against common sense[20] or even, in the case of his evolving immigration bans on Islamic countries, cast "political correctness" as dangerous in the American war on terror.[21] Americans were ushered to move on.

And move on they have. In studies of millennials, 88 percent condemn racial preferences as unfair, and 70 percent are even willing to label affirmative action initiatives as prejudiced despite "historical inequalities."[22] The past does not seems to matter anymore. Perhaps no other group has been more eager to move on from racial debates than white southerners. Republican support over the years for protecting the "heritage" symbolized by the Confederate flag,[23] for example, or the party's refusal to rewrite Section 4b of the Voting Rights Act (VRA) that was recently struck down by the Supreme Court, has validated that desire time and time again. Thus, no matter the cost, buying into the philosophy of colorblind individualism that was marketed and sold throughout the Long Southern Strategy is worth the price, for it wipes both the historical slate and the white conscience clean, gaslighting persistent racial inequities via the myth of a post-racial America.

IN "A MORE PERFECT UNION," the landmark speech on race that incensed Pat Buchanan, then candidate Obama attempted to reach out to white Americans by addressing the implication of this gaslighting. He knew that coded language had masked racial appeals with fiscal conservatism and ideological stances in support of small government. Moreover, he knew that it had been done so successfully and for so long, that many who adopted those attitudes were unaware of their racial roots. Thus, he warned that "to wish away the resentments of white Americans, to label them as misguided or even racist, without recognizing they are grounded in legitimate concerns," only "widens the racial divide."[24] Perhaps even more important, Obama recognized that the embrace of colorblindness had also obscured the facts of continued racial inequality so fully that programs to help (or even perceived as helping) minority Americans now seem unfair to many whites. In turn, white resentment rises when policies to level a playing field they already believe to be level are enacted. Ironically, it was when whites were made to participate in the leveling that the concept of colorblindness exploded.

During the 1970s, public school districts attempted to comply with *Brown v. Board* and achieve integration via busing students to various locations. Whereas the 1954 court ruling had eliminated de jure, or legal, codified segregation, Jim Crow housing settlement patterns maintained a barrier between whites and blacks, and these residential patterns dictated school assignments. Thus, in order to enforce de jure integration, districts had to tackle the elusive, intangible, cultural sources of de facto segregation. It was this slippery slope that caused an enormous uproar, particularly in the South. With a long history of circumventing laws that challenged white supremacy, white southerners balked at the notion that lifestyle choices and traditions could be scrutinized by the federal government.

For the most part, President Nixon, who faced this crisis during his administration, adopted a stance of "benign neglect," choosing primarily to avoid such dicey issues as often as possible.[25] When he could not avoid it, most notably when he faced southern audiences, he transformed the issue from one of civil rights to the scope of the federal government. In a 1968 television interview broadcast in the Carolinas, he warned: "'When you . . . say that it is the responsibility of the federal government and the federal courts to, in effect, act as local school districts in determining how we carry . . . out [the *Brown* decision] and then use the power of the federal treasury to withhold funds or give funds in order to carry it out, then I think we are going too far.'"[26] Additionally, Nixon deferred to local school districts in early 1969 regarding timetables for implementation of desegregation plans, an effort that "was not lost on Southerners."[27] In the wake of the 1971 *Swann v. Charlotte-Mecklenburg* case, in which the Supreme Court endorsed busing as a means to "achieve a realistic level of desegregation," Nixon was advised to "keep the liberal writers convinced that we are doing what the Court requires, and our conservative Southern friends convinced that we are not doing more than the Court requires."[28] Nevertheless, despite his effort to skate the middle—despite the smoke and mirrors of coded language—the busing issue did not go quietly into the night, particularly among the white southern voters whom the GOP had decided to chase.

Facing competition from pro-segregationist, Alabama Governor George Wallace in the 1972 primaries, Nixon intensified his rhetoric opposing federal intervention, and, in the aftermath of Wallace's primary victory in Florida, Nixon demanded a moratorium: "the majority of Americans of all races want more busing stopped and better education started."[29] The statement sounded several key dog whistles. It deflected the racial discrimination issue inherent in ongoing segregation by focusing instead on "better education." The zero-sum dynamic resurfaces, in which better education and integration become mutually exclusive, and it implies that whites are suffering from these efforts to overcome de facto segregation. Moreover, by using the phrase "the majority of all Americans," whites in the South did not have to defend accusations of being aberrant or uniquely problematic; rather, they were part of the national mainstream. That same spirit of defensiveness had led delegations from seven southern states to found the Unified Concerned Citizens of American (UCCA) anti-busing organization. Calling their anti-busing efforts the "great crusade," the UCCA proclaimed itself non-racist and insisted on equal treatment of northern states where residential segregation patterns remained unchanged.[30] Not only was it time to embrace colorblindness, the South, despite its history, should not be scrutinized as a greater offender—or so many claimed.

Nixon's "benign neglect"[31] of federal enforcement of civil right policies extended to the 1965 VRA as well, which his administration attempted to destroy when it came up for a renewal vote two years into his first term by portraying it too as an unnecessary overstep of federal power. Section 4b of the VRA, which established a formula for determining counties that had the most egregious records of black disenfranchisement and required those areas to submit all election laws for federal approval, was chastised for unfairly micro-managing an aspect of state and local control. Outrage regarding the unfair scrutiny proved particularly intense when under the original formula, the entire states of Alabama, Georgia, Louisiana, Mississippi, South Carolina, Virginia, and Alaska became "covered jurisdictions." (The Senate's rejection of Nixon's two white southern Supreme Court nominees, Harrold Carswell and Clement Haynsworth, were also framed as unfair and anti-southern.) The message took root. White southern Republicans attacked President Gerald Ford for his "quarter-loaf" concession to apply the VRA to all fifty states "administratively" but refusing to support a legislative corrective. Ford's was a weak Southern Strategy, penned Rowland Evans and Robert Novak, quoting GOP southerners as saying that Ford's effort was "a chicken way to do it."[32] Not only was the federal government interfering beyond its jurisdiction, but also the South was being singled out unfairly. Conservative southern intellectuals even launched a new magazine in 1979 called *The Southern Partisan* to protest such federal scrutiny of the South. Writers for the magazine, including Mel Bradford (a professor of literature at the University of Dallas who would be considered by Reagan for head of the National Endowment for the Humanities), chastised the "wrongheaded, government-impost spirit of egalitarianism" and "ridiculed the political correctness they identified with civil rights."[33]

Over three decades later, the Supreme Court finally agreed, striking Section 4b of the VRA in 2013, contending that the regions it covered were subject to unfair scrutiny. The majority argued that the VRA had done its job and was no longer necessary as written. The court also challenged Congress to rewrite the section with a formula that would reflect contemporary discriminatory voting practices. Congress has not responded. In the oral arguments of the case, Chief Justice John Roberts asked, "it is the government's submission that the citizens of the South are more racist than citizens in the North?"—a question that tipped his hand. However, it was Justice Antonin Scalia's comments that suggested the place of the VRA in the larger conservative cosmology. When discussing the voting record on VRA renewals (in 2006 Senate approval was unanimous), Scalia said: "Now, I don't think that's [the unanimous vote is] attributable to the fact that it is so much clearer now that we need this. I think it is attributable, very likely attributable, to a phenomenon that is called perpetuation of racial entitlement. It's been written about. Whenever a society adopts racial entitlements, it is very difficult to get out of them through the normal political processes."[34] Even voting protections are deemed an unfair advantage for black Americans.

In contrast, "high minority turnout does not prove an absence of discrimination," argued Spence Overton in his article "Against a 'Post-Racial' Voting Rights Act." In fact, he continued, "rather it often triggers discrimination,"[35] citing gerrymandering and voting wait times (a national average of 23 minutes for African Americans compared to 19 minutes for Latinos and 12 minutes for whites) and voter identification laws that have surged in the South and throughout the rest of "post-racial" America. Even now, in the wake of his loss in the popular vote, Trump insists that massive voter fraud, which he falsely attributed to illegal immigrants, accounted for the discrepancy. He even launched the White House Commission on Election Integrity to investigate and appointed Hans von Spakovsky, arguably the most vocal promoter of the threat of American voter fraud, to the commission.[36]

Apparently, government oversight is only needed when the white vote is threatened. Back in the 1980s, Reagan cemented this coded "small government" rhetoric in his inaugural address.[37] "Our government has no power except that granted it by the people," Reagan announced. "It is time to check and reverse the growth of government, which shows signs of having grown beyond the consent of the governed. It is my intention to curb the size and influence of the Federal establishment."[38] In doing so, Reagan seemed to channel Goldwater, who during the floor debate on the 1964 Civil Rights Act, cloaked his opposition in terms of this danger, while repeatedly insisting that he was "unalterably opposed to discrimination." Specifically, he objected to Titles II and VII of the bill that required federal oversight. "This bill would require the creation of a Federal police force of mammoth proportions," he warned, concluding that "if my vote be misconstrued, let it be, and let me suffer the consequences."[39] Goldwater was highlighting this important shift from legal equality to proactive efforts to close the gaps between the races in tangible ways supported by federal enforcement power with real teeth. The coded language advocating small government seemed to take hold almost immediately. In a poll conducted by the *Rome News-Tribune* in Georgia, for example, local citizens expressed extreme frustration with the passage of the bill. However, they expressed their opposition not to the notion of black equality but to big government. "The public accommodations feature is an open invitation to complete government dictatorship," wrote local minister Rev. Thomas Wheelis. Bill Blaylock, another local who worked for Georgia Power, proclaimed that "with the passage of this bill, you are no longer a free citizen—you are now a slave of the federal government."[40]

The influence of both the coded language and its appeal in the South proved lasting. In her 2000 summary of scholarship exploring the source of racial policy attitudes, Maria Krysan cites over half a dozen studies finding that "people who prefer a limited government or identify their ideology as conservative tend to oppose equal treatment policies" and "government spending on blacks."[41] Among party activists in the South, the partisanship associated with the support for government services and particularly government aid to minorities is undeniable, with political scientist Jay Barth finding a 22-point gap between white Democrats and Republicans as of 2001.[42] Similar gaps remain present among white southerners and white non-southerners. Table 3.1 shows the 2010 and 2012 geographic and identity breakdown of white Americans' attitudes regarding whether or not it is the federal government's responsibility to provide for minorities access to jobs, housing, education, healthcare, and treatment by the courts that is equal to whites.

Self-described southerners disagree most vehemently at levels that are significantly distinct from non-southern whites in every category in 2012 and in four of five categories in 2010 (housing is the exception). The levels of opposition are followed closely by whites who live in the South. The greatest resistance is to the most directly economic efforts: federal support for equal jobs and housing, with healthcare services a close third. Regardless, a clear majority of white southerners reject the idea that the federal government has a role in providing for equality in any area other than equal treatment by the courts, whether it be employment, education, housing, or healthcare. So "small government" meant declaring efforts to promote equality or to enforce equal treatment and access as not the responsibility of the federal government. That attitude dovetailed with ease into the old calls for states' rights and the newer proclamations of colorblindness.

REAGAN FURTHER SANITIZED the GOP's coded message. As a state politician, he had been more direct, campaigning against housing regulations by arguing that they violated a property owner's choice "to discriminate against Negroes."[43]

Table 3.1 Percent Reporting That Providing the Following Is Not
the Responsibility of the Federal Government, Among Whites, 2010–2012

	2010			
	Non-South	South	Non-southern	Southern
Jobs equal in quality to whites	69.4	71.0	68.9	73.5
Schools equal in quality to whites	49.0	51.2	48.8	53.4
Housing equal in quality to whites	67.3	66.6	66.2	68.8
Health care services equal to whites	56.9	58.8	55.2	64.7
Treatment by the courts and police equal to whites	40.4	43.8	40.2	45.8

	2012			
	Non-South	South	Non-southern	Southern
Jobs equal in quality to whites	63.5	66.6	63.7	68.0
Schools equal in quality to whites	45.0	53.8	46.6	54.8
Housing equal in quality to whites	60.9	69.6	63.4	68.0
Health care services equal to whites	51.3	59.1	52.1	61.0
Treatment by the courts and police equal to whites	41.2	44.7	39.6	49.8

Data are from the 2010 and 2012 Blair Center Polls.

As president, however, he transformed opposition to affirmative action efforts into a progressive-sounding cry for fairness to all races. The language of fairness is almost impenetrable and can easily be co-opted from pro–civil rights advocates. The government should not tolerate "favoring or disfavoring individuals because of their skin color," announced William Bradford Reynolds, the head of the Civil Rights Division of Reagan's Justice Department.[44] Using this rhetoric of colorblindness, Reagan's administration portrayed the parties as at war, but now with Republicans as the upholders of fairness and Democrats as the proponents of bias. By the end of Reagan's term, nearly 71 percent of all Americans (and 85 percent of Republicans) disagreed with the statement that "we should make every effort to improve the position of blacks and minorities, even if it means giving preferential treatment." By 2009, one year into the first term of the first African American presidency, opposition had only dropped six points.[45]

Perhaps nothing fueled the political rhetoric of colorblindness and gave credence to the assertion that America had reached a post-racial era more than Obama's election. Success of an individual, of course, while signaling progress to some degree, cannot single-handedly dissolve structural racism. Director Spike Lee, when interviewed about the death of Eric Garner at the hands of white police officers in New York City, confirmed this notion emphatically. "You can't just think I'm so successful that I've reached another realm," Lee told audiences. With regards to Obama's election ushering in an era of post-racialism," Lee simply stated, "That's bullshit."[46] On the other hand, Obama has suffered from leftist criticism that his own rhetoric and policy positions often strengthened this perception. He has opted, journalist Tim Stanley observed, "to play the role not of a black president but a president who happens to be black."[47] Others wonder what choice Obama had if he wanted to pass key parts of his agenda, particularly when critics on the right promote the idea that revisiting race only serves to incite racial divisions. That idea implies that racism fades away when it is ignored, but that only works for those who are not its target.

The partisan drive behind the myth of post-racialism remains just as powerful in the twenty-first century. Elected officials, such as Representative Mo Brooks of Alabama, have accused Democrats of "waging a war on whites"; "I'm one of those who does not believe in racism," Brooks claims. "Race is immaterial."[48] However, these denials are not limited to personal evaluations or abstract assessments of the country writ large. In many ways, denial is most damaging when applied to institutions because it means that they do not need to change. For example, in a 2014 poll conducted by the Public Religion Institute, 45 percent of all Americans surveyed agreed that "police officers generally treat blacks and other minorities the same as whites." Among Democrats, that number drops to 27 percent. Republicans, on the other hand, believe the police are colorblind, to the tune of 66 percent. For those who watch conservative media outlet Fox News, the number swells yet again to 71 percent. Whites, of course, respond to these questions from their own "standpoint" of whiteness. More than half (52 percent) believe that justice is, indeed, colorblind, compared to only 30 percent of non-whites.[49] So, the reasoning goes, if the justice system is considered fair, then additional federal efforts to correct racial inequities in that institution or in any other are no longer needed.

The impact of the colorblind message of the Long Southern Strategy had a dramatic and lasting effect nationwide because it did not rely solely on the absolute superiority embedded in whiteness. While it gave whites a way to wash their hands of race, it was wrapped in a non-racist package that had much broader appeal. Looking back, Gallup's Spring polls of 1965 show that 72 percent of whites (only those living outside of the South were included) approved of then president

Lyndon Johnson's efforts, believing he was "pushing civil rights 'about right' or 'not fast enough.'"[50] The Blair Center Polls of both 2010 and 2012, as shown in Figure 3.1, report responses to a similar question—"is there too much, the right amount, or too little attention paid to race these days?"—as the one posed by Gallup nearly 45 years ago.

In this recent snapshot, for whites who live outside of the South, the comparable answer has dropped almost 30 points, with roughly 15 percent claiming "too little" attention is paid to race, around 30 percent saying it is the "right amount," and the clear majority indicating that "too much" attention is being paid to race. However, the numbers are even higher in the geographic South, with 60 percent in 2012 holding the "too much" perspective, for example. The attitudes among whites who identify as southern are both more extreme and significantly distinct from their non-southern counterparts, with 65.1 percent claiming that the attention paid to race is "too much." To that end, despite ongoing racial violence and economic and political disparities, most whites, particularly southern whites, seem to have bought the myth of a post-racial, colorblind America.

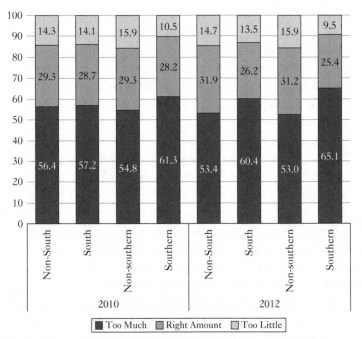

FIGURE 3.1 Percent Responses to: "Is There Too Much, the Right Amount, or Too Little Attention Paid to Race These Days?" Among Whites, 2010–2012

Data are from the 2010 and 2012 Blair Center Polls.

SINCE THE PUSH for colorblindness developed hand in hand with distrust of and restrictions on the federal government, modern ideological conservatism and racial animus are difficult to separate. Halting integration efforts could be justified by critics or politicians as curbing unchecked federal power. After all, the transporting of students across what had functioned as a strict color line for generations became the symbol of "too much" attention focused on race—of a shift beyond equal opportunity to equal outcome, of a swing from political and rhetorical legalities to boots-on-the-ground change. Critics could rail against federal encroachment on states' rights, they could massively resist, or they could advocate that such pro-action was unnecessary because Americans had moved beyond race. From Gerald Ford's hedging on busing, to George W. Bush's refusing to attend the NAACP's convention for the first five years of his presidency,[51] to John McCain[52] and Bob Dole's opposition to affirmative action in general (Dole contended that race-based preferences "were dividing Americans instead of bringing us together"[53]), the GOP's vision of a colorblind country mythologized a reconciled and reconstructed America and did so for political purposes. Even Mitt Romney, who called on Donald Trump to denounce the white supremacist rally held in Charlottesville, Virginia, in 2017, and who repeatedly touted the civil rights records of his father (who left the 1964 Republican convention because of Goldwater's racial politics), still quipped on the campaign trail in 2012 that "no one's ever asked to see my birth certificate."[54] That dig at Barack Obama's American citizenship, particularly when juxtaposed against his anti-racist claims, seems to function as a distorting code in and of itself. Denying, deflecting, masking, were ammunition in the GOP's efforts to go hunting where the ducks were, and in post–civil rights America, they made the state of race relations hard to decipher.

In the 1980s, David Sears published two studies, one with Ethnocentrism scholar Donald Kinder, and the other with Harris Allen, trying to discern what "new racism" might look like. They specifically examined white opposition to busing, since the issue seemed to be spark some kind of shift from support for civil rights ideals in the abstract to resistance to their application. Sears developed the Symbolic Racism scale—now often referred to as the Racial Resentment scale—to ascertain the beliefs that were driving this new wave of resistance. The scale includes eight questions, though four are most often used. Each is posed as a statement with respondents indicating agreement or disagreement along a 5-point Likert scale. They are: "Irish, Italians, Jewish and many other minorities overcame prejudice and worked their way up. Blacks should do the same without any special favors" (Q1); "Generations of slavery and discrimination have created conditions that make it difficult for blacks to work their way out of the lower class" (Q2); "Over the past few years, blacks have gotten less than they deserve"

(Q3); and "It's really a matter of some people not trying hard enough; if blacks would only try harder they could be just as well off as whites" (Q4). The conclusion of those early articles showed that Symbolic Racism/Racial Resentment was a significant predictor of opposition to busing, and that the issue of busing was functioning "as a symbol evoking Symbolic Racism no matter what the phase of busing controversies the individual is in—or indeed if her or she is many miles and/or years away from direct contact with its realities."[55]

Over the years, perhaps no other theory of racial animus other than Ethnocentrism has provided as much explanatory power as Racial Resentment/ Symbolic Racism. The key to the scale's success is that it is measuring exactly what the Long Southern Strategy was doing to change the racial conversation in a way that benefited the white voters in the South whose support they wanted. Nevertheless, the scale is not without criticism. In the early 1990s, for example, when surveys revealed a significant drop-off in the number of white Americans citing race as a dire problem in America,[56] some scholars contended that rather than reflecting some kind of "new racism," these attitudes actually indicated a growing colorblindness (or "race-neutral attitudes"—the moniker used by several political scientists).[57] Still others have suggested that opposition to race-targeted policies reflect white Americans' frustration with the welfare state or with the federal government in general.[58] Some claim it is a lack of political sophistication or knowledge of the system that contributes to "new racism," not some aspect of ongoing prejudice.[59] Most recently, Edward Carmines, Paul Sniderman, and Beth Easter, argue that the measure of Symbolic Racism is "fundamentally flawed because it may be conflated with the measurement of attitudes toward racial policies."[60] They contend that policy preferences toward, for example, affirmative action are not the same as one's personal views on race. But if that racial animus was directed and channeled and socialized politically—which is how Symbolic Racism is defined, as a product of socialization—via coded language and dog whistles, the distinction seems irrelevant. In fact, the conflation seems to prove the point.

Sears and his colleagues have defended the measure of Symbolic Racism/ Racial Resentment repeatedly in leading political science and psychology journals. Statistical testing has shown it to be internally consistent and unique with "construct, predictive, and discriminant validity."[61] It lives and breathes as a separate mindset from ideological conservatism, visions of limited government, anti-egalitarianism, and its predecessor, Old-Fashioned Racism. Though data crunchers have noted it functions distinctly too from measures of individualism, Sears and P. J. Henry indicated that it does incorporate some aspects of that particular cosmology. The blending is the story. In that same defensive stance, Sears and Henry identify the four fundamental themes—not the specific questions, but the underlying belief—embodied in the Symbolic Racism scale. The belief is diagrammed this way: "(1) racial discrimination is no longer a serious obstacle to blacks' prospects for a good life, so that (2) blacks continuing disadvantages are largely due to their unwillingness to work hard enough. As a result, both their (3) continuing demands and (4) increased advantages are unwarranted."[62] It may be called Symbolic Racism, but it cuts through the GOP's merging of economic and racial policies, through Goldwater's focus on the "individual," and through Reagan's rhetoric of fairness and colorblindness. In one of his most recent studies, Sears, writing with Joshua Rabinowitz, Jim Sidanius, and Jon Krosnick, attempted to distinguish Racial Resentment from attitudes toward government and, specifically, attitudes toward what are seen as redistributive government policies. Controlling for such beliefs, they still find Racial Resentment to be predictive of white opposition to government efforts to aid African Americans.[63]

Simply put, Symbolic Racism/Racial Resentment measures what is really post-racial racism. It remains powerfully predictive of clear-cut racial issues, such as opposition to busing and to black political candidates.[64] However, it also proves just as powerful in understanding white attitudes toward coded issues like "law and order" policies. A 2013 study by international social scientists using American National Election Survey data found that a one-point increase in a white American's Symbolic Racism score increased the likelihood of the respondent having a gun at home by 50 percent and supporting the carry of concealed handguns by 28 percent.[65] In 2006, Sears and colleagues Eva Green and Christian Staerkle found that "high levels of Symbolic Racism are associated with support for tough, punitive crime policies and with opposition to preventative policies."[66] Unsurprisingly, Gary Segura and Ali Valenzuela found that Racial Resentment diminished Obama's share of the white vote in 2008, particularly in the Deep South.[67]

The Long Southern Strategy played a role in perpetuating these attitudes. After all, as political historians Earl Black and Merle Black have observed, Goldwater and Reagan often drew all-white audiences in the South.[68] Those speeches to those white southern audiences are, in fact, part of that socialization critical to this measure of post-racial racism, and the Blair Center Polls consider the contemporary impact of this long socialization. Whites who live in the South and those who claim a southern identity still report higher Racial Resentment scores than other white Americans with self-identification as southern, proving more powerful here too than geography. To get an idea of the identity-based gaps, Figure 3.2A shows the mean, overall Racial Resentment scores toward African Americans in both 2010 and 2012. Additionally, although the Racial Resentment scale is specifically designed to capture attitudes toward African Americans, altering a few phrases and labels allows the questions to be directed toward

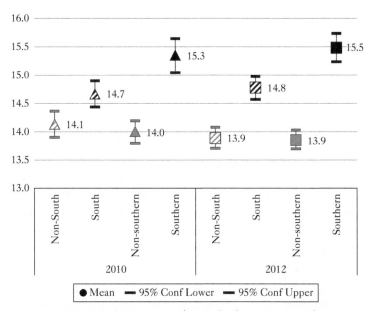

FIGURE 3.2A Mean Racial Resentment (Toward African Americans) Scores, Among Whites, 2010–2012

Data are from the 2010 and 2012 Blair Center Polls.

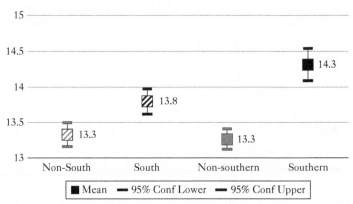

FIGURE 3.2B Mean Racial Resentment (Toward Latinos) Scores, Among Whites, 2012

Data are from the 2012 Blair Center Poll.

Latinos. In 2012, the Blair Center Poll experimented with a measure of Latino Symbolic Racism, and the overall means are shown in Figure 3.2B. As previously mentioned, each of the four questions comprising the scale is scored from 1 to 5, for a potential overall score ranging from 4 to 20.

In 2010, Southern white respondents had a mean Racial Resentment score toward African Americans of 15.3, significantly higher than the mean for non-southern white respondents at 14. Moreover, since the 95 percent confidence intervals do not overlap (the bars above and below the mean), the differences are particularly distinct and highly unlikely to have happened by chance. Similar patterns emerge in 2012 as well. Respondents who identify themselves as southern express the highest mean Racial Resentment score toward African Americans, and the gap between southern identity and non-southern identity is significant and greater than the regional geographic gap between the South and the non-South. The experimental Racial Resentment scores toward Latinos are somewhat lower than the Racial Resentment scores toward African Americans across the board, but the difference between respondents who identify as southern to those who do not is still present and significant. The mean score for non-southern whites stood at 13.3 compared to 14.3 for whites who claim a southern identity.

Beyond just a comparison of means, there are important distinctions between southern whites and non-southern whites in terms of where they fall along the Racial Resentment scale. The midpoint of the Racial Resentment scale is 12, which would indicate a neutrality of sorts regarding these questions. Scores below 12 reflect an "overall" lack of Racial Resentment, while scores above 12 indicate its presence. Figures 3.3A and 3.3B compare the percentage of whites in each subgroup who fall into these three categories. High numbers of white Americans express Racial Resentment in every subgroup, though the percentage is significantly higher—almost 80 percent—among those who claim a southern identity. While only 20 percent of non-southern whites do not harbor such feelings, that number among southern whites falls to single digits. The majority of white Americans also report Racial Resentment toward Latinos, though, again, among white southerners such feelings are significantly more widely shared (63.8 percent). Thus, in terms of the long-term impact of discrimination toward Latinos and the degree of their contemporary disadvantages, the response pattern and gaps are similar. The Long Southern Strategy may not have addressed Latinos specifically, but colorblindness does not see blackness or brownness, nor the structural racism that continues to affect both.

Additionally, in an effort to see the impact of various demographics on these attitudes, least squares regression models predicting Racial Resentment toward African Americans is presented in Table 3.2A and toward Latinos in Table 3.2B for whites grouped by both southern identification and by geography. In terms of Racial Resentment toward both African Americans and Latinos, education, party identification, and ideology are significant across the board. The less educated, more conservative, and more strongly Republican, the more likely the respondent is to have bought this myth of post-racialism hook, line, and sinker.

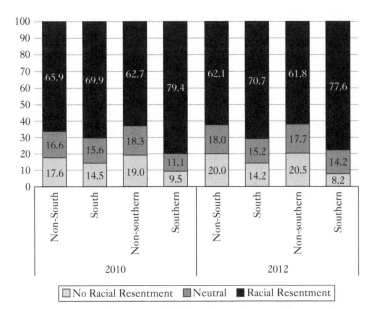

FIGURE 3.3A Percent Above, At, and Below the Midpoint of the Racial Resentment (Toward African Americans) Scale, Among Whites, 2010–2012

Data are from the 2010 and 2012 Blair Center Polls.

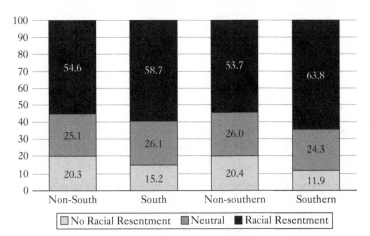

FIGURE 3.3B Percent Above, At, and Below the Midpoint of the Racial Resentment (Toward Latinos) Scale, Among Whites, 2012

Data are from the 2012 Blair Center Poll.

Table 3.2A Predicting Racial Resentment (Toward African Americans),
Among Whites, 2012

	Non-South	South	Non-southern	Southern
Age	−0.005	−0.004	−0.001	−0.007
(toward older)	(0.006)	(0.006)	(0.005)	(0.008)
Education	−0.649****	−0.714****	−0.674****	−0.616****
(toward more educated)	(0.098)	(0.109)	(0.086)	(0.137)
Income	0.040**	−0.02	0.049***	−0.074***
(toward wealthier)	(0.024)	(0.025)	(0.020)	(0.032)
Married	−0.198	0.191	−0.207	0.289
	(0.190)	(0.204)	(0.164)	(0.261)
Female	−0.236*	−0.099	−0.065	−0.611***
	(0.172)	(0.187)	(0.150)	(0.237)
Unemployed	−0.337	−0.594*	−0.489**	−0.375
	(0.309)	(0.365)	(0.267)	(0.488)
Fundamentalist	0.155	−0.256	−0.195	−0.003
	(0.231)	(0.223)	(0.203)	(0.262)
Party Identification	0.346****	0.407****	0.459****	0.233***
(toward Republican)	(0.069)	(0.079)	(0.061)	(0.096)
Ideology	0.749****	0.715****	0.628****	0.817****
(toward conservative)	(0.078)	(0.087)	(0.068)	(0.112)
Constant	11.209****	12.178****	11.048****	13.349****
	(0.515)	(0.537)	(0.444)	(0.676)
N	1282	1080	1738	587
R Squared	0.272	0.266	0.258	0.234
Adjusted R Squared	0.268	0.260	0.254	0.223

Note: Standard errors in parentheses * p<= .10, ** p<= .05, *** p<= .01, **** p<.001
Data are from the 2012 Blair Center Poll.

Southern white women are significantly less likely to hold Racial Resentment attitudes toward both African Americans and Latinos. Household income also seems to play a role, though in very different ways among those who identify as southern and those who do not. Among white southerners, lower income levels increase the likelihood of Racial Resentment toward both African Americans and Latinos, but among non-southerners, higher incomes significantly predict this type of racial animus. Unemployment is actually significant in predicting

Table 3.2B Predicting Racial Resentment (Toward Latinos), Among
Whites, 2012

	Non-South	South	Non-southern	Southern
Age	−0.003	0.010**	0.004	0.008
(toward older)	(0.005)	(0.005)	(0.004)	(0.007)
Education	−0.439****	−0.404****	−0.466****	−0.280**
(toward more educated)	(0.089)	(0.096)	(0.077)	(0.124)
Income	0.032*	0.012	0.069****	−0.077***
(toward wealthier)	(0.022)	(0.022)	(0.018)	(0.029)
Married	−0.162	0.126	−0.213*	0.397**
	(0.171)	(0.179)	(0.145)	(0.241)
Female	−0.115	−0.303**	0.02	−0.882****
	(0.156)	(0.164)	(0.133)	(0.216)
Unemployed	−0.691***	0.075	−0.492**	0.094
	(0.283)	(0.325)	(0.241)	(0.444)
Fundamentalist	0.354**	−0.298*	0.172	−0.417**
	(0.210)	(0.196)	(0.182)	(0.240)
Party Identification	0.351****	0.346****	0.406****	0.253***
(toward Republican)	(0.062)	(0.069)	(0.054)	(0.087)
Ideology	0.536****	0.537****	0.460****	0.647****
(toward conservative)	(0.070)	(0.076)	(0.061)	(0.102)
Constant	10.833****	10.481****	10.151****	11.542****
	(0.471)	(0.471)	(0.397)	(0.617)
N	1274	1067	1724	580
R Squared	0.232	0.216	0.227	0.200
Adjusted R Squared	0.227	0.210	0.223	0.189

Note: Standard errors in parentheses * $p <= .10$, ** $p <= .05$, *** $p <= .01$, **** $p < .001$
Data are from the 2012 Blair Center Poll.

lower Racial Resentment levels toward just Latinos, and only among whites who live outside of the South or who do not identify as southern.

Finally, it is worth noting that significant gaps between southern and non-southern whites also exist on all four sub-questions, as shown in Figures 3.4A, 3.4B, and 3.4C. A greater percentage of self-identified white southerners dismiss the long-term impact of the historic discrimination and segregation faced by African Americans (questions 1 and 2) to a double-digit degree, both in 2010

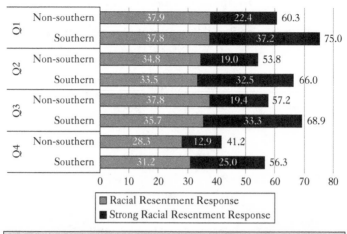

QI. Italians, Jewish and many other minorities overcame prejudice and worked their way up. Blacks should do the same without any special favors.
Q2. Generations of slavery and discrimination have created conditions that make it difficult for Blacks to work their way out of the lower class.
Q3. Over the past few years, Blacks have gotten less than they deserve.
Q4. It's really a matter of some people not trying hard enough; if Blacks would only try harder they could be just as well off as Whites.

FIGURE 3.4A Percent of Racial Resentment Responses (Toward African Americans) by Individual Questions, Among Whites, 2010

Data are from the 2010 Blair Center Poll.

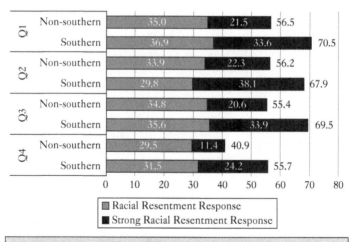

Q1. Italians, Jewish and many other minorities overcame prejudice and worked their way up. Blacks should do the same without any special favors.
Q2. Generations of slavery and discrimination have created conditions that make it difficult for Blacks to work their way out of the lower class.
Q3. Over the past few years, Blacks have gotten less than they deserve.
Q4. It's really a matter of some people not trying hard enough; if Blacks would only try harder they could be just as well off as Whites.

FIGURE 3.4B Percent of Racial Resentment Responses (Toward African Americans) by Individual Questions, Among Whites, 2012

Data are from the 2012 Blair Center Poll.

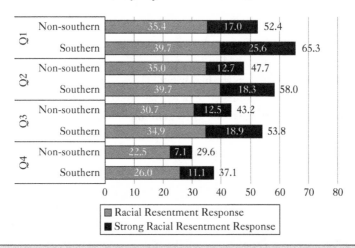

Q1. Irish, Italians, Jewish and many other minorities overcame prejudice and worked their way up. Latinos should do the same without any special favors.
Q2. Generations of discrimination have created conditions that make it difficult for Latinos to work their way out of the lower class.
Q3. Over the past few years, Latinos have gotten less than they deserve.
Q4. It's really a matter of some people not trying hard enough; if Latinos would only try harder they could be just as well off as whites.

FIGURE 3.4C Percent of Racial Resentment Responses (Toward Latinos) by Individual Questions, Among Whites, 2012

Data are from the 2012 Blair Center Poll.

and in 2012, and a greater portion of them do so strongly. The pattern remains unaltered when whites are asked about contemporary inequity and how it should be overcome (questions 3 and 4), resulting in equally wide gaps. White Americans who claim a southern identity also give racially resentful responses to questions about Latinos in higher numbers than white Americans who do not claim a southern identity, and they do so on every question with greater intensity. Moreover, just as they did in the Racial Resentment questions toward African Americans, questions 1 and 2 regarding the unique historic roots of Latino disadvantages draw the largest numbers of white southerners expressing racial animus. A significant portion of white Americans, and the vast majority of white southerners, will not acknowledge past oppression nor its legacy—and for a great many of them the denial is forceful. Colorblindness, in this sense, seems retroactive and revisionist.

IF WHITE SOUTHERNERS think that too much attention has been paid to race, believe that efforts to stem those inequities are no longer the responsibility of the federal government, and score high on the Racial Resentment scale, then

the colorblindness campaign must affect other policies aimed at leveling the racial playing field as well. After all, as Thomas and Mary Edsall note in their book
Chain Reaction: The Impact of Race, Rights, and Taxes on American Politics, "the
centerpiece of this assault was the highly publicized, sustained Republican attack
on affirmative action; on race-based quotas, goals, and timetables; on minority set-
asides; on race-norming (race-based scoring) in employment testing; on race-based
university admissions policies; and on other forms of racial preference."[69] That assault was a major part of the Long Southern Strategy, which capitalized on white
racial angst and perpetuated it. Such attitudes are not merely a holdover from the
Jim Crow era; they remain prevalent and increasingly divisive, and even more so
when connected to one's personal identification and stoked by partisanship.

In his book *The Partisan Sort: How Liberals Became Democrats and
Conservatives Became Republicans*, Matthew Levendusky explores the way in
which party identification aligns with ideology, arguing that party elites drive this
process and the masses follow via cues. Of particular relevance is Levendusky's
comparison of sorting in the North versus sorting in the South. He finds that
the people in each region moved parallel to each other—except on racial issues.
Specifically, policy attitudes toward two affirmative action issues caused only a
7 percent shift in the North from 1972 to 2004. However, in the South, among
whites, opposition to affirmative action constituted a 26 percent shift, further
aligning conservatives with the Republican Party.[70] Levendusky focused on geographic divisions, as have James Kuklinski, Michael Cobb, and Martin Gilens,
authors of the 1997 study "Racial Attitudes in the New South" that appeared in
the *Journal of Politics*. In their expansive study, Kuklinski, Cobb, and Gilens consider the intangible, emotional elements of southern racial animus, employing
a list experiment to test white anger toward affirmative action. They find that
98 percent of whites who live in the South expressed anger when questioned
about "black leaders asking for affirmative action," compared to 42 percent in the
non-South.[71]

If opposing affirmative action, like opposing busing, became the means to
halt true racial equality—not just equality of opportunity, but also equality of
outcome—then southern identity should live and breathe there too. Figure 3.5
shows an ongoing distinctiveness between whites who claim a southern identity
and those who do not regarding their attitudes toward government programs
that attempt to close the gap between whites and blacks. In 2010 and 2012, approximately 43 percent and 41 percent respectively of white southerners oppose "employers and colleges making an extra effort to find and recruit qualified
minorities," a significant departure from non-southerners. Opposition rates
are also higher among non-southerners—34.1 percent in 2010 and 34.9 percent in 2012. Moreover, less than a quarter of white Americans across the board

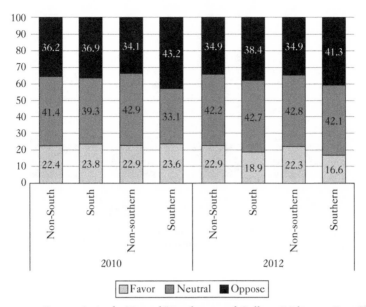

FIGURE 3.5 Percent Attitudes Toward "Employers and Colleges Making an Extra Effort to Find and Recruit Qualified Minorities," Among Whites, 2010–2012

Data are from the 2010 and 2012 Blair Center Polls.

report supporting affirmative action programs, with only 16.6 percent of white southerners approving of them in 2012.

This lack of support may, in fact, stem from the belief that affirmative action programs—even at the college level—are no longer needed. Accordingly, the 2010 Blair Center Poll asked respondents, "Do African Americans have more opportunity, about the same, or less opportunity than whites?" Figure 3.6 reports white responses to that question by geography and identity. The clear majority of whites in all four groups do not see structural inequities and think that African Americans and whites have "about the same" opportunities. The percentage is significantly higher among respondents who live in South (61.6 percent) and who identify as southern (61.7 percent), as compared to their non-South and non-southern counterparts. Moreover, a slightly greater percentage of respondents from the South (22.2 percent) and whites who identify as southern (24.2 percent) think that blacks actually have "more opportunities" than whites—though it is important to note that this is still less than one-fourth of these subgroups. That particular attitude had been growing ever since the Supreme Court's decision in *Regents of the University of California v. Bakke* (1978), in which the court declared quotas unconstitutional, admitted white student, Allan Bakke, and limited the consideration of race in higher education

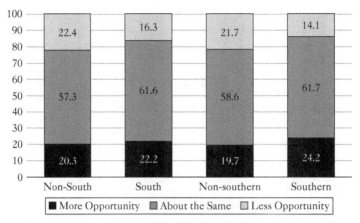

FIGURE 3.6 Percent Responses to: "Do You Think African Americans Have More Opportunity, About the Same, or Less Opportunity Than Whites?" Among Whites, 2010 Data are from the 2010 Blair Center Poll.

admissions to instances with a compelling state interest. The sentiment was underscored by the way in which the Court chose to highlight sixteen African American students admitted as part of UC-Davis Medical School's special admissions program who all had lower grade point averages than Bakke. However, thirty-six white students were also admitted with lower GPAs and five applicants were admitted because of family legacies and donor support.[72] Arguably, justice was not colorblind there. Objections even to the limited use of race-based admissions remain ongoing with federal courts upholding some state bans on affirmative action though still allowing for their use in higher education.[73] The persistent challenges reflect the perspective that the post-racial playing field is not only even, but also tilted against whites. Thus, affirmative action is not seen as a means to achieve racial equality, but a means to reverse the racial hierarchy.

FEAR OF A reversed racial hierarchy might be a dividing line among whites— a fear that polarized the electorate during this most recent election cycle. For example, a 2016 *Washington Post*–ABC News poll noted specifically that more Americans (40 percent) believed African Americans and Latinos were still "losing out because of preferences for whites," compared to 28 percent who believed whites were receiving the short end of the stick. However, among registered voters who supported Donald Trump, the pattern was reversed, with 44 percent believing that preferences for African Americans and Latinos were hurting whites and only 16 percent recognizing the persistence of structural racism.[74] Trump's victory might have quieted some of these fears, perhaps similar to the post-election plummet of white economic pessimism, but it did not put a dent in the colorblind desire to move past race.

According to the 2016 Blair Center Poll taken in the weeks after Trump's victory, the majority of white Americans still believe that too much attention is paid to race—in fact, certain subgroups believe that in increasingly higher numbers than the sample in 2012. However, opposition to affirmative action in higher education dipped slightly from Obama-era levels. Figure 3.7 juxtaposes these responses. There is a single-digit gap between whites who identify as southern (37.8 percent) and whites who do not (32.8 percent) on opposition to affirmative action. Further, this five-point gap was similar in 2010 and 2012. However, in 2016, 69.3 percent of whites who identify as southern said that "too much" attention is being paid to race, up from 61.3 percent in 2010 and 65.1 percent in 2012, and significantly higher—13 points—than whites who do not identify as southern.

Looking closely at the measure of Racial Resentment in 2016, Figure 3.8A reveals the persistence of this southern identity gap as well. At first glance, the news is promising. The mean Racial Resentment score among southern whites has dropped from 15.5 in 2012 (the midpoint of the scale is 12) to 14.9. However,

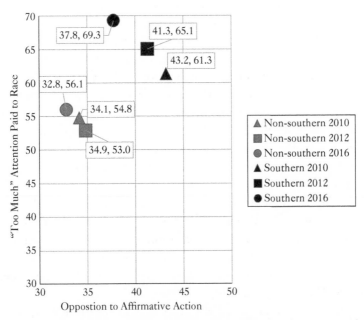

FIGURE 3.7 Percent Reporting "Too Much" Attention Is Paid to Race and Who "Oppose" or "Strongly Oppose" Affirmative Action, Among Whites, 2010–2016

Data are from the 2010, 2012, and 2016 Blair Center Polls.

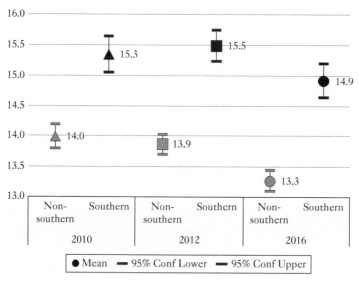

FIGURE 3.8A Mean Racial Resentment (Toward African Americans) Scores, Among Whites, 2010–2016

Data are from the 2010, 2012, and 2016 Blair Center Polls.

the mean for non-southern whites has also dropped from 13.9 to 13.3, edging ever closer to neutral. Therefore, the gap remains significant.

The distribution of white respondents along the scale, as shown in Figure 3.8B, provides sharper contrast. For southern whites, the percentage who fall above the midpoint in the scale has dropped from 77.6 to 75.1 percent, yet among whites who do not claim a southern identity, only 56.4 percent have overall scores indicating Racial Resentment. That is still, of course, the clear majority, but some aspect of southern identity when claimed by whites seems to lock in racial animus to a significant degree, while whites who reject that label seem to move in the other direction. Perhaps more important, in 2016, among non-southern whites, over a quarter (27.7 percent) fall under the midpoint, while only 12 percent of southern whites do. One group remains entrenched; the other is shifting.

On the individual questions, these persistently significant gaps widen to double digits, peaking at 24 points on question 4, as shown in Figure 3.8C. Southern whites overwhelming reassert that inequity is the fault of African Americans. They do not work hard enough, they insist, which is the exact blend of colorblind belief in post-racialism and overt racial stereotypes. This is not even resentment; really, it is just a new way of saying the same old thing. Question 1, in a similar vein, tries to historicize this idea that African Americans, like other past immigrant communities, do not need "favors" to advance or, as it implies, to

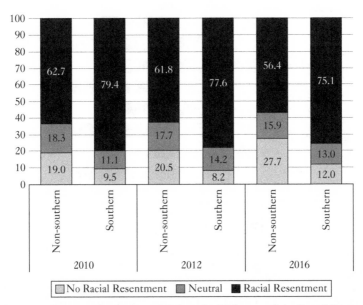

FIGURE 3.8B Percent Above, At, and Below the Midpoint of the Racial Resentment (Toward African Americans) Scale, Among Whites, 2010–2016

Data are from the 2010, 2012, and 2016 Blair Center Polls.

assimilate. To that statement—"Italians and Jews overcame prejudice and worked their way up. Blacks should do the same"—71.1 percent of whites who identify as southern express agreement, compared to 70.6 percent in 2012. However, whites who do not identify as southern dropped from 56.4 percent who expressed agreement with the statement in 2012, to only 52.8 percent in late November 2016. What was a 14-point gap based on southern white identity grew to an 18-point gap. Slavery cannot be compared in any way to immigration, which was, itself, immeasurably challenging. However, one was human bondage, and such severity leaves a darker legacy.

To that specific notion, in 2016, slightly fewer white "southerners" (64.7 percent) disagreed that "generations of slavery and discrimination have made it hard for blacks to work their way out of the lower class" than in 2012 (67.9 percent). Once again, whites who do not identify as southern dropped from 56.2 percent disagreeing with that statement in 2012 to 49.3 percent in 2016. The biggest change in Racial Resentment occurs in contemporary assessments of the idea that "In the last few years, blacks have gotten less than they deserve." Close to 70 percent of whites who identify as southern disagreed with that statement in 2012. Now, in 2016, the number has fallen to 63.1 percent. However, among non-southern whites, the decline is much steeper—from 55.4 percent disagreeing in

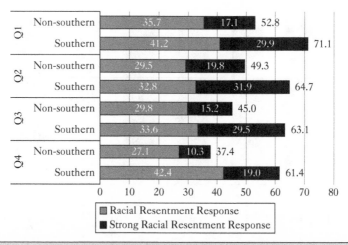

Q1. Italians, Jewish and many other minorities overcame prejudice and worked their way up. Blacks should do the same without any special favors.
Q2. Generations of slavery and discrimination have created conditions that make it difficult for Blacks to work their way out of the lower class.
Q3. Over the past few years, Blacks have gotten less than they deserve.
Q4. It's really a matter of some people not trying hard enough; if Blacks would only try harder they could be just as well off as Whites.

FIGURE 3.8C Percent of Racial Resentment Responses (Toward African Americans) by Individual Questions, Among Whites, 2016

Data are from the 2016 Blair Center Poll.

2012 to 45 percent in 2016, from the majority to the minority. It is important to note too that the portion of white southerners and non-southerners in 2016 who report strong Racial Resentment to these questions is smaller than in 2012.

If the overall levels of Racial Resentment have dipped or the intensity has softened as Trump enters the White House and Obama exits, it could be for a host of reasons. It might reflect a shift back from Racial Resentment to Old-Fashioned Racism, where racist appeals need not be coded.[75] Alternatively, it could be a polarization of racial animus, with some whites growing increasingly racist while others grow increasingly less racist. Or it could be the "selective consciousness" of whiteness, as John D. Foster describes in his recent study of white racial discourse. Foster deconstructs the way in which whites talk about race—how they frame their own white identity and how they describe their interactions with African Americans. He finds that whites are "selectively conscious" of their whiteness, employing it often in times when advantageous while downplaying its relevance when attacked.[76] Whiteness is framed as under siege when it needs to be. And when it does not, colorblindness rules the day.

THE 2010 CENTENNIAL issue of *The Crisis*, the NAACP's historic magazine, carried the headline "Putting "Post-Racial' to Rest."[77] Lawrence Bobo, W. E. B. Du Bois Professor of the Social Sciences at Harvard, agreed, warning that "declarations of having arrived at the post-racial moment are premature."[78] During NPR's one-year post-2008 election coverage, Duke University Professor Mark Anthony Neal offered a more devastating critique when he claimed that the conversation on race in America is worse than stagnant; rather it "has gone backwards."[79] Leading public intellectuals such as Ta-Nehisi Coates have pointed to the ongoing double standard faced by African Americans, including President Obama who has to be "twice as good" and "half as black" to be successful in today's America.[80] This double standard is evidence for the dissolution of the term post-racialism altogether, which Touré insists is a label "for a concept that doesn't exist."[81] These assertions made by Bobo and Coates and Touré were validated in the November 15, 2016, issue of the *New York Times Magazine*, which, in light of the highly charged racial atmosphere of the presidential election, announced "The End of the Postracial Myth."[82] Yet, election results muddied these waters as well, with analysts noting that some of the gains made by Trump were in pockets of the country that previously voted for Obama. This, naturally, led many pundits to insist that racial animus could not be the source of this support. However, as the author, Nikole Hannah-Jones argues, "What's missing from the American conversation on race is the fact that people don't have to hate black people or Muslims or Latinos to be uncomfortable with them, to be suspicious of them, to fear their ascension as an upheaval of the natural order of things. A smart demagogue plays to those fears under the guise of economic anxieties. Things not as good as you hoped? These folks are the reason."[83] Thus, as historian Robin Kelley reminds the readers, "Race always plays a role. It never disappears."[84] It will continue to play a role because proclamations of colorblindness, whether well intended or not, will not dissolve magically persistent racial inequities. Moreover, it will not disappear because it works as a tool for white political mobilization.

Tim Wise chronicles the ongoing gaps between white Americans and black and brown Americans in his book *Dear White America: Letter to a New Minority*. The net worth of white families remains, on average, 20 times and 18 times that of African American and Latino families respectively.[85] Wise has also chronicled discrepancies in pay, interview callbacks, unemployment rates, imprisonment rates, and police search-and-seizure stops, among countless other metrics in his popular works.[86] He asks repeatedly in the face of these statistics, how can anyone consider America post-racial? What is even more disturbing, as *Salon* contributor Sean McElwee notes, "is that in all of these areas, we have actually seen previous progress eroded."[87] Even the United Nations Human Rights Council Report from 2008 calls on the US government to "intensify its efforts to enforce federal civil rights laws" and to educate law enforcement officials in order to combat racial profiling.[88] An imperfect union it remains.

The answer to Wise's question about how claims of post-racialism persist is that the rhetoric of colorblindness promoted by the Long Southern Strategy, and the moral imperative contained within it, gave birth to and nourished this myth. Worse, colorblindness—because it contains no mechanism to explain ongoing racial inequities—implies that racial disparities are based on hard work and sheer objective talent. These gaps are "rationalized as legitimate, warranted, earned, and deserved."[89] The fight for equality gets reframed by the GOP as support for racial preference, and small government becomes the justification for Republicans to apply the brakes. Both further entangle southern white identity with conservative ideology and party identification.

Nixon used this new framework to halt executive enforcement of civil rights legislation and to make transformative nominations to the Supreme Court. He knew his nominations would ensure that the Supreme Court would be "a body less likely to interpret the Constitution in ways that encouraged the enforcement of affirmative action and de facto integration, either in policies of busing, of residential desegregation, or of minority preferences."[90] Gerald Ford supported the 1971 Higher Education Act, which put off "any federal court order requiring busing for racial, sexual, religious or socioeconomic balance until all appeals . . . had been exhausted."[91] George H. W. Bush vetoed the 1990 Civil Rights Act,[92] calling it a quota bill. And, of course, Reagan co-opted Dr. Martin Luther King Jr.'s language of colorblindness, giving white southerners an abstract way to bury race as a policy issue, which has long-term implications. "Colorblindness is a dog whistle," Ian Haney López writes. "It invokes a higher principle, yet also communicates sympathy for supposedly imperiled whites."[93] Now Trump inflames the racial divide, this time with whites as victims.

Cultural critics such as Ruth Frankenberg have pointed to the effects of the myth of post-racialism on education. Classroom curricula aimed at promoting multiculturalism are "watered down" by institutional "practices and policies that arise out of classical 'color-blindness.'"[94] Consequently, white millennials, who have been accused of being "racially apathetic," still advocate and believe in post-racialism.[95] That may be changing now as public clashes over Confederate memorials, NFL protests, and the plight of the Dreamers all consume the electorate. Thus, the legacy of the Long Southern Strategy is, indeed, long, and it must be acknowledged because the type of racial animus it promotes will not just die off. Rather, it is an almost impossible fight against the status quo racial hierarchy when many do not believe it exists. Yet it is a necessary fight because the choice to perpetuate the myth of post-racial America, to respond to the dog whistles of small government, to point to symbolic change while ignoring the facts of structural racism, or to resent efforts to address racial inequality, is not choosing to be colorblind. It is choosing to be blind.

PART II

Operation Dixie Family Values

*The majority of southern women convinced themselves that
God had ordained that they be deprived of pleasure, and
meekly stuffed their hollowness with piety, trying to believe the
tightness they felt was hunger satisfied.*

—LILLIAN SMITH[1]

In its quest to win over white voters in the American South, the GOP played
a full house of racial cards, but these were not the only cards they played. They
could not secure the region for their party on white racial resentment alone.
Realignment from solidly blue to solidly red requires tectonic shifts. The Civil
Rights Movement was, indeed, a cultural earthquake for white southerners, but
so too was the Women's Movement that followed. Similar to the way in which
the GOP and the Democratic Party danced around the issue of race-based civil
rights, touting almost matching platforms in the 1950s, both parties' leading
candidates in the 1970s held matching positions against abortion and for the
Equal Rights Amendment (ERA) despite factions on each side organizing in opposition. The Republican Party actually reinstated support for the ERA, which
it introduced in the 1940s,[2] into its platform after staying mum on the issue in
the 1960s due to pressure from labor organizations concerned about its impact
on labor laws.[3] Despite that reassertion, by 1976, with Second-Wave Feminism
in full swing, conservatives in the GOP threatened to establish a third party if
incumbent president Gerald Ford failed to move to the right on several key issues, including women's rights. First Lady Betty Ford had been a vocal advocate
of the ERA, and public opinion polls conducted in 1976 indicated that pro-
feminist GOP members liked her for her advocacy.[4] But a new, conservative
anti-feminist wing of the party—organized by Phyllis Schlafly—took root and
blossomed in the GOP in the years leading up to Ford's eventual loss and Ronald
Reagan's successful bid. The late Schlafly, when interviewed in 2011, still echoed
the same sentiments as she did to her "Blue Eagle Forum" readers. "A lot of people

don't understand what feminism is," she complained, "They think it is about advance and success for women, but it's not that at all. It is about power for the female left. And they have this ridiculous idea that American women are oppressed by the patriarchy and we need laws and government to solve our problems."[5]

This anti-feminism campaign—or the "other" Women's Movement as it has been described—made its own waves in the late 1970s when the International Women's Year (IWY) events and meetings took place across the country, culminating in the 1977 National Women's Conference in Houston. Much of Schlafly's army who showed up en masse had southern roots, where demonization of feminism and the denial of sexism—the foundation of what social scientists now call "Modern Sexism"—was as necessary to protecting southern white culture as Jim Crow. As southern historian James Cobb notes, "ERA stood for 'Exceedingly Radical Amendment', an Alabama Baptist woman warned."[6] The cult of southern white womanhood, the ideal of a pure and fragile southern white woman who must be protected, particularly from African American men, had been preserved since the Antebellum era because it served as the primary, yet false, justification for slavery,[7] lynchings,[8] and white supremacy in general. The southern white lady was also a "symbol of white men's power." She was "carefully placed on a moral pedestal within the privacy of the home, well out of the realm of politics and public power."[9] As a result, the gender and racial hierarchies in white southern culture were inextricable and enforced both socially and from the pulpit. As Tanya Melich argues in her 1996 book *The Republican War against Women*, "long before the birth of the Moral Majority, Schlafly's women of the Religious Right had become fixtures in the capitols of southern states where they clutched their Bibles and exhorted legislators to understand that 'women weren't meant by the Lord to be equal.'"[10] Tapping into "The Not-So-New Southern Sexism" (chapter 4), Schlafly inspired them to protest and march against their own equality—which had been cast as unnecessary or a threat to their own privileges—and to do so under the banner of "family values."

The pitch rang clear to many across the country, but nowhere was it more embraced than among white southerners, for whom traditional gender roles remained as sacrosanct as white privilege. Even women's educational opportunities, particularly in the South, have been constructed to support gender norms and preserve women's space, which in turn, preserves male (and white) power.[11] Since the two were mutually constructed, not only have the struggles against racial and gender inequality been "ever-intertwined," so too has the backlash that seems always to follow.[12]

Long considered "divine agents of social stability,"[13] some white women in the South became political reactionaries in the face of changing racial norms, but others—and perhaps with a greater degree of intensity—did so in the face of changing gender roles. That instinct toward reactionary resistance to change seemed almost hard-wired among white southerners. Even feminist leaders saw it. Karen DeCrow of the National Organization for Women pointed to the solidly anti-feminist South, where the ERA failed in every state except Texas. "They may call it the new South," she lamented, "but as far as I'm concerned they still vote like the old South. These are the same states that voted to keep slavery."[14] GOP leaders recognized that impulse—and just in time. Republicans had ceded not only the White House, but also some of their southern ground back to the Democrats in the 1976 election due to the fact that the Democrats had nominated a southern, white, evangelical peanut farmer, Georgia Governor Jimmy Carter. The backlash to the IWY and the ERA, and the "political baptism" of these southern white women,[15] offered the GOP "a new Southern Strategy."[16]

The Betty Ford feminists warned the Republican Party that turning its back on women would ensure its demise;[17] however, misogyny can be coded too.[18] Patriarchy can be masked by projecting rugged masculinity, and anti-feminism was already cloaked in support for "family values." Such bravado found a ready-made audience in the South. The region, after all, remains distinct from the rest of the country for the lax "domestic violence statutes, the acceptance of corporal punishment in the schools, and the use of the death penalty," not to mention extensive gun ownership and vanishing gun control regulations. Such policies reflect "the proprietary right to control the family"[19] so fundamental to southern white masculinity. Promoted most notably by Reagan's cowboy image and rhetoric, the Long Southern Strategy's coded misogyny reinforced masculine leadership traits while relegating women to the confines of a protected pedestal. Feminism was deemed aberrant and extreme or unnecessary. And to many white southerners, it was. While this southern white notion of femininity had remained virtually static over time, masculine ideals in the white South morphed from the honorable gentleman, agrarian farmer archetype to the rebel outlaw to the "good ole boy" with a healthy dose of "muscular evangelicalism."[20] Like whiteness, masculinity evolved depending on the threat level to "The Southern White Patriarchy" (chapter 5). Thus, an increased aggressiveness was required as both African Americans and women entered the workforce and asserted their rights—a double threat, or so it seemed to many. In that context, appeals to traditional gender roles, whether via hostility to feminism, praise to a traditional female ideal, condescension toward a female equal, vigorous performances of manliness, or invocations of honor[21] attracted southern white voters.

Yet such overtures, even if only to win elections, have consequences beyond the ballot box and beyond southern borders. Although the ERA was defeated, the Women's Movement achieved significant legal victories in such areas as sexual harassment and divorce laws. However, women's gains were taken by many as men's losses in a gender-based, zero-sum game. As Senator Sam Ervin insisted in a speech to the Tennessee Bar Association regarding the 1964 Civil Rights Act (to which gender was added as a protected class in an unsuccessful effort to sink the bill), "equality coerced by law" and "freedom of the individual"[22] could not coexist. When those threats became reality, the GOP's appeal to southern white traditionalists validated backlash men's groups that began forming across the country in response to Second-Wave Feminism.[23] Calling themselves Men's Rights Associations (MRA), these organizations—similar to white accusations of reverse racism—co-opted the rhetoric of feminists,[24] protested affirmative action policies that help women, and asserted their own claims of gender discrimination. Like Schlafly's anti-feminism, this men's rights ideology is a false equivalency to women's liberation.

Ignoring this major component of the Long Southern Strategy has contributed to another significant falsehood. Post-election analysis of Ronald Reagan's 1980s sweeping victory revealed a gender gap that favored the Democrats. Feminists, in turn, used the gender gap as leverage to insist upon the place of women in electoral "political calculations."[25] A women's voting bloc might force candidates to take more progressive stances on women's issues. Moreover, they pushed for a female vice-presidential candidate, which they got in Geraldine Ferraro's 1984 Democratic nomination. In turn, GOP insiders like Lee Atwater reiterated the warnings of feminist Republicans about the fate of the party. Reagan's campaign team polled 45,000 American women voters, and based on their answers, classified them into sixty-four categories, with each category given names like "Bettys" or "Helens."[26] What Schlafly's movement had taught them and what their survey research confirmed was that not all women embraced feminism. Richard Wirthlin, Reagan's pollster who undertook the $100,000 study under the direction of Michael Deaver, then secretary of transportation Elizabeth Dole, and secretary of health and human services Margaret Heckler[27] reported that many women "were turned off by Democrats' talking of ERA and abortion as the only issues of concern to women." They learned that they should not turn their backs on all women, just the "liberated" ones.

That critical aspect of the Long Southern Strategy is what gave rise to "The Myth of the Gender Gap" (chapter 6). The myth was based on the assumption that women, inspired by Second-Wave Feminism, were voting and identifying with Democrats in greater numbers from the mid-1980s forward because the GOP had abandoned the ERA and women's rights in general. This assumption has two critical flaws. First, the gap was created not only by women, but also by men who, in terms of partisanship, just happened to be heading in the opposite direction. In 1999, Karen Kaufman and John R. Petrocik reported in the *American Journal of Political Science* that the gender gap resulted from the movement of white men to the Republican Party, who were lured by its commitment to "family values" and an inerrant belief in male authority.[28] The second flaw is that the gender gap is not universal, though too often it has been presumed to be. Louis Bolce's scholarship had actually highlighted that point ten years earlier specifically on the issue of race, noting that Reagan did not have a "woman problem" in general, but a non-white woman problem.[29] Similarly, Reagan did not have a "white woman problem," he had a non-southern white woman problem. White southern women, many of whom had embraced the Republican Party on the initial appeals to white racial angst, may have slipped back to the Democratic Party under native-son Carter, but they were attracted to the GOP's anti-feminism and "family values." Many of them were lured by the masked misogyny, which served to protect their privilege whether real or aspirational. Moreover, as the GOP's support for traditional gender roles became increasingly wrapped in scripture and championed from the pulpit, many southern white women were willing to convert once more.

Southern white women actually deflate the gender gap, which is driven by non-white women and non-southern white women. Anti-feminist, southern white women are, in many important ways, a whole different category of white women. In terms of an intersectional approach, in which race and gender are considered in tandem, many southern white women have "whiteness" in common with other white women, but they see and experience their gender in a radically different way. Despite clear privileged differences, white feminists may share more common political ground with feminists of color than with white anti-feminists—that is how stark the distinction is. Those white anti-feminist women are more concentrated in the South, though they are by no means exclusive to it. And that part of the story has not been told enough. For example, in their 1992 study of thirteen states with female candidates on the ballot for statewide office, Eric Plutzer and John Zipp found that in eight of those states the gender of the voter was significantly related to support for the female candidates[30]—so women were more likely to vote for other women. In 1997, Kathleen Dolan affirmed these conclusions, finding a major gender gap in support for female candidates, most notably at the national level.[31] However, Plutzer and Zipp did not look at any races in the South. Dolan did not consider region either, and it turns out that in the political arena, support for women by white women is not a southern thing. These anti-feminist southern white women have too often been missed, and yet they are the bridge between the racial appeals of the original Long Southern Strategy and the political ascent of the Christian Right, both topics that have dominated the debates about realignment.

Southern historian Glenda Gilmore pointed to the long-term damage of this dynamic in her address to the Southern Conference on Women's History, entitled "But She Can't Find Her [V. O.] Key." Highlighting not only the political silence of southern women, but also the silence of historians and political scientists of the South on the impact of gender in their respective fields, Gilmore laments the loss of those important voices. In the future, she argues, "no one should be able to write about southern white men without writing about gender and race." Just as the

South cannot exist without the North, so too, Gilmore notes, "you cannot be man without woman."[32] The parties each took a different path at the fork in the road that feminism and anti-feminism presented. The GOP recognized, that this "new" issue, not only "provided a link with fundamentalist churches," but also "mobilized a group, traditional homemakers, that had lost status over the past two decades and was feeling the psychological effects of the loss."[33] They felt alienated in a liberated world. Whereas integration had felt like a loss to many white southerners, changing gender roles threatened others, and for many in a much more personal way. So the Republicans chose the route that would solidify their southern base, not just among men, but among women too, a silent majority shoring up support for a vulnerable patriarchy and the privilege it provides.

4

The Not-So-New Southern Sexism

*To Woman, lovely woman of the Southland, as pure and
chaste as this sparkling water, as cold as this gleaming ice, we
lift this cup, and we pledge our hearts and our lives to the protection of her virtue and chastity.*

—CARL CARMER[1]

IN THE AFTERMATH of her speech at the 1996 Republican National
Convention, potential first lady Elizabeth Dole's presentation style, in which
she traversed the whole stage without a podium, was lauded as Oprah-like and
incredibly likeable. She acknowledged the departure from tradition and confided
in the audience: "I'm going to be speaking to friends and, secondly, I'm going
to be speaking about the man I love,"[2] hence the strategic informality. After the
speech, her approval numbers jumped by seven points to 58 percent—a double-
digit lead over then first lady Hillary Clinton.[3] Many thought she had succeeded
in humanizing her husband, and Peter Jennings proclaimed the speech to be "an
impressive piece of stagecraft."[4] Despite her own accomplishments—which included graduating *Phi Beta Kappa* from Duke University, where she was elected
student body president,[5] earning her law degree at Harvard, one of only twenty-
four women in the 1962 class of over five hundred,[6] being named secretary of
transportation and labor under Ronald Reagan, and serving as president of the
Red Cross—Elizabeth Dole insisted that her husband was her strength, her "Rock
of Gibraltar."[7] She denounced any characterization of herself as ambitious, rather
playing up a southern belle image in which she personified traditional notions of
femininity. "It's her beauty, her poise, her ability to move well in a man's world,"[8]
noted an Atlanta woman who heard her speak on the stump during her husband's
presidential campaign. She became, in effect, her husband's Southern Strategy,[9]
adhering to the "male formula"[10] of political success by embodying publicly the
stereotypical but enduring submissive role of southern white womanhood. In
doing so, she made Bob Dole more palatable as a candidate in the increasingly
Republican South.

This stereotype of southern white womanhood and femininity is anything but new, and manipulating it for political gain became a critical, yet ignored, part of the Long Southern Strategy. Southern white womanhood was described as distinct from both the ideal northern woman imbued with a Protestant work ethic[11] and from the "tough, strong, and courageous" western women.[12] In many ways, the stereotype strips women of their power, intelligence, and strength, casting them as delicate and in need of constant protection. Southern white men manufactured that vulnerability to justify the strict laws segregating the races; white women could not defend themselves against predatory black men, or so the story goes. The pedestal was erected to mask these racial motivations, constructing a superficial, adorned, hollow definition of southern femininity that proliferates. Contemporary media representations of southern white women will offer twenty reasons why "if you've never dated a southern girl you are absolutely missing out."[13] Fashion magazines and blogs chronicle the beauty routine of the "true Southern woman" whose appearance seems both perfect and effortless, while offering the reader dozens of products to recreate her look.[14] Television programing throughout the Women's Movement and beyond portrayed southern white women as homemakers with impeccable manners and "downhome southern living as emblematic of all that is good about America."[15] Beauty pageants have long been and continue to be staples in southern culture, and even those that grant scholarship money often still sit in judgment of women's physical appearances.

This portrayal of femininity came under increased scrutiny amidst the second-wave feminist movement of the 1970s. During that time, Florence King published what many believed to be a comedic, satirical exposé of gender relations in the American South called *Southern Ladies and Gentlemen*. King described the pedestal upon which southern white womanhood was erected and the repercussions that such elevation caused southern women. In chapter 3, entitled "Would Youall [*sic*] Be Good Enough to Excuse Me While I Have an Identity Crisis: The Cult of Southern Womanhood," she designates five simultaneous images that a southern white woman must portray. "She is required," King proclaims, "to be frigid, passionate, sweet, bitchy, and scatterbrained—all at the same time."[16] Perhaps her colloquial or bawdy language—particularly about sex, which comprises a significant portion of the book—accounted for the book's reception as sensationalistic. However, beneath King's brazen accusations regarding the ongoing existence of the "Melanie syndrome,"—the self-sacrificial temperament named for *Gone With the Wind*'s martyr—or the "Blue Angel Syndrome," in which men rebel against the "untouchable pristine creature" and "woman worship"[17] that perpetuates this cult, lurked darker, more serious gender dynamics on a collision course with partisan politics.

The cult of southern white womanhood clashed not only with the women's suffrage movement of the 1920s, but also with modern efforts to secure an Equal Rights Amendment (ERA) to the US Constitution for women's equality. In the initial fight to ratify the Nineteenth Amendment guaranteeing universal woman suffrage, eight of the nine states that originally rejected the amendment and only ratified it decades after its implementation are in the American South, and the ERA remains unratified in ten of those same eleven states of the former Confederacy. Only Texans passed it. Tennessee initially did so but later repealed the vote.[18] The feminist loss, however, was a major GOP gain, as the Republican establishment realized that traditional gender roles could be the next strategic issue that could reignite realignment. The fuel driving the opposition is rooted in the "sacred womanhood" that, as southern writer Lillian Smith warned, "culturally stunted" women by insisting that they perch "on lonely pedestals" and play "statue."[19] Though these fights may seem distant historically, the myth of southern white womanhood is not a relic of the past; rather, the powerful image perseveres and has meaning even now.

As Nina Baym writes in her collection of essays, *Feminism and American Literary History*, if the myth has power, then it has real—that is, material— effects, and these effects have been measured. Jean Twenge, for example, tested the "Attitudes Toward Women" scale developed in 1972 and consisting of twenty-five items such as "Swearing and obscenity are more repulsive in the speech of a woman than of a man"; "Women should take increasing responsibility for leadership in solving the intellectual and social problems of the day"; and "Women should worry less about their rights and more about becoming good wives and mothers."[20] Over twenty-five years (1970–1995), Twenge found that undergraduate students in the South reported more conservative responses (agreement or disagreement based on the posed statement) that echo the "southern tradition" that Lillian Smith described.[21] The 1995 General Social Survey (GSS) data, as analyzed by Tom Rice and Diane Coates, confirmed this ongoing regional conservatism when respondents faced questions not only on the employment of women, but also on the effectiveness of women in politics.[22] Still, another over-time GSS study—this one reaching forward to 1998—found whites who lived in the South expressing more conservative attitudes toward the ability of a working mother to create "a warm and secure relationship" with her children. In addition, opinions in the South were more likely to affirm that "it is much better for everyone involved if the man is the achiever outside the home and the woman takes care of the home and family."[23] Even as recently as 2014, Virginia legislators attempted to revive the ERA and secure passage in their state, only to have it pass in the Senate but fail in the House of Delegates, and then to have Republican state senators rescind their support and defeat the measure again in

2015.[24] Similar efforts in Arkansas have met the same fate.[25] So deeply ingrained is the notion of southern white femininity that it persists despite such dramatic changes in the lives of American women.

The depth results largely from the religious emphasis on traditional gender roles, which grew only more intense when challenged by Second-Wave Feminism. During the 1970s and 1980s, the Southern Baptist Convention (SBC) "placed adherence to biblical gender norms at the heart of theological orthodoxy."[26] Moreover, in 1998, Southern Baptists amended their encyclical "Faith and Message" to cite female submission specifically.[27] Accordingly, southern white women often buy into these stereotypes themselves and "reinforce the patriarchal order,"[28] sometimes at great personal cost. In their 1986 study Jacqueline Boles and Maxine Atkinson found that 70 percent of southern white women still described the ideal lady as "simple, good, submissive, mannerly, humble, kind, economical, generous, hospitable, and calm," but they also overwhelmingly felt as if they are failing to reach that ideal.[29] They cannot climb atop the mythological pedestal, but many still strive to do so. Cherry Good argues in the *Journal of American Studies* that southern women "prolong the myth" to protect their own privileges. They play a role to maintain social and moral acceptance. To stay in character, so to speak, means perfecting the art of dissembling. "This ability to dissemble," Good writes, "to cloak the steely strength with the delicate covering of a magnolia bud, is passed on from mother to daughter at a tender age."[30] And no one played that role better on the national stage than Elizabeth Dole who, even with all of her career accomplishments, somehow did not threaten the southern "good ole boys"[31] or the southern belles, for that matter—at least not when she was the doting spouse of the presidential candidate. When she ran herself in 2000, she struggled to raise money even to compete in the GOP primary.[32]

That is reflective of the GOP's Long Southern Strategy, which included appeals to traditional gender roles in order to pick off southern white voters. Threats to this ideal southern white femininity provided opportunities for the GOP to reinforce the myth of fragile southern white womanhood. Early legal battles regarding the inclusion of sex in the 1964 Civil Rights Act (CRA), for example, addressed the feasibility of equality between men and women coexisting with protections for women from mandated military service or workplace hazards—a question that set off alarm bells among many white southerners.[33] The push for the ERA, the elevation of feminism and family to the center stage of American politics, and the eventual emergence of serious female political candidates ultimately made women's rights a decidedly partisan issue. In due course, the GOP's messaging, often subtle and coded, tapped into and perpetuated a Modern Sexism, characterized by a distrust of ambitious women (condemned in 2016 as "nasty"[34]), a demonization of feminism in general, and a growing resentment toward the tangible and intangible ways in which changes to women's roles affected the workplace, the home, and the family.[35] Nowhere were those roles, which were increasingly seen as limited and sexist, more embedded than in the hearts and minds of southern whites where traditional femininity, first constructed to rationalize white supremacy and privilege, remains revered and not, in any way, new.

THE MYTH OF southern white womanhood, in order to maintain its power and longevity, has been bent and twisted over time to suit political whims.[36] The result is a contradictory message in which women are both esteemed and virtuous, yet "better suited to simpler positions," notes modern blogger Holly Baer in her personal essay "My Failures as a Southern Woman."[37] Margaret Ripley Wolfe, writing in the *Journal of Popular Culture*, drew the same conclusions nearly forty years earlier, pointing to the paradox by which women were praised as "discerning about human relations, sympathetic, and compassionate, given to suffering in silence, a natural teacher, and a wise counsellor for her family." However, despite being a "paragon of virtue," women "still needed their [men's] direction."[38] Kent Anderson Leslie's 1986 study traced the roots of this definition via a systematic analysis of the Antebellum writings by Thomas Dew, George Fitzhugh, and William Harper, classifying five elements of southern white female identity based on their descriptive language. Present consistently in their writings were:

(1) characteristics that validate a theory of the innate physical weakness of woman, i.e., she is weak, delicate, soft;

(2) behaviors that negate authenticity, i.e., she is nervous, fickle, capricious, meek, timid, cheerful, charming, animating, and ornamental, having "fine feelings unchecked by considerations of interest or of calculations of remote consequences";

(3) traits required by motherhood in a difficult situation, i.e., she is quiet, forbearing, patient, sympathetic;

(4) symbolic states, i.e., she is pure and virtuous; and

(5) behaviors that clearly acknowledge that someone else is in power, i.e., she is dependent, diffident, and obedient.[39]

The expectation of emotional strength, yet physical weakness, of ethical clarity yet worldly confusion, allowed southern white men to be taken care of at home and never challenged in public.

Of course, the image of the Antebellum white southern lady did not remain stagnant for generations, but rather it morphed over time. Elite white southern women, for example, ran their family plantations during the Civil War[40]—similar to the way women supplemented the workforce during World War II—and the experience called into question the illusion of southern women as delicate, fragile, and vaporous.[41] Widows had to maintain their new authority during Reconstruction, but others, such as the women in Colorado County, Texas, profiled by Angela Boswell in her chapter "Married Women's Property Rights and the Challenge to the Patriarchal Order," ceded their new power back to their husbands after the war. Such women, Boswell writes, "showed little interest in using the laws already available to them to challenge the prevailing social system, much less organizing to push for even greater reforms." Rather, she concludes, "Supported by law and custom, this group of southern women returned to the Antebellum ideal of marriage and to male authority over wives, family, and property."[42] On the other hand, in the industrializing towns of the South, lower-income women joined the textile labor force, for example, in droves, comprising by 1880, 40 percent of the employees in four southern states.[43] Other scholars such as Jane Turner Censer highlight additional ways in which southern women redefined their roles during Reconstruction when the prohibition of slave labor forced women to embrace "technology" and to reduce birth rates in order to manage household duties.[44]

Household duties, despite the myth of the delicate white southern woman, proved no leisurely task. In this sense, the myth alludes to something more imagined than real. For the vast majority of white southern women were not part of the plantation elite, and their "women's work" as defined by historian Sara Evans, encompassed "gardening, caring for cows and poultry, spinning, weaving, sewing, baking, preserving, and cheese making as well as the routine duties of meal preparation, housecleaning, and child rearing."[45] In truth, the household in an agricultural society functioned as the "dominant unit of production,"[46] and women proved invaluable, equal partners in that enterprise. Despite the shared workload or perhaps because of it, guarding male authority was accomplished by promoting female weakness and neediness and relegating women to oversee an idealized notion of home and family. Over time, as Anna Gavanas writes in her work on fatherhood in America, "domesticity and family involvement became associated with femininity in the nineteenth-century market economy."[47] Accordingly, the idea of the pedestal reflected a "bourgeois ideology of domesticity"—elusive and unrealistic for the majority of southern white women—that "propounded the radical separation of public and private spheres and the unswerving identification of men with the former and women with the latter."[48] The pedestal, though unattainable for most southern white women, became a romanticized privilege to which many aspired, an identity connected to status. For epitomizing not just femininity, but sacred, domestic, privileged femininity, remained the brass ring for many southern white women.

Consequently, forays into political life by southern white women were primarily ornamental. When GOP presidential nominee Barry Goldwater, for example, stopped in Alabama as part of his southern campaign tour in 1964, he was greeted by seven hundred girls from every county in the state dressed in long white gowns and waving American flags. "Some unsung Alabama Republican impresario had hit upon an idea of breathtaking simplicity," wrote Richard Rovere in his account for *The New Yorker*, "to show the country the 'lily-white' character of Republicanism in Dixie by planting the bowl with a great field of white lilies—living lilies, in perfect bloom, and gorgeously arrayed."[49] This superficial, sacred femininity was the public face of this self-cultivated regional depiction of gender roles. Threats and challenges to it were met with unapologetic displays like that which greeted Goldwater. After all, the entire social structure hinged on maintaining this traditional way of life. Adherence could only be absolute. Or as Joel Williamson once wrote: a "good" white southern woman "cannot be a little bit bad, or a little bit masculine, any more than she can be a little bit black."[50]

The negative repercussions of the pedestal extend well beyond this notion of dissembling and are, perhaps, more dangerous than absolutism. Limiting women's influence to the home afforded them a "moral passivity" of sorts, insulated from the business of slavery, war, and, later, Jim Crow.[51] Gender functioned as a buffer, creating a privileged distance from the moral questions that plagued the nation. This passive femininity reflected the desires of a white male patriarchy that appeased southern white women by championing their moral superiority while simultaneously ignoring it. The myth carried yet another cost: isolation. As noted by Antebellum historian Elizabeth Fox-Genovese, "southern society discouraged women from developing many of the characteristics identified as typical of northeastern women—networks, bonds, voluntary associations, mother's clubs."[52] Relegated to the private sphere by their gender and elevated by their race, white southern women were often alienated from their peers and, of course, segregated from black southern women altogether.[53] Protests for suffrage, reproductive rights, equal pay, child custody protections, and no-fault divorce require collective action and political socialization, and those things happen in shared space. There are exceptions of course, such as Lucy M. Stanton, who recognized the commodity of her whiteness and used it to forge common ground with white men in her public advocacy for white supremacy.[54] Still, most southern white women functioned in wholly dependent relationships—yet another price paid for perching atop the pedestal. Virginia Foster's 1971 article "The Emancipation of Pure, White, Southern Womanhood" said it plainly: "it was having a man look after you and provide for you that was necessary and the lack of one . . . meant a life of poverty as well as pity."[55] This dependence, of course, made a patriarchal society possible and kept it protected long after progressive changes confronted this very notion.

Dependence, isolation, and moral passivity, create a bubble in which such women were protected and privileged, yet politically unengaged. Moreover, that combination ensures the pedestal stays intact and allows stereotypes of southern white women to thrive. In fact, data collected as late as 1992 as part of the University of North Carolina's Southern Focus Polls demonstrate the lingering strength of what may seem an old myth to many. Comparing women who identify as southern to women who do not—all of whom reside in the geographic South—shows that southernness may be more cultural than residential, particularly in terms of gender stereotypes. As shown in Table 4.1, even twenty-five years ago, within the South, the clear majority of non-southern white women believe in this myth of southern white womanhood. They report that in their minds, southern women are less career-oriented (66 percent), less feminist (65.3 percent), less independent (59.5 percent), and less assertive (58.6 percent) than American women in general.

To be fair, high percentages of white women who do identify as southern described themselves in mostly the same way. The differences between southern white women and non-southern white women are statistically significant in every category except their assessments of how career-oriented they believe southern women to be. The majority on both sides indicate that southern women are less focused on careers. Actually, self-identified southern white women seem to be in fairly close agreement with what non-southern white women believe about them. In addition to being less career-oriented (51.8 percent), they also say that southern women are less feminist (50.9 percent), less independent (42.1 percent), and less assertive (52.2 percent). Moreover, both women who identify as southern and women who do not classified southern women to be friendlier (88.4 percent and 68.2 percent, respectively) than American women as a whole. Perceptions are more varied regarding how strong-willed and self-centered southern women are—with those who identify as southern giving themselves more positive marks.

Still, overall, among those who live in the South, the myth of southern white womanhood is accepted by outsiders, legitimized by insiders, and persistent well beyond expectations. Surely too, such stereotypes exist outside of the region's borders. Although popular assessments of the graciousness of southern women and the pronouncements of southern hospitality and beauty—"gorgeously arrayed"—may seem like praise, they celebrate an identity structure that oppresses the very women it claims to honor. Even Dole herself, after describing her substantial accomplishments, pivoted to her role as a proud wife who is "truly in awe of his [Bob Dole's] problem-solving abilities."[56] Smiling and deferential,

Table 4.1 Percent Reporting "Southern Women" Are "More," "Less," or "No Different" from American Women on the Following Traits, Among White Women Who Live in the Geographic South, 1992

		Non-southern	Southern
Career-oriented	Southern Women More	6.1	17.7
	Southern Women Less	66.0	51.8
	No Difference	27.9	30.5
Friendly	Southern Women More	68.2	88.4
	Southern Women Less	12.1	3.7
	No Difference	19.8	7.9
Feminist	Southern Women More	14.9	28.9
	Southern Women Less	65.3	50.9
	No Difference	19.9	20.3
Strong-willed	Southern Women More	27.2	59.3
	Southern Women Less	38.8	18.9
	No Difference	34.0	21.7
Independent	Southern Women More	13.1	35.3
	Southern Women Less	59.5	42.1
	No Difference	27.5	22.6
Self-centered	Southern Women More	35.2	16.5
	Southern Women Less	30.3	61.8
	No Difference	34.5	21.8
Assertive	Southern Women More	18.4	35.1
	Southern Women Less	58.6	52.2
	No Difference	23.0	12.7

Data are from the Fall 1992 Southern Focus Poll, South Survey available at http://www. thearda.com/Archive/Sfocus.asp/.

and too often silent altogether, southern white women remain, in many ways, trapped in a myth of their own making.

IN THE AFTERMATH of the 1964 CRA, affirmative action programs began to build a bridge from the private to the public sphere for American women. The entrance of women into the modern workplace threatened southern gender dynamics perhaps more so than in other parts of the country. The powerful lure of "bourgeois domesticity" had been reinforced throughout the twentieth century by decades of advertising that portrayed women's place within the home (even though studies show that this decreased over time)[57] and continuously dependent on men. The elevation of the homemaker to the moniker "domestic engineer" and the explosion of home economics programs served to adjust the tone of gender dynamics without really changing the basic power structure. This was not a new technique in the South; in fact, it struck a familiar chord. The head of household title bestowed on women in the Antebellum era, proclaims Fox-Genovese, proved similarly manipulative, forming "the basis for the illusion of equality as citizens that informed the political culture of white men."[58] Even as Second-Wave Feminism made many American men culturally conscious of gender inequities or at least aware of the true workload that "domestic engineers" carried daily, labor in the home remained the work of women. In the late 1980s, Julie Press and Eleanor Townsley published findings revealing that a "reporting gap" existed in studies of domestic labor. The National Survey of Families and Households conducted in 1988 and the diaries recorded in 1985 as part of the American's Use of Time project show that the rhetoric of equality and the reality of sharing "homemaking" work are still quite distinct.[59]

Resentment accompanied that awareness and often surfaced as digs and critical comments about working women that reduced them to their ornamental or superficial function. President Richard Nixon, for example, was reported to have criticized White House correspondent Helen Thomas for wearing pants. He even asked her to turn around to see if the pants were flattering, reducing her to an object to be admired.[60] Nixon received little pushback if any for the remark. Decades later, President George W. Bush drew minor criticism for a similarly gendered quip when he commented on Nancy Pelosi's ascendance as the first female Speaker of the House by quipping that he had sent her names of decorators for her new office, implying that cosmetic concerns would or even should trump her substantive agenda.[61] Even John McCain during his 2008 presidential campaign told crowds at the Sturgis motorcycle rally that he was volunteering his wife Cindy, the former Junior Rodeo Queen of Arizona in 1968,[62] to enter their biker beauty pageant.[63] McCain may not have realized that the competition included nudity, but he still decided to promote her looks. Moreover, Donald Trump at his initial meeting with the newly elected French president and his wife, Brigitte Macron, proclaimed to her, "you're in such good shape,"[64] repeating this tendency to prioritize public appearance in evaluations of women. Trump has a long and well-documented history of objectifying women via his ownership and promotion of beauty pageants, not to mention his comments about an American model and actress caught on tape during an interview with *Access Hollywood* that resurfaced during the campaign.

Such offhand comments objectify women and render their contribution artificial, though the latter example presents more severe incidences of sexual harassment that are not exclusive to either party. In more extreme cases, such objectification encourages women's silence, which is another increasingly unsustainable condition of femininity. Literary scholar Diane Roberts called this the "problem of the modern feminine" that she finds running throughout the work of the most famous of southern novelists, William Faulkner. Addressing the character of Caddy in *The Sound and the Fury*, for example, Roberts describes the character's tendency to silence herself due to the fact that she lives in a world in which "speaking is pollution for women."[65] It remained risky and often carried a hefty price, particularly among southerners and within the GOP, even in the wake of women's liberation. First Lady Betty Ford ran headfirst into this issue when she responded frankly to a series of questions on a *60 Minutes* interview during her husband's administration. Probed about her opinion on *Roe v. Wade*, as well as asked to speculate on what she would do hypothetically if her daughter had an extramarital affair, Ford appeared neither shocked nor flustered, praising *Roe* and promising understanding for her daughter. Though her own husband claimed to admire her honesty and her opinions, he cited the interview as contributing to his loss to Jimmy Carter in 1976.[66]

The antipathy toward outspoken women exposed how shallow the consciousness-raising about gender equity has been. Even when politically correct lip service was paid to the issue, it seems to have masked a true commitment to change, at least to a degree that remains influential now. Similar to the rhetoric of colorblindness and the demonization (and feminization) of the poor as entitled "welfare queens," the rhetoric of women's equality preceded substantive changes in attitudes, particularly among southerners where the "proper" place of women had been cemented into southern white identity for generations. Moreover, just as scholars reported declines in overtly racist attitudes (Old-Fashioned Racism in which African Americans are deemed lazy, unintelligent, and untrustworthy), in the decades following the Civil Rights Movement, so too were Americans, men and women, less likely to condone or to express overt notions of female inferiority. However, measures of modern racism, such as Symbolic Racism, uncovered ongoing racial resentment and frustration with affirmative action programs, and new measures of "Modern Sexism" have done the same.

In 1995, Janet Swim, Kathryn Aikin, Wayne Hall, and Barbara Hunter introduced a scale to measure this new expression of Modern Sexism. At its core, the scale seeks to uncover whether the respondent believes in the ongoing discrimination against women, expresses hostility to women's push for equality, and/or resents efforts made to help women overcome past discrimination.[67] Prior to the development of the Modern Sexism scale, scholars utilized the Attitudes Toward Women Scale (AWS), which was created in the early 1970s and focused directly on women's "roles, rights, and responsibilities." The AWS functioned a bit differently from Old-Fashioned Racism in that it does not assign negative stereotypes to women; rather, it quantified the degree to which a respondent buys into gendered separate spheres. Still, as those boundaries were challenged, AWS, with its fifty-five items, proved a useful way to assess whether these long-held notions were starting to shift in America. That being said, women entering the workforce in droves—with affirmative action programs and scholarships helping women advance—catalyzed a new set of emotions, much different from a gendered belief and cosmology. These emotions included distrust, frustration, and resentment, as women chipped away at the American patriarchy. Thus, the AWS has a "ceiling effect" influenced by "social desirability."[68] However, the Modern Sexism scale seemed to capture more accurately contemporary feelings about women in the workplace.

As previously mentioned, Jean Twenge found in her over-time study of the AWS that well into the 1990s, people who lived in the South continued to report a stronger commitment to the traditional roles of women than the rest of the country.[69] Therefore, it is no surprise that measures of Modern Sexism would also reveal a regional distinctiveness. Modern Sexism, as measured in the 2012 Blair Center Poll, included five statements, with which respondents could strongly disagree, disagree, be neutral, agree, or strongly agree. The statements read as follows: "Many women are actually seeking special favors, such as hiring policies that favor them over men, under the guise of asking for 'equality'" (Q1); "Most women interpret innocent remarks or acts as being sexist" (Q2); "Feminists are seeking for women to have more power than men" (Q3); "When women lose to men in a fair competition, they typically complain about being discriminated against" (Q4); and "Discrimination against women is no longer a problem in the United States" (Q5). The responses, as reported in in Figure 4.1A and Figure 4.1B, were each scored from 1 to 5, for a potential overall score ranging from 5 to 25, with 15 as the midpoint. In Figure 4.1A, the mean scores for white Americans are provided, as well as the upper and lower 95-percent confidence intervals for those means. Whites who live outside of the South or who do not claim a southern

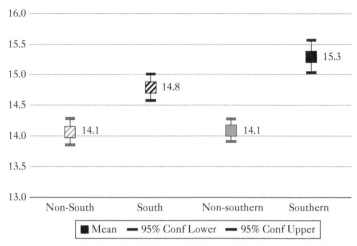

FIGURE 4.1A Mean Modern Sexism Scores, Among Whites, 2012
Data are from the 2012 Blair Center Poll.

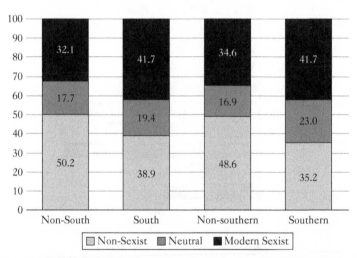

FIGURE 4.1B Percent Above, At, and Below the Midpoint of the Modern Sexism Scale, Among Whites, 2012
Data are from the 2012 Blair Center Poll.

identity have a mean Modern Sexism score of 14.1, slightly below the midpoint. These scores are significantly lower than whites who live in the South, among whom the average is 14.8. Moreover, whites who embrace southern identity have significantly higher scores, reporting an average above the midpoint at 15.3.

Figure 4.1B provides the percent distribution of respondents in each subgroup who fall above, below, or at the midpoint of the scale. The percentage of whites with scores higher than 15 is greatest among those who live in the South and among those who identify as southern, both at about 42 percent. Moreover, the greatest percentage of respondents at the midpoint on this scale are southerners, with approximately 23 percent of southerners indicating a neutral score. In total, 65 percent of white southerners reported a neutral or sexist score on the Modern Sexism scale. Only 35.2 percent of southern whites fall into the non-sexist category, with scores below the midpoint, compared to 48.6 percent of non-southern whites.

Beyond just averages on the overall scale, the specific questions in the scale provide useful comparisons between these gaps, which southern identity seems specifically to exacerbate. Figure 4.2 presents the percent of whites who "agree" and "strongly agree" with each question included in the Modern Sexism scale.

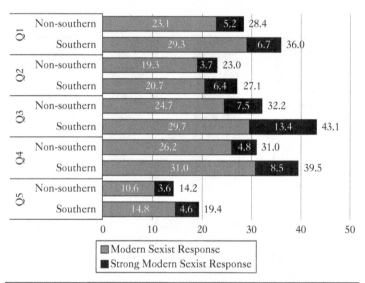

Q1: Many women are actually seeking special favors, such as hiring policies that favor them over men, under the guise of asking for "equality."
Q2: Most women interpret innocent remarks or acts as being sexist.
Q3: Feminists are seeking for women to have more power than men.
Q4: When women lose to men in a fair competition, they typically complain about being discriminated against.
Q5: Discrimination against women is no longer a problem in the United States.

FIGURE 4.2 Percent of Modern Sexist Responses by Individual Questions, Among Whites, 2012

Data are from the 2012 Blair Center Poll.

For every question in the scale, a significantly greater percentage of southern respondents give sexist responses. Across all questions, the sexist gap between southern whites and non-southern whites varies from 4.1 percent to 11 percent. The notion that "feminists are seeking for women to have more power than men" provokes the sharpest renouncement by 43.1 percent of southern whites, as compared to 32.1 percent of non-southern whites.

Elizabeth Dole was quoted during her 2000 run for president as saying she was not running as a woman, but rather was a woman running, suggesting that the public advancement of gender equity for its own sake was unpalatable to GOP audiences.[70] Moreover, just as the rhetoric of colorblindness convinced many voters that they lived in a post-racial America, so too do the vast majority of whites, particularly southern whites, believe that America is post-sexist. Thus, any efforts to rectify or level the playing field tilted by institutionalized sexism or by the effects of motherhood, for that matter, on workplace advancement are deemed "favors." If women have special needs, then they should not be in the workplace. They should remain on their pedestal, or so the ideology goes. This complex upkeep of southern white gender roles requires, then, for southern women to resent feminism or women's advancement right alongside men, and even to resent the programs that would facilitate these changes.[71] Though potentially surprising to some, data from the 2012 Blair Center Poll reveals exactly that. Figures 4.3A and 4.3B show the mean Modern Sexism scores of just white women.

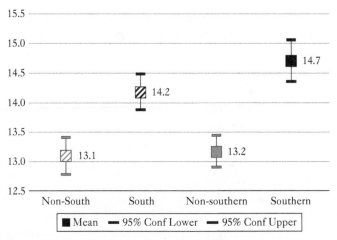

FIGURE 4.3A Mean Modern Sexism Scores, Among White Women, 2012
Data are from the 2012 Blair Center Poll.

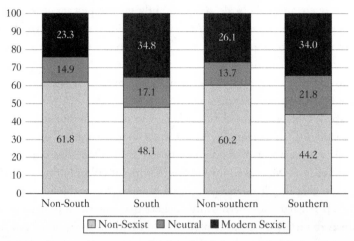

FIGURE 4.3B Percent Above, At, and Below the Midpoint of the Modern Sexism Scale, Among White Women, 2012

Data are from the 2012 Blair Center Poll.

White women who live outside of the South have a mean Modern Sexism score of 13.1, and white women who do not call themselves southern fall closely behind at 13.2. However, among white women who reside in the South, the mean Modern Sexism score jumps significantly to 14.2, and for white women who identify as southern, it is significantly higher still at 14.7, with an upper confidence interval that ticks above the midpoint of the scale. Perhaps even more revealing are the distributions of women across the scale as shown in Figure 4.3B. Only 23.3 percent of women outside of the South fall into the Modern Sexist category, with a vast majority, 61.8 percent, falling below the midpoint and in the non-sexist classification. Among white women who live in the South, 34.8 percent are above the midpoint, with only 48.1 percent in the non-sexist range. The percentage of white women who identify as southern who fall into the sexist category is slightly less at 34 percent, but the percentage in the non-sexist category is also less, at 44.2 percent, meaning that a larger portion were neutral (21.8 percent). Although neutral may seem innocuous as a response, it means that non-sexist southern white women are in the minority. The rest of their community is either undecided on such issues as whether or not discrimination against women still exists or they believe that it does not.

There is also a substantive breakdown of white women's responses to the individual questions in the Modern Sexism scale, as shown in Figure 4.4. Again, compared to white women who do not identify as southern, those who do have a significantly higher percentage giving a Modern Sexist, or strongly Modern Sexist

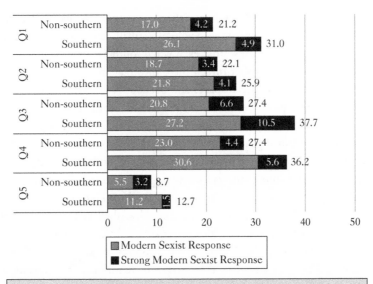

FIGURE 4.4 Percent of Modern Sexist Responses by Individual Questions, Among White Women, 2012

Data are from the 2012 Blair Center Poll.

response. These significant gaps between these two groups of white women range from 3.8 percent to 10.3 percent. Again, the largest negative reaction is to question 3, which inquires as to agreement or disagreement that "Feminists are seeking for women to have more power than men," with question 4 a close second. Question 4 specifically states, "when women lose to men in a fair competition, they typically complain about being discriminated against," and 36.2 percent of southern white women agree with that statement. Another 39.7 percent— not shown in the figure—are neutral on this question, with only one-quarter of southern white women disagreeing. So only one-fourth of southern white women trust other women not to blame falsely gender discrimination when they lose, which indicates very little shared women's consciousness, if much at all. A significant portion of southern white women seem to have a vested interest in rejecting feminism and pledging some level of allegiance or at least neutrality to the southern white patriarchy.

SOUTHERN WOMEN HAVE been socialized to support the patriarchy and to obey their husbands, a tendency that sociologists still find present at the end of the twentieth century.[72] So much so that even when southern white women gained power in the wake of wars that forced them into male roles, at war's end, they often retuned to their gendered spaces and occupations.[73] Some of the greatest progressive efforts in pursuit of women's equality had to be reframed in the South to play to this pedestal mythology so deeply ingrained. Anti-suffragettes in the South praised traditional gender roles, claiming that it was a privilege for women to be protected from having to make "a public display" of themselves by voting.[74] To some degree, the same sentiment drove opposition to the ERA five decades later and the country took notice. In 1975 the *New York Times* ran an article that pointed to the myth of southern womanhood—described as "the South's historical fascination with the romantic ideal; men are meant to wield power; women are made to be protected and idealized"[75]—as the key reason why the Women's Movement stalled in the region. This version of femininity "was certainly no blueprint for building mature, decisive, independent women."[76]

Some of the conservative organizations that rose in opposition to Second-Wave Feminism called themselves the WWWW, standing for "Women Who Want to Be Women,"[77] and STOP ERA, which stood for "Stop Taking Our Privileges." STOP ERA was comprised of conservative women, and some men, who fought to protect women's privileged role as homemaker, insisting they did not want to "step down from the pedestal."[78] Not working was deemed not just a privilege but a right by anti-ERA advocates.[79] Women were not victims, and housework was not "slavery,"[80] proclaimed anti-feminist leader and spokeswoman Phyllis Schlafly. Moreover, by the 1970s, Schlafly argued, technology had lightened the duties of women, thereby heightening their privilege. Women were blessed to be taken care of by their husbands and blessed to be mothers. GOP presidential nominees such as Mitt Romney seemed to embody this philosophy. His wife, Ann Romney,[81] had her husband won, would have been the first first lady born in the twentieth century to have never worked outside of the home (beyond the duties that resulted from her husband's elections to public office). Mamie Eisenhower would be the most recent precedent, and she was born in 1896.[82] This was the same vision that Anne Romney, herself, promoted in her speech at the 2012 Republican National Convention, glorifying mothers as the hardest-working members of the family. "It's the moms of this nation—single, married, widowed—who really hold this country together,"[83] she proclaimed, emphasizing that most important women's role, which rang loud and clear among southern audiences.

The STOP ERA movement gained traction with southern women, not only because it portrayed women as special and privileged, but also because it championed biblical roles for women, channeling an evangelical energy of sorts.

This was particularly effective in the South where one of the primary sources of socialization was the church. In the wake of Second-Wave Feminism, Southern Baptist leadership doubled down on their institutional commitment to traditional gender roles. The greatest threat came from the rise of evangelical feminists who pushed for equal treatment within the church, including "egalitarian readings of scripture" and the ordination of women.[84] In 1974, Letha Scanzoni and Nancy Hardesty outlined this progressive vision in their book, *All We're Meant to Be*— a vision which spread the evangelical egalitarian position throughout many southern congregations. The concepts of "masculine" and "feminine" resulted from "cultural conditioning," the authors explained, not biological differences and, thus, were not ordained by God.[85] They supported their argument with passages from scripture demonstrating the historic role of women in the church, and they likened support for a gendered hierarchy to support for slavery repeatedly. "Those who declare that the gospel offers women spiritual equality in Christ but not in this world," Scanzoni and Hardesty insisted, "find themselves arguing along with [those] who wrote in defense of slavery."[86] Their detractors codified their beliefs first in the 1987 Danvers Statement, which warned that straying from the God-given gender hierarchies would "backfire in the crippling of Biblically faithful witness."[87] Four short years later, anti-egalitarians published their own 500-page manifesto, *Recovering Biblical Manhood and Womanhood*, edited by John Piper and Wayne Gruden.[88] The manifesto proved influential, and in 1998, the Southern Baptist Executive Council issued a revision to their "Baptist Faith and Message," which instructed wives to "take the initiative to subject themselves to their husbands."[89] Throughout all the progressive legislation and cultural change facing Americans in the 1960s and 1970s, this addendum—called the "Doctrine of Wifely Submission"—was the first revision in thirty-five years, and gender was the only subject addressed.

In the decades that followed, more restrictions would come. In 1995, for example, on a date later nicknamed Black Wednesday, the Southern Baptist Theological Seminary, against the support of students and faculty, rejected female ordination in any capacity. They insisted, from that point forward, that only faculty who believed in male-only ordination would be hired. Women were unsuited to pastoral leadership positions, insisted the SBC.[90] Extreme wings of the Southern Baptist community argued that women should, instead, undertake the education of their children and pushed for homeschooling. One particular group, Vision Forum, contends that Christians should not participate in public education because it is not divinely ordained and because such schools are "sub-Christian at best and anti-Christian at worst."[91] Doug Phillips, the leader of the Boerne Christian Assembly in San Antonio, Texas, and the son of Howard Phillips who worked in the Nixon administration, started the group. They have rejected what they refer to as "the working-woman philosophy of the late 20th century" and the "feministic philosophy of the anti-complementarian, pro-egalitarian household leadership."[92]

Anti-ERA advocates promoted Bible-backed gender definitions and portrayed "Christian" and "feminism" as incompatible—a notion that contemporary men's rights groups continue to promote. The "Shattered Man" website, for example, insists that Christian feminist is "an oxymoron."[93] The dramatic shift of more women into the workplace (by the mid-1980s, less than one-half of American families were two-parent households with traditional gender roles including the male breadwinner and the female homemaker)[94] fueled this angst. Such angst, in turn, catalyzed a morally righteous nostalgia for the "normal" family. Many believed that women's entrance into the public sphere would alter forever the religiously sanctioned private sphere. One could not be both a working woman and a homemaker, many argued, which was a false dichotomy in and of itself, but one that had mass appeal. Beyond the protection of white southern privilege, anti-feminism caught national fire when it played offense, positioning itself as part of a broader pro-family movement. For those who did not want to touch women's liberation or organize in direct opposition to it, the pro-family frame proved more accessible and less political to women, many of whom in the South saw politics as beyond the scope of their domestic responsibilities. It felt like an urgent fight too, as sexual permissiveness (particularly among teenagers),[95] sup-port for cohabitation (by 1976–1977 almost half of college freshmen supported cohabitation before marriage), and the doubling of the divorce rate between 1965 and 1975[96] seemed to spell the demise of traditional family values.

An annotated bibliography of the ERA, covering the tumultuous years from 1976 to 1985, includes close to one hundred scholarly works that address the potential impact of the ERA on the "family" unit.[97] The pro-family argument galvanized supported in an unprecedented manner, convincing GOP leaders of its power to sway debate. [98] Moreover, when the pro-family rhetoric needed some kind of definitive authority, politicians turned to the Bible and the pulpit, redefining the party for the foreseeable future. Robert Self describes the potency of this religious injection in this way: "Antifeminism and breadwinner conserv-atism would not have achieved the political leverage and longevity they did without the formidable institutional resources of conservative Christianity."[99] As Sally Gallagher notes in her 2004 article "Where Are the Antifeminist Evangelicals? Evangelical Identity, Subcultural Location, and Attitudes toward Feminism," nowhere was this more true than in the American South,[100] particu-larly among people who identified with the region and wore their southernness alongside their faith. Republican Party leaders and candidates had been speaking with a white southern "accent," of sorts, on issues related to race, but via their

Southern Baptist Strategy, the GOP practically became "born again" southern. The conversion worked, as Daniel Williams has explained: "Across the South, socially conservative Democratic women began to view the federal government as a threat to family, and conservative Republicans as their allies."[101]

Understanding the variables that influenced and continue to influence this anti-feminist perspective among white women remains critical to assessing the way in which the Long Southern Strategy realigned the South with the Republican Party. Table 4.2 analyzes exactly this, as much as such a thing can be measured. Estimating least squares regression models to predict Modern Sexism scores reveals that the variables influencing these attitudes among non-southern and southern women are quite different. For white women who do

Table 4.2 Predicting Modern Sexism, Among White Women, 2012

	Non-southern Women	Southern Women
Age	−0.001	−0.032***
(toward older)	(0.008)	(0.011)
Education	−1.039****	−0.441**
(toward more educated)	(0.145)	(0.212)
Income	−0.048	0.028
(toward wealthier)	(0.034)	(0.050)
Married	0.392*	−0.012
	(0.262)	(0.396)
Unemployed	−0.176	0.27
	(0.434)	(0.849)
Fundamentalist	0.32	1.098***
	(0.334)	(0.387)
Party Identification	0.297***	0.274**
(toward Republican)	(0.096)	(0.138)
Ideology	0.787****	0.134
(toward conservative)	(0.11)	(0.168)
Constant	12.254****	14.765****
	(0.784)	(1.087)
N	862	298
R Squared	0.262	0.112
Adjusted R Squared	0.255	0.088

Note: Standard errors in parentheses * p<= .10, ** p<= .05, *** p<= .01, **** p<.001
Data are from the 2012 Blair Center Poll.

not claim a southern identity, it is a function of politics, with conservatism and party identification as Republican significantly increasingly the probability of higher Modern Sexism scores. Party identification is significant for white women who claim a southern identity, though slightly less significant than among non-southern white women, and ideology is not significant at all. However, in this 2012 sample, that may be because white women who claim a southern identity are almost exclusively conservative already. For them, fundamentalism—measured here as a belief in biblical literalism—significantly predicts their resentment toward working women and their negative depiction of feminists. Age is significant as well, but only for southern white women. In this case, the older they become, the less likely they are to hold these attitudes. That could reflect generational differences, or it could indicate that the cultural conditioning of this myth of southern white womanhood still occurs for younger generations and erodes only with the life experience that comes with the passage of time. For both groups of women, education is also a negative predictor, meaning that higher educational attainment results in lower scores on the Modern Sexism scale, though the effect is slightly less significant for southern white women.

This could be the result of education functioning differently in the white South for much of the region's history. The educational system nationwide, of course, was originally a gendered system emphasizing not "male-male sameness, but male-female differences."[102] Nevertheless, the practice continued well into the twentieth century in the South, with the University of Virginia, for example, fully admitting women in 1970. Even in southern colleges that permitted female students much earlier, curricula were often gender segregated with a "classical curriculum"—the "core of traditional training for leadership"—being reserved for men.[103] The education of white southern women, described most thoroughly by Anne Frior Scott in her landmark book *The Southern Lady* and summarized succinctly by Jacqueline Boles and Maxine P. Atkinson, "consisted primarily of training in correct behavior, for intelligence in a woman was more distressing than pleasing to a man."[104] As late as the 1970s, human rights activists in Jimmy Carter's administration, such as Mississippi-born Pat Derian, lamented the lack of education for women in the South. "Southern women, both black and white, are undereducated," she insisted, and "very few actually finish college, and those that do are paid as if they had not gone at all."[105] But part of that wound, at least for whites, is self-inflicted. After all, if a sizeable portion of white women who claim a southern identity also defend and protect traditional gender roles and the privileges that they associate with those roles, then they remain an obstacle to women's full equality, an immovable weight holding a traditional patriarchy in place.

WHITE WOMEN WHO live in the South have come under renewed scrutiny in the wake of the 2016 election for their overwhelming support of Donald Trump's candidacy. Trump, himself came under fire for his promotion of beauty pageants, specifically, as well as for his evaluation of women in general based on their attractiveness. Those with whom he has sparred publicly, whether it be celebrities like Rosie O'Donnell or candidates like Carly Fiorina, are first denounced based on their looks.[106] All of this reflects a vision of women as ornamental, at best. Yet the criticism of Trump in this regard seemed fleeting and half-hearted, and it did not turn off white voters, particularly those in the South—not even women; for many of them, such objectification was familiar.[107] The cult maintains a powerful following and the stereotypes remain rooted deeply in the minds and expectations of southern white women.

However, even well before this most recent election cycle, southern white women, both by geography and identity, have not been vocal advocates of women's equality to the same degree as women outside of the region. The failure to ratify women's suffrage, nor the ERA, in most southern states speaks to that, as well as the lack of successful candidates competing for national office. Thus, it is no surprise to see, as noted in Figure 4.5A, that the mean Modern Sexism score in the 2016 Blair Center Poll for white women who claim a southern identity is still significantly higher (14.6) than for white women (13.2) who reject that label. And, as noted in Figure 4.5B, almost half (45.4 percent) of these women—compared to only 29.7 percent of non-southern white women—fall above the

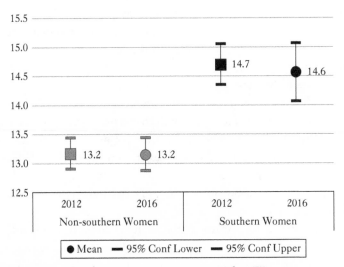

FIGURE 4.5A Mean Modern Sexism Scores, Among White Women, 2012–2016
Data are from the 2012 and 2016 Blair Center Polls.

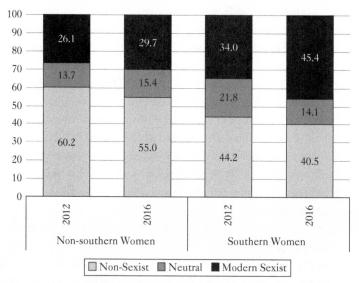

FIGURE 4.5B Percent Above, At, and Below the Midpoint of the Modern Sexism Scale, Among White Women, 2012–2016

Data are from the 2012 and 2016 Blair Center Polls.

midpoint of the Modern Sexism scale, indicating a widespread resentment and distrust of working women and feminists in general, even now.

The gaps between these two groups on the individual questions on the Modern Sexism scale are all significant and in 2016 range from 4.2 points at the lowest to 13.5 points at the greatest, as seen in Figure 4.6. That widest gap still reflects the distinct attitudes between southern and non-southern white women on their response to feminism, with 41.3 percent of the former distrusting feminists and their pursuit of equality. It is important to note too that the question that draws the lowest percentage of sexist responses is the notion that discrimination is no longer a problem for women. Only 16.4 percent of southern white women agree with that statement, and yet a large percentage of them think that women complain too quickly about discrimination and misinterpret innocent comments as sexist. In many ways, such denial and the distrust of working women that underscores that denial is rooted in their southern identity, which became highly politicized as the Republican Party turned southern itself.

Finally, in 2016, getting married and having children is important or very important to a significantly greater percentage of southern white women than non-southern white women, as seen in Figure 4.7. In fact, it seems almost inseparable from the identity label "southern," wherein 77 percent of the women

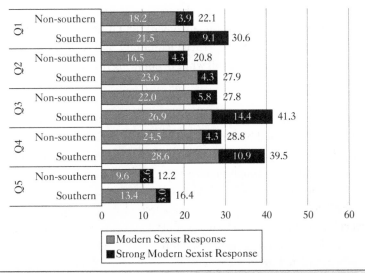

Q1: Many women are actually seeking special favors, such as hiring policies that favor them over men, under the guise of asking for "equality."
Q2: Most women interpret innocent remarks or acts as being sexist.
Q3: Feminists are seeking for women to have more power than men.
Q4: When women lose to men in a fair competition, they typically complain about being discriminated against.
Q5: Discrimination against women is no longer a problem in the United States.

FIGURE 4.6 Percent of Modern Sexist Responses by Individual Questions, Among White Women, 2016

Data are from the 2016 Blair Center Poll.

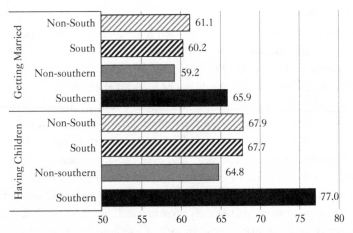

FIGURE 4.7 Percent Reporting That Getting Married and Having Children Is "Very Important" or "Important" to Them, Among White Women, 2016

Data are from the 2016 Blair Center Poll.

who claim it also indicate that having children is important to them, as is getting married (65.9 percent). To win these women, the GOP played up traditional gender roles, including both a superficial femininity, as well as the primary role of women as wives and mothers, all while denouncing the alternative as that of a "nasty woman."

EVEN FOR THOSE who seemingly defy the boundaries of southern white womanhood, the cultural power of it abides. In her comparison of the political paths of Hillary Rodham Clinton and Elizabeth Dole, Karrin Vasby Anderson illuminates this point. Though pundits often credited their twelve-year age gap as the source for their different leadership styles (noting that Clinton came of age during the Women's Movement),[108] there is a secondary, more significant identity difference. A southern woman by place of birth and persona, Dole often greeted southern audiences by claiming that she was finally in a place where she did not need to be translated by an interpreter to the audience.[109] Her southern charm was coupled by a consistent deference to her husband that helped him secure southern voters. Capitulation was still required. Asserting her own power, despite her clear ability to yield it, would violate the confines of traditional gender roles, and catalyze resentment not realignment. That resentment was, indeed, growing—especially for white southerners—as some women entered the workforce and upset the delicate social structure in which women's inequality and domesticity were presented as a privilege.

This persistent southern belle story of fragility and submissiveness remains one of the primary tenets of southern white identity and a critical component of southern distinctiveness. The political manipulation of it is too often ignored, partially because of the silence it creates, but also because of the ironic way in which it functions. Southern white women have "had to inhabit a pedestal—a notoriously small space in which to maneuver—yet many things have been done in their name, on their behalf: Jim Crow laws, lynchings, and a rigid class system were maintained in the South partly out of fear that the purity of white women would somehow be compromised by the right to vote."[110] They have been the motive for violence toward and oppression of African Americans. It is important to note, however, that some southern white women recognized their role in maintaining their own oppression and even the oppression of others. Antilynching activists in the early twentieth-century South implored privileged white women to acknowledge that their own socially constructed weakness and need for protection was being used to justify these spectacle homicides.[111] Yet, this ideal had power. Though, in many ways, the cult of southern white womanhood has "denied white women significant activity," leaving too many of those who adhere to it isolated, dependent, and politically passive. The cultural pull of the pedestal is just too powerful. That power comes from the fact that keeping southern white women in the shadows of public life was reinforced at the pulpit. The SBC, specifically, reaffirmed traditional gender roles when confronted with Second-Wave Feminism. Thus, privilege, patriarchy, and religion are soldiers in the fight against the ERA. And the anti-ERA position becomes part of the compounded identity structure of Christian, pro-family, GOP, white, southern womanhood.

Republican candidates celebrated traditional femininity and attacked feminists who betrayed it, and white southerners joined their party. After all, protecting southern belle privilege protects male privilege, which goes hand-in-hand with protecting white privilege. Choosing to violate the image of sacred womanhood is still met with stiff resistance and, sometimes, crass insults. South Carolina state senator Katrina Shealy, for example, came under attack in February 2015, when her male colleague described her as a "lesser cut of meat"—referring to the biblical notion of Eve being made from Adam's rib.[112] From the demonization of feminists and the objectification of women by the GOP's most recent, successful presidential nominee (part of an extended partisan history of this behavior)[113] to contemporary blogs that still define the proper behavior of southern women,[114] the cultural stronghold of southern white femininity is not new, and it shows little sign of letting go. The Long Southern Strategy and the partisan Modern Sexism it fueled purposefully tightened the grip.

5

Southern White Patriarchy

*To stand on his head in a bar, to toss down a pint of raw
whiskey in a gulp, to fiddle and dance all night, to bite off the
nose or gouge out the eye of a favorite enemy, to fight harder,
love harder than the next man, to be known eventually far
and wide as a hell of a fellow—such would be his focus.*

—W. J. CASH[1]

DURING THE SECOND presidential debate of the 2012 election season, GOP hopeful and former Massachusetts governor Mitt Romney set social media ablaze by uttering the phrase, "binders full of women." The expression launched a Facebook group, countless memes, and even the occasional Halloween costume. It came in response to a question posed by moderator Candy Crowley regarding pay equity for women. Romney's answer—which did not address pay equity—focused on the process by which his gubernatorial administration had selected cabinet members. "All the applicants seemed to be men," claimed Romney, so "I went to a number of women's groups and said, 'Can you help us find folks?' and they brought us whole binders full of women."[2] A note of surprise lurked beneath his statement, as if he had been unaware of the scores of qualified women in the public sector. Not only did the statement prove to be false (he had not initiated the effort), but "he managed to conjure an image confirming every feminist's worst fears."[3] Women were objects, filed away, as invisible as his answer on equal pay for equal work. Romney's comment was not aggressively sexist, rather it hinted at the way in which masculinity is rooted in superiority and privilege. The same spirit engendered his scolding tone when Crowley dared question the specific math of his proposed budget deficit reduction plan.[4] Romney's defensive penchant for condescension harkened back to his earlier debate against Shannon O'Brien in the 2002 Massachusetts governor's race. In response to O'Brien's question regarding the inconsistencies in his views on abortion, Romney pointed his finger at her and called her behavior "unbecoming."[5] The accusation that a female challenging a male was somehow unseemly exposed the way in which notions of male authority have saturated American political culture. Ten years prior, in a

1992 interview with the *New York Times* about Hillary Clinton's impact on Bill Clinton's presidential chances, former president Richard Nixon quoted Cardinal de Richelieu who claimed, "intellect in a woman is unbecoming."[6] This was not as crass as when Nixon characterized his 1950 US Senate opponent, Helen Gahagan Douglas, as "pink right down to her underwear."[7]

Romney's comment was much more subtle, but his attitude toward the female debate moderator in general sparked commentary that labeled him "Mitt the Jerk." Or as Amy Sullivan writes, "Mitt the man gets his way by talking over you," and he "can go from charming to testy in two seconds flat because while he has tolerated you as a female colleague, he will not allow you to disrespect him and his authority."[8] This kind of "faux chivalry"[9] functions as indirect and coded support for a patriarchal system and the traditional gender roles inherent in that system, to which the GOP appealed as it chased southern white voters throughout the Long Southern Strategy. After all, the pedestal upon which sacred southern white womanhood stood and, in many ways, continues to stand is buttressed by an equally sacred notion on southern masculinity. Moreover, just as the myth of the fragile southern white woman offered an ersatz justification for racial oppression and segregation, it simultaneously functioned as the foil to a patriarchy defined by a distorted notion of honor, a penchant for violence, and male righteousness.

Southern masculinity, like whiteness, has always adapted to the conditions of the times, proving it to be a politically malleable identity. The chivalrous southern white gentlemen of the Antebellum era, for example, reflected the aristocratic myth needed to dignify a plantation system built on human bondage. Yet in the aftermath of Confederate defeat, this gentleman farmer gave way to a "masculine martial ideal," as the "rough and tumble violence of earlier decades became insufficient evidence of manliness."[10] Defeated or challenged men must be more assertive, more dominant in order to restore honor to their families and their society. For example, racial change in the post–World War II era, including early civil rights victories in the court system and desegregation efforts by Harry Truman's executive pen, catalyzed a southern white masculinity crisis expressed, as Steve Estes argues, via massive resistance. "In the 1950s," editor Trent Watt surmises, "southern white men faced a stiff challenge for control of a social order that they had dominated since the turn of the century." Consequently, in an all-out effort to "retain their economic and social authority," southern white men, many of whom were members of White Citizens' Councils, "demonized black men's sexuality" while bestowing on themselves "ideals of whiteness, honor, and manhood" that often turned violent.[11]

Such imagined honor can rationalize a host of sins, and when it is threatened, the retaliation, whether by force, by vote, or by a shift in public opinion, is swift.

In this context, Second-Wave Feminism—including the public focus on women's rights and authority over their own bodies, the recognition of institutionalized sexism that created unequal pay for equal labor, and the heightened awareness of sexual harassment in the workplace—picked a bleeding scab. Kristin Anderson contends that this retaliatory response comes from the "center stage problem" in which "those who are used to being at the center of everything important in society are moved from the center." The group members—in this case, men— Anderson notes, "experience a threat and therefore are motivated to re-assert their privilege."[12] The influx of women into male-dominated spaces, as well as the surge of female success in school,[13] triggered this perception of endangerment, whereby the advancement of women signals the decline of men. Contemporary social movement theorists have long argued that some sort of shared, collective, even imagined identity underscores both social movements and the counter-movements that they call to arms.[14] In this case, feminism spurred not only a defiant anti-feminism with which many white southern men and women identified, but also a men's rights campaign that portrayed men as victims of reverse discrimination and promoted a dominant, defensive, even angry, masculinity that was all too familiar to southern white audiences.

The southern white patriarchy infiltrates cultural, religious, and political life so deeply that it can almost go unnoticed. Comments as subtle as Romney's "binders full of women" reflect it and quietly enforce it. But Romney did not win. Four years later, such patriarchy and misogyny seem almost celebrated—even championed—by both GOP candidate Donald Trump and the large audiences he draws, many of whom are women. In fact, attacking women's rights became the primary topic at the first GOP primary debate in August 2015.[15] Rather than suffering from his sexist comments,[16] Trump garnered some female admirers for—as Republican pundit, Taylor Brown has argued—"sounding like he's got a pair."[17] Perhaps, most dramatically, the emergence of the crass, sexualized term, "cuckservative" during the 2016 presidential primaries best captures this prevailing spirit. The term merges the words cuckold and conservative. "Cuckold" is a derogatory term used for a man whose wife or girlfriend is an adulteress. It also refers to a genre of pornography in which a woman has sex with another man in front of her husband. Such scenes are often racialized, depicting sex between a white woman and an African American man. The Alt-Right co-opted the term to attack the masculinity of their opponents on the left as well as men in their own circles—cuckservatives—whom they consider weak and emasculated.[18] In a broader sense, the slur is used to ridicule white men who have been humiliated by women or black men. Radio personality Rush Limbaugh employed the term to characterize Republican leaders and to praise Donald Trump for not being an "average, ordinary, cuckolded Republican."[19] The disparaging term weds all that is "toxic" about white supremacy and misogyny into one insult.

From the popularity of southern rock to the subservience of women preached from the pulpits of Southern Baptist ministers (a reason that Jimmy Carter has cited as motivating his decision to leave the church)[20] to the Neo-Conservatives fighting against what K. Michael Prince has called "the emasculated South,"[21] all serve in some way as a hyper-masculine stopgap to feminist efforts for inclusion and progress. Moreover, since the "entire social order"—or at least the community who identifies as southern—"has sanctioned their rule and called it moral,"[22] southern white males still overwhelmingly dominate southern politics. Thus, the conviction that the southern white patriarchy is inherently right or ordained and challenges to it are inherently wrong remains firm. The fact that forward progress is made in spite of such cultural objection fuels the belief that in the post–civil rights era, men are drawing the short stick. And that belief is easily politicized. The reassertion of southern white masculinity becomes party strategy, creating along the way a new, even more refined, dog whistle that perpetuated the oppressive southern belle mythology while promoting a fraternal, white, southern, male "badassness."[23]

THE NOTION OF a shared fraternal identity has characterized American life and southern life, in particular, for most of the nation's history. At its core is a notion of male exceptionality, and it is that sense of entitlement and privilege that needs constant protection through what Dana Nelson calls the "imagined reconstruction of fraternity."[24] Nelson envisions that process as operating "in a state of melancholy, a false and unhealthy nostalgia for a uniform, brotherly state of unity and wholeness that never in fact did or even could exist."[25] Perhaps, a wistful sadness does underscore the performance of American and southern masculinity, but in the wake of women organizing for equal rights, its primary function is to establish a unified front that will conserve and maintain the status quo patriarchy at all costs. It is a defensive play based on a zero-sum game outlook on gender relations in which the advancement of women can only be achieved by the demotion of men.[26]

Even before the recognized start of the second-wave feminist movement, as gender barriers began to bend and bow to progressive pressure, male victimization rhetoric blossomed. In one of its earliest expressions, Norman Mailer's *The White Negro*, published in 1959, deconstructs the white hipster, an archetype that reflects "the anxieties associated with normative masculine identities."[27] In addition, stretching into recent years, arguments regarding "The War Against Boys," and cries to "Save the Males" proliferate.[28] Hannah Rosin's 2010 article "The End of Men," published in *The Atlantic*, pivots from the statistical finding that

American couples prefer having female children versus male children[29] (this preference is inconsistent with Gallup polling data). Nevertheless, this perception that girls are favored "resonates with those who believe that feminism has gone too far."[30] In the space between Mailer's imaginative depiction of an imploding white patriarchy and a well-established resentment toward feminism, the issue became highly politicized throughout the country and with a distinct intensity in the South.

This male anxiety of the twentieth century has slowly given way to a masculine anger, stemming primarily from a perceived loss of economic power. Many white males believe that women were allowed to "invade" their workplaces.[31] The stratification of wealth in America, and the resulting dissolution of the middle class, only heightened this sense that American men were less able to provide for their families and climb the economic ladder. In 2003, Jonathan Mahler charted the loss of middle class jobs by white males in his foreboding *New York Times* article, "Commute to Nowhere." Now women are perceived as invading not just the workplace, but also the sacred "all-male bastions of sports, the military, and military schools."[32] This vision of female encroachment in the modern era, as cultural critic Michael Kimmel writes, has "reached a fevered pitch, fueling everything from the Boy Scouts and a sports craze to nativist anti-immigrant politics and efforts to prevent women's suffrage and women's entry into the public arenas, lest their presence make it harder for men to prove their manhood."[33] All of these manifestations are rooted in a profound anger, argues Kimmel, that spans behaviors as extreme as insurrectionism to hissing "with venomous anger when their corporation or law firm hires a woman or a minority," or "exploding in 'sensitivity' workshops about how 'diversity' and affirmative action are really reverse discrimination."[34]

Political scientists such as Susan Tolchin pointed to the rise of anger as a source of political attitudes in the 1990s, which she contends reflects a growing distrust of government. "The psychological roots of anger," she states, are "feelings of deprivation, injustice, confusion, and betrayal,"[35] all of which many white males experienced as women and African Americans became increasingly prominent in that public arena and equally protected by court rulings. Political anger, moreover, is easily manipulated, particularly because it stems, as Robert Jay Lifton argues in *The Protean Self*, from "bewilderment about values" and "is a way of seeking fundamental truths, all in the name of a past of perfect harmony that never was."[36] The political anger underscoring this imagined fraternity challenged political scientists to consider the psychological impact that engaged and organized women and minority voters who fall "outside of the white male circle of concern"[37] would have on those inside the "circle." Of course, the election of Barack Obama, and his place in the inner circle of power, catalyzed anger among many white Americans, including now president Trump. Trump became one of the leading voices in the "birther" movement, which sought to delegitimize Obama's citizenship, and thus, his presidency. That same rage ignited chants of "lock her up," demoting his female opponent, Hillary Clinton, from major-party nominee to criminal.

At the core of this sense of betrayal, distrust, and anger is the loss of privilege—not just white privilege, but also male privilege. This is, perhaps, most clearly demonstrated by a series of experiments conducted by psychologist Brenda Major and her colleagues who attempted to isolate and quantify the sense of male entitlement among college students. In short, male and female students were assigned a specific task. Upon completing the task, students were required to list how much money they thought they should be paid for their labor. In a second experiment, male and female students were presented with an open-ended assignment. When they felt they had sufficiently completed the project, the total labor time was recorded. The experiments found that men wanted more money for the same labor and spent less time on the work than women.[38] The currency of privilege could be dollars or hours, but it was ever present. Thus, the threat to white male privilege whether real or perceived drives fear, fuels anger, and gives rise to a rhetoric of victimhood. "Feminist" professors are accused of "indoctrinating students into a 'cult.'"[39] The judicial system is portrayed as having "degenerated into an appendage of feminist intrigue."[40] And Men's Rights Associations (MRA) blame the "quasi-totalitarian domination of the media in respect of gender issues by feminist advocates and their sympathizers,"[41] as the source of reverse discrimination against men in the workplace and men in the family. These MRAs really gained traction as they grappled with "fatherhood politics," decrying the unfair advantage mothers are given in custody trials as an example of the reverse discrimination that modern men have endured. Even beyond family court issues, fatherhood in and of itself was inevitably altered when (or in some cases, if) traditional notions of motherhood give way to a progressive multidimensional mom.[42] Many white American men are left resentfully licking their wounds in a changing world where the deck is seemingly stacked against them.

In fact, simultaneous to the second wave, men's liberation organizations sought to free men from the oppressive demands of masculinity, promoting self-help programs that encouraged men to reject the "prescribed package of behaviors and traits."[43] One advocate, Herb Goldberg, believed modern expectations of masculinity to be responsible for the "disease of disconnection"[44] experienced by American men. Goldberg, among others, blamed women for this plight of manliness. He insisted that "women supported, encouraged, and demanded that men act this way." In many ways, particularly among white southerners, he was right. Women's support propped up the patriarchy. However, that admission quickly approaches the slippery slope whereby feminist attacks on the patriarchy are deemed hypocritical and unjust. The latter implies that men are "the *real* victims in American society," a sentiment echoed by the National Coalition of Men (formerly the Coalition for Free Men), Men's Rights, Inc., and Men Achieving Liberation and Equality (MALE), all of which arose as a backlash to Second-Wave Feminism.[45] Co-opting the language of the Civil Rights Movement, MRAs push for equal access and gender blindness[46] and have made inroads in several states regarding joint custody and paternity rights.

These organizations are not relics of the past. They have shifted from conservative to reactionary in spirit, and some of their members have found support among the Alt-Right.[47] The advent of social media has provided virtual meeting space for likeminded men to voice their frustration at their perceived loss of status and victimization. Nicknamed the "manosphere," these websites and chat rooms give anonymity and license to male anger and, as a result, are now monitored by anti-hate watch groups such as the Southern Poverty Law Center.[48] Their 2012 report details the way in which these sites propose a false, angry, often violent narrative about the way in which women have manipulated their way into power. Those who venture into this space, notes historian Robert Menzies, are "quickly rewarded with a torrent of diatribes, invectives, atrocity tales, claims to entitlement, calls to arms, and prescriptions for change in the service of men, children, God, the past, the future, the nation, the planet, and all other things non-feminist."[49] The Southern Poverty Law Center profiles several key sites including "Alcuin," which compares feminists to Nazis, stating that "just as the Nazis had to create a Jewish conspiracy as a way to justify mass slaughter, so feminists have to create patriarchy to justify mass slaughter of innocent unborn, and the destruction of men and masculinity."[50] Feminists have made rape, according to the site, "a political crime," and the whole "female-supremacist hate movement"—as labeled on the site "The Counter Feminist"—"must be opened to the disinfecting sunlight of the world's gaze and held to a stern accounting for its grievous transgressions."[51] The False Rape Society, MensActivism, A Voice for Men, and hosts of other virtual fraternities, spew this rhetoric into cyberspace, fueling the myth of feminist misandry and reverse gender discrimination.[52]

Sociologist Michael Kimmel provides an anecdote in the second edition of his cultural history *Manhood in America*, in which he describes his experience as a panelist on a television talk show. The episode, entitled "A Black Woman Stole My Job," featured three white males who expressed anger that affirmative action programs had robbed them of employment opportunities, making them the victims of reverse discrimination. In his commentary on the show, Kimmel asked the men "to consider just one word in the title of the show: the word 'my.'"[53] The sense that the job belonged to these men revealed, in its simplest form, the notion of male entitlement. That sense of entitlement means that equality is tantamount to loss, to denial, to victimhood. James Cameron's 2001 study of undergraduates at St. Mary's University in Nova Scotia found that men with high scores on the Modern Sexism scale were more likely to perceive themselves as being discriminated against. Their resentment toward women colored their impression of justice. The same was true for men who reported that their masculinity was very important to them; the more central the gender identification for men, the higher the levels of perceived discrimination, among white men specifically.[54] Even nostalgic counterarguments about self-made men who pull themselves up by their bootstraps—a favorite character in the GOP's Long Southern Strategy—feed into the men's rights storyline by dismissing the opportunities that have been and still are granted without question to many white men.

This sense of persecution is perhaps felt most strongly when assumptions of privileges are embedded so deeply as to be rendered invisible, which, of course, has long been true in the white South. Buried or shielded, this sense of persecution, like the perceived threat that gave rise to it, becomes, over time and with political prodding, pervasive, ideological, and inextricable from one's own identity. Considering the long-term impact of this dynamic, Figure 5.1 offers the battery of reverse racial discrimination questions disaggregated by gender and southern identity. A higher percentage of whites who identify as southern compared to whites who do not report experiencing discrimination based on their race. However, southern white males, who are significantly more likely to report such experiences compared to southern white women across all questions, are driving that gap. For example, in 2012, 29.5 percent of non-southern men and 25.8 percent of non-southern women believed they have been called names or insulted because of their whiteness. Among southern women, the rate falls in the middle of the non-southern men and non-southern women at 27.5 percent. However, among southern white men it climbs to 41.9 percent.

Yet, as Figure 5.1 clearly shows, the specific experiences of discrimination are never reported in numbers as high as the percent who report general discrimination in the abstract. That general experience is reported by 37.2 and 37.1 percent of non-southern men and women respectively—almost an exact match. However, between southern women and southern men there is a significant gap of 18.5 points. Southern white women (38 percent) hover at a level equal to non-southerners, while southern white men surge to 56.5 percent. This is not to say that white male angst is limited to only southern whites, but the combination of being both southern and male among whites proves a significant and potent combination across the board for perceiving reverse discrimination. That may be in part because the very essence of southern white identity for men meant

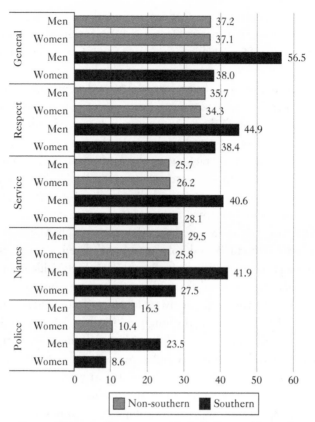

FIGURE 5.1 Percent Reporting Experience with the Following Types of Reverse Racial Discrimination, Among Whites, by Gender, 2012

Data are from the 2012 Blair Center Poll.

domination of both women and African Americans, and civil rights victories threatened both power structures.

SUPPORT FOR A southern white patriarchy, much like the pedestal of white, female purity, stood at the core of the Antebellum South and was inseparable from the Lost Cause narrative that buoyed support for the Civil War. Even before secession, the southern version of masculinity was already distinct from the self-made northern notion, as Lorri Glover demonstrates in her case study of the Ball family of South Carolina. Elite southern white males prioritized their reputations over their academic achievements, claimed Glover, and needed what Edward Hooker, a northern tutor of southern male students, described as "a different sort of management."[55] Deemed willful, southern sons required strict supervision and discipline in order to protect the cherished traits of family honor and status. Southern gentility, noted Bertram Wyatt-Brown, mimicked the British elites' "mastery of quite subtle marks of status—the proper accent, the right choice of words and conversational topics, the appropriate attire, the acquaintance with various kinds of social proprieties and other rules not easy to follow with aplomb."[56] However, this code proved problematic in the white South, particularly as westward growth expanded the plantation system beyond the older, established patriarchies in Virginia and South Carolina. Established or not, the nouveau plantation elite performed masculinity for the sake of building relationships and accruing social and political power. The fixation with outward appearances and lineage functioned as armor in a culture increasingly criticized and deemed aberrant for its protection of slavery. That protection required, moreover, "white gentry solidarity," and a vigilant commitment to "physical and emotional mastery of women" and racial superiority,[57] all of which was coated in southern "honor."

Looking beyond elite society, journalist W. J. Cash described the southern white male masses a bit differently, characterizing them as "individualistic, independent, and resentful of authority."[58] Moreover, the strict social code required lower-class white males to show deference to the elite, a practice that often fostered internal resentment and a desire for upward mobility.[59] This notion of honor proved an antidote for that distrust,[60] and so it became the common language of southern white men among whom it forged solidarity. Honor, however, is not a rational bond based on mutual interests, but rather it is primed with emotion. The southern white man "did not (typically speaking) think; he felt; and discharging his feelings immediately, he developed no need for intellectual culture in its own right."[61] That emotionalism remains distinctive well into the modern era, as noted by sociologists Kenneth Wilson and Patricia Yancey Martin. Their 1988 study of southern families as compared to northern families found that southern husbands and wives were less likely to confront domestic conflicts rationally, and they consider this "disinclination to discuss problems" as a "major legacy of patriarchy in southern family life."[62] This emotive nature was studied again in 1996, when white male students at the University of Michigan participated in an experiment in which they were divided into groups based on their native residence. When called an "asshole" by a stranger, southerners were more likely than non-southerners to be "(a) more likely to think their masculine reputation was threatened, (b) more upset (as shown by a rise in cortisol levels), (c) more physiologically primed for aggression (as show by a rise in testosterone levels), (d) more cognitively primed for aggression, and (e) more likely to engage in aggressive and dominant behavior."[63] At the core of the analysis, conducted by Dov Cohen, Richard Nisbett, Brian Bowdle, and Norbert Schwarz, lies the notion of honor and the insult-defense trigger associated with its deep, historic connection to white southern male identity.

Contemporary cultural ethnographers have labeled this defensiveness as "rebel manhood"—a popular archetype, for example, in southern rock music. This modern rebel masculinity is still expressed by "protesting authority figures" and "dominating women."[64] In this sense, the modern rebel is a direct descendant of the southern white male rebels who once wore Confederate gray. The rebels in uniform are emblematic not only of an ideology of honor and willful aggression, but also of a hawkish southern white masculinity. After all, in southern white culture, war was perceived as something "that turned boys into men."[65] However, losing the Civil War combined with the threat of Reconstruction, specifically, turned many men into combatants and further entrenched southern white masculinity with militarism or a "martial ideal."[66] True southern men, despite rank, needed to be "warriors willing to engage in violence in order to preserve their southern and Christian honor."[67] Nancy MacLean best illustrates this darker militarism, also cloaked in honor, in her book on the Ku Klux Klan entitled *Behind the Mask of Chivalry*. The merged militarism and masculinity of the Klan is described in detail. In addition to elaborate ranks and obsession with hierarchy, leaders repeatedly instructed Klan members that their "organization was 'not a lodge,' but 'an army of Protestant Americans.'"[68] Despite the simplistic association of the Klan with racial violence, it promoted virulently hostile positions on birth control and reproductive rights as well as sexual morality. Indeed, MacLean's most important point is that much of the Klan's reactionary conservatism was "a deeply gendered phenomenon."[69] Deeply gendered. Deeply white. Deeply southern. Deeply distinctive. And now, deeply political.

Even outside of the Ku Klux Klan, a militaristic, robust Christian manhood was not without its damaging repercussions, and in its most grievous manifestations, it pushed some southern white men toward violence. Studies have blamed everything from the region's higher temperatures to the psychology of herding economies to debilitating poverty for the persistent high levels of violence in the South.[70] Surely, the mental faculties necessary to subjugate slaves required a significant capacity for and tolerance of extreme violence.[71] Wyatt-Brown, the leading authority on southern honor, cites sociologist Émile Durkheim on the subject; "crimes," Wyatt-Brown surmises, "reflect the culture of a people."[72] During the Reconstruction era and up until about 1915, some studies have shown, for example, that the homicide rate in certain parts of the South stood at ten times the national average.[73] This penchant for violence and vengeance is justified by southerners who point to its effectiveness in socializing children or who blame patriarchal clashes between households.[74] Here that "tender skin to criticism," as noted by historian Fletcher Green, makes many white southerners retaliate because they believe that some "insult damaged their appearance of strength and masculinity in the eyes of another."[75] A taste for violence—or a "southern subculture of violence," as some scholars have called it[76]—and vengeance is prevalent in the laws and social customs of the South as well, including support for corporal punishment in schools and the death penalty in the justice system.[77] It has even been referenced in relation to the training of southern cops.[78] Rates of gun ownership and/or carrying guns for self-defense have long been found to be higher in the South and linked to a culture of defensiveness, honor, and violence.[79] Of course, as both sociologist John Shelton Reed and historian Sheldon Hackney have observed, many of these markers are intertwined; the use of guns, mixed with corporal punishment, might indeed affect homicide rates.[80]

The "virile heroism,"[81] or projected hyper-masculinity, championed by and required of white southern men clearly extended well beyond Appomattox. Even when not expressed by a violent, hooded organization, civic groups such as the League of the South also encouraged a "true and proper manhood," in which southern white men aggressively defended southern white traditions from external threats by actively critiquing the "contemporary American political, social, and economic order."[82] Threats to southern, white, male dominance have taken many forms. Southern white men, for example, gave each other great latitude in handling racial conflicts. The practice stretched back to slavery, where "personal discretion" was granted to "those who killed maimed or assaulted slaves belonging to someone else,"[83] particularly if the slave was less than subservient in any way. A retaliation culture formed to protect the masters from insurrectionism,[84] and many aspects of that culture continued for generations. For example, the notion that white leaders and judges could not handle racial conflict on their own terms—as granted by the "home rule" that President Woodrow Wilson had restored to the New South—elicited cries of interposition, spurred the writing of manifestos, and encouraged standing-in-doorways theatrics, all to maintain not just Jim Crow, but white, southern, male authority.

To outsiders, these actions seem extreme, reckless, and even barbaric. However, many southern white men still express the need for "violence in preventing future harm," in higher numbers than even their non-white neighbors do.[85] Many still operating out of a distorted sense honor, compensate, and resist such threats by flexing their power publicly, no matter how irrational it seems. Trump constantly comparing the size of the crowds at his inauguration, for example, and his use of Twitter for self-congratulations or for insulting his critics, are all attempts to flex—to assert a "toxic masculinity"[86] that his supporters seem not to mind. In fact, some like that Trump does not apologize, but rather doubles down on promoting his own successes or attacking those seen as enemies both on social media and at his rallies. The bully pulpit of social media has turned off some

Americans, but to others, his defiance reflects their own temperament—and one that is celebrated in southern white culture—for which they also do not want to apologize. Ironically, during the 1964 presidential campaigns, incumbent president Lyndon Johnson criticized his opponent, Barry Goldwater, for this kind of stubborn, extremist masculinity without ever saying his name. Johnson's famous Daisy campaign ad depicted the impact of such recklessness and a penchant for war as a nuclear explosion occurs near a young girl picking flowers.[87] However, this allusion to militaristic, hotheadedness may have actually endeared Goldwater to white southern men and women. Even John McCain, the GOP-nominee for president in 2008, was described in that moment as "the standard bearer for conventional manhood: stubborn, controlling, shoot-from-the-hip, inflexible,"[88] though he was later considered more moderate and willing to compromise. Still, this strain of masculinity, particularly as new threats such as immigration are manufactured, is a part of the white southern attraction to the GOP.

Over a decade into the twenty-first century, the marker of self-proclaimed southern identity does indeed affect the attitudes of white men toward what has been described as a "threat" issue. Figure 5.2 compares, for example, support and opposition of American men to strict immigration laws like those in Arizona (made famous by Sheriff Joe Arpaio), including the ability for officers to request legal IDs at any time.[89] The overwhelming majority—81.8 percent in 2010 and 80.7 percent in 2012—of southern white men support such strict immigration policies, significantly higher than the 63.4 percent in 2010 and 60.6 percent in

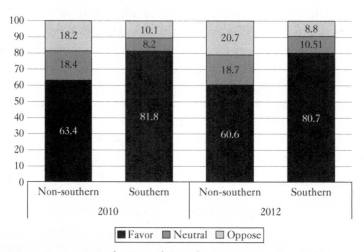

FIGURE 5.2 Percent Attitudes Toward "Tougher Immigration Laws Like in Arizona," Among Whites, 2010–2012

Data are from the 2010 and 2012 Blair Center Polls.

2012 of non-southern white men. It is important to recognize, however, that the vast majority of all white men support such aggressive immigration enforcement. Among men who call themselves southern, the desire to curb this threat and to reassert dominance over immigrants is practically universal and highly significant.

JUST AS THREATENING to the southern white patriarchy as slave rebellions or integration or now immigration stood the potential loss of power over women. That threat had endless manifestations. If women were rumored—and white men often spread these rumors (even circulating fake speeches by black leaders)[90]—to prefer African American men sexually, white southern males retaliated by lynching. If women were seen as surpassing men in school, then progressive universities and the media became the enemy.[91] Moreover, when women questioned church doctrine, they were re-oppressed from the pulpit. Although they are most often associated with protecting racial supremacy, southern white masculinity, militarism, and misogyny also underscore anti-feminism. This is not to say, of course, that southern men did not or do not value southern women—as the definition of misogyny would imply. Rather, the advancement of women as a group threatened the multifaceted privileges that many southern white men enjoy, regardless of the esteem in which they may have personally held the women in their lives.

These individual relationships allowed southern white men to deny their resentment toward women as a collective in similar ways to the paradox inherent in white claims of a post-racial state or a personal denial of racial animus simply because one has black friends or colleagues. The "invisible knapsack" of privilege is maintained by this deniability, and the gendered component is equally powerful among many white southerners. Just as Peggy McIntosh created a list of questions to identify white privilege in her 1988 book *White Privilege: Unpacking the Invisible Knapsack*, along with Barry Deutsch, she created an equally powerful list probing male privilege. These statements include, for example, "If I fail in my job or career, I can feel sure this won't be seen as a black mark against my entire sex's capabilities"; "If I choose not to have children, my masculinity will not be called into question"; "I can be loud with no fear of being called a shrew. I can be aggressive with no fear of being called a bitch"; and "Chances are my elected representatives are mostly people of my own sex. The more prestigious and powerful the elected position, the more likely this is to be true."[92] The purpose of the list, of course, is to both point to the way in which gender, despite personal relationships, functions as a collective identity, and to unearth how deeply embedded male advantages are in American and southern culture. In this regard, feminism, if it were to debunk the myth of sacred southern white womanhood, would topple the southern white patriarchy and the male privileges associated with it. That kind of threat required a dramatic public performance to assert traditional values, as Craig Friend and Lorri Glover note in the introduction to their edited volume *Southern Manhood*. "Conflicts over manhood necessarily took place before the community,"[93] they argue, and in this case, both the southern religious and the political arenas offered the biggest stages.

In his essay "A New Kind of Patriarchy," Seth Dowland points to the rise of feminism and homosexual rights in the 1970s and 1980s as triggering the Southern Baptist Convention's (SBC) resurgent commitment not only to the submissiveness of women, but also to a robust masculinity. In this vein, indecision was considered weak, and liberal Christians who were "waffling" on issues such as female ordination were characterized as such. Moreover, feminist arguments that gender roles were socially and culturally constructed undermined this authority, and in response, the SBC "introduced a new kind of patriarchy." Whereas in the past, male authority "relied on social custom and unspoken guidelines to maintain order, this new patriarchy sanctioned masculine privilege through explicit reference to scripture."[94] Those scriptures and the spirit they represented underscored much of the Republican rhetoric for men to reclaim America, a push that included not just support for social conservatism, but also for a hawkish, aggressive foreign policy. This type of manhood and womanhood has been re-canonized in the Southern Baptist church, and the guide to it can still be downloaded at the Southern Baptist Theological Seminary website.[95] The conflation of these issues (including the most recent framing of the war on terror as a Christian crusade of sorts)—the way in which religion buttresses such attitudes, the way in which the church itself became such a prominent advocate for the GOP, and the way in which evangelicalism proves so prolific in the South—ensure that white southern identity, white southern Christianity, and white southern patriarchy all become mutually reinforcing.

Thus, it is no surprise that measures of Modern Sexism—a resentment toward and distrust of working women and feminists—indicate high agreement among southern white men. As shown in Figure 5.3A and Figure 5.3B from the 2012 Blair Center Poll, white men who claim a southern identity have the highest mean Modern Sexism score at 16, significantly higher than non-southern white men at 15. Since the midpoint of the scale is 15, this indicates that on average these men agree that feminists are trying to gain power over men or that women are quick to blame sexism. Figure 5.3B presents their distribution across the scale. Approximately half (50.2 percent) of southern white men fall into the Modern Sexist category, while another 24.3 percent are neutral, leaving only one-quarter of this group reporting non-sexist scores. Non-southern white men, on the other

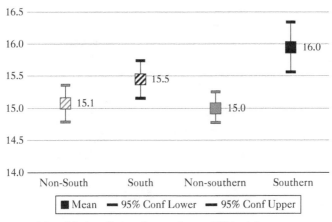

FIGURE 5.3A Mean Modern Sexism Scores, Among White Men, 2012
Data are from the 2012 Blair Center Poll.

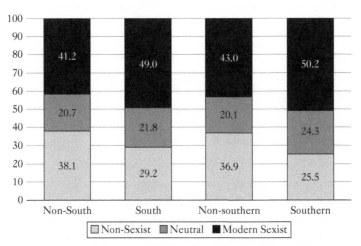

FIGURE 5.3B Percent Above, At, and Below the Midpoint of the Modern Sexism Scale, Among White Men, 2012
Data are from the 2012 Blair Center Poll.

hand, are less likely to be neutral or sexist, and more likely (36.9 percent) to fall into the non-sexist range.

On the individual Modern Sexism questions, the pattern is the same with white men who claim a southern identity, giving Modern Sexist and strong Modern Sexist responses significantly more often than white men who reject the southern label. As shown in Figure 5.4, those gaps between southern and non-southern men are 4.5 points at minimum, and 12.2 points at their maximum.

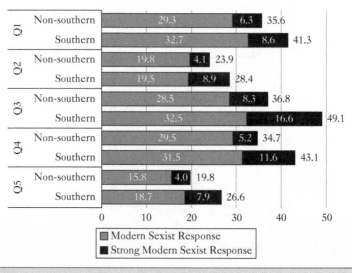

FIGURE 5.4 Percent of Modern Sexist Responses by Individual Questions, Among White Men, 2012

Data are from the 2012 Blair Center Poll.

Just as among southern white women, questions 3 and 4 elicit the largest portion of sexist responses from southern white men. Almost half (49.1 percent) of white men who identify as southern (compared to 36.8 percent of nonsouthern white men) believe that feminists are trying to obtain more power than men, not equality. Moreover, 43.1 percent of southern white men believe that women complain about discrimination when they lose a fair fight to men, and over one-quarter, 26.6 percent, of these men believe that "discrimination against women is no longer a problem in the United States." On a bit of a softer question that asks whether respondents agree that "obstacles that made it hard for women to get ahead are largely gone," a 2016 Pew poll found that 56 percent of American men agree. That number falls to only 23 percent among Republican men, notes the Pew study.[96] All of which speaks to the negative reaction of many men to the women's marches that followed the inauguration of Donald Trump in January 2017 or to the persistent lack of legislative action on equal pay initiatives.

Just like that of southern white women, the Modern Sexism of southern white men is not driven by the same variables as for white men who do not claim the southern label. As shown in Table 5.1, education is highly significant and negative for non-southern white men, meaning the higher the educational attainment, the lower the level of Modern Sexism. However, education is not significant for southern white men. Here too, it could be a reflection of the gendered educational programs so long running in the region. The more conservative one is ideologically, the more likely one is to have higher Modern Sexism scores, for both groups of men, though party identification (in this case as one becomes more Republican) is only significant among non-southern white men. Just as was the case with ideology among southern white women, this may be the result of how

Table 5.1 Predicting Modern Sexism, Among White Men, 2012

	Non-southern Men	Southern Men
Age	−0.011**	−0.009
(toward older)	(0.006)	(0.012)
Education	−0.482****	−0.208
(toward more educated)	(0.125)	(0.218)
Income	−0.015	−0.116**
(toward wealthier)	(0.03)	(0.052)
Married	−0.594***	−0.514
	(0.243)	(0.417)
Unemployed	−0.362	2.795****
	(0.414)	(0.727)
Fundamentalist	0.115	−0.563*
	(0.301)	(0.436)
Party Identification	0.390****	0.18
(toward Republican)	(0.092)	(0.164)
Ideology	0.712****	0.666****
(toward conservative)	(0.1)	(0.182)
Constant	12.881****	14.360****
	(0.595)	(0.984)
N	847	276
R Squared	0.247	0.206
Adjusted R Squared	0.240	0.183

Note: Standard errors in parentheses * p<= .10, ** p<= .05, *** p<= .01, **** p<.001

Data are from the 2012 Blair Center Poll.

little variation there is in partisanship among white men who claim a southern identity since they are overwhelmingly Republican. Being married makes white men who do not claim a southern identity less sexist, but that is not true for southern white men. On the other hand, unemployment is highly significant and positive among southern white men, while income is significant and negative, though neither is true among non-southern white men. This indicates that being unemployed and of lower income are both associated with higher Modern Sexism scores, which could reflect job competition and economic angst among white southern males. After all, the 1964 Civil Rights Act (CRA) that sought to end employment discrimination was not just impactful for African American job seekers in the formerly Jim Crow South. Women, included in its protections, also benefited. Moreover, in the South, white women had not been prohibited fully from college admissions or, in many cases, from obtaining professional degrees, even if they did not always put them to use in the workplace. Those who did have the credentials and wanted to work had the protection to do so, despite southern white cultural and religious norms that discouraged it.

THIS REASSERTION OF the patriarchy extended well beyond the test of Second-Wave Feminism, as can be seen in the rise of what could be called the religious version of an MRA, Promise Keepers, a multidenominational, spiritual men's group that surged in popularity in the 1990s. The organization met in football stadiums, establishing a mass, team-like comradery among men who sought to reassert their privilege in a world in which "their occupational betrayal and civic betrayal had been compounded by a powerful sense of domestic betrayal."[97] Women in the workplace changed men's self-conceptions, threated men's self-worth, and rendered visible men's assumed privileges. Promise Keepers audiences were encouraged to reclaim their manhood. Preachers offered scripted sample conversations that men should have with their wives, such as: "Honey, I've made a terrible mistake. I've given you my role. I gave up leading this family, and I forced you to take my place."[98] The notion that men had voluntarily given up their power, of course, robbed women of their agency in their own fight for equality and propagated the misogynistic characterization of women as too weak, indecisive, or overwhelmed to lead their own families—or their own lives for that matter. Women were expected to graciously cede their independence to their husbands and take up traditional duties of keeping house and rearing children.

Political leadership reflected this same vision of masculinity. Ronald Reagan's 1980 campaign reinforced traditional gender roles by embedding them in his pro-family, hawkish rhetoric.[99] As *Rolling Stone* reporter William Greider argued, "Ronald Reagan looks like a 'real man'. He stands up to the commies.

He loves rockets. He even dresses up like a cowboy. In every dimension, his political personality embodies the nostalgic idea of masculinity." [100] Looking like a wimp, after all, was the ultimate political kiss of death, at least it was for Michael Dukakis when 1988 Republican nominee George H. W. Bush ran a devastating campaign ad against him featuring images of Dukakis riding in a tank[101]—images that made him look diminutive in size and not manly enough to be commander-in-chief. Moreover, in the wake of the terrorist attacks of 9/11,[102] "virile heroism" and nationalism flooded the manosphere. Men's rights meets patriotism in a quest to reassert power and dominance. The masculine posturing becomes not only a strategy to counter feminism, but also an asset in the developing holy war against jihad. Researchers combing George W. Bush's rhetoric before and after 9/11 found countless examples of a conscious and injected masculinity for just this reason,[103] and no strategy could hardly be more effective than that to southern white audiences.

Perhaps even more important—unlike Gerald Ford who did have the college athlete manliness characteristic[104] but was married to a feminist—Reagan's masculinity is dramatized by contrast. First Lady Nancy Reagan exuded traditional femininity, embodying the role of submissive, adoring wife who is never threatening. Reagan's "anti-feminist stance," noted Zilla Eisenstein, "underlines the militaristic mentality of strengthening America: restrengthen the authority of the father and one will reestablish the 'moral mother' and the 'moral society.'"[105] The dynamic can even be superficial and still have an impact, as former president Nixon advised the Clintons in that same 1992 interview with the *New York Times*. "If the wife comes off as too strong and too intelligent," Nixon warned, "then the husband looks like a wimp."[106] In addition, Bob Dole, when running against Bill Clinton for his second term, had been equally quick to emphasize that his own wife, Liddy Dole, despite being president of the Red Cross, would not be in charge of healthcare.[107] Being upstaged by one's wife would not play well for a GOP candidate in the South.

This projection of white southern hyper-masculinity, however, has not retained its power through the backing of men alone, as can be seen in the Modern Sexism scores reported by white southern women. In other words, many of these southern white women dislike feminism because it threatens their own sense of femininity, but also because they embrace a culture that promotes a certain kind of masculinity too. These are the women who like that Trump "has a pair." Feminist activist and writer Ruth Rosen locates the same anti-feminist, pro-hyper-masculinity ideology among women who support and have held leadership roles in the Tea Party. "To put it bluntly," Rosen writes, "some women love men who love guns, love men who hate government and loathe taxes, or love men who are not afraid to voice racist and xenophobic feelings."[108] Sometimes the enthusiasm for such rhetoric and even action bubbled over. Historically, southern white women themselves actually have higher rates of violent activity than non-southern women.[109] Nisbett and Cohen document this contradictory southern femininity and describe the way in which "women actively participate in a culture of honor." The "steel magnolia" southern female archetype is both "highly feminine" and "capable of toughness." They note, in extreme cases, white southern women are much more likely, statistically, to commit homicide than a non-southern female comparison group.[110] And hierarchal, patriarchal armies like the Klan did, indeed, count women among their members. Even when they were not members officially, women in several noted cases pressured the Klan to attack men who broke the marital contract by which women who "performed their marital obligations" were entitled to protection by white southern men.[111] Whether women liked this dynamic or whether they enabled it, under the code of honor and chivalry, the privileges afforded to southern white womanhood by this "rebel manhood" were voraciously defended.

The 1994 Southern Focus Poll conducted at the University of North Carolina exposed the ongoing support for notions of chivalry and protection among both white men and white women who identify as southern (they also all resided in the geographic South). As shown in Figure 5.5, when asked who should pay on a date, almost all southern whites, 88.5 percent of southern men, and 83.8 percent of southern women held fast to traditional notions of chivalry and indicated that men should pay. Almost all southern men (91.7 percent) also believed that the male should function as a protector in the marriage. Only 68.4 percent of southern women agreed—a significant difference—though that attitude is still held by an overwhelming majority of women. However, in a more direct question—asking southern couples whether or not husbands should have the main "say-so" in the marriage—the numbers expressing agreement drop dramatically, but also have almost the exact rate of support from southern men (31.8 percent) and southern women (30.5 percent). Perhaps by 1994, that question was recognized as somewhat sexist, but this remains a sizeable (and equal) portion of both men and women willing to support absolute male authority publicly. In some sense these questions suggest that, at least two decades ago, southern white women overwhelmingly supported the public privileges (protection and paying on a date) associated with southern white traditional gender roles, but they were divided when it comes to power dynamics within the private family. Moreover, their attitudes were not significantly distinct from southern white men on two of the questions—paying on a date and on the ultimate authority of husbands— meaning the southern white sexes were aligned to some degree on gender role issues like these.

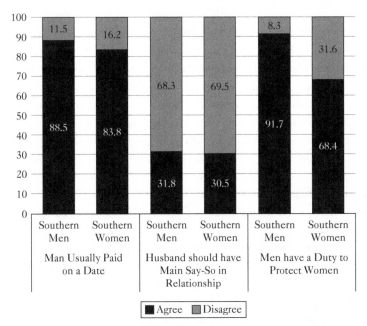

FIGURE 5.5 Percent Agreement Regarding Gender Roles, Among White Men and Women Who Identify as Southern, 1994

Data are from the Spring 1994 Southern Focus Poll, South Survey available at http://www. thearda.com/Archive/Sfocus.asp/.

Such attitudes took center stage during the debate over the Equal Rights Amendment (ERA), when anti-feminist crusader Phyllis Schlafly promoted it as an economic advantage. "In America," Schlafly wrote, "a man's first significant purchase is a diamond for his bride, and the largest financial investment of his life is a home for her to live in." American women, she insisted, were benefiting from "a tradition of special respect for women which dates back to the Christian Age of Chivalry."[112] The specialness of Christianity met the specialness of womanhood, just as masculine authority and Christian authority would prove mutually reinforcing in Promise Keepers. The desire to protect the southern white way of life, including these visions of femininity and masculinity, rallied conservative women to attend and in many cases overtake the Status of Women Commissions and the state meetings that took place during the International Women's Year (IWY) in 1975. In Mississippi, for example, while only 250 anti-feminist registered for the state IWY meeting, 1,500 showed up, startling the feminists, and ensuring majorities on several committees. Supported primarily by church organizations, these anti-ERA crusaders arrived in large groups via church transportation. They called themselves Mississippians for God, Family, and Country, and they defeated not only the ERA, but also several resolutions regarding federal and state childcare and gay and lesbian rights. Feminists in Mississippi—and throughout the South and the country—were condemned for "ruining the Christian based fiber on which everything worthwhile in the country is based."[113]

In the middle of the fight against the ERA, the pro-masculine, anti-feminist spirit among southern whites revealed a racist streak. For example, anti-feminists who organized coups of the state IWY meetings included several wives of noted Ku Klux Klan members.[114] So that they might use white angst to rally more supporters, anti-feminists argued that the inclusion of sex into the 1964 CRA would result in women being hired solely for affirmative action purposes.[115] These policies, which traditionally were aimed at racial minorities, reinforced the narrative that women were victims of discrimination. Moreover, the anti-ERA advocates decried the feminist labeling of housework as "domestic slavery," a phrase that linked white southern homemakers with the institution of African-American bondage—a comparison that many white southerners rejected vehemently. Newspaper reporters covering the state meetings, such as Bill Minor of the *New Orleans Time Picayune*, observed that the southern anti-ERA efforts represented a "new form of anti-black militancy of the White Citizen's Councils and the Ku Klux Klan." This militancy, however, had not been the exclusive purview of white men. As Elizabeth McCrae demonstrates in her book *Mothers of Massive Resistance: White Women and the Politics of White Supremacy*, southern white women often performed "the mundane and the persistent" tasks "that make movements"[116]—including the anti-integration campaigns during the civil rights conflicts of the 1950s and 1960s. This time that militancy was expanded to oppose "liberalism in any form" and this, in turn, "provided a ready-made framework for its decisive rejection of the women's movement and gay and lesbian rights in this era," writes historian Robert Self. He continues, "So too did the white South's long tradition of protecting white womanhood from threats both sexual and racial."[117] Thus, the new militancy against feminism was simultaneously hyper-masculine and hyper-feminine, and primed for partisanship.

WITH SUCH A long history of anti-feminism and an elevation of southern white masculinity, it is no surprise that high Modern Sexism levels would be part of southern white identity. It is also no surprise that in the wake of a two-term African American president, and with the first female nominee from a major party on the ballot, Modern Sexism levels increased for many. As presented in Figure 5.6A, in the 2016 Blair Center Poll conducted after the presidential election, the mean Modern Sexism score for white men who claim a southern identity ticked slightly upward from 16 in 2012 (as shown in Figure 5.3A) to 16.2 in 2016. On the other hand, the mean for non-southern white men dropped from 15

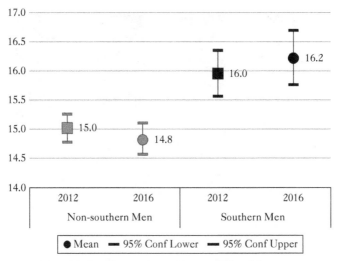

FIGURE 5.6A Mean Modern Sexism Scores, Among White Men, 2012–2016
Data are from the 2012 and 2016 Blair Center Polls.

to 14.8, making for almost a 1.5-point southern identity gap that remains highly significant.

Figure 5.6B also shows that the percentage of southern white men who fall above the midpoint of the Modern Sexism scale, and thus into the "Modern Sexist" category, has increased from 50.2 percent in 2012 (as shown in Figure 5.3B) to 55.9 percent in 2016, and the gap between this group and white men who do not call themselves southern is now over 15 points. Moreover, in 2016 the percentage of white southern men who fall into the non-sexist category has also risen from 25.5 in 2012 to 29.8 points—but there is still a double-digit gap with non-southern white men. The neutral category, thus, has shrunk. Such sexism is more polarizing among southern white men in 2016.

In terms of the individual questions in the Modern Sexism scale, there has been a rise of 10 points in sexist responses to question 2, which probes agreement with the notion that "most women interpret innocent remarks or acts as being sexist." That jump, from 28.4 percent in 2012 (as shown in Figure 5.4) to 38.8 percent in 2016 among southern white men, speaks not only to a general distrust of women, but more specifically to the belief in men being victimized by women's over-sensitivity to sexism or even to political correctness when it comes to gender. As shown in Figure 5.7, the fact that nearly 40 percent of this community (and 27.6 percent of non-southern white men) believe that statement to be true speaks to a serious misunderstanding of what constitutes sexism and even sexual harassment in the first place, a point that is reflected in the downplaying, for example,

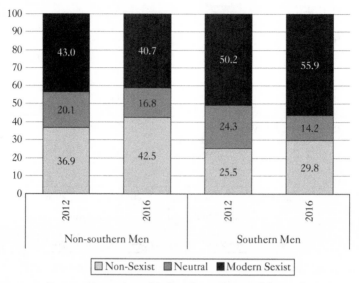

FIGURE 5.6B Percent Above, At, and Below the Midpoint of the Modern Sexism Scale, Among White Men, 2012–2016

Data are from the 2012 and 2016 Blair Center Polls.

of Trump's *Access Hollywood* tape and the characterization of his comments as "locker-room" talk.

On question 3 regarding the negative view of feminists, the percent of southern white men reporting that attitude now stands at 53.3 percent, up from 49 percent in 2012. The gaps between southern white men and non-southern white men, which are significant across all questions in 2016, have also widened in the past four years. The gaps ranged from 4.5 points to 12.1 points in 2012, and in 2016, they range from 9.4 points to 14.6 points. Overall, white men as a whole reported more Modern Sexist attitudes in 2016, but the size and degree of that shift up the scale was much greater among white men who call themselves southern, and it has policy implications.

Locker-room talk is often dismissed as sexual bravado even though it is laced with violence. On the other hand, perhaps it is actually violence masked as sexual bravado. As Nesbit and Cohen found so many years ago, that penchant for violence has distinguished the South as a region for generations, whether it be by measures of homicides or domestic violence or lynchings or state-sanctioned executions. This level of violence may be caused by the high rate of gun ownership or it may contribute to attitudes toward gun control in the sense that people feel the need for self-protection; some studies have shown that stricter gun control may be perceived as a threat to masculinity.[118] Southern identity, even in 2016,

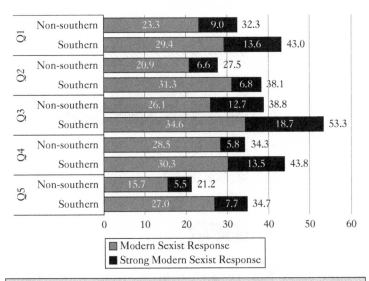

FIGURE 5.7 Percent of Modern Sexist Responses by Individual Questions, Among White Men, 2016

Data are from the 2016 Blair Center Poll.

also makes white men significantly more likely to oppose restrictions on semi-automatic weapons compared to non-southern white men, as seen in Figure 5.8A.

On issues related to background checks, like most national polls, there is little disagreement. Yet, southern white men are still more likely to oppose such reforms. Gun ownership, of course, has been heavily politicized for much of southern history, from fear of armed slave rebellions, to tales of defeat in the Civil War and the confiscation of Confederate weapons, to debates about whether or not newly freed slaves could own weapons. Ronald Reagan was actually the first presidential candidate that the National Rifle Association endorsed, and it did a great deal to seal his hyper-masculine image and win him friends in the South. That image of armed protection and bravado appeals to a lot of southern white women too, who have also been shown to be more likely to carry guns.[119] As shown in Figure 5.8B, there are statistically significant gaps between white women who identify as southern and those who do not, even when the percentages are small. Only 9 percent of southern white women are against mandatory background checks,

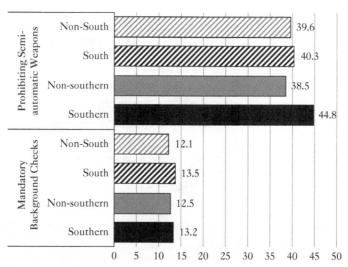

FIGURE 5.8A Percent Who "Disagree" or "Strongly Disagree" with the Following Types of Gun Control, Among White Men, 2016

Data are from the 2016 Blair Center Poll.

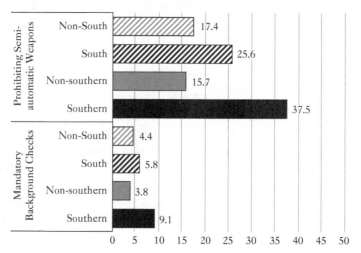

FIGURE 5.8B Percent Who "Disagree" or "Strongly Disagree" with the Following Types of Gun Control, Among White Women, 2016

Data are from the 2016 Blair Center Poll.

which is lower than all male groups, but almost twice as high as non-southern white women. A greater number (37.5 percent) of southern white women are opposed to the prohibition of semi-automatic weapons, almost 22 percent more than non-southern women (15.7 percent) and almost on par with non-southern men (38.5 percent). So there is still, indeed, something in that southern white label for many men and women that makes them protective to some degree of hyper-masculinity and its symbols.

Data from 2016 present another important shift, which may be related to Donald Trump's victory. In the weeks after the election, as shown in Figures 5.9 and 5.10, the gaps between whites who identify as southern and those who do not on how often they perceive themselves to be victims of reverse racial discrimination closed considerably, as did the gaps between southern white men and southern white women. All groups are responsible for the shift. However, non-southern white men, non-southern white women, and southern white

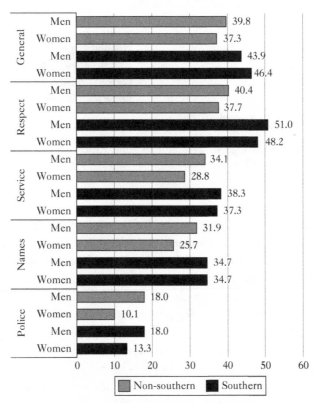

FIGURE 5.9 Percent Reporting Experience with the Following Types of Reverse Racial Discrimination, Among Whites, by Gender, 2016

Data are from the 2016 Blair Center Poll.

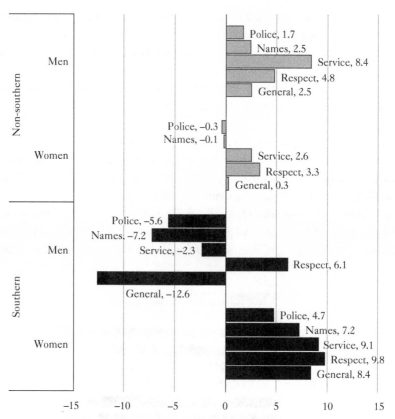

FIGURE 5.10 Net Change in Percent Reporting Experiences of Reverse Racial Discrimination, Among Whites, by Gender, 2012–2016

Data are from the 2012 and 2016 Blair Center Polls.

women all reported more experience with discrimination in almost every category. Among southern white women, the percentage experiencing disrespect because of their whiteness jumped almost ten points. However, southern white men, though they still reported the highest levels in almost every category, moved in the opposite direction dramatically. For example, among southern white men the percentage reporting general experiences with reverse discrimination dropped 12.6 points. Moreover, of all the gaps between southern white men and southern white women that were significant in 2012 on this issue, only two (being disrespected or targeted by police) remain significantly distinct in 2016. Perhaps, like the dropping rates in economic pessimism among whites post-election, surveys reveal that many men felt reassured by Trump's candidacy or re-empowered in some way[120]—undoubtedly, his victory proved even more affirming. On the other hand, white women received intense criticism on social media and from pundits for being the cause of Hillary Clinton's loss. Even though most southern white women are Republican, there was an assumption that some would cross over and vote for the first female major party nominee, or at least they might do so after Trump's past misogynistic comments were revealed on the *Access Hollywood* tape. Usually overlooked, these southern white women might be feeling intense scrutiny from women's political organizations that formed in the months after the election, planning marches and recruiting female candidates to run for office in 2018. In that environment, as their power within the GOP's base comes to light, they are revealed to be a pillar propping up the southern white patriarchy.

THOUGH THESE MUTUALLY reinforcing visions of southern white masculinity and femininity developed initially from traditional divisions of labor, particularly in a system that remained agriculturally based longer than most, they have given way over time to a "cultural misogyny." David Gilmore distinguishes between these two concepts clearly. "Patriarchal traditionalism," he explains, "is a matter of defining women's proper place within a broader constellation of political beliefs." Women safely tucked in a binder. However, the cultural cosmology that develops, he argues, "is a specifically emotive sensibility that feeds off phobias, terrors, and fantasies, regardless of a women's position in the social structure."[121] Throughout southern history, these fantasies—of slave insurrection, of miscegenation, of female authority—have heightened this sense of threat and caused, in many ways, a doubling-down by conservatives bent on protecting the status quo at all costs. Of course, the more unyielding the notion of masculinity, the more likely men, many of whom are under pressure to perform it as well, become blinded to its power and react emotionally to challenges that threaten institutional and cultural patriarchy. In southern culture, the pressure proved more intense due to the inseparable requirements of protecting male supremacy and white supremacy, and doing so all under the guise of an Antebellum-holdover definition of honor resurrected by modern religious organizations.

The cost of maintaining these traditional gender roles is high, particularly as progress continues to be made, albeit slowly, in American society. Michael Kimmel, in his book *Angry White Men*, discusses the price, contending that men forced to base their entire worth in their work success suffer from stress, loneliness, and isolation.[122] For many white southern men, that worth was not based solely on money, but also on status, reputation, racial dominance, and the ability to keep feminist ideas at bay—seemingly impossible tasks in the wake of the seismic shifts reverberating from the Civil Rights and Women's Movements. Thus, the anger may be greater, the feelings of discrimination more widespread, and the perception of threats more intense. And feminism was the most intense kind of threat. After all, as Glenda Gilmore asks in *Gender and Jim Crow*, "if patriarchy ceases to limit women, is it still a patriarchy?"[123] One cannot exist without the other. In that regard, many southern white women see themselves not as victims of, but rather as defenders of the southern white patriarchy. The anti-ERA campaign galvanized support from these conservative, anti-feminist, and newly politicized women by championing chivalry and the need for women (and thus whiteness) to be protected by men. And so the southern code of honor, the religious assertion of manhood, and the misogyny embedded in southern white identity—even when masked by romanticized notions of chivalry and masculine protection[124]—all provided an opportunity to attract southern voters. The GOP would capitalize on that opportunity, making it yet another component of the Long Southern Strategy to win the hearts and minds and loyalty of southern whites. After all, keeping up the myth of southern white womanhood via a southern white hyper-masculinity melded gender roles, southern identity, and whiteness into one powerful construct that responds to a long list of political dog whistles, some of them obvious, but many as deeply buried and coded as the patriarchy itself.

6

The Myth of the Gender Gap

*"Grab'em by the pussy" was the line that was supposed to have
ended Donald Trump's campaign for presidency. Instead it
turned out to be one of the most astonishing and successful
strategies for the highest office. In a campaign based on racism,
misogyny and bullying, Trump proved that boasting about
sexually assaulting women, far from ruining a man's career,
can boost it; and white women voted for him in droves.*

—HADLEY FREEMAN[1]

WHEN GOP PRESIDENTIAL nominee John McCain selected Alaska Governor
Sarah Palin as his running mate in 2008, the choice was hailed as a progressive step
forward for conservative women who had seen their best hope, Elizabeth Dole,
sidelined by the party eight years earlier. Liddy Dole had been somewhat quiet
on women's rights, embracing instead the non-threatening persona emblematic
of southern white womanhood, which ultimately made her a great asset for her
husband's campaign and deemed her own candidacy safe but inane. The choice
of Palin, a former second-runner-up for Miss Alaska,[2] however, represented a
new level of GOP commitment to gender-baiting as part of the Long Southern
Strategy. Palin promoted an anti-feminism that rejected efforts to achieve
women's equality and a post-sexist America to which both conservative men and
women were drawn. She played on the resentment and anger—Nicole Wallace
nicknamed her the "rage whisperer"[3]—that conservatives felt toward civil rights
efforts across the board. Palin denied the racism of the Tea Party in her Facebook
posts, demonized President Barack Obama for "palling around with terrorists,"[4]
and questioned Obama's citizenship. Her brand of "mama grizzly" or "frontier"
feminism[5] resurrected so much of what conservative activist Phyllis Schlafly and
the anti–Equal Rights Amendment (ERA) movement built three decades earlier,
including her condemnation of pro-choice women, the "bra burning militancy
of Hillary Clinton and Gloria Steinem,"[6] and the Lily Ledbetter Act for Equal
Pay, which she claimed was intended to line the pockets of Democratic trial
lawyers.[7] At the Susan B. Anthony List breakfast in 2010, even after her defeat,

Palin continued to reframe the history of American feminism by staking claim to the suffragettes and earlier women's rights activists as part of a direct lineage leading to her anti-feminist feminism.[8] That same spirit defeated the ERA in southern states and, in fact, has not died. In ways coded and brazen, Sarah Palin functioned as McCain's Southern Strategy,[9] attracting not only conservative male voters who championed her type of feminism[10] but also a somewhat forgotten and overshadowed community of white southerners—conservative women.

They have been overlooked because the well-established cult of southern white womanhood fenced them in the domestic sphere. Women's participation in the political system in general, even after securing the vote in 1920, was often ignored. Those who tried to enter the political arena faced what Kathleen Hall Jamieson, one of the leading scholars on women and American politics, called the "double bind."[11] Women must conform to traditional gender roles to avoid threatening male colleagues, yet the traditional femininity they embrace can "curtail their options and circumscribe their power."[12] The double bind propagates the absence of women in positions of authority so fully that discussions of gender often vanish. Denying women power, in effect, silences their concerns. That silence renders the impact of patriarchal institutions invisible. Southern white women have been relegated to the sidelines of public life for so long that many deny it, accept it, or defend it at their own expense. In fact, their defense of traditional gender roles during the debate over the ERA would break this silence—but not in support of progressive legislation for women.

The inclusion of gender in the Civil Rights Act of 1964 opened political and economic doors for women but it was also seen as an encroachment of federal authority, a dog whistle continuously sounded since the Civil War. The addition is well known as a last-minute move made by Representative Howard W. Smith of Virginia. Many of his critics argue that as "a conservative Southern opponent of federal civil rights," his amendment was an effort to ensure failure of the bill.[13] Moreover, the court system, condemned by many white southerners for its judicial activism, not only opened the door, but also threw open several windows for women throughout the 1970s and early 1980s. The Fourteenth Amendment's equal protection clause—ratified to give citizenship to newly freed slaves after the Civil War—was applied to women, as was the 1963 Fair Labor Standards Act. Also, numerous custody and child support laws were enforced that benefited women.[14] All of these changes leading up to and throughout the International Women's Year events (IWY) of 1975 catalyzed countless state and federally funded commissions on the status of women. However, for those southern white women who may have sympathized with second-wave feminists, any inclination for change found little encouragement. As Ashli Quesinberry Stokes contends in her study of women's liberation newsletters in the South—of which there were few—"seeing images of brutal civil rights beatings and National Guard activity, to the frequency of editorials decrying everything from the ERA to the antiwar movement, white southern women had clear evidence that any action undertaken to challenge the status quo was unwelcome."[15] However, men were not the only ones to complain. Rather, these initiatives met forceful objection in the South (lawsuits would even follow),[16] and southern white women led the resistance.

Federal encroachment was not the only source of fuel behind the anti-ERA fight—and, eventually, the GOP's Long Southern Strategy. Phyllis Schlafly's creation of the anti-feminist ideology and her fight for its recognition and parity politicized and organized southern white women by legitimizing their culture. Female leadership and participation were valid, but only in the service of the preservation of conservative values—especially when those values were under attack by feminists, the federal government, and increasingly, the Democratic Party. This was pointedly true for many southerners because the lens through which they viewed the fight for the ERA and other women's initiatives was the same lens through which they had watched the Civil Rights Movement unfold. Both campaigns were "misinterpreted by many southerners, who thought that the federal government was destroying the things they held most dear—their families, their wives and husbands, their homes, their traditional way of life."[17] The conservative, reactionary impulse against feminism received reinforcement not only from Schlafly's validation of anti-feminism, but also from southern Christian moralism. The resulting pro-family, pro-Christianity rhetoric insisted upon traditional gender roles and opposed reproductive rights, like abortion and even birth control, the two fundamental premises on which equality for women hinged. Strategically, some ERA supporters tried to downplay their support for legal abortion and for lesbian rights as well—clearly seen as an affront to religious conservatives—but to no avail. The lines were drawn and religious southern white, anti-feminist women transformed themselves into activists.

The ongoing existence of a large community of "Modern Sexist" southern white women may speak volumes about the past cultural production of southern identity, but it also has a significant impact on the country's political future in many ways that have been misunderstood. The resurgence of American feminism marked the beginning of a gender gap in electoral politics, which garnered perhaps more attention than any other political statistic related to women ever has. By the 1980s, feminists argued that women were voting for Democrats in much higher numbers than men were voting for Democrats. The advantage, in time, even pushed Democrats to support progressive female candidates. However, the trend was not universal because anti-feminism remains deeply burrowed into southern whiteness. Thus, when geography and identity are brought to bear on the myth of the gender gap, it looks remarkably different. Where it does not disappear completely, it is often reversed, with southern white women proving more conservative than southern white men and dramatically more so than American women as a whole. Palin's anti-feminist feminism gave a voice to those women in 2012. Donald Trump's attacks on Hillary Clinton as a "nasty woman" amplified it. Both, in their own way, offered the contemporary version of a message that worked for the long strategy of turning and keeping the South red. The distinct combination of the historical commitment to traditional gender roles, underscored by fundamentalist religion, and the constant squelching of protests for change, gave the GOP another way to go hunting where the ducks were and still are.

THE BACKLASH TO Second-Wave Feminism gained traction in the South for a number of telling reasons, all of which connected in some way to the tangled history of southern white identity and its maturing alliance with the GOP. Yet, the misunderstanding of or lack of attention to this backlash—this "other women's movement"—is exactly what gave rise to the myth of the gender gap, the ramifications of which are still ongoing. As previously mentioned, the anti-feminist community was not partisan initially, as both Republicans and Democrats endorsed the ERA in the 1950s, 1960s, and in 1972. By 1976, however, fractures in the GOP became visible on women's issues, with President Gerald Ford openly supporting the ERA and backed by the feminists in the Republican Women's Task Force. The budding STOP ERA (Stop Taking Our Privileges) movement organized by Schlafly supported primary challenger Ronald Reagan, and, perhaps most important, wanted the GOP to drop the ERA officially from the party platform.

These anti-feminist advocates worked around the clock at the convention, convincing the deciding vote, Joe Usry of Oregon, that he could be a Ford supporter—particularly since he was a fundamentalist Christian minister—and still oppose a party endorsement of the ERA.[18] The success of STOP ERA took the Ford administration, as well as feminists in both parties, by complete surprise. However, when Ford defeated Reagan for the GOP nomination and then Democratic nominee Jimmy Carter (with white southern support) defeated the Republicans altogether, this budding anti-feminism may have seemed short-lived. Attention to anti-feminism was eclipsed four years later by media coverage of the gender gap—whereby more women were found to be voting for the Democratic Party than men—despite the fact that the majority of both voted for Reagan. Yet, these conservative women (and men) would ultimately defeat the ERA by blocking ratification, leaving the amendment three states short. Such was the power of Phyllis Schlafly's flock.

Schlafly, whether she realized it or not, was an integral part of the Long Southern Strategy. She came to prominence via the self-published polemic

A Choice Not an Echo, in which she chastised GOP elites for functioning as "kingmakers" and selecting candidates at the convention who did not reflect the true conservatism of the people. She urged Republicans to support Senator Barry Goldwater's bid for the nomination because he would stand up to the establishment elite. Without much advertisement, the book sold close to 2 million copies in the summer of 1964 and clearly contributed to Goldwater's successful nomination (scholarly estimates indicate that 26 percent of readers swayed their vote and pointed to Schlafly's manifesto as the reason). However, it was her ability to organize and politicize women in opposition to their own equality that changed the American and southern political landscapes. In her book *Republican Women*, Catherine Rymph argues that the fleeting feminist GOP moment did not spring forth from a true party feminist consciousness, but rather the party's effort to broaden its appeal to new voters—until Schlafly's work showed the party faithful that standing against women's equality would bring in more voters than standing up for it.

Schlafly and her supporters in STOP ERA undertook both stylistic and substantive techniques to establish and grow the anti-feminist wing of the Republican Party that appealed to white southerners. And though *A Choice Not an Echo* did not delve into women's issues or gender roles, the key to understanding Schlafly's most important stylistic move lay in her criticism of bipartisanship. Specifically, Schlafly condemned Nelson Rockefeller for crossing the party line so often that it seemed like he worked for both parties. These elites, she, argued operate in secrecy and betray true grassroots Republican values. Schlafly saw the two parties as black and white, with little, if any, gray, and this dichotomous outlook or "us vs. them" mentality became her most effective weapon in her war against the ERA. Since both parties backed the ERA originally, since IWY women's commissions were organizing across the country, and since even the White House launched its own women's advisory group under Ford, the cause of feminism seemed to have no opposition. Feminism was framed as an unquestionable worldview whose time had come—a step forward in the evolution of human rights. Thus, all of the women on the National IWY commission were pro-ERA advocates[19] and feminists, or so Schlafly complained. But feminism, she insisted, was an opinion, an ideology, a singular perspective.

Schlafly set up anti-feminism as a false equivalency to feminism. And it worked. After all, if feminism is choice, then the real foil to feminism is sexism, but that label would not gain women's support. Two conservative women's organizations, the International Women's Federation and the Conservative Women's Association, still condemn feminists for not representing all women.[20] However, in the 1970s, the argument was newly popularized, which Schlafly primarily did through her speeches and writings in her "Blue Eagle Forum." The argument allowed anti-feminists to insist upon having an equal number of seats at the table. They also wanted equal money, particularly if taxes were being spent in support of feminism. When Schlafly and her colleagues proved unsuccessful at having the pro-ERA IWY commission stripped of its funding, they established the IWY Citizens' Review Committee (CRC). This watchdog organization tracked every dollar spent at the state and national level, insisting on equal spending for the anti-ERA perspective and on equal representation at state conventions and at the National Women's Conference to be held in Houston in 1977.[21] By defining her followers in opposition to feminism, Schlafly utilized a rhetorical frame familiar and deeply popular among white southerners, whose very identity functioned exactly the same way. Femininity and masculinity. Black and white. North and South. Women were forced to take one side or another. Many white southern women became, in effect, highly politicized and strategic political actors in a fight to protect the myth of southern womanhood and the traditional gender roles associated with it.

If that oppositional identity structure did not ring familiar enough to white southern audiences, casting anti-feminists as soldiers in a substantive battle for morality surely would. The debate over abortion rights bolstered the anti-feminist appeal throughout the Bible Belt. Within a year of the 1973 *Roe v. Wade* decision, anti-abortion activists routinely marched on Washington on the anniversary of the decision, pleading for an amendment forcing the reversal of the decision.[22] According the scholar Laura Kalman, the fight for the ERA and support for reproductive freedom became equally important and somewhat inseparable to feminists.[23] In fact, using oral history interviews, Richard Hughes demonstrates the way the 1960s Civil Rights Movement shaped the anti-abortion movement, in which the rhetoric of the rights of the unborn caught fire and created yet another partisan fracture.[24] Some scholars have even suggested that anti-abortion sentiment is what actually motivated efforts to block the ERA, which conservatives, they contend, believed would strengthen the pro-choice position in the eyes of the court.[25] As early as 1970 in California, GOP organizers actively advocated outside of Catholic churches for parishioners to change their registration from Democrat to Republican in the wake of the state Democratic Party's pro-choice stance.[26] However, if reproductive rights and the ERA became inseparable to feminists, then opposition to the ERA and the pro-life stance proved mutually fortifying to anti-feminists, particularly when cloaked in religiosity.

Whether instigated by a perceived threat to traditional gender roles or by the legalization of abortion or both, the injection of religion into the anti-ERA campaign had long-lasting effects on the Republican Party. White southerners who realigned with the GOP over feminism pushed the whole party rightward. Public opinion polls in 1975 and 1976 showed that a majority of Americans believed reproductive rights should be left to women and their doctors.[27] The ground started shifting, however, as the debate over the ERA intensified and spilled into additional questions of faith. First Lady Betty Ford took a pro-choice stance, while her husband, President Ford, maintained his pro-life position, symbolizing not only a divide in the White House, but also a divide in a Republican Party beginning to dig its heels into the anti-abortion ground. Even four decades since the legalization of abortion, the Republican Party continues to politicize the issue to score points, particularly among evangelicals in the South. Mitt Romney, for example, faced a potential uphill battle in 2012 as a Mormon campaigning in the Bible Belt. Despite having been pro-choice at one point, Romney flip-flopped publicly on the issue (what was successful in Massachusetts would not work in the South). Stories of Romney's commitment to the pro-life stance, including one in which Romney pressured a fellow Mormon woman not to have an abortion even though her life was being compromised by the pregnancy,[28] may have helped woo white southern voters, particularly conservative southern white women.

The GOP's continued embrace of southern white religiosity via these "pro-family" anti-feminists trickled down throughout the party. As Matthew Levendusky demonstrates in his book *The Partisan Sort: How Liberals Became Democrats and Conservatives Became Republicans*, acceptance of abortion rights (calculated by an index of six questions about abortion), even by non-religious GOP members, has weakened over time.[29] The same religiosity, of course, underscored opposition to homosexual rights, which became leverage for anti-ERA advocates who saw the eventual, though controversial, inclusion of lesbians signaled by Betty Friedan's public acceptance of the community at the 1977 National Women's Conference in Houston.[30] Regardless of whether abortion and gay rights influenced opinions on the ERA or whether the ERA influenced opinions on abortion and gay rights, the combination further alienated the parties from each other and fueled the culture wars. This trifecta unified and motivated opposition to the Women's Movement. Schlafly warned anti-feminists that the ERA would result in federal funding for abortions and the legalization of gay marriage, despite court rulings such as *Maher v. Doe* (1977) and *Baker v. Nelson* (1971), respectively, that found otherwise.[31] Moreover, the powerful conflation of these issues was not short-lived. In her study of attitudes from 1988 to 2000, Karen Kaufman, for example, shows that the combination of abortion protections, female equality, and gay rights exerted a significant influence on women in terms of their party allegiance.[32]

That influence, however, cuts both ways and not evenly across the country. Understanding the way that abortion and gay rights were politicized by anti-feminism reveals clues to this myth of the gender gap. Even looking at attitudes in the 2012 Blair Center Poll among white Americans sheds light on the subject.

Figure 6.1A shows contemporary regional and identity differences on abortion attitudes by gender. Outside of the geographic South, only 29.2 percent of women believe that abortion should rarely or never be legal, significantly less than 44.5 percent of women who live in the South.

The difference is much greater and still highly significant when southern identity is considered, with 28.7 percent of non-southern white women opposing almost all forms of legal abortion, compared to a clear majority, 55.4 percent, of southern white women. The gaps between men, both by geographic residence or regional identification, are much smaller though they are still significant. In part, the myth of the gender gap was built on the assumption that American women nationwide support protection of these rights at higher rates than men. Thus, ignoring the regional variation is why the myth of the gender gap persists. Opposition to gay marriage, as of 2012, follows a similar pattern, as shown in Figure 6.1B. Living in the South and, even more so, identifying as southern, significantly increases white women's opposition to gay marriage. In terms of identity, the gap between non-southern and southern white women is over 30 points.

In terms of how these attitudes contribute to the ongoing myth of the gender gap is best shown in Figure 6.2, in which the gaps between men and women in each subgroup are presented for both abortion and gay marriage attitudes. In terms of abortion, this traditional gender gap—in which women are more liberal than men—stands at 8.3 points among whites who live outside of the geographic South. However, below the Mason-Dixon line, the gap does not merely shrink, it actually goes in the opposite direction. There is a 4.3-point "reverse" gender

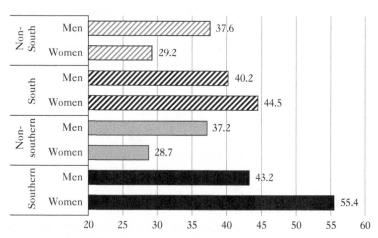

FIGURE 6.1A Percent Reporting Abortion Should "Rarely" or "Never" Be Legal, Among Whites, by Gender, 2012

Data are from the 2012 Blair Center Poll.

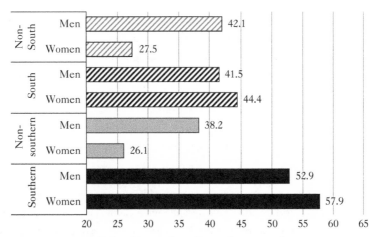

FIGURE 6.1B Percent Who "Oppose" or "Strongly Oppose" Gay Marriage, Among Whites, by Gender, 2012

Data are from the 2012 Blair Center Poll.

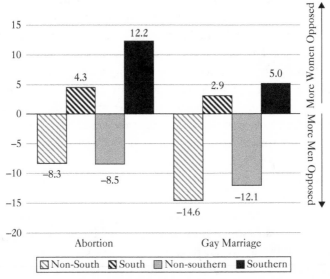

FIGURE 6.2 Percent Gender Gaps (Women Minus Men) in Opposition to Abortion and Gay Marriage, Among Whites, 2012

Data are from the 2012 Blair Center Poll.

gap with women in the South proving more conservative and more opposed to abortion than men. The same striking pattern is more significant when southern identity is considered. Among non-southern whites, there is an 8.5-point traditional gap, but among whites who call themselves southern there is a 12.2-point gender gap in the opposite direction. Southern white women are the most opposed to abortion, significantly more so than southern white men. A similar pattern holds for attitudes toward gay marriage. Outside of the geographic South and among non-southerners, the traditional gender gap swells to 14.6 and 12.1 points respectively, with women significantly less likely to oppose gay rights. However, white women who live in the South and white women who claim a southern identity are more conservative than their male counterparts, reporting a 2.9 and a 5-point reverse gender gap. Like the anti-feminists before them, they continue to pull the GOP to the right.

EVEN THOUGH THE gender gap received national attention when analysis of the 1980 election revealed that American women had begun to favor Democrats more than American men and by noticeable margins, what caused and continues to cause the gender gap remains a heated debate. As research on the gender gap broadened, political psychologists contended that due to the caretaker and nurturer role that many women fulfilled, they reported more liberal attitudes on what were coined "compassion" issues—policies related to education, children, healthcare, inequality, etc. Other social scientists dismissed the "compassion" distinctiveness of women, arguing instead that the division of labor caused the gender gap. In other words, because women were still primarily functioning within the domestic sphere, their self-interest and political opinions would reflect that fact.[33] So women supposedly held more liberal positions on education because they were the ones volunteering at the schools, signing the permission slips, running the parent-teacher organizations, and so on. To some degree, the tendency of women to align with the increasingly liberal Democratic Party was overblown. They were voting more Democratic than men, but more women and men overall had voted for Reagan. Still the media, as well as scholarly interest persisted.

Scholars argued that the gender gap resulted from an increase of women participating in the labor force.[34] Thus, more women were paying into Social Security and dealing with minimum wages and employer benefits, and even work-place harassment—all issues that drove an increased interest in public policies. Of course, causality is an issue here, as Jeff Manza and Clem Brooks questioned whether more women were entering the labor force because of a growing "feminist consciousness" or whether their experiences in the workplace were creating this consciousness and thus affecting their political views.

The decline of marriage was even cited as a factor contributing to the gender gap because men, as primary breadwinners, became wealthier after divorce, while women—many of whom had never worked—became poorer. The increase of women in poverty, the research suggests, affected political attitudes toward social entitlement programs, thus influencing the gender gap.[35] Additional findings related to the gender gap have shown that, at times, women have expressed more concern for the national economy than men, who are individual "pocketbook" voters.[36] More women, logically, have been found to support issues that specifically affect women.[37] In addition, the gender gap has been found to have a significant impact on foreign policy goals and the means to achieve those goals, with women proving less hawkish than men.[38] Still others, such as Kaufmann and Warren Miller, argued, and fairly early on, that the gap was actually the result of men moving to the Republican Party, some of whom may have been attracted to Reagan's masculinity and anti-feminist rhetoric and switched party allegiances.[39] Terrel Rhodes recognized that both parties had a hand in the gender gap. He pointed out that "although a strategy by the Democrats to appeal to women voters has provided positive results for the party, the success of the Republican party and its candidates in appealing to males, particularly White male voters, has proven to be even more successful in the South."[40] This more complex narrative does note the significance of the South, but the main actors are limited to only white men.

All of these findings are surely part of the gender gap as it exists in parts of the country, but little research covers why, in light of all of those reasons, so many white women in the South turned away from the Democratic Party. Though the samples are limited, the white women did exactly what white men in the South did, turning red over the course of the Long Southern Strategy. Ignoring southern white women not only results in a misperceived universality of the American gender gap, but it also concludes the Southern Strategy prematurely, which creates a shortsighted interpretation of southern realignment. Beyond that, the myth of the gender gap has additional unintended consequences. Despite Reagan's 1980 victory, feminists used the new gender gap to promote the importance of female voters within the Democratic Party because they did not want the party to abandon the ERA as the Republican Party had done. The self-promotion worked, and Women's Movement organizers succeeded, albeit temporarily, in cementing their standing within the party and advocating for female candidates and feminist issues.[41] This, beyond the fight over the ERA, further shaped the Democratic Party's image in a way that conflicted with many aspects of the southern white label, not just for men, but also for women. It also harkens back to Schlafly's framing of anti-feminism as a false equivalency to feminism. Rather than redefine feminism for themselves or even offer their own moderate positions and alternative views within the movement, anti-feminists demonized it and created an alt-identity that mirrored southern white identity. As the Democratic Party became more associated with feminism and more women began to run for office under its banner, identity politics drove anti-feminists to the GOP.

In her 1988 article "Feminists and the Gender Gap," Pamela Johnston Conover examines exactly this, dissecting female voters into feminist and non-feminist subgroups. The findings are pretty remarkable. Employing a measure of feminist "identity"—based on two core tenets of identity: (1) "a sense of membership" and (2) "a sense of psychological attachment to the group"—Conover examines public opinion differences between men and women. In a series of multivariate regressions, she finds that "feminist identity" has a significant impact on such fundamental notions as egalitarianism, racial animus, moral traditionalism, sympathy for the disadvantaged, and sex roles. "On the political values," she contends, "the effects of a feminist identity are as strong as or stronger than all of the other variables except party identification. And, on the more basic value orientations, a feminist identity has an even stronger impact, an impact which rivals, and in some instances exceeds, that of party identification."[42] She concludes with this punch, "There is not so much a gap between men and women as there is a gap between men and feminist women."[43] Only three years later, Elizabeth Cook and Clyde Wilcox examined not just feminist women, but also feminist men.[44] Though there are fewer feminist men, as of 2004, feminism in men is attributable to the same variables as in women—education, age, religious affiliation, and political identification.[45] Moreover, in 2016, Leonie Huddy and Johanna Wilmann presented new research digging into this notion of feminist identity, questioning "why the feminist partisan gap in American politics has received modest attention in recent years."[46] Alongside that important assertion lies the need to study anti-feminism as well, particularly in terms of regional identity, because diametrically opposed to feminist identity lies the pedestal of southern white womanhood, the proponents of which would resist and resent changes to the gender status quo.

This sense of resentment and hostility toward feminists created a whole other type of gender gap—a candidate gender gap, with few progressive white women in the South running for office. The candidate gender gap also underscores the white male political monopoly still very much intact in the South. During the push for ERA ratification, female Florida state senator Lori Wilson connected these historic dots. On April 13, 1977, on the Senate floor, she admonished her colleagues, proclaiming that:

> I've a feeling we've been down this 'ole road before. Ya'll took the wrong turn last time.... In all 10 of these Southern states, ERA remains in trouble. Why? Because the good old boys in the Southern legislatures traditionally do not consider people [sic] issues like ERA on their merit. They consider only what it might do to their own manliness or their own money-ness, or their man-power. At work. At home. Yes, even at play. Let's look at the historic pattern. The good old boys in Southern politics refused to give up their slaves ... until the rest of the nation whipped them on the battlefields. The good old boys refused to approve the 19th Amendment

granting women the right to vote until the rest of the nation whipped them in the legislative halls elsewhere across this land. The good old boys fought the 1964 Civil Rights Act down to their last axe handles until the rest of the nation whipped them in the courtrooms, and on the streets, and at the polls . . . with legal power, and armed power and PEOPLE POWER. And now, on the last remaining issue of human rights, civil rights, people rights, and equal rights, the good old boys are summoning all their remaining, but weakening power for one last hurrah. The good old boys are trying desperately to hold on to the power they have given one another, or taken from one another. Well let me assure you that the good old boys in this Senate and elsewhere in the South are clutching at pseudo power, that will not last.[47]

But it has lasted primarily because it is so fundamental to southern identity. In her essay "Can the Flower of Southern Womanhood Bloom in the Garden of Southern Politics?," Sue Tolleson-Rinehart, writing at the tail end of the twentieth century, considers the long-term implications of the cult of southern womanhood, southern white patriarchy, and anti-feminism on women entering public life. Lori Wilson in Florida was the exception in the 1970s, far from the rule. The South, Tolleson-Rinehart insists, "remains the region least hospitable to the election of women to office." Without hesitation, she asserts that "the reasons for this are intricately and inextricably bound to those notions of southern womanhood."[48]

In general, white women in the South have a history of low political and civic participation dating back to Antebellum times. Unlike communities of women in the North who established "bonds of womanhood" through their reform work (including abolitionism), southern white women "most often accepted their place in the patriarchal order." Moreover, the reform work undertaken by women in the North is what awoke many "to their own powerlessness in politics and the law and to work together for change."[49] This is not to say that there are not examples of southern white women who fought against slavery[50] or for temperance[51] or have driven other social justice reform movements. Indeed, not all southern white women were absorbed solely by family life;[52] some joined women's clubs[53] and many have rejected key elements of the "southern lady" archetype.[54] Still, without a mass level of group activism, efforts to open up the political sphere to women often failed. As early as the days of Reconstruction, when southern states redrafted their state constitutions, hardly any requests for women's suffrage (usually initiated to enhance white political power in some way) passed committee.[55] Women's equality efforts were difficult enough when white women in the South were disengaged, but that paled in comparison to how difficult (and how ironic) it was when they mobilized against it, as they did when faced with the ERA.

In her 1974 landmark book *Political Woman*, Jeane Kirkpatrick described four hypothetical constraints that explain this persistent disengagement. "The paucity of women in political life" resulted from "physiological constraints," "cultural constraints," "role constraints," and "male conspiracy."[56] The physical distinctiveness of women—that is, their lack of aggressiveness and decision-making ability—is easily dismissed. Yet, a belief in these differences, combined with a culture that reinforces such constraints, proves powerful. Add the "role constraints" imposed by historically limited access to the public sphere and the "male conspiracy" to maintain male power by supporting these divisions and beliefs,[57] and the path from pedestal to politics seems long. So long that as late as 2000, an analysis of the American National Election Survey data revealed that region remained a significant negative predictor of female political participation. Moreover, it is not a generational holdout. Irrespective of age, women who live in the South were and are less likely to vote.[58]

The resistance to women voting became a resistance to women working became a resistance to women running for public office, particularly if the motive is feminist in nature. Women voting to protect the patriarchy, or working outside of the home out of absolute financial necessity, or being appointed to fill the political seat of a husband who has died, proved acceptable because they did not conflict with notions of southern white femininity and privilege instilled for generations. In fact, anthropological fieldwork conducted by Susan Middleton-Keirn in the mid-1980s attempted to define southern white perceptions of modern femininity in the aftermath of Second-Wave Feminism. Her research, published as "Magnolias and Microchips: Regional Subcultural Constructions of Femininity," exposes the new political tenets layered onto sacred southern womanhood. Persistent attitudes among the "magnolias" predictably include "husbands should be head of the household," "femininity is essential," and "no woman's life is complete until she marries and has children." Breadwinning is socially sanctioned only when required and only in certain professions. "Women who participate in the women's movement are unhappy misfits," and only 7 percent of southern women call themselves feminists.[59] The "magnolias" deem equal rights as either already achieved—visions of a post-sexist America—or unnecessary. Good (non-nasty) women remain backstage. They "were not supposed to display themselves; only prostitutes and actresses did that."[60] If pursuing a career equaled a public display, then pursuing a political career was center stage under neon lights.

A new crop of Southern Republican legislators who took office in the mid-1990s echoed these antiquated sentiments regarding the potential for female leadership. Newt Gingrich, the New Right Republican and future Speaker of the

House from Georgia, lambasted his opposing candidate, State Senator Virginia Shephard, an ongoing ERA advocate. His campaign ads, for example, stated that "Newt will take his family to Washington and keep them together. Virginia will go to Washington and leave her husband and children in the care of the nanny."[61] Reagan had pointed to similar doomsday scenarios in his stance against the ERA, insisting that women would be forced to put their children in daycare. He also praised his second wife Nancy Reagan for quitting acting when they got married because she recognized that staying home would be "fair" to him.[62] Both Reagan and Gingrich's anti-feminism included little discussion of policy issues, just character attacks that attracted both white southern men and white southern women. They signaled the "magnolias'" assertion that feminists were misfits who were breaking the social, familial, even biblical, contract.

The long legacy of the cult of southern womanhood, its major role in southern white identity formation, the GOP's decision to amplify the anti-feminist messaging, and the growing strength of the GOP in the region overall, maintained high levels of both male and female Modern Sexist attitudes and support for a gender status quo. Though racial animus is often cited as the source of regional realignment, the debate over gender roles has become a powerful component of partisan polarization. So much so that in hypothetical contests in which Republican women run, David King and Richard Matland have shown that Democrats are more likely to vote for them than their own party is.[63] The debate only intensifies when the office sought by a female is the highest office in the country. Support for a female president has been measured by Gallup and Pew for decades. Gallup first posed the question in 1937 showing only one-third of Americans polled supporting the notion. That number reached 87 percent in 2003, with over 90 percent of younger voters indicating they would vote for a female presidential candidate.[64] Pew's 2007 poll found support remained at 87 percent, up from 53 percent when they debuted the question in 1969.[65] Regardless of these high numbers in public opinion surveys, women who have run for national executive office have often faced a sexist backlash. Of course, none were successful. In the spring of 2008, as Hillary Clinton campaigned for the Democratic presidential nomination, Matthew Streb, Barbara Burrell, Brian Frederick, and Michael Genovese published a telling article regarding Americans' real feelings about the possibility of a female president. Just as research in the 1980s showed that men were more likely to express support for sharing household duties than they were to actually take on more household duties, here too social desirability seems to be skewing the overwhelming majorities found by Gallup and Pew. This team of researchers found that 26 percent of the population actually expresses anger or upset feelings in response to a female president, suggesting that support is highly exaggerated.[66] Anger jumps significantly among people who live in the South to almost one-third of the population.

Leonnie Huddy and Nayda Terkildsen, as well as David Lubin and Sarah Brewer, explain yet another aspect of the perception of progress that masks southern white sexism.[67] In their study of southern elections, they find that the level of office to which the candidate aspires is relevant to the potential for voters to support a woman. Male traits—such as aggression—are preferred by people who live in the South when evaluating candidates for national offices, but female traits are deemed acceptable for lower-level, compassion-based county and state positions. Hillary Clinton's political star rose based on her efforts in the educational arena in Arkansas, a more acceptable policy category for a woman. Going outside of those limitations, invites criticism. For example, Geraldine Ferraro, the first female nominee for vice president, felt condescended to in her 1980 debate against George H. W. Bush specifically when discussing world affairs. Bush's tone was patronizing, noted Ferraro, as if he needed to educate her about foreign policy.[68] Ferraro's levelheaded, diplomatic, and nuanced responses did not warrant Bush's tone. It was as if she had broken some unarticulated rule by expressing an informed opinion on the masculine subject of national security and international affairs. A few election cycles later, George W. Bush reframed women's interest in foreign policy to make it more compatible with traditional gender roles. He sought the support and votes of what his campaign team called "security moms"[69]—conservative, often southern, white women who were focused on defeating terrorism and protecting their families at home.

In many ways, very little has changed since Jeanne Hurlbert's landmark 1989 GIS-based analysis of southern distinctiveness (based on geographic residence) concluded that people who live in the South are significantly less likely to vote for a female for president.[70] Nearly a quarter century later, the 2012 Blair Center Poll examined how impending a woman president seemed to white Americans. Figure 6.3 shows the percentage of respondents who expect to see a female president in their lifetime by both geographic region and regional identity. As expected, white Americans who call themselves southerners were significantly less likely to believe a woman will run the country in the decades to come. It is important to note that among no group is this pessimism expressed by more than one-third of the respondents. Southern white women are the highest at 32.2 percent. Nevertheless, there are important distinctions. Despite assumptions, the differences between white men and women who live in the South or who identify as southern are not statistically significant. However, for whites who live outside of the South or who do not claim a southern identity, responses between the sexes are significantly different. Perhaps the regional and identity divide reflects a social environment in which the idea of a female president just seems too far-fetched. Or perhaps

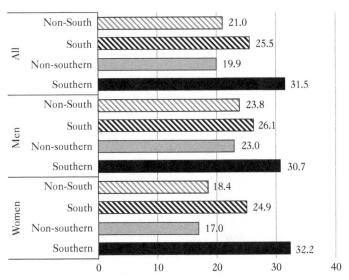

FIGURE 6.3 Percent Who Do Not Expect to See a Female President in Their Lifetime, Among Whites, by Gender, 2012

Data are from the 2012 Blair Center Poll.

pessimism among white southerners, both men and women, demonstrates how the very notion of a female president threatens an ideology initiated in the Antebellum South that persists in modern times, having been tapped into and perpetuated by the Republican Party's Long Southern Strategy to turn the region red via identity politics.

Table 6.1 presents a logistic regression model examining which variables significantly predict optimism or doubt regarding the possibility of a female president. For every group of white Americans, higher educational attainment makes one significantly more optimistic about electing a future female president, though among white southerners it is less significant. Moreover, for whites in the non-South or those who do not identify as southern, being married makes one significantly more likely to believe in the possibility of a woman in the Oval Office, but being Republican and/or fundamentalist has the opposite effect. However, among whites who live in the South and among those who call themselves southern, neither marriage, nor party identification, nor fundamentalism is significant, which may reflect the fact that there is less variation in the South and among southerners regarding those variables. Income, however, is significant, with wealthier white women in the South or who identify as southern being more likely to believe in the possibility of a female president. Age is significant across the board, with older Americans—for whom "in their lifetime" is shorter—being

Table 6.1 Predicting Belief in a Future Female President, Among Whites, 2012

	Non-South	South	Non-southern	Southern
Age	−0.026****	−0.020****	−0.019****	−0.035****
(toward older)	(0.005)	(0.005)	(0.004)	(0.006)
Education	0.292****	0.298****	0.324****	0.201**
(toward more educated)	(0.086)	(0.089)	(0.075)	(0.114)
Income	0.002	0.037**	0.008	0.043*
(toward wealthier)	(0.021)	(0.021)	(0.018)	(0.028)
Married	0.327**	−0.008	0.310**	−0.151
	(0.163)	(0.168)	(0.142)	(0.221)
Female	0.130	0.050	0.179*	−0.044
	(0.151)	(0.157)	(0.133)	(0.201)
Unemployed	−0.317	−0.260	0.030	−0.717**
	(0.274)	(0.299)	(0.249)	(0.389)
Fundamentalist	−0.626****	0.02	−0.343**	−0.080
	(0.174)	(0.172)	(0.155)	(0.212)
Party Identification	−0.206****	−0.061	−0.242****	0.064
(toward Republican)	(0.058)	(0.062)	(0.052)	(0.079)
Ideology	−0.036	−0.264****	−0.079*	−0.263***
(toward conservative)	(0.067)	(0.073)	(0.060)	(0.096)
Modern Sexism	−0.072****	−0.083****	−0.071****	−0.083***
	(0.022)	(0.025)	(0.019)	(0.032)
Constant	3.801****	3.732****	3.590****	4.066****
	(0.550)	(0.588)	(0.476)	(0.771)
N	1250	1052	1697	571
Pseudo R Squared	0.113	0.096	0.111	0.102

Note: Standard errors in parentheses * p<=.10, ** p<=.05, *** p<=.01, **** p<.001
Data are from the 2012 Blair Center Poll.

less likely to believe they will see a female president. The only other significant and negative predictor of doubt in a future woman president across all groups is distrust and resentment of working women—that is, Modern Sexism. Plotting the results of this logistic regression in a predicted probability chart shows the relationships between Modern Sexism, southern identity, and expecting to see a female president more clearly. At the low end of the Modern Sexism scale, as

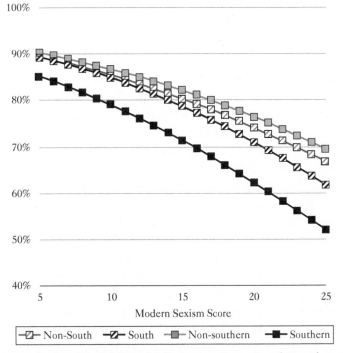

FIGURE 6.4 Predicted Probability of Believing in a Future Female President, Among Whites, Across Modern Sexism Scale, 2012

Data are from the 2012 Blair Center Poll.

shown in Figure 6.4, the predicted probability is very high that the respondent will expect to see a female president.

The probability of expecting to see a female president, however, drops precipitously as the level of Modern Sexism grows. Among those who score at the highest end of the Modern Sexism scale, their probability of expecting to see a female president drops below 70 percent among non-southerners, below 67 percent among whites living in the non-South, below 62 percent for whites living in the South, and below 53 percent among whites who claim a southern identity. Even in this generic, nonpartisan question, the same pattern persists in which southern identity and Modern Sexism flex their collective and mutually reinforcing muscles in support of traditional gender roles—roles that do not include a woman president, particularly if she is seen as fighting for women.

IN 2016, THE idea of a female president was not an abstraction, but a real possibility. In the end, whites who live in the South, particularly white women, played a big part in Hillary Clinton's loss. In some ways, they voted as data predicted. As

Mary McThomas and Michael Tesler demonstrate, in 2012 Modern Sexism had a larger negative effect on Clinton's favorability than on Democrats in general, even though Clinton's popularity had increased in her role as secretary of state. Several years earlier, analyzing the 2005 American National Election Studies data, Tesler and David Sears also found Modern Sexism to be "a strong and independent predictor" of Clinton's favorability.[71] Despite these critical findings, the mainstream assumption that white women would vote for the first female major-party nominee persisted. That assumption, which has been challenged by scholars, persists at large because it is based on a non-South, non-southern view of the country, exactly as the myth of the gender gap is. The anti-feminism that shocked many feminists in the 1970s shocked just as many people in 2016.

Too often, sexism as it related to the notion of a female president focused singularly on whether a woman could serve as commander-in-chief or on characteristics such as decisiveness and resolve under pressure. Hillary Clinton, however, seemed to many to have overcome the negative stereotypes of women in this regard, and because of that the impact of sexism on the election received less attention, particularly during the campaigns, and sometimes met outright denial. Clinton's success at overcoming that traditional notion of sexism obscured the fact that the anti-feminist backlash to the Women's Movement of the 1970s had ushered in this secondary or new attitude called Modern Sexism. This kind of sexism does not reflect the belief that a woman cannot succeed as commander-in-chief, but captures resentment toward a woman who can. And it reflects distrust toward her for wanting that kind of power. That Schlafly's anti-feminism morphed into a demonization of feminism as the enemy of "family values," and that such Modern Sexism proliferates, is due in part to having been adopted and nurtured as a key tenet of conservative, partisan ideology. As such, campaign strategists and pollsters would have been wise to account for not only traditional attitudes toward women, but also for hostile sexism,[72] as well as for Modern Sexism in pre-election polling, just as Racial Resentment was considered when Barack Obama was on the ballot in 2008 and 2012.

The 2016 Blair Center Poll shows just how impactful Modern Sexism, conflated with southern identity and whiteness, was in the 2016 election. As shown in Figure 6.5A and 6.5B, it is a distinguishing marker even in the presidential primaries. White respondents who report voting in the primary elections overwhelmingly supported Trump as compared to all other candidates. White voters who identify as southern chose Trump at a significantly higher rate of 48.3 percent, 16.4 percent more than non-southern white voters. On the other hand, of all primary voters, 25.9 percent of non-southern whites cast for Clinton, while significantly fewer (11.2 percent) southern whites claim to have chosen her.

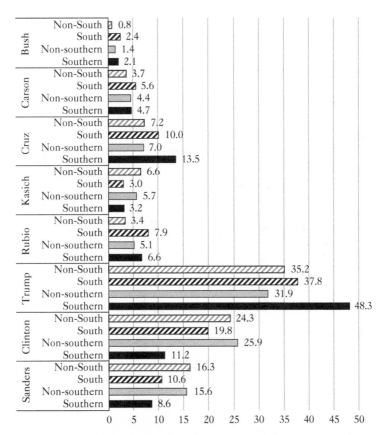

FIGURE 6.5A Percent Vote for Presidential Primary Candidates, Among Whites, 2016
Data are from the 2016 Blair Center Poll.

Moreover, among whites, as Figure 6.5B reveals, the gender gap needs a regional revision. More men than women supported both Cruz and Kasich in
every subgroup, while Rubio's supporters almost reached gender parity. However,
among Trump supporters, outside of the geographic South, significantly more
men (a gap of 11.8 percent) chose him than women. Among whites who live in
the South, that gap drops to an insignificant 1.3 points. Among whites who do not
identify as southern, 9.6 percent more men chose Trump in the primary—again,
a significant gender gap. However, among those who do identify as southern,
2 percent more women than men voted for Trump—a reverse gender gap in primary voting. It is the fact that the difference between southern white men and
southern white women in terms of their early support for Trump is statistically
insignificant that begins to debunk this myth of the gender gap. Looking at the
Democratic candidates, among those who voted in primaries, more women than

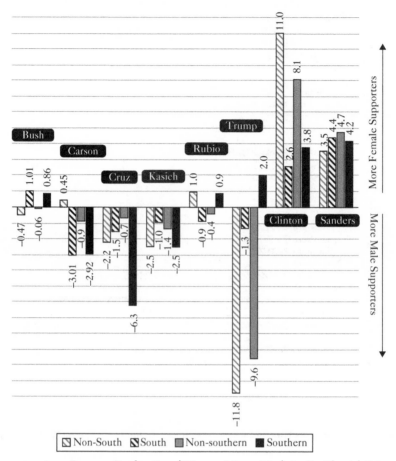

FIGURE 6.5B Percent Gender Gap (Women Minus Men) in Presidential Primary Supporters by Candidate, Among Whites, 2016

Data are from the 2016 Blair Center Poll.

men voted for Sanders and Clinton in every subgroup. However, the size of the gender gaps varies dramatically—but only for Clinton. Outside of the South and among non-southern whites, the gender gaps are significant at 11 and 8.1 points respectively, but for whites who live in the South or consider themselves southern, the gender gaps in support for Clinton fall to an insignificant 2.6 and 3.8 percent, respectively.

In the general election, white support heavily favored Donald Trump, as shown in Figure 6.6A, but, again, regional distinctiveness is dramatic and significant. Ten percent more whites who live in the South reported voting for Trump, but when the electorate is disaggregated by those who identify as southern and those who do not, that gap widens to 24.1 percent among whites.

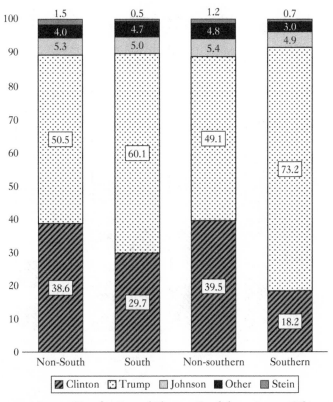

FIGURE 6.6A Percent Vote for General Election Candidates, Among Whites, 2016
Data are from the 2016 Blair Center Poll.

The gender breakdown in Figure 6.6B is important too. More women voted for Clinton than men, and more men voted for Trump than women in every group. However, only 21.9 percent of southern white women report voting for Clinton, which is significantly more than the 14 percent of southern white men who did so. Yet that 21.9 percent of southern white women who voted for Clinton is lower than the percentage of men who supported Clinton both inside and outside of the geographic South, as well as among non-southern whites. Southern white men, followed closely by southern white women, drove support for Trump at the highest rates.

Those individual gender gaps within each candidate's body of support are highlighted in Figure 6.6C, showing how strikingly different the gender dynamics are among southern and non-southern whites voters. The gender gap in support for Clinton, for example, is cut roughly in half by region and regional identity. Moreover, the negative gender gaps in support for Trump are three to

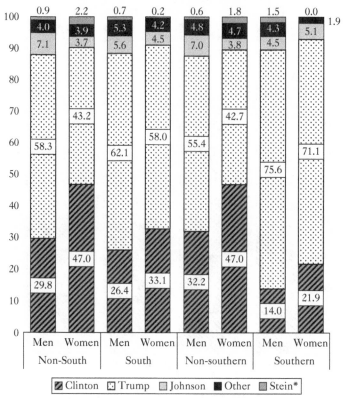

FIGURE 6.6B Percent Vote for General Election Presidential Candidates, Among Whites, by Gender, 2016

Data are from the 2016 Blair Center Poll.

four times larger outside of the South and among non-southerners, meaning that white women who live in the South or who claim a southern identity supported Trump at rates much closer to their male counterparts than white women who do not live in the South or do not claim a southern identity. Even among the small percentage of respondents who voted for Jill Stein, such gaps are relevant. More men supported her than women, but only in the South or among white southerners. Outside of the South and among non-southern whites, more of her support came from women.

Beyond just the gender of these voters, their Modern Sexism scores matter as well. In Figure 6.6D, only the percent support for Trump and Clinton is presented, alongside the mean Modern Sexism score for each group of voters. Among non-southern white men who voted for Trump (at a rate of 55.4 percent),

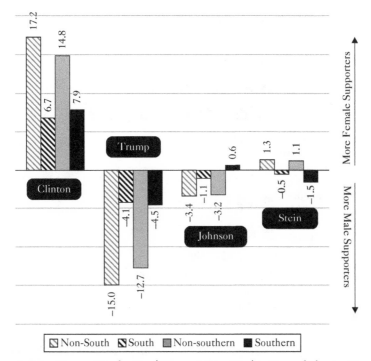

FIGURE 6.6C Percent Gender Gap (Women Minus Men) in General Election Voters by Candidate, Among Whites, 2016
Data are from the 2016 Blair Center Poll.

for example, the mean Modern Sexism score was 16.5, only 0.5 points higher than southern white women who voted for Trump, though they did so at the much higher rate of 71.1 percent. Southern white men who voted for Trump, did so at the highest rate (75.6 percent) and had the highest mean Modern Sexism score (17.3). Non-southern white women are the only group in which the majority did not report voting for Trump. Of the 42.7 percent who did, however, their average Modern Sexism score was 15.8, above the midpoint of the scale. The pattern is reversed among Clinton supporters. Non-southern white women voted for her at a rate of 47 percent and had a mean Modern Sexism score of 10.1, compared to southern white women, of whom only 21.9 percent voted for her. Among those who did, their mean Modern Sexism score was just as low, at 10.2. The resentment and distrust of working women and feminists clearly affected her candidacy and her success among white voters. Modern Sexism is significant for every group, with higher scores making white Americans more likely to vote for Trump and lower scores making them more likely to vote for Clinton. When looking only at the two major party candidates, perhaps what is most startling is the comparison

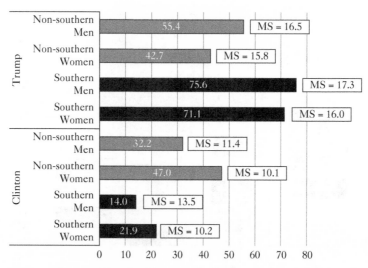

FIGURE 6.6D Percent Vote for Trump and Clinton, Among Whites, with Mean Modern Sexism Scores for Those Voters, 2016

Data are from the 2016 Blair Center Poll.

between the 71.1 percent of southern white women who voted for Trump and that 21.9 percent of southern white women who voted for Clinton. The difference in their average Modern Sexism scores is a startling 5.8 points.

The 2016 election cycle also presented the opportunity to examine another kind of gender gap—the candidate gender gap—which will become increasingly important as female presidential candidates become more common. The candidate gender gap, as measured here, is the percentage of votes for a male candidate (typically the only option and thus the norm) minus the percentage of votes for a female candidate, which in the 2016 general election would include both Clinton and Stein. In Figure 6.7, the candidate gender gap is presented on the vertical axis while the mean Modern Sexism score is presented across the horizontal axis.

Circles are the markers for male subgroups, while diamonds mark female subgroups by both geography and identity. At the bottom left of the figure, where the candidate gender gap is the smallest and the mean Modern Sexism score is the lowest, are non-southern white women and white women who do not live in the geographic South, and they are virtually indistinguishable. In the middle—with both a higher candidate gender gap (meaning more voted for a male candidate than a female candidate) and a higher Modern Sexism mean—are non-southern white men and white men who do not live in the geographic South. Slightly lower and toward the left of them are white women who live in the South, and slightly above them and to the right are white men who live in the South. White

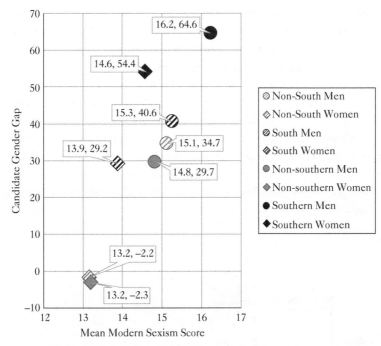

FIGURE 6.7 Mean Modern Sexism Score by Candidate Gender Gap (Percent Vote for Male Candidates Minus Percent Vote for Female Candidates), Among Whites, by Gender, 2016

Data are from the 2016 Blair Center Poll.

women living in the South have a slightly smaller candidate gender gap (though it is very close) and a lower mean Modern Sexism score than non-southern white men. White men who live in the South have a higher candidate gender gap and a higher mean Modern Sexism score than their non-southern and non-South male counterparts.

However, at the top of the figure are women and men who identify as southern. Southern white women report a 54.4-point candidate gender gap (compared to 13.2 points for non-southern white women), and their mean Modern Sexism score stands at 14.6, the highest of all female groups and only 0.2 points lower than non-southern white men. White men who identify as southern have the highest mean Modern Sexism score (16.2) and report the most extreme candidate gender gap, with 64.6 percent more votes cast for a male candidate than for a female candidate in the 2016 general election. That is more than double the gap for non-southern white men (29.7 points). It is the combination of southern identity and gender and Modern Sexism that seems to explode these significant gaps among white Americans.

Finally, following the election, there was a substantial amount of attention given to differences between the voting patterns of married and single women. Post-election, Hillary Clinton herself mentioned that, particularly in the Republican Party, there is still a "sort of ongoing pressure to vote the way that your husband, your boss, your son, whoever, believes you should."[73] Regardless of party identification, that is particularly true when it comes to region and regional identity. In that vein, if southern white sexism and patriarchy are alive and well, and the culture of southern white womanhood and anti-feminism have preserved allegiance to traditional gender roles, then marriage—an institution for many in which those traditional roles are embodied most personally—should have some relationship to vote choice. Figure 6.8 shows how influential both marriage and southern white identity are in this regard.

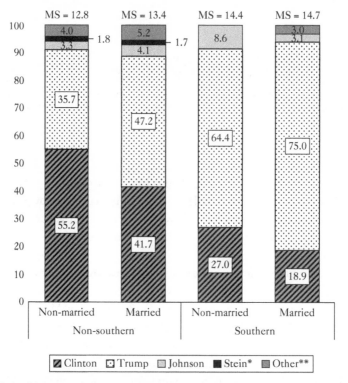

*Stein did not receive any votes from southern white women, non-married or married.
** No southern non-married white women voted "other."

FIGURE 6.8 Percent Vote for General Election Candidates, Among White Women, by Marital Status with Mean Modern Sexism Scores, 2016
Data are from the 2016 Blair Center Poll.

Among non-married, non-southern white women, who have a mean Modern Sexism score of 12.8, 55.2 percent voted for Hillary Clinton, the only subgroup to give her a majority. However, among non-married southern white women, that support dropped to 27 percent, and the mean Modern Sexism score is significantly higher at 14.4. Among non-southern, married women (mean Modern Sexism score for this group is 13.4), 41.7 percent reported voting for Clinton, but among southern married women (mean Modern Sexism for this group is significantly higher at 14.7), the vote for Clinton plummeted significantly to 18.9 percent with 75 percent voting for Trump. That is a 22.8 percent decline in support for Clinton compared to non-southern white women who are also married. Marriage as an institution tends to make white women more conservative in this sense. However, identifying as southern proves to be an "institution" all its own, and it compounds this anti-feminist distrust and partisanship with interest.

WHEN STUDIED IN hindsight, public opinion polls show that support for the ERA was actually very unstable over time and that the rise of the anti-ERA forces swung opinion dramatically against the amendment.[74] Southern white women were a big part of that. And that was a big part of the Long Southern Strategy. Looking back, it seems as though the anti-ERA, anti-feminists got lost somewhere beneath the larger umbrella that covered Americans who expressed "discontent over social and moral issues,"[75] including abortion and the *Engel v. Vitale* (1973) decision that removed prayer from school. Too much change and way too fast, their grassroots support seemed to suggest. However, their specific cause of anti-feminism was more than a voice of discontent. It reduced women's equality to a distasteful option, to which they were the moral, "family values" alternative. The irony is that the "massive resistance" to the ERA[76] is what politicized many of these women, and many of their institutions of faith permitted their participation and even encouraged their efforts to stand against their own equality. Their powerful uprising, as Marjorie Spruill shows, would lay the foundation for the Christian Coalition and Moral Majority that reasserted Republican dominance at the end of the twentieth century.[77]

For many white southerners, the advocacy of reproductive rights by female politicians and social leaders triggered resistance to women in power by resuscitating the Antebellum white man's "terror of losing jurisdiction over women's bodies."[78] Feminist campaigns for both abortion rights and gay rights catalyzed scripture-based opposition, while legislation for equal employment and pay for women, as well as efforts to elect female candidates to high government offices, threatened jurisdiction over women in general. "Family values" anti-feminism served as the legitimate counter-ideology deserving of equal seats at the table. Taking their cue from Schlafly, the GOP took the opportunity to celebrate traditional gender roles and demonize feminism and feminists as part of a Long Southern Strategy. Republican women and groups such as the Independent Women's Forum[79] work alongside numbers of Christian organizations and still attempt to court female voters on the basis of religion and family values whether packaged in subtle Elizabeth Dole–like ways or in the brash and bold style of the grizzly Sarah Palin.

Two years after her defeat as the vice-presidential running mate to John McCain in 2012, Palin actually announced that she was a feminist, but her feminist label reflected anti-feminist positions on a host of issues. So successful had the "other woman's movement" been that it was now eclipsing feminism and taking its name, at least for this GOP leader. In trying to describe Palin's outlook, Michelle Rodino-Colocino noted that "Palinite feminism justifies women's domination under capitalism and patriarchy by inverting a reality already inverted by the systems of domination—giving her advocates yet another false bargain.[80] Like Schlafly, she co-opts the language of equality (much as the Men's Rights Associations have done) and denies ever-present gender inequities (much as the colorblind rhetoric did for racial inequities). Though pseudo-feminist in nature, this bargain was struck with the help of southern white women who organized to defend the right for their pedestal to be upheld. For many of them, feminists, like Hillary Clinton, were enemies to their entire way of life.

Democrats continue to criticize the GOP for its "war on women,"[81] but among many white southerners—men and women—it is a war they support. There are white women who are feminists and there are white women who are not, and they are a different political faction altogether, just as Reagan's pollsters recognized.[82] These anti-feminist women have received little scholarly attention, but they are a major part of why feminist candidates struggle in the South, why political participation levels remain low among white women in the South, why the white South is less likely to vote for a female presidential candidate, why the ERA failed, why the gender gap is not universal, why the 2016 election turned out the way that it did, and why and how the Long Southern Strategy realigned the South with the Republican Party.

PART III

Politics and the Pulpit

White nationalism isn't simply an extremist political ideology. It is an alt-religious movement that provides its adherents with its own twisted version of what all religions supply to adherents: identity, a personal sense of who I am; community, a social sense of where I belong; and purpose, a spiritual sense of why my life matters.

—BRIAN D. MCLAREN[1]

With higher levels of attendance and activity,[2] there is no better place for politicking than in the Christian churches that blanket the American South. They are full of voters sitting at rapt attention each and every week—or for some denominations, like Southern Baptists, multiple times per week. Their membership is both spiritual and social. The institution, in many parts of the region, is the central community structure by which society is organized and cultural norms are upheld. Indeed, southern religion was not just a category. It was lived, often inherited, bound so deeply to family history and southern culture, that over time it ensured a mutual dependence. Advanced data analytics researchers actually attempted to explain the persistence of regional patterns of religious belief. They concluded that what accounts for the religiosity of a region is how deeply the residents connect their faith to their identity.[3] This is why political appeals to southern identity helped convert religious voters to the Republican Party.

Even though southern religiosity has received substantial scholarly attention, political scientists, cultural critics, and even religious historians have struggled over the last forty years to untangle various religious terms such as evangelicalism and fundamentalism in general,[4] let alone within the southern white population.[5] Since the 1980s, scholars have used the "Bebbington quadrilateral" and its four key tenets—biblicism (Bible as the ultimate authority), crucicentrism (the belief that Jesus died on the cross to atone for human sin), activism (missionary and social reform), and conversionism—to define evangelicalism,[6] though its popularity as a metric is fading. There are some members of the Southern Baptist Convention (SBC) who do not like being called evangelicals because they think it is too intertwined with the term fundamentalist, preferring the label "conservatives."[7] The term fundamentalist is equally complex. In general, fundamentalism has often been seen as a stricter sect under the larger umbrella of evangelical Protestantism.[8] Differences remain, however, between fundamentalists who are well-versed in doctrinal beliefs,[9] and fundamentalists who are less well-versed in formal theology—a kind of cultural fundamentalist. Southern church activity, in particular, observes Hill, has been less "formulative or theological" and more practical.[10] Other scholars measure high and low fundamentalism based on how many vices such as gambling are considered sins.[11] There are intrinsic and extrinsic southern fundamentalists, psychologists note, either for whom religion is utilitarian or reflects internal devoutness, respectively.[12] Even fundamentalist Southern Baptists, who have ruled the governing convention since 1979, still bicker over definitions of orthodoxy and heresy.[13]

There are countless fractures and contradictions and points of overlap. On the one hand, "primitive Baptists" in the nineteenth century not only believed in predestination, but also rejected any kind of clerical elite. Rather they were "an obstinate resistance movement among the poor whites against the condescending leadership of their betters."[14] On the other hand, dispensational premillennialists[15] were primarily concerned with end times. The southern version of fundamentalism, contends historian Samuel Hill, "carefully sifts the biblical material and systemizes it into a series of truths around the central commission to save souls,"[16] tying it to evangelicalism in a common fight. And there are neo-evangelists[17] who were fundamentalists who preferred to re-engage with world affairs in the hopes of converting Americans. There is also, of course, variation in the theological climate of individual churches, which has been shown to have an impact on the political outlooks of the members,[18] all of which makes analysis of the Bible Belt challenging.

However, "the southern way of religion" seemed to blur the lines between these labels. In turn, the evangelical movement "crossed denominational lines without erasing them."[19] And the "evangelical" label—and with it the need to broadcast faith and multiply believers and create purified, moral communities[20]—became a more formative identity marker than denomination. Evangelicals are evangelicals because to them the label affirms a set of cultural and political associations and forms of belonging in various "imagined" communities that they find desirable to affirm. Enter fundamentalism, which now does not function solely as a set of theological beliefs, but rather as an inflexible attitude,[21] so much so that for many it "serves as a badge of identity."[22]

Perhaps they are best understood as lifestyle brands, worn to signal status or membership—who they are and with whom they belong. That is why evangelicalism and fundamentalism have been easy to monetize in America[23] and why they create social bubbles. It is also why they were so easy to politicize, particularly in the South; southernness and partisanship are lifestyle brands too.

That religious fortress of the Bible Belt took generations to build, with evangelical tent revivals laying the cornerstone. Early settlers, many in rural isolation, desired a direct spiritual experience and craved community. The Protestant and, specifically, Baptist belief in a personal relationship with God, and the evangelical focus on the spiritual rewards in the afterlife, offered them both. Nevertheless, such wants, and the distinct religious prescription that fed them, were not without emotional side effects. The desire for certainty that accompanied war and lost causes and social upheaval turned the sacred into a safeguard of white southern identity. Religious philosopher Peter Berger contends that all religion provides "an illusion of certainty," warning that it "can even function as the supreme fiction that sanctifies all other fictions,"[24] and so the church became the protector, both inside and outside of the sanctuary, of the racial and gender hierarchies without which the southern white way of life would collapse.

Historically, many southern white churches have not been places of comfort. In fact, as Ernest Kurtz observes in his essay "The Tragedy of Southern Religion," "through all these—slavery, defeat, poverty, and more—the southern white Christian churches have remained singularly blind to the nature and meaning of tragedy and thus also to the significance of suffering."[25] Fear, defensiveness, distrust, and conformity have too often been their currency. Conformity, specifically, necessitated a strict moral code, while evangelicalism required proselytizing and conversion. Together they established a sacred canopy in the region, whereby homogeneity and the sheer volume of believers shields them from pluralism, diversity, or competing ideas. Therefore, when change does come, it is often met with shock, resistance, and a reactionary backlash. For example, when modernism, science, and Darwinism threatened Victorian morals, gender norms, and white supremacy, fundamentalism surged. The inerrancy of the Bible pushed evangelical protestants toward absolutism, a tendency all too familiar in the black and white world of the patriarchal South. The Civil Rights Movement, Second-Wave Feminism, and gay rights would incite the same defiance decades later. It is this recipe of Protestant, evangelical, fundamentalist moralism, and "The Not-So-New Southern Religion" (chapter 7) it creates that made white southerners such an easy mark in the Long Southern Strategy.

Unlike evangelicalism's focus on otherworldly affairs, fundamentalism has been politicized often and with great ease[26]—from the southern Protestant antipathy toward Al Smith's 1928 candidacy[27] as the first Roman Catholic contender, all the way to the rise of the Christian Right and the Moral Majority of the late twentieth century. However, for most of their history, religious fundamentalists remained underground. Like evangelicals, which many of them were, fundamentalists tended to believe that "if the world is doomed and believers are assured of escape in the Rapture, political action seems hardly necessary."[28] Yet, buried in the conversion intent of evangelicalism is the requirement to "take up the sword of the Lord, especially when the world seems ready." Thus, when faced with the social changes of the 1970s, believers came to see "that 'lifestyle' concerns were important political issues."[29] More so than any other denomination, Southern Baptists led the way. Southern Baptist churches have been characterized as individualistic[30] and in favor of decentralization,[31] but under the umbrella of SBC, they mirror a political party, in and of themselves. However, their impact on politics would have been less intense were it not for the fundamentalist takeover of the SBC in the late 1970s and 1980s. Feeling alienated by moderates and frustrated by the non-engagement of many SBC pastors in opposition to women's rights, gay rights, and civil rights in general, biblical literalists successfully orchestrated and executed a plan to seize power of the SBC from the top down.

When they won, these champions of "Southern White Fundamentalism" (chapter 8) did not reach across the aisle to moderates; they exiled them. They dissolved the SBC lobbying organization, which had primarily aimed to protect freedom of religious practice, and replaced it with a team who pushed for the establishment of Christian values in every pocket of the government. The shift is significant because, as Christopher Ellison and Marc Musick argue in their study of southern intolerance, fundamentalism "typifies a more general preoccupation with issues of authority and obedience." This fixation makes fundamentalists not only see "institutional authority figures as inherently legitimate," but also renders conformity as "intrinsically virtuous" and "social and ideological diversity as warranting suspicion and even hostility."[32] So when the SBC leadership marched head first into the partisan culture wars, believing "they are called to permeate and help mold the institutions of their society in an effort to stem the tide of cultural decay,"[33] the congregation went with them. The literalists delved into presidential politics immediately when Adrian Rogers, the SBC president elected at the fundamentalist coup, came out publicly for Ronald Reagan, claiming that "God was real to the candidate, who had had a personal experience when he invited Christ into his life."[34]

That being said, the SBC did not stumble into politics; fundamentalists were guided by a Long Southern Strategy to secure the region for the GOP. For example, Nixon's staff, as Kevin Kruse notes, brought conservative and fundamentalist clergy into the White House, including, at the suggestion of Billy Graham, inviting Carl Bates, SBC president in 1971, to deliver a sermon in the East Room.[35] Having been offered a seat at the table of power, the SBC, despite the hesitation of even some Republican leaders, made church and state one and the same, and an extreme version at that. Policy positions on abortion and gay marriage, among others, grew increasingly absolute. New SBC codes were adopted that re-emphasized the submissive role of women in a Christian marriage. Such appeals to traditional gender roles were anything but new for white southerners. After all, as Ted Ownby notes, the white southern patriarchy was built on "hot-blooded" violence and power, and yet the spreading sacred religious canopy sought to curb "the sinfulness of male culture."[36]

In many ways, politics offered an outlet for that hot-blooded ambition and a path of influence. Believers needed to act quickly too, as they were under attack from a host of enemies. "We have lost our nation," proclaimed W. A. Crisswell, former SBC president, in his speech at the 1988 convention, "to the liberals, humanists, and atheists, and infidels."[37] Thus, evangelical fundamentalism came to characterize not just southern religious identity—and not just any fundamentalism, but a decidedly political fundamentalism. "The political solidarity of the South," wrote Dwight Dorough in *The Bible Belt Mystique*, "was conceived in an atmosphere of religious tension."[38] Moreover, to insulate their members from such corruption, fundamentalists created an entire subculture complete with Christian films, books, radio stations, television programs, and news. In turn, the all-consuming and isolating nature of southern fundamentalist and evangelical culture—even in seemingly secular activities—allowed for absolutist stances to proliferate.

The SBC, however, was not alone. In countless other religious organizations both inside the South and beyond its borders, fundamentalist Christian ministers and congregants entered the political arena. From Jerry Falwell's Moral Majority to the broader Christian Right, all pushed for a new social conservatism. The GOP, in turn, advocated for a hands-off government approach to economic policies and entitlements, while insisting on government oversight and regulation of the "family values" issues of marriage and reproduction. By doing so, they dissolved denominational differences, overcame direct third-party challenges from Christian Right leaders, and even softened the "born-again" litmus test for candidates. Softening that litmus test of Christian authenticity is not an easy thing to do, particularly when the purists, sometimes called high-commitment fundamentalists or evangelicals, were the first to shift to the GOP.[39] They did so at a steeper rate if they were regular church attenders[40] and if they lived in the South.[41] More recently, the hardcore believers have been called creedal Christians, and now they are challenged in the political arena by the mass of what is being called cultural Christians. These cultural Christians were shaped from commodity Christianity and the social status provided by the southern religious identity label. Some have argued that the distinction became clear in the Republican primary contests of 2016, when creedal Christians[42] sought a candidate such as Ted Cruz with an authentic Christian pedigree and a reputation as a moral crusader.[43] On the other hand, cultural Christians (or moderately active church members who have been shown to be less tolerant)[44] seemed more willing to overlook the absence of a candidate's authentic record of re-ligious belief if the candidate's policy stances support conservative policies. Trump was able to pass as a Christian in the first southern primary in South Carolina[45] because Christianity is not just a belief system. It is a culture that the GOP alliance with the Christian Right helped to create. According to historian Molly Worthen, evangelicals also "craved an intellectual authority that would quiet disagreement and dictate a plan for fixing everything that seemed broken with the world."[46] For many, and to the chagrin of others, politics served that function, and the party of "family values" provided a partisan home for all of them.

To that end, the religiosity of the contemporary GOP is not solely a reflection of the rising saliency of moral issues; that is "The Myth of Social Conservatism" (chapter 9). Rather, the Christian Right, of which southern whites were and are the primary base, expanded its vision beyond such debates into policy battles over the environment, the economy, and immigration, to name a few. There is a new militancy[47] to the vision, whereby every issue becomes part of the evangelical cos-mology in a spirit of Christian nationalism that has long been part of the southern white mind.[48] As far back as the Civil War, many white southerners believed that "through defeat God was readying them for future victory."[49] Southern religion is rooted in the image of a phoenix rising from the ashes that would save the nation.[50] That future includes a global fight against terrorism and Islam, and it requires a hawkishness that is now often wrapped in scripture. So complete is the southern white fundamentalist Republican merger that the good and evil dichotomy so historically critical to southern white culture now underscores a partisan foreign policy, laced with racism and misogyny, the consequence of a Long Southern Strategy to convert the hearts, minds, souls, and voters of the Bible Belt.

7

The Not-So-New Southern Religion

Its consciousness of its own pains and sorrows, of the gallantry
and chivalry of its sons, of its mistakes and sufferings, of its
superiority to the worst calamities which came to it, of its
ability to build a civilization out of ashes, makes the present
South worth far more both to the nation and to itself. Having
had such experiences, it has become not merely a loyal part of
the nation, but something more. That something more is the
wisdom and the strength and a certain depth of soul which
the South has acquired through the bitterness of trials which
purged it of dross and have healed without hate. We do well
to treasure the lessons of the history of our section. It is to con-
serve the spiritual dynamic with which God has equipped us
for building in our own section a great Christian civilization
and aiding to the same end in the other sections of our beloved
country.

—VICTOR IRVINE MASTERS[1]

THOUGH RARELY REMEMBERED as one of the more religious American presidents, Richard Nixon performed religion—particularly southern religion—better than most. He built a friendship and partnership with Billy Graham, the South's most famous preacher, before and throughout his presidency, a move that must be considered part of the GOP's Long Southern Strategy. Playing the race card may have been most prominent in Nixon's campaign efforts in the region, but his appearance alongside Graham, particularly at the height of campus unrest during the Vietnam War, endeared him to southern white voters as well. Graham's traveling ministry, in the great tradition of southern evangelical revivals, attracted mass audiences. In May 1970, in the wake of the shootings at Kent State, Nixon wanted to make a campus visit—any campus visit—that would provide positive optics.[2] Speaking at Graham's service at the University of Tennessee, at that time the largest public university in the South, offered him a perfect opportunity. The event drew a crowd of 100,000,[3] including some protestors carrying signs marked

"Thou Shall Not Kill,"[4] as well as substantial regional and national publicity in part because it was held in the football stadium, which had never hosted any event other than a game.[5] Though Graham was not in the habit of having politicians speak at his services, Nixon did just that. He immediately expressed relief that there were "more on one side than the other"[6] with respect to protestors versus supporters, but he could have just as easily been referencing believers versus non-believers. Nixon went on to describe the United States as a "nation under God."[7] Both the "us vs. them" rhetoric and the nationalistic visual, in which church and state were simultaneously promoted, reflected the unique brand of southern religiosity, one that Graham hoped to politicize in an effort to grow his movement. To that effort, Graham built a close relationship with Nixon. He not only called the president with policy tips,[8] but he also met personally with George Wallace in 1972[9] and asked him to drop out of the presidential race and support Nixon. Graham understood the power of the church in southern culture, and Nixon recognized the power of Graham's "evangelical mediation of race and politics"[10] and the "reassurances of the old South"[11] that the preacher provided.

What Graham knew and what is still true in many parts of the South is that the church remains the central institution defining, organizing, and politicizing its surrounding community. Over time, that has created a moral bubble of sorts. This "sacred canopy" drapes over the region, where there is a common cosmology—even a language—that is intractable from southern white identity. In 1976, for example, when journalists and pundits greeted Democratic presidential nominee Jimmy Carter's self-identification as a "born-again Christian" with bewilderment, southern audiences understood not only the terminology, but also the lifestyle and view of the world to which Carter ascribed and belonged.[12] Because underneath Carter's theological assertion lay a shared religious culture rooted in the evangelical fervor that swept through the Antebellum South and became increasingly potent—even exported to other parts of the country or what John Shelton Reed observed as "the Southernization of American religion"[13]—in the modern era. In that vein, any contemporary assessment of the South and its relationship to national politics requires unearthing the causes and conditions that initiated and maintained such distinct religiosity. Historian Ted Ownby pinpointed the nature of southern religious distinctiveness by cautioning readers to "bear in mind that having a religious identity seemed to be more of a cultural requirement in the South than in the rest of the country."[14] So looming is the shadow of the southern steeple, Reed insisted, that "even those Southerners who don't go to church at least know which one they're not going to."[15] In general, as a block, white southerners were more evangelical, protestant, fundamentalist, and moralist than the rest of the country, all of which has had—and still has—significant political ramifications.

Despite the fact that religion has proved so critical to southern white identity, wide scholarly attention took root primarily in the post-Carter era, as if the national spotlight on the native Georgian illuminated that which hid in plain sight. Tracing the evangelical and fundamentalist fervor of white southerners to its source, Samuel Hill, Kenneth Bailey, John Boles, and Donald Matthews,[16] among others, recovered a distinct religious history for the region. With only 20 percent of whites who lived in the South claiming a church membership in the years before the Civil War, the region remained virtually untouched by America's First Great Awakening. Rather, a civil religion of sorts guided society and provided some sort of comfort or meaning for life.[17] During and after the Civil War, the Lost Cause narrative of southern Confederate nationalism became this civil religion's creed, a public statement of faith based on the ideology of white supremacy and a defense of slavery[18] that was even built into the liturgy of southern church services.[19] Though evangelicalism (a label that some Southern Baptist leaders called a "Yankee" word),[20] with its insistence on conversion, did eventually capture white southern audiences, first in the 1830s and then more fervently in the 1920s, it did not do so in the traditional reformist package. Rather, evangelicals won over white southerners by championing biblical principles regarding the submissive role of women in the family[21] and by the literalism of the Genesis story of creation. Hence, an appeal to patriarchy and heteronormative behavior[22] and an insistence on biblical literalism were well in place as the anchors holding down the sacred canopy that covers so much of the region even now.

These anchors were needed because the white southern way of life was constantly threatened, whether by surrender, by Reconstruction, by modernization, or by the civil rights movements, broadly defined. As twelve southern writers contended in the introduction to their 1930 Agrarian manifesto, *I'll Take My Stand*, religion in the South provided a sense of control in an inscrutable world.[23] At times when criticism of the region proved prolific—both after catastrophic defeat[24] and during the media scrutiny of the twentieth century[25]—evangelical religion, particularly with the added layer of fundamentalism, turned, as Nancy Ammerman has noted, "powerlessness into power." Faith was armor and defense. That notion that "although human power is worthless in the Fundamentalist economy, God's power can accomplish anything"[26] mollified many white southerners despite their circumstances. In that sense, southern white religiosity matured alongside a sectional consciousness[27] with each influencing the other. Engulfed into a broadened southern white identity construct, unifying lower- and middle-class southern whites, evangelical Protestantism and fundamentalism functioned just as Clifford Geertz theorized—as a cultural system.[28]

Thus, when Senator Barry Goldwater and his Long Southern Strategy successors went hunting for disaffected white southern voters, they bagged a flock of evangelicals whether they originally intended to or not. Such a cultural system translated easily into a political cultural system, which is why Billy Graham has been called the "most politically sophisticated" preacher "since Williams Jennings Bryan."[29] He hitched his wagon to Nixon and let Nixon summon the not-so-new southern religion from the stump, pulling more Democrats steadily his way.[30] And it is why, nearly one-half century later, GOP candidate, now-president, Donald Trump brought the evangelical minister son of Billy Graham, Franklin Graham, to the campaign stump. This time, however, the rally belonged not to the preacher, but to the politician. Trump did not need to borrow Graham's stage; he had his own. To that stage southern fundamentalist leaders came with their endorsements, having traveled down a well-worn path carved out by the Long Southern Strategy.

NOTED HISTORIAN JOHN B. Boles opened his article "The Southern Way of Religion" by describing "the cultural primacy of religion" in which church—specifically evangelical Protestantism—served as the constant backdrop to his southern upbringing. Prayer remained a fixture at school, at football games, at Rotary Club meetings, at rodeos, and at every gathering in between these events. Official church services took up most of the day on Sunday and Wednesday evenings as well, and weeklong traveling revivals came through regularly. "Every person I was taught to respect," Boles observed, "was a church member."[31] The constant religious activity throughout the South shapes both the identity of those who call themselves southerners and the impression that identity makes on the rest of the country. There are geographic pockets in the region that seemingly function with little or no separation between church and state, remaining somehow beyond, for example, the reach of the Supreme Court's ban on prayer in public schools. The theology claimed by southern denominations may not be that different from denominations nationwide, but the daily fervor and saturation in the region renders it a world all its own.

Southern historian Charles Reagan Wilson attributes southern religious distinctiveness to four characteristics, none of which is unique in and of itself, and none of which developed at the same time as another. However, when they are all finally present en masse, they set apart "the southern way of religion." Moralist, fundamentalist, evangelical Protestantism[32] as a combination classifies this southern kingdom within the American church, and the details of its evolution reveal why it was particularly susceptible to politicization as part of the GOP's Long Southern Strategy. Compared to the rest of the country, the vast majority of counties in the states of the former Confederacy have 25–49.9 percent of their population reporting a church membership, with some counties reporting even higher numbers.[33] The overwhelming majority of those church members were and are southern Protestants, and these southern Protestants are more dogmatic than their counterparts outside of the region.[34] Thus, it is not only the distinct history of southern white religiosity, nor the sheer volume of southern white believers, but also the intensity of their beliefs that laid the groundwork for a partisan political movement.

The history of southern religious distinctiveness offers a prescription of sorts for harnessing its political power. That distinctiveness stretches back to colonial settlement when the new world of the Americas heightened the Protestant and Catholic rivalry plaguing European powers.[35] English Protestant reformers on their "errand into the wilderness" settled alongside Anglicans in Virginia and Spanish and French Catholics along the coast. However, the Great Awakening of the early eighteenth century, which tore through the colonies with the fire-and-brimstone rhetoric of such leaders as George Whitefield, Gilbert Tennant, and Jonathan Edwards, failed to seep fully into southern soil.[36] The errand in the South was more individualistic in nature. The homestead proved more sacred than church buildings (even some religious rituals took place in the home),[37] and what high-church presence did exist waned in the aftermath of the American Revolution. As settlers headed westward into a rural, frontier South, they sought a "powerful emotional faith," and "Methodists, Baptists, and Presbyterians soon emerged as dominant denominations among people whose religious needs had been earlier unmet."[38] That need for an emotional faith has been attributed to the violence, loneliness, and the "hard, bitter, monotonous life" of the frontier and the "socially and emotionally starved pioneers"[39] that toiled in seclusion.

Not only did the strain of rural life make the South receptive to more emotive religions, the sparse population made regular church and worship services virtually impossible. Thus, when the tent revivals that would become a staple of southern culture were pitched, crowds of all denominations and no denominations gathered to the tune of tens of thousands. This evangelical nature of these revivals made conversion their first priority. Reports of similarly massive crowds at tent revivals throughout the South in the summer of 1801 described "inexplainable [*sic*] conversions and miraculous transformations of entire communities." At McCready's Gasper River Presbyterian Church in North Carolina, "listeners were literally and figuratively struck down by feelings of sinfulness and forgiveness and rose up shouting and singing with joy, certain they had undergone a genuine conversion."[40] This type of experiential Christianity spread like wildfire throughout what is sometimes called the "South's Great Awakening,"[41] making it a social touchstone in a region that was growing increasingly culturally isolated. The awakening was swift. Southern Baptists, in particular, seized on this conversion and expansion aspect of evangelicalism, growing at a rate seven times faster than northern Baptists.[42] Methodist membership almost doubled in a six-year period from 1801 to 1807.[43]

Such evangelical, religious transformations were successful not only because conversion was the primary goal, but also because of the core belief in "direct access to God's grace." Such access was necessary in the rural South, but it also stressed an individualism that was not without political side effects. For Baptists, specifically, individualism underscores the bedrock principle of "soul competency."[44] The idea is that each individual soul is competent to make its own choices without mediation—a sharp contrast to Catholicism, for example.[45] Spiritual independence, however, is accompanied by a sense of responsibility for one's own salvation that is hard, at times, to bear or to compartmentalize. White southerners, contends Ted Ownby, became "obsessed"[46] with personal righteousness, which, in some cases, morphed into an external vetting by some southern churches of the morality of their members.[47] Policing personal behavior with an unyielding code of good and evil, coupled with the mission to proselytize and convert, became integral parts of the "southern way of religion."

The 2007 Baylor Religion Survey finds the same strictness and moral demands still dwelling in the southern pews. Table 7.1 compares the regions, revealing that a statistically significantly greater percentage of white residents

Table 7.1 Percent Reporting Their Current Place of Worship "Strongly Discourages" or "Forbids" the Following Activities, Among Whites, 2007

	Non-South		South	
	Strongly Discourages	Forbids	Strongly Discourages	Forbids
Pornography	27.9	66.6	22.6	74.2
Gambling	40.7	17.1	45.1	32.9
Wearing Revealing Clothing	46.5	11.6	53.5	13.3
Premarital Sex	41.6	39.1	43.9	44.3
Living Together Before Marriage	38.6	34.4	40.7	39.1
Contraception	14.3	23.7	11.4	16.6
Displays of Wealth	26.7	3.1	30.1	6.3

Data are from the 2007 Baylor Religion Survey available at https://www.baylor.edu/baylorreligionsurvey/.

in the South indicate that their current place of worship "forbids" or "strongly discourages" a range of activities. Virtually all residents in the South report that their church disapproves of pornography, with 74.2 percent forbidding it and another 22.6 percent strongly discouraging it, compared to 66.6 percent and 27.9 percent, respectively, of whites in the non-South. A similar pattern follows for church attitudes on premarital sex and living together before marriage, and in each case, a higher percentage of whites who live in the South described their churches as having this strict moral code of conduct. Only on the issue of using contraception do fewer respondents who live in the South, as compared to those who do not, describe their churches as actively opposing the practice. Moreover, only about one-third of respondents report that their church takes a stand against displays of wealth, with even fewer doing so in the non-South than in the South.

The largest gap between how whites in the South and whites living outside of the South describe the moral positions of their places of worship comes on the issue of gambling. There is a smaller percentage who indicate that their place of worship fully prohibits gambling (32.9 percent), yet when combined with those who say their religious institution strongly discourages it (45.1 percent), the total reaches 80 percent. That total is 20 points higher than what is reported by non-South whites. This gap and the overall pattern reflects a particular strain of moral obedience and mission that runs deep in the states below the Mason-Dixon line, where religion functions as a social and emotional touchstone.

WHEN CHURCH MEMBERSHIP or leadership or even just social standing in the community becomes conditional based on personal morality, then a culture of exclusivity—of "us vs. them"—proliferates. On one hand, that exclusivity re-enforces the certainty that many evangelicals have of their own value, much in the same way that white privilege perpetuates white value. They "see themselves," opines John Stratton Hawley, "as a holy remnant of an idealized past and as the vanguard of a future yet to be revealed."[48] As the vanguard of the future, southern evangelicalism often encourages an apocalyptic cosmology laid out in biblical prophecy in which believers will be victorious.[49] On the other hand, personal righteousness and moral vetting also foster a distrust of outsiders—and this is on top of the distrust that many Protestant denominations had toward the existence of a divine middle man through whom one must go to reach God so common in high church denominations. This distrust of outsiders, institutions, and expertise are all rational side effects of this "southern way of religion," but they bleed into "secular" cosmologies too. As late as 2006, the South as a region has been shown to be statistically, significantly less trusting overall than the rest of the country.[50] This tendency toward distrust would actually play an important role in the GOP efforts to win over southern evangelicals, specifically during then vice president

George H. W. Bush's 1988 campaign, in which evangelical Pat Robertson entered the race. Bush hired Doug Wead who wrote "The Red Memo," a strategy for subtly wooing evangelical voters which included a list of two hundred influential evangelical leaders (Billy Graham held the top spot) to "target." Wead insisted that since Bush was an outsider, leaders like Jerry Falwell would need to be "privately reassured from time to time of the Vice President's personal friendship."[51]

The difficulty of managing this notion of distrust as well as the responsibility of "soul competency" was mitigated by the sense of certainty that accompanied evangelical morality and righteousness. Specifically, pre-millennialist theology[52] provided a sense of certainty in an uncertain world—not to mention a significant role and result for these chosen believers. And when the fear and the chaos of the outside world seemed particularly acute, comfort came from belief in a God who "knows whom they should marry, which jobs they should take, and how they should make each decision; God knows what will happen it the world tomorrow and when everything will come to an end."[53] Since it heightened belief, southern homilies often encouraged such fear and anxiety about the world beyond the evangelical community. "In many instances," notes John Boles in his history of southern revivals, "fear was used to shake congregations away from indifference."[54] Thus, for many southern evangelicals grasping for that sense of certainty, the "God of Thunder," as southern writer John Crowe Ransom described, must be obeyed.[55]

The rise and spread of fundamentalism lifted the burden of evangelical belief by confirming the inerrancy of biblical prophecy, among other absolutes. Surrendering all control to this evangelical vision of God, after all, requires constant discipline. The narrative that encourages such discipline—just like the narrative of evangelical exclusivity—centers on believers being right and therefore set apart from non-believers. Such certainty mitigates the desire to cooperate with other institutions; if "all others are wrong, whatever they may claim about themselves; they are ultimately deceptive and evil, doomed to divine condemnation." In such an extreme cosmology, "compromise," continues Sam Hill, "is thus a vice, not a virtue in the moral universe of a fundamentalist," particularly if fundamentalism arrived in the South at a time of extreme cultural angst.

To some degree, fundamentalism also brought a political edge to evangelical Protestantism. It actually arrived, in many ways, from the North, as ministers such as Robert McQuilkin and Lewis Chafer traveled across the region, arguing against societal changes and liberalizing theologies.[56] Consumerism[57] and progressivism, challenges to Victorian gender roles, and higher textual criticism of the Bible, among other issues, triggered cultural anxiety that was both religious and secular. The key beliefs of the modern fundamentalist movement, as declared at the Niagara Bible Conference in 1895, included belief in "(1) the authority and inerrancy of Scripture; (2) the Virgin Birth and deity of Christ; (3) Christ's substitutionary atonement; (4) Christ's physical resurrection; and (5) the Second Coming and his earthly, millennial reign."[58] Some southerners wrote for *The Fundamentals: A Testimony to the Truth*, the doctrinal creed published in twelve volumes between 1910 and 1915.[59] However, others such as J. Frank Norris resisted joining the northern World Christian Fundamentalists Association. Rather, Norris advocated for decentralization, encouraging clergy to focus on their local churches.[60]

Keeping the fight local, however, would be increasingly hard to do. Three million copies[61] of *The Fundamentals* reached ministers and congregants. This penchant for localism was quickly abandoned, most notably, when parents perceived that their college-aged children had begun to question the Genesis story of creation because of their exposure to the teaching of evolution. In response, a widespread anti-evolution movement—which foreshadowed future grassroots, religious, political movements yet to come—became the defining issue catalyzing biblical literalism among southern Protestant evangelicals. Even seemingly moderate communities, such as Dayton, Tennessee (there were more members of the local Masonic Lodge in Dayton than regular churchgoers),[62] home of the infamous 1925 Scopes trial that pitted William Jennings Bryan's biblical literalism against Clarence Darrow's scientific experts, were gripped by the charge of fundamentalism.[63] The trial elicited negative media scrutiny of both white southerners and of biblical literalism. For example, Charles Francis Potter, a Unitarian Minister who was pro-evolution, criticized the biblical literalists for their insularity, for not being "aware of the existence of any other religions than their own."[64]

These fundamentalists in the South even got a nickname. Journalist and critic of the South H. L. Mencken first employed the moniker "Bible Belt" during the height of the conflict between evolutionary science and religious fundamentalism, using it to describe the large swath of southern biblical literalists. That term was the nicest thing Mencken ever wrote about them. In the wake of such intense public scrutiny, biblical literalism became, for many, a daily shield against criticism of a backward South.[65] Behind that shield, fundamentalists, rather than continue fighting for changes in the public arena, created their own network of private, Protestant, evangelical, southern schools and colleges—even graduate programs at institutes such as the Dallas Theological Seminary. Here believers were protected from "the penetration of liberalism,"[66] which, in many ways, helped to maintain this southern religious distinctiveness over time. Certainty, after all, has power, particularly when it goes unchallenged in safe and private spaces.

According to the 2007 Baylor Religion Survey, as well as a 2010 version of the survey that repeated some of the same questions, many of these aspects

of regional religious distinctiveness remain firmly intact as well. As seen in
Table 7.2A, the region has a significantly greater percentage of white residents
who have no doubt that God exists (74.7 percent in 2007 and 66.9 percent
in 2010), and who absolutely believe in the devil, heaven, hell, Armageddon,
angels, demons, and the rapture. In every category in 2007, the gap is around
20 points. In the 2010 survey—which, of course, has a completely different
group of respondents—the gaps are closer to 10 points on these questions,
but they are still statistically significant. In 2007, respondents were also asked
whether they believed that teaching one's morality to others and converting
others to one's faith were necessary to being a good person. Among white
residents in the South, 37.2 percent said that teaching their morals was very important, compared to 31.6 percent among whites living outside of the South.
On the notion of converting others, 20.9 percent of whites in South insisted
that was of highest importance, compared to only 8.7 percent of whites in the

**Table 7.2A Percent Agreement with the Following Statements Regarding
Religious Beliefs, Among Whites, 2007, 2010**

	2007		2010	
	Non-South	South	Non-South	South
Have no doubt that God exists	57.6	74.7	58.7	66.9
Absolutely believe in the devil	45.1	66.1	48.0	58.7
Absolutely believe in heaven	54.0	75.3	57.3	66.1
Absolutely believe in hell	44.3	65.4	46.6	56.1
Absolutely believe in Armageddon	22.3	41.8	23.6	39.8
Absolutely believe in angels	51.8	72.7	53.6	64.4
Absolutely believe in demons	36.3	58.3	40.4	51.6
Absolutely believe in the rapture	22.1	48.0	n/a	n/a
Strongly agree that evil comes from the devil	14	29.7	n/a	n/a
In order to be a good person it is very important to teach others your morals	31.6	37.2	n/a	n/a
In order to be a good person it is very important to convert others to your religious beliefs	8.7	20.9	n/a	n/a

Data are from the 2007 and 2010 Baylor Religion Surveys available at https://www.baylor.
edu/baylorreligionsurvey/.

non-South—and those percentages are among all people surveyed, even those who are not religious. That 20.9 percent, combined with another 23.3 percent who say converting others is somewhat important, shows just how much of an evangelical spirit still exists in the region as a whole.

This distinct and significant regional religiosity is also reflected in how many whites in the South report having had specific religious experiences, as shown in Table 7.2B. Roughly 30 percent of respondents in the South say they have witnessed a miraculous, physical healing, compared to 17.8 percent in the non-South. Over half (52.6 percent) of whites in the South claim that they have felt called by God to do something, a number that drops to 38.2 percent among whites living outside of the region. Significantly greater percentages of whites in the South compared to the non-South also report that they have received their own miraculous healing, have heard the voice of God speaking to them, have been protected by their guardian angel, or have spoken in tongues, than those surveyed who live outside of the region. Only on the question of whether they have ever felt at one with the universe, did a smaller number of whites in the South answer yes.

Perhaps most important, on the notion of religious conversion, 33.5 percent of all of those surveyed in the South indicate having personally experienced conversion, which is the same percentage reported in the 1940s, but in that case among all Americans.[67] Without recognizing this consistent religiosity in the white South and the need for the certainty that fundamentalist, evangelical belief fulfilled, a

Table 7.2B **Percent Reporting to Have Had the Following Religious Experiences, Among Whites, 2007**

	Non-South	South
Witnessed a miraculous, physical healing	17.8	30.4
Received a miraculous, physical healing	10.9	19.7
Spoke or prayed in tongues	5.3	9.2
Felt called by God to do something	38.2	52.6
Heard the voice of God speak to me	14.3	24.5
Was protected from harm by my guardian angel	50.6	57.5
Had a religious conversion experience	22.1	33.5
Felt at one with the universe	22.7	16.4

Data are from the 2007 Baylor Religion Survey available at https://www.baylor.edu/baylorreligionsurvey/.

major—and eventually politicized—component of southern distinctiveness gets lost.[68]

OVERALL, THE NOT-SO-NEW southern religiosity, much like southern white identity in general, satisfies this appetite for certainty, conformity, and even social status. However, the price of doing so is increased cultural defensiveness, anxiety, fear, and distrust—all of which are easily manipulated toward political ends. The desire for conformity, specifically, was perhaps more important in southern white society than in any other part of the country because it was central to maintaining both southern racial and gender hierarchies. To some degree, however, the Protestant faith in general rejected a notion of church hierarchy, so a different ranking was needed. Historian Eugene Genovese argues that southern religion enforced a divinely sanctioned[69] hierarchy of individuals based on their godliness and morality, and whiteness (Genovese concedes that "their viewpoint has often accompanied racism").[70] The southern white social code had, in fact, already been based on "God's providence in nature and human history,"[71] signaled by the divine ordination of white supremacy that "bonded planter and yeoman in a common world view."[72] The conformity that religion imposed on the region is as old as the region itself. Religious discipline created social solidarity that, in many ways, facilitated the survival of, for example, the Virginia colonists,[73] who actually built their church services to enforce this social order.[74] So constant has the pressure been that the impulse now is practically second nature, with many southern religious fundamentalists well into the twentieth century insisting that even civil disobedience (including protesting Jim Crow) was against God's will.[75]

Over time, this impulse to conform as part of the culture of southern religion creates a sacred canopy that covers many southern communities and shields them from diverse influences. Hill describes this block astutely: "We deem it legitimate to speak of a transdenominational 'southern church,' embracing what may be called 'popular southern Protestantism.' Whereas only the Southern Baptist Convention (SBC) stands as an institutional embodiment of it, its character permeates and constitutes the life of many others."[76] Thus, despite different labels, there exists a "remarkable homogeneity" among the white southern faithful led mostly by Baptists and Methodists[77] that is reinforced via the vehicle of evangelical conversion.[78] The more like-minded individuals in the community, the less likely competing ideas are able to penetrate this sacred canopy.

The term "sacred canopy," first coined by Peter Berger, refers to the "sacred cosmos" that is established by man-made religion,[79] which gives order to the universe and to which individuals and communities can grow desperately attached.[80] Conversion can strengthen the bubble, but attachment to it grows when it is challenged,[81] with believers doubling down on their commitment to southern,

Protestant, fundamentalist, evangelical morals. The earliest waves of southern evangelicals fostered a sense of urgency to convert both Anglicans and the unchurched when challenged by new settlers.[82] Southern clergymen expressed intense devotion, for example, to the Confederate cause, particularly when it seemed to be lost.[83] Jefferson Davis, president of the Confederacy, called for fasting in the middle of the Civil War, summoning some sort of spiritual rebel nationalism.[84] And when Stonewall Jackson died, some religious faithful contended that the South needed redemption from God if it were ever to be victorious.[85] Yet all of that doubt, in times so dire, gave rise to a religious reconstruction of sorts[86] in which the civil religion of the Lost Cause "publicly reaffirmed social solidarity" and condemned "Yankee heretics as anarchists and madmen."[87] Solidarity is, after all, often built by common enemies, and in this way, the southern white religiosity is not-so-new as well. Anti-Catholic attitudes in the 1960s proved more common in the South.[88] Even as late as the 1970s, urbanization and in-migration—not to mention Second-Wave Feminism—altered southern demographics. The accompanying diversity of religious practice[89] seemed only to strengthen the sacred canopy, solidifying and politicizing southern evangelical fundamentalism in the very moment in which other options finally became more viable.

Conversion may increase church membership and challenges to shared religious beliefs may strengthen members' attachment, but expanding the coverage of the sacred canopy beyond the church walls required building a separate, secular world entirely. Southern evangelicals and fundamentalists had already constructed a network of seminaries and religious colleges throughout the twentieth century in an effort to shield believers from the encroachment of modernism. Institutions like Williams Jennings Bryan College, for example, was founded in 1930, in Dayton, Tennessee, in the aftermath of that critical Scopes Trial and went on to house the Center for Origins Research, a database that promoted creationism and intelligent design in its various incarnations.[90] A private educational system soon gave way to fundamentalist publishing and broadcasting outlets, oftentimes led by Southern Baptists who were concerned with the secularization of American culture and frustrated with the moderation of their own SBC leadership.[91] Christian radio programming, for example, grew exponentially from the 1970s forward. From 1972 to 1997 specifically, the number of Christian radio stations grew from 399 to 1,648, accompanied by 257 Christian television stations.[92] Efforts to revive the Campus Crusade for Christ organizations also sparked in the late 1970s,[93] and the construction of Christian theme parks[94] and the publication of children's books acclimated young evangelicals and fundamentalists into a subculture all its own. The overwhelmingly popular *Left Behind* novels, written by major Christian Right leader and Southern Baptist Tim LaHaye and published in the 1990s, contained embedded and explicit references to the biblical book of Revelation and to "the coming Rapture, Tribulation, and a final battle between good and evil."[95] Fundamentalists, particularly in the South, turned their private faith into a shared and lived culture; they "contributed to a process," argues Douglas Abrams, "that diminished religion to a commodity for consumption or an experience to bring happiness."[96]

Christian popular culture quickly and readily became Christian popular political culture. Even the earliest of those radio stations and television programs—including Jerry Falwell's *Old Time Gospel Hour* and Pat Robertson's *700 Club*—bent political news to religious ears, making the rise of a Christian Right possible.[97] Now as media scholar Chip Berlet notes, these programs have led to or have become (like the still-running *700 Club*) "right wing alternative information networks."[98] The news is different. The analysis is different. Even statistics are different if they come from a Christian Right–based think tank. The National Empowerment Television network founded by Paul Weyrich (who also started the Heritage Foundation), provides a studio in Washington, DC, where "Republican members of congress and sympathetic talk show hosts can tape broadcasts for national distribution," and his Free Congress Foundation whose goal is to "mobilize conservative Christians" has also attempted to "develop a political philosophy" of "cultural conservatism."[99]

This separate subculture bonded believers while insulating them from nonbelievers, all of which propped up this sacred canopy. Well into the twenty-first century, these practices remain a distinct feature of the region, as captured in the 2007 and 2010 Baylor Religion Surveys. Table 7.3 shows the geographic gap between whites who live in the South and whites who live outside of the South on a series of shared religious activities. A significantly greater percentage of whites who live in the South, both in 2007 and 2010, engage in Bible studies or Sunday school and witness to their communities. Among whites who live in the South, around 36 percent read their Bible or other sacred books about weekly, if not more, compared to about 23 percent of whites in the non-South both in 2007 and in 2010. They are significantly more likely to tithe to their churches, to volunteer at their churches, and to volunteer in the community on behalf of their churches. Whites living in the South are also more likely to have most or all of their close friends attend their same church—a clear nod to a more cohesive flock in the region. The consistency of that religiosity is apparent in the high percentage (68.9 percent) of whites in the South who report attending church weekly as a child, and in the even higher number (80.9 percent) indicating that, as a young person, they had been somewhat or very religious.

Touching one's childhood, community service, finances, and friendships, religion in the South is, in many ways, an all-encompassing and often insulating

Table 7.3 **Percent Participation in Religious or Faith-Based Activities, Among Whites, 2007, 2010**

	2007		2010	
	Non-South	South	Non-South	South
Tithe (Yes)	32.7	43.2	n/a	n/a
Amount given (>$5000)	10.2	17.5	n/a	n/a
Friends at the same church (most or all)	16.6	22.0	n/a	n/a
Bible study of Sunday school (at least once in the last month)	30.5	50.0	26.3	36.5
Witnessed with friends (at least once in the last month)	44.5	55.4	31.4[*]	41.7[*]
Witnessed with strangers (at least once in the last month)	24.4	33.4		
Community Bible study (at least once in the last month)	5.6	12.7	12.6	21.2
Read the Bible or another sacred book (about weekly or more)	22.3	36.9	23.5	35.8
Pray (a few times per week or more)	58.4	70.2	55.8	69.0
Religious at age 12 (somewhat or very religious)	71.5	80.9	n/a	n/a
Church attendance at age 12 (about weekly or more)	57.0	68.9	n/a	n/a
Volunteer at church (one hour or more per month)	26.2	34.4	n/a	n/a
Volunteer in community on behalf of church (one hour of more per month)	23.2	30.0	n/a	n/a

[*] In 2010, the questions were combined in the survey (witnessed with friends or strangers).

Data are from the 2007 and 2010 Baylor Religion Surveys available at https://www.baylor.edu/baylorreligionsurvey/.

lifestyle. This insulation—as noted in the sacred canopy hypothesis, which Ted Jelen compares to Elisabeth Noelle-Neumann's concept of a "spiral of silence,"[100]— has a tangible impact on policy attitudes as well. For example, the proportion of conservative Protestants in a state has a direct effect on gender attitudes among whites, even after controlling for specific denominations, practices, and theological beliefs.[101] Writing in 1972, John Lee Eighmy surmised it this way: "Southern Baptist churches tend to reflect the values held by their surrounding culture rather than to prompt critical assessment of those values."[102] The "paucity of options"[103] created by the sacred canopy, in turn, makes the church the only game in town—which serves to reinforce the self-perpetuating sacred canopy. Religious dissent, just as it had been described in the Old South, functions not just as a theological dispute or questioning, but is part and partial to the "disruption of the community."[104] And disruption of the community—even for seemingly secular reasons, is cast as religious dissent. That dynamic made white southern identity—past and present—and all the baggage it carries, inseparable from "the way of Southern religion." To challenge any aspect of it is to challenge it all.

SUCH DOGMATIC OR fundamentalist belief, in general, has been statistically associated with "prejudice, authoritarianism," and "superstition,"[105] and in that sense religion often became entangled with the other key elements of southern identity, most notably whiteness. What remains is a collective religiosity inseparable from southern culture so commanding that that even Bible Belt Catholics functioned differently than did their fellow Catholics beyond the Mason-Dixon line.[106] This shared religious culture with its distinct worldview becomes, in effect, normative, even absorbed into southern white identity,[107] and self-protective. Defined against the behavior and beliefs of non-fundamentalists, these southerners not only objected to a host of non-religious issues related to modernity, but they were also easily swayed by partisan rhetoric. Moreover, they found strength in numbers, establishing the National Association of Evangelicals (NAE) in 1942. Via the NAE, "southern fundamentalists found a new media-savvy spokesperson" who eventually championed Christianity over communism during the Cold War and even "seized on race as another issue to circle conservative wagons."[108] A defensive posture was not solely aimed abroad. For many southern white believers, faith buttressed a "regional self-esteem"[109] in which southerners, under criticism in the secular world, praised themselves for being God-fearing, Bible-reading, warm-hearted people. That self-conception cuts across all of these factions and labels and would prove politically powerful.

In the South, the emotional need to trumpet religious superiority played harmoniously alongside the evangelical emphasis of conversion and fundamentalist absolutism, and it sprung from a "spiritual and psychological need to reaffirm southern identity" again and again.[110] Daniel Hummel argued that the post–War War II era was characterized by a revivalist nationalism, reflected by the relationships between such ministers as Billy Graham, Bill Bright (founder of Campus Crusade for Christ), and Falwell. From his anti–Equal Rights

Amendment (ERA) rallies or his "I Love America" bicentennial extravaganza to his endorsement of Gerald Ford, Falwell "hit on the same evangelical themes that had animated revivalism since World War II: moral decline, coming judgment, the unlimited potential of redemption for both the individual and the nation."[111] GOP politicians followed suit. In that same vein, Ronald Reagan's 1980 campaign took on a revivalist spirit under the banner "Make America Great Again." One of his campaign staffers described Reagan this way: "he's a man with a message who want to make converts."[112] Validating that evangelical cosmology became a requirement of sorts among GOP candidates, though some were more complimentary than others. In 1996, Bob Dole acquiesced to evangelical policies being included on the GOP platform,[113] a symbolic gesture compared to Reagan's all-out embrace. In 2008, John McCain, who struggled to win over evangelicals and admitted his distaste for pandering to religious voters, included a story on the campaign trail that came as close to a religious "testimony" that he would give. Reflecting on his time as a prisoner of war during Vietnam, McCain described a Christmas morning in which a fellow captive soldier came up to him "and drew a cross in the dirt with his sandal." As McCain reflected, "for a minute there, there were just two Christians worshipping together. I'll never forget that moment."[114] He would go on to include the story in his campaign ads.[115]

George W. Bush, on the other hand, often frankly recounted his personal religious conversion during his campaign speaking engagements. The conversion occurred for him at the age of forty, when he took a walk with Billy Graham who "planted the seed," Bush confessed to a Texas audience, that made him "recommit his heart" to Jesus.[116] On the campaign trail in 2012, Mitt Romney gave the commencement address at Falwell's Liberty University, telling the crowd, "What you believe, who you value, how you live, matters."[117] Romney, a devout Mormon, demonstrated the power of that public validation despite denominational differences, so much so that it is now required. As scholars have noted, the "religious Solid South preceded the political Solid South," and some predict that "the first will apparently outlast the latter,"[118] though neither show signs of collapse, particularly when they reinforce each other.

In terms of contemporary strength in numbers, there seems little evidence of collapse, at least regionally. Southern Baptists remain the largest denomination nationally, the vast majority of whose adherents live in the geographic South. The group accounts for 24.3 percent of geographic southerners by church records as of 2000, though self-identification raises that number to 32.4 percent.[119] In some southern states, such as Alabama and Mississippi, over 40 percent of the population belong to this most prominent denomination.[120] Table 7.4 includes data from both the Baylor Religion Surveys of 2007 and 2010, with their geographic divisions, and the 2010 and 2012 Blair Center Polls in which southern identity

Table 7.4 Percent Religious Identification, Among Whites, 2007, 2010, 2012

Baylor Religion Survey	2007		2010	
	Non-South	South	Non-South	South
Baptist (among all)	5.8	28.5	6.9	26.6
Baptist (among those with a religious affiliation)	6.7	32.6	8.4	29.1
Identifies as Fundamentalist	15.9	24.0	13.6	19.2
Identifies as Born Again	31.4	54.8	31.7	48.4
Identifies as Evangelical	24.6	34.9	24.1	28.0
Biblical literalist	16.2	31.7	15.7	30.8
Fundamentalist Combination (Identifies as either Fundamentalist, Born Again, or Evangelical or believes in a literalist interpretation of the Bible)	39.8	61.2	39.9	52.8

Blair Center Poll	2010			
	Non-South	South	Non-southern	Southern
Baptist (among all)	8.5	21.9	10.1	28.0
Baptist (among those with a religious affiliation)	9.9	25.0	12.1	29.8
Biblical literalist	22.7	35.1	22.0	44.8

Blair Center Poll	2012			
	Non-South	South	Non-southern	Southern
Baptist (among all)	9.3	27.0	10.0	39.4
Baptist (among those with a religious affiliation)	11.9	32.9	12.8	45.3
Biblical literalist	20.1	30.6	18.7	41.0

Data are from the 2010 and 2012 Blair Center Polls as well as the 2007 and 2010 Baylor Religion Surveys available at https://www.baylor.edu/baylorreligionsurvey/.

and religious belief—at least biblical literalism—seem to go hand in hand. In terms of understanding the religious affiliations in the South, the strength of the Baylor Religion Surveys are that they include multiple self-identification categories that are not mutually exclusive. Respondents are not only asked to which denomination they belong, they are also asked if they identify as fundamentalist, as born again, and/or as an evangelical. Those questions (along with probing respondents' views on the Bible) are presented with a geographic regional breakdown. Across every comparison, the differences between whites living in the South and those who do not, or between whites who identify as southern compared to those who do not, are statistically significant.

Among whites in the South who reported some sort of denominational affiliation, around 30 percent are Baptist, which is about the same amount who believe in a literal interpretation of the Bible. Among those who live outside of the South, Baptist affiliation drops to single digits and the number of biblical literalists are cut in half, compared to those in the South. Those who live in the South are also more likely to identify as fundamentalist (24 percent in 2007 and 19.2 percent in 2010), born again (54.8 percent in 2007 and 48.4 percent in 2010) and evangelical (34.9 percent in 2007 and 28 percent in 2010), than those living outside of the region. In an effort to explore just how pervasive such belief and religious self-identification is in the South, all of these variables are combined into a single measure, called here "fundamentalist combination," which includes any respondent identifying with one of these labels (fundamentalist, evangelical, or born again), or believing in biblical literalism. To that end, among whites who live in the South, 61.2 percent in 2007 and 52.8 percent in 2010 fall under this broader canopy.

Moreover, the 2010 and 2012 Blair Center Polls have the advantage of having measures for both geographic South and identification as a southerner; however, they only contain a measure for biblical literalism. According to the 2012 Blair Center Poll, 30.6 percent of those who live in the South believe in a literal reading of the Bible compared to 20.1 percent of those who live beyond the region's borders. The number spikes to 41 percent among whites who claim a southern identity and drops to 18.7 percent among whites who do not, resulting in a 22.3-point gap. Denominational affiliation follows a similar trend with nearly three times the number of Baptists living in the geographic South than in the non-South across all polls. However, among whites who claim a southern identity, as captured in the 2012 Blair Center Poll, the percentage who also self-identify as Baptist jumps to 39.4 percent (compared to just 27 percent in the geographic South), indicating that the Bible Belt is both a place and a state of belonging.

IN GENERAL, SOUTHERN religious distinctiveness, based on the combination of Protestantism, evangelicalism, fundamentalism, and eventually moralism, has survived over the region's dynamic history exactly because it became inextricable from southern white identity. "Sectionalism," Kenneth Bailey notes, "has perhaps been perpetuated more explicitly in the southern churches than in any other institutions."[121] The southern way of life and the southern way of religion grew up together. Antebellum Protestants made concessions to permit slavery, when evangelicalism "discovered that it could not both expand its influence in Southern culture, continuing its growth among the whites, and stand for freedom for the blacks."[122] During the Civil War, the concessions led to permanent schisms, as southern Protestant denominations broke with their non-southern wings—specifically in the Baptist and Methodist organizations—over slavery. Throughout the twentieth century, they have withstood additional challenges from non-southern wings of their churches, specifically avoiding, as George Maddox and Joseph Fichter note, "the three tendencies clearly discernible in American Protestantism outside the South," with those being: "a concern for unity of the church, a liberalizing theology, and an increasing emphasis upon social aspects of religion." Reform and progressivism did not characterize the southern church, rather the "old-time religion" prevailed, despite war and the "advance of industry, urbanization, and education."[123] Religious historian Samuel Hill offered similar sentiments regarding the regional splits of major faiths; he wrote: "'Mainline' Yankee churches stood as a model of what to avoid and prevent."[124]

A nineteenth-century Southern Baptist clergyman once proclaimed directly that "We do not believe that 'all men are created equal,'"[125] a sentiment that underscored additional defenses of anti-miscegenation and segregation laws. Henry Lyon, an Alabama pastor, was known for his sermon "Why Racial Integration Is UnChristian," which emphasized "the white South's most profound conceptions of the proper social ordering."[126] Using their most coded language, ministers contended that the biblical notion of the equality of man was referring to their souls, which, of course, would be equal in the afterlife. However, others used racial purity to explain great human catastrophes, signifying the absolute necessity of white supremacy. As Jane Dailey writes, "White ministers and laymen across the South offered a biblically-based history of the world that accounted for all of the significant tragedies of human history, from the Fall and the Flood through the Holocaust, in terms of race relations." Moreover, "binding the narrative together and linking the catastrophes of the past with the integrated apocalypse to come," miscegenation became, as Dailey notes, "the chief sin in the service of the anti-Christ."[127]

The most violent expression of maintaining this sacred racial purity at all costs were lynchings, often occurring when whites accused (often falsely) black men of violating white women. Scholars such as Walter White and Arthur Raper have shown both that "the religion of southern whites was the fundamental basis for their emotion-driven compulsion to lynch blacks," and that the location of the lynching occurred most often in areas with high-church membership numbers.[128] White even describes a horrific lynching via burning after which spectators yelled "Glory be to God!"[129] Moreover, countless white southern churchgoers, seminary faculty, even ministers, such as C. E. Matthews who ran Fort Worth's Travis Avenue Baptist Church, were members of the Ku Klux Klan.[130] Rory McVeigh, Klan historian, describes the way in which the Klan recruited at Protestant churches. "Klan recruiters," he notes, "offered clergymen free membership, complimentary subscriptions to Klan publications, and a promise to actively promote the supremacy of Protestant Christianity."[131] White Citizen Councils, the later version of such bastions of white supremacy, also "pressured local congregations to maintain segregation in church life," including Baptist leaders in South Carolina, Alabama, and Mississippi, among other states.[132] This blurred the lines between faith and racism and made them both integral parts of southern white identity.

Scholars attempting to understand what they saw as the hypocrisy of many church leaders grappled with the way in which religious institutions failed to denounce Jim Crow. They pointed to southern culture as holding these churches in "cultural captivity." This perspective, noted Paul Harvey, portrayed white southerners, as "slumbering in a reactionary form of evangelicalism," excusing to a certain degree, "stiff-necked deacons and ushers" who "stood cross-armed at church house doors, defending segregation now, segregation forever."[133] Nevertheless, that culture was inextricable from firmly accepted theological dogma in which white supremacy was viewed as a "fundamental law of nature," and thus part of "God's eternal laws as fixed in the stars."[134] Some ministers relied heavily on the second half of Acts 17:26, which insisted that although God "created the whole human race so that they could occupy the entire earth" (a point championed by integrationists), he also "decreed how long each nation shall flourish and what the boundaries of its territory should be." The South was white territory, and any changes would have to come from the divine.[135] The social construction of this racial hierarchy was rarely questioned by laypersons, who had lived under this system their entire lives—a system elevated to the status of sacred.[136] Segregation was religion and "most ministers," surmised Harvey, "knew when to keep quiet." Many, as one southern churchgoer explained, "hid their heads in the sand and spoke the language of the people in the church even if they didn't believe it."[137] Their role, before the reactionary fundamentalists took over, was to conserve the status quo, particularly when the biblical support for segregation from ministers seemed contrived or inconsistent.[138] Often called the "folk theology of segregation," the acceptance of this system exposes how mutually reinforcing social norms and cosmology were for southern white believers.

For some white clergy, the Civil Rights Movement seemed at times a distant issue. Nancy Ammerman's research on seventy-two Alabama congregations revealed that localism, or how isolated the congregation remained from larger governing bodies, influenced whether or not they became active in the Civil Rights Movement.[139] However, larger denominational umbrella organizations, such as the General Assembly of the Southern Presbyterian Church, confronted the issue head-on and faced internal battles for decades. In the years leading up to *Brown v. Board*, for example, L. Nelson Bell, Billy Graham's father-in-law and the founder of the *Southern Presbyterian Journal*, took a strong stand against forced integration, with the operative word being "forced." Anything forced violated God's will and plan, a stance supported most vehemently by fundamentalists within the denomination to whom inerrancy was indisputable.[140] In the wake of *Brown*, civil disobedience was criticized with the same logic, with protesters accused of disobeying not only state laws but also God's laws.[141] However, even that represented a subtle shift—from unflinching biblical support for white supremacy to a rejection of desegregation efforts. Moreover, that shift was a stark contrast from the whole-scale theological endorsement of slavery, and it angered secular leaders of massive resistance. Ironically, or perhaps in a way that foreshadowed the GOP efforts to tighten the political-religious coalition in the South, when segregationists lost the battle, they cast blame on southern church leaders for not being militant enough in their resistance.[142] And those who were willing to take a stronger stand, such as Jerry Falwell, who not only had African American protestors taken out of his church, but also had them arrested,[143] would rise to power and political influence when fundamentalism ruled the day.

The legacy of this racially loaded cosmology, this folk theology of segregation, remains long after the rhetoric has quieted. The SBC still grapples with its racist past. In recent years, it has entertained resolutions for racial reconciliation.[144] Under the new leadership of Russell Moore, the president of the Ethics and Religious Liberty Commission of the SBC, it voted to reject the Confederate flag.[145] Additionally, a resolution condemning white supremacy and the Alt-Right passed after substantial controversy. Alt-Right leader Richard Spencer responded on Twitter, denouncing the "cucked SBC."[146] The complex dynamics within the SBC on racial issues indeed has a long history that is still unfolding. The dynamics are complex among individual members too. A 1964 study of southern fundamentalists lends further evidence to the mutually reinforcing relationship of southern white identity and southern religious identity. Dividing fundamentalists into two groups, Joe Feagin found that "intrinsic" fundamentalists, who exhibit high attendance and for whom "his creed is part of his personality," do not exhibit high levels of prejudice. However, those "extrinsic" fundamentalists, who are infrequent attenders and for whom "religion serves a more external function—like social status—are more likely to be prejudiced."[147] One decade later, Richard Gorsuch and Daniel Aleshire offered similar findings in which non-fundamentalists and those who held less tightly to the "value traditions of society at large" were less racially tolerant.[148] Still others exposed the role of concern for "social status" as predictive of prejudice among southern churchgoers,[149] and protecting that social status was paramount. In addition, Ted Jelen found in 1987 that fundamentalists were the most intolerant (in this case toward homosexuality), and that they were "significantly more likely to translate personal values into demands for the legal enforcement of those values."[150] Even as late as 2010, "religious racism" has been found to be "tied to basic life values of social conformity and respect for tradition."[151] So if many church members belong to gain social status, which scholars have noted,[152] then their beliefs reflect their need to conform to the social status quo and to protect that sense of belonging. Theoretically, if the status quo of society changes—or if the church institution changes its position—they will follow.

Thus, when the SBC dropped its anti-integration rhetoric for the most part in the 1970s, it had to find another outlet to protect the status quo, as well as its own power. "For religious conservatives," argues Paul Harvey, "patriarchy has supplanted race as the defining first principle of God-ordained order."[153] The SBC's relationship to women and to feminism in general became, in additional to biblical inerrancy, a linchpin for fundamentalists. And that is critically important in terms of the Long Southern Strategy. Racism and racially coded rhetoric may have driven many white southerners to the GOP, but they did not stay there. In order to win them back after the administration of one of their own, Jimmy Carter, the GOP trumpeted the "family values" mantra to woo social conservative voters. In order to cross from racial politics to religious politics, they built a bridge on the backs of feminists. In fact, of all of the cultural issues arising during the 1970s and 1980s, the partisan gap was widest and grew only wider on the ERA specifically and on evaluations of the Women's Movement in general.[154] Among mainline Protestants nationwide, women's rights was the first social/cultural issue significantly correlated with partisanship.[155]

Many evangelicals and fundamentalists in general considered feminism a crisis. The 1977 National Women's Conference in Houston "shocked" conservative religious women, who comprised roughly 20 percent of those in attendance. They characterized the event as a "Marxist/lesbian circus."[156] They began to organize. Leaders of the anti-feminist countermovement contended that women's liberation would lead to unisex restrooms, integrated prison facilities, the legalization of homosexuality, the requirement that women register for the draft, the abolition of sodomy and adultery laws, the absolution of requirements that husbands support their families, the loss of a wife's rights to her husband's social security benefits, the abolition of single-sex schools, the jeopardizing of churches and church colleges because they refused to admit women or homosexuals to the clergy and the establishment of abortion as a constitutional right.[157]

For conservative evangelicals and fundamentalists, the entire movement posed a direct threat to the church, and because the potential ramifications were seen as affecting every family in some way or another, the saw themselves as "under siege."[158] And women led the resistance, "establishing women's groups and prayer chapters, as well as antipornography and right-to-life campaigns,"[159] which, in turn, became part of the network that would support the burgeoning political umbrella of the Christian Right. Pastors took their example to heart, encouraging congregants to bring stamped envelopes to services so they could all write their congressional delegations in opposition to the ERA.[160] The SBC had the resources—to the tune of $10 billion in assets[161] and a $150 million dollar operating budget[162] in the 1980s—and they used that money and power to try to influence national elections. They called out Carter, specifically, over his support and endorsement of the National Women's Conference and the ERA.[163]

Perhaps most devastating was the way in which the religious attacks on antifeminism shamed women for asserting themselves, for having a self to assert in the first place. Phyllis Schlafly, the leader of the STOP ERA movement, expressed her loathing toward her own gender and wrapped it all in Genesis:

> The women in the Garden of Eden freely decided to tamper with God's order and ignore His rules. She sought her own self-fulfillment. She decided to do things her way, independent of God's commandment. She even persuaded the man to join in her "liberation" from God's law. Sin thus entered the world, bringing fear, sickness, pain, anger, hatred, danger, violence, and all varieties of ugliness.[164]

The SBC agreed with Schlafly and at their 1984 convention adopted a resolution characterized as "blaming women for the sin of the world." The actual language declared: "While Paul commends women and men alike in other roles of ministry and services, he excludes women from pastoral leadership to preserve a submission God requires because the man was first in creation and the woman was first in the Edenic fall."[165] The declaration even stood up to a failed effort to change it in 1994.[166] If women were the cause of all the world's problems, then their submission was the only antidote to God's forgiveness. In 1988, a study of the rhetoric of clergy revealed that abortion and "women's roles" ranked among the most frequent issues mentioned publicly by both fundamentalists and evangelicals.[167] Even as recently as 2004, analysis of the messaging put out by the SBC concludes that it still insists that "the proper gender order includes women in submissive spousal relations as they take care of children and stay out of the pulpit."[168]

At the heart of the motivation for men to re-emphasize the submissiveness of women as ordained by the Bible, lies the need for dominance, argues Karen McCarthy Brown in her 1994 essay "Fundamentalism and the Control of Women." In addition, Brown theorizes that it is the "us vs. them" structure of modern fundamentalist identity that makes fundamentalists hyper-aware of the "other" against which their values and beliefs are defined. That fixation, she contends, drives their efforts to bridle the "others" within their own organization—in this case, the women.[169] Moreover, the culture of honor and often violence so prevalent in the Antebellum South was, in many ways, absorbed into evangelicalism. Southern white male culture, as Ted Ownby has demonstrated, relied on "hunting, drinking, carousing in town, attending professional entertainments, mocking preachers, and generally raising hell."[170] However, during the Civil War, the religious military press promoted the image of a "manly Christian." "The belief in Providence," they reasoned, "gave the Christian solider the confidence to face any battle or foe without flinching, exhibiting courage that other warriors could admire."[171] That manliness, however, maintained its authority. So even when the evangelical revivals that swept through the South in the nineteenth century attempted to civilize and to purify southern male souls, they still functioned as leaders of a church body-at-large that often policed society. It was a quick jump then from "church discipline to disciplining society as a whole"[172] without flinching.

Southern Baptist clergywomen, the first of whom, Addie Davis, was ordained in Durham, North Carolina, in 1964,[173] were often scapegoated as the cause of the division within the SBC,[174] and many feminists became victims of a fundamentalist purge in that organization.[175] Moreover, the SBC, including female members who supported the patriarchy, contributed significantly to the demonization of feminism in general. Religious women, argues Michael Linesch, obtained "power through powerlessness,"[176] a concept deeply familiar to the paradoxical nature of the cult of southern white womanhood. Women who adhere to the doctrine of submissiveness are then usually given more of a voice in the family.

In case studies of one Texas Women's Bible Class, many white Southern Baptist women vocally supported the notion of the male head of the household concept, for example, while still exerting their own authority within the domestic sphere.[177] They draw boundaries and live within them, allowing patriarchal institutions like the SBC to function without their interference. Their focus is individual not collective—personal, not political. As another example of these manufactured boundaries, Dr. Dorothy Patterson, who worked at the Southwestern Baptist Theological Seminary, chose only to teach female students because "it would be unbiblical for a woman to teach men."[178] Patterson's area of expertise is women's studies. Her husband, Paige Patterson, was one of the leading architects of the fundamentalist takeover—also called the "conservative resurgence" of the SBC initiated in 1979. Paige Patterson served as a past president of the SBC from 1998 to 2000. He also served as president of the Southeastern Baptist Theological Seminary for eleven years and as president of the Southwestern Baptist Theological Seminary for fifteen years until he was fired in May 2018 for suppressing rape allegations made by female students during his tenure at both institutions.[179]

In an interview with her own mother, Susan Shaw, author of *God Speaks to Us, Too: Southern Baptist Women on Church, Home, & Society*, probes the subject of gender equality in the church. "If I were younger," her mom said, "I might believe that. I can see women in leadership positions in the church, maybe under a pastor, as assistant or something like that, but not the head of the church." "To me," she continued, "the pastor is the head of the church under Christ, and even though God is no respecter of persons . . ." Shaw notes her mother's reaction: "The irony of what she was saying struck her." Her mother's response speaks to the cultural power of religious fundamentalism and the social construction of gender. "I guess," she confessed, "it's just because of the way I was raised, and my age, and everything, that I just don't believe a women should be the pastor of a church."[180]

The "everything" of which she speaks is the white southern identity built historically on a foundation of both white supremacy and male authority. In fact, Donald Matthews notes in his history of religion in the Old South that "the field of tension between southern lady and Evangelical woman . . . sometimes disappeared in a conflation of ideals." They seemed and still seem complementary, almost twin identities.[181] This submissive identity is reinforced, not only in the pew, but also in the vast Christian media empire. Books and book series, including *The Power of a Praying* (insert: wife, parent, teen, mom, etc.) and *There's No Place Like Home: Steps to Becoming a Stay-at-Home Mom*, reinforce traditional, biblical, and southern gender roles. *The Journal for Biblical Manhood and Womanhood* provides audio recordings of key essays, as well as manuals that can be downloaded from their website.[182]

Yet the impact of maintaining these identities, of propping up both white supremacy and the institutional patriarchy and of submitting to its political will, is devastating in measurable ways. Over time, assessments of the educational attainment of white American women from the 1970s to the late 1990s show that a Baptist affiliation is a highly significant and negative predictor of educational advancement. For both young and older women, being Baptist, and the expectations for "family, marriage and child bearing," means they are less likely to get a degree.[183] Over the course of the same period, fundamentalists were also shown to be less accepting of women in politics—an aversion mimicking the reluctance to have female pastors.[184] In 2017, the Tennessee Baptist Convention expelled First Baptist Church of Jefferson City from its organization because it had a woman as a pastor—so the aversion is not a relic of the past.[185] Well into the twenty-first century, racial attitudes, as well as measures of resentment toward women in the workplace, shed light on the way in which race, gender, fundamentalism, and southern identity remain tightly braided.

In terms of race, the 2012 Blair Center Poll, as shown in Figure 7.1, finds important gaps between not only southern identity, but also fundamentalist belief (defined here as respondents who believe in biblical literalism). Among non-southerners, non-fundamentalists have a significantly lower average Racial Resentment score (13.6), compared to fundamentalists who have a slightly higher mean Racial Resentment score of 14.7. So being a biblical literalist does influence racial animus, moving the respondents up the scale a full point. However, southern identity significantly widens the gaps. Southern white

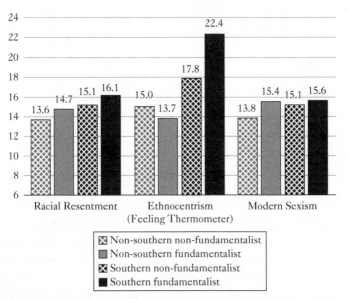

FIGURE 7.1 Mean Racial Resentment, Ethnocentrism, and Modern Sexism Scores, Among Whites, by Fundamentalism (Biblical Literalism), 2012

Data are from the 2012 Blair Center Poll.

non-fundamentalists reporting a mean Racial Resentment score of 15.1, compared to southern fundamentalists with the highest score of 16.1.

In yet another measure of racial animus—Ethnocentrism—southern identity dramatically divides the racial attitudes of fundamentalists throughout the country. The mean level of feeling thermometer–based Ethnocentrism (measured here by how "warmly" the respondent feels about whites minus the average of how "warmly" they feel about African Americans and Latinos) for non-southern fundamentalists is 13.7, which is actually lower than non-southern, non-fundamentalists. This means that for white Americans who do not identify as southern, being a biblical literalist actually shrinks the difference they feel between themselves and other races. However, for fundamentalists who identify as southern, that gap reaches 22.4 degrees, which is significantly higher than all non-southern whites and also significantly higher than southern non-fundamentalists. So, fundamentalism itself is a very different thing for those who embrace southern white culture—it compounds this view of "us vs. them."

Modern Sexism scores, on the other hand, reveal a commonality among fundamentalists nationwide. Non-southern fundamentalists and southern fundamentalist have mean Modern Sexism scores of 15.4 and 15.6 respectively; both are high and the difference between the scores of the two groups is statistically insignificant. Whites who claim a southern identity but who are not fundamentalists are slightly lower at 15.1. However, non-southern, non-fundamentalists have an even lower score of just 13.8. Therefore, this resentment toward feminists and distrust of working women is both part of southern identity and part of fundamentalist belief. Subscribing to both moves one significantly up the scale into the "sexist" category; subscribing to neither drops one well into the "non-sexist" camp. Numbers like those are why the family values mantra established in opposition to feminism and co-opted by the GOP during the debate over the ERA became part of the Long Southern Strategy, as well as the rallying cry of the Moral Majority and the Christian Right, the result of which would solidify the realignment of the South with the Republican Party.[186]

THE SOUTHERN WAY of religion seems to persist even though numerous reports indicate that fewer Americans are participating in organized religion. On one hand, the 2016 Blair Center Poll finds that among whites who live in the South or who claim a southern identity, the percentage of Baptists has also declined slightly since 2012. Baptists constitute 22.7 percent of whites in the geographic South, down from 27 percent. Among whites who identify as southern, 35 percent are Baptists, down from 39.4 percent in 2012. One the other hand, Baptist is still the most frequently chosen denomination among these subgroups. However, denomination is, perhaps, not as important as whether one embraces the Christian fundamentalist "brand." Accordingly, in the 2016 Blair Center Poll, respondents were asked not only if they believed in a literal interpretation of the Bible, but also whether or not they identified as a Christian fundamentalist. The results point, once again, to the difficulty in measuring religiosity without consideration of regionalism. When examining fundamentalist belief in 2016, 21.3 percent of white Americans living outside of the South believe in a literal interpretation of the Bible, compared to 28.7 percent of whites living in the geographic South. Here again, when southern identity is considered, that number dips to 20.3 percent for non-southerners and jumps to 37.9 percent of whites who claim a southern identity—a 17.6-point gap. However, this gap in a literalist interpretation of the Bible as a definition of fundamentalism is surpassed by

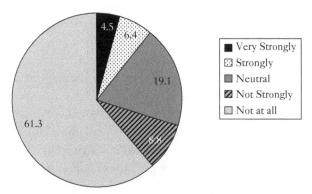

FIGURE 7.2A Percent Responses to: "How Strongly Do You Think of Yourself as a Christian Fundamentalist?" Among Non-southern Whites, 2016

Data are from the 2016 Blair Center Poll.

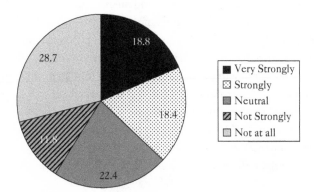

FIGURE 7.2B Percent Responses to: "How Strongly Do You Think of Yourself as a Christian Fundamentalist?" Among Southern Whites, 2016

Data are from the 2016 Blair Center Poll.

assessing whether the respondent identifies as a Christian fundamentalist, as seen in Figures 7.2A and 7.2B. Whereas only 10.9 percent of white Americans who do not identify as southern "strongly" or "very strongly" identify as a Christian fundamentalist, among southern whites that number jumps significantly to 37.2 percent—a gap of 26.3 points.

Moreover, examining these two measure of fundamentalism side by side reveals that only 34.7 percent of non-southern whites who are bib-lical literalists also identify as a Christian fundamentalist. However, among southern whites, 66.4 percent of biblical literalists also identify as Christian fundamentalists. In southern white culture, fundamentalism is both a the-ological point of view and an identity for two-thirds of the community. That being said, there are still roughly one-third of both non-southern and southern whites who identify as Christian fundamentalists but who do not believe in a literal interpretation of the Bible. This is actually a small fraction of non-southern whites since only 10 percent of them identify as Christian fundamentalists in the first place. However, for southern whites, it is more significant. In order to compare more accurately the impact of religiosity on political attitudes, both those who believe in biblical literalism and/or those who identify as Christian fundamentalists should be included. In 2016, 49.7 percent of whites who identify as southern fall under this broader defi-nition of fundamentalism (similar to the Baylor Religion Surveys of 2007 and 2010), compared to 24.1 percent among whites who do not identify with the southern label.

In 2016, the overwhelming majority of fundamentalists (the broader measure is used throughout the analysis of the 2016 data), by both definitions, still be-lieve that it is important to live a religious life, as shown in Figure 7.3. Among non-southern whites, 80.1 percent of fundamentalists indicate it is "impor-tant" or "very important" to do so, and among southern white fundamentalists, 86.5 percent agree. Even among non-fundamentalists, 32 percent of non-southern whites and 40.2 percent of southern whites assign importance to religion. In ad-dition, there are still more in each subgroup who say it is "somewhat important." However, among fundamentalists overall, a mere 3.3 percent and 1.5 percent of non-southern and southern whites respectively indicate that living a religious life is of "no importance." It is that answer that really separates fundamentalists from non-fundamentalists among whom only 41.1 percent and 31.3 percent of non-southern and southern whites respectively assign no personal significance to religion.

Religion, for fundamentalists, is a way of life, and for white southerners, it remains knotted to other components of that way of life, including racial an-imus and Modern Sexism. In 2016, the Racial Resentment, Ethnocentrism,

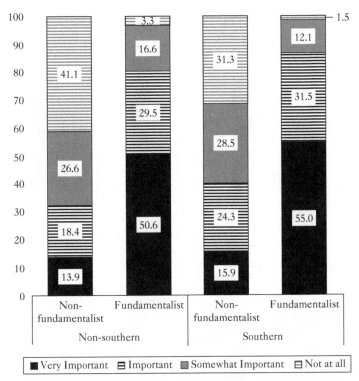

FIGURE 7.3 Percent Responses to: "How Important Is It to You Personally to Live a Religious Life?" Among Whites, by Fundamentalism (Biblical Literalism and/or Self-identified), 2016

Data are from the 2016 Blair Center Poll.

and Modern Sexism levels have shifted some among fundamentalists and non-fundamentalists, as shown in Figure 7.4. However, in 2016 when the more in-clusive measure of fundamentalism—which included biblical literalists and/or those who self-identified as a Christian fundamentalist—is utilized, these shifts occurred in exactly the same direction even when limiting fundamentalism to the 2012 definition of biblical literalism. Racial Resentment means are down slightly in all subgroups, but for both southern and non-southern fundamentalists, the drop is less than half of one point, while among non-fundamentalists, the decrease is 0.7 points for white southerners and one full point for white non-southerners.

Ethnocentrism scores, whereby one's "warmth" toward African Americans and Latinos is subtracted from one's "warmth" toward whites, has declined dra-matically for non-southern, non-fundamentalists, to a score of 7.7 points (it was 15 points in 2012 among biblical literalists only). Non-southern fundamentalists have an average score of 12.1 points, though this too is down slightly (1.5 points)

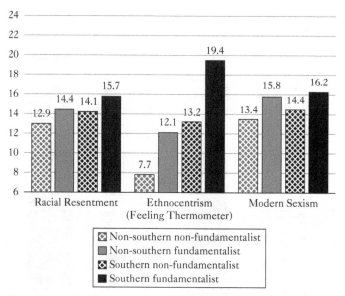

FIGURE 7.4 Mean Racial Resentment, Ethnocentrism, and Modern Sexism Scores, Among Whites, by Fundamentalism (Biblical Literalism and/or Self-identified), 2016 Data are from the 2016 Blair Center Poll.

from 2012. Southern non-fundamentalists are only slightly higher at 13.2, a 4.6-point change, and southern fundamentalists still have a significantly higher "us vs. them" score at 19.4 points, a drop from 22.4 in 2012.

However, despite this downward trend across the board, the gaps that fundamentalism catalyzes are larger in 2016. Among non-southerners in 2012, fundamentalists had an Ethnocentric score 1.3 points lower than non-fundamentalists, but in 2016 fundamentalists are 4.4 points higher. For whites who claim a southern identity, the gap between fundamentalists and non-fundamentalists has grown from 4.6 points to 6.2 points, with fundamentalists being significantly more Ethnocentric. In terms of Modern Sexism scores, in 2016, non-fundamentalists were less sexist than in 2012, while fundamentalists were more sexist—both for non-southern and southern whites. Among white Americans who do not call themselves southern, the mean Modern Sexism score of non-fundamentalists dropped 0.4 points, while it increased 0.4 points among fundamentalists. Among southern whites, non-fundamentalist scores dropped 0.6 points, while fundamentalists increased 0.7 points to the significantly highest score of 16.2. Thus, fundamentalism, in terms of anti-feminist sentiment and resentment toward working women, proves more polarizing than ever. To that end, fundamentalism, whether by biblical belief or self-labeled, and southern white identity are still significantly snared in the oldest southern traditions of white superiority and patriarchal authority.

FOR THE HISTORIANS who turned to the much-neglected subject of southern religion,[187] the process of explaining the "way of southern religion" has been self-revelatory.[188] To live in the Bible Belt is to understand, whether from inside the church or as an outsider, the cultural power that private faith now has in the public arena. Southern white churches have been the source of political resistance to change,[189] the constant and steady defender of a conservative tradition.[190] Though for most of its history, politics has played second fiddle to faith,[191] they are in many ways indistinguishable now, with religious identity bleeding into southern identity and vice versa, feeding their common distinctiveness. The Protestant personal relationship to God or the "soul competency" of the Baptists[192] combined with the evangelical fervor and the "gospel working up"[193] to convert and multiply the church's flock, combined with the fundamentalist efforts to hold the modern world at bay,[194] produced a regional moralism[195] that was ripe for the GOP's picking. The result must be understood as a surprisingly unified social movement of southern religion,[196] blanketed by a "sacred canopy" that holds the region in "cultural captivity"[197] in which political problems are essentially religious and moral problems.[198]

The sacred canopy insulates southern fundamentalists from external societal and cultural shifts, protecting not just religious values but the social hierarchy too. So social change, not just theological changes, sets white southern fundamentalism at odds with modern life in ways that seem destabilizing. The world outside of the sacred canopy feels hostile, and that feeling lies at the core of reactionary politics. For white fundamentalists who cling to a southern identity, this feeling of threat is exacerbated by challenges to racial and gender hierarchies upon which the southern label was constructed—and those are anything but new. Such was the case in the aftermath of the Civil War, when evangelical religion merged with the civil religion of the Lost Cause, giving white southerners a touchstone in a world without slavery.[199] "The 'southernness' of religion in the South, like the South itself," argued Donald Matthews, "is affected by race and the section's history of racial consciousness."[200] Race, after all, had created the SBC in the first place, splitting the denomination by region on issues of equality.[201] When confronted again with societal changes in the early twentieth century, white southern evangelical fundamentalists, losing their authority in public schools over Bible reading and the teaching of evolution, for example, retreated from the cause of majoritarianism and built, instead, a society in their image.[202] Only when the sheer force of cultural change became insurmountable would the SBC soften its position on race. But it merely unclenched one fist while clenching the other, shifting its sacred massive resistance to women's liberation.[203] Traditional Christian, southern white women rallied against feminists, with fundamentalists leaders such as Jerry Falwell actively campaigning with them.[204] So southern white fundamentalism, for many, came already assembled with racial animus and patriarchy. That conflation has been reinforced politically so that candidates now can utilize one to catalyze another. All remain as easy to perform now—even for candidates as removed from southern white fundamentalism as Donald Trump seemed to be—as they were when Nixon took the stage alongside Billy Graham. And it must have been a good performance because five months into Trump's administration, Jerry Falwell Jr. proclaimed that in Trump, "evangelicals have found their dream president."[205]

In an effort to win southern voters, the GOP embraced the old southern religion turning the church faithful into the party loyal. By the time Ronald Reagan was elected, southern fundamentalism would be the primary variable accounting for regional distinctiveness.[206] By the end of his second term, fundamentalism and intolerance would be significantly correlated in the General Social Survey data for people who lived in the South,[207] and the percent of religious evangelicals voting Republican doubled nationwide.[208] The GOP seemed more and more likely to stand for "God's Own Party," as Daniel Williams notes in the title of his book by the same name.[209] But in many ways, the arc of southern religion has done little but bend until it circles back around to where it started. The evangelicals of the old South, after all, envisioned themselves to be part of a moral community juxtaposed against non-believers.[210] Just as religion functions as a cultural identity, particularly in the Bible Belt, then it is also the story of what it means to be a white southerner then and now. "The airwaves in the South on any Sunday morning," Boles observes, "are filled with the sermons that might have been preached in 1894 or 1794. The technology is newer than the theology, and the emphasis is still on the lonely sinner, not the complex society."[211] Thus, southern religious identity is built on the foundation of whiteness and patriarchy both in content and in structure, which is polarizing, definitive, unflinching, partisan, and reflective of a Long Southern Strategy.

8

Southern White Fundamentalism

When it comes to a woman who has chosen to marry,
who is to be a helper to her husband, I cannot say that
Scripture allows her, much less encourages her, to become his
commander-in-chief.

—DOROTHY PATTERSON[1]

IN THE SUMMER of 1976, Gerald Ford became the first American president to speak at a meeting of the Southern Baptist Convention (SBC), which praised him in a formal resolution.[2] President Richard Nixon had received a similar accolade in 1971 for setting up a federal commission to help parochial schools,[3] but Ford's decision to speak in person signaled a shift in the Republican Party. In order to maintain their inroads in the South, particularly when faced with native son Jimmy Carter as the Democratic rival[4] for the White House, the GOP made a conscious move to make its relationship with the SBC more official. In his address, Ford did not skimp on the religious rhetoric; rather, he painted a broad picture of the United States as a Christian nation[5] since its inception. He anointed Congressman Brooks Hays, as well as Thomas Jefferson and Abraham Lincoln, as saints and praised Baptists as the "fabric of America."[6] Perhaps more important, Ford extolled the SBC for its ability to "overcome its enemies of the world."[7] His successors would follow suit. Ronald Reagan addressed a crowd of 17,000 members of the Religious Roundtable, including many SBC leaders, at Reunion Arena in Dallas just a few months before the 1980 election. At the rally (which a young Mike Huckabee,[8] future GOP presidential contender, helped organize), Reagan promised the crowd, "I know you can't endorse me, but I endorse you."[9] Addressing the SBC convention by satellite in 2002, President George W. Bush proclaimed, "You're believers, and you're patriots, faithful followers of God and good citizens of America. And one day, I believe that it will be said of you, 'Well done, good and faithful servants.'"[10] Before him, his father, President George H. W. Bush, made an emotional appeal to the group in 1991, breaking into tears when confessing to the crowd how prayer got him through the Gulf War. The audience gave him a standing ovation and shouted, "Amen."[11] And Donald Trump, in the 2016 primaries, posted a video on Facebook of the Bible that his mother inscribed to him, as if to suggest he was a card-carrying member of their club.[12] Yet, it was Ford who initiated the tradition and who went on to speak to the National Religious Broadcasters and the National Association of Evangelicals,[13] repeating the same message and always reminding the audience that his own son was in seminary, making Ford an insider.[14]

The targeted speeches have been cast as part of Ford's two-prong religious strategy[15] to maintain Republican momentum in the South, with the second being broader appeals laced with scripture and spoken in "Baptese."[16] There was, indeed, a coded language of religiosity, which GOP leaders would learn to speak fluently if they wanted to win these southern voters. However, that language grew increasingly absolutist in nature, and that was the result of an explosive conflict within the SBC that, at the time of Ford's speech, loomed on the horizon. At the heart of the conflict was the fact that fundamentalists and biblical literalists were angry and felt pushed aside by moderates within the SBC. Frustrated for years, in 1979 the fundamentalists fashioned a takeover in a moment in which they believed that America was on a slippery moral slope. The coup, however, was not limited to a simple change in leadership. Complete with the purging of moderates (it has been called a painful "ethnic cleansing")[17] and the installation of more conservative, even reactionary doctrines, the new SBC was the perfect battlefield for the last leg of the Long Southern Strategy.[18]

So when W. A. Crisswell, a past president of the SBC whose election would spark a fundamentalist surge, appeared in campaign ads for Ford,[19] as opposed to a card-carrying SBC moderate like Carter, it signaled not just that the GOP was courting religious voters, but rather that it was courting a certain kind of religious voter. Under fundamentalist leadership, many Southern Baptists transformed their personal moral code to a public moral crusade. White southern churchgoers had, of course, always taken stricter positions on moral issues such as Prohibition. In 1959, for example, 74 percent of Methodists in the South supported "total abstinence, national prohibition" of alcohol, roughly 10 points higher than Methodists outside of the South.[20] In the 1970s, white southern fundamentalists turned to political controversies regarding gay rights and reproductive rights, all in a partnership with the GOP and all in an effort to fight back against a liberalizing American society.[21] In turn, the southern white church became very partisan very fast. By 1993, partisanship and faith had become so intertwined, that the SBC leadership tried to block the seating of convention delegates—or "messengers" as they are called—from President Bill Clinton's home church. And in 2016 when Russell Moore, the head of the Ethics and Religious Liberty Commission of the SBC, took a strong stand against GOP nominee Donald Trump, labeling him a huckster and denouncing him for his treatment of women,

Moore faced demands for his resignation. Donald Trump himself called Moore a "nasty man" on Twitter.

The feeling of alienation that drove fundamentalists to take over the SBC and to purge those who dared to disagree extended beyond the confines of the convention, transforming the political landscape. By the time that Newt Gingrich and his "Contract for America" took office in 1995, the culture wars between "angry white men"[22] and the rest of the country seemed firmly in place. One adjective short, "angry white men" included many fundamentalists, who saw themselves increasingly living a life in opposition to the rest of American culture,[23] and many wanted their country back—a reactionary spirit that the GOP championed. Gone was the evangelical aversion to worldly concerns. Gone was moderation both in church and in state;[24] rather, fundamentalists fought for the legal enforcement of their values[25] without compromise, defining themselves in opposition to a host of contemporary policy issues in the GOP's final push to turn the South red.

THE SHIFT TO a politically active religiosity did, of course, have its roots in past conflicts. The SBC had flexed its political muscles in the early twentieth century on major conflicts regarding Prohibition, evolution, and even integration.[26] However, this was a new beast altogether. As political issues either threatened the institutional power of the church or challenged traditions that needed to be upheld, a southern religious bloc began to rally and organize. It would go on to build an infrastructure that included "parents' networks, legal defense funds, and lobbying groups."[27] One such early trigger issue arose from the Supreme Court decisions banning prayer in schools in *Engel v. Vitale* (1962) and school Bible devotionals in *Abington v. Schempp* (1963). At first, the SBC publicly backed the decisions, perhaps because they were hesitant to build a political alliance with Catholics who were fighting the prayer in school decisions vehemently. However, some Protestants feared that Catholics were gaining too much power in the wake of President John Kennedy's election to the presidency.[28] The SBC also recognized that the rulings were not being enforced and worried that bringing attention to them would warrant executive action,[29] surely reminiscent of President Dwight Eisenhower's federal intervention in the Little Rock Central High School desegregation showdown a few years earlier.

However, in the end, when additional attempts to actually amend the Constitution—thus forcing a Supreme Court reversal—failed, the religious faithful promised action. The 1966 Dirksen Amendment, which prohibited the government from banning "any school, school system, educational institution or other public building supported in whole or in part through the expenditure of public funds from providing for or permitting the voluntary participation by students or others in prayer,"[30] failed by close margins (nine votes shy of the two-thirds needed to pass the Senate). The failure prompted southern religious leaders such as Billy Graham to vow a public political fight from churchgoers. By the first Reagan administration, the SBC would pass a series of resolutions encouraging the Supreme Court to shift from a separationist perspective to the "accomodationist doctrine" in which students' free exercise was paramount.[31] Southern religiosity would be playing offense as opposed to defense.

The transformation of evangelical fundamentalists from politically inactive to a 66 percent self-reported turnout rate in 1984 remains one of the most radical shifts in modern American politics. Nearly three-fourths of those voters chose Ronald Reagan despite the fact that only half claimed a Republican affiliation.[32] By 1988, turnout among biblical literalists hit 73 percent—up from 34 percent in 1964—as voting was encouraged from the pulpit.[33] From 1980 to 2000, the percent of Southern Baptist ministers who claimed a GOP party identification increased from 27 to 85 percent,[34] and research has shown predictably that the climate of the church has a strong political impact on its members.[35] After all, the demographic characteristics of these "doctrinally conservative Christians" were more representative of non-voters that active politicos. They were, in the years preceding the politicization of the SBC, "more likely to have lower levels of education, to live in rural areas, to live in the South, and to be female than the population at large"[36] (though leadership, of course, was the exclusive purview of men).

Scholarly assessments have changed little over the years, with whiteness and rurality and lower incomes still defining the community.[37] The connection to regionalism remains formidable as well, and still, at the end of the twentieth century, over 50 percent of self-proclaimed fundamentalists were born and raised and continued to live in the South.[38] According to the 2012 Blair Center Poll, 56.2 percent of fundamentalists live in the geographic South, and like their counterparts outside of the South, they continue to be relatively older, less educated, and have lower incomes than non-fundamentalists. However, as previously shown, white fundamentalists who live in the South and those who claim a southern identity are more than twice as likely to be Baptists (47.1 percent and 56.1 percent respectively) compared to non-South (21.9 percent) and non-southern (21.5 percent) white fundamentalists. All of which means that the Southern Baptist church still carries the biggest stick not only in the region, but within the fundamentalist community throughout the country. Using that stick to shape American politics would take a Long Southern Strategy.

There was one problem. Comparing fundamentalists—not just clergy—in the South and the non-South, as Tod Baker, Robert Steed, and Laurence Morehead did in the early 1980s, revealed not only an education and income gap, but also a persistent party gap—and not in the GOP's favor. Evangelicals who lived in the

South were still more likely to be affiliated with the Democratic Party (54.4 percent) compared to those in the non-South (43.4 percent).[39] The majority had not turned fully red yet. Some or many may have voted for a GOP presidential candidate, but they had not changed their party affiliation. That being said, 55 percent of whites in the South compared to 36 percent in the non-South did classify themselves as ideologically conservative.[40] If the GOP could align itself with that southern version of conservatism, then perhaps, southern white fundamentalism could solidify its base there. It would go on to do exactly that. In 2012, as shown in Figure 8.1, the GOP did have clear majorities both among fundamentalists nationwide, with the greatest support coming from below the Mason-Dixon line.

For white fundamentalists—measured in 2012 as biblical literalists—who live outside of the South, 55 percent identify as Republicans, with 12.9 percent of those considering themselves "strongly Republican." White fundamentalists who live in the South align themselves with the GOP at the rate of 65.7 percent, with almost 20 percent identifying as "strongly Republican." White fundamentalists who identify as southern are slightly less Republican as a whole (62.3 percent), but the percentage who "strongly" identify as Republican climbs to 24.1 percent. Southern white identity, in this case, alongside biblical literalism, creates a partisan intensity. It is important to note also that non-fundamentalist whites who live in the South are not majority Republican, reaching only 38.1 percent. Whites

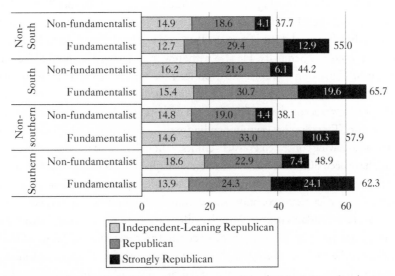

FIGURE 8.1 Percent Republican by Fundamentalism (Biblical Literalism), Among Whites, 2012

Data are from the 2012 Blair Center Poll.

who identify as southern but are not fundamentalists get closer, at 48.9 percent. But being fundamentalist too puts them clearly in the GOP's corner.

MUCH OF THIS politicization could not have occurred without the transformation of the SBC in the 1970s and 1980s. The irony, of course, is that the large Bible Belt voting bloc that results from the fundamentalist takeover of the SBC and the rising Christian Right required a collective structure and hierarchy deeply familiar to southerners, but altogether rejected by Baptist principles of independence. Even more ironic is that the fact that the SBC was established in 1845 because of its rejection of oversight rules governing the appointment of missionaries abroad. The Home Missionaries agency, which vetted missionaries and oversaw their placement, decided to take a position of neutrality on the question of slavery in the decades leading up to the Civil War, as the debate intensified and grew increasingly violent. When a southern candidate was rejected based on his slave-owning status—which, of course, violated this neutrality principle— southern Baptists formed their own governing body. Even neutrality proved too overbearing. By the 1970s, with over 14 million SBC members,[41] moderation would soon be cast aside as well.

Technically, the takeover of the SBC by fundamentalists began over a meeting between Paul Pressler and Paige Patterson at Café Du Monde in New Orleans in 1967. At that time Patterson was a doctoral student at New Orleans Baptist Theological Seminary. He would eventually serve as president of Crisswell College, the Southeastern Baptist Theological Seminary, the Southwestern Baptist Theological Seminary, and the SBC itself. However, in 2018, based on comments he made downplaying the sexual abuse of women, Patterson was fired from the Southwestern Baptist Theological Seminary. He also withdrew from giving a keynote address at the 2018 SBC meeting.[42] Pressler was a former Texas state representative who would go on to serve as a Judge on the Texas 14th Circuit Court of Appeals. However, in 2018, Pressler was accused by multiple men of molesting and raping them when they were minors. There are civil lawsuits pending in those cases, one of which also names Patterson as having concealed Pressler's crimes,[43] though most of the claims of sexual assault have been dismissed due to the relevant statute of limitations.[44] Back in 1967, however, their goal was to control the SBC, and through their strategic planning and the Pressler-Patterson coalition, they accomplished this feat in ten years.[45]

Still, the fundamentalist impulse did not materialize from thin air. Others have pointed to the battles over the interpretation of Genesis that consumed the SBC in the 1960s.[46] Afraid of the cultural changes unfolding throughout the country and implemented or validated by the courts, the literalist wing of the SBC feared what they saw as a slippery slope toward moderation within their own faith group. This would leave no pocket of their lives where conservatism and their specific brand of moralism remained status quo—a pocket where they were in the majority. That general fear has been dissected by scholars often and with great skill. While some cite the inerrancy of the Bible[47] and theology as sources of the strain, others point to racism, to the threat of integration, to the rise of feminism, to government control, or to the culture wars as a whole as fueling the fundamentalist plot. And it was, indeed, a plot. By the time the dust had settled and "the fundamentalists (who termed themselves 'conservatives') achieved a complete victory, the 'moderates' (whom the polite fundamentalists referred to as 'liberals' but other conservatives called 'rats' and 'skunks') charged that the fundamentalists were leaders of the Inquisition, but they were routed."[48]

In truth, the SBC moderates were not unfamiliar to challenges from the fringe, and the organization as a whole did not stumble into politics in the 1970s. The Landmarkers, one of the four groups that first fed into the SBC coalition in the nineteenth century, insisted on the exclusivity of the Baptist faith as the "true church," which could be traced back the New Testament. They insisted that all baptism be conducted by Baptists, and labeled any other an "alien immersion." The extremism extended to opinions on communion and church leadership, and eventually some left the SBC in 1905.[49] In the 1920s, debate regarding the validity of evolution as opposed to the Old Testament account of creation forced members of the SBC to take a stand on biblical literalism. As a compromise of sorts the SBC adopted the Baptist Faith and Message of 1925, stating that the "Holy Bible was written by men divinely inspired, and is a perfect treasure of heavenly instruction; that it has God for its author, salvation for its end, and truth, without any mixture of error."[50] This somewhat blended creed satisfied those "who believed that the denomination needed to declare its doctrinal position," while "those who objected to creeds found the statement ambiguous enough to merit their acquiescence."[51]

In the aftermath of World War II, the National Association of Evangelicals (NAE), "abandoning the traditional term 'fundamentalist' in favor of the more optimistic-sounding 'evangelical.'" stirred controversy by dipping its toes in the political waters. Among other efforts, the NAE pushed for the protection of evangelical preachers' rights to broadcast their programs on the federal airwaves, they sought to curb the commercial promotion of alcohol, they argued against the centralization of public schooling to protect local control, and they made a major push against communism.[52] Most recently, Kevin Kruse argued that the religious fervor of the post–World War II era was less about anti-communism and more about a kind of Christian-based corporatism aimed at rescinding much of the New Deal policies and culture.[53] The NAE was not alone on in the political arena. In 1946, the SBC launched a full-time Washington-based lobbying firm, first called the Joint Committee on Public Relations (changed to "Public Affairs" a few years later), which was supported by moderates and focused primarily on protecting religious liberty and the separation of church and state.[54] They had a political arm, but its purpose (until the late 1970s) was to keep faith and government at an arm's length. In the 1960s, anti-Catholic sentiment pitted the SBC against Kennedy,[55] perhaps not as militantly as some religious groups since moderates were still in control of the organization, but flexing their political muscles all the same.

In this sense, the fundamentalist uprising and the politicization that followed should not have come as a surprise. It is the harvest of seeds sown across the decades. In 1963, for example, a pastor at the Midwestern Baptist Theological Seminary named Ralph Elliot resigned after his book *The Message of Genesis* stirred serious controversy among Southern Baptist leaders.[56] The book, which offered a more liberal interpretation of the Old Testament, threatened literalists, forcing the SBC to issue a more strongly worded version of the "Baptist Faith and Message" statement almost forty years after its initial publication. Holding the factions together under one umbrella in a decade marked by rapid-fire societal changes proved impossible. In 1968, "in the midst of that year of the assassinations of Martin Luther King, Jr. and Robert Kennedy, the police riot at the Democratic convention, the height of student protests in the Vietnam War, and the beginning of feminist organization," southern Baptists chose fundamentalist W. A. Crisswell, the pastor at that time of First Baptist Church in Dallas, as their president.[57] While in office, Crisswell published *Why I Preach That the Bible Is Literally True*, marking the commencement of a battle royale.[58] Perhaps if these theological battles over the Bible had not taken place simultaneous to the radical cultural changes taking place across the country and particularly in the South, then Crisswell's ascendancy would have stayed relevant only within the SBC itself. However, his success motivated other fundamentalists to organize and to revamp the mission of the SBC and the Joint Committee on Public Affairs, as well as countless other committees that they would soon run and through which they would champion Christian morality in governmental process and policies. Protecting religious freedom shifted toward establishing religion—Southern Baptist Christianity—in as many ways as possible.

Essentially, the SBC only exists as a real convention for a few days each year at the annual meeting. Congregations choose "messengers" to attend and vote on issues and elections. These "messengers" are not seen as traditional representatives of their congregations, but rather they are supposed to "listen when God speaks directly to them."[59] Thus, the wheeling and dealing for leadership positions need not involve congregations at home, but instead takes place in real time during the convention. This key structural element proved critical in the fundamentalist takeover of the SBC and explains, in many ways, how one minor contingency gained so much power so quickly. As previously mentioned, when Paul Pressler and Paige Patterson plotted their attack, they recognized that they did not need a true grassroots uprising. They needed to lobby hard at the convention and successfully elect a fundamentalist president because that president would have the power to nominate other fundamentalists to the SBC Committee on Committees. The Committee on Committees would nominate fellow literalists to the Committee on Nominations, and the Committee on Nominations would then select fundamentalists as "like-minded trustees and directors to Southern Baptist agencies and institutions who would hire like-minded staff." Pressler admitted that the pyramid, trickle-down strategy was aggressive: "we are going for the jugular. We are going for . . . trustees of all our institutions, who are not going to sit there like a bunch of dummies and rubber stamp everything that's presented to them."[60]

At the 1979 convention held in Houston, Texas, the Pressler-Patterson strategy was put into action. They held a strong pre-campaign conducted in fifteen states aimed at selecting the right "messengers." They had a noticeable presence at the actual convention too. "Pressler, Patterson, and others occupied a command post in 'sky-boxes' above the convention floor and maintained contact with the floor beneath through an elaborate communications network,"[61] and they succeeded easily. Their candidate, Adrian Rogers of Bellevue Baptist Church in Memphis, Tennessee, won a six-way race on the first ballot. They have won most elections since, including Patterson's own in 1998. The success shocked many who would come to recognize the significance of the SBC's race to the right, but the power of politics should never be underestimated. These "messengers," as their name suggests, were believed to be decidedly different from political delegates, un-bound to any community, and responsible only to a higher power. Nevertheless, in the absence of other persuasive voices, a plotted and sophisticated campaign such as the Patterson-Pressler coalition is virtually unstoppable.

The willingness to mimic public-sphere political wheeling and dealing in the scared sphere reflected how urgent many conservatives felt it was to stem the tides of change erupting in the 1960s and 1970s. The loss of control that many white men felt as racial and gender barriers were being toppled, or at least bent, fu-eled the desire to establish a definitive command over the SBC. Analysis of key documents coming out of the SBC during this transition period reveal the ob-session with the enforcement of traditional women's roles in regards to careers, sexuality, and reproduction, with female pastors being specifically targeted.[62] Anthony Hankins contends in *Uneasy in Babylon: Southern Baptist Conservatives in American Culture* that the motivation came from the fact that these leaders, "as young men, moved outside the South intellectually, and in some cases geographically.... They became convinced that the South was no longer immune to diversity, pluralism, and secularism, and they began to mobilize."[63] The "us" became fundamentalist Southern Baptists and the "them" became everyone else— even including moderate Baptists, with each SBC election presenting opposing slates of candidates in what foreshadowed the contemporary partisan dynamics in American politics.[64] Fundamentalists felt discriminated against in their own place of worship, so they remade the SBC in their image.

From the "self-righteousness of Evangelical exclusiveness"[65] in the Old South to the Baptist tradition as dissenters from persecution,[66] to the lost causes of all things southern, the SBC was primed for victimization. And it can be a deep well to draw from. Religious activism can spring from discrimination or even the perception of discrimination, as it has throughout human history. What might be perceived as "instruments of acquiescence" (in this case, organized religion), claims Fred Harris in his work on the influence of religion on the political activism of African Americans, "may actually serve as disguised forms of resistance."[67] In this case the congregants were white southern literalists—many of whom already felt alienated by changes to the racial dynamics in the region— and the SBC would be their commandeered, armored tank of resistance. These feelings of reverse racial persecution merged for many with a perception of religious persecution, and those feelings would linger long after the takeover of the SBC. In fact, activating those feelings has become an integral part of keeping the religious-political bond tied every so tightly. Perhaps the most poignant contemporary example is the perceived "war on Christmas" that many Republicans proclaim, including 2012 presidential nominee Mitt Romney who told campaign audiences, "I believe that we should be able to have religious ornamentation and celebration in the public square. Whether that's a manger or a menorah, or representatives of other faiths, it is important for us as a society to recognize that we look to God for many of our blessings."[68] Donald Trump took the sentiment a step further on the campaign trail, insisting he would "end the War on Christmas,"[69] and fanning the flames of anti-Christian bias.

This sense of persecution, which a Public Religion Research Institute/ Brookings Institution poll found to be present in eight of ten white evangelical Protestants,[70] can be seen even in a comparison of white fundamentalists and non-fundamentalists in terms of how many report experiences of reverse racism. According to the 2012 Blair Center Poll, as seen in Figure 8.2, a significantly higher percentage of white fundamentalists, both non-southern and southern, perceive that they have been discriminated against based on their race than do non-fundamentalists across a battery of questions. In addition, southern fundamentalists have the greatest percentage of respondents reporting reverse discrimination in general (47 percent). Similarly, almost 48 percent of

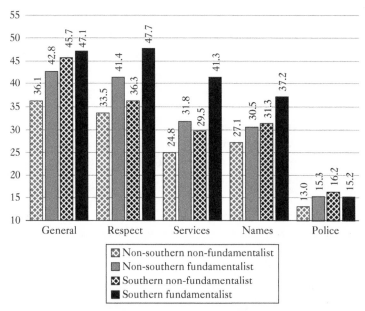

FIGURE 8.2 Percent Reporting Experiences with the Following Types of Reverse Racial Discrimination, Among Whites, by Fundamentalism (Biblical Literalism), 2012

Data are from the 2012 Blair Center Poll.

white southern fundamentalists feel they are treated with less respect than other people, 41 percent claim to receive poorer service than other people at restaurants or stores, and 37 percent report being called names or insulted based on their race. Moreover, name-calling is the only category where there is no significant difference between fundamentalists and non-fundamentalists among those who identify as southern. Non-southern non-fundamentalists, on the other hand, perceive the least amount of discrimination, with only 36.1 percent reporting to experiencing reverse discrimination in general.

In this sense, for many southern white fundamentalists, their frustration with moderates, which prompted their politicization within the SBC, may have merged with their frustration with post–civil rights social changes and political correctness, fueling a complex, intersectional alienation. In terms of feeling targeted for their fundamentalist beliefs alone, which GOP political rhetoric emphasizes, fundamentalists and evangelicals may sense that they are disliked by a lot of Americans and have been for a long time. In their 1996 study, for example, Louis Bolce and Gerald De Maio found that a significant portion (35 percent) of the agnostic American population held "very negative" or "negative" feelings toward fundamentalists, while only 11 percent held them in a "positive" or "very positive" light.[71] That antipathy to fundamentalists is a political force as well, as the scholars note in a study in which they report that 70 percent of those with negative views of fundamentalists voted for Democrat Al Gore in 2000.[72] The fundamentalist takeover would damage the SBC brand in the eyes of many outsiders, but that hostility would only heighten this multidimensional sense of persecution so familiar to southern white audiences.

TO BE FAIR, there were moderates who fought valiantly (but failed) to protect the SBC from what they saw as deeply politicized extremism. The Southern Baptist Alliance, for example, organized in 1986 after failing once again to recapture leadership for moderates, promoted seven key principles, at the heart of which was the individual freedom of churches and members and the "calling of men and women to ministry." Social justice advocacy, modern biblical interpretation, and servant leadership values were championed, though many grieved for what they feared was the permanent loss of their beloved institution to fundamentalists.[73] Most moderates failed to believe that the fundamentalist surge was anything more than a momentary interruption (77 percent initially expected "no concrete effects from the takeover").[74] The Baptist media, according to Louis Moore at the *Houston Chronicle*, "treated the controversy as a Watergate-like scandal to be exposed and stamped out."[75] The takeover was seen as a political conspiracy that did not reflect the truth of the membership, and so many worked diligently to stay unified despite the change in leadership. However, the confidence in a reconciliation waned with each passing year. In 1985, 33 percent of SBC members surveyed were "hopeful, see signs of reconciliation" with only 6 percent "grieving that SBC has been lost." By 1988, only 14 percent remained optimistic, while 47 percent reported mourning the loss.[76] The moderates who had run the SBC for generations were "bitterly resented" by fundamentalists for cooperating with "people who held nontraditional theological and social views."[77] The fundamentalists who had felt excluded, according to religious historian David Striklin, then excluded moderates when they got their first taste of power.

Within ten years, fundamentalists, according to plan, had seized majority control of the SBC committees. Moderates made a last stand of sorts in Dallas in 1986 without much success. The next year in St. Louis at the 1987 convention, the Peace Committee, created to foster cooperation between the warring factions, issued a report that more or less blamed both sides for getting too political.[78] Fundamentalist Adrian Rogers was elected once again to the SBC presidency, with 60 percent of the vote, and the convention sermon, delivered by Jerry Vines, doubled down on inerrancy. "If one cannot believe what the Bible says about history," professed Vines, "one cannot believe what it says about eternity. And if one does not believe what it says about creation, one cannot be sure of what it says about salvation."[79] Perhaps the nail in the coffin for moderates, and there are many that could be chosen, arose at the San Antonio convention in 1988 when Resolution No. 5 passed by a vote of 10,950 to 9,050. The resolution, sponsored by fundamentalist leaders, established the power and "authority of the pastor," which for Baptists flies in the face of the founding principle of individualism. Nevertheless, the fundamentalists believed that individualism, also called the "priesthood of the believer," allowed moderates (whom they called "liberals") to "believe anything they wanted to believe and still be loyal Southern Baptists." Pastors would no longer simply serve as inspiration to a community of equal believers, they would rule over them.[80]

The political ambitions of the SBC leadership quickly began to eclipse their sacred purpose. They turned their attention also to the Baptist Joint Committee on Public Affairs (BJC), which had painstakingly garnered a reputation for moderation and for supporting the separation of church and state. The SBC Executive Committee withdrew funding from the BJC "because it would not cooperate with the fundamentalist agenda to restore publicly-led prayer in schools, government vouchers to attend religious schools and other right wing political/religious goals."[81] Specifically, from 1989 to 1993, funding for the BJC decreased from $448,400 to $0, and the Christian Life Commission (CLC) was empowered instead to recommend "the SBC's position on moral and ethical issues" and to lobby and organize accordingly. Whereas the BJC focused solely on issues related to religious liberty, the CLC broadened its scope and the political influence of the SBC dramatically.[82] The BJC was not the only organization singled out by the fundamentalists. The Home Mission Board, the Foreign Mission Board, the Sunday School Board, as well as the press and educational wings of the organization, were heavily scrutinized.[83] The tactics of the new SBC were difficult for any moderates to survive. Ideological tests, scrutiny of seminaries, and a growing "list of activities, associations, and beliefs that constituted deviation from approved Southern Baptist standards was slowly being lengthened,"[84] all in an effort to purge "liberals" from the organization as a whole under the fundamentalist regime. Not only were seminary students granted official permission by the SBC Executive Board to tape their professor's lectures in an effort to catch heretics, the board also terminated the editors at the Associated Baptist Press for negative coverage of the fundamentalists' rise to power.[85]

At the heart of the purge remained the notion of biblical inerrancy, which worked because it forced members to take sides. The issue was black and white and the "gray" belief in divine inspiration or in interpretation was simply non-fundamentalist, period. Inerrancy, as Rob James and Gary Leazer contend, makes "no's" look weak and less committed. "The inerrancy issue has worked as a yes/ no question, like 'Have you stopped beating your wife,'" they argued. And, "a moderate with any honesty," they contend, "cannot answer that question without appearing to lack faith in scripture's spiritual perfection, even though he or she believes in the Bible just as much as the fundamentalist questioner."[86] This purifi- cation strategy (or a least forced obedience), utilized a "rhetoric of exclusion" that merged, according to Carl Kell and Ray Camp, the "rhetoric of fundamentalism" and the "rhetoric of inerrancy."[87] It also played on fears—fear of abandonment, fear of persecution, fear of social rejection—which in turn forced the moderates who were not purged into taking a more conservative stance. The threat was not limited to those on the opposite side of the battlefields of the culture wars, but ex- tended within their own ranks. The price of membership became ideological and theological extremism, a technique part and parcel to white southern identity that is, of course, based on a definitive group belonging at the extreme exclusion of others.

The dissidents, despite the fact that they reflected a long-standing streak of progressives in the SBC, were drowned out.[88] For lifetime SBC members, such as Paul Simmons, the takeover was personally painful. Considering him- self a religious exile, he wrote, in a collection entitled *Exiled: Voices of the Southern Baptist Convention Holy War*, that "I was there. I did my best to keep it from happening!"[89] His story joins countless others, compiled in the years after the "war," which, perhaps more than anything else, illustrates the power of belonging associated with religion, particularly in the South. Simmons compares himself to the Dalai Lama,[90] kicked out of his homeland. Others described the experience as "a lot like dying."[91] William Faulkner described this type of dying when he mourned the loss of the moderate stance on integration. "But where will we go," he wrote in his "Letter to the North" that appeared in *Life* magazine in 1956, "if the middle becomes untenable? If we have to va- cate it in order to keep from being trampled?" Moderates either left the SBC, or they moved to the right theologically, publicly, and politically. The trickle- down fundamentalist takeover did exactly that to the SBC and its millions of members.

This absolutism has political ramifications as well. As the SBC and fundamentalists grew increasingly politicized, the GOP became, via the Long Southern Strategy, the only acceptable partner. Looking, for example, at the 2012 presidential election reveals not only that fundamentalists overwhelm- ingly identified as Republican, but also they were more likely to vote with the party at the ballot box. As shown in Table 8.1, non-fundamentalists outside of the South or who do not consider themselves southern, but who do identify as

Table 8.1 Percent Party Identification and Vote for Romney, by Fundamentalism (Biblical Literalism), Among Whites, 2012

		Republican	Republican vote for Romney	Independent	Independent vote for Romney
Non-South	Non-fundamentalist	37.7	85.4	18.4	35.1
	Fundamentalist	55.0	94.4	20.1	36.8
South	Non-fundamentalist	44.2	94.3	21.0	54.3
	Fundamentalist	65.7	97.7	20.7	84.7
Non-southern	Non-fundamentalist	38.1	88.6	18.3	34.4
	Fundamentalist	57.9	94.6	21.8	44.4
Southern	Non-fundamentalist	48.9	91.3	25.0	77.4
	Fundamentalist	62.3	100.0	19.4	87.1

Data are from the 2012 Blair Center Poll.

Republican, voted for the GOP nominee Mitt Romney at the rates of 85.4 percent and 88.6 percent respectively. These are high rates, but they are significantly lower than fundamentalist Republicans. White fundamentalist Republicans who live in the South, for example, voted for the party at the rate of 99.2 percent, and for white fundamentalist Republicans who also call themselves southern, support for Romney was unanimous in this Blair Center Poll sample. These high rates of party loyalty among fundamentalists in general, especially those who live in the South or those who identify as southern, are particularly powerful since those white subgroups are so large in number.

Moreover, such absolute party loyalty among fundamentalists in the region tends to pull the middle—where non-Republican fundamentalists might reside—ever rightward. In this case, the vote choice made by true independents (those who do not report leaning toward either party) is telling, though the sample sizes get fairly small at this point. Overall, roughly 20 percent of each subgroup claims no allegiance or leaning to either of the two major parties, with southern white non-fundamentalists at the highest level (25 percent). Despite the relative consistency of the independent rate across subgroups, the vote choice made by independents in 2012 varies significantly. For example, of the 20.1 percent of white fundamentalists living outside of the South and who call themselves independents, only 36.8 percent voted for the Republican nominee. Fundamentalist independents who live in South, however, chose Romney at a rate of 84.7 percent, a significant 47.9 percent difference. Additionally, 87.1 percent of fundamentalist independents who identify as southern also voted with the GOP. Even non-fundamentalist independents in the South (54.3 percent) or who identify as southern (77.4 percent) voted for Romney, though at significantly lower rates than their fundamentalist counterparts. That is how successful the Long Southern Strategy turned out to be in marrying the GOP and the SBC. It too made it impossible for a middle to hold.

THE LEGACY OF the SBC's purging of moderates not only shows up at the ballot box, but also surfaces in the fact that the organization's issue positions showed—expectedly—little moderation. White southern identity has always been based on extreme positioning—racial purity, massive resistance to integration, secession—so such stances struck a familiar chord. And fanaticism works hand in hand with alienation. Faulkner's letter did not end with his prediction about the collapse of the middle. He saw several steps down the road, positing that white southerners in the era beyond civil rights would transition from oppressor to oppressed. "So the underdog," he speculated, "will be that white embattled minority who are our blood and kin." That perceived zero-sum game of racial dominance easily translated to religious authority. Absolutism and victimization came to characterize the SBC and would spill over into its politics, particularly on policy issues that threatened fundamentalist values. Political engagement was no longer a choice; it was a requirement. Specifically, under fundamentalist leadership, Resolution No. 8 that passed at that 1988 San Antonio "nail in the coffin" convention mandated political activism on the issue of abortion. That political kettle had almost reached full boil in the fifteen years since the decision in the Texas-based case *Roe v. Wade* had been handed down.

Angela Wilson notes that "it comes as little surprise that one of the most fervent sexual religious battles in American history was sparked off in the South."[92] The fight, of course, did not stay regional. Within three years of the Supreme Court's decision in *Roe v. Wade*, abortion became a major issue in the 1976 presidential campaign. President Nixon made no comment when *Roe* was handed down, but Ford, then serving as House Minority Leader, authored an unsuccessful amendment to revoke the ruling. By the time Ford took center stage as the GOP nominee, however, Catholic pro-life advocacy groups pushed the party platform toward a wholescale pro-life position.[93] Still, Carter as a "born-again" Christian carried the majority of Southern Baptist voters. The support proved temporary, as Republicans continued to seize on the mobilization of white Protestant evangelical fundamentalists on these trigger moral issues.

The fact that Carter won the support of the SBC over the new pro-life platform of the GOP, however, did not indicate the SBC stance on abortion was moderate or becoming more moderate. Rather, the SBC had already started taking a more extreme stance on abortion beginning in 1971. During that decade, they shifted from opposing abortion but making exceptions for rape, incest, severe fetal deformities, or the life of the mother, to passing resolutions using the terminology "unborn persons" with only a threat to the mother's life as an acceptable concession.[94] This shift, in large part, explains why in the South, as a whole, opposition has remained the most conservative nationally for forty years.[95] Such a conservative pro-life stance also helped forge common ground between demographic groups and denominations with varying motivations. Research has shown, for example, that the educated religious faithful opposed abortion on the grounds of the "sanctity of life," while fundamentalists feared that legal abortion would lead to sexual promiscuity.[96] However, by the early 1980s, analysis of the SBC and the National Council of Catholic Bishops (NCCB) reveals that both organizations were expressing a common anti-choice stance.[97] As a result of that shift, absolute adherence to a pro-life position and pro-life leadership became required of GOP national contenders because of the growing power of the southern white base. Even Bob Dole, the 1996 presidential nominee of the party, helped fundamentalists block the appointment of a pro-choice physician, Henry Foster, to Surgeon General.[98] John McCain, born an Episcopalian in Arizona, went so far in his 2008 effort to campaign as a Southern Baptist (though ministers claimed he had not been baptized) that he publicly insisted that *Roe* be overturned.[99] Four years later, in the lead-up to the 2012 contest, Mitt Romney also reversed course on abortion,[100] rather than commit political suicide in the South by arguing for moderation on the issue.

This increasingly radical stance on abortion also reflected the misogyny of the SBC and its resistance to what was seen as women's authority over their own bodies. The resulting reassertion of the patriarchy in the SBC had additional repercussions as well, as it was coupled by a reassertion of the Christian definition of marriage. The equally absolutist battle against gay rights was connected to women's liberation, and much like female submission, it was backed up by scripture, which in this case interpreted homosexuality as sin. The misogyny and anti-gay bigotry bled together easily. Ted Jelen, perhaps the most prolific political science scholar who studied the effects of southern religion, finds fundamentalism having a significant impact on tolerance levels in general, including toward homosexuals.[101] Moreover, fundamentalism, specifically, has been shown to be a significant predictor of prejudice against gay men and women, even after controlling for other measures that evaluate orthodoxy or authoritarianism.[102] Southern fundamentalists were the first to mobilize[103] and they played "the 'queer card,'" notes Rita Whitlock, "because, unlike outright racial or sexist sentiments, they can do so without penalty of public outcry."[104] At that time, homophobic discrimination need not be coded.

As late as the Carter administration, politicians felt little pressure to respond to gay rights. However, as protests increased in the early 1970s, cities across the country responded by passing anti-discrimination ordinances to protect gay Americans, launching the National Gay Task Force, and initiating peaceful demonstrations in places like Greenwich Village. The American Psychiatric Association even declassified homosexuality as a mental disorder in 1973.[105] In response, the SBC went on the attack, petitioning against Gay Pride Day and ratifying official resolutions against homosexuality. Support for the anti-gay position grew stronger as the GOP and fundamentalist Christians grew increasingly co-dependent. In the 1990s, for example, subgroups like the American Family Association continued to attack homosexuals as "a threat to society," issuing literature to their members, insisting that gay Americans are not "normal, healthy, everyday people" and that they are not "an oppressed minority" with the need to have their civil rights protected.[106] In 2004, the Louisiana televangelist Jimmy Swaggart delivered a speech in Toronto on the issue of gay marriage that soon circulated throughout Christian media outlets and signaled a new absolutism. In it, Swaggart equated same-sex marriage with a sin so severe as to be punishable by death. "I've never seen a man in my life I wanted to marry," he proclaimed, "and I'm going to be blunt and plain: If one ever looks at me like that, I'm going to kill him and tell God he died."[107] That same year, religious voters helped to pass thirteen state constitutional amendments to ban gay marriage,[108] while voting George W. Bush into his second term. And though there has been widespread opposition to gay rights across a variety of faith groups, a 2013 Public Religion Research Institute poll shows that only among white evangelical Protestants do more people favor (56 percent) allowing small business owners to refuse services to the gay and lesbian community than people who oppose (39 percent) such policies.[109]

A backward glance indicates that the fundamentalist takeover of the SBC changed a great deal more than just church leadership. By simultaneously purging moderates while politicizing the remainder of the flock, the SBC cultivated rigid and absolutist voters, and the GOP's Long Southern Strategy called them to the polls. Thus far, it has been a permanent shift in which white southern culture, particularly patriarchy, melds with white southern faith and white southern politics. As seen in Figure 8.3A, the percentage of white respondents from the 2012 Blair Center Poll who favor or oppose gay marriage is affected by both southern identity and fundamentalism. There are significant differences in the percentages of fundamentalist respondents who oppose gay marriage compared to the percentages of non-fundamentalists who oppose gay marriage. Among white Americans who do not call themselves southern, 52.9 percent of fundamentalists "strongly oppose" gay marriage, with

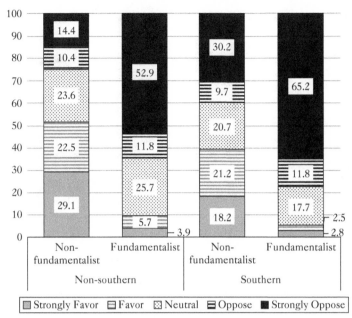

FIGURE 8.3A Percent Attitudes Toward Gay Marriage, Among Whites, by Fundamentalism (Biblical Literalism), 2012

Data are from the 2012 Blair Center Poll.

another 11.8 percent who "oppose" it for a total of 64.7 percent. However, for non-southern whites who are not fundamentalists, "strong" opposition stands at 14.4 percent and "opposition" at 10.4 percent, for a total of 24.8 percent—a significant gap of nearly 40 points when compared to non-southern fundamentalists. Among southern white respondents, the opposition is higher. For southern white fundamentalists, 65.2 percent "strongly oppose," and an additional 11.8 percent "oppose," for a total of 77 percent, 13 points higher than non-southern fundamentalists. Southern whites who are not fundamentalists, however, "strongly oppose" gay marriage at a rate of 30.2 percent, and "oppose" at a rate of 9.7 percent, for a total just shy of 40 percent. This is higher than non-southern, non-fundamentalists by 15.2 points. But the gap between southern fundamentalists and southern non-fundamentalist is close to 40 points, just as it is among non-southerners.

There are similar patterns in the 2012 Blair Center Poll when looking at attitudes toward abortion. As seen in Figure 8.3B, there are dramatic differences between fundamentalists and non-fundamentalists. Looking first at non-southern respondents, 58.7 percent of non-fundamentalists reported that "by

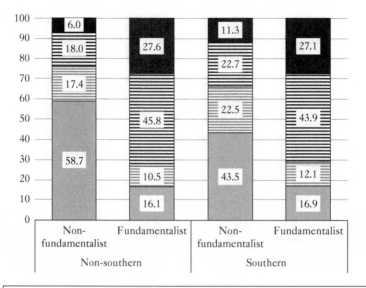

FIGURE 8.3B Percent Attitudes Toward Abortion, Among Whites, by Fundamentalism (Biblical Literalism), 2012

Data are from the 2012 Blair Center Poll.

law, a woman should always be able to obtain an abortion as a matter of personal choice," while only 16.1 percent of fundamentalists agreed with that position. Among southern respondents, 43.5 percent of non-fundamentalists hold this least restrictive view that abortion should always be legal, which is 15 percent less than their non-southern counterparts (58.7 percent) and 23.6 points higher than southern white fundamentalists, only 16.9 percent of whom share that opinion. That rate, 16.9 percent of southern white fundamentalists, is actually 0.08 percent higher than non-southern white fundamentalists. At the other end of the spectrum, the pattern is the same too, with southern white fundamentalists slightly less likely to say abortion should never be legal (27.1 percent) than non-southern white fundamentalists (27.6 percent), though the difference is statistically insignificant. However, among the non-fundamentalists, identifying as southern makes one nearly twice as likely (11.3 percent to 6.0 percent) to hold this strictest anti-abortion position. So that extreme pro-life position, now a litmus test for GOP contenders, wins the candidate a lot of fundamentalist friends, and among white southerners, it draws a crowd even outside of the fundamentalist community, making it a wise investment that still pays off on Election Day.

IN 2016, SOUTHERN fundamentalists—inclusive to those who are biblical literalists and those who self-identify as Christian fundamentalists—are still twice as likely to be Baptist (46.3 percent) as non-southern fundamentalists (21 percent), securing the SBC's role as the engine driving the political-religious train. Despite that demarcation, southern and non-southern white fundamentalists remain demographically similar. They are still slightly older and with lower incomes than non-fundamentalists. They are less educated, a finding supported by a 2014 Pew survey, which revealed that only 19 percent of SBC members had a college degree.[110] Partisanship still creates a divide, with 80.2 percent of southern white fundamentalists identifying as Republican, compared to 66.4 percent of non-southern fundamentalists—still a sizeable majority, but a gap nonetheless. In similar fashion, non-southern fundamentalists, as shown in Figure 8.4, still report experiences of reverse racial discrimination more often than non-southern non-fundamentalists, except in terms of discrimination by the police, and

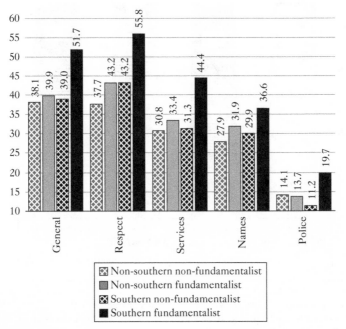

FIGURE 8.4 Percent Reporting Experience with the Following Types of Reverse Racial Discrimination, Among Whites, by Fundamentalism (Biblical Literalism and/or Self-identified), 2016

Data are from the 2016 Blair Center Poll.

southern fundamentalists still do so at significantly higher rates than southern non-fundamentalists in nearly every category, from facing discrimination by the service industry to being disrespected.

The most common experience of discrimination—being disrespected—was reported by 55.8 percent of southern white fundamentalists, compared to 43.2 percent of their non-southern counterparts. That number is slightly higher than what non-southern fundamentalists reported in 2012 (41.4 percent)—which is fairly consistent across the battery of questions for this group. However, for the southern white fundamentalists, the percent reporting being disrespected based on their race in 2016 (55.8 percent), is over 8 points higher than in 2012 (47.7 percent), and these 2016 shifts are consistent even when examining the narrower measure of fundamentalism—biblical literalism—that was used in 2012. Somehow, religious angst and racial angst still bleed together for many white Americans, particularly those who identify as southern.

Perhaps because of this increased perception of discrimination, or perhaps because of the presence of a staunch defender of women's reproductive rights

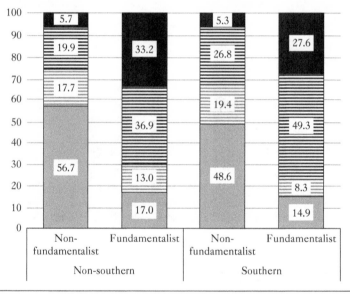

FIGURE 8.5A   Percent Attitudes Toward Abortion, Among Whites, by Fundamentalism (Biblical Literalism and/or Self-identified), 2016

Data are from the 2016 Blair Center Poll.

at the top of the Democratic ticket, southern fundamentalists in 2016 reported more absolutist abortion attitudes than in 2012, as shown in Figure 8.5A. In 2016, 76.9 percent of southern fundamentalists reported that abortion should never be legal or only legal in the cases of rape, incest, or danger to the mother's life, which is almost 6 points higher than four years prior, and is significantly higher southern non-fundamentalists.

Attitudes among non-southern fundamentalists have moved in the opposite direction. Whereas in 2012, 73.4 percent of non-southern fundamentalists held one of these two strictest views on abortion, that number has dropped to 71.1 percent in 2016, though the portion of that 71.1 percent who fall in to the "never legal" category is slightly higher in 2016 (32.8 percent) than in 2012 (27.6 percent). Among non-fundamentalists, those who believe abortion should always be legal are near or above majorities in 2016, with 56.7 percent of non-southerners supporting unrestricted legality and 48.6 percent of southern non-fundamentalists. All of these patterns are consistent even if the 2016 sample is limited to biblical literalists, revealing again how significantly fundamentalism, no matter the measure, and southernness can alter one's political worldview.

For many of Trump's religious voters, abortion was cited as the main reason for supporting his candidacy in the hope that he would appoint a pro-life justice to the empty seat on the Supreme Court. Figure 8.5B considers, for each subgroup, the percent who believe in an absolute ban on abortion alongside the percent who supported the GOP nominees in both 2012 and 2016. Non-fundamentalist non-southern whites are consistent both in 2012 and 2016, with roughly 6 percent believing that abortion should never be legal and giving around 41–43 percent of their votes to the GOP nominee. Southern white fundamentalists are also consistent but at the opposite end of the spectrum, with about 27 percent supporting an absolute ban on abortion without exceptions and voting for the Republican presidential nominee at a rate of almost 88 percent, both in 2012 and 2016. However, there is movement among non-southern fundamentalists and southern non-fundamentalists. In 2012, both of these groups voted for the GOP candidate to the tune of 71 percent, though their respective opposition to all abortion ranged from 11.3 percent for non-fundamentalists who do claim a southern identity to 27.6 percent of fundamentalists who do not claim a southern identity. That being said, in 2016, support for the GOP candidate dropped by double digits among southern white non-fundamentalists to 57.4 percent, as did opposition to all abortions, which fell to 5.3 percent. On the other hand, non-southern white fundamentalists increased their support for the GOP-nominee to 75 percent, up 3.6 points, and the percentage of those who believed abortion should never be legal also increased to 33.2 percent, up 5.6 points. Perhaps the most important thing to notice is that at the extreme ends of the graph—the top

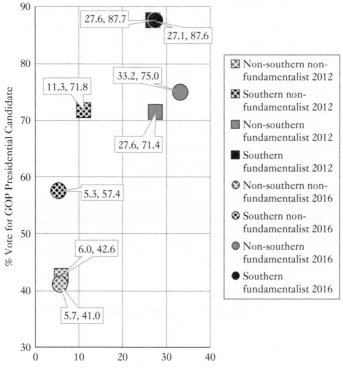

FIGURE 8.5B Percent Who Believe Abortion Should "Never" Be Legal and Percent Vote for GOP Presidential Nominee, by Fundamentalism (Biblical Literalism in 2012 and Biblical Literalism and/or Self-identified in 2016), 2012–2016

Data are from the 2012 and 2016 Blair Center Polls.

right and the bottom left—sit southern fundamentalists and non-southern, non-fundamentalists respectively, pointing to how significantly each label influences the ballot box.

The partisanship of fundamentalists has also proved more extreme in the wake of the 2016 election. As shown in Figure 8.6, now 80.2 percent of southern white fundamentalists (the inclusive definition) define themselves as "strongly Republican," "Republican," or "Independent-leaning-Republican," with 26.1 percent reporting the most intense affiliation. This is a substantial increase from the 62.3 percent Republican overall in 2012. Among white fundamentalists in the non-South, the South, and among whites who do not identify as southern, the percentage carrying the GOP label has risen as well, though by about 10 points, less than the almost 18-point jump among southern white fundamentalists.

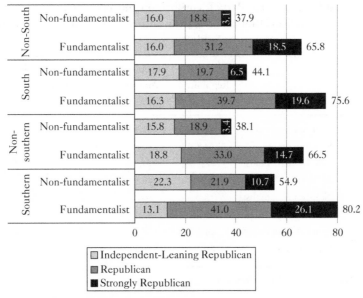

FIGURE 8.6 Percent Republican by Fundamentalism (Biblical Literalism and/or Self-identified), Among Whites, 2016

Data are from the 2016 Blair Center Poll.

All patterns are consistent irrespective of the broader fundamentalist measure in 2016.

As shown in Table 8.2, this growing percentage of self-identified Republicans and Republican-leaners voted for the GOP nominee in 2016 at slightly lower levels than they did in 2012. Among Republican southern white fundamentalists, for whom Romney was a unanimous choice, support for Trump dipped to 96.6 percent, while among non-southern, non-fundamentalist, white Republicans, support dropped to 80.8 percent, down 7.3 points from 2012.

Moreover, whereas roughly 20 percent of every subgroup identified as true independents in 2012 (with southern, non-fundamentalists slightly higher at 25 percent), in the 2016 sample, that number has changed among fundamentalists. Among fundamentalist whites in the non-South, it has fallen to 15.4 percent—making sample sizes even smaller—and for fundamentalist whites living in the geographic South it has fallen to 14 percent independent. Independents now make up 17 percent of non-southern fundamentalists, and among southern white fundamentalists, that middle has shrunk to just 9.7 percent. Maybe the partisan stakes seem higher now. Maybe polarization is causing more white Americans to lean away from that pure middle. That being said, among whites living outside of the South, independent support for Trump was greater than it was for

Table 8.2 Percent Party Identification and Vote for Trump,
by Fundamentalism (Biblical Literalism and/or Self-identified), Among
Whites, 2016

		Republican	Republican Vote for Trump	Independent	Independent Vote for Trump
Non-South	Non-fundamentalist	37.9	82.6	20.4	43.4
	Fundamentalist	65.8	89.9	15.4	56.4
South	Non-fundamentalist	44.1	81.3	23.3	28.3
	Fundamentalist	75.6	96.3	14.0	55.0
Non-southern	Non-fundamentalist	38.0	80.8	21.8	36.9
	Fundamentalist	66.4	90.9	17.0	48.6
Southern	Non-fundamentalist	54.9	85.2	18.8	40.0
	Fundamentalist	80.2	96.6	9.7	66.3

Data are from the 2016 Blair Center Poll.

Romney among both non-fundamentalists (43.4 percent) and fundamentalists (56.4 percent) by about 8 points and almost 20 points respectively. However, among independents in the geographic South, support for Trump dropped to 28.3 percent among non-fundamentalists (roughly half of what Romney received), and to 55 percent among fundamentalists, a drop of nearly 30 points. Support proved fairly stable from 2012 to 2016 among non-southern white independents, both non-fundamentalists and fundamentalists, with 36.9 and 48.6 percent voting for Trump respectively. Finally, among southern whites who identify as independents, Trump received only 40 percent of the vote from non-fundamentalists and 66.3 percent from fundamentalists, drops of 37.4 points and 20.8 points respectively. All of these shifts are true in 2016 for the biblical literalist measure of fundamentalism as well.

Thus, the middle was less supportive of Trump, but the middle is shrinking. Fundamentalists are more Republican than ever, and that increase perhaps helped to offset the fact that Republicans were slightly less likely to vote for Trump than for Romney four years earlier. That is how powerful the GOP brand has become, particularly for white fundamentalists—and southern white fundamentalists even more so. It can carry the nominee, no matter who he is. And Trump was still able to win the majority of white fundamentalist independents in the South, the non-South, and among self-identified southerners. The only fundamentalist independents from whom Trump did not receive a majority of votes were those who do not claim a southern identity. He came up short at 48.6 percent, which shows that even in that narrow population outside of the two-party system, southern identity exerts an influence.

Panning out to the entire electorate, the power of the fundamentalist designation in combination with southern white identity comes into sharper focus. Throughout the 2016 campaign, pundits and journalists alike questioned how religious voters would respond to the Trump candidacy. After all, Trump has been divorced twice, a factor that for most of American history—until Reagan was elected—was considered fatal for those seeking the presidency. Moreover, Trump had little previous involvement in any church or religious organization, begging the question of whether or not Ted Cruz's or John Kasich's primary voters, both of whom were openly religious candidates, would cast their vote for Trump in the general election. Overall, regardless of party identification, of the white fundamentalists (either measure) in the 2016 Blair Center Poll sample, 85.6 percent claim to have voted in the general election, and of those who voted, 80.2 percent voted for Trump, compared to 12.8 percent for Clinton. The non-southern white fundamentalists who voted split 75 percent for Trump to 16.5 percent for Clinton, but for southern white fundamentalists, the split was wider, with Trump receiving 87.7 percent of the vote, compared to single digits, 7.1 percent, for Clinton—an 80-point gap. Among non-fundamentalist white southerners, that 80-point gap collapses to 27 points, with 57.4 percent reporting they voted for Trump and 30.3 percent for Clinton. However, among white Americans who do not identify as southern or as Christian fundamentalists (or subscribe to biblical literalism), the gap is reversed, with Trump winning 41 percent of the vote to Clinton's 46.7 percent. In a very real sense, southernness and fundamentalism are—in terms of this election—as divisive as partisanship itself, the product (and in many ways, the goal) of the Long Southern Strategy.

SINCE BAPTISTS ARE twice as prominent in the South as they are in any other part of the country,[111] the story of what has happened to the SBC, in many ways, is the story of the region. The fundamentalist takeover of the SBC in the 1970s and 1980s shifted both faith and politics ever rightward. Fundamentalists became fully engaged in policy conflicts and political campaigns, operating from a cosmology in which they are the forces of good in constant battle against the forces of evil.[112] They were defined in opposition not just to non-believers, but also to moderates, independents, and anyone and anything who stands somewhere in the middle of the culture wars. The extremist political positions arose from the fundamentalist crusade to conquer the SBC from top to bottom, capturing first the presidency of the organization and then appointing only fundamentalists to committees until the whole substructure reflected their values. Perhaps the most striking aspect of the coup was the way in which a relatively small percentage of SBC members managed to take power and hold it.[113]

Contrary to common practice, fundamentalists in the SBC did not succeed by compromise or coalition-building. They passed resolutions in their committees enforcing a belief in the inerrancy of the Bible and in the submissiveness of women both in the church and at home.[114] They spied on, accused, and interrogated members, purging all who dare speak of moderation of any kind. Having felt alienated in the decades before the takeover and fed up with the accommodationist stances they believed moderate Baptists were taking on progressive social changes, when their turn came, fundamentalists played hardball, using the threat of exclusion to turn conservatives into reactionaries. That desire to purge reveals just how alienated fundamentalists felt, not only for past decades in the SBC, but also in a rapidly changing American society. That spirit would live on in the larger Christian Right, which has been supported primarily by a section of the population who continues to feel threatened.[115]

This perceived alienation fueled fundamentalists' drive to organize and to bend the country to their liking. School prayer may have catalyzed the evangelical desire for conversion, but by the 1980s, the anti-abortion, anti-feminist, and anti-homosexuality grounds[116] were clearly staked out as part of the GOP's religious messaging in a Long Southern Strategy.[117] The unification of the religious faithful, particularly in the South, around these "family values" issues[118] and anything tangentially related—and more recently, the right to live those values even in the wake of progressive changes—accounts for the collective political power of fundamentalists. As they became increasingly politicized, religiosity became a litmus test for politicians who courted their favor. Gerald Ford, when faced with running against one of their own, strengthened his appeal by showing up at the SBC in person, and Bob Dole, when faced with running against Southern Baptist Bill Clinton, made sure to attend some Baptist services.[119]

The foray of such groups as the SBC into the public arena changed politics forever, as 1964 GOP presidential nominee Barry Goldwater warned. "Mark my word," Goldwater insisted, "if and when these preachers get control of the [Republican] party, and they're sure trying to do so, it's going to be a terrible damn problem. Frankly, these people frighten me. Politics and governing demand compromise."[120] Goldwater knew that a marriage of the two would mean absolutist religious beliefs could turn into absolutist politics. Southern white fundamentalism, led by the SBC, in particular, became both absolutist and ambitious because the issues at hand threatened the core tenets of every layer of the southern white way of life. And that means that the many shades of gray inherent in governance, in policy-making, in the human endeavor for that matter, are lost somewhere in a middle that cannot hold.

9

The Myth of the Social Conservative

Our culture is superior. Our culture is superior . . . because our religion is Christianity and that is the truth that makes men free. . . . We cannot raise a white flag in the cultural war because that war is who we are.

—PAT BUCHANAN[1]

IN THE WAKE of the terrorist attacks on September 11, 2001, President George W. Bush addressed a mournful and anxious nation at the National Cathedral. Regarded as one of the most religious of modern presidents,[2] Bush's evangelicalism was on full display in his interpretation of the tragedy. He believed, rather than resulting from resentment toward America for its long-term involvement in the Middle East, that the country "had been attacked for its values."[3] Once focused primarily on domestic issues, including his faith-based initiatives, Bush was writing himself into this messianic worldview as the leader of the country that now must "answer these attacks and rid the world of evil."[4] Bush's tendency to merge his spiritual autobiography and American history stretched back to his early days in politics when he stopped drinking and used religion to compose "a story to make his life make sense."[5] He did not shy away from asking Texas preachers to "lay hands" on him after being elected governor,[6] or from opening each Cabinet meeting as president with a prayer,[7] or from "witnessing" to other world leaders.[8] Now, after the 9/11 attack, the president's grandiose vision[9] became a justification for war. In his State of the Union address the following January, Bush described the "axis of evil," which included the countries of Iraq, North Korea, and Iran, specifically, but also gathered all suspected terrorist organizations under a rhetorical umbrella. The three-word moniker harkened back to the axis powers of World War II,[10] against which the allies had triumphed, with the evil notion adding a moral cause to a righteous Christian nation's foreign policy.

Social conservatism, cultivated as part of the religious arm of the Long Southern Strategy, evolved into something much broader and more dangerous too. Over a stretch of three tumultuous decades, the Christian Right would inject religion into virtually every domestic and international policy issue, extending its efforts far beyond the bedrocks of abortion and gay marriage. The myth of social conservatism limits the understanding of how interconnected these broader beliefs are for so many in the Grand Old Party. The absolutist spirit promoted by the Southern Baptist Convention (SBC) on domestic issues spilled over into contemporary attitudes toward American foreign policy. Evil, after all, is itself an absolute, allowing for little if any diplomacy.[11] And if "the root of all evil is moral relativism," then it is an easy sell to southern white evangelicals already believing themselves as being persecuted by the American media or political correctness in the ongoing culture wars.[12] As Andrew Preston notes in his book *Sword of the Spirit, Shield of Faith: Religion in American War and Diplomacy*, "To evangelicals, America's national and international weaknesses were inextricably linked." From their vantage point, and with the "blessed assurance,"[13] the cause of American Christianity, particularly for the more extreme and dominant southern white fundamentalists, becomes that of "a nation at war."[14] The ultimate "us vs. them" proved so powerful that even as the country turned against the Iraq war, evangelical leaders continued to support it.[15] Now the dog whistles sound a harmonic combination of "'militarism, masculinism, and messianic zeal.'"[16]

That degree of widespread politicization required more than just an activated SBC. The rise of the larger Christian Right would prove that the American party system is "exceptionally open to penetration by social movements," eventually shaping the GOP platform and nominating process and seizing control of several party organizations at the state and local level.[17] For many Republicans, particularly the campaign strategists, the relationship with evangelicals was tactical only—an effort to compete nationally by solidifying their stronghold in the South. However, each increased level of power or influence was met by higher demands from the Christian Right. By the 1990s, Richard Land, head of the Ethics and Religious Liberty Commission—the public policy division of the SBC—expressed what many fundamentalists were feeling when he told the GOP that "the go-along, get-along strategy is dead. No more engagement. We want a wedding ring, we want a ceremony, we want a consummation of the marriage."[18] The bold stance may have seemed presumptuous, especially since the very notion that "religion and radical politics can be compatible pursuits in American society," argues Anthony Orum, "has stirred considerable controversy."[19] In fact, they proved quite compatible particularly in the South, where church, often the primary institution in many southern communities, and religion seem to structure electoral order, defined by Byron Shafer as "a stable political relationship between the social base, intermediary organizations, and government institutions."[20] The "southern way of religion" found its political voice and planned to use it.

Research has shown that the fundamentalist and evangelical churches in the South and throughout the country went along on the political ride willingly. An examination of Protestant churches from 1972 to 1998 shows an increased willingness to disseminate political messages to congregations and, more important, that the "climate of opinion" and political socialization offered by the church was reflected back in the political opinions of the members "beyond what could otherwise be predicted from personal commitment to traditional values."[21] Hosting conservative evangelical ministers such as Jerry Falwell, who credited himself for "breaking the psychological barrier that religion and politics don't mix,"[22] for example, "propounded" the ideology and position issues of those in attendance.[23] By 1998, 75 percent of evangelical Protestants agreed that "it is important for organized religious groups to stand up for their beliefs in politics."[24]

The Christian Right has included many organizations that have risen and fallen and (some) risen again over time, including the Moral Majority, the Christian Voice, the Religious Roundtable, Conservative Women for America, and the Christian Coalition (which helped Republicans take over Congress in 1994). As of the early 1990s, about half of the people of faith represented by the Christian Right are Baptists, with mainline Protestants coming in at roughly 25 percent and Pentecostals at 15 percent. The rest are disseminated among other denominations.[25] Political unification of this community of believers, including the SBC so dominant in the South, with other Protestant denominations under the umbrella of the Christian Right required common issue positions, financial resources, and some semblance of shared culture. The 1970s and 1980s saw the rise of the mass media empire of evangelicals, including television outlets such as the Christian Broadcasting Network, which was capable of raising substantial amounts of money for GOP candidates,[26] providing a common cultural touchstone. That unity, coupled with increased influence in the party, empowered these religious conservatives. They no longer sought only to protect freedom of exercise, now they wanted the state to endorse "God designed institutions like the family and the church to run under certain authority structures."[27] Such a call rang familiar to white southerners who had sought the sanctioning of their own racial and gender hierarchies time and time again. The Christian Right would prove to be at peak strength below the Mason-Dixon line.[28]

Winning the hearts and minds and souls of the white southern faithful was a critical and sustained component of the Long Southern Strategy. From symbolic gestures such as President Ronald Reagan's speech-ending line, "God Bless America,"[29] to more concrete changes such as Richard Nixon's White House church services (to which corporate CEOs were invited),[30] to Donald Trump having evangelical pastors pray over him in the Oval Office and in front of photographers,[31] the GOP courted white southern evangelicals and fundamentalists consistently over time. To maintain their loyalty at the ballot box, the GOP repackaged "secular" issues regarding the environment, the economy, and even war as issues of religious-political concern. Donald Matthews once wrote that Antebellum southern whites "converted God to their society,"[32] but in this case, the GOP converted the Christian Right, particularly southerners, to its society. Thus, support for "family values" melds into support for all things Republican, including a hawkish foreign policy, and all somehow get wrapped in scripture. It also melds into an opposition to Democrats so intense that the Christian faith of Democratic candidates is denied or rejected. For example, Barack Obama's Christianity was questioned repeatedly throughout his presidency until, eventually, the majority of the GOP (many of whom are part of the religious right) asserted that he was a Muslim.[33] John McCain made headlines when he publicly denounced such rumors during the middle of his campaign, but they took root nonetheless. On the other hand, this conflation of partisanship and Christian religiosity also gave Republican candidates a pass, so to speak, if their sacred credentials were lacking. To that end, the myth of the social conservatism is that religious voters were engaged solely because of their commitment to moral, religious values. However, many were or became red on all kinds of issues. And many are willing to overlook religious pedigree for the GOP label, wearing their partisanship alongside their southern and religious identities into their battle for a Christian America.

EVEN BEFORE THE fundamentalist takeover of the SBC in the late 1970s, there were signs of a brewing religious political storm. From the 1940s to the 1960s, for example, some "conservative Protestants began to identify the GOP as the party of anti-communism and a Protestant-based moral order," notes Daniel Williams. Of course, conservative Protestants in the South split from their northern counterpart over issues of slavery and segregation, demonstrating long ago that social concerns could, indeed, trump denominational loyalty. Many southern fundamentalists had also supported third-party, Dixiecrat candidate Strom Thurmond in 1948, showing their willingness to break with the national Democratic Party. Perhaps most notably, fundamentalists and evangelicals had rejected John Kennedy as a Catholic but primarily under the guise of his "softness on Communism," a foreshadowing of their potential to unite, to code their language, to influence campaign politics, and to commit to seeing a like-minded man of faith in the White House.[34] Religious fundamentalists and evangelicals could, in fact, affect the ballot box.

Early on, George Wallace's presidential campaigns both in 1968 and 1972 exposed the power of "us vs. them," absolutist rhetoric as another calling card for white southerners—and one that might work among religious believers. Though Wallace's appeal had more to do with race than religion explicitly, he honed the technique of positive polarization, meaning rather than define one's

own candidacy or movement by one's own principles, the candidate or movement defines itself in opposition to other principles or cultural forces. Hippie
agitators, communists, and liberals got a lot of heat from Wallace, as did moderation on almost any issue, not unlike the SBC fundamentalist crusade that loomed
around the corner. While only 16 percent of Baptists in the non-South cast for
Wallace in 1968, almost three times that many (48 percent) of Southern Baptists
supported his candidacy.[35] Further analysis of the southern fundamentalist support of Wallace showed that education had no effect or influence.[36] It was not
white southern ignorance; it was white southern faith, making southern churches
critical sites of political promise, adept at taking sides.

Perhaps the most overt early test of how useful and politically pliant southern
fundamentalism could be came at the hands of Nixon's advisers. When student
protests over the administration's covert bombing of Cambodia chipped away
at Nixon's approval ratings, his advisers attempted to manipulate the SBC at
its 1970 convention. In an effort to stop the public opinion bleeding, they had
Nixon send a congratulatory telegram to the Foreign Mission Board of the SBC
for its 125 years of service. Flattered, the convention messengers did not just steer
clear of criticizing the president or even stay neutral on the subject. Rather, they
approved a resolution supporting Nixon's policy in Vietnam.[37] By the time Jimmy
Carter was elected in 1976, the SBC and a growing coalition of Christian Right
organizations would not only expect a lot more from the White House than a
telegram, but they would also start to lean on one party in particular.

The Christian Right's ascension to the height of influence may have shocked
pundits and journalists who were not aware of the dance it had been having with
the GOP for decades. Evangelicals nationwide, who had supported the "born-
again Christian" Carter, began the slow move toward the Republican Party just
two years later, disappointed with the southern Democrat's unwillingness to
practice what he preached, so to speak.[38] In January 1980, hoping to mend fences,
Carter's son's minister, Robert Maddow of First Baptist Church in Calhoun,
Georgia, arranged a meeting with leaders of the Religious Right who were turning
their backs on the president, including Falwell, Pat Robertson, an SBC preacher
who established the Christian Broadcasting Network, and James Robison, another SBC preacher who headed up the Religious Roundtable.[39] The meeting
proved unsuccessful in silencing Carter's religious critics, but it demonstrated the
breakneck rise to power of this new Christian Right that the invitation had been
extended in the first place.

By the Republican Convention that following summer, Falwell was
functioning as a major powerbroker, successfully getting the national party platform to include "endorsements of constitutional amendments to restore prayer
in schools and prohibit abortion, as well as a denunciation of the ERA [Equal

Rights Amendment], which the GOP had officially supported for forty years."
"It is right down the line," one observer told the *Washington Post*, "an evangelical platform."[40] Nominee Ronald Reagan, despite not having a reputation as
a devout man of faith—particularly in contrast to Carter—adopted the language and rhetoric of the pulpit.[41] Most observers predicted that the Christian
Right would see through Reagan's superficial religious appeals, but they were
wrong.[42] Evangelicals voted him into office, including white southern religious
conservatives who broke decades of Democratic Party allegiance. Historian
Eugene Genovese contends that Reagan's southern support was based on two key
beliefs. "First, as a matter of principle," Genovese notes that southerners "saw socialism, big government, and the welfare states as the main enemy" against which
Reagan would fight, and secondly, "Reagan takes traditionalist ground on social
values and stresses family, church, and local community, rather than the state."[43]
The anti–welfare state message echoes the coded language of economic policies
aimed at protecting white privilege that Barry Goldwater initiated. However, the
"family values" principle, first championed by the anti-feminist defense of traditional gender roles, also drew in religious southerners as it expanded to cover a
host of moral behaviors.

The problem came when the Christian Right's political agenda, like the SBC,
exiled moderation in favor of fundamentalism. Reagan could do little, if anything,
to please them without alienating moderately religious Protestants, Catholics, or
non-believers. He quoted scripture and made symbolic gestures, like nominating
James Watt as his secretary of the interior. Watt did not believe that the government needed to protect public lands, for example, because he observed that a
"number of the predictions in the biblical book of Revelations [*sic*] appeared to
be coming to pass" and the "accuracy of these predictions led Watt to believe that
the end of the world, as foretold in Revelations [*sic*], was imminent."[44] But the
Christian Right leaders wanted more. They wanted everything. In 1988, after two
terms trying to push Reagan ever rightward, Pat Robertson launched his own,
albeit unsuccessful, bid for the GOP presidential nomination.

Robertson's campaign, as Daniel Williams notes, "shocked the GOP establishment," not only because evangelicals and fundamentalists had been recruited
to support the Republican Party (not to take it over), but also because "never before had the party's presidential aspirants had to run against someone who spoke
in tongues and practiced faith-healing."[45] Robertson's campaign was both well-
funded and well-organized,[46] but it still represented an extreme wing of Christian
conservatism, relying on "Pentecostal and charismatic support."[47] His failure to
win outright even a single primary highlighted two major lessons regarding the
merger of religion and politics. For the GOP, the fact that Robertson ran at all
meant that evangelicals would have to be consciously catered to in order that they

stay in the party fold. For the Christian Right, the loss highlighted that unity across Christian faiths, and the strength in numbers that a more inclusive platform of social conservatism would provide, was more important than the authenticity or denominational specificity of their candidate's beliefs.

Whereas the first iteration of the movement was "rendered ineffective in part because of the effects of religious particularism,"[48] the Christian Right that coalesced in the 1990s and forward, particularly in the South, was aligned by a broader political ideology, irrespective of ecumenical differences or even candidate authenticity. Based on a study of Virginia politics, there is a sense that "Christian conservatives recognize each other as political allies in an intraparty factional struggle," and they choose less on the personal beliefs of the candidate and more on the "specific issues that constitute their agenda."[49] This politics of consolidation proved effective in Texas and Florida too.[50] Though accepted in some ways now, this type of interdenominational political cohesion—which Falwell actually attempted originally—is radical for fundamentalists who waged their own war for authority.[51] However, it is not unusual in the South, and perhaps that is one of the reasons that it grew so powerful there. Southern white supremacy had long required a cohesion among the economic and social classes for the sake of racial hierarchy, so southern white fundamentalism—with the same power structure—could surely tear down fences particularly in times of battle. After all, denominational differences proved irrelevant in fundamentalist support for George Wallace's candidacy, which, of course, was explicitly about whiteness.[52] Differences had to be set aside. Winning did not require absolute religious legitimacy on the part of the candidate at the top of the ticket; it required allegiance to the policies of social conservatism.

This conditioning has been so powerful that the 2012 GOP nominee's religion seemed of little concern to fundamentalists. Mitt Romney's status as a Mormon would have been considered by many as non-Christian or even membership in a cult, as the denomination was called by the SBC. However, southern white fundamentalist evaluations of Romney's faith, as shown in Figure 9.1A, reflect either a clear softening of such denominational classifications or a blind eye to them. Polled the week after the 2012 election, the majority of southern white fundamentalists (51.5 percent) said they believed that Romney was a Christian, significantly higher than the 38.9 percent of fundamentalists who do not identify as southern. Southern whites were also the least likely to give a definitive no to Romney's status as a Christian at the rates of 13.3 percent for non-fundamentalists and 16.2 percent for fundamentalists. The percentage saying "no" was higher among non-southern whites, at 20.7 percent for non-fundamentalists and 26.8 percent for fundamentalists.

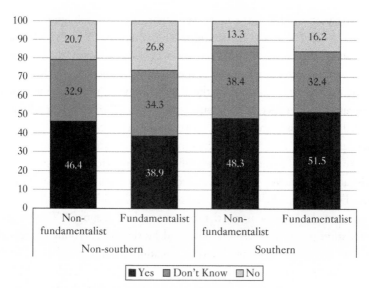

FIGURE 9.1A Percent Responses to: "Do You Believe Mitt Romney Is a Christian?" by Fundamentalism (Biblical Literalism), Among Whites, 2012

Data are from the 2012 Blair Center Poll.

These numbers signpost a couple of crucial points about the relationship between party politics and the pulpit in contemporary elections. First and foremost, there is a double-digit gap between southern and non-southern fundamentalists regarding their belief that Romney is a Christian, with southerners much more accepting. Yet—and secondly—still only the slightest majority of those southern white fundamentalists classified Romney as Christian. That means that 49.5 percent of them either did not know if he was Christian or thought he was not, and yet, Romney received 86.7 percent of the vote from that community. Non-southern fundamentalists are less likely to wash away denominational differences, with the majority, in their case 61.1 percent being uncertain of or rejecting the notion of Romney being a Christian. However, they too voted overwhelmingly for him (71.1 percent). Third, it is worth noting that fundamentalists were also more likely than non-fundamentalists across the board to answer no, which means many know that Mormonism is rarely classified as Christian.

This is all the more striking when reflecting back at white attitudes toward Barack Obama's religious faith. In the 2010 Blair Poll, while Obama was in office, but before Romney emerged as a 2012 presidential contender, white Americans were asked to identify Obama's religious denomination. As show in Figure 9.1B, the results indicate that the powerful combination of fundamentalist belief and southern identity significantly heighten the popularity of such false views. Only

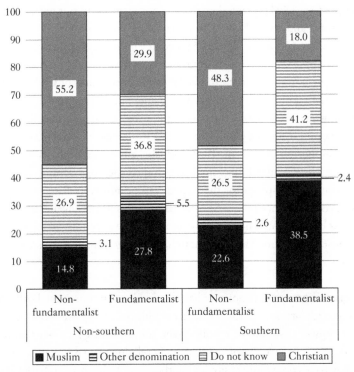

FIGURE 9.1B Percent Responses to: "Do You Happen to Know What Religion Barack Obama Belongs to?" Among Whites, by Fundamentalism (Biblical Literalism), 2010 Data are from the 2010 Blair Center Poll.

18 percent of southern white fundamentalists (measured in 2010 as a belief in biblical literalism) correctly noted that Obama was a Christian, compared to 48.3 percent of southern non-fundamentalists. Among whites who do not identify as southern, 29.9 percent of fundamentalists said Obama was Christian, compared to 55.2 percent of non-fundamentalists. In 2010, however, the question was more open-ended, allowing respondents to say more than if Obama was a Christian or not, but rather to connect him to another faith group. Among southern white fundamentalists, almost 40 percent said he was a Muslim, as did 27.8 percent of non-southern fundamentalists and 22.6 percent of southern non-fundamentalists. Only 14.8 percent of white Americans who do not believe in a literal interpretation of the Bible and who do not identify as southern incorrectly assigned a Muslim faith to Obama.

All of these points indicate that the Christian label has been politicized. For some fundamentalists it is strategic to designate a candidate as not belonging even when they authentically share a common faith category. For others, for candidates they support, the label is granted even if it is not accurate. In this regard, the label is so expansive and amorphous as to cover anyone who is considered conservative in some way. Or the GOP label has become more important than any other. As far back as the Goldwater campaign in 1964, these southern fundamentalists alluded to the impulse of accepting GOP candidates' claims of Christianity, regardless of their authenticity. Southern fundamentalists remained virtually silent when Goldwater announced a Catholic running mate, an important shift considering their opposition to Kennedy in 1960.[53] Whiteness and Christian morality had to be supported in tandem. The GOP label enveloped both. By 2012, social conservatism as a political ideology had trumped theology completely. In fact, during Romney's campaign for the Republican nomination, Richard Land, the SBC lobbyist, announced on C-SPAN that though some evangelicals would not vote for Romney because he was a Mormon, most evangelicals were skeptical of him because he was "not Mormon enough," meaning he had strayed *too far* from social conservatism.[54]

THE WILLINGNESS TO unify politically despite denominational differences, to back a candidate despite the particulars of his own religiosity, to broaden the sacred canopy to cover even Catholics (who started voting majority Republican in 2000),[55] and even to support a Mormon (a religion once deemed a cult by the SBC) may have come more easily for southerners. As historian Charles Reagan Wilson notes, modern religion in the South has "drawn from the beliefs and practices of folk religion," creating a kind of southern "evangelical cauldron" in which "scriptural literalism, consciousness of God's providence in human affairs, evangelism, informality, emotionalism, sectarianism, egalitarianism, isolation of church facilities if organized, and demonstrative performance style"[56] brew. He argues that because of the way in which identity and culture and religion have merged, most southern "true believers" see contemporary denominations as "artificial divisions." That enveloping notion of religion for white southerners—its popularity and familiarity and folkness—made unity on "family values" issues natural, easy, and powerful at the ballot box, particularly when waged against a common partisan enemy. The GOP, thus, need only to expand the definition of "family values" or portray a policy position as some kind of war on faith to activate the flock. White southerners, after all, were professionals in the game of identity politics.

At the 1992 GOP convention, Republican Party leaders portrayed "family values" as under attack by the immoral Democratic ticket. Vocalized most aggressively by Pat Buchanan,[57] the identity politics game plan not only denigrated the Democratic team of Bill Clinton and Al Gore for being the most pro-lesbian ticket in history, but he also denounced Hillary Clinton alongside her husband for their "radical feminist" policy positions. "The agenda that Clinton and Clinton would impose on America," Buchanan surmised, included "abortion on demand, a litmus test for the Supreme Court, homosexual rights, discrimination against religious schools, women in combat units. . . ." It was against those positions that Christians must stake their political ground more fervently than ever. Even if the GOP nominee is not of their own inner religious circle, they must see themselves as soldiers in a battle so great as to render denominational concerns and theological differences irrelevant. "There is a religious war going on in this country for the soul of America," he warned, and "it is a cultural war as critical to the kind of nation we shall be as the Cold War itself, for this war is for the soul of America. And in that struggle for the soul of America, Clinton and Clinton are on the other side, and George Bush is on our side."[58] The high stakes set by Buchanan's speech made the Clinton victory seem all the more dire for the religious right, who quickly turned their attention to the 1994 midterm elections and Newt Gingrich's "Contract for America." Their efforts produced landslide congressional victories for the GOP though the "contract" had little to do with religious policy positions.[59] Rather, the successful rout demonstrated how the Christian Right could unify and support even "secular" policy issues if framed as part of a partisan culture war in which a Republican Congress functioned as a dam holding back the liberal Clinton tide.

Republicans, although they benefited significantly from activating southern white fundamentalists, also learned to be careful what they wished for. The very Americans—"cockroaches issuing out from underneath the baseboard of the South,"[60] remarked presidential son Neil Bush—whom they had courted wanted not just any seat, but the one at the head of the table. And even though Pat Robertson was turned away from that seat, the organizations he helped build remained ambitious. Buoyed by their successful congressional takeover, the Christian Coalition asked the GOP to scratch its back in return by publicly supporting their 1995 addendum, the "Contract with the American Family." Speaker of the House Newt Gingrich and Senate Majority Leader Trent Lott, both southerners, were present for its unveiling. The plan, "designed as a supplement to the Republican Party's 'Contract with America,' included a 'religious equality' amendment to the Constitution, as well as provisions to provide family tax credits, to slash federal spending for the arts, humanities, and education, to protect 'parental rights,' and to restrict abortion."[61] Refusal to meet these demands, in the wake of such strong electoral support, seemed futile.

Social conservatism and "family values" would prove impossible to contain. By 1996, the relationship between the Christian Right and the GOP had grown so strong that it was inconceivable for nominee Bob Dole to forgo attending the coalition's "Road to Victory Conference" and plead for their support, despite his hesitation that he would look "like a pawn."[62] So complete was the merger that it resulted in a lawsuit by the Federal Election Commission that same year when it discovered that the Christian Coalition was funneling money straight to GOP candidates, a violation of their tax status.[63] They were quickly becoming both their financial and electoral base. The GOP would have to find a way to keep evangelicals unified and loyal to the party establishment, particularly in the South where the Christian Right dominated state Republican parties in eight southern states throughout the 1990s, and by 2000, would wield power over ten of eleven total.[64]

Though Dole and George H. W. Bush struggled to manage an electorate that included a strong and empowered evangelical base, their successor would find the key to balancing the relationship between the party and the pulpit. George W. Bush became a born-again Christian in the mid-1980s. In 1985, he was living in Midland, Texas, when many oilmen and business leaders were struggling from the stagflation and economic downturns that led to Reagan's election to the presidency. Bush was invited to join a weekly Bible study group, and it became a refuge for him and other businessmen who had suffered financially and psychologically during the economic downturn of the early 1980s.[65] Based on this experience, the younger Bush became his father's outreach to the Christian Right. "He was perfect for the role," noted Republican strategist Karl Rove's biographers; "He spoke their language and was not shy about recounting his own conversion experience with evangelical leaders."[66] More important, George W. Bush, because he was part of the evangelical community, knew how all-encompassing its culture had become. There were no political issues, really, that could not be brought under a "family values" or protection of religion umbrella. Even more important, from his Bible study, Bush understood the relationship between achievement—particularly wealth and power—and evangelical faith. The desire for material progress tapped into the longing for both conformity and certainty so prevalent in southern religion. The gospel of wealth makes sacred the pursuit of wealth and glorifies the elite as blessed and thus worthy of being followed, as was preached by numerous Southern Baptist ministers.[67] Both the reach of born-again religious ideology and its conception of financial success—not to mention his "new accent, thicker and softer, a true son of the South"[68]—would help Bush carry and deepen the GOP's hold on the red South.

In the wake of his father's re-election loss in 1992, Bush and Rove went back to Texas with their eyes set on the governorship, both having realized that "to govern on behalf of the corporate right, they would have to appease the Christian right."[69] Running against then governor Ann Richards, Bush put his plan into action. Rove's electoral strategy included recruiting as many evangelical voters as possible while Bush wore his faith on his sleeve. He had "learned from his dad the peril of ignoring the Christian right; he talked about faith-based social services and the right to life."[70] In response, evangelical Christians showed up en masse at the 1994 Texas Republican convention in Fort Worth. According to Lou Dubose, Jan Reid, and Carl M. Cannon, authors of the book *Boy Genius*:

> Christian Right delegates filled the convention center two blocks from the hotel where John Kennedy spent the night of November 21, 1963. Prayer breakfasts drew bigger crowds than hospitality suites. The virtuous William Bennett came in first in the presidential straw vote. Texas Senator Phil Gramm won only 8 percent of the pool because he was soft on defense of the unborn. Every winning candidate (and most losing candidates) for party office praised God and excoriated abortion. And U.S. Senator Kay Bailey Hutchinson was booed when she stood up to address the convention. Not because of anything she said in her speech, but because she openly supported women's reproductive rights.[71]

Such public declarations of faith signaled an acceptance, even an expectation, of Republican religiosity. In addition, fundamentalist Christians at the state convention did not hesitate to push for a pro-life gubernatorial platform. However, that was not all that they wanted. In a move that foreshadowed the course that this marriage of politics and faith would take, evangelical delegates did not limit their policy demands to the traditional "moral issues" of abortion or gay marriage; rather, they advocated for "the repeal of the Clean Air Act and the Endangered Species Act, the end of the state's authority to compel children to attend school, a repeal of the minimum wage, and a return to the gold standard."[72] Evangelical politics was expanding beyond its original rallying cries, branching into policy debates that seemed far more secular than scriptural in an effort to protect wealth and even whiteness.

Moreover, it was the "secular" issues among the SBC members that had the strongest impact on members' identification as conservative Republicans.[73] Social conservatism or the "increased salience of traditional moral issues," as Ted Jelen notes, is not the complete story.[74] Here is where the white southernness of the Christian Right becomes so significant. The economic positions taken by the GOP in the decades after the Civil Rights Movement, such as welfare reform, are racially loaded, meant to regulate or eliminate money for those deemed "undeserving" while railing against regulation on capitalism for inhibiting the accumulation of wealth. Southern Baptists had long been "complacent about the exploitation of the economically disadvantaged," contends David Stricklin,[75] choosing the preservation of whiteness over the populist impulse. Organized labor, a major struggle that failed miserably in the South, found little support conceptually by Southern Baptists. "Their church," insists Nancy Ammerman, "does not attempt to overcome their powerlessness." Workers instead resign to their fate. "They join the union if they have to," Ammerman argues, "but if there is a strike, they may ask God's help in crossing the picket lines. It would be unthinkable to ask God's help in taking over the plant." Preachers simply don't speak about "God being active in structuring economic activity."[76] The silence, in this sense, is tailor-made for conservative ideology bent on protecting the status quo.

This economic-religious dynamic accounts for why some scholars, such as Daniel Williams, have argued that the Sunbelt had an equally powerful influence on the rise of the Christian Right. Specifically, William singles out Falwell as emblematic of the collision of the Bible Belt and the Sunbelt, both of which defined the modern Republican Party. Falwell's ideology, proclaims Williams, "was forged in the political climate of the rapidly growing Sunbelt, a region whose corporate leaders and megachurch pastors shared a deep suspicion of federal regulation, believing that the national government was a threat to the sanctity of the home and the health of the economy."[77] Williams credits Falwell's hands-off approach to economics and pro-business evangelicalism with the fact that Falwell witnessed private industry be the "principle source of economic uplift for his previously impoverished community" during the early years of the Cold War. However, to their detractors, the Christian Right's anti-regulatory and anti-federal encroachment positions were seen as ways that televangelists in particular could grow their personal fortunes while shielded from the IRS. Of course, the anti–federal intervention rhetoric conjures up a defense of states' rights to white southern congregations. Non-compulsory school attendance laws, as advocated in the 1994 Texas gubernatorial platform, harken back to similar legislation across the South in the wake of *Brown v. Board*, allowing white families to opt out of compulsory school attendance, and thus, out of integration. In this case, the opt-out protects evangelical and fundamentalist children from the secular culture of public schools and from the rules of the Federal Department of Education, which is seen as federal overreach in the same way that IRS regulations were.

Contemporary exposés of GOP preachers and politicians highlight the way in which a religious defense of wealth remains par for the course. Sarah Posner's book *God's Profits: Faith, Fraud, and the Republican Crusade for Values Voters*, for example, examines how contemporary ministers line their own pockets with "for-profit church-related enterprises" that are not only tax-exempt but unreported. "Where profit-driven church meets the cornerstone of conservative economic ideology," she concludes, "televangelists have been enriching themselves in an unregulated marketplace trading on God, the culture of personality, and American dreams of riches and success."[78] In her commentary on Ted Haggard, the former head of the National Association of Evangelicals (NAE) who resigned after a drug and homosexual scandal, Lynne Stuart Parramore put it more bluntly. "Getting Christianity and elite economics together on the same page," she warns, "is useful in signaling that policies that serve the rich are simply articles of faith, the dispute of which is akin to arguing with a literal interpretation of the Bible."[79]

Here identity politics is played in two fundamental ways. The ability of the GOP to convince poor white southerners specifically to vote against their economic self-interest has been questioned repeatedly. The common answer is that poor white southerners vote socially, on moral issues, as opposed to economic policies. However, for many the "economic" is "religious," just as the "economic" is racial—particularly if it is framed that way.[80] Perhaps a desire to identify with success and wealth even when it is solely aspirational contributes to this partisan loyalty. In addition, it is an elevation of financial success, under the nickname "gospel of wealth," as indicative of morality, leadership, and power that may bind poor white southerners to GOP candidates so far removed from their own hardships. This is an aspect of Southern Baptist theology that had mass appeal in places like California to which many southerners migrated in search of economic opportunity from the 1930s to the 1960s. These southern transplants helped to spread this "southern way of religion" well beyond the borders of the South, as Darren Dochuk describes in detail in his book *From Bible Belt to Sun Belt: Plain-Folk Religion, Grassroots Politics, and the Rise of Evangelical Conservatism.*[81] Via the Long Southern Strategy, these economic policies, as well as a host of other domestic policy initiatives, became part of the moral cosmology, part of the merger of religion and politics, and part of the GOP's nationalization of southern identity. That is the price of identity politics. Once established, it can be directed against anything, leaving self-destructive, counterintuitive partisan allegiances in its wake.

The Christian Right–laced GOP at various times has taken hard stances in support of the death penalty,[82] and fundamentalists, particularly those in the South, have expressed a general unwillingness "to admit of [*sic*] scientific advances."[83] Conservative Protestants have played a role in support for the Confederate flag,[84] and the GOP has called for immigration to be limited to Christians only.[85] And so the myth of social conservatism is that it is limited to "family values" politics, but it is so deeply and deliberately entangled with southern identity and its historic baggage, that now it is about a lot more than taking a stand against feminists and abortion and homosexuality. The Baylor Religion Survey, which includes measures for identifying as fundamentalist, born-again, and/or evangelical, as well as a measure for biblical literalism, also posed questions on "secular" political and policy issues. Using a combined, inclusive measure of all respondents who identified in one of these religious categories provided a deeper understanding of the way both fundamentalism—in a broad sense—and region (the survey does not include a southern identity variable) influence attitudes toward seemingly non-religious policies. Table 9.1 reports the 2007 data—and one data point from 2010 when fewer such questions were asked.

Table 9.1 Percent Responses to the Following Secular Statements/ Questions, Among Whites, by Fundamentalism,* 2007, 2010

		Non-South		South	
		Non-Fund.	Fund.	Non-Fund.	Fund.
2007	Federal government should abolish the death penalty (strongly disagree)	28.8	35.9	41.7	44.3
2007	Federal government should declare English the national language (strongly agree)	44.0	58.2	52.9	72.9
2007	Federal government should punish criminals more harshly (strongly agree)	22.4	30.7	34.8	43.1
2007	Federal government should enact stricter gun laws (strongly disagree)	15.7	21.1	23.6	26.0
2010	Government bailout of major banks and corporations (always wrong)	22.2	35.9	18.7	54.7
2007	You have dated a person of another race (no)	61.6	69.2	58.6	78.3
2007	Trust immigrants (not at all or only a little)	29.2	29.1	32.8	37.1
2007	Men are better suited for politics (strongly agree)	3.7	16	6.2	19.2

*In Baylor 2007 and 2010, fundamentalist includes those who believe in a literal interpretation of the Bible and/or who identified as fundamentalist, born again, or evangelical. In the 2010 Blair Center Poll, fundamentalist includes respondents who reported a literal interpretation of the Bible.

Data are from the 2007 and 2010 Baylor Religion Surveys available at https://www.baylor.edu/baylorreligionsurvey/.

A significantly greater percentage of white fundamentalists who live in the South oppose the federal government abolishing the death penalty (44.3 percent) or enacting stricter gun laws (26 percent) compared to non-fundamentalists in the South, among whom 41.7 percent and 23.6 percent strongly disagree on these issues respectively. Fundamentalists who live in the South also strongly agree at higher levels than fundamentalists outside of the South that the federal government should declare English as the national language (72.9 percent) and punish criminals more harshly (43.1 percent). They are also more likely to indicate that government bailouts for major banks and corporations are always wrong (54.7 percent) and that men are better suited for politics (19.2 percent). White fundamentalists who live in the South also admit that they do not trust immigrants to the tune of 37.1 percent, and they are the most likely to have dated exclusively in their own race (78.3 percent). Fundamentalists who live in the South have the highest number of people (even when the total is small) holding the most extreme opinions on every one of these non-religious questions. Moreover, their attitudes are significantly distinct from non-fundamentalists in the South across the board and from fundamentalists outside of the South on every issue except gun control. This highlights the spillover of religion into politics, particularly in the South, well beyond the key political causes traditionally identified with social conservatism.

A more recent example from the 2012 Blair Center Poll exposes this fundamentalist gap on the issue of healthcare. When asked whether they favor or oppose "current efforts at health care reform," which at that time meant the Affordable Care Act, southern white fundamentalist reported the highest levels of opposition, as shown in Figure 9.2. With nearly three-fourths (73.6 percent) opposing the reform, southern white fundamentalists viewed this issue more negatively than southern white non-fundamentalists (63 percent). Moreover, southern white fundamentalists who "strongly opposed" the issue outnumbered southern white non-fundamentalists 49.9 percent to 35.9 percent respectively. Among non-southerners, there is also a strong divide between fundamentalists and non-fundamentalists, with 59.5 percent of the former opposing healthcare reform compared to 38.9 percent of the latter. At 59.5 percent opposition, non-southern fundamentalists are significantly less opposed than southern fundamentalists, but still more opposed than southern non-fundamentalists. Indeed, religious fundamentalism, in and of itself, impacts attitudes toward this seemingly non-religious legislation.

THE CONVERSION OF fundamentalist evangelicals to politicos influenced attitudes beyond the domestic arena. The righteousness of "the southern way of religion" as expanded in the Christian Right agenda heightened a belief that the

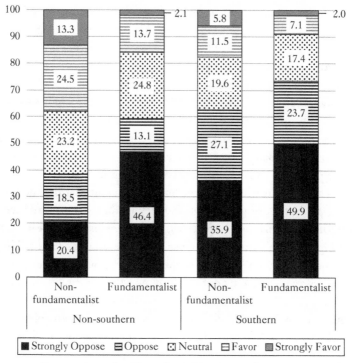

FIGURE 9.2 Percent Attitudes Toward Health Care Reform, Among Whites, by Fundamentalism (Biblical Literalism), 2012

Data are from the 2012 Blair Center Poll.

direction of the nation is off course and in need of correction. There is almost a separatist, even nationalistic streak, and southern white believers stand at the helm. It is not their first attempt to steer the country toward righteousness. Just as the religion of the Lost Cause functioned both spiritually and culturally as a means of massive resistance to a changing way of life for southern whites, so too did Christian conservatism become a shield against a diversifying American landscape. Ammerman has written about the all-consuming identity construct that is religious fundamentalism, the embodiment of which requires extreme "discipline" in order to "sustain a fundamentalist view of the world."[86] That view insists upon fundamentalists worrying "a good deal about our [the United States'] collective standing before God."[87] The country's "moral fiber" is entrusted to them and, as Ammerman continues, "they are willing to enter politics if necessary to protect the social territory."[88]

Southern white Christians had entered that territory before, sanctifying slavery across many denominational lines.[89] Though some struggled initially with the issue, eventually Baptists, Methodists, and Presbyterian ministers in the South supported and protected slavery as part of the social order of the nation, fighting against the abolitionist campaigns of their fellow denominations in the North (who were not necessarily racial progressives but made a distinction between slavery and what they saw as "less harmful" prejudice)[90] and even theorizing slavery as compatible with Christian theology.[91] Catholics in the South, held in "cultural captivity," acquiesced to slavery, choosing not to minister to slaves, in the hopes that it would "stave off nativism and anti-Catholic attacks."[92] Support for human bondage seemed, in fact, sacred and nationalistic. As the preacher of the Chillicothe Presbytery in Mississippi reasoned in 1836, "if slavery be a sin, then, verily three fourths of all Episcopalians, Methodists, Baptists, and Presbyterians, in eleven States of the Union 'are of the devil.'"[93] Donald Matthews has also noted that evangelical anti-slavery fervor often dissipated when slaveholders converted to Christianity even "without their conversion to emancipationism."[94] In turn, when they promoted their new Christian values,[95] the status of slavery as a sin remained unclear. In a document published in *Christian History* in 1992, entitled "Why Christians Should Support Slavery: Key Reasons Advanced by Church Leaders," among all of the scriptural references to a divine condonation of slavery, the notion of a Christian nationalism proved most prominent.[96]

However, the Civil War was not the only war that gave rise to a Christian nationalism of sorts. Evangelical ministers believed that the early events of World War I, for example, were following biblical prophecies signaling end times, forcing "radical evangelicals to reconcile their beliefs about the future with the realities of their obligations to a nation at war."[97] In the early decades of the Cold War, the NAE began to lobby the GOP, believing the party to be tougher on communism.[98] Southern religious leaders such as Bob Jones Jr., president of the university named after his father, followed suit, hosting a forum in 1951 of international diplomats critical of communism. Jones offered the capstone address emblematic of his "Christian Americanism" in which he demanded that the United States take a harder line against the "raging wolves of the Kremlin."[99] Even Christian Women of America (CWA) encouraged members to help their husbands stand against communist subversives.[100] Methodist Deacon Ralph Lord Roy surmised the connection this way: "They see the issue in theological terms. One is God, who leads the legions of good. The other is Satan . . . who is the father of Communism . . . spreading modernism and disbelief across our land."[101] This dichotomy fell on welcome ears in the South, and Alabama Governor George Wallace was one of many politicians who would invoke this battle cry to woo southern voters.[102]

There have, of course, been moments when a broader "Christian Americanism" gripped the nation at large. The addition of "In God We Trust" on US currency and "under God" into the Pledge of Allegiance under President Eisenhower's tenure occurred right after Reverend Billy Graham "went to Washington and made Congress his congregation." Religious services at the Capitol, the founding of the National Day of Prayer, and presidential speeches laced with scripture resulted from Graham's efforts.[103] Eisenhower, of course, proved the first GOP candidate—though a moderate one—to break the solidly Democratic South, winning seven of eleven states of the former Confederacy in 1952 and six in his re-election bid four years later. However, in the decades that followed, the civil rights revolution both in the streets and in the courts challenged any singular vision of America, rocking southern white fundamentalists, in particular, back on their heels. Over time, the GOP would help them stand back up. After all, the demand for the country to reassert its status as a "Christian Nation," Gary Wills has argued, grew most insistent "when the statement was no longer true."[104]

Since that moment, Christian Right political activism has left no stone unturned in its quest to save the country. The South has been home to their most far-reaching, comprehensive political influence. Just as the SBC fundamentalists knew that control of their committee system would solidify their power, the Christian Right did not ignore state and local politics. For example, in the wake of the 1994 congressional GOP victories and for the rest of the 1990s, Religious Right candidates in the South proved victorious in 59 percent of US House, Senate, and state gubernatorial contests in which they ran. They won roughly half of the southern governorships, as the GOP "finally succeeded in getting conservative voters to bring their behavior for down-ticket offices in line with votes for the presidency."[105] At the grassroots level, the Christian Right distributed voting guides throughout congregations in order to inform and direct voters to full slates of candidates. In Texas alone, the Christian Right disseminated 2 million guides, and get-out-the-vote volunteers contacted 50,000 potential voters in the 1998 midterm elections.[106] The movement is, according to Michael Linesch, much more sophisticated than many noticed, complete with "candidate 'hit lists,' moral 'report cards,' and 'Christian political action manuals.'"[107]

Additionally, just as the Christian Right has advocated for America as a Christian nation, it has simultaneously—particularly when progressive policies have been enacted—lobbied for the free exercise of religion in an almost libertarian manner.[108] Labeled their "offensive" and "defensive" agendas,[109] the Christian Right has worked (on offense) with the Republican Party to amend state constitutions, most notably in the South, to define marriage as exclusively heterosexual and to protect religious Americans, such as county clerks, from participating in homosexual marriages. None of this political activity speaks to a dissolving Christian Right, but rather a movement that has adapted and broadened beyond simply electing a Christian Right president to a comprehensive engagement in the entire political system—at every level. Their role, notes John Green, Mark Rozzell, and Clyde Wilcox, has been both to compete politically and to be "a source of controversy,"[110] to present a unified obstacle to the liberal changes they see as destroying the country.

In 1998, a Republican Congress, lobbied hard by the Christian Coalition, the NAE, and the SBC, passed legislation protecting Christians living overseas, aptly called the International Religious Freedom Act.[111] In the early years of a new century, President George W. Bush funded the cause of Christian nationalism, as the Department of Health and Human Services granted roughly $30 million in federal appropriations to religious organizations in 2002 alone as part of the president's faith-based initiatives.[112] The funding was controversial, yet as of 2015, according to Public Policy Polling, over 57 percent of Republicans assert that Christianity should be the religion of the United States.[113] Beyond just funding it, Donald Trump lauded Christian nationalism explicitly, insisting that Americans want "one beautiful nation, under God" at the 2017 National Prayer Breakfast[114] and emphasized its historical roots: "When the Pilgrims landed at Plymouth," he reminded a crowd at Liberty University, "they prayed."[115] As shown in Figure 9.3, approximately 38.7 percent of non-southern fundamentalists reported that it is important to be a Christian in order to be an American, while only 12.3 percent of non-southern, non-fundamentalists said that being a

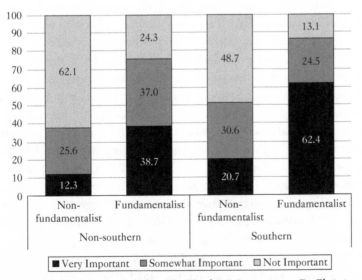

FIGURE 9.3 Percent Responses to: "Do You Think It Is Important to Be Christian to Be Fully American?" Among Whites, by Fundamentalism (Biblical Literalism), 2012
Data are from the 2012 Blair Center Poll.

Christian was important. Among southern fundamentalist respondents, however, that percentage skyrockets to 62.4 percent who claim that it is important to be a Christian in order to be an American, which is not only a significant increase over non-southern fundamentalists of 23.7 percent, but is also 41.7 points greater than southern whites who are not fundamentalists. Bible Belt morality turned into social conservatism. Traditionally "secular" issues became religious issues with Christian values asserted as decidedly American.

THE LONG SOUTHERN Strategy that politicized evangelical fundamentalism even on seemingly secular issues at home has also promoted a hawkish foreign policy propped up by a blended partisan and religious cosmology. The evangelical strain that is so prominent in the southern wing of the Christian Right has always championed a conversion mission in which they "carry their faith to the ends of the earth." Many American evangelicals, specifically, have viewed the entire national experiment (the "city on a hill") as redemptive with a "political responsibility to bring law and liberty to other lands." The Southern Baptists declared at their 1919 convention that "America is in fact God's new Israel for the race of men . . . divinely chosen, preserved with providential purpose, prospered with world power, and pledged to a divine mission."[116] From Jerry Falwell's support of the GOP on defense spending in the early days of the Moral Majority,[117] military preparedness[118] and military aggression[119] have been political undercurrents of the Christian Right.

The penchant for violence, also part of this hawkish stance, is a strongly southern phenomenon—there is a positive correlation between percent conservative Protestant population and homicide rates, but only in the South[120]—and is clearly influential to the way in which the "redeemer nation"[121] status of America is conceptualized by the Christian Right. "The approach to foreign policy taken by religious conservatives," contends Michael Linesch, has been "a particularly confrontational and combative version of this redemptive international impulse."[122] Any candidate seen as soft on foreign policy risks defeat. For example, Gerald Ford suffered when he used religious rhetoric to support his plan for mercy for conscientious objectors to the Vietnam War. Only weeks after his inauguration, Ford quoted from Psalm 23 imploring all Americans "who ever asked for goodness and mercy in their lives, whoever sought forgiveness for trespasses, to join in rehabilitating all the casualties of all the tragic conflicts that passed."[123] Ford used the Bible, but he did not use it in the right way. Hawkishness, to some degree, is part of the Christian Right's self-conception, and the rhetoric of fundamentalists, the SBC, and even the Moral Majority has often been militaristic. Fundamentalists are described as having "taken the sword of the Lord in hand to face off against the modern world."[124] So-called moderates who were purged from the SBC after the fundamentalist takeover called themselves refugees from war.[125] The Moral Majority was an "army."[126] Politics was merely a battle plan; foreign policy is a crusade in which amnesty is weakness.

The Christian Right foreign policy vision requires an evil empire[127] against which these battles must be waged, and the most recent incarnation is the Middle East in general. Israel is a victim in-kind, of which Christian fundamentalists and Republican politicians[128] have become increasingly supportive. Bob Dole, for example, in an effort to align his politics with that of the religious right when he launched a presidential bid in 1996, reversed his positions on not only abortion and guns, but also strengthened his defense of Israel, even releasing a statement to that effect after meeting with Netanyahu during his campaign.[129] Christian Coalition leader Ralph Reed, who co-founded the organization Stand for Israel, has stated that "Christians have the potential to be the most effective constituency influencing a foreign policy since the end of the Cold War . . . they are shifting the center of gravity in the pro-Israel community to become a more conservative and Republican phenomenon."[130] John McCain's running mate in 2008, Sarah Palin, told her church congregation in Wasilla, Alaska, that the war in Iraq is "a task that is from God," a point that was picked up by Muslim news bloggers.[131] From the crusade against Sharia law and its alleged spread to America,[132] to the overwhelming accusations of Obama's Muslim sympathies and even his own adherence to Islam, to proposed immigration policies that admit only Christian Syrian refugees to the country,[133] to Ohio Governor John Kasich's desire to convert the Middle East to Christianity,[134] all speak to a tangled partisan and Christian Right worldview that debunks the narrow definition of the social conservative.

Data from the Baylor Religion Surveys of 2007 and 2010 show just how great the geographic gap is for foreign policy issues as well as Christian nationalism, as seen in Table 9.2. There are statistically significant gaps between fundamentalists who live in the South and fundamentalists living outside of the South on all of these issues. Among white fundamentalists in the geographic South, 67.6 percent believe that war is not wrong at all or that it is only wrong sometimes, which drops to 58.8 percent among fundamentalists living outside of the South, to 43.7 percent among non-fundamentalists living inside of the South, and to the lowest level, 37.4 percent, among non-fundamentalists living outside of the region. Fundamentalists who live in the South are also the most likely to strongly agree that the federal government should expand its authority to fight terrorism (35.7 percent) and that going to war in Iraq was the right decision (30.3 percent). The majority of white fundamentalists (54.2 percent) living in the South also indicate that the media portrayal of religion made them

Table 9.2 Percent Responses to the Following Foreign Policy/Nationalism Statements/Questions, Among Whites, by Fundamentalism,* 2007, 2010

Baylor Religion Survey	Non-South		South	
	Non-Fund.	Fund.	Non-Fund.	Fund.
2007 How do you feel about the morality of war? (not wrong at all or only wrong sometimes)	37.4	58.8	43.7	67.6
2007 Federal government should advocate Christian values (strongly agree)	6.2	34.0	8.3	45.8
2007 Federal government should declare the United States a Christian nation (strongly agree)	2.3	16.4	4.0	25.6
2007 Federal government should expand its authority to fight terrorism (strongly agree)	17.5	23.8	22.0	35.7
2007 Going to war in Iraq was the right decision (strongly agree)	9.0	24.1	18.2	30.3
2010 Has the media portrayal of religion made you believe that more Muslims are terrorists? (yes)	29.5	40.2	26.5	54.2

Blair Center Poll	Non-southern		Southern	
	Non-Fund.	Fund.	Non-Fund.	Fund.
2010 The President's handling of the war on terror (strongly oppose)	7.4	15.6	15.5	24.0
2010 The President's handling of the war in Afghanistan (strongly oppose)	7.5	12.6	13.1	19.5
2010 The President's handling of the war in Iraq (strongly oppose)	6.8	13.4	11.6	19.8

*In Baylor 2007 and 2010, fundamentalist includes those who believe in a literal interpretation of the Bible or who identified as fundamentalist, born again, or evangelical. In the 2010 Blair Center Poll, fundamentalist includes respondents who reported a literal interpretation of the Bible.

Data are from the 2010 Blair Center Poll as well as the 2007 and 2010 Baylor Religion Surveys available at https://www.baylor.edu/baylorreligionsurvey/.

believe that more Muslims are terrorists, as asked in the Baylor Religion Survey in 2010.

The 2010 Blair Center Poll, which only includes biblical literalism as its measure of fundamentalism, asked three questions regarding approval of the president's—at that time Obama's—handling of the war on terror, the war in Afghanistan, and the war in Iraq. Since the Blair Center Polls measure both residence in the geographic South and identification as a southerner, these questions—albeit specific to one president—do provide for deeper investigation into the relationship between southern identity and fundamentalist belief and foreign policy attitudes. White fundamentalists who identify as southern were the most strongly opposed to the president's handling of all three of these wars, more so than whites who identify as southern but who are not fundamentalists and more than fundamentalists who do not identify as southern, and those gaps are significant for all three questions. White Americans who are neither fundamentalists nor southern reported the lowest levels of strong opposition to how the president was managing these military conflicts. Returning to the questions posed in the 2007 Baylor Religion Survey, Table 9.2 also reveals that fundamentalists who live in the South have higher numbers of respondents who strongly agree that the federal government should advocate Christian values (45.8 percent) and that the federal government should declare the United States a Christian nation (25.6 percent)—and those are just the percentages reporting the most extreme category of agreement. Though the measures all have their limitations, there seems to be some merger of Christian exceptionalism and southern exceptionalism and American exceptionalism, which may reflect the taste not only for hawkish candidates, but also for Christian nationalist believers in the GOP's new home base in the South. The Long Southern Strategy now seems to be at play on the global stage.

THE REASON DEBUNKING the myth of the social conservatism is critical is because it invalidates many assessments of American religious voters, particularly among those who claim a southern identity. The two primary false assumptions are that fundamentalism solely influences religious policy issues, which of course it does, but not exclusively, and, second, that its influence is limited to domestic issues. In terms of the influence of fundamentalism on attitudes toward "secular," domestic policies, data from the 2016 Blair Center Poll examine fundamentalists' attitudes toward climate change, as shown in Figure 9.4.

Southern white fundamentalists disagree that global warming is the result of human activity at a rate of 36.8 percent, with non-southern fundamentalists a close second at 31.9 percent. The gap between southern white fundamentalists

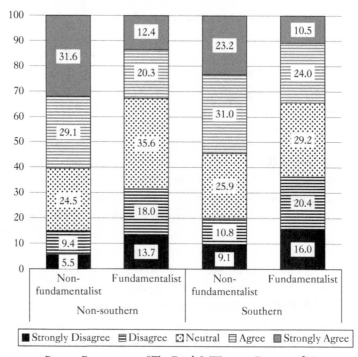

FIGURE 9.4 Percent Responses to: "The Earth Is Warming Because of Human Activity," Among Whites, by Fundamentalism (Biblical Literalism and/or Self-identified), 2016 Data are from the 2016 Blair Center Poll.

and southern white non-fundamentalists is 17.3 points. There are similar patterns when assessing public opinion regarding security issues, both at home and abroad. As seen in Figure 9.5, there is a statistically significant gap between southern white fundamentalists and non-fundamentalists in their support for building a wall across the southern border of Mexico. Among southern fundamentalists, support stands at 63.7 percent, more than twice that of non-southern fundamentalists at 31 percent. For white Americans who do not identify as southern, fundamentalism proves a decisive wedge on this issues as well, with roughly half (51.1 percent) of fundamentalists supporting the building of a wall, compared to 25.9 percent of non-fundamentalists. Yet, both support levels are also lower than among their southern counterparts.

The environment and immigration are not the only two issues that have become entangled with fundamentalist belief. Public opinion among white Americans on gun reform, as noted in the 2007 Baylor Religion Survey, is impacted by fundamentalism. In fact, advocacy for gun rights is being used by politicians in Texas to reach evangelical voters[135]—that is

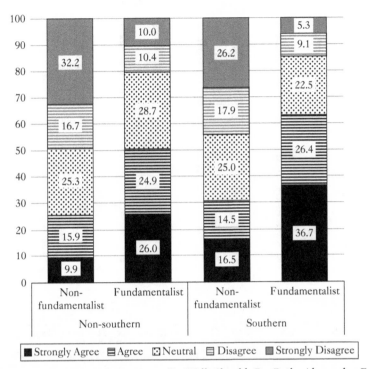

FIGURE 9.5 Percent Responses to: "A Wall Should Be Built Along the Entire
Border with Mexico," Among Whites, by Fundamentalism (Biblical Literalism and/or
Self-identified), 2016

Data are from the 2016 Blair Center Poll.

how powerful Second Amendment politics has become within certain religious
communities, particularly those who feel under attack. As shown in Figure 9.6,
in 2016, when asked the degree to which they agree with the banning of semi-
automatic weapons, among fundamentalists who identify as southern, 27.1 percent strongly disagree, while another 17.8 percent disagree. Among southern
non-fundamentalists, strong disagreement drops to 17.8 percent, and among
non-southern fundamentalists it ticks back up to 19 percent. Among those who
are neither fundamentalist, nor southern, only 12 percent disagree so vehemently.

The same pattern persists in Figure 9.7, which reports the result of
respondents being asked if they agree with sending ground troops to Syria and
Iraq to combat ISIS. While 33.5 percent of southern fundamentalists agreed,
that number dropped to 17.2 percent among southern non-fundamentalists.
Similarly, among non-southerners there is a drop in support from
fundamentalists (26.9 percent) to non-fundamentalists (18.2 percent) agreeing
with the idea of troop deployment.

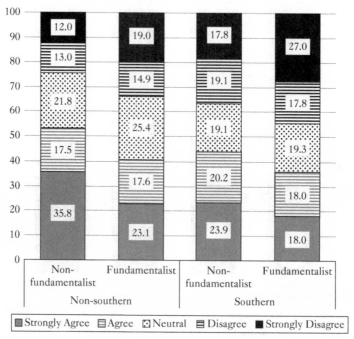

FIGURE 9.6 Percent Attitudes Toward Banning Automatic Weapons, Among Whites, by Fundamentalism (Biblical Literalism and/or Self-identified), 2016
Data are from the 2016 Blair Center Poll.

In addition to these persistent divides on these domestic and foreign policy issues, the myth of social conservatism included an assumption that authentic Christian belief—and practice even—would be required of any candidate seeking the support of religious fundamentalists. Yet, as noted in 2012, only half of southern fundamentalists believed Mitt Romney was a Christian, though they still overwhelmingly voted for him. The same is true—perhaps to an even greater degree—in 2016, as seen in Figure 9.8. Only 41.7 percent of southern white fundamentalism claimed that Donald Trump was a Christian, with half (50.4 percent) saying they did not know, and 8.9 percent denying he was. Among southern white non-fundamentalists, again, the majority (52.4 percent) said they did not know, while 22 percent said he was not. Only 25.6 percent of southern non-fundamentalists affirmed Trump's Christianity, a significant drop from southern fundamentalists, and yet they too overwhelming indicated voting for him. Among non-southern whites, belief in Trump's Christianity is also higher among fundamentalists (32.3 percent) compared to non-fundamentalists (23.7 percent), though, again, this is less than their southern counterparts. Overall, these rates are lower than belief in Romney's Christianity

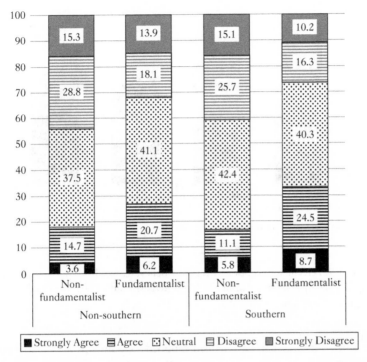

FIGURE 9.7 Percent Attitudes Toward Sending Ground Troops to Fight ISIS in Iraq and Syria, Among Whites, by Fundamentalism (Biblical Literalism and/or Self-identified), 2016

Data are from the 2016 Blair Center Poll.

in 2012, and yet, Trump received close to the same portion of the vote from white fundamentalists, both southern and non-southern, than Romney did four years earlier, as shown in Figure 9.9. Also included is the rate at which white Americans in both 2012 and in 2016 said it was important to be Christian to be American, mapped along with percent vote for the Republican candidate in both elections.

In an almost linear fashion, Christian nationalism and GOP vote go hand in hand. Non-southern non-fundamentalists report almost identical rates of support for both Romney and Trump and in terms of a belief in Christian nationalism from 2012 to 2016, reporting the lowest numbers in both regards. In the middle are the subgroups who carry one of the two markers—southernness or fundamentalism, but not both. A little over half of southern non-fundamentalists believe it is important to be Christian to be American across both years, though their support for the GOP candidate dropped from 71.8 percent in 2012 to 57.4 percent in 2016. While among non-southerners who are fundamentalists,

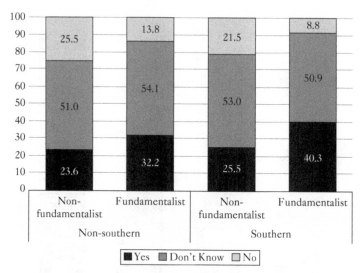

FIGURE 9.8 Percent Responses to: "Do You Believe Donald Trump Is a Christian?" Among Whites, by Fundamentalism (Biblical Literalism and/or Self-identified), 2016 Data are from the 2016 Blair Center Poll.

agreement with Christian nationalism dropped 5.5 points from 75.7 percent in 2012 to 70.2 percent in 2016, but vote for Trump stood at 75.5 percent, up from Romney's portion of 71.4 percent.

Southern white fundamentalists land at the uppermost point of the grid, with 86.9 percent and 83 percent belief in Christian nationalism in 2012 and 2016 respectively, and supporting Romney at a rate of 87.6 percent and Trump at 87.7 percent. The pattern is unchanged when the 2016 measure of fundamentalism is limited to only biblical literalists, as it was in 2012. Regardless, the invisible line that seems to slope steeply upward from non-southern, non-fundamentalists to southern fundamentalists shows just how tightly wedded fundamentalism and southern identity and Christian nationalism and the Republican Party have become, regardless of whether or not the policy issue has a religious bent and irrespective of their nominee's Christian authenticity. The Christian right is just the right, especially for white southerners.

THE HISTORY OF how an American region became more Protestant, more evangelical, more fundamentalist, and more moralist than the rest of the country may explain a great deal about the distinctiveness of southern culture, but it is the recent events in the Bible Belt that explain the politics that divide southerners and Americans at large. The rise of a unified Christian Right, which was both created and, at times, resented by GOP leadership, changed both southern religion and politics

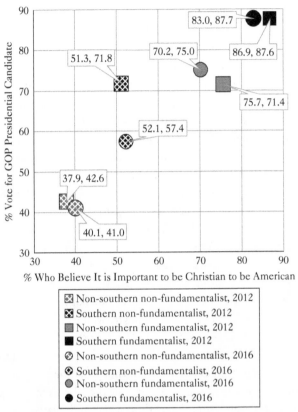

FIGURE 9.9 Percent Who Believe It Is Important to Be Christian to Be American and Percent Vote for Nominee, by Fundamentalism (Biblical Literalism in 2012 and Biblical Literalism and/or Self-identified in 2016), 2012–2016

Data are from the 2012 and 2016 Blair Center Polls.

at a foundational level. The denominational unity necessary to build a sustainable and influential movement required evangelicals and fundamentalists to focus on their shared Christian culture, rather than their theological differences with fellow Protestants, and later with Catholics too, among others. Faith became ideology and ideology became faith. "Conservative Christians at the grassroots," leaders of the religious media reasoned, must "simply organize themselves according to their politics rather than their particular denominations."[136] And organize they did. Southern white fundamentalism insisted on its reactionary righteousness, asserting its power to shape debates over public policy nationwide.

The ambition once activated was hard to control. As Sara Diamond characterizes the movement in her book-length treatment *Not by Politics Alone: The Enduring Influence of the Christian Right*, the rise reflected for many ministers and church leaders that "a taste of power is enticing, but one taste is never enough."[137] There were, indeed, failures, most notably the unsuccessful presidential bid made by Pat Robertson, and there were disappointments when candidates they supported, such as Reagan, did not deliver on their promises. But the Christian Right learned an important lesson from these obstacles. Religious authenticity of a politician paled in comparison to a commitment to the policy positions that aligned with the values of the Christian Right—or against the values that they denounce. That realization, coupled with denominational unity, made it a force with which the GOP has to reckon. The power may be more than the current Republican leaders bargained for.

Yet it is the GOP, as part of the Long Southern Strategy, who breathed political life into this community and resuscitated it time and time again via the posturing of identity politics. This shared Christian culture was under siege and the only armor was their partisan loyalty. Theirs was the party of moral righteousness and personal success. Such a merger of political outlooks and religious convictions is not accomplished by voter guides alone; rather, the Christian Right became, in many ways, its own political ideology, mixed from southern white identity and the Republican messaging regarding threats to that very identity. The relationship between the GOP and the Christian Right, in turn, became so co-dependent that Republicans had to constantly channel collective anger at societal changes and maintain a sense of urgency regarding the country's moral compass. That urgency, over time, accounts for the all-encompassing nature of the Christian Right agenda and the myth of social conservatism. The myth was that such religious-political activism could be controlled or limited to sacred domestic concerns. However, traditional social conservative issues gave way to economic policies and regulation policies, and ultimately to a specific vision of global warfare that requires a commitment to American Christian nationalism. Victory meant all-out victory, a full vision of a Christian nation protecting a Christian world from the axis of evil.

The GOP benefited greatly from this expansion. After all, there is an "advantage to zealotry," in that "conservative Protestantism is a system of beliefs that encourages enthusiastic support. It supposes a simple world of good and evil; it asserts certainty and castigates doubts; it divides people into believers and apostates; and it requires people to spread the Word."[138] And spread the word they did. This pull to the right led by southern evangelicals and championed by the GOP has shifted the entire political playing field, and self-proclaimed conservatives outnumber self-proclaimed liberals in the majority of the United States.[139] Nevertheless, there is a cost and a sense that there is no going back. GOP politicians, particularly in the South, can't merely be conservative on most issues, they must be conservative—or perform that conservatism as Donald

Trump did repeatedly—on almost all issues or risk not being invited to the party,[140] so to speak. Senator Barry Goldwater, who turned the GOP's head southward in the first place, balked at this exact tendency in a speech entered into the Congressional Record in 1981. "I'm frankly sick and tired of the political preachers across this country telling me as a citizen," Goldwater proclaimed, "that if I want to be a moral person, I must believe in 'A,' 'B,' 'C,' and 'D.' Just who do they think they are? And from where do they presume to claim the right to dictate their moral beliefs to me?"[141] His indictment reveals just how far the GOP has moved since his candidacy. Now, not only have the demarcations between denominations vanished, so too has the line between the Republican Party and the Christian Right, between what was once called social conservatism and a new all-encompassing cosmology and foreign policy wrapped in religion—between church and state for that matter. All burn away while a crusader nation, built by a Long Southern Strategy to capitalize on southern white cultural defeat, attempts to rise from its ashes.

Conclusion

AN ECHO, NOT A CHOICE

Let us face the facts. This is a harvest. It is the crop of things sown.

—RALPH MCGILL[1]

IN HER 1964 best-selling exposé,[2] Phyllis Schlafly described how an elite faction within the Republican Party had plotted and schemed to nominate faux conservatives whose policy positions were but echoes of their liberal opponents' positions. In order to win, she insisted, the Grand Old Party needed to offer a distinct choice to the American people, reflected in both the party's presidential nominee and its platform. At the heart of her conspiratorial polemic, however, beat a radical rebuke of the inevitability of progress. Schlafly's arc toward a moral universe was not linear. Rather, she called for a reactionary about-face on progressive social changes. Republicans, she argued, had trekked down that path much slower than Democrats had but, nonetheless, they were taking the same route. Schlafly questioned not only the course of the path, but also its very existence, demanding Republicans strike out on their own. Barry Goldwater would adopt her mantra, announcing to audiences that he offered a choice, not an echo, ushering in a new partisan polarization that would crumble the coalition politics of the New Deal.[3] Goldwater's Operation Dixie set in motion the partisan realignment of the white South, a region that "never indigenously fostered a free press, freedom of expression or movement, or any of the liberal values that were taken for granted elsewhere." Schlafly's path, it turned out, led directly to the white South where for many conserving a white patriarchy remained sacrosanct. For, as Chris Ladd contends, "If you [the South] have formed a perfect society in terms of culture, race, and religion, there is no such thing as 'progress.' Progress is a perversion, since every change is a descent from the ideal."[4]

Rather than arguing over exactly how to implement civil rights legislation, Republican candidates questioned the role of the federal government in enforcing such laws in the first place or insisted that government should be colorblind.

Mitt Romney, for example, spoke at the NAACP national convention in 2012 and announced that, if elected, he would eliminate Obamacare, knowing that the boos from the audience would win him applause from some key white voters.[5] Such deflections were, in fact, choices, seemingly polite and abstract, that had everything to do with halting the march to racial equality while pretending not to be about that at all. White southerners and Americans, for that matter, were less likely to stereotype negatively African Americans in this new politically correct era, but many simultaneously elevated their evaluation of whiteness; the gap between how they view whites and people of color may have shifted, but the absolute value or size of that gap is preserved. Whiteness thus remains a vantage point by which one sees both others and sees the world. Moreover, as a social construction, whiteness has meaning only when it is defined in opposition to an "other," which makes it hollow, malleable, and politically valuable. As a result, as V. O. Key Jr. surmised, "Whites used whiteness,"[6] as did political parties. Threats to white privilege, for example, whether manufactured or real, could spark action at the ballot box in favor of candidates who would conserve institutional inequities. After all, in a mythological post-racial America, affirmative action becomes reverse racism, persistent attention to race stokes Racial Resentment, and inequality becomes the just reward for the undeserving takers. But it did not have to be that way. Both parties could have championed civil rights, which was not predestined to be a partisan issue.

Nor was the Equal Rights Amendment (ERA). Feminism was the freedom to choose, and the ERA was an attempt to tear down the obstacles that stood in the way of making that choice. Phyllis Schlafly, however, invalidated that premise, insisting that feminism was an ideology and anti-feminism was an equally valid ideology that deserved equal representation and time. Her support exploded among southern white women who had bought into the myth of southern white womanhood, willing to endure its limitations for the privileges it afforded them. Atop that pedestal, many could be morally passive about public life and policy, protected from the hardships of the external world, even as they suffered the internal hardships that accompany that kind of powerlessness. This brand of southern white femininity was mirrored by a robust masculinity, bull-headed, quick-tempered, and authoritative. George Wallace epitomized such stubborn masculinity when he promised in his campaign to make the "government quit pussy-footing around,"[7] just as George W. Bush embodied a somewhat more benevolent version in his Texas rancher persona.[8] Such bravado assuaged male insecurities and protected patriarchal structures, which many white southerners felt were sanctioned by scripture. As Paul Harvey has explained, "by the 1960s and 1970s, Southern whites lost much of their traditional theological undergirding for their race politics, but they found new inspiration in the defense of gender roles. In the process the conservatives jettisoned the familiar racial arguments for racial hierarchy, replacing the now discredited views with a renewed and updated defense of gendered hierarchies."[9]

Many southern white women lauded such masculine defiance, so much so that their distrust of feminists and resentment toward working women, as seen in their Modern Sexism scores, is on par with non-southern white men and only slightly trails southern white men. That anti-feminist, hyper-masculine protection of privilege-on-a-pedestal debunks the myth of the gender gap as a universal phenomenon. To look at the gender gap without considering the impact of regional identity is not only to miss its full complexity, but also, in many ways, to allow white southerners to mute it nationally. The bipartisan ERA, and the movement that propelled it, became another casualty of polarization to the point that now Republicans and Democrats do not even agree on what constitutes sexual harassment.[10] That divergence began when the GOP embraced the false equivalency of anti-feminism, dropped the ERA from its platform, and campaigned on "family values" to solidify their southern white base.[11] In this case, however, echoes between candidates—even across the aisle—would have sufficed because feminism itself was based on choice, no matter how vehemently Schlafly proclaimed otherwise.

The "family values" slogan that emerged from the anti-feminist campaign became the mantra of the Christian Right, as religious voters in many southern states became politicized (or re-politicized) over debates about women's rights, gay marriage, and prayer in schools. Social changes such as these sounded a midnight alarm throughout their sacred canopy, just as the teaching of evolution had done a half-century earlier. The certainty of evangelical belief, including believers' status as God's chosen people, the mission to convert, and the fundamentalist belief in the inerrancy of the Bible all contributed to a "southern way of religion" that was partly a theological phenomenon, but even more so a cultural one. Just as Schlafly condemned inaction for greasing the slippery slope of progress rather than conserving the status quo or, better yet, reversing it, fundamentalists within the Southern Baptist Convention (SBC) staged a coup to control the organization. They forced moderates who they thought echoed the moral permissiveness of non-believers to make a choice. The all-consuming nature of southern fundamentalism and evangelicalism—even in seemingly "secular" activities—and the often-isolated status that accompanied it allowed an extremist stance to proliferate. And white southern identity, and all of its baggage, only further entrenched some of these communities in extremism. The fundamentalists did not just take over the SBC, they hijacked its culture and lifestyle.

The absolutism in terms of religious doctrine gave way to an absolutism in public policy attitudes, while the lobbying arm of the SBC moved from advocating for religious freedom to advancing the establishment of religion. Less than two decades after what was deemed a shockingly religious and off-putting keynote speech made by Tennessee Governor and SBC member Frank Clement at the 1956 Democratic Convention,[12] Rev. Billy Graham proclaimed at Richard Nixon's inauguration that "we recognize, O Lord, that in Thy sovereignty Thou has permitted Richard Nixon to lead us at this momentous hour of our history."[13] That actually seems like a slippery slope. Forty years later, George W. Bush explained his efforts in the Middle East by claiming, "I am driven with a mission from God."[14] This promotion of Christian values in the public arena turned social conservatives, across denominations, into all-out conservatives, not just on religious issues like abortion, but on a broad and seemingly odd range of "secular" domestic issues. Moreover, the myth of social conservatism obscured a streak of global Christian nationalism that influenced attitudes toward American foreign policy. Faith could have remained integral to both parties, as could the separation of church and state, but the choice to woo southern white voters meant meeting them in the pews.

Still, as many observers of the 2016 race began to connect the Southern Strategy to Donald Trump, their focus was primarily on race, noting how immigrants were receiving the blunt force of these overtly racial appeals. They also primarily described Trump as a modern manifestation of a once-dead spirit that had come back to life. Jeet Heer at *The New Republic*, in trying to explain the role that racism was having in Trump's rise to power, argued that "the Southern Strategy was the original sin that made Donald Trump possible."[15] He is right. It is the starting point, but the transgressions have been constant and wide-ranging. This is not a case of biting the serpent's apple and suffering consequences down the road. This is eating that apple and many more, in a multitude of varieties, constantly. To turn the South red, the GOP had to capitalize on white racial angst, on anti-feminism, and on fundamentalist, evangelical fervor. They needed all three groups of voters; because it turns out, they are not necessarily one and the same.

The 2016 Blair Center Poll confirms, for example, that not all white Americans who express Racial Resentment also express resentment toward working women and feminists. In an effort to examine religious fundamentalism alongside Modern Sexism and Racial Resentment, an experimental "Christian Fundamentalism" scale is created from six questions regarding attitudes toward evolution, abortion, the inerrancy of the Bible, the personal importance of living a religious life, how strongly one identifies as a Christian fundamentalist, and whether being a Christian is an important part of being an American. Overall scores range from 6 to 24, with the midpoint of the scale being 15. When examining the percentage of white Americans who are above the midpoint of the scale, just like the fact that not all whites who express high racial animus are

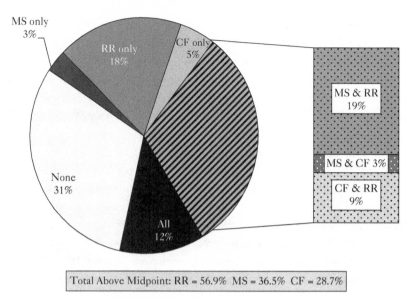

Total Above Midpoint: RR = 56.9% MS = 36.5% CF = 28.7%

FIGURE C.1A Percent Above the Racial Resentment, Christian Fundamentalism, and Modern Sexism Scales, All Combinations, Among Non-southern Whites, 2016

Data are from the 2016 Blair Center Poll.

also sexist, not all Christian fundamentalists have bought into post-racialism or the untrustworthiness of feminists. As shown in Figure C.1A, which specifically describes non-southern whites, the largest portion (31 percent) of whites do not have scores above the midpoints of any of these scales. There are 18 percent who express Racial Resentment solely. The percentages of those who scored above the midpoint for either Modern Sexism or Christian Fundamentalism alone were in the single digits. Roughly one-third of non-southern whites have high scores in two of three categories, with the most popular combination being high sexism and high racism. Only 12 percent of non-southern whites, which represents roughly 75 percent of the country, report the trifecta of high scores.

Among those who claim a southern identity, those proportions are significantly different, though the assumption that all three labels are interchangeable is still incorrect. As seen in Figure C.1B, only one-third of southern whites report high levels of all three—racist, sexist, as well as fundamentalist—attitudes simultaneously. The other third of the pie (34 percent) express two of the three, but in this case, the combination of Racial Resentment and Modern Sexism (16 percent) is equally popular to the combination of Racial Resentment and Christian Fundamentalism. And still there are those who fall above the midpoint on only one of these scales—1 percent are only Modern

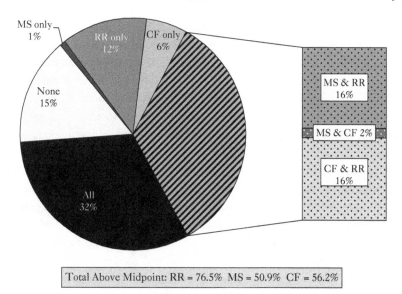

Total Above Midpoint: RR = 76.5% MS = 50.9% CF = 56.2%

FIGURE C.1B Percent Above the Racial Resentment, Christian Fundamentalism, and Modern Sexism Scales, All Combinations, Among Southern Whites, 2016

Data are from the 2016 Blair Center Poll.

Sexists, 6 percent are only Christian fundamentalists, and 12 percent only express high Racial Resentment levels. Only 15 percent of southern whites hold none of these attitudes, which is significantly lower than non-southern whites (31 percent).

Though this is only a snapshot of one election cycle, it demonstrates exactly why the Long Southern Strategy was, in fact, long, and why all three components of the strategy were necessary to build a solid red base in the states of the old Confederacy. While whites in the Deep South may have been quick converts to Goldwater because those states had the highest population of African Americans and would be the most impacted by civil rights changes, they did not represent enough of the region's population to cause realignment alone. White racial angst, of course, exists throughout the region[16]—and the nation, for that matter—but the saliency required to catalyze party defection was not universal throughout the South. Other issues mattered as much, more, or instead of racial animus to other pockets or subgroups of whites. Thus, scholarship that focuses exclusively on the distinctiveness of the Deep South may, as Jonathon Knuckey notes, be limited,[17] just as scholarship exclusively about race and southern politics or gender and southern politics or religion and southern politics is limited. Rather, all three choices mattered.

And they still matter. Choosing to exploit the racial angst and fear of feminism and evangelical righteousness that already existed in the South is one thing, but perpetuating those angsts is another. That means that the GOP has a vested interest in keeping those emotions running high. In fact, if part of self-identification requires a consciousness about one's own community, then the Long Southern Strategy may have extended the life of southernness, as it still spans generations.[18] Furthermore, reaching out to white southern voters is one thing, but remaking the party in their image is another. It means that conservatism has been redefined on the basis of white southern identity, and that definition becomes the baseline ideology for Republicans across the country. In that vein, recent polling indicates that Racial Resentment, for example, makes white Americans more supportive of the Confederate flag and makes them feel warmer toward southerners in general.[19] Moreover, the resurgence of Lost Cause symbols have, in many ways, helped white southerners and their sympathizers identify with Trump.[20] Just as the southern "way of religion" was sold to the nation at large via the SBC and the Moral Majority and, eventually, the Christian Right (some of Jerry Falwell's largest audiences were in Los Angeles, California),[21] these symbols reflect the fact that southern identity was disseminated throughout the country, at least in part, via the Long Southern Strategy.

The stark polarization that resulted from these partisan choices unraveled the New Deal coalition.[22] It also redivided white Americans not just along the Mason-Dixon line, but across the imagined fault line of southern identity. Southern whites are now the social group least likely to identify as Democrats.[23] Other white Americans have and will continue to sort themselves accordingly as well. As a result of these choices and the sorting that followed, the distribution of white Americans who harbor Racial Resentment or Modern Sexism or identify with Christian Fundamentalism is no longer even across the parties. Outside of the South, white defections from the Democratic Party to the GOP are much lower,[24] because the concentration of voters who hold these racist, sexist, and/or fundamentalist beliefs is much higher in the South. Some have deemed this the Republican Party's White Strategy and warned that it will sink the party, citing the California GOP as evidence.[25] However, the strategy is multidimensional, and Republicans have won in the South, so much so that one-party politics is the name of the game yet again in most of the southern states. Moreover, because of this sorting, when Republicans win nationally now, there is not enough opposition to such prejudice and absolutism within the party to fully suppress it.

Figure C.2 shows just how polarizing these three choices have been in terms of party identification. The triangular marker represents the members of the group who have scores above the midpoint of the various scales, while the circular

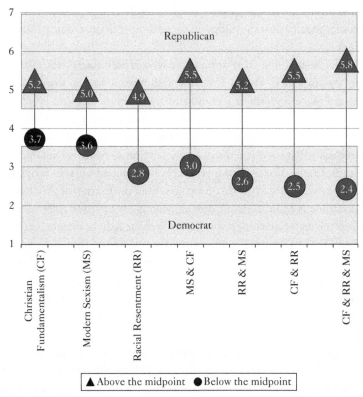

FIGURE C.2 Mean Party Identification of Respondents Who Score Above and Below the Midpoints of the Christian Fundamentalism, Modern Sexism, and Racial Resentment Scales, Among Whites, 2016

Data are from the 2016 Blair Center Poll.

marker represents the members of the same group who have scores below the midpoint of the various scales. The placement of each marker reflects the average party identification of that subgroup across a seven-point scale that runs from Strong Democrat (1) to Strong Republican (7). Pure independent individuals would score a 4, and a group mean that is independent would fall between 3.5 and 4.5. White Americans below the midpoint of the experimental Christian Fundamentalism scale fall into that category, as do those below the midpoint of the Modern Sexism scale. For those below the Racial Resentment scale or below the midpoints in any combination of the scales, their average party identification is in the Democratic range. For every scale, and every possible combination of scales, those above the midpoint, on average, are Republicans. Those who are above the midpoint of the Racial Resentment scale and the Christian Fundamentalist scale and the Modern Sexism scale have the highest average party identification at 5.8, which is 3.4 points higher (the full range is only seven points) than those who fall below the midpoint on all three scales at a solidly Democratic 2.4 points.

This allegiance to the GOP from those who express Racial Resentment and Modern Sexism and Christian Fundamentalism must be maintained. Partisan victories are made to seem tantamount to the survival of white privilege and patriarchy and a Christian America. Much of that urgency, however, is a con, based on manufactured threats, or a false equivalency, or the fantasy of a zero-sum game. Christianity is still the majority religion in America, the opposite of feminism is sexism (because feminism is choice), and advantages for people of color do not necessitate white disadvantages. Even the fixation of the South with small government and the accompanying rallying cry of states' rights developed only when the region seemingly lost power over the federal government.[26] Yet it works because the alternative—losing—is cast as suffering. The consequences of defeat are being forced to live in a world that does not reflect one's values, a society that is reconstructed and in which the winner's ideals are imposed. Often those defeats have proved shocking in the white South, whether they came at the hands of Union troops, the Supreme Court, or even voters in a presidential election. The sacred canopy, for example, insulates such homogenous communities to the point that the legalization of gay marriage seems sudden, radical, and surely imposed by a powerful, fringe minority. This, by the way, is the root of the admiration that some extreme southern evangelicals feel for Russian president Vladimir Putin, whom they see as having rolled back gay rights in his country.[27] In the wake of such shocking events, the national culture seems unrecognizable to many southern whites. In this changed world, they feel like they have no voice and no control.[28] Many of them never did, but their race and gender and religion were reflected by their leaders, which reinforced the illusion. And feeling powerless and subjugated, whether it be to integration, or military occupation, or political correctness, remains the recipe for the politics of resentment, with which southern whites are well acquainted.

Such resentment can fuel denial. Before the Civil War, for example, some white southerners proclaimed that *Uncle Tom's Cabin* was completely fraudulent.[29] Moreover, in the years after the Civil War white southern elites balked at the "outrage mills," newspapers that relentlessly churned out articles exposing continued oppression of newly freed slaves. These "outrage mills" delayed white southerners from re-establishing their control by keeping federal intervention on the table. Thus, they were denounced as biased or altogether "fake news." The entire elite southern social system from its inception was built on a self-proclaimed notion of aristocracy that was as inauthentic as the moonlight-and-magnolias image that romanticized it. The Lost Cause propaganda that it generated to ameliorate the wounds of war and surrender, complete with memorials to the Confederate patriots who served gallantly in this "War Between the States," was a placebo, curing little of the resentment that festered. In recent decades, for example, the Christian Right, broadly conceived, has also offered counter-narratives with their own news broadcasts highlighting false stories of the war on Christians.[30]

In response, southern whiteness becomes a defensive identity, which manifests in a number of important ways, from memorializing the southern version of the past to pointing out the hypocrisy of the other side to creating a false equivalency even when there was or is no other side. So when Trump, in his defense of the Robert E. Lee statue in Charlottesville, Virginia, claims that there is "literally no difference" between Lee and George Washington—both "owned slaves," both "rebelled against the ruling government," "both were great men, great Americans, great commanders," and both "saved America"—he is equating Confederate nationalism and American patriotism. He is equating the defense of slavery with the revolutionary cause of independence and scolding the media for not getting the parallel.[31] Trump's comments echoed Nixon's complaints about the "regional bias"[32] he claimed had blocked his southern Supreme Court nominees. Both validate one of the oldest and deepest sources of that resentment—the belief that the white South is unjustly demonized or ridiculed by those who live beyond its boundaries—which spreads like kudzu in a climate of denial. Often special animosity has been aimed toward the media, because the media makes denial so much harder to maintain. Both the anti-feminists[33] and the SBC charged the media and academics[34] with liberal bias on numerous occasions.[35] Perhaps most directly—until Trump hit the campaign trail—George Wallace politicized that sense of inferiority by insisting that there was a full media conspiracy against the good people of the South. "The average citizen in this county," he once told a Florida crowd, "has more intelligence and sense in his little finger than the editor of the *New York Times* has in his whole head."[36] That sentiment undoubtedly grew further entrenched whenever Democrats flaunted the moral high ground and accused the candidates or their supporters of racism or sexism or bigotry of any sort.[37]

Such defensiveness easily deflates into victimhood, and victimhood is where resentment grows—resentment that can be mobilized politically.[38] White southerners had long perceived themselves as subjects of federal overreach or scapegoats for national problems. They are under siege,[39] unjustly attacked by a biased media, or not taken seriously, or their history is being erased. This rhetoric of group victimization that Wallace used to mobilize his supporters[40] resurfaces when the values those voters enshrined are no longer privileged exclusively. Reminiscent of the tent revivals of the past, both this rhetoric of victimization and defensiveness draw big crowds. Conversion narratives are popular too because the convert offers a sense of righteousness.[41] The late Zell Miller, a former Democratic senator from Georgia, for example, gave the keynote at the Republican National Convention in 2004. In it he reviewed decades of Democratic Party policy decisions interjected with the repeating chorus, "They were wrong."[42] Such converts have been abandoned by the Democrats, and have had no choice but to defect. Such conversions, including Strom Thurmond's 1964 about-face, were a constant occurrence as the solidly blue South turned red. Righteousness, just like the certainty that evangelical fundamentalism had provided, eased the pain of all of the lost causes, whatever they may be. However, righteousness can also trigger blind ambition and a thirst for vengeance, especially in a culture that feels so prone to ridicule and even defeat. "We are as hurt at criticism of our region," wrote Lillian Smith, "as if our own name were called aloud by the critic. We have known guilt without understanding it, and there is no tie that binds men closer to the past and each other than that."[43] Such is the topography and power of southern white identity.

Criticism, victimization, and resentment also make strange bedfellows—or so it can seem to outside observers. Though the Long Southern Strategy played on three different types of social angst—racial, gender-role, and religious—the "us vs. them" technique used in each case, muddied the waters, so to speak, in two important ways. First, the Long Southern Strategy made southern white political behavior seem strange or irrational even though it is not. For example, southern white women voted overwhelmingly against the first female major-party nominee for the presidency, to the surprise of many. Southern whites also vote against their economic self-interest, with some even railing against "Obamacare" despite desperately needing better access to healthcare. Second, the Long Southern Strategy had a crossover effect, whereby common enemies created friends. For example, the 1994 Republican Contract for America, promoted by southern congressional leaders, did not directly mention the Christian Right; however, campaigns on its behalf and on behalf of the candidates who endorsed it focused on "God, guns, and gays."[44] Others have pointed out that the fringe Alt-Right is just as misogynistic as it is racist.[45] Christians have been found to be more likely to believe that poverty results from a lack of effort.[46] The waters were and are muddy. So much so that even those who were not above the midpoint of the Racial Resentment scale, for example, may be neutral on it. Moreover, those who are not Modern Sexists may not be turned off by those who are. The common wisdom is that sounding such dog whistles will activate some voters, but doing so will repel others. However, after four decades of the Long Southern Strategy, the partisan umbrella has made many white southerners tolerant of the intolerance of others, and that has made normal bedfellows of many whites nationwide.

Table C.1 lists every possible combination on the Racial Resentment, Modern Sexism, and Christian Fundamentalism scales. Respondents fall above the scale, below the scale, or are neutral on the scale. The percentage of those in each category is listed, and a running total is presented in the adjacent column. If a candidate is outwardly racist, or sexist, or openly Christian fundamentalist, or uses rhetoric to that effect, they will activate only 12.3 percent of whites in the non-South and only 11.5 percent of those who do not identify as southern. However, among whites who live in the South, 20.9 percent are potentially activated, and among those who claim a southern identity, such rhetoric reaches a like-minded audience of 32.1 percent. Moreover, if those who are neutral in one of the three categories but who are high in the other two are likely to be attracted to such rhetoric (despite that neutrality in one area), then the audience share increases quite a bit. In the states of the former Confederacy, that audience would be 28.1 percent of whites, and among those who claim a southern identity, that share grows to 42.3 percent—reaching almost half by playing to the far right end of the spectrum. Additionally, if one also includes those who are above the midpoint on two of the three scales and low on the other, or if they are high on one scale and neutral on the other two, the national white audience reaches near majority (49.4), reaches a clear majority in the geographic South (53.7 percent), and reaches a supermajority of whites who identify as southern (68.9 percent).

Those highest numbers, of course, are only among whites who claim a southern identity. That being said, according to the 2016 Blair Center Poll, 76.7 percent of self-proclaimed southerners voted in the primaries, with 78.4 percent of those who participated choosing to vote in the Republican primary. Thus, there is a lot of bang for a GOP candidate's buck in activating angst and fear and resentment. This is particularly true if one wants to lead the pack in a crowded race coming out of the new "SEC Primary," a nickname referencing the region's largest collegiate athletic conference.[47] Cue the big crowds, chants, rivalry, inflammatory rhetoric, and reactionary policy promises that are hardly coded anymore. Donald Trump did exactly that. This southern Super Tuesday is not a sporting event, contrary to its moniker, but it might as well be. In Georgia's Republican presidential primary, "Trump won evangelicals. He won the wealthy. He won men. He won women. He won the college-educated. In fact," as was reported in the *Atlanta Journal Constitution*, "the New York billionaire won nearly every category of Georgia voter with an appeal that cut across demographics, regardless of age, education level, gender, religious belief or degree of conservatism." When the polls closed, Trump had "won more votes than any other Republican candidate ever in a Georgia presidential primary."[48]

Table C.1 Percent (with Running Totals) Above, At, and Below the Midpoint of the Modern Sexism, Racial Resentment, and Christian Fundamentalism Scales, Among Whites, 2016

			All		Non-South		South		Non-southern		Southern	
			%	Total	%	Total	%	Total	%	Total	%	Total
MS ↑	RR ↑	CF ↑	14.9	14.9	12.3	12.3	20.9	20.9	11.5	11.5	32.1	32.1
MS =	RR ↑	CF ↑	2.7	17.6	2.2	14.5	3.8	24.8	2.0	13.4	6.1	38.2
MS ↑	RR ↑	CF =	1.9	19.5	1.6	16.1	2.5	27.3	1.8	15.2	2.4	40.6
MS ↑	RR =	CF ↑	2.0	**21.5**	2.5	**18.6**	0.8	**28.1**	1.6	**16.8**	1.8	**42.4**
MS ↓	RR ↑	CF ↑	7.4	28.9	7.2	25.8	8.0	36.1	6.8	23.6	10.2	52.6
MS =	RR ↑	CF =	0.9	29.8	0.8	26.6	1.0	37.1	0.8	24.4	1.2	53.8
MS =	RR =	CF ↑	1.6	31.4	1.5	28.1	1.8	39.0	1.6	26.0	1.8	55.6
MS ↑	RR ↑	CF ↓	16.6	48.0	17.6	45.7	14.2	53.1	16.9	42.9	13.3	68.9
MS ↑	RR =	CF =	0.0	48.0	0.0	45.7	0.0	53.1	0.0	42.9	0.0	68.9
MS ↑	RR ↓	CF ↑	1.4	**49.4**	1.8	**47.5**	0.6	**53.7**	1.6	**44.5**	0.0	**68.9**
MS ↓	RR ↑	CF =	0.9	50.3	0.6	48.1	1.5	55.3	1.0	45.6	1.1	70.0
MS ↓	RR =	CF ↑	1.1	51.4	0.8	48.9	1.9	57.2	0.7	46.2	3.3	73.3
MS =	RR ↑	CF ↓	3.4	54.8	3.7	52.6	2.7	59.9	3.8	50.1	1.4	74.7
MS =	RR =	CF =	0.6	55.4	0.8	53.4	0.0	59.9	0.6	50.7	0.0	74.7
MS =	RR ↓	CF ↑	0.4	55.8	0.3	53.7	0.7	60.6	0.6	51.3	0.0	74.7
MS ↑	RR =	CF ↓	1.5	57.3	1.6	55.3	1.3	61.9	1.7	53.0	0.9	75.6
MS ↑	RR ↓	CF =	0.3	57.7	0.4	55.7	0.1	62.1	0.4	53.3	0.0	75.6
MS ↓	RR ↑	CF ↓	11.3	69.0	11.1	66.8	11.8	73.9	12.3	65.7	8.6	84.2
MS ↓	RR =	CF =	0.1	69.1	0.2	67.0	0.0	73.9	0.1	65.8	0.0	84.2
MS ↓	RR ↓	CF ↑	2.1	71.2	2.1	69.1	2.0	75.9	2.4	68.2	0.9	85.1
MS =	RR =	CF ↓	2.4	73.5	2.4	71.5	2.3	78.2	2.5	70.7	1.8	87.0
MS =	RR ↓	CF =	0.0	73.6	0.0	71.5	0.1	78.3	0.1	70.8	0.0	87.0
MS ↑	RR ↓	CF ↓	1.0	74.5	1.0	72.5	0.9	79.1	1.1	71.9	0.4	87.3
MS ↓	RR =	CF ↓	3.5	78.1	3.6	76.1	3.4	82.5	4.0	75.8	2.0	89.4
MS ↓	RR ↓	CF =	0.7	78.8	0.7	76.8	0.7	83.2	0.5	76.4	1.3	90.7
MS =	RR ↓	CF ↓	0.9	79.6	1.1	77.8	0.5	83.8	1.0	77.4	0.3	90.9
MS ↓	RR ↓	CF ↓	20.4	100	22.1	100	16.2	100	22.6	100	9.0	100
N=			2088		1094		948		1547		485	

Data are from the 2016 Blair Center Poll.

To get a sense of the bigger picture, the questions that comprise the Racial Resentment scale and the Modern Sexism scale and this experimental Christian Fundamentalist scale were combined into what is called here the Long Southern Strategy (LSS) scale, and its impact is undeniable. Figure C.3 presents the average LSS score across region, regional identity, party identification, and for Trump voters, revealing that much of the variation in southern politics hinges on these three choices made by the GOP to court those who held tightly to that white southern way of life. The scale ranges from 15 to 69, with a midpoint of 42. Whites who live in the South are above the midpoint, but the gap is relatively small when measured against whites who live beyond the borders of the old Confederacy. However, southern identity expands this gap significantly, with southern whites averaging a score of 46, which is now almost the exact same average as Republicans nationally. Trump supporters fall only 1 point higher, at a score of 47 on average compared to non-Trump

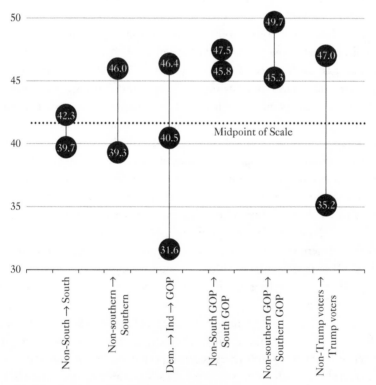

FIGURE C.3 Mean LSS Scores, Among Whites, 2016
Data are from the 2016 Blair Center Poll.

voters at 35.2. It turns out that southern identity is the chasm between two Americas.

In a logit model predicting vote for Trump in the general election, as shown in Table C.2, the impact of these choices is visible as well. Even controlling for demographics, party identification, and a host of other variables, Racial Resentment and Modern Sexism are significant predictors of voting for Trump among all white Americans, though the effect is greatest among whites who identify as southern. However, only among whites who either live in the South or call themselves southern is Christian Fundamentalism a significant predictor of voting for Trump.

There are other critical differences as well. Unemployment and income are slightly significant, but unemployment made whites in the South and whites who identify as southern less likely to vote for Trump; higher incomes, on the other hand, made them more likely to vote for Trump. Gender is slightly significant, but only among whites who call themselves southern, with white women being more likely to vote for Trump. It is important to note as well that being married significantly decreases one's likelihood of voting for Trump—but only among whites who either live outside of the South or among whites who do not identify as southern. Moreover, for every group except white southerners, support for Trump is significantly hampered by increased education levels. Among white southerners, education has no effect, nor does having a liberal ideology. For many of them, rather than political ideology, "southern" is their way of looking at the world.

The models also point to another complexity regarding the persistent nature of southern white identity. For every group except southern whites, age is a significant predictor of voting for Trump, with older white Americans being more likely to do so. That seems logical if racism and sexism are playing a role because it reinforces the common assumption that older white Americans are the bearers of such old-fashioned prejudices. That assumption about age and racism and sexism leads to a secondary assumption that such prejudices will diminish with the passage of time. However, despite optimistic theories (John Dollard professed in 1949 that "Americans instinctively hate the caste system and will not too long abide it"),[49] younger southern whites are not significantly less likely to vote for Trump. Time may not have eroded such attitudes. Perhaps the Long Southern Strategy would not let it.

With this in mind, it becomes easier to see that in the wake of the passage of the Civil Rights Act and the Voting Rights Act, hearts and values may not have changed among white southerners as was expected. Rather, at least some white southerners believed that rising to power again—winning again—would be possible and would mean reactionary change, turning the clock backward, erasing

Table C.2 Predicting General Election Vote for Trump, Among Whites, 2016

	Non-South	South	Non-southern	Southern
Age	0.023****	0.013**	0.017****	0.012
(toward older)	(0.007)	(0.007)	(0.006)	(0.011)
Education	−0.533****	−0.422***	−0.509****	−0.299
(toward more educated)	(0.141)	(0.166)	(0.119)	(0.252)
Income	0.005	0.049*	0.004	0.087**
(toward wealthier)	(0.033)	(0.035)	(0.026)	(0.052)
Married	−0.492**	−0.105	−0.497**	0.433
	(0.260)	(0.269)	(0.215)	(0.388)
Female	−0.215	0.235	−0.167	0.512*
	(0.234)	(0.241)	(0.189)	(0.394)
Unemployed	0.72	−0.950*	0.426	−1.736**
	(0.685)	(0.581)	(0.509)	(0.829)
Party Identification	1.013****	1.037****	0.971****	1.151****
(toward Republican)	(0.104)	(0.110)	(0.084)	(0.160)
Ideology	0.267**	0.228**	0.369****	−0.02
(toward conservative)	(0.119)	(0.117)	(0.095)	(0.176)
Racial Resentment	0.229****	0.240****	0.224****	0.249****
	(0.042)	(0.044)	(0.033)	(0.077)
Modern Sexism	0.117****	0.108***	0.101****	0.164***
	(0.033)	(0.036)	(0.027)	(0.056)
Christian	−0.007	0.112****	0.027	0.096**
Fundamentalism	(0.028)	(0.029)	(0.023)	(0.042)
Constant	−9.566****	−12.010****	−9.874****	−13.260****
	(1.033)	(1.208)	(0.831)	(2.090)
N	936	816	1325	419
Pseudo R Squared	0.572	0.573	0.557	0.584

Note: Standard errors in parentheses * p<= .10, ** p<= .05, *** p<= .01, **** p<.001
Data are from the 2016 Blair Center Poll.

the previous losses, and silencing the critics. GOP candidates who hinted at that or took a policy position that at least stemmed the tide of change pulled southern white voters. But over the decades since, as the Republican Party emphasized an "us vs. them" America, preached policy absolutes, accused the media of liberal bias, prioritized identity over the economy, insisted that the southern way of life was under attack, promised that southern white fears were right and southern white anger was justified, and championed a politics of vengeance, it remade itself in the southern image. In doing so, it nationalized southern white identity.

The combination of bait the GOP used to catch southern whites was tailored to the region, but it is still bait to all who are hungry. So calls for states' rights, law and order, fiscal conservatism, colorblindness, anti-feminism, men's rights, and Christian nationalism can summon a southern white majority, but other Americans are beckoned too. When dissecting Trump's share of the white vote, in fact, those who had scores above the midpoint of the Racial Resentment, Modern Sexism, and this Christian Fundamentalism scale, or some combination therein, accounted for 95 percent of his total white support. The only distinguishing characteristic of the remaining 5 percent seems to be an above average household income. That explains why, over time, at the national level, Republican candidates had no choice but to echo all three of those dog whistles in order to win. Those who did not or could not lost.

The Long Southern Strategy also helps to explain why Confederate flags fly in Iowa and why white supremacists gathered around a statue of Robert E. Lee to march in Charlottesville, Virginia, in 2017. It explains why rural voters[50] and poor southern whites vote against their economic self-interest. It explains why there has been such a surge in "negative partisanship," as highlighted in Alan Abramowitz's *The Great Alignment*, in which "a growing number of Americans have been voting against the opposing party rather than for their own."[51] It explains why white evangelicals are the only religious group still supporting Trump,[52] and why they applauded his decision to recognize Jerusalem as the capital of Israel[53] (it may even explain why Trump made the decision in the first place). It explains why one of the most successful Russian attempts to influence the 2016 election via social media was their fake "Heart of Texas" Facebook page, which championed secession and grew to over 250,000 followers.[54] It explains why Phyllis Schlafly endorsed Trump early in the primaries, and why Trump gave the eulogy at her funeral two months before his election. It explains why Trump demonized Christine Blasey Ford at a rally in Mississippi, and why the crowd chanted back, "Lock her up!"[55] It explains why the majority of Republican women (51 percent) and Republican men (65 percent) were "barely" or "not at all" outraged by Trump's assertion that he could grab women "by the pussy"[56] and why there is a partisan gap in support for #MeToo.[57] It explains why there is a "resistance." It explains why there is a resistance to the "resistance." It explains why a "blue wave" of Democratic voters in 2018 toppled GOP regimes in Kansas, Wisconsin, and in the Sunbelt's Orange County, California, but why statewide victories in Texas, Georgia, and Florida were still slightly out of reach and will take an equally long strategy to achieve. It explains why 75 percent of white women in Georgia voted against Stacey Abrams for governor.[58] It explains why there are white Americans who voted for Obama but would not vote for Hillary Clinton. It explains why, despite decades of media coverage of the gender gap in favor of Democrats, according to the strictly geographic measure in the 2016 Blair Center Poll, 47 percent of white women who live outside of the South voted for Clinton and 43 percent for Trump. However, in the states of the old Confederacy, only 33 percent of white women voted for Clinton, while 58 percent chose Trump.[59] It explains why political scientists need to measure geography and identity (Clinton's vote shared drops to 21.9 percent among white women who identify as southern). It explains why running to the far right helped Trump emerge as the GOP nominee from a crowded field. It explains why Trump won.

Trump's victories both in the GOP primaries and in the general election come with expectations from many of his voters. Winning, they think, should silence the accusations of racism, sexism, ignorance, or hate that have been lobbed their way—accusations that are anything but new in the white South. But it has not. That, in turn, has amped up the denial and resentment for many. Abraham Lincoln actually recognized this "sore winner" dynamic, as noted by journalist Heath Digby Parton, when white southerners, despite the concessions made to allow slavery to continue in the decades prior to the Civil War, seemed persistently enraged. In his 1860 speech at Cooper Union in New York, Lincoln asked the crowd, "What will it take to satisfy them?" His answer: "This, and this only: cease to call slavery wrong, and join them in calling it right."[60] For many, their righteousness needs validation, which is why the partisan screen and fake news proliferate, and why political correctness, which is seen as endorsing the liberal worldview, has become the new enemy. But righteousness only needs validation when it is based on manufactured threats or false equivalencies or orchestrated outrage or bogus notions of supremacy. Trump's victory did not mean that his opposition had surrendered, because democracy is not war, despite the fact that the Long Southern Strategy has made it seem that way. Rather it is the harvest of seeds planted, of choices made in the GOP deal to win southern white voters, the echoes of which continue to reverberate across America.

APPENDIX A

Survey Instruments

2010 Blair Center Poll

Variable	Question	Coding of Responses
Affirmative Action	The following is a list of issues that we often hear about in the news. In general do you favor or oppose the following: Employers and colleges making an extra effort to find and recruit qualified minorities.	1=Strongly favor; 2=Favor; 3=Neither; 4=Oppose; 5=Strongly oppose
Approval of president's handling of: –War on terrorism –War in Afghanistan –War in Iraq	The following is a list of issues that we often hear about in the news. In general do you favor or oppose the following: The president's handling of the war on terrorism; The president's handling of war in Afghanistan; The president's handling of war in Iraq	1=Strongly favor; 2=Favor; 3=Neither; 4=Oppose; 5=Strongly oppose
Attention paid to race	In general, would you say that there is there too much, too little, or about the right amount of attention paid to race and racial issues these days?	1=Too little; 2=About the right amount; 3=Too much
Competition for jobs –African Americans –Latinos	Some have suggested that whites are in competition with other groups, particularly when it comes to getting jobs. To what extent do you believe that you have a lot of competition, some competition, just a little competition, or none at all with each of the following groups? African Americans; Latinos	1=None at all; 2=Just a little competition; 3=Some competition; 4=A lot of competition
Denomination	With what religious tradition do you most closely identify?	1=Baptist; 2=Protestant; 3=Catholic; 4=Mormon; 5=Jewish; 6=Muslim; 7=Hindu; 8=Buddhist 9=Pentecostal; 10=Eastern Orthodox; 11=Other Christian; 12=other, Non-Christian; 13=none
Ethnocentrism (Feeling Thermometer measure)	Feeling Thermometer Evaluations of: Whites; African Americans; Latinos	Respondents' Feeling Thermometer evaluation of whites minus the average of their feeling thermometer evaluation of African Americans and their feeling thermometer evaluation of Latinos

Variable	Question wording	Coding
Ethnocentrism (Racial Stereotype measure)	Old-Fashioned Racism/ Racial Stereotype measure toward: Whites; African Americans; Latinos	Respondents' total Racial Stereotype evaluation of whites minus the average of their Racial Stereotype evaluation of African Americans and their Racial Stereotype evaluation of Latinos
Feeling Thermometer Evaluations -Whites -African Americans -Latinos	We'd like to get your feelings toward some people and groups in the news these days. Please rate the following people or groups on a thermometer that runs from 0 to 100 degrees. A rating above 50 means that you feel favorable and warm toward them. A rating below 50 means that you feel unfavorable and cool toward them. A rating right at the 50-degree mark means you don't feel particularly warm or cold: Whites; African Americans; Latinos	Unfavorable/Cold to Favorable/Warm
Fundamentalism (biblical literalism)	Which of these statements comes closest to describing your feelings about the Bible?	0=The Bible is the inspired Word of God, but not everything in it should be taken literally; The Bible is a book written by men and is not the Word of God. 1=The Bible is the actual Word of God and is to be taken literally, word for word.
Future outlook -Personal -Country -Whites -South	We are also interested in peoples' perspective on the future and whether they believe things are getting better or worse. When you think of the following people and groups, do you think things will get much better or much worse in the future? Your own personal situation; The country; Whites; The South	1=Much worse; 2=Somewhat worse; 3=Neither/neutral; 4=Somewhat better; 5=Much better
Gay Marriage	The following is a list of issues that we often hear about in the news. In general, do you favor or oppose the following: Allowing homosexual couples to legally marry	1=Strongly favor; 2=Favor; 3=Neither; 4=Oppose; 5=Strongly oppose
Healthcare reform concerns: -Rationing -Delays -Quality -Taxes -Socialism -Euthanasia -Undeserved	To what extent are you concerned that recent/President Obama's proposed reforms may lead to the following: Healthcare rationing; Long delays in getting needed medical treatment; Substantial drop in quality of healthcare; Taxes being raised for average Americans; These reforms will lead to socialism; Euthanasia ("mercy killing") of elderly patients; Benefits to people that do not work hard enough to deserve it	Five-point response scale ranging from 1=Not at all concerned to 5=Extremely concerned with 3=Neither/neutral

Variable	Question	Coding
Immigration	The following is a list of issues that we often hear about in the news. In general, do you favor or oppose the following: Tougher immigration laws like the one in Arizona	1=Strongly oppose; 2=Oppose; 3=Neither; 4=Favor; 5=Strongly favor
Obama's religion	Thinking about Barack Obama's religious beliefs . . . Do you happen to know what Barack Obama's religion is? Is he: Christian, Jewish, Muslim, Buddhist, Hindu, Atheist, Agnostic, Something else, Don't know	1=Christian; 2=Don't know 3=Jewish; Buddhist; Hindu; Atheist; Agnostic; or Something else; 4=Muslim
Opportunities for African Americans	Thinking about the opportunities that most White people have these days, do you feel that the following groups have more, less, or about the same opportunities in life: African Americans.	1=Less opportunity; 2=About the same; 3=More opportunity
Party identification	Generally speaking, do you usually think of yourself as a Democrat, Republican, or Independent?	1=Strong Democrat; 2=Democrat; 3=Independent-leaning Democrat; 4=Independent; 5=Independent- leaning Republican; 6=Republican; 7=Strong Republican
Prospective personal economic evaluation	We are also interested in how people are getting along financially these days. Thinking about your own economic situation, what do you think your financial situation will be a year from now?	1=Worse off; 2=Just about the same; 3=Better off
Racial Resentment toward African Americans –Overcame prejudice (Q1) –Generations of slavery (Q2) –Less than deserved (Q3) –Try harder (Q4)	To what extent do you agree or disagree with the following statements? (Q1) Irish, Italians, Jewish, and many other minorities overcame prejudice and worked their way up, blacks should do the same without any special favors; (Q2) Generations of slavery and discrimination have created conditions that make it difficult for blacks to work their way out of the lower class; (Q3) Over the past few years, blacks have gotten less than they deserve; (Q4) It's really a matter of some people not trying hard enough; if blacks would only try harder they could be just as well as whites.	Q1 and Q4: 1=Strongly disagree; 2=Disagree; 3=Neither; 4=Agree; 5=Strongly agree Q2 and Q3: 1=Strongly agree; 2=Agree; 3=Neither; 4=Disagree; 5=Strongly disagree. Answers were summed to create a single scale with scores that range from 4–20. The midpoint of the scale is 12. The scale has an alpha of .82.
Racial Stereotypes/ Old-Fashioned Racism –Work ethic –Intelligence –Trustworthiness	In general, where would you rate the following groups in terms of: How hard-working they are? How intelligent they are? How trustworthy they are? Whites; African Americans; Latinos	Seven-point scale ranging from 1=Hard-working to 7=Lazy; 1=Intelligent to 7=Unintelligent; 1=Trustworthy to 7=Untrustworthy. Answers were summed to create a single scale with scores that range from 3–21. The scale has an alpha of .91 for stereotypes of African Americans; .83 for stereotypes of Latinos; and .85 for stereotypes of whites.

Variable	Question	Coding of Responses
South	11 states of the former Confederacy	1=Alabama; Arkansas; Florida; Georgia; Louisiana; Mississippi; North Carolina; South Carolina; Tennessee; Texas; Virginia 0=other states.
Southern identity	In general, how strongly do you think of yourself as any of the following? Southerner	0=Not at all; Not strongly; Neither/neutral 1=Strongly; Very strongly
White identity	In general, how strongly do you think of yourself as any of the following? White	1=Not at all 2=Not strongly; 3=Neither/neutral; 4=strongly; 5=Very strongly

2012 Blair Center Poll

Variable	Question	Coding of Responses
Abortion	Which one of the opinions below best agrees with your view about abortion?	1=By law, a woman should always be able to obtain an abortion as a matter of personal choice. 2=The law should permit abortion for reasons other than rape, incest, or danger to the woman's life, but only after the need for the abortion has been clearly established. 3=The law should permit abortion only in case of rape, incest, or when the woman's life is in danger. 4=By law, abortion should never be permitted.
Affirmative Action	The following is a list of issues that we often hear about in the news. In general do you favor or oppose the following: Employers and colleges making an extra effort to find and recruit qualified minorities	1=Strongly favor; 2=Favor; 3=Neither; 4=Oppose; 5=Strongly oppose
Age	Age in years	18–93
Attention paid to race	In general, would you say that there is there too much, too little, or about the right amount of attention paid to race and racial issues these days?	1=Too little; 2=About the right amount; 3=Too much
Christian to be American	When you think of what it means to be fully "American" in the eyes of most Americans, do you think it is very important, somewhat important, or not important to be Christian?	1=Not important; 2=Somewhat important; 3=Very important

Variable	Question	Coding
Competition for jobs – African Americans – Latinos	Some have suggested that whites are in competition with other groups, particularly when it comes to getting jobs. To what extent do you believe that you have a lot of competition, some competition, just a little competition or none at all with each of the following groups? African Americans; Latinos	1=None at all; 2=Just a little competition; 3=Some competition; 4=A lot of competition
Denomination	With what religious tradition do you most closely identify?	1=Catholic; 3=Baptist; 4=Pentecostal; 5=Other Protestant; 6=Mormon; 7=Jewish; 8=Don't identify with a denomination; 9=Muslim; 10=Buddhist; 12=other
Discrimination -General -Respect -Services -Names -Police	In your day-to-day life, how often do any of the following things happen to you because of your racial or ethnic background? You experience discrimination; You are treated with less respect than other people; You received poorer service than other people at restaurants and stores; You are called names or insulted; You have been unfairly stopped by police.	1=Never; 2=Once in a while; 3=Fairly often; 4=Very often
Education	Highest level of education attained	1=Less than high school; 2=High school; 3=Some College; 4=Bachelor's degree or higher.
Ethnocentrism (Feeling Thermometer measure)	Feeling Thermometer Evaluations of: Whites; African Americans; Latinos	Respondents' Feeling Thermometer evaluation of whites minus the average of their feeling thermometer evaluation of African Americans and their feeling thermometer evaluation of Latinos
Ethnocentrism (Racial Stereotype measure)	Old-Fashioned Racism/Racial Stereotype measure toward: Whites; African Americans; Latinos	Respondents' total Racial Stereotype evaluation of whites minus the average of their Racial Stereotype evaluation of African Americans and their Racial Stereotype evaluation of Latinos
Feeling Thermometer Evaluations of: –Whites –African Americans –Latinos	We'd like to get your feelings toward some people and groups in the news these days. Please rate the following people or groups on a thermometer that runs from 0 to 100 degrees. A rating above 50 means that you feel favorable and warm toward them. A rating below 50 means that you feel unfavorable and cool toward them. A rating right at the 50-degree mark means you don't feel particularly warm or cold: Whites; African Americans; Latinos	Unfavorable/Cold to Favorable/Warm

Federal government responsibility to ensure equality: -Jobs -Schools -Housing -Health services -Courts/Police	Do you believe it is the responsibility of the federal government to make sure that minorities have equality with Whites in each of the following areas, even if it means you will have to pay more in taxes? Jobs; Schools; Housing; Health services; Treatment by the courts and police	0=Not the Responsibility of the Federal Government. 1=Responsibility of the Federal Government
Female president	Do you believe you will see a woman as the American president in your lifetime?	0=No; 1=Yes
Fundamentalism (biblical literalism)	Which of these statements comes closest to describing your feelings about the Bible?	0=The Bible is the inspired Word of God, but not everything in it should be taken literally; The Bible is a book written by men and is not the Word of God. 1= The Bible is the actual Word of God and is to be taken literally, word for word.
Gay marriage	The following is a list of issues that we often hear about in the news. In general, do you favor or oppose the following: Allowing homosexual couples to legally marry	1=Strongly favor; 2=Favor; 3=Neither; 4=Oppose; 5=Strongly oppose
General Election vote	In the 2012 presidential election, who did you vote for?	1=Barack Obama; 2=Mitt Romney; 3=Other
Global warming	Is there solid evidence the earth is warming?	1=Yes because of human activity; 2=Yes because of natural patterns; 3=Yes but don't know the reason; 4=No
Healthcare reform	There has been a great deal of discussion recently about healthcare reform. In general how do you feel about President Obama's approach to/recent approaches to healthcare reform?	1=Strongly oppose; 2=Oppose; 3=Neither; 4=Support; 5=Strongly support
Ideology	Generally speaking, do you usually think of yourself as a Liberal, Conservative, or Moderate?	1=Strong liberal; 2=liberal; 3=Moderate-leaning liberal; 4=Moderate; 5=Moderate-leaning conservative; 6=Conservative; 7=Strong conservative

Immigration	The following is a list of issues that we often hear about in the news. In general, do you favor or oppose the following: Tougher immigration laws like the one in Arizona	1=Strongly oppose; 2=Oppose; 3=Neither; 4=Favor; 5=Strongly favor
Income (household)	Total Household Income Per Year	1=\$5,000 to \$7,499; 2=\$7,500 to \$9,999; 3=\$10,000 to \$12,499; 4=\$12,500 to \$14,999; 5=\$15,000 to \$19,999; 6=\$20,000 to \$24,999; 7=\$25,000 to \$29,999; 8=\$30,000 to \$34,999; 9=\$35,000 to \$39,999; 10=\$40,000 to \$49,999; 11=\$50,000 to \$59,999; 12=\$60,000 to \$74,999; 13=\$75,000 to \$84,999; 14=\$85,000 to \$99,999; 15=\$100,000 to \$124,999; 16=\$125,000 to \$149,999; 17=\$150,000 to \$174,999; 18=\$175,000 or more
Married	Marital Status	1=Married; 0=Widowed; Divorced; Separated; Never Married; or Living with Partner
Modern Sexism –Favors (Q1) –Remarks (Q2) –Power (Q3) –Complain (Q4) –Discrimination (Q5)	To what extent to do you agree or disagree with the following statements?: (Q1) Many women are actually seeking special favors, such as hiring policies that favor them over men under the guise of asking for "equality"; (Q2) Most women interpret innocent remarks or acts as being sexist; (Q3) Feminists are seeking for women to have more power than men; (Q4) When women lose to men in a fair competition, they typically complain about being discriminated against; (Q5) Discrimination against women is no longer a problem in the United States.	1=Strongly disagree; 2=Disagree; 3=Neither; 4=Agree; 5=Strongly agree Answers were summed to create a single scale with scores that range from 5–25. The midpoint of the scale is 15. The alpha of the scale is .8.
Party identification	Generally speaking, do you usually think of yourself as a Democrat, Republican, or Independent?	1=Strong Democrat; 2=Democrat; 3=Independent-leaning Democrat; 4=Independent; 5=Independent- leaning Republican; 6=Republican; 7=Strong Republican
Prospective personal economic evaluation	We are also interested in how people are getting along financially these days. Thinking about your own economic situation, what do you think your financial situation will be a year from now?	1=Worse off; 2=Just about the same; 3=Better off

Variable	Question wording	Coding
Racial Resentment toward African Americans —Overcame prejudice (Q1) —Generations of slavery (Q2) —Less than deserved (Q3) —Try harder (Q4)	To what extent do you agree or disagree with the following statements? (Q1) Irish, Italians, Jewish, and many other minorities overcame prejudice and worked their way up, blacks should do the same without any special favors; (Q2) Generations of slavery and discrimination have created conditions that make it difficult for blacks to work their way out of the lower class; (Q3) Over the past few years, blacks have gotten less than they deserve; (Q4) It's really a matter of some people not trying hard enough; if blacks would only try harder they could be just as well off as whites.	Q1 and Q4: 1=Strongly disagree; 2=Disagree; 3=Neither; 4=Agree; 5=Strongly agree Q2 and Q3: 1=Strongly agree; 2=Agree; 3=Neither; 4=Disagree; 5=Strongly disagree Answers were summed to create a single scale with scores that range from 4–20. The midpoint of the scale is 12. The scale has an alpha of .84.
Racial Resentment toward Latinos —Overcame prejudice (Q1) —Generations of discrimination (Q2) —Less than deserved (Q3) —Try harder (Q4)	To what extent do you agree or disagree with the following statements? (Q1) Irish, Italians, Jewish, and many other minorities overcame prejudice and worked their way up, Latinos should do the same without any special favors; (Q2) Generations of discrimination have created conditions that make it difficult for Latinos to work their way out of the lower class; (Q3) Over the past few years, Latinos have gotten less than they deserve; (Q4) It's really a matter of some people not trying hard enough; if Latinos would only try harder they could be just as well off as whites.	Q1 and Q4: 1=Strongly disagree; 2=Disagree; 3=Neither; 4=Agree; 5=Strongly agree Q2 and Q3: 1=Strongly agree; 2=Agree; 3=Neither; 4=Disagree; 5=Strongly disagree Answers were summed to create a single scale with scores that range from 4–20. The midpoint of the scale is 12. The scale has an alpha of .77.
Racial Stereotypes/ Old-Fashioned Racism —Work ethic —Intelligence —Trustworthiness	In general, where would you rate the following groups in terms of: How hard-working they are? How intelligent they are? How trustworthy they are? Whites; African Americans; Latinos	Seven-point scale ranging from 1=Hard-working to 7=Lazy; 1=Intelligent to 7=Unintelligent; 1=Trustworthy to 7=Untrustworthy Answers were summed to create a single scale with scores that range from 3–21. The scale has an alpha of .88 for stereotypes of African Americans; .81 for stereotypes of Latinos; and .84 for stereotypes of whites.
Romney's Religion	Do you believe that Mitt Romney is a Christian?	1=Yes; 2=No; 3=Don't know
South	11 states of the former Confederacy	1=Alabama; Arkansas; Florida; Georgia; Louisiana; Mississippi; North Carolina; South Carolina; Tennessee; Texas; Virginia 0=other states
Southern identity	In general, how strongly do you think of yourself as any of the following? Southerner	0=Not at all; Not strongly; Neither/neutral 1=Strongly; Very strongly

		0=Working as a paid employee; Working, self-employed; Not working, retired; Not working, disabled; Not working, other 1=Not working, on temporary layoff; Not working, looking for work
Unemployed/Looking for work	Current employment status	
White identity	In general, how strongly do you think of yourself as any of the following? White	1=Not at all 2=Not strongly; 3=Neither/neutral; 4=Strongly; 5=Very strongly
Woman	Respondent's sex	1=Woman; 0=Man

2016 Blair Center Poll

Variable	Question	Coding of Responses
Abortion	Which one of the opinions below best agrees with your view about abortion?	1=By law, a woman should always be able to obtain an abortion as a matter of personal choice. 2=The law should permit abortion for reasons other than rape, incest, or danger to the woman's life, but only after the need for the abortion has been clearly established. 3=The law should permit abortion only in case of rape, incest, or when the woman's life is in danger. 4=By law, abortion should never be permitted.
Affirmative Action	The following is a list of issues that we often hear about in the news. In general do you favor or oppose the following: Employers and colleges making an extra effort to find and recruit qualified minorities	1=Strongly favor; 2=Favor; 3=Neither; 4=Oppose; 5=Strongly oppose
Age	Age in years	18–91
Attention paid to race	In general, would you say that there is there too much, too little, or about the right amount of attention paid to race and racial issues these days?	1=Too little; 2=About the right amount; 3=Too much
Ban assault rifles	The following is a list of policy positions that we often hear about in the news. In general, do you agree or disagree with the following: It should be illegal to manufacture, sell, or possess semi-automatic guns known as assault rifles.	1=Strongly agree; 2=Agree; 3=Neither; 4=Disagree; 5=Strongly disagree

Background checks	The following is a list of policy positions that we often hear about in the news. In general, do you agree or disagree with the following: Background checks should be required for gun shows and private sales.	1=Strongly agree; 2=Agree; 3=Neither; 4=Disagree; 5=Strongly disagree
Biblical literalist	Which of these statements comes closest to describing your feelings about the Bible?	0=The Bible is the inspired Word of God, but not everything in it should be taken literally; The Bible is a book written by men and is not the Word of God. 1=The Bible is the actual Word of God and is to be taken literally, word for word.
Children, importance	How important is each of the following to you personally? Having children	1=Not at all important; 2=Somewhat important; 3=Important; 4=Very important
Christian fundamentalist identity	In general, how strongly do you think of yourself as any of the following? Christian fundamentalist	1=Not at all; 2=Not strongly; 3=Neither/neutral; 4=strongly; 5=Very strongly
Christian Fundamentalism scale	Experimental scale including the following variables: Christian fundamentalist identity; Biblical literalism; Evolution; Abortion; Christian to be American; and Religious life, importance	Answers were summed to create a single scale with scores that range from 6–24. The midpoint of the scale is 15. The alpha of the scale is .85.
Christian to be American	When you think of what it means to be fully "American" in the eyes of most Americans, do you think it is very important, somewhat important, important, or not important to be Christian?	1=Not at all important; 2=Somewhat important; 3=Important; 4=Very important
Competition for jobs –African Americans –Latinos	Some have suggested that whites are in competition with other groups, particularly when it comes to getting jobs. To what extent do you believe that you have a lot of competition, some competition, just a little competition or none at all with each of the following groups? African Americans; Latinos	1=None at all; 2=Just a little competition; 3=Some competition; 4=A lot of competition
Denomination	With what religious tradition do you most closely identify?	1=Catholic; 2=Assemblies of God; 3=Baptist; 4=Pentecostal; 5=Other Protestant; 6=Mormon; 7=Jewish; 8=Don't identify with a denomination; 9=Muslim; 10=Buddhist; 11=other
Discrimination –General –Respect –Services –Names –Police	In your day-to-day life, how often do any of the following things happen to you because of your racial or ethnic background? You experience discrimination; You are treated with less respect than other people; You received poorer service than other people at restaurants and stores; You are called names or insulted; You have been unfairly stopped by police.	1=Never; 2=Once in a while; 3=Fairly often; 4=Very often

	Description	Coding
Education	Highest level of education attained	1=Less than high school; 2=High school; 3=Some College; 4=Bachelor's degree or higher
Ethnocentrism (Feeling Thermometer measure)	Feeling Thermometer Evaluations of: Whites; African Americans; Latinos	Respondents' Feeling Thermometer evaluation of whites minus the average of their Feeling Thermometer evaluation of African Americans and their Feeling Thermometer evaluation of Latinos
Evolution	Which of these comes closest to your views? Humans and other living things have . . .	1=Evolved over time due to natural processes; 2=Evolved over time, but don't know how; 3=Evolved over time guided by a supreme being; 4=Created by a supreme being in their present form since the beginning of time
Feeling Thermometer evaluations of: –Black Lives Matter –Police/Law enforcement	We'd like to get your feelings toward some people and groups in the news these days. Please rate the following people or groups on a thermometer that runs from 0 to 100 degrees. A rating above 50 means that you feel favorable and warm toward them. A rating below 50 means that you feel unfavorable and cool toward them. A rating right at the 50-degree mark means you don't feel particularly warm or cold. Black Lives Matter; Police/Law enforcement	Unfavorable/Cold to Favorable/Warm
Feeling Thermometer Evaluations of: Whites, African Americans, Latinos	We'd like to get your feelings toward some people and groups in the news these days. Please rate the following people or groups on a thermometer that runs from 0 to 100 degrees. A rating above 50 means that you feel favorable and warm toward them. A rating below 50 means that you feel unfavorable and cool toward them. A rating right at the 50-degree mark means you don't feel particularly warm or cold: Whites; African Americans; Latinos	Unfavorable/Cold to Favorable/Warm
Fundamentalist Combination	Combination of being those who identify as a Christian fundamentalist and/or believe in a literal interpretation of the Bible	0=The Bible is the inspired Word of God, but not everything in it should be taken literally or The Bible is a book written by men and is not the Word of God AND "not at all," "not strongly," or "neutral" response to identification as a Christian fundamentalist. 1=The Bible is the actual Word of God and is to be taken literally, word for word AND/OR "strongly" or "very strongly" identify as a Christian fundamentalist.

Variable	Question wording	Coding
Global warming	Is there solid evidence the earth is warming?	1=Yes because of human activity; 2=Yes because of natural patterns; 3=Yes but don't know the reason; 4=No
General Election vote	In the 2016 presidential election, who did you vote for?	1=Hillary Clinton; 2=Donald Trump; 3=Gary Johnson; 4=Jill Stein; 5=other
Ideology	Generally speaking, do you usually think of yourself as a Liberal, Conservative, or Moderate?	1=Strong liberal; 2=Liberal; 3=Moderate-leaning liberal; 4=Moderate; 5=Moderate-leaning conservative; 6=Conservative; 7=Strong conservative
Income (household)	Total Household Income Per Year	1=\$5,000 to \$7,499; 2=\$7,500 to \$9,999; 3=\$10,000 to \$12,499; 4=\$12,500 to \$14,999; 5=\$15,000 to \$19,999; 6=\$20,000 to \$24,999; 7=\$25,000 to \$29,999; 8=\$30,000 to \$34,999; 9=\$35,000 to \$39,999; 10=\$40,000 to \$49,999; 11=\$50,000 to \$59,999; 12=\$60,000 to \$74,999; 13=\$75,000 to \$84,999; 14=\$85,000 to \$99,999; 15=\$100,000 to \$124,999; 16=\$125,000 to \$149,999; 17=\$150,000 to \$174,999; 18=\$175,000 or more
Long Southern Strategy scale	Experimental scale that combines all of the questions in the Racial Resentment toward African Americans scale, the Modern Sexism scale, and the experimental Christian Fundamentalism scale	Answers were summed to create a single scale with scores that range from 15–69. The midpoint of the scale is 42. The scale has an alpha of .89.
Marriage, importance	How important is each of the following to you personally? Being married	1=Not at all important; 2=Somewhat important; 3=Important; 4=Very important
Married	Marital status	1=Married; 0=Widowed; Divorced; Separated; Never Married; or Living with Partner
Mexico wall	The following is a list of policy positions that we often hear about in the news. In general, do you agree or disagree with the following: A wall should be built along the entire border with Mexico.	1=Strongly disagree; 2=Disagree; 3=Neither; 4=Agree; 5=Strongly agree
Modern Sexism –Favors (Q1) –Remarks (Q2) –Power (Q3) –Complain (Q4) –Discrimination (Q5)	To what extent to do you agree or disagree with the following statements?: (Q1) Many women are actually seeking special favors, such as hiring policies that favor them over men under the guise of asking for "equality"; (Q2) Most women interpret innocent remarks or acts as being sexist; (Q3) Feminists are seeking for women to have more power than men; (Q4) When women lose to men in a fair competition, they typically complain about being discriminated against; (Q5) Discrimination against women is no longer a problem in the United States.	1=Strongly disagree; 2=Disagree; 3=Neither; 4=Agree; 5=Strongly agree Answers were summed to create a single scale with scores that range from 5–25. The midpoint of the scale is 15. The scale has an alpha of .88.

Variable	Question wording	Coding
Party identification	Generally speaking, do you usually think of yourself as a Democrat, Republican, or Independent?	1=Strong Democrat; 2=Democrat; 3=Independent-leaning Democrat; 4=Independent; 5=Independent-leaning Republican; 6=Republican; 7=Strong Republican
Primary vote	In your state's 2016 presidential primary/caucus, did you vote for:	1=Jeb Bush; 2=Ben Carson; 3=Ted Cruz; 4=John Kasich; 5=Marco Rubio; 6=Donald Trump; 7=Hillary Clinton; 8=Bernie Sanders; 9=other
Prospective personal economic evaluation	We are also interested in how people are getting along financially these days. Thinking about your own economic situation, what do you think your financial situation will be a year from now?	1=Worse off; 2=Just about the same; 3=Better off
Racial Resentment toward African Americans –Overcame prejudice (Q1) –Generations of slavery (Q2) –Less than deserved (Q3) –Try harder (Q4)	To what extent do you agree or disagree with the following statements? (Q1) Irish, Italians, Jewish, and many other minorities overcame prejudice and worked their way up, blacks should do the same without any special favors; (Q2) Generations of slavery and discrimination have created conditions that make it difficult for blacks to work their way out of the lower class; (Q3) Over the past few years, blacks have gotten less than they deserve; (Q4) It's really a matter of some people not trying hard enough; if blacks would only try harder they could be just as well off as whites.	Q1 and Q4: 1=Strongly disagree; 2=Disagree; 3=Neither; 4=Agree; 5=Strongly agree Q2 and Q3: 1=Strongly agree; 2=Agree; 3=Neither; 4=Disagree; 5=Strongly disagree Answers were summed to create a single scale with scores that range from 4–20. The midpoint of the scale is 12. The scale has an alpha of .84.
Racial Stereotypes/ Old-Fashioned Racism –Work ethic –Intelligence –Trustworthiness	In general, where would you rate the following groups in terms of: How hard-working they are? How intelligent they are? How trustworthy they are? Whites; African Americans; Latinos	Seven-point scale ranging from 1=Hard-working to 7=Lazy; 1=Intelligent to 7=Unintelligent; 1=Trustworthy to 7=Untrustworthy Answers were summed to create a single scale with scores that range from 3–21. The scale has an alpha of .87 for stereotypes of African Americans; .82 for stereotypes of Latinos; and .84 for stereotypes of whites.
Religious life, importance	How important is each of the following to you personally? Living a religious life	1=Not at all important; 2=Somewhat important; 3=Important; 4=Very important
South	11 states of the former Confederacy	1=Alabama; Arkansas; Florida; Georgia; Louisiana; Mississippi; North Carolina; South Carolina; Tennessee; Texas; Virginia 0=other states
Southern identity	In general, how strongly do you think of yourself as any of the following? Southerner	0=Not at all; Not strongly; Neither/neutral 1=Strongly; Very strongly

Variable	Question	Coding of Responses
Syria and Iraq	The following is a list of policy positions that we often hear about in the news. In general, do you agree or disagree with the following: The U.S. should send ground troops to fight Islamic militants in Iraq and Syria.	1=Strongly disagree; 2=Disagree; 3=Neither; 4=Agree; 5=Strongly agree
Trump's Religion	Do you believe that Donald Trump is a Christian?	1=Yes; 2=No; 3=Don't know
Unemployed/Looking for work	Current employment status	0=Working as a paid employee; Working, self-employed; Not working, retired; Not working, disabled; Not working, other 1=Not working, on temporary layoff; Not working, looking for work
White identity	In general, how strongly do you think of yourself as any of the following? White	1=Not at all; 2=Not strongly; 3=Neither/neutral; 4=strongly; 5=Very strongly
Woman	Respondent's sex	1=Woman; 0=Man

2007 Baylor Religion Survey		
Variable	**Question**	**Coding of Responses**
Biblical literalist	Which one statement comes closest to your personal beliefs about the Bible?	1=The Bible means exactly what it says. It should be taken literally, word-for-word, on all subjects. 0=The Bible is perfectly true, but it should not be taken literally, word-for-word. We must interpret its meaning; The Bible contains some human error; The Bible is an ancient book of history and legends; I don't know.
Christian nation	To what extent do you agree or disagree that the federal government should declare the United States a Christian nation?	1=Strongly disagree; 2=Disagree; 3=Undecided; 4=Agree; 5=Strongly agree
Christian values	To what extent do you agree or disagree that the federal government should advocate Christian values?	1=Strongly disagree; 2=Disagree; 3=Undecided; 4=Agree; 5=Strongly agree
Church attendance at 12	By your best estimate, how often did you attend religious services at age 12?	1=Never; 2=Less than once a year; 3=Once or twice a year; 4=Several times a year; 5=Once a month; 6=2–3 times a month; 7=About weekly; 8=Weekly; 9=Several times a week
Church friends	How many of your friends attend your place of worship?	1=None; 2=A few; 3=About half; 4=Most; 5=All

Variable	Question	Coding
Convert others	How important is it to do the following if one wishes to be a good person? Convert others to your religious faith	1=Not important; 2=Not very important; 3=Somewhat important; 4=Very important
Dated (another race)	Have you ever dated or been romantically involved with a person of another race?	0=No; 1=Yes
Death penalty	To what extent do you agree or disagree that the federal government should abolish the death penalty?	1=Strongly disagree; 2=Disagree; 3=Undecided; 4=Agree; 5=Strongly agree
Denomination	With what religious family do you most closely identify?	Denominations are coded irregularly; Baptist=12; Other options: Adventist; African Methodist; Asian folk religion; Assemblies of God; Bible; Brethren; Buddhist; Catholic/Roman Catholic; Christian & Missionary Alliance; Christian Reformed; Christian Science; Church of Christ; Church of God; Church of the Nazarene; Congregational; Disciples of Christ; Episcopal/Anglican; Hindu; Holiness; Jehovah's Witnesses; Jewish; Latter-day Saints; Lutheran; Mennonite; Methodist; Muslim; Orthodox (Eastern; Russian; Greek); Pentecostal; Presbyterian; Quaker/Friends; Reformed Church of America/Dutch Reformed; Salvation Army; Seventh-day Adventist; Unitarian Universalist; United Church of Christ; Non-denominational Christian; No religion; Other; Don't know
Devil causes evil	Please indicate your level of agreement with the following statements about evil in the world: Most evil in the world is caused by the Devil.	1=Strongly disagree; 2=Disagree; 3=Undecided; 4=Agree; 5=Strongly agree
English as national language	To what extent do you agree or disagree that the federal government should declare English the national language?	1=Strongly disagree; 2=Disagree; 3=Undecided; 4=Agree; 5=Strongly agree
Fundamentalist Combination	Combination of those who identify as fundamentalist, or born again, or evangelical, and/or believe in a literal interpretation of the Bible	0=Those who believe "The Bible is the inspired Word of God, but not everything in it should be taken literally" or "The Bible is a book written by men and is not the Word of God" AND who indicate that the terms fundamentalist, born again, and evangelical describe their religious identity "not at all," "not strongly," or "neutral"; 1=Those who believe "The Bible means exactly what it says. It should be taken literally, word-for-word, on all subjects" AND/OR those who believe the terms fundamentalist, born again, or evangelical describe their religious identity "well" or "very well"

God exists	Which one statement comes closest to your personal beliefs about God?	1=I have no doubts that God exists; 2=I believe in God, but with some doubts; 3=I sometimes believe in God; 4=I believe in a higher power or cosmic force; 5=I don't know and there is no way to find out; 6=I am an atheist
Gun control	To what extent do you agree or disagree that the federal government should enact stricter gun laws?	1=Strongly disagree; 2=Disagree; 3=Undecided; 4=Agree; 5=Strongly agree
Iraq War	Please indicate your level of agreement with the following statements about world events: Going to war in Iraq was the right decision.	1=Strongly disagree; 2=Disagree; 3=Undecided; 4=Agree; 5=Strongly agree
Men better suited for politics	Please indicate your level of agreement with the following statements about men's and women's roles: Most men are better suited emotionally for politics than most women.	1=Strongly disagree; 2=Disagree; 3=Undecided; 4=Agree; 5=Strongly agree
Moral stances of church/place of worship: -Pornography -Gambling -Premarital sex -Cohabitation -Contraception -Revealing clothing -Displays of wealth	By your best guess, how would your current place of worship feel about each of the following behaviors? Pornography; Gambling; Premarital sex; Cohabitation; Use of contraception; Wearing revealing clothing; Displays of wealth	1=Forbids; 2=Strongly discourages; 3=Somewhat discourages; 4=Isn't concerned; 5=Encourages
Morality of war	How do you feel about the morality of war?	1=Always wrong; 2=Almost always wrong; 3=Only wrong sometimes; 4=Not wrong at all
Pray/Meditate	About how often do you pray or meditate outside of religious services?	1=Never; 2=Only on certain occasions; 3=Once a week or less; 4=A few times a week; 5=Once a day; 6=Several times a day
Punish Criminals	To what extent do you agree or disagree that the federal government should punish criminals more harshly?	1=Strongly disagree; 2=Disagree; 3=Undecided; 4=Agree; 5=Strongly agree
Religious Activity -Bible study/Sunday school -Witness to friends -Witness to strangers -Community Bible study	How often did you participate in the following religious or faith-based activities in the last month? Religious education programs, such as Bible study or Sunday school; Witnessing/sharing your faith with friends; Witnessing/sharing your faith with strangers; Community Bible study not affiliated or sponsored by a congregation (e.g., in the community or workplace)	1=Not at all; 2=One to two times; 3=Three to four times; 4=Five or more times

Variable	Question	Coding
Religious at 12	How personally religious were you at age 12?	1=Not at all religious; 2=Not too religious; 3=Somewhat religious; 4=Very religious
Religious beliefs –Devil/Satan –Heaven –Hell –Armageddon –Angels –Demons –Rapture	In your opinion, does each of the following exist? Devil/Satan; Heaven; Hell; Armageddon; Angels; Demons; Rapture	1=Absolutely not; 2=Probably not; 3=Probably; 4=Absolutely
Religious experiences: –Witnessed a healing –Received healing –Spoke in tongues –Felt called –Heard God –Guardian angel –Religious conversion –One with universe	Please indicate whether or not you have ever had any of the following experiences: I witnessed a miraculous, physical healing; I received a miraculous, physical healing; I spoke or prayed in tongues; I felt called by God to do something; I heard the voice of God speaking to me; I was protected from harm by a guardian angel; I had a religious conversion experience; I felt at one with the universe.	0=No; 1=Yes
Religious identity –Fundamentalist –Born Again –Evangelical	How well do the following terms describe your religious identity? Fundamentalist; Born Again; Evangelical	0=Not at all; Not very well; Undecided 1=Somewhat well; Very well
Sacred book	Outside of attending religious services, about how often do you read the Bible, Koran, Torah, or other sacred book?	1=Never; 2=Less than once a year; 3=Once or twice a year; 4=Several times a year; 5=Once a month; 6=2–3 times a month; 7=About weekly; 8=Weekly; 9=Several times a week or more often
South	Census definition	1=Alabama; Arkansas; Delaware; District of Columbia; Florida; Georgia; Kentucky; Louisiana; Maryland; Mississippi; North Carolina; Oklahoma; South Carolina; Tennessee; Texas; Virginia; West Virginia 0=All other states

Variable	Question	Coding of Responses
Teach morals	How important is it to do the following if one wishes to be a good person? Teach others your morals	1=Not important; 2=Not very important; 3=Somewhat important; 4=Very important
Terrorism	To what extent do you agree or disagree that the federal government should expand its authority to fight terrorism?	1=Strongly disagree; 2=Disagree; 3=Undecided; 4=Agree; 5=Strongly agree
Tithe	Do you tithe (give a fixed percentage of your income) to your current place of worship?	0=No; 1=Yes
Tithe (amount)	During the last year, approximately how much money did you and other family members in your household contribute to your current place of worship?	1=Under $500; 2=$500–$999; 3=$1,000–$1,999; 4=$2,000–$2,999; 5=$3,000–$3,999; 6=$4,000–$4,999; 7=$5,000–$5,999; 8=$6,000–$6,999; 9=$7,000–$7,999; 10=$8,000–$8,999; 11=$9,000–$9,999; 12=$10,000 or more
Trust immigrants	How much would you say that you trust the following people or groups? Immigrants	1=Not at all; 2=Only a little; 3=Some; 4=A lot
Volunteer at church	About how many hours per month do you volunteer for your place of worship?	1=None; 2=One to two hours; 3=Three to four hours; 4=Five to ten hours; 6=Eleven or more hours
Volunteer in community	About how many hours per month do you volunteer for the community, through your place of worship?	1=None; 2=One to two hours; 3=Three to four hours; 4=Five to ten hours; 6=Eleven or more hours

2010 Baylor Religion Survey

Variable	Question	Coding of Responses
Bailout of banks	How do you feel about the morality of the following? Government bailout of major banks and corporations	1=Always wrong; 2=Almost always wrong; 3=Only sometimes wrong; 4=Not wrong at all
Biblical literalist	Which one statement comes closest to your personal beliefs about the Bible?	1=The Bible means exactly what it says. It should be taken literally, word-for-word, on all subjects. 0=The Bible is perfectly true, but it should not be taken literally, word-for-word. We must interpret its meaning; The Bible contains some human error; The Bible is an ancient book of history and legends; I don't know

Variable	Question	Coding
Denomination	With what religious family, if any, do you most closely identify?	Denominations are coded irregularly; Baptist=12; Other options: Adventist; African Methodist; Anabaptist; Asian Folk Religion; Assemblies of God; Baha'i; Baptist; Bible Church; Brethren; Buddhist; Catholic/Roman Catholic; Christian & Missionary Alliance; Christian Reformed; Christian Science; Church of Christ; Church of God; Church of the Nazarene; Congregational; Disciples of Christ; Episcopal/Anglican; Hindu; Holiness; Jehovah's Witnesses; Jewish; Latter-day Saints; Lutheran; Mennonite; Methodist; Muslim; Orthodox (Eastern, Russian, Greek); Pentecostal; Presbyterian; Quaker/Friends; Reformed Church of America/Dutch Reformed; Salvation Army; Seventh-day Adventist; Sikh; Unitarian Universalist; United Church of Christ; Non-denominational Christian; No religion; Other (please specify); Don't know
Fundamentalist Combination	Combination of those who identify as fundamentalist, or born again, or evangelical, and/or believe in a literal interpretation of the Bible	0=Those who believe "The Bible is the inspired Word of God, but not everything in it should be taken literally" or "The Bible is a book written by men and is not the Word of God" AND who indicate that the terms fundamentalist, born again, and evangelical describe their religious identity "not at all," "not strongly," or "neutral" 1=Those who believe "The Bible means exactly what it says. It should be taken literally, word-for-word, on all subjects" AND/OR those who believe the terms fundamentalist, born again, or evangelical describe their religious identity "well" or "very well"
God exists	Which one statement comes closest to your personal beliefs about God?	1=I have no doubts that God exists; 2=I believe in God, but with some doubts; 3=I sometimes believe in God; 4=I believe in a higher power or cosmic force; 5=I don't know and there is no way to find out; 6=I am an atheist; 7=I have no opinion
Media portrayal of Muslims	Media portrayals of religious traditions and beliefs have made you: Believe that Muslims are more likely to be terrorists	1=No; 2=Yes

Pray	About how often do you spend time alone praying outside of religious services?	1=Never; 2=Only on certain occasions; 3=Once a week or less; 4=A few times a week; 5=Once a day; 6=Several times a day
Religious activity –Bible study/Sunday school –Witness –Community Bible study	How often did you participate in the following religious or faith-based activities in the last month? Religious education programs, such as Bible study or Sunday school; Witnessing/sharing your faith; Community Bible study not affiliated or sponsored by a congregation (e.g., in the community or workplace)	1=Not at all; 2=One to two times; 3=Three to four times; 4=Five or more times
Religious beliefs –Devil/Satan –Heaven –Hell –Armageddon –Angels –Demons	In your opinion, does each of the following exist? Devil/Satan; Heaven; Hell; Armageddon; Angels; Demons	1=Absolutely not; 2=Probably not; 3=Probably; 4=Absolutely
Religious identity –Fundamentalist –Born Again –Evangelical	How well do the following terms describe your religious identity? Fundamentalist; Born Again; Evangelical	0=Not at all; Not very well; Undecided 1=Somewhat well; Very well
Sacred book	Outside of attending religious services, about how often do you read the Bible, Koran, Torah, or other sacred book?	1=Never; 2=Less than once a year; 3=Once or twice a year; 4=Several times a year; 5=Once a month; 6=2–3 times a month; 7=About weekly; 8=Weekly; 9=Several times a week or more often
South	Census definition	1=Alabama; Arkansas; Delaware; District of Columbia; Florida; Georgia; Kentucky; Louisiana; Maryland; Mississippi; North Carolina; Oklahoma; South Carolina; Tennessee; Texas; Virginia; West Virginia 0=all other states

1992 Southern Focus Poll, South Sample

Variable	Question	Coding of Responses
Assertive	Would you say that Southern women are more assertive or less assertive than American women in general?	1=Southern women more; 2=Southern women less; 3=No difference
Career-oriented	Would you say that Southern women are more career-oriented or less career-oriented than American women in general?	1=Southern women more; 2=Southern women less; 3=No difference
Feminist	Would you say that Southern women are more feminist, that is, sympathetic to the Women's Movement, or less feminist than American women in general?	1=Southern women more; 2=Southern women less; 3=No difference
Friendly	Would you say that Southern women are more friendly or less friendly than American women in general?	1=Southern women more; 2=Southern women less; 3=No difference
Independent	Would you say that Southern women are more independent or less independent than American women in general?	1=Southern women more; 2=Southern women less; 3=No difference
Self-centered	Would you say that Southern women are more self-centered or less self-centered than American women in general?	1=Southern women more; 2=Southern women less; 3=No difference
Southern identity	Do you consider yourself a Southerner, or not?	1=Yes; 0=No
Strong-willed	Would you say that Southern women are more strong-willed or less strong-willed than American women in general?	1=Southern women more; 2=Southern women less; 3=No difference
White	What race do you consider yourself?	1=White; 0=all other races
Woman	Respondent's sex	1=Woman; 0=Man

Sample Sizes

INTRODUCTION

Figure/Table	Source	Year	Variable	Sample Sizes
I.1	ANES	1964–2016	Vote for Democrat, South only	1964 n=177, 1968 n=183, 1972 n=280, 1976 n=290, 1980 n=221, 1984 n=237, 1988 n=203, 1992 n=292, 1996 n=235, 2000 n=214, 2004 n=145, 2008 n=474, 2012 n=800, 2016 n=777
Figure I.2	ANES	1964–2016	Party identification as Democrat, South only	1964 n=282, 1968 n=310, 1972 n=544, 1976 n=540, 1980 n=360, 1984 n=407, 1988 n=392, 1992 n=482, 1996 n=388, 2000 n=369, 2004 n=215, 2008 n=676, 2012 n=1,173, 2016 n=1,135
Figure I.3A	ANES	1964–2016	Party identification (mean), South only, Men only	1964 n=129, 1968 n=142, 1972 n=243, 1976 n=239, 1980 n=159, 1984 n=182, 1988 n=186, 1992 n=234, 1996 n=173, 2000 n=154, 2004 n=113, 2008 n=298, 2012 n=588, 2016 n=380
Figure I.3B	ANES	1964–2016	Party Identification (mean), South only, Women only	1964 n=153, 1968 n=168, 1972 n=301, 1976 n=301, 1980 n=201, 1984 n=225, 1988 n=206, 1992 n=248, 1996 n=214, 2000 n=215, 2004 n=102, 2008 n=377, 2012 n=585, 2016 n=410

CHAPTER 1

Figure/Table	Source	Year	Variable	Sample Sizes
Figure 1.1A	Blair	2010	White FT evaluations of whites	Non-South n=784, South n=773, Non-southern n=1,082, Southern n=444
	Blair	2012	White FT evaluations of whites	Non-South n=1,264, South n=1,043, Non-southern n=1,679, Southern n=576
Figure 1.1B	Blair	2012	White RS evaluations of whites:	
	Blair	2012	– Work ethic	Non-South n=1,330, South n=1,119, Non-southern n=1,803, Southern n=606
	Blair	2012	– Intelligence	Non-South n=1,316, South n=1,109, Non-southern n=1,789, Southern n=597
	Blair	2012	– Trustworthiness	Non-South n=1,309, South n=1,106, Non-southern n=1,780, Southern n=593
Figure 1.2.A	Blair	2012	White identity	Non-southern n=1,811
Figure 1.2B	Blair	2012	White identity	Southern n=607
Figure 1.3	Blair	2010	White FT evaluations of whites	See Figure 1.1A

	Blair	2010	White FT evaluations of African Americans	Non-South n=779, South n=772, Non-southern n=1,077, Southern n=444
	Blair	2010	White FT evaluations of Latinos	Non-South n=778, South n=763, Non-southern n=1,069, Southern n=442
	Blair	2012	White FT evaluations of whites	See Figure 1.1A
	Blair	2012	White FT evaluations of African Americans	Non-South n=1,259, South n=1,044, Non-southern n=1,692, Southern n=577
	Blair	2012	White FT evaluations of Latinos	Non-South n=1,250, South n=1,041, Non-southern n=1,684, Southern n=573
Figure 1.4A	Blair	2010	Ethnocentrism (FT measure)	Non-South n=771, South n=757, Non-southern n=1,060, Southern n=439
	Blair	2012	Ethnocentrism (FT measure)	Non-South n=1,244, South n=1,027, Non-southern n=1,670, Southern n=567
Figure 1.4B	Blair	2010	Ethnocentrism (RS measure)	Non-South n=787, South n=772, Non-southern n=1,086, Southern n=448
	Blair	2012	Ethnocentrism (RS measure)	Non-South n=1,277, South n=1,094, Non-southern n=1,755, Southern n=577
Figure 1.5	Blair	2010	Immigration	Non-southern n=1,128, Southern n=466
	Blair	2012	Immigration	Non-southern n=1,813, Southern n=611
Figure 1.6	Blair	2010	White FT evaluations of whites	See Figure 1.1A
	Blair	2010	White identity	Non-southern n=1,127, Southern n=464
	Blair	2012	White FT evaluations of whites	See Figure 1.1A
	Blair	2012	White identity	See Figures 1.2A & 1.2B
	Blair	2016	White FT evaluations of whites	Non-southern n=1,809, Southern n=548
	Blair	2016	White identity	Non-southern n=1,870, Southern n=573
Figure 1.7	Blair	2016	FT evaluations of Black Lives Matter	Non-South n=1,284, South n=1,094, Non-southern n=1,796, Southern n=549
	Blair	2016	FT evaluations of police	Non-South n=1,289, South n=1,099, Non-southern n=1,804, Southern n=551
Figure 1.8	Blair	2016	Mexico wall	Non-South n=1,345, South n=1,128, Non-southern n=1,861, Southern n=570

363

CHAPTER 2

Figure/Table	Source	Year	Variable	Sample Sizes
Table 2.1	Blair	2010	Healthcare concerns:	
	Blair	2010	– Rationing	Non-South n=816, South n=802, Non-southern n=1,121, Southern n=466
	Blair	2010	– Delays	Non-South n=818, South n=802, Non-southern n=1,123, Southern n=466
	Blair	2010	– Quality	Non-South n=813, South n=805, Non-southern n=1,119, Southern n=467
	Blair	2010	– Taxes	Non-South n=819, South n=804, Non-southern n=1,126, Southern n=466
	Blair	2010	– Socialism	Non-South n=815, South n=805, Non-southern n=1,122, Southern n=466
	Blair	2010	– Euthanasia	Non-South n=816, South n=803, Non-southern n=1,123, Southern n=466
	Blair	2010	– Undeserved	Non-South n=818, South n=804, Non-Southern n=1,124, Southern n=466
Figure 2.1	Blair	2010	Future outlook:	
	Blair	2010	– Personal	Non-South n=818, South n=802, Non-southern n=1,128, Southern n=466
	Blair	2010	– Country	Non-South n=817, South n=801, Non-southern n=1,125, Southern n=466
	Blair	2010	– South	Non-South n=809, South n=797, Non-southern n=1,116, Southern n=466
	Blair	2010	– Whites	Non-South n=816, South n=801, Non-southern n=1,126, Southern 464
Figure 2.2	Blair	2012	Competition with African Americans	Non-South n=1,328, South n=1,104, Non-southern n=1,787, Southern n=601
	Blair	2012	Competition with Latinos	Non-South n=1,330, South n=1,109, Non-southern n=1,797, Southern n=596
Figure 2.3	Blair	2012	Experiences of racial discrimination:	
	Blair	2012	– General	Non-South n=1,334, South n=1,123, Non-southern n=1,808, Southern 604
	Blair	2012	– Respect	Non-South n=1,338, South n=1,122, Non-southern n=1,811, Southern n=604
	Blair	2012	– Services	Non-South n=1,341, South n=1,123, Non-southern n=1,815, Southern n=604
	Blair	2012	– Names	Non-South n=1,337, South n=1,123, Non-southern n=1,810, Southern n=602
	Blair	2012	– Police	Non-South n=1,333, South n=1,123, Non-southern n=1,806, Southern n=604
Figure 2.4	Blair	2010	Prospective personal economic outlook	Non-southern n=1,132, Southern n=465
	Blair	2012	Prospective personal economic outlook	Non-southern n=1,817, Southern n=608
	Blair	2016	Prospective personal economic outlook	Non-southern n=1,869, Southern n=571

Figure 2.5	Blair	2010	Competition with African Americans	Non-southern n=1,117, Southern n=464
	Blair	2010	Competition with Latinos	Non-southern n=1,109, Southern n=458
	Blair	2012	Competition with African Americans	See Figure 2.2
	Blair	2012	Competition with Latinos	See Figure 2.2
	Blair	2016	Competition with African Americans	Non-southern n=1,856, Southern n=571
	Blair	2016	Competition with Latinos	Non-southern n=1,856, Southern n=571

CHAPTER 3

Figure/Table	Source	Year	Variable	Sample Sizes
Table 3.1	Blair	2010	Responsibility of Federal Government to ensure racial equality in access to:	
	Blair	2010	– Jobs	Non-South n=816, South n=803, Non-southern n=1,124, Southern n=466
	Blair	2010	– Schools	Non-South n=818, South n=804, Non-southern n=1,127, Southern n=466
	Blair	2010	– Housing	Non-South n=810, South n=805, Non-southern n=1,120, Southern n=465
	Blair	2010	– Healthcare	Non-South n=813, South n=804, Non-southern n=1,126, Southern n=462
	Blair	2010	– Courts and police	Non-South n=820, South n=801, Non-southern n=1,128, Southern n=462
	Blair	2012	Responsibility of Federal Government to ensure racial equality in access to:	
	Blair	2012	– Jobs	Non-South n=1,327, South n=1,113, Non-southern n=1,794, Southern n=604
	Blair	2012	– Schools	Non-South n=1,326, South n=1,107, Non-southern n=1,790, Southern n=601
	Blair	2012	– Housing	Non-South n=1,325, South n=1,107, Non-southern n=1,789, Southern n=601
	Blair	2012	– Healthcare	Non-South n=1,325, South n=1,103, Non-southern n=1,787, Southern n=600
	Blair	2012	– Courts and police	Non-South n=1,326, South n=1,107, Non-southern n=1,788, Southern n=603
Figure 3.1	Blair	2010	Attention paid to race	Non-South n=824, South n=806, Non-southern n=1,132, Southern n=464
	Blair	2012	Attention paid to race	Non-South n=1,338, South n=1,134, Non-southern n=1,802, Southern n=611
Figure 3.2A	Blair	2010	Racial Resentment, African Americans (mean)	Non-South n=810, South n=794, Non-southern n=1,114, Southern n=463
	Blair	2012	Racial Resentment, African Americans (mean)	Non-South n=1,311, South n=1,119, Non-southern n=1,783, Southern n=606

Figure 3.2B	Blair	2012	Racial Resentment, Latinos (mean)	Non-South n=1,302, South n=1,104, Non-southern n=1,767, Southern n=599
Figure 3.3A	Blair	2010	Racial Resentment, African Americans (distribution)	See Figure 3.2A
	Blair	2012	Racial Resentment, African Americans (distribution)	See Figure 3.2A
Figure 3.3B	Blair	2012	Racial Resentment, Latinos (distribution)	See Figure 3.2B
Table 3.2A	Blair	2012	Racial Resentment, African Americans, (model)	Samples sizes included in table
Table 3.2B	Blair	2012	Racial Resentment, Latinos (model)	Sample sizes included in table
Figure 3.4A	Blair	2010	Racial Resentment, African Americans (individual questions):	
	Blair	2010	– Overcame prejudice (Q1)	Non-southern n=1,127, Southern n=465
	Blair	2010	– Generations of slavery (Q2)	Non-southern n=1,124, Southern n=465
	Blair	2010	– Less than deserved (Q3)	Non-southern n=1,124, Southern n=465
	Blair	2010	– Try harder (Q4)	Non-southern n=1,121, Southern n=464
Figure 3.4B	Blair	2012	Racial Resentment, African Americans (individual questions):	
	Blair	2012	– Overcame prejudice (Q1)	Non-southern n=1,803, Southern n=607
	Blair	2012	– Generations of slavery (Q2)	Non-southern n=1,805, Southern n=607
	Blair	2012	– Less than deserved (Q3)	Non-southern n=1,802, Southern n=606
	Blair	2012	– Try harder (Q4)	Non-southern n=1,810, Southern n=607
Figure 3.4C	Blair	2012	Racial Resentment, Latinos (individual questions):	
	Blair	2012	– Overcame prejudice (Q1)	Non-southern n=1,779, Southern n=602
	Blair	2012	– Generations of discrimination (Q2)	Non-southern n=1,788, Southern n=602
	Blair	2012	– Less than deserved (Q3)	Non-southern n=1,789, Southern n=600
	Blair	2012	– Try harder (Q4)	Non-southern n=1,779, Southern n=602
Figure 3.5	Blair	2010	Affirmative Action	Non-South n=818, South n=805, Non-southern n=1,126, Southern n=466
	Blair	2012	Affirmative Action	Non-South n=1,339, South n=1,126, Non-southern n=1,811, Southern n=611
Figure 3.6	Blair	2010	African Americans' opportunities	Non-South n=812, South n=802, Non-southern n=1,120, Southern n=462

Figure 3.7	Blair	2010	Attention paid to race	See Figure 3.1
	Blair	2010	Affirmative Action	See Figure 3.5
	Blair	2012	Attention paid to race	See Figure 3.1
	Blair	2012	Affirmative Action	See Figure 3.5
	Blair	2016	Attention paid to race	Non-southern n=1,859, Southern n=572
	Blair	2016	Affirmative Action	Non-southern n=1,858, Southern n=566
Figure 3.8A	Blair	2010	Racial Resentment, African Americans (mean)	See Figure 3.2A
	Blair	2012	Racial Resentment, African Americans (mean)	See Figure 3.2A
	Blair	2016	Racial Resentment, African Americans (mean)	Non-southern n=1,865, Southern n=571
Figure 3.8B	Blair	2010	Racial Resentment, African Americans (distribution)	See Figure 3.2A
	Blair	2012	Racial Resentment, African Americans (distribution)	See Figure 3.2A
	Blair	2016	Racial Resentment, African Americans (distribution)	Non-southern n=1,865, Southern n=571
Figure 3.8C	Blair	2016	Racial Resentment, African Americans (individual questions):	
	Blair	2016	– Overcame prejudice (Q1)	Non-southern n=1,869, Southern n=572
	Blair	2016	– Generations of slavery (Q2)	Non-southern n=1,868, Southern n=572
	Blair	2016	– Less than deserved (Q3)	Non-southern n=1,870, Southern n=572
	Blair	2016	– Try harder (Q4)	Non-southern n=1,866, Southern n=571

CHAPTER 4

Figure/Table	Source	Year	Variable	Sample Sizes
Table 4.1	SFP	1992	Stereotypes of southern women:	
	SFP	1992	– Career-oriented	Non-southern n=71, Southern n=188
	SFP	1992	– Friendly	Non-southern n=76, Southern n=194
	SFP	1992	– Feminist	Non-southern n=68, Southern n=190
	SFP	1992	– Strong-willed	Non-southern n=71, Southern n=188
	SFP	1992	– Independent	Non-southern n=74, Southern n=190
	SFP	1992	– Self-centered	Non-southern n=68, Southern n=190
	SFP	1992	– Assertive	Non-southern n=73, Southern n=178
Figure 4.1A	Blair	2012	Modern Sexism (mean)	Non-South n=1,284, South n=1,102, Non-southern n=1,752, Southern n=593
Figure 4.1B	Blair	2012	Modern Sexism (distribution)	See Figure 4.1A
Figure 4.2	Blair	2012	Modern Sexism (individual questions):	
	Blair	2012	– Favors (Q1)	Non-southern n=1,786, Southern n=600
	Blair	2012	– Remarks (Q2)	Non-southern n=1,782, Southern n=598
	Blair	2012	– Power (Q3)	Non-southern n=1,776, Southern n=600
	Blair	2012	– Complain (Q4)	Non-southern n=1,780, Southern n=601
	Blair	2012	– Discrimination (Q5)	Non-southern n=1,777, Southern n=598
Figure 4.3A	Blair	2012	Modern Sexism, Women only (mean)	Non-South n=653, South n=564, Non-southern n=875, Southern n=308
Figure 4.3B	Blair	2012	Modern Sexism, Women only (distribution)	See Figure 4.3A
Figure 4.4	Blair	2012	Modern Sexism, Women only (individual questions):	
	Blair	2012	– Favors (Q1)	Non-southern n=899, Southern n=312
	Blair	2012	– Remarks (Q2)	Non-southern n=896, Southern n=310
	Blair	2012	– Power (Q3)	Non-southern n=893, Southern n=312
	Blair	2012	– Complain (Q4)	Non-southern n=893, Southern n=313
	Blair	2012	– Discrimination (Q5)	Non-southern n=890, Southern n=312

Figure/Table	Source	Year	Variable	Sample Sizes
Table 4.2	Blair	2012	Modern Sexism, Women only (model)	Sample sizes included in table
Figure 4.5A	Blair	2012	Modern Sexism, Women only (mean)	See Figure 4.3A
	Blair	2016	Modern Sexism, Women only (mean)	Non-southern n=930, Southern n=313
Figure 4.5B	Blair	2012	Modern Sexism, Women only (distribution)	See Figure 4.3A
	Blair	2016	Modern Sexism, Women only (distribution)	See Figure 4.5A
Figure 4.6	Blair	2016	Modern Sexism, Women only (individual questions):	
	Blair	2016	– Favors (Q1)	Non-southern n=932, Southern n=313
	Blair	2016	– Remarks (Q2)	Non-southern n=932, Southern n=313
	Blair	2016	– Power (Q3)	Non-southern n=933, Southern n=313
	Blair	2016	– Complain (Q4)	Non-southern n=933, Southern n=313
	Blair	2016	– Discrimination (Q5)	Non-southern n=932, Southern n=314
Figure 4.7	Blair	2016	Importance of getting married, Women only	Non-South n=690, South n=577, Non-southern n=940, Southern n=311
	Blair	2016	Importance of having children, Women only	Non-South n=688, South n=577, Non-southern n=940, Southern n=310

CHAPTER 5

Figure/Table	Source	Year	Variable	Sample Sizes
Figure 5.1	Blair	2012	Experiences of racial discrimination, Men only:	
	Blair	2012	– General	Non-southern n=893, Southern n=286
	Blair	2012	– Respect	Non-southern n=895, Southern n=286
	Blair	2012	– Services	Non-southern n=898, Southern n=286
	Blair	2012	– Names	Non-southern n=897, Southern n=285
	Blair	2012	– Police	Non-southern n=892, Southern n=286
	Blair	2012	Experiences of racial discrimination, Women only:	
	Blair	2012	– General	Non-southern n=914, Southern n=318
	Blair	2012	– Respect	Non-southern n=916, Southern n=318
	Blair	2012	– Services	Non-southern n=918, Southern n=318

	Blair	2012	– Names	Non-southern n=913, Southern n=317
	Blair	2012	– Police	Non-southern n=914, Southern n=318
Figure 5.2	Blair	2010	Immigration, Men only	Non-southern n=539, Southern n=240
	Blair	2012	Immigration, Men only	Non-southern n=900, Southern n=290
Figure 5.3A	Blair	2012	Modern Sexism, Men only (mean)	Non-South n=632, South n=538, Non-southern n=877, Southern n=285
Figure 5.3B	Blair	2012	Modern Sexism, Men only (distribution)	See Figure 5.3A
Figure 5.4	Blair	2012	Modern Sexism, Men only (individual questions):	
	Blair	2012	– Favors (Q1)	Non-southern n=887, Southern n=288
	Blair	2012	– Remarks (Q2)	Non-southern n=886, Southern n=287
	Blair	2012	– Power (Q3)	Non-southern n=883, Southern n=288
	Blair	2012	– Complain (Q4)	Non-southern n=887, Southern n=288
	Blair	2012	– Discrimination (Q5)	Non-southern n=887, Southern n=285
Table 5.1	Blair	2012	Modern Sexism, Men only (model)	Sample sizes included in table
Figure 5.5	SFP	1994	Man paid on dates, Southern only	Men n=265, Women n=370
	SFP	1994	Husband should have main say-so, Southern only	Men n=264, Women n=364
	SFP	1994	Men have a duty to protect women, Southern only	Men n=263, Women n=363
Figure 5.6A	Blair	2012	Modern Sexism, Men only (mean)	See Figure 5.3A
	Blair	2016	Modern Sexism, Men only (mean)	Non-southern n=921, Southern n=258
Figure 5.6B	Blair	2012	Modern Sexism, Men only (distribution)	See Figure 5.3A
	Blair	2016	Modern Sexism, Men only (distribution)	See Figure 5.6A
Figure 5.7	Blair	2016	Modern Sexism, Men only (individual questions):	
	Blair	2016	– Favors (Q1)	Non-southern n=926, Southern n=258
	Blair	2016	– Remarks (Q2)	Non-southern n=925, Southern n=258

	Blair	2016	– Power (Q3)	Non-southern n=922, Southern n=258
	Blair	2016	– Complain (Q4)	Non-southern n=926, Southern n=258
	Blair	2016	– Discrimination (Q5)	Non-southern n=926, Southern n=258
Figure 5.8A	Blair	2016	Mandatory background checks, Men only	Non-South n=655, South n=551, Non-southern n=925, Southern n=258
	Blair	2016	Ban semi-automatic weapons, Men only	Non-South n=655, South n=551, Non-southern n=925, Southern n=258
Figure 5.8B	Blair	2016	Mandatory background checks, Women only	Non-South n=691, South n=579, Non-southern n=937, Southern n=314
	Blair	2016	Ban semi-automatic weapons, Women only	Non-South n=689, South n=576, Non-southern n=933, Southern n=313
Figure 5.9	Blair	2016	Experiences of racial discrimination, Men only:	
	Blair	2016	– General	Non-southern n=926, Southern n=257
	Blair	2016	– Respect	Non-southern n=927, Southern n=257
	Blair	2016	– Services	Non-southern n=927, Southern n=257
	Blair	2016	– Names	Non-southern n=927, Southern n=257
	Blair	2016	– Police	Non-southern n=927, Southern n=257
	Blair	2016	Experiences of racial discrimination, Women only:	
	Blair	2016	– General	Non-southern n=934, Southern n=314
	Blair	2016	– Respect	Non-southern n=935, Southern n=314
	Blair	2016	– Services	Non-southern n=934, Southern n=314
	Blair	2016	– Names	Non-southern n=935, Southern n=313
	Blair	2016	– Police	Non-southern n=937, Southern n=314
Figure 5.10	Blair	2012	Experiences of racial discrimination, gender gaps	See Figure 5.1
	Blair	2016	Experiences of racial discrimination, gender gaps	See Figure 5.9

CHAPTER 6

Figure/Table	Source	Year	Variable	Sample Sizes
Figure 6.1A	Blair	2012	Abortion, Men only	Non-South n=651, South n=539, Non-southern n=894, Southern n=287
	Blair	2012	Abortion, Women only	Non-South n=683, South n=584, Non-southern n=908, Southern n=318
Figure 6.1B	Blair	2012	Gay marriage, Men only	Non-South n=655, South n=543, Non-southern n=899, Southern n=290
	Blair	2012	Gay marriage, Women only	Non-South n=686, South n=581, Non-southern n=913, Southern n=321
Figure 6.2	Blair	2012	Abortion, gender gap	See Figure 6.1A
	Blair	2012	Gay marriage, gender gap	See Figure 6.1B
Figure 6.3	Blair	2012	Female president, all	Non-South n=1,333, South n=1,125, Non-southern n=1,798, Southern n=607
	Blair	2012	Female president, Men only	Non-South n=647, South n=539, Non-southern n=887, Southern n=288
	Blair	2012	Female president, Women only	Non-South n=686, South n=586, Non-southern n=911, Southern n=319
Table 6.1	Blair	2012	Female president (model)	Sample sizes included in table
Figure 6.4	Blair	2012	Female president (plot)	See Table 6.1
Figure 6.5A	Blair	2016	Primary vote, all	Non-South n=939, South n=801, Non-southern n=1,271, Southern n=435
Figure 6.5B	Blair	2016	Primary vote, gender gaps	
	Blair	2016	Primary vote, Men only	Non-South n=452, South n=400, Non-southern n=616, Southern n=202
	Blair	2016	Primary vote, Women only	Non-South n=487, South n=401, Non-southern n=635, Southern n=233
Figure 6.6A	Blair	2016	General Election vote, all	Non-South n=1,122, South n=941, Non-southern n=1,548, Southern n=478

Figure/Table	Source	Year	Variable	Sample Sizes
Figure 6.6B	Blair	2016	General Election vote, Men only	Non-South n=545, South n=475, Non-southern n=781, Southern n=221
	Blair	2016	General Election vote, Women only	Non-South n=577, South n=466, Non-southern n=767, Southern n=257
Figure 6.6C	Blair	2016	General Election vote, gender gaps	See Figure 6.6B
Figure 6.6D	Blair	2016	Trump and Clinton vote by gender	See Figure 6.6B
	Blair	2016	Modern Sexism (mean), Trump voters, Men only	Non-southern n=426, Southern n=167
	Blair	2016	Modern Sexism (mean), Trump voters, Women only	Non-southern n=324, Southern n=181
	Blair	2016	Modern Sexism (mean), Clinton voters, Men only	Non-southern n=250, Southern n=31
	Blair	2016	Modern Sexism (mean), Clinton voters, Women only	Non-southern n=357, Southern n=56
Figure 6.7	Blair	2016	Modern Sexism (mean), Men only	See Figure 5.6A
	Blair	2016	Modern Sexism (mean), Women only	See Figure 4.5A
	Blair	2016	General election vote, Men only	See Figure 6.6B
	Blair	2016	General election vote, Women only	See Figure 6.6B
Figure 6.8	Blair	2016	Modern Sexism (mean), Non-southern Women only	Married n=541, Non-married n=389
	Blair	2016	Modern Sexism (mean), Southern Women only	Married n=185, Non-married n=128
	Blair	2016	General election vote, Non-southern Women only	Married n=466, Non-married n=301
	Blair	2016	General election vote, Southern Women only	Married n=164, Non-married n=94

CHAPTER 7

Figure/Table	Source	Year	Variable	Sample Sizes
Table 7.1	Baylor	2007	Pornography	Non-South n=624, South n=299
	Baylor	2007	Gambling	Non-South n=590, South n=292
	Baylor	2007	Revealing clothes	Non-South n=598, South n=285
	Baylor	2007	Premarital sex	Non-South n=617, South n=288

	Baylor	2007	Cohabitation	Non-South n=608, South n=282
	Baylor	2007	Contraception	Non-South n=518, South n=232
	Baylor	2007	Displaying wealth	Non-South n=497, South n=241
Table 7.2A	Baylor	2007	God exists	Non-South n=909, South n=377
	Baylor	2007	Devil exists	Non-South n=914, South n=375
	Baylor	2007	Heaven exists	Non-South n=923, South n=375
	Baylor	2007	Hell exists	Non-South n=917, South n=374
	Baylor	2007	Armageddon exists	Non-South n=886, South n=366
	Baylor	2007	Angels exist	Non-South n=917, South n=374
	Baylor	2007	Demons exist	Non-South n=908, South n=371
	Baylor	2007	Rapture exists	Non-South n=878, South n=363
	Baylor	2007	Devil causes evil	Non-South n=913, South n=380
	Baylor	2007	Teach morals	Non-South n=922, South n=383
	Baylor	2007	Convert others	Non-South n=921, South n=384
	Baylor	2010	God exists	Non-South n=747, South n=398
	Baylor	2010	Devil exists	Non-South n=754, South n=396
	Baylor	2010	Heaven exists	Non-South n=758, South n=399
	Baylor	2010	Hell exists	Non-South n=752, South n=394
	Baylor	2010	Armageddon exists	Non-South n=732, South n=384
	Baylor	2010	Angels exist	Non-South n=753, South n=394
	Baylor	2010	Demons exist	Non-South n=753, South n=392
Table 7.2B	Baylor	2007	Witnessed a healing	Non-South n=914, South n=377
	Baylor	2007	Received a healing	Non-South n=914, South n=380
	Baylor	2007	Spoken in tongues	Non-South n=917, South n=384
	Baylor	2007	Felt called	Non-South n=915, South n=383

	Baylor	2007	Heard God	Non-South n=911, South n=382
	Baylor	2007	Protected by guardian angel	Non-South n=914, South n=375
	Baylor	2007	Experienced a religious conversion	Non-South n=908, South n=378
	Baylor	2007	Felt at one with the universe	Non-South n=905, South n=377
Table 7.3	Baylor	2007	Tithe	Non-South n=584, South n=254
	Baylor	2007	Amount given as tithe	Non-South n=550, South n=247
	Baylor	2007	Friends at your church	Non-South n=636, South n=283
	Baylor	2007	Bible study or Sunday school	Non-South n=671, South n=306
	Baylor	2007	Witness to friends	Non-South n=672, South n=305
	Baylor	2007	Witness to strangers	Non-South n=666, South n=302
	Baylor	2007	Community Bible study	Non-South n=668, South n=307
	Baylor	2007	Read Bible or sacred book	Non-South n=924, South n=389
	Baylor	2007	Pray	Non-South n=931, South n=386
	Baylor	2007	Religious at age 12	Non-South n=896, South n=372
	Baylor	2007	Church attendance age 12	Non-South n=932, South n=387
	Baylor	2007	Volunteer in church	Non-South n=920, South n=383
	Baylor	2010	Volunteer in community	Non-South n=918, South n=386
	Baylor	2010	Bible study or Sunday School	Non-South n=744, South n=381
	Baylor	2010	Witness to friends or strangers	Non-South n=742, South n=377
	Baylor	2010	Community Bible study	Non-South n=739, South n=371
	Baylor	2010	Read Bible or sacred book	Non-South n=759, South n=401
	Baylor	2010	Pray	Non-South n=762, South n=402
Table 7.4	Baylor	2007	Baptist	Non-South n=925, South n=386
	Baylor	2007	Baptist (among those with affiliation)	Non-South n=805, South n=338
	Baylor	2007	Biblical literalist	Non-South n=920, South n=376
	Baylor	2007	Fundamentalist	Non-South n=848, South n=360

	Survey	Year	Measure	Sample sizes
	Baylor	2007	Born again	Non-South n=864, South n=377
	Baylor	2007	Evangelical	Non-South n=855, South n=362
	Baylor	2007	Fundamentalist combination	Non-South n=938, South n=391
	Baylor	2010	Baptist	Non-South n=759, South n=401
	Baylor	2010	Baptist (among those with affiliation)	Non-South n=622, South n=367
	Baylor	2010	Biblical literalist	Non-South n=758, South n=397
	Baylor	2010	Fundamentalist	Non-South n=682, South n=339
	Baylor	2010	Born again	Non-South n=702, South n=368
	Baylor	2010	Evangelical	Non-South n=691, South n=344
	Baylor	2010	Fundamentalist combination	Non-South n=769, South n=407
	Blair	2010	Baptist	Non-South n=817, South n=809, Non-southern n=1,128, Southern n=463
	Blair	2010	Baptist (among those with affiliation)	Non-South n=697, South n=708, Non-southern n=941, Southern n=436
	Blair	2010	Biblical literalist	Non-South n=822, South n=810, Non-southern n=1,132, Southern n=468
	Blair	2012	Baptist	Non-South n=1,359, South n=1,129, Non-southern n=1,817, Southern n=607
	Blair	2012	Baptist (among those with affiliation)	Non-South n=1,059, South n=928, Non-southern n=1,416, Southern n=528
	Blair	2012	Biblical literalist	Non-South n=1,346, South n=1,131, Non-southern n=1,804, Southern n=607
Figure 7.1	Blair	2012	Racial Resentment (mean), Non-southern only	Non-fundamentalist n=1,439, Fundamentalist n=329
	Blair	2012	Racial Resentment (mean), Southern only	Non-fundamentalist n=355, Fundamentalist n=246
	Blair	2012	Ethnocentrism (FT measure), Non-southern only	Non-fundamentalist n=1,370, Fundamentalist n=287
	Blair	2012	Ethnocentrism (FT measure), Southern only	Non-fundamentalist n=341, Fundamentalist n=222
	Blair	2012	Modern Sexism (mean), Non-southern only	Non-fundamentalist n=1,417, Fundamentalist n=320

Figure/Table	Source	Year	Variable	Sample Sizes
	Blair	2012	Modern Sexism (mean), Southern only	Non-fundamentalist n=349, Fundamentalist n=238
Figure 7.2A	Blair	2016	Fundamentalist identity, Non-southern only	n=1,870
Figure 7.2B	Blair	2016	Fundamentalist identity, Southern only	n=566
Figure 7.3	Blair	2016	Importance of religious life, Non-southern only	Non-fundamentalist n=1,418, Fundamentalist n=443
	Blair	2016	Importance of religious life, Southern only	Non-fundamentalist n=286, Fundamentalist n=283
Figure 7.4	Blair	2016	Racial Resentment (mean), Non-southern only	Non-fundamentalist n=1,418, Fundamentalist n=447
	Blair	2016	Racial Resentment (mean), Southern only	Non-fundamentalist n=287, Fundamentalist n=283
	Blair	2016	Ethnocentrism (FT measure), Non-southern only	Non-fundamentalist n=1,371, Fundamentalist n=420
	Blair	2016	Ethnocentrism (FT measure), Southern only	Non-fundamentalist n=281, Fundamentalist n=266
	Blair	2016	Modern Sexism (mean), Non-southern only	Non-fundamentalist n=1,409, Fundamentalist n=443
	Blair	2016	Modern Sexism (mean), Southern only	Non-fundamentalist n=287, Fundamentalist n=283

CHAPTER 8

Figure/Table	Source	Year	Variable	Sample Sizes
Figure 8.1	Blair	2012	Party identification, Non-South only	Non-fundamentalist n=1,060, Fundamentalist n=270
	Blair	2012	Party identification, South only	Non-fundamentalist n=776, Fundamentalist n=330
	Blair	2012	Party identification, Non-southern only	Non-fundamentalist n=1,457, Fundamentalist n=330
	Blair	2012	Party identification, Southern only	Non-fundamentalist n=355, Fundamentalist n=247
Figure 8.2	Blair	2012	Experiences of racial discrimination, Non-southern only:	
	Blair	2012	– General	Non-fundamentalist n=1,460, Fundamentalist n=330
	Blair	2012	– Respect	Non-fundamentalist n=1,461, Fundamentalist n=333
	Blair	2012	– Services	Non-fundamentalist n=1,463, Fundamentalist n=336
	Blair	2012	– Names	Non-fundamentalist n=1,462, Fundamentalist n=331
	Blair	2012	– Police	Non-fundamentalist n=1,459, Fundamentalist n=330
	Blair	2012	Experiences of racial discrimination, Southern only:	
	Blair	2012	– General	Non-fundamentalist n=351, Fundamentalist n=247
	Blair	2012	– Respect	Non-fundamentalist n=351, Fundamentalist n=247

Blair	2012	– Services	Non-fundamentalist n=351, Fundamentalist n=247
Blair	2012	– Names	Non-fundamentalist n=351, Fundamentalist n=245
Blair	2012	– Police	Non-fundamentalist n=351, Fundamentalist n=247
Table 8.1	2012	Party identification	See Figure 8.1
Blair	2012	Republican vote for Romney, Non-South only	Non-fundamentalist n=333, Fundamentalist n=128
Blair	2012	Republican vote for Romney, South only	Non-fundamentalist n=279, Fundamentalist n=179
Blair	2012	Republican vote for Romney, Non-southern only	Non-fundamentalist n=452, Fundamentalist n=163
Blair	2012	Republican vote for Romney, Southern only	Non-fundamentalist n=150, Fundamentalist n=131
Blair	2012	Independent vote for Romney, Non-South only	Non-fundamentalist n=102, Fundamentalist n=24
Blair	2012	Independent vote for Romney, South only	Non-fundamentalist n=74, Fundamentalist n=34
Blair	2012	Independent vote for Romney, Non-southern only	Non-fundamentalist n=140, Fundamentalist n=30
Blair	2012	Independent vote for Romney, Southern only	Non-fundamentalist n=34, Fundamentalist n=28
Figure 8.3A	2012	Gay marriage, Non-southern only	Non-fundamentalist n=1,459, Fundamentalist n=336
Blair	2012	Gay marriage, Southern only	Non-fundamentalist n=358, Fundamentalist n=248
Figure 8.3B	2012	Abortion, Non-southern only	Non-fundamentalist n=1,454, Fundamentalist n=332
Blair	2012	Abortion, Southern only	Non-fundamentalist n=354, Fundamentalist n=246
Figure 8.4	2016	Experiences of racial discrimination, Non-southern only:	
Blair	2016	– General	Non-fundamentalist n=1,415, Fundamentalist n=445
Blair	2016	– Respect	Non-fundamentalist n=1,418, Fundamentalist n=445
Blair	2016	– Services	Non-fundamentalist n=1,416, Fundamentalist n=445
Blair	2016	– Names	Non-fundamentalist n=1,417, Fundamentalist n=445
Blair	2016	– Police	Non-fundamentalist n=1,417, Fundamentalist n=447
Blair	2016	Experiences of racial discrimination, Southern only:	
Blair	2016	– General	Non-fundamentalist n=289, Fundamentalist n=283
Blair	2016	– Respect	Non-fundamentalist n=289, Fundamentalist n=283
Blair	2016	– Services	Non-fundamentalist n=289, Fundamentalist n=283

	Blair	2016	– Names	Non-fundamentalist n=289, Fundamentalist n=281
	Blair	2016	– Police	Non-fundamentalist n=289, Fundamentalist n=283
Figure 8.5A	Blair	2016	Abortion, Non-southern only	Non-fundamentalist n=1,410, Fundamentalist n=446
	Blair	2016	Abortion, Southern only	Non-fundamentalist n=279, Fundamentalist n=283
Figure 8.5B	Blair	2012	Abortion	See Figure 8.3B
	Blair	2016	Abortion	See Figure 8.5A
	Blair	2012	Vote for Romney, Non-southern only	Non-fundamentalist n=1,099, Fundamentalist n=238
	Blair	2012	Vote for Romney, Southern only	Non-fundamentalist n=246, Fundamentalist n=183
	Blair	2016	Vote for Trump, Non-southern only	Non-fundamentalist n=1,181, Fundamentalist n=368
	Blair	2016	Vote for Trump, Southern only	Non-fundamentalist n=229, Fundamentalist n=249
Figure 8.6	Blair	2016	Party identification, Non-South only	Non-fundamentalist n=1,005, Fundamentalist n=347
	Blair	2016	Party identification, South only	Non-fundamentalist n=732, Fundamentalist n=407
	Blair	2016	Party identification, Non-southern only	Non-fundamentalist n=1,418, Fundamentalist n=451
	Blair	2016	Party identification, Southern only	Non-fundamentalist n=289, Fundamentalist n=283
Table 8.2	Blair	2016	Party identification	See Figure 8.6
	Blair	2016	Republican vote for Trump, Non-South only	Non-fundamentalist n=328, Fundamentalist n=209,
	Blair	2016	Republican vote for Trump, South only	Non-fundamentalist n=290, Fundamentalist n=275
	Blair	2016	Republican vote for Trump, Non-southern only	Non-fundamentalist n=475, Fundamentalist n=270
	Blair	2016	Republican vote for Trump, Southern only	Non-fundamentalist n=138, Fundamentalist n=206
	Blair	2016	Independent vote for Trump, Non-South only	Non-fundamentalist n=129, Fundamentalist n=30
	Blair	2016	Independent vote for Trump, South only	Non-fundamentalist n=89, Fundamentalist n=35
	Blair	2016	Independent vote for Trump, Non-southern only	Non-fundamentalist n=188, Fundamentalist n=44
	Blair	2016	Independent vote for Trump, Southern only	Non-fundamentalist n=25, Fundamentalist n=18

CHAPTER 9

Figure/Table	Source	Year	Variable	Sample Sizes
Figure 9.1A	Blair	2012	Romney's religion, Non-southern only	Non-fundamentalist n=1,455, Fundamentalist n=336
	Blair	2012	Romney's religion, Southern only	Non-fundamentalist n=358, Fundamentalist n=247
Figure 9.1B	Blair	2010	Obama's religion, Non-southern only	Non-fundamentalist n=881, Fundamentalist n=245
	Blair	2010	Obama's religion, Southern only	Non-fundamentalist n=257, Fundamentalist n=209
Table 9.1	Baylor	2007	Death penalty, Non-South only	Non-fundamentalist n=554, Fundamentalist n=362
	Baylor	2007	Death penalty, South only	Non-fundamentalist n=150, Fundamentalist n=235
	Baylor	2007	English as national language, Non-South only	Non-fundamentalist n=558, Fundamentalist n=365
	Baylor	2007	English as national language, South only	Non-fundamentalist n=150, Fundamentalist n=235
	Baylor	2007	Punish criminals, Non-South only	Non-fundamentalist n=554, Fundamentalist n=362
	Baylor	2007	Punish criminals, South only	Non-fundamentalist n=149, Fundamentalist n=233
	Baylor	2007	Gun control, Non-South only	Non-fundamentalist n=555, Fundamentalist n=363
	Baylor	2007	Gun control, South only	Non-fundamentalist n=150, Fundamentalist n=234
	Baylor	2010	Government bailout of banks, Non-South only	Non-fundamentalist n=453, Fundamentalist n=301
	Baylor	2010	Government bailout of banks, South only	Non-fundamentalist n=185, Fundamentalist n=212
	Baylor	2007	Dated another race, Non-South only	Non-fundamentalist n=502, Fundamentalist n=329
	Baylor	2007	Dated another race, South only	Non-fundamentalist n=137, Fundamentalist n=214
	Baylor	2007	Trust immigrants, Non-South only	Non-fundamentalist n=544, Fundamentalist n=357
	Baylor	2007	Trust immigrants, South only	Non-fundamentalist n=148, Fundamentalist n=229
	Baylor	2007	Men better suited for politics, Non-South only	Non-fundamentalist n=556, Fundamentalist n=367
	Baylor	2007	Men better suited for politics, South only	Non-fundamentalist n=152, Fundamentalist n=234

Figure 9.2	Blair	2012	Healthcare reform, Non-southern only	Non-fundamentalist n=1,462, Fundamentalist n=330
	Blair	2012	Healthcare reform, Southern only	Non-fundamentalist n=354, Fundamentalist n=248
Figure 9.3	Blair	2012	Christian to be American, Non-southern only	Non-fundamentalist n=1,451, Fundamentalist n=333
	Blair	2012	Christian to be American, Southern only	Non-fundamentalist n=357, Fundamentalist n=247
Table 9.2	Baylor	2007	Morality of war, Non-South only	Non-fundamentalists n=557, Fundamentalists n=368
	Baylor	2007	Morality of war, South only	Non-fundamentalists n=151, Fundamentalist n=233
	Baylor	2007	Christian values, Non-South only	Non-fundamentalist n=554, Fundamentalist n=363
	Baylor	2007	Christian values, South only	Non-fundamentalist n=149, Fundamentalist n=233
	Baylor	2007	Christian nation, Non-South only	Non-fundamentalist n=553, Fundamentalist n=363
	Baylor	2007	Christian nation, South only	Non-fundamentalist n=150, Fundamentalist n=233
	Baylor	2007	Terrorism, Non-South only	Non-fundamentalist n=551, Fundamentalist n=363
	Baylor	2007	Terrorism, South only	Non-fundamentalist n=148, Fundamentalist n=233
	Baylor	2007	Iraq War, Non-South only	Non-fundamentalist n=558, Fundamentalist n=366
	Baylor	2007	Iraq War, South only	Non-fundamentalist n=150, Fundamentalist n=237
	Baylor	2010	Media portrayal of Muslims, Non-South only	Non-fundamentalist 444, Fundamentalist n=299
	Baylor	2010	Media portrayal of Muslims, South only	Non-fundamentalist n=183, Fundamentalist n=212
	Blair	2010	Obama's handling of terrorism, Non-southern only	Non-fundamentalist n=871, Fundamentalist n=244
	Blair	2010	Obama's handling of terrorism, Southern only	Non-fundamentalist n=258, Fundamentalist n=201
	Blair	2010	Obama's handling of Afghanistan, Non-southern only	Non-fundamentalist n=877, Fundamentalist n=246
	Blair	2010	Obama's handling of Afghanistan, Southern only	Non-fundamentalist n=258, Fundamentalist n=205
	Blair	2010	Obama's handling of Iraq, Non-southern only	Non-fundamentalist n=875, Fundamentalist n=246
	Blair	2010	Obama's handling of Iraq, Southern only	Non-fundamentalist n=257, Fundamentalist n=208
Figure 9.4	Blair	2016	Global warming, Non-Southern only	Non-fundamentalist n=1,418, Fundamentalist n=438
	Blair	2016	Global warming, Southern only	Non-fundamentalist n=289, Fundamentalist n=283

Figure/Table	Source	Year	Variable	Sample Sizes
Figure 9.5	Blair	2016	Mexico wall, Non-southern only	Non-fundamentalist n=1,416, Fundamentalist n=444
	Blair	2016	Mexico wall, Southern only	Non-fundamentalist n=287, Fundamentalist n=282
Figure 9.6	Blair	2016	Ban semi-automatic weapons, Non-southern only	Non-fundamentalist n=1,414, Fundamentalist n=444
	Blair	2016	Ban semi-automatic weapons, Southern only	Non-fundamentalist n=287, Fundamentalist n=283
Figure 9.7	Blair	2016	Syria, Non-southern only	Non-fundamentalist n=1,411, Fundamentalist n=443
	Blair	2016	Syria, Southern only	Non-fundamentalist n=287, Fundamentalist n=283
Figure 9.8	Blair	2016	Trump's religion, Non-southern only	Non-fundamentalist n=1,425, Fundamentalist n=452
	Blair	2016	Trump's religion, Southern	Non-fundamentalist n=288, Fundamentalist n=285
Figure 9.9	Blair	2012	Christian to be American	See Figure 9.3
	Blair	2012	Vote for Romney	See Figure 8.5B
	Blair	2016	Christian to be American, Non-southern only	Non-fundamentalist n=1,420, Fundamentalist n=442
	Blair	2016	Christian to be American, Southern only	Non-fundamentalist n=286, Fundamentalist n=283
	Blair	2016	Vote for Trump	See Figure 8.5B
Conclusion				
Figure C.1A	Blair	2016	Modern Sexism, Racial Resentment, and Christian Fundamentalism scales	Non-southern n=1,547
Figure C.1B	Blair	2016	Modern Sexism, Racial Resentment, and Christian Fundamentalism scales	Southern n=485

Figure C.2	Blair	2016	Party identification for 3 categories of Modern Sexism, Racial Resentment, and Christian Fundamentalism scales	Christian Fundamentalism (above) n=701; Christian Fundamentalism (below) n=1,284; Modern Sexism (above) n=965; Modern Sexism (below) n=1,158; Racial Resentment (above) n=1,499; Racial Resentment (below) n=636; Modern Sexism & Christian Fundamentalism (above) n=519; Modern Sexism & Christian Fundamentalism (below) n=733; Racial Resentment & Modern Sexism (above) n=797; Racial Resentment & Modern Sexism (below) n=533; Christian Fundamentalism & Racial Resentment (above) n=521; Christian Fundamentalism & Racial Resentment (below) n=465; Christian Fundamentalism & Racial Resentment & Modern Sexism (above) n=311; Christian Fundamentalism & Racial Resentment & Modern Sexism (below) n=424
Table C.1	Blair	2016	Modern Sexism, Racial Resentment, and Christian Fundamentalism scales	All whites n=2,088; Non-South n=1,094; South n=948; Non-southern n=1,547; Southern n=485
Figure C.3	Blair	2016	Mean LSS scores	Non-South n=1,094; South n=948; Non-southern n=1,547; Southern n=485; Democrat n=686; Independent n=355; Republican n=1,044; Non-South Republican n=514; South Republican n=539; Non-southern Republican n=716; Southern Republican n=332; Non-Trump voters n=1,417; Trump voters n=941
Table C.2	Blair	2016	Vote for Trump (model)	Sample sizes included in table

APPENDIX C

Significance Tests (one-tail)

INTRODUCTION

Figure/Table	Source	Year	Variable	Comparison Groups	p <=
Figure I.1	ANES	1964–2016	Vote for Democrat, South only	N/A	N/A
Figure I.2	ANES	1964–2016	Party identification as Democrat, South only	N/A	N/A
Figure I.3A Figure I.3B	ANES	1964–2016	Party identification (mean), South only		
	ANES	1964	Party identification (mean), South only	Women vs. Men	.325
	ANES	1968	Party identification (mean), South only	Women vs. Men	.120
	ANES	1972	Party identification (mean), South only	Women vs. Men	.040
	ANES	1976	Party identification (mean), South only	Women vs. Men	.411
	ANES	1980	Party identification (mean), South only	Women vs. Men	.258
	ANES	1984	Party identification (mean), South only	Women vs. Men	.178
	ANES	1988	Party identification (mean), South only	Women vs. Men	.019
	ANES	1992	Party identification (mean), South only	Women vs. Men	.010
	ANES	1996	Party identification (mean), South only	Women vs. Men	.002
	ANES	2000	Party identification (mean), South only	Women vs. Men	.008
	ANES	2004	Party identification (mean), South only	Women vs. Men	.385
	ANES	2008	Party identification (mean), South only	Women vs. Men	.044
	ANES	2012	Party identification (mean), South only	Women vs. Men	.370
	ANES	2016	Party identification (mean), South only	Women vs. Men	.189

CHAPTER 1

Figure/Table	Source	Year	Variable	Comparison Groups	p <=
Figure 1.1A	Blair	2010	White FT evaluations of whites	Non-South vs. South	.041
	Blair	2010	White FT evaluations of whites	Non-southern vs. Southern	.000
	Blair	2012	White FT evaluations of whites	Non-South vs. South	.117
	Blair	2012	White FT evaluations of whites	Non-southern vs. Southern	.000
Figure 1.1B	Blair	2012	White RS evaluations of whites:		
	Blair	2012	– Work ethic	Non-South vs. South	.020
	Blair	2012	– Work ethic	Non-southern vs. Southern	.136
	Blair	2012	– Intelligence	Non-South vs. South	.499
	Blair	2012	– Intelligence	Non-southern vs. Southern	.043
	Blair	2012	– Trustworthiness	Non-South vs. South	.197
	Blair	2012	– Trustworthiness	Non-southern vs. Southern	.301
Figure 1.2A	Blair	2012	White identity, Non-southern only		
Figure 1.2B	Blair	2012	White identity, Southern only	Non-southern vs. Southern	.000
Figure 1.3	Blair	2010	White FT evaluations of whites	See Figure 1.1A	
	Blair	2010	White FT evaluations of African Americans	Non-South vs. South	.094
	Blair	2010	White FT evaluations of African Americans	Non-southern vs. Southern	.128
	Blair	2010	White FT evaluations of Latinos	Non-South vs. South	.319
	Blair	2010	White FT evaluations of Latinos	Non-southern vs. Southern	.025
	Blair	2012	White FT evaluations of whites	See Figure 1.1A	
	Blair	2012	White FT evaluations of African Americans	Non-South vs. South	.182
	Blair	2012	White FT evaluations of African Americans	Non-southern vs. Southern	.391
	Blair	2012	White FT evaluations of Latinos	Non-South vs. South	.311
	Blair	2012	White FT evaluations of Latinos	Non-southern vs. Southern	.013

Figure/Table	Source	Year	Variable	Comparison Groups	p <=
Figure 1.4A	Blair	2010	Ethnocentrism (FT measure)	Non-South vs. South	.267
	Blair	2010	Ethnocentrism (FT measure)	Non-southern vs. Southern	.000
	Blair	2012	Ethnocentrism (FT measure)	Non-South vs. South	.086
	Blair	2012	Ethnocentrism (FT measure)	Non-southern vs. Southern	.000
Figure 1.4B	Blair	2010	Ethnocentrism (RS measure)	Non-South vs. South	.062
	Blair	2010	Ethnocentrism (RS measure)	Non-southern vs. Southern	.000
	Blair	2012	Ethnocentrism (RS measure)	Non-South vs. South	.211
	Blair	2012	Ethnocentrism (RS measure)	Non-southern vs. Southern	.000
Figure 1.5	Blair	2010	Immigration	Non-southern vs. Southern	.000
	Blair	2012	Immigration	Non-southern vs. Southern	.000
Figure 1.6	Blair	2010	White FT evaluations of whites	See Figure 1.1A	
	Blair	2010	White identity	Non-southern vs. Southern	.000
	Blair	2012	White FT evaluations of whites	See Figure 1.1A	
	Blair	2012	White identity	See Figures 1.2A & 1.2B	
	Blair	2016	White FT evaluations of whites	Non-southern vs. Southern	.000
	Blair	2016	White identity	Non-southern vs. Southern	.000
Figure 1.7	Blair	2016	FT evaluations of Black Lives Matter	Non-South vs. South	.000
	Blair	2016	FT evaluations of Black Lives Matter	Non-southern vs. Southern	.000
	Blair	2016	FT evaluations of police	Non-South vs. South	.001
	Blair	2016	FT evaluations of police	Non-southern vs. Southern	.000
Figure 1.8	Blair	2016	Mexico wall	Non-South vs. South	.000
	Blair	2016	Mexico wall	Non-southern vs. Southern	.000
CHAPTER 2					
Table 2.1	Blair	2010	Healthcare concerns:		
	Blair	2010	– Rationing	Non-South vs. South	.027

	Blair	2010	– Rationing	Non-southern vs. Southern	.000
	Blair	2010	– Delays	Non-South vs. South	.009
	Blair	2010	– Delays	Non-southern vs. Southern	.000
	Blair	2010	– Quality	Non-South vs. South	.004
	Blair	2010	– Quality	Non-southern vs. Southern	.000
	Blair	2010	– Taxes	Non-South vs. South	.133
	Blair	2010	– Taxes	Non-southern vs. Southern	.000
	Blair	2010	– Socialism	Non-South vs. South	.001
	Blair	2010	– Socialism	Non-southern vs. Southern	.000
	Blair	2010	– Euthanasia	Non-South vs. South	.001
	Blair	2010	– Euthanasia	Non-southern vs. Southern	.000
	Blair	2010	– Undeserved	Non-South vs. South	.030
	Blair	2010	– Undeserved	Non-southern vs. Southern	.000
Figure 2.1	Blair	2010	Future outlook:		
	Blair	2010	– Personal	Non-South vs. South	.395
	Blair	2010	– Personal	Non-southern vs. Southern	.149
	Blair	2010	– Country	Non-South vs. South	.467
	Blair	2010	– Country	Non-southern vs. Southern	.014
	Blair	2010	– South	Non-South vs. South	.425
	Blair	2010	– South	Non-southern vs. Southern	.027
	Blair	2010	– Whites	Non-South vs. South	.440
	Blair	2010	– Whites	Non-southern vs. Southern	.016
Figure 2.2	Blair	2012	Competition with African Americans	Non-South vs. South	.001

	Blair	2012	Competition with African Americans	Non-southern vs. Southern	.000
	Blair	2012	Competition with Latinos	Non-South vs. South	.052
	Blair	2012	Competition with Latinos	Non-southern vs. Southern	.000
Figure 2.3	Blair	2012	Experiences of racial discrimination:		
	Blair	2012	– General	Non-South vs. South	.000
	Blair	2012	– General	Non-southern vs. Southern	.000
	Blair	2012	– Respect	Non-South vs. South	.037
	Blair	2012	– Respect	Non-southern vs. Southern	.011
	Blair	2012	– Services	Non-South vs. South	.000
	Blair	2012	– Services	Non-southern vs. Southern	.000
	Blair	2012	– Names	Non-South vs. South	.027
	Blair	2012	– Names	Non-southern vs. Southern	.000
	Blair	2012	– Police	Non-South vs. South	.001
	Blair	2012	– Police	Non-southern vs. Southern	.052
Figure 2.4	Blair	2010	Prospective personal economic outlook	Non-southern vs. Southern	.214
	Blair	2012	Prospective personal economic outlook	Non-southern vs. Southern	.000
	Blair	2016	Prospective personal economic outlook	Non-southern vs. Southern	.036
Figure 2.5	Blair	2010	Competition with African Americans	Non-southern vs. Southern	.057
	Blair	2010	Competition with Latinos	Non-southern vs. Southern	.387
	Blair	2012	Competition with African Americans	See Figure 2.2	
	Blair	2012	Competition with Latinos	See Figure 2.2	
	Blair	2016	Competition with African Americans	Non-southern vs. Southern	.000
	Blair	2016	Competition with Latinos	Non-southern vs. Southern	.076

CHAPTER 3

Figure/Table	Source	Year	Variable	Comparison Groups	p <=
Table 3.1	Blair	2010	Responsibility of Federal Government to ensure racial equality in access to:		
	Blair	2010	– Jobs	Non-South vs. South	.248
	Blair	2010	– Jobs	Non-southern vs. Southern	.034
	Blair	2010	– Schools	Non-South vs. South	.188
	Blair	2010	– Schools	Non-southern vs. Southern	.050
	Blair	2010	– Housing	Non-South vs. South	.381
	Blair	2010	– Housing	Non-southern vs. Southern	.155
	Blair	2010	– Healthcare	Non-South vs. South	.215
	Blair	2010	– Healthcare	Non-southern vs. Southern	.000
	Blair	2010	– Courts and police	Non-South vs. South	.086
	Blair	2010	– Courts and police	Non-southern vs. Southern	.021
	Blair	2012	Responsibility of Federal Government to ensure racial equality in access to:		
	Blair	2012	– Jobs	Non-South vs. South	.057
	Blair	2012	– Jobs	Non-southern vs. Southern	.029
	Blair	2012	– Schools	Non-South vs. South	.000
	Blair	2012	– Schools	Non-southern vs. Southern	.000
	Blair	2012	– Housing	Non-South vs. South	.000
	Blair	2012	– Housing	Non-southern vs. Southern	.020
	Blair	2012	– Healthcare	Non-South vs. South	.000
	Blair	2012	– Healthcare	Non-southern vs. Southern	.000
	Blair	2012	– Courts and police	Non-South vs. South	.042
	Blair	2012	– Courts and police	Non-southern vs. Southern	.000
Figure 3.1	Blair	2010	Attention paid to race	Non-South vs. South	.476
	Blair	2010	Attention paid to race	Non-southern vs. Southern	.005

	Blair	2012	Attention paid to race	Non-South vs. South	.001
	Blair	2012	Attention paid to race	Non-southern vs. Southern	.000
Figure 3.2A	Blair	2010	Racial Resentment, African Americans (mean)	Non-South vs. South	.001
	Blair	2010	Racial Resentment, African Americans (mean)	Non-southern vs. Southern	.000
	Blair	2012	Racial Resentment, African Americans (mean)	Non-South vs. South	.000
	Blair	2012	Racial Resentment, African Americans (mean)	Non-southern vs. Southern	.000
Figure 3.2B	Blair	2012	Racial Resentment, Latinos (mean)	Non-South vs. South	.000
	Blair	2012	Racial Resentment, Latinos (mean)	Non-southern vs. Southern	.000
Figure 3.3A	Blair	2010	Racial Resentment, African Americans (distribution)	See Figure 3.2A	
	Blair	2012	Racial Resentment, African Americans (distribution)	See Figure 3.2A	
Figure 3.3B	Blair	2012	Racial Resentment, Latinos (distribution)	See Figure 3.2B	
Table 3.2A	Blair	2012	Racial Resentment, African Americans, (model)	Significance tests included in table	
Table 3.2B	Blair	2012	Racial Resentment, Latinos (model)	Significance tests included in table	
Figure 3.4A	Blair	2010	Racial Resentment, African Americans (individual questions):		
	Blair	2010	– Overcame prejudice (Q1)	Non-southern vs. Southern	.000
	Blair	2010	– Generations of slavery (Q2)	Non-southern vs. Southern	.000
	Blair	2010	– Less than deserved (Q3)	Non-southern vs. Southern	.000
	Blair	2010	– Try harder (Q4)	Non-southern vs. Southern	.000
Figure 3.4B	Blair	2012	Racial Resentment, African Americans (individual questions):		
	Blair	2012	– Overcame prejudice (Q1)	Non-southern vs. Southern	.000
	Blair	2012	– Generations of slavery (Q2)	Non-southern vs. Southern	.000
	Blair	2012	– Less than deserved (Q3)	Non-southern vs. Southern	.000
	Blair	2012	– Try harder (Q4)	Non-southern vs. Southern	.000
Figure 3.4C	Blair	2012	Racial Resentment, Latinos (individual questions):		
	Blair	2012	– Overcame prejudice (Q1)	Non-southern vs. Southern	.000
	Blair	2012	– Generations of discrimination (Q2)	Non-southern vs. Southern	.000

Figure	Source	Year	Variable	Comparison	p
	Blair	2012	– Less than deserved (Q3)	Non-southern vs. Southern	.000
	Blair	2012	– Try harder (Q4)	Non-southern vs. Southern	.000
Figure 3.5	Blair	2010	Affirmative Action	Non-South vs. South	.488
	Blair	2010	Affirmative Action	Non-southern vs. Southern	.009
	Blair	2012	Affirmative Action	Non-South vs. South	.000
	Blair	2012	Affirmative Action	Non-southern vs. Southern	.000
Figure 3.6	Blair	2010	African Americans' opportunities	Non-South vs. South	.004
	Blair	2010	African Americans' opportunities	Non-southern vs. Southern	.001
Figure 3.7	Blair	2010	Attention paid to race	See Figure 3.1	
	Blair	2010	Affirmative Action	See Figure 3.5	
	Blair	2012	Attention paid to race	See Figure 3.1	
	Blair	2012	Affirmative Action	See Figure 3.5	
	Blair	2016	Attention paid to race	Non-southern vs. Southern	.000
	Blair	2016	Affirmative Action	Non-southern vs. Southern	.162
Figure 3.8A	Blair	2010	Racial Resentment, African Americans (mean)	See Figure 3.2A	
	Blair	2012	Racial Resentment, African Americans (mean)	See Figure 3.2A	
	Blair	2016	Racial Resentment, African Americans (mean)	Non-southern vs. Southern	.000
Figure 3.8B	Blair	2010	Racial Resentment, African Americans (distribution)	See Figure 3.2A	
	Blair	2012	Racial Resentment, African Americans (distribution)	See Figure 3.2A	
	Blair	2016	Racial Resentment, African Americans (distribution)	See Figure 3.8A	
Figure 3.8C	Blair	2016	Racial Resentment, African Americans (individual questions):		
	Blair	2016	– Overcame prejudice (Q1)	Non-southern vs. Southern	.000
	Blair	2016	– Generations of slavery (Q2)	Non-southern vs. Southern	.000
	Blair	2016	– Less than deserved (Q3)	Non-southern vs. Southern	.000
	Blair	2016	– Try harder (Q4)	Non-southern vs. Southern	.000

CHAPTER 4

Figure/Table	Source	Year	Variable	Comparison Groups	p <=
Table 4.1	SFP	1992	Stereotypes of southern women:		
	SFP	1992	– Career-oriented	Non-southern vs. Southern	.014
	SFP	1992	– Friendly	Non-southern vs. Southern	.000
	SFP	1992	– Feminist	Non-southern vs. Southern	.027
	SFP	1992	– Strong-willed	Non-southern vs. Southern	.000
	SFP	1992	– Independent	Non-southern vs. Southern	.001
	SFP	1992	– Self-centered	Non-southern vs. Southern	.000
	SFP	1992	– Assertive	Non-southern vs. Southern	.005
Figure 4.1A	Blair	2012	Modern Sexism (mean)	Non-South vs. South	.000
	Blair	2012	Modern Sexism (mean)	Non-southern vs. Southern	.000
Figure 4.1B	Blair	2012	Modern Sexism (distribution)	See Figure 4.1A	
	Blair	2012	Modern Sexism (distribution)	See Figure 4.1A	
Figure 4.2	Blair	2012	Modern Sexism (individual questions):		
	Blair	2012	– Favors (Q1)	Non-southern vs. Southern	.000
	Blair	2012	– Remarks (Q2)	Non-southern vs. Southern	.000
	Blair	2012	– Power (Q3)	Non-southern vs. Southern.	.000
	Blair	2012	– Complain (Q4)	Non-southern vs. Southern	.000
	Blair	2012	– Discrimination (Q5)	Non-southern vs. Southern	.000
Figure 4.3A	Blair	2012	Modern Sexism, Women only (mean)	Non-South vs. South	.000
	Blair	2012	Modern Sexism, Women only (mean)	Non-southern vs. Southern	.000
Figure 4.3B	Blair	2012	Modern Sexism, Women only (distribution)	See Figure 4.3A	
	Blair	2012	Modern Sexism, Women only (distribution)	See Figure 4.3A	

Figure/Table	Source	Year	Variable	Comparison Groups	p <=
Figure 4.4	Blair	2012	Modern Sexism, Women only (individual questions):		
	Blair	2012	– Favors (Q1)	Non-southern vs. Southern	.000
	Blair	2012	– Remarks (Q2)	Non-southern vs. Southern	.000
	Blair	2012	– Power (Q3)	Non-southern vs. Southern	.000
	Blair	2012	– Complain (Q4)	Non-southern vs. Southern	.000
	Blair	2012	– Discrimination (Q5)	Non-southern vs. Southern	.001
Table 4.2	Blair	2012	Modern Sexism, Women only (model)	Significance tests included in table	
Figure 4.5A	Blair	2012	Modern Sexism, Women only (mean)	See Figure 4.3A	
	Blair	2016	Modern Sexism, Women only (mean)	Non-southern vs. Southern	.000
Figure 4.5B	Blair	2012	Modern Sexism, Women only (distribution)	See Figure 4.3A	
	Blair	2016	Modern Sexism, Women only (distribution)	See Figure 4.5A	
Figure 4.6	Blair	2016	Modern Sexism, Women only (individual questions):		
	Blair	2016	– Favors (Q1)	Non-southern vs. Southern	.000
	Blair	2016	– Remarks (Q2)	Non-southern vs. Southern	.003
	Blair	2016	– Power (Q3)	Non-southern vs. Southern	.000
	Blair	2016	– Complain (Q4)	Non-southern vs. Southern	.000
	Blair	2016	– Discrimination (Q5)	Non-southern vs. Southern	.000
Figure 4.7	Blair	2016	Importance of getting married, Women only	Non-South vs. South	.230
	Blair	2016	Importance of getting married, Women only	Non-southern vs. Southern	.052
	Blair	2016	Importance of having children, Women only	Non-South vs. South	.259
	Blair	2016	Importance of having children, Women only	Non-southern vs. Southern	.000

CHAPTER 5

Figure/Table	Source	Year	Variable	Comparison Groups	p <=
Figure 5.1	Blair	2012	Experiences of racial discrimination, Men only:		
	Blair	2012	– General	Non-southern vs. Southern	.000

	Blair	2012	– Respect	Non-southern vs. Southern	.012
	Blair	2012	– Services	Non-southern vs. Southern	.000
	Blair	2012	– Names	Non-southern vs. Southern	.000
	Blair	2012	– Police	Non-southern vs. Southern	.065
	Blair	2012	Experiences of racial discrimination, Women only:		
	Blair	2012	– General	Non-southern vs. Southern	.067
	Blair	2012	– Respect	Non-southern vs. Southern	.293
	Blair	2012	– Services	Non-southern vs. Southern	.406
	Blair	2012	– Names	Non-southern vs. Southern	.111
	Blair	2012	– Police	Non-southern vs. Southern	.173
	Blair	2012	Experiences of racial discrimination, Non-southern only:		
	Blair	2012	– General	Women vs. Men	.156
	Blair	2012	– Respect	Women vs. Men	.001
	Blair	2012	– Services	Women vs. Men	.121
	Blair	2012	– Names	Women vs. Men	.084
	Blair	2012	– Police	Women vs. Men	.000
	Blair	2012	Experiences of racial discrimination, Southern only:		
	Blair	2012	– General	Women vs. Men	.000
	Blair	2012	– Respect	Women vs. Men	.007
	Blair	2012	– Services	Women vs. Men	.001
	Blair	2012	– Names	Women vs. Men	.001
	Blair	2012	– Police	Women vs. Men	.000
Figure 5.2	Blair	2010	Immigration, Men only	Non-southern vs. Southern	.000
	Blair	2012	Immigration, Men only	Non-southern vs. Southern	.000
Figure 5.3A	Blair	2012	Modern Sexism, Men only (mean)	Non-South vs. South	.035
	Blair	2012	Modern Sexism, Men only (mean)	Non-southern vs. Southern	.000

Figure 5.3B	Blair	2012	Modern Sexism, Men only (distribution)	See Figure 5.3A	
Figure 5.4	Blair	2012	Modern Sexism, Men only (individual questions):		
	Blair	2012	– Favors (Q1)	Non-southern vs. Southern	.006
	Blair	2012	– Remarks (Q2)	Non-southern vs. Southern	.020
	Blair	2012	– Power (Q3)	Non-southern vs. Southern	.000
	Blair	2012	– Complain (Q4)	Non-southern vs. Southern	.002
	Blair	2012	– Discrimination (Q5)	Non-southern vs. Southern	.005
Table 5.1	Blair	2012	Modern Sexism, Men only (model)	Sample sizes included in table	
Figure 5.5	SFP	1994	Man paid on dates, Southern only	Women vs. Men	.197
	SFP	1994	Husband should have main say-so, Southern only	Women vs. Men	.383
	SFP	1994	Men have a duty to protect women, Southern only	Women vs. Men	.000
Figure 5.6A	Blair	2012	Modern Sexism, Men only (mean)	See Figure 5.3A	
	Blair	2016	Modern Sexism, Men only (mean)	Non-southern vs. Southern	.000
Figure 5.6B	Blair	2012	Modern Sexism, Men only (distribution)	See Figure 5.3A	
	Blair	2016	Modern Sexism, Men only (distribution)	See Figure 5.6A	
Figure 5.7	Blair	2016	Modern Sexism, Men only (individual questions):		
	Blair	2016	– Favors (Q1)	Non-southern vs. Southern	.000
	Blair	2016	– Remarks (Q2)	Non-southern vs. Southern	.003
	Blair	2016	– Power (Q3)	Non-southern vs. Southern	.000
	Blair	2016	– Complain (Q4)	Non-southern vs. Southern	.000
	Blair	2016	– Discrimination (Q5)	Non-southern vs. Southern	.000
Figure 5.8A	Blair	2016	Mandatory background checks, Men only	Non-South vs. South	.017
	Blair	2016	Mandatory background checks, Men only	Non-southern vs. Southern	.037
	Blair	2016	Ban semi-automatic weapons, Men only	Non-South vs. South	.265
	Blair	2016	Ban semi-automatic weapons, Men only	Non-southern vs. Southern	.018

Figure 5.8B	Blair	2016	Mandatory background checks, Women only	Non-South vs. South	.019
	Blair	2016	Mandatory background checks, Women only	Non-southern vs. Southern	.001
	Blair	2016	Ban semi-automatic weapons, Women only	Non-South vs. South	.000
	Blair	2016	Ban semi-automatic weapons, Women only	Non-southern vs. Southern	.000
Figure 5.9	Blair	2016	Experiences of racial discrimination, Men only:		
	Blair	2016	– General	Non-southern vs. Southern	.140
	Blair	2016	– Respect	Non-southern vs. Southern	.001
	Blair	2016	– Services	Non-southern vs. Southern	.092
	Blair	2016	– Names	Non-southern vs. Southern	.026
	Blair	2016	– Police	Non-southern vs. Southern	.001
	Blair	2016	Experiences of racial discrimination, Women only:		
	Blair	2016	– General	Non-southern vs. Southern	.070
	Blair	2016	– Respect	Non-southern vs. Southern	.000
	Blair	2016	– Services	Non-southern vs. Southern	.000
	Blair	2016	– Names	Non-southern vs. Southern	.039
	Blair	2016	– Police	Non-southern vs. Southern	.196
	Blair	2016	Experiences of racial discrimination, Non-southern only:		
	Blair	2016	– General	Women vs. Men	.366
	Blair	2016	– Respect	Women vs. Men	.126
	Blair	2016	– Services	Women vs. Men	.048
	Blair	2016	– Names	Women vs. Men	.010
	Blair	2016	– Police	Women vs. Men	.000
	Blair	2016	Experiences of racial discrimination, Southern only:		
	Blair	2016	– General	Women vs. Men	.293
	Blair	2016	– Respect	Women vs. Men	.065

Figure/Table	Source	Year	Variable	Comparison Groups	p <=
	Blair	2016	– Services	Women vs. Men	.344
	Blair	2016	– Names	Women vs. Men	.337
	Blair	2016	– Police	Women vs. Men	.088
Figure 5.10	Blair	2012	Experiences of racial discrimination, gender gaps	See Figure 5.1	
	Blair	2016	Experiences of racial discrimination, gender gaps	See Figure 5.9	

CHAPTER 6

Figure/Table	Source	Year	Variable	Comparison Groups	p <=
Figure 6.1A	Blair	2012	Abortion, Men only	Non-South vs. South	.003
	Blair	2012	Abortion, Men only	Non-southern vs. Southern	.031
	Blair	2012	Abortion, Women only	Non-South vs. South	.000
	Blair	2012	Abortion, Women only	Non-southern vs. Southern	.000
	Blair	2012	Abortion, Non-South only	Women vs. Men	.007
	Blair	2012	Abortion, South only	Women vs. Men	.047
	Blair	2012	Abortion, Non-southern only	Women vs. Men	.001
	Blair	2012	Abortion, Southern only	Women vs. Men	.009
Figure 6.1B	Blair	2012	Gay marriage, Men only	Non-South vs. South	.371
	Blair	2012	Gay marriage, Men only	Non-southern vs. Southern	.000
	Blair	2012	Gay marriage, Women only	Non-South vs. South	.000
	Blair	2012	Gay marriage, Women only	Non-southern vs. Southern	.000
	Blair	2012	Gay marriage, Non-South only	Women vs. Men	.000
	Blair	2012	Gay marriage, South only	Women vs. Men	.300
	Blair	2012	Gay marriage, Non-southern only	Women vs. Men	.000
	Blair	2012	Gay marriage, Southern only	Women vs. Men	.153

Figure 6.2	Blair	2012	Abortion, gender gap	See Figure 6.1A	
	Blair	2012	Gay marriage, gender gap	See Figure 6.1B	
Figure 6.3	Blair	2012	Female president, all	Non-South vs. South	.005
	Blair	2012	Female president, all	Non-southern vs. Southern	.000
	Blair	2012	Female president, Men only	Non-South vs. South	.181
	Blair	2012	Female president, Men only	Non-southern vs. Southern	.005
	Blair	2012	Female president, Women only	Non-South vs. South	.003
	Blair	2012	Female president, Women only	Non-southern vs. Southern	.000
	Blair	2012	Female president, Non-South only	Women vs. Men	.008
	Blair	2012	Female president, South only	Women vs. Men	.330
	Blair	2012	Female president, Non-southern only	Women vs. Men	.001
	Blair	2012	Female president, Southern only	Women vs. Men	.344
Table 6.1	Blair	2012	Female president (model)	Significance tests included in table	
Figure 6.4	Blair	2012	Female president (plot)	See Table 6.1	
Figure 6.5A	Blair	2016	Primary vote, all		
	Blair	2016	– Bush	Non-South vs. South	.005
	Blair	2016	– Bush	Non-southern vs. Southern	.150
	Blair	2016	– Carson	Non-South vs. South	.031
	Blair	2016	– Carson	Non-southern vs. Southern	.406
	Blair	2016	– Cruz	Non-South vs. South	.020
	Blair	2016	– Cruz	Non-southern vs. Southern	.000
	Blair	2016	– Kasich	Non-South vs. South	.001
	Blair	2016	– Kasich	Non-southern vs. Southern	.021
	Blair	2016	– Rubio	Non-South vs. South	.000
	Blair	2016	– Rubio	Non-southern vs. Southern	.121

Blair	2016	– Trump	Non-South vs. South	.127
Blair	2016	– Trump	Non-southern vs. Southern	.000
Blair	2016	– Clinton	Non-South vs. South	.013
Blair	2016	– Clinton	Non-southern vs. Southern	.000
Blair	2016	– Sanders	Non-South vs. South	.001
Blair	2016	– Sanders	Non-southern vs. Southern	.000
Figure 6.5B	Blair	2016	Primary vote, gender gaps	
	Blair	2016	Primary vote, Men only	
	Blair	2016	– Bush	Non-South vs. South	.150
	Blair	2016	– Bush	Non-southern vs. Southern	.408
	Blair	2016	– Carson	Non-South vs. South	.010
	Blair	2016	– Carson	Non-southern vs. Southern	.221
	Blair	2016	– Cruz	Non-South vs. South	.118
	Blair	2016	– Cruz	Non-southern vs. Southern	.000
	Blair	2016	– Kasich	Non-South vs. South	.004
	Blair	2016	– Kasich	Non-southern vs. Southern	.168
	Blair	2016	– Rubio	Non-South vs. South	.001
	Blair	2016	– Rubio	Non-southern vs. Southern	.327
	Blair	2016	– Trump	Non-South vs. South	.202
	Blair	2016	– Trump	Non-southern vs. Southern	.004
	Blair	2016	– Clinton	Non-South vs. South	.494
	Blair	2016	– Clinton	Non-southern vs. Southern	.000
	Blair	2016	– Sanders	Non-South vs. South	.003

Figure 6.5B (Cont.)					
	Blair	2016	– Sanders	Non-southern vs. Southern	.005
			Primary vote, Women only		
	Blair	2016	– Bush	Non-South vs. South	.007
	Blair	2016	– Bush	Non-southern vs. Southern	.123
	Blair	2016	– Carson	Non-South vs. South	.450
	Blair	2016	– Carson	Non-southern vs. Southern	.335
	Blair	2016	– Cruz	Non-South vs. South	.044
	Blair	2016	– Cruz	Non-southern vs. Southern	.030
	Blair	2016	– Kasich	Non-South vs. South	.019
	Blair	2016	– Kasich	Non-southern vs. Southern	.030
	Blair	2016	– Rubio	Non-South vs. South	.010
	Blair	2016	– Rubio	Non-southern vs. Southern	.117
	Blair	2016	– Trump	Non-South vs. South	.008
	Blair	2016	– Trump	Non-southern vs. Southern	.000
	Blair	2016	– Clinton	Non-South vs. South	.002
	Blair	2016	– Clinton	Non-southern vs. Southern	.000
	Blair	2016	– Sanders	Non-South vs. South	.017
	Blair	2016	– Sanders	Non-southern vs. Southern	.005
			Primary vote, Non-South only		
	Blair	2016	– Bush	Women vs. Men	.214
	Blair	2016	– Carson	Women vs. Men	.357
	Blair	2016	– Cruz	Women vs. Men	.098
	Blair	2016	– Kasich	Women vs. Men	.063
	Blair	2016	– Rubio	Women vs. Men	.206

Figure 6.5B (*Cont.*)				
Blair	2016	– Trump	Women vs. Men	.000
Blair	2016	– Clinton	Women vs. Men	.000
Blair	2016	– Sanders	Women vs. Men	.071
Blair	2016	Primary vote, South only		
Blair	2016	– Bush	Women vs. Men	.179
Blair	2016	– Carson	Women vs. Men	.033
Blair	2016	– Cruz	Women vs. Men	.238
Blair	2016	– Kasich	Women vs. Men	.217
Blair	2016	– Rubio	Women vs. Men	.323
Blair	2016	– Trump	Women vs. Men	.349
Blair	2016	– Clinton	Women vs. Men	.182
Blair	2016	– Sanders	Women vs. Men	.023
Blair	2016	Primary vote, Non-southern only		
Blair	2016	– Bush	Women vs. Men	.462
Blair	2016	– Carson	Women vs. Men	.218
Blair	2016	– Cruz	Women vs. Men	.314
Blair	2016	– Kasich	Women vs. Men	.146
Blair	2016	– Rubio	Women vs. Men	.372
Blair	2016	– Trump	Women vs. Men	.000
Blair	2016	– Clinton	Women vs. Men	.001
Blair	2016	– Sanders	Women vs. Men	.011
Blair	2016	Primary vote, Southern only		
Blair	2016	– Bush	Women vs. Men	.268
Blair	2016	– Carson	Women vs. Men	.079
Blair	2016	– Cruz	Women vs. Men	.030

	Blair	2016	– Kasich	Women vs. Men	.074
	Blair	2016	– Rubio	Women vs. Men	.362
	Blair	2016	– Trump	Women vs. Men	.337
	Blair	2016	– Clinton	Women vs. Men	.108
	Blair	2016	– Sanders	Women vs. Men	.062
Figure 6.6A	Blair	2016	General Election vote, all		
	Blair	2016	– Clinton	Non-South vs. South	.000
	Blair	2016	– Clinton	Non-southern vs. Southern	.000
	Blair	2016	– Trump	Non-South vs. South	.000
	Blair	2016	– Trump	Non-southern vs. Southern	.000
	Blair	2016	– Johnson	Non-South vs. South	.384
	Blair	2016	– Johnson	Non-southern vs. Southern	.308
	Blair	2016	– Stein	Non-South vs. South	.013
	Blair	2016	– Stein	Non-southern vs. Southern	.186
	Blair	2016	– other	Non-South vs. South	.199
	Blair	2016	– other	Non-southern vs. Southern	.054
Figure 6.6B	Blair	2016	General Election vote, Men only		
	Blair	2016	– Clinton	Non-South vs. South	.115
	Blair	2016	– Clinton	Non-southern vs. Southern	.000
	Blair	2016	– Trump	Non-South vs. South	.105
	Blair	2016	– Trump	Non-southern vs. Southern	.000
	Blair	2016	– Johnson	Non-South vs. South	.166
	Blair	2016	– Johnson	Non-southern vs. Southern	.094
	Blair	2016	– Stein	Non-South vs. South	.372

Figure 6.6B (Cont.)					
Blair	2016	– Stein	Non-southern vs. Southern	.104
Blair	2016	– other	Non-South vs. South	.178
Blair	2016	– other	Non-southern vs. Southern	.394
General Election vote, Women only					
Blair	2016	– Clinton	Non-South vs. South	.000
Blair	2016	– Clinton	Non-southern vs. Southern	.000
Blair	2016	– Trump	Non-South vs. South	.000
Blair	2016	– Trump	Non-southern vs. Southern	.000
Blair	2016	– Johnson	Non-South vs. South	.257
Blair	2016	– Johnson	Non-southern vs. Southern	.182
Blair	2016	– Stein	Non-South vs. South	.013
Blair	2016	– Stein*	Non-southern vs. Southern	N/A
Blair	2016	– other	Non-South vs. South	.405
Blair	2016	– other	Non-southern vs. Southern	.026
General Election vote, Non-South only					
Blair	2016	– Clinton	Women vs. Men	.000
Blair	2016	– Trump	Women vs. Men	.000
Blair	2016	– Johnson	Women vs. Men	.007
Blair	2016	– Stein	Women vs. Men	.048
Blair	2016	– other	Women vs. Men	.465
General Election vote, South only					
Blair	2016	– Clinton	Women vs. Men	.013
Blair	2016	– Trump	Women vs. Men	.099
Blair	2016	– Johnson	Women vs. Men	.224
Blair	2016	– Stein	Women vs. Men	.154

Blair	2016	– other	Women vs. Men	.230
Blair	2016	General Election vote, Non-southern only		
Blair	2016	– Clinton	Women vs. Men	.000
Blair	2016	– Trump	Women vs. Men	.000
Blair	2016	– Johnson	Women vs. Men	.003
Blair	2016	– Stein	Women vs. Men	.024
Blair	2016	– other	Women vs. Men	.490
Blair	2016	General Election vote, Southern only		
Blair	2016	– Clinton	Women vs. Men	.014
Blair	2016	– Trump	Women vs. Men	.135
Blair	2016	– Johnson	Women vs. Men	.389
Blair	2016	– Stein*	Women vs. Men	N/A
Blair	2016	– other	Women vs. Men	.065
Figure 6.6C	Blair	2016	General Election vote, gender gaps	See Figure 6.6B
Figure 6.6D	Blair	2016	Trump and Clinton vote by gender	See Figure 6.6B
Blair	2016	General Election vote for Trump, Non-southern Men only	Modern Sexism	.000
Blair	2016	General Election vote for Trump, Southern Men only	Modern Sexism	.000
Blair	2016	General Election vote for Trump, Non-southern Women only	Modern Sexism	.000
Blair	2016	General Election vote for Trump, Southern Women only	Modern Sexism	.000
Blair	2016	General Election vote for Clinton, Non-southern Men only	Modern Sexism	.000
Blair	2016	General Election vote for Clinton, Southern Men only	Modern Sexism	.000
Blair	2016	General Election vote for Clinton, Non-southern Women only	Modern Sexism	.000

Figure	Author	Year	Description	Comparison	p-value
	Blair	2016	General Election vote for Clinton, Southern Women only	Modern Sexism	.000
Figure 6.7	Blair	2016	Modern Sexism (mean), Men only	See Figure 5,6A	
	Blair	2016	Modern Sexism (mean), Women only	See Figure 4,5A	
	Blair	2016	General Election vote, Men only	See Figure 6.6B	
	Blair	2016	General Election vote, Women only	See Figure 6.6B	
	Blair	2016	General Election vote, Candidate gender gap		
	Blair	2016	General Election vote for a female candidate, Men only	Non-South vs. South	.080
	Blair	2016	General Election vote for a female candidate, Men only	Non-southern vs. Southern	.000
	Blair	2016	General Election vote for a female candidate, Women only	Non-South vs. South	.000
	Blair	2016	General Election vote for a female candidate, Women only	Non-southern vs. Southern	.000
	Blair	2016	General Election vote for a female candidate, Non-South only	Women vs. Men	.000
	Blair	2016	General Election vote for a female candidate, South only	Women vs. Men	.009
	Blair	2016	General Election vote for a female candidate, Non-southern only	Women vs. Men	.000
	Blair	2016	General Election vote for a female candidate, Southern only	Women vs. Men	.052
Figure 6.8	Blair	2016	Modern Sexism (mean), Non-southern Women only	Married vs. Non-married	.018
	Blair	2016	Modern Sexism (mean), Southern Women only	Married vs. Non-married	.304
	Blair	2016	Modern Sexism (mean), Non-married Women only	Non-southern vs. Southern	.001
	Blair	2016	Modern Sexism (mean), Married Women only	Non-southern vs. Southern	.001
	Blair	2016	General Election vote for Clinton, Non-southern Women only	Married vs. Non-married	.000
	Blair	2016	General Election vote for Clinton, Southern Women only	Married vs. Non-married	.067
	Blair	2016	General Election vote for Clinton, Non-married Women only	Non-southern vs. Southern	.000

Figure 6.8 (Cont.)					
	Blair	2016	General Election vote for Clinton, Married Women only	Non-southern vs. Southern	.000
	Blair	2016	General Election vote for Trump, Non-southern Women only	Married vs. Non-married	.001
	Blair	2016	General Election vote for Trump, Southern Women only	Married vs. Non-married	.036
	Blair	2016	General Election vote for Trump, Non-married Women only	Non-southern vs. Southern	.000
	Blair	2016	General Election vote for Trump, Married Women only	Non-southern vs. Southern	.000
	Blair	2016	General Election vote for Johnson, Non-southern Women only	Married vs. Non-married	.284
	Blair	2016	General Election vote for Johnson, Southern Women only	Married vs. Non-married	.031
	Blair	2016	General Election vote for Johnson, Non-married Women only	Non-southern vs. Southern	.019
	Blair	2016	General Election vote for Johnson, Married Women only	Non-southern vs. Southern	.279
	Blair	2016	General Election vote for Stein, Non-southern Women only	Married vs. Non-married	.480
	Blair	2016	General Election vote for Stein, Southern Women only*	Married vs. Non-married	N/A
	Blair	2016	General Election vote for Stein, Non-married Women only*	Non-southern vs. Southern	N/A
	Blair	2016	General Election vote for Stein, Married Women only*	Non-southern vs. Southern	N/A
	Blair	2016	General Election vote for other, Non-southern Women only	Married vs. Non-married	.208
	Blair	2016	General Election vote for other, Southern Women only**	Married vs. Non-married	N/A
	Blair	2016	General Election vote for other, Non-married Women only**	Non-southern vs. Southern	N/A
	Blair	2016	General Election vote for other, Married Women only	Non-southern vs. Southern	.121

CHAPTER 7

Figure/Table	Source	Year	Variable	Comparison Groups	p <=
Table 7.1	Baylor	2007	Pornography	Non-South vs. South	.011
	Baylor	2007	Gambling	Non-South vs. South	.000
	Baylor	2007	Revealing clothes	Non-South vs. South	.014
	Baylor	2007	Premarital sex	Non-South vs. South	.037
	Baylor	2007	Cohabitation	Non-South vs. South	.050
	Baylor	2007	Contraception	Non-South vs. South	.001
	Baylor	2007	Displaying wealth	Non-South vs. South	.011
Table 7.2A	Baylor	2007	God exists	Non-South vs. South	.000
	Baylor	2007	Devil exists	Non-South vs. South	.000
	Baylor	2007	Heaven exists	Non-South vs. South	.000
	Baylor	2007	Hell exists	Non-South vs. South	.000
	Baylor	2007	Armageddon exists	Non-South vs. South	.000
	Baylor	2007	Angels exist	Non-South vs. South	.000
	Baylor	2007	Demons exist	Non-South vs. South	.000
	Baylor	2007	Rapture exists	Non-South vs. South	.000
	Baylor	2007	Devil causes evil	Non-South vs. South	.000
	Baylor	2007	Teach morals	Non-South vs. South	.042
	Baylor	2007	Convert others	Non-South vs. South	.000
	Baylor	2010	God exists	Non-South vs. South	.001
	Baylor	2010	Devil exists	Non-South vs. South	.003
	Baylor	2010	Heaven exists	Non-South vs. South	.003

Table 7.2B	Baylor	2010	Hell exists	Non-South vs. South	.002
	Baylor	2010	Armageddon exists	Non-South vs. South	.000
	Baylor	2010	Angels exist	Non-South vs. South	.000
	Baylor	2010	Demons exist	Non-South vs. South	.002
	Baylor	2007	Witnessed a healing	Non-South vs. South	.000
	Baylor	2007	Received a healing	Non-South vs. South	.000
	Baylor	2007	Spoken in tongues	Non-South vs. South	.005
	Baylor	2007	Felt called	Non-South vs. South	.000
	Baylor	2007	Heard God	Non-South vs. South	.000
	Baylor	2007	Protected by guardian angel	Non-South vs. South	.013
	Baylor	2007	Experienced a religious conversion	Non-South vs. South	.000
	Baylor	2007	Felt at one with the universe	Non-South vs. South	.006
Table 7.3	Baylor	2007	Tithe	Non-South vs. South	.002
	Baylor	2007	Amount given as tithe	Non-South vs. South	.006
	Baylor	2007	Friends at your church	Non-South vs. South	.005
	Baylor	2007	Bible study or Sunday school	Non-South vs. South	.000
	Baylor	2007	Witness to friends	Non-South vs. South	.000
	Baylor	2007	Witness to strangers	Non-South vs. South	.000
	Baylor	2007	Community Bible study	Non-South vs. South	.001
	Baylor	2007	Read Bible or sacred book	Non-South vs. South	.000
	Baylor	2007	Pray/meditate	Non-South vs. South	.000
	Baylor	2007	Religious at age 12	Non-South vs. South	.003
	Baylor	2007	Church attendance age 12	Non-South vs. South	.000
	Baylor	2007	Volunteer in church	Non-South vs. South	.001
	Baylor	2007	Volunteer in community	Non-South vs. South	.029

	Baylor	2010	Bible study or Sunday school	Non-South vs. South	.000
	Baylor	2010	Witness to friends or strangers	Non-South vs. South	.002
	Baylor	2010	Community Bible study	Non-South vs. South	.001
	Baylor	2010	Read Bible or sacred book	Non-South vs. South	.000
	Baylor	2010	Pray/meditate	Non-South vs. South	.000
Table 7.4	Baylor	2007	Baptist	Non-South vs. South	.000
	Baylor	2007	Baptist (among those with affiliation)	Non-South vs. South	.000
	Baylor	2007	Biblical literalist	Non-South vs. South	.000
	Baylor	2007	Fundamentalist	Non-South vs. South	.001
	Baylor	2007	Born again	Non-South vs. South	.000
	Baylor	2007	Evangelical	Non-South vs. South	.000
	Baylor	2007	Fundamentalist combination	Non-South vs. South	.000
	Baylor	2010	Baptist	Non-South vs. South	.000
	Baylor	2010	Baptist (among those with affiliation)	Non-South vs. South	.000
	Baylor	2010	Biblical literalist	Non-South vs. South	.000
	Baylor	2010	Fundamentalist	Non-South vs. South	.011
	Baylor	2010	Born again	Non-South vs. South	.000
	Baylor	2010	Evangelical	Non-South vs. South	.088
	Baylor	2010	Fundamentalist combination	Non-South vs. South	.000
	Blair	2010	Baptist	Non-South vs. South	.000
	Blair	2010	Baptist	Non-southern vs. Southern	.000
	Blair	2010	Baptist (among those with affiliation)	Non-South vs. South	.000
	Blair	2010	Baptist (among those with affiliation)	Non-southern vs. Southern	.000
	Blair	2010	Biblical literalist	Non-South vs. South	.000
	Blair	2010	Biblical literalist	Non-southern vs. Southern	.000

	Blair	2012	Baptist	Non-South vs. South	.000
	Blair	2012	Baptist	Non-southern vs. Southern	.000
	Blair	2012	Baptist (among those with affiliation)	Non-South vs. South	.000
	Blair	2012	Baptist (among those with affiliation)	Non-southern vs. Southern	.000
	Blair	2012	Biblical literalist	Non-South vs. South	.000
	Blair	2012	Biblical literalist	Non-southern vs. Southern	.000
Figure 7.1	Blair	2012	Racial Resentment, Non-southern only	Non-fundamentalist vs. Fundamentalist	.000
	Blair	2012	Racial Resentment, Southern only	Non-fundamentalist vs. Fundamentalist	.000
	Blair	2012	Racial Resentment, Non-fundamentalist only	Non-southern vs. Southern	.000
	Blair	2012	Racial Resentment, Fundamentalist only	Non-southern vs. Southern	.000
	Blair	2012	Ethnocentrism (FT measure), Non-southern only	Non-fundamentalist vs. Fundamentalist	.170
	Blair	2012	Ethnocentrism (FT measure), Southern only	Non-fundamentalist vs. Fundamentalist	.018
	Blair	2012	Ethnocentrism (FT measure), Non-fundamentalist only	Non-southern vs. Southern	.023
	Blair	2012	Ethnocentrism (FT measure), Fundamentalist only	Non-southern vs. Southern	.000
	Blair	2012	Modern Sexism, Non-southern only	Non-fundamentalist vs. Fundamentalist	.000
	Blair	2012	Modern Sexism, Southern only	Non-fundamentalist vs. Fundamentalist	.068
	Blair	2012	Modern Sexism, Non-fundamentalist only	Non-southern vs. Southern	.000
	Blair	2012	Modern Sexism, Fundamentalist only	Non-southern vs. Southern	.344
Figure 7.2.A	Blair	2016	Fundamentalist identity, Non-southern only	Non-southern vs. Southern	.000
Figure 7.2.B	Blair	2016	Fundamentalist identity, Southern only	Non-southern vs. Southern	
Figure 7.3	Blair	2016	Importance of religious life, Non-southern only	Non-fundamentalist vs. Fundamentalist	.000
	Blair	2016	Importance of religious life, Southern only	Non-fundamentalist vs. Fundamentalist	.000
	Blair	2016	Importance of religious life, Non-fundamentalist only	Non-southern vs. Southern	.006
	Blair	2016	Importance of religious life, Fundamentalist only	Non-southern vs. Southern	.068
Figure 7.4	Blair	2016	Racial Resentment, Non-southern only	Non-fundamentalist vs. Fundamentalist	.000

Figure/Table	Source	Year	Variable	Comparison Groups	p <=
	Blair	2016	Racial Resentment, Southern only	Non-fundamentalist vs. Fundamentalist	.000
	Blair	2016	Racial Resentment, Non-fundamentalist only	Non-southern vs. Southern	.000
	Blair	2016	Racial Resentment, Fundamentalist only	Non-southern vs. Southern	.000
	Blair	2016	Ethnocentrism (FT measure), Non-southern only	Non-fundamentalist vs. Fundamentalist	.000
	Blair	2016	Ethnocentrism (FT measure), Southern only	Non-fundamentalist vs. Fundamentalist	.001
	Blair	2016	Ethnocentrism (FT measure), Non-fundamentalist only	Non-southern vs. Southern	.000
	Blair	2016	Ethnocentrism (FT measure), Fundamentalist only	Non-southern vs. Southern	.000
	Blair	2016	Modern Sexism, Non-southern only	Non-fundamentalist vs. Fundamentalist	.000
	Blair	2016	Modern Sexism, Southern only	Non-fundamentalist vs. Fundamentalist	.000
	Blair	2016	Modern Sexism, Non-fundamentalist only	Non-southern vs. Southern	.001
	Blair	2016	Modern Sexism, Fundamentalist only	Non-southern vs. Southern	.051

CHAPTER 8

Figure/Table	Source	Year	Variable	Comparison Groups	p <=
Figure 8.1	Blair	2012	Party identification, Non-South only	Non-fundamentalist vs. Fundamentalist	.000
	Blair	2012	Party identification, South only	Non-fundamentalist vs. Fundamentalist	.000
	Blair	2012	Party identification, Non-southern only	Non-fundamentalist vs. Fundamentalist	.000
	Blair	2012	Party identification, Southern only	Non-fundamentalist vs. Fundamentalist	.000
	Blair	2012	Party identification, Non-fundamentalist only	Non-South vs. South	.000
	Blair	2012	Party identification, Fundamentalist only	Non-South vs. South	.000
	Blair	2012	Party identification, Non-fundamentalist only	Non-southern vs. Southern	.000
	Blair	2012	Party identification, Fundamentalist only	Non-southern vs. Southern	.019
Figure 8.2	Blair	2012	Experiences of racial discrimination, Non-southern only:		
	Blair	2012	– General	Non-fundamentalist vs. Fundamentalist	.029
	Blair	2012	– Respect	Non-fundamentalist vs. Fundamentalist	.000

Blair	2012	– Services	Non-fundamentalist vs. Fundamentalist	.001
Blair	2012	– Names	Non-fundamentalist vs. Fundamentalist	.046
Blair	2012	– Police	Non-fundamentalist vs. Fundamentalist	.225
Blair	2012	Experiences of racial discrimination, Southern only:		
Blair	2012	– General	Non-fundamentalist vs. Fundamentalist	.004
Blair	2012	– Respect	Non-fundamentalist vs. Fundamentalist	.012
Blair	2012	– Services	Non-fundamentalist vs. Fundamentalist	.011
Blair	2012	– Names	Non-fundamentalist vs. Fundamentalist	.149
Blair	2012	– Police	Non-fundamentalist vs. Fundamentalist	.076
Blair	2012	Experiences of racial discrimination, Non-fundamentalist only:		
Blair	2012	– General	Non-southern vs. Southern	.000
Blair	2012	– Respect	Non-southern vs. Southern	.027
Blair	2012	– Services	Non-southern vs. Southern	.044
Blair	2012	– Names	Non-southern vs. Southern	.003
Blair	2012	– Police	Non-southern vs. Southern	.091
Blair	2012	Experiences of racial discrimination, Fundamentalist only:		
Blair	2012	– General	Non-southern vs. Southern	.001
Blair	2012	– Respect	Non-southern vs. Southern	.116
Blair	2012	– Services	Non-southern vs. Southern	.029
Blair	2012	– Names	Non-southern vs. Southern	.174
Blair	2012	– Police	Non-southern vs. Southern	.091
Blair	2012	Republican, Non-South only	Non-fundamentalist vs. Fundamentalist	.000
Blair	2012	Republican, South only	Non-fundamentalist vs. Fundamentalist	.000
Blair	2012	Republican, Non-southern only	Non-fundamentalist vs. Fundamentalist	.000
Blair	2012	Republican, Southern only	Non-fundamentalist vs. Fundamentalist	.001

Table 8.1

Table 8.1 (*Cont.*)					
	Blair	2012	Republican, Non-fundamentalist only	Non-South vs. South	.003
	Blair	2012	Republican, Fundamentalist only	Non-South vs. South	.004
	Blair	2012	Republican, Non-fundamentalist only	Non-southern vs. Southern	.000
	Blair	2012	Republican, Fundamentalist only	Non-southern vs. Southern	.142
	Blair	2012	Independent, Non-South only	Non-fundamentalist vs. Fundamentalist	.267
	Blair	2012	Independent, South only	Non-fundamentalist vs. Fundamentalist	.456
	Blair	2012	Independent, Non-southern only	Non-fundamentalist vs. Fundamentalist	.068
	Blair	2012	Independent, Southern only	Non-fundamentalist vs. Fundamentalist	.053
	Blair	2012	Independent, Non-fundamentalist only	Non-South vs. South	.086
	Blair	2012	Independent, Fundamentalist only	Non-South vs. South	.427
	Blair	2012	Independent, Non-fundamentalist only	Non-southern vs. Southern	.002
	Blair	2012	Independent, Fundamentalist only	Non-southern vs. Southern	.238
	Blair	2012	Republican vote for Romney, Non-South only	Non-fundamentalist vs. Fundamentalist	.006
	Blair	2012	Republican vote for Romney, South only	Non-fundamentalist vs. Fundamentalist	.011
	Blair	2012	Republican vote for Romney, Non-southern only	Non-fundamentalist vs. Fundamentalist	.015
	Blair	2012	Republican vote for Romney, Southern only***	Non-fundamentalist vs. Fundamentalist	N/A
	Blair	2012	Republican vote for Romney, Non-fundamentalist only	Non-South vs. South	.001
	Blair	2012	Republican vote for Romney, Fundamentalist only	Non-South vs. South	.016
	Blair	2012	Republican vote for Romney, Non-fundamentalist only	Non-southern vs. Southern	.178
	Blair	2012	Republican vote for Romney, Fundamentalist only ***	Non-southern vs. Southern	N/A
	Blair	2012	Independent vote for Romney, Non-South only	Non-fundamentalist vs. Fundamentalist	.437
	Blair	2012	Independent vote for Romney, South only	Non-fundamentalist vs. Fundamentalist	.002
	Blair	2012	Independent vote for Romney, Non-southern only	Non-fundamentalist vs. Fundamentalist	.153
	Blair	2012	Independent vote for Romney, Southern only	Non-fundamentalist vs. Fundamentalist	.164

	Blair	2012	Independent vote for Romney, Non-fundamentalist only	Non-South vs. South	.006
	Blair	2012	Independent vote for Romney, Fundamentalist only	Non-South vs. South	.000
	Blair	2012	Independent vote for Romney, Non-fundamentalist only	Non-southern vs. Southern	.000
	Blair	2012	Independent vote for Romney, Fundamentalist only	Non-southern vs. Southern	.001
Figure 8.3A	Blair	2012	Gay marriage, Non-southern only	Non-fundamentalist vs. Fundamentalist	.000
	Blair	2012	Gay marriage, Southern only	Non-fundamentalist vs. Fundamentalist	.000
	Blair	2012	Gay marriage, Non-fundamentalist only	Non-southern vs. Southern	.000
	Blair	2012	Gay marriage, Fundamentalist only	Non-southern vs. Southern	.001
Figure 8.3B	Blair	2012	Abortion, Non-southern only	Non-fundamentalist vs. Fundamentalist	.000
	Blair	2012	Abortion, Southern only	Non-fundamentalist vs. Fundamentalist	.000
	Blair	2012	Abortion, Non-fundamentalist only	Non-southern vs. Southern	.000
	Blair	2012	Abortion, Fundamentalist only	Non-southern vs. Southern	.457
Figure 8.4	Blair	2016	Experiences of racial discrimination, Non-southern only:		
	Blair	2016	– General	Non-fundamentalist vs. Fundamentalist	.361
	Blair	2016	– Respect	Non-fundamentalist vs. Fundamentalist	.121
	Blair	2016	– Services	Non-fundamentalist vs. Fundamentalist	.380
	Blair	2016	– Names	Non-fundamentalist vs. Fundamentalist	.008
	Blair	2016	– Police	Non-fundamentalist vs. Fundamentalist	.204
	Blair	2016	Experiences of racial discrimination, Southern only:		
	Blair	2016	– General	Non-fundamentalist vs. Fundamentalist	.002
	Blair	2016	– Respect	Non-fundamentalist vs. Fundamentalist	.014
	Blair	2016	– Services	Non-fundamentalist vs. Fundamentalist	.001
	Blair	2016	– Names	Non-fundamentalist vs. Fundamentalist	.109
	Blair	2016	– Police	Non-fundamentalist vs. Fundamentalist	.002
	Blair	2016	Experiences of racial discrimination, Non-fundamentalists only:		
	Blair	2016	– General	Non-southern vs. Southern	.056

	Blair	2016	– Respect	Non-southern vs. Southern	.046
	Blair	2016	– Services	Non-southern vs. Southern	.104
	Blair	2016	– Names	Non-southern vs. Southern	.143
	Blair	2016	– Police	Non-southern vs. Southern	.236
	Blair	2016	Experiences of racial discrimination, Fundamentalists only:		
	Blair	2016	– General	Non-southern vs. Southern	.009
	Blair	2016	– Respect	Non-southern vs. Southern	.003
	Blair	2016	– Services	Non-southern vs. Southern	.001
	Blair	2016	– Names	Non-southern vs. Southern	.220
	Blair	2016	– Police	Non-southern vs. Southern	.005
Figure 8.5A	Blair	2016	Abortion, Non-southern only	Non-fundamentalist vs. Fundamentalist	.000
	Blair	2016	Abortion, Southern only	Non-fundamentalist vs. Fundamentalist	.000
	Blair	2016	Abortion, Non-fundamentalist only	Non-southern vs. Southern	.017
	Blair	2016	Abortion, Fundamentalist only	Non-southern vs. Southern	.004
Figure 8.5B	Blair	2012	Abortion	See Figure 8.3B	
	Blair	2016	Abortion	See Figure 8.5A	
	Blair	2012	General Election vote for Romney, Non-southern only	Non-fundamentalist vs. Fundamentalist	.000
	Blair	2012	General Election vote for Romney, Southern only	Non-fundamentalist vs. Fundamentalist	.000
	Blair	2012	General Election vote for Romney, Non-fundamentalist only	Non-southern vs. Southern	.000
	Blair	2012	General Election vote for Romney, Fundamentalist only	Non-fundamentalist vs. Fundamentalist	.000
	Blair	2016	General Election vote for Trump, Non-southern only	Non-fundamentalist vs. Fundamentalist	.000
	Blair	2016	General Election vote for Trump, Southern only	Non-fundamentalist vs. Fundamentalist	.000
	Blair	2016	General Election vote for Trump, Non-fundamentalist only	Non-southern vs. Southern	.000
	Blair	2016	General Election vote for Trump, Fundamentalist only	Non-southern vs. Southern	.000

Figure 8.6	Blair	2016	Party identification, Non-South only	Non-fundamentalist vs. Fundamentalist	.000
	Blair	2016	Party identification, South only	Non-fundamentalist vs. Fundamentalist	.000
	Blair	2016	Party identification, Non-southern only	Non-fundamentalist vs. Fundamentalist	.000
	Blair	2016	Party identification, Southern only	Non-fundamentalist vs. Fundamentalist	.000
	Blair	2016	Party identification, Non-fundamentalist only	Non-South vs. South	.000
	Blair	2016	Party identification, Fundamentalist only	Non-South vs. South	.001
	Blair	2016	Party identification, Non-fundamentalist only	Non-southern vs. Southern	.000
	Blair	2016	Party identification, Fundamentalist only	Non-southern vs. Southern	.000
Table 8.2	Blair	2016	Republican, Non-South only	Non-fundamentalist vs. Fundamentalist	.000
	Blair	2016	Republican, South only	Non-fundamentalist vs. Fundamentalist	.000
	Blair	2016	Republican, Non-southern only	Non-fundamentalist vs. Fundamentalist	.000
	Blair	2016	Republican, Southern only	Non-fundamentalist vs. Fundamentalist	.000
	Blair	2016	Republican, Non-fundamentalist only	Non-South vs. South	.005
	Blair	2016	Republican, Fundamentalist only	Non-South vs. South	.002
	Blair	2016	Republican, Non-southern only	Non-southern vs. Southern	.000
	Blair	2016	Republican, Fundamentalist only	Non-southern vs. Southern	.000
	Blair	2016	Independent, Non-South only	Non-fundamentalist vs. Fundamentalist	.021
	Blair	2016	Independent, South only	Non-fundamentalist vs. Fundamentalist	.000
	Blair	2016	Independent, Non-southern only	Non-fundamentalist vs. Fundamentalist	.014
	Blair	2016	Independent, Southern only	Non-fundamentalist vs. Fundamentalist	.001
	Blair	2016	Independent, Non-fundamentalist only	Non-South vs. South	.078
	Blair	2016	Independent, Fundamentalist only	Non-South vs. South	.288
	Blair	2016	Independent, Non-fundamentalist only	Non-southern vs. Southern	.130
	Blair	2016	Independent, Fundamentalist only	Non-southern vs. Southern	.003
	Blair	2016	Republican vote for Trump, Non-South only	Non-fundamentalist vs. Fundamentalist	.011

Figure/Table	Source	Year	Variable	Comparison Groups	p <=
	Blair	2016	Republican vote for Trump, South only	Non-fundamentalist vs. Fundamentalist	.000
	Blair	2016	Republican vote for Trump, Non-southern only	Non-fundamentalist vs. Fundamentalist	.003
	Blair	2016	Republican vote for Trump, Southern only	Non-fundamentalist vs. Fundamentalist	.000
	Blair	2016	Republican vote for Trump, Non-fundamentalist only	Non-South vs. South	.338
	Blair	2016	Republican vote for Trump, Fundamentalist only	Non-South vs. South	.004
	Blair	2016	Republican vote for Trump, Non-fundamentalist only	Non-southern vs. Southern	.124
	Blair	2016	Republican vote for Trump, Fundamentalist only	Non-southern vs. Southern	.010
	Blair	2016	Independent vote for Trump, Non-South only	Non-fundamentalist vs. Fundamentalist	.101
	Blair	2016	Independent vote for Trump, South only	Non-fundamentalist vs. Fundamentalist	.003
	Blair	2016	Independent vote for Trump, Non-southern only	Non-fundamentalist vs. Fundamentalist	.077
	Blair	2016	Independent vote for Trump, Southern only	Non-fundamentalist vs. Fundamentalist	.047
	Blair	2016	Independent vote for Trump, Non-fundamentalist only	Non-South vs. South	.012
	Blair	2016	Independent vote for Trump, Fundamentalist only	Non-South vs. South	.455
	Blair	2016	Independent vote for Trump, Non-fundamentalist only	Non-southern vs. Southern	.382
	Blair	2016	Independent vote for Trump, Fundamentalist only	Non-southern vs. Southern	.105

CHAPTER 9

Figure/Table	Source	Year	Variable	Comparison Groups	p <=
Figure 9.1A	Blair	2012	Romney's religion, Non-southern only	Non-fundamentalist vs. Fundamentalist	.009
	Blair	2012	Romney's religion, Southern only	Non-fundamentalist vs. Fundamentalist	.136
	Blair	2012	Romney's religion, Non-fundamentalist only	Non-southern vs. Southern	.002
	Blair	2012	Romney's religion, Fundamentalist only	Non-southern vs. Southern	.001
Figure 9.1B	Blair	2010	Obama's religion, Non-southern only	Non-fundamentalist vs. Fundamentalist	.000
	Blair	2010	Obama's religion, Southern only	Non-fundamentalist vs. Fundamentalist	.000
	Blair	2010	Obama's religion, Non-fundamentalist only	Non-southern vs. Southern	.015
	Blair	2010	Obama's religion, Fundamentalist only	Non-southern vs. Southern	.002

Table 9.1					
	Baylor	2007	Death penalty, Non-South only	Non-fundamentalist vs. Fundamentalist	.000
	Baylor	2007	Death penalty, South only	Non-fundamentalist vs. Fundamentalist	.000
	Baylor	2007	Death penalty, Non-fundamentalist only	Non-South vs. South	.007
	Baylor	2007	Death penalty, Fundamentalist only	Non-South vs. South	.000
	Baylor	2007	English as national language, Non-South only	Non-fundamentalist vs. Fundamentalist	.000
	Baylor	2007	English as national language, South only	Non-fundamentalist vs. Fundamentalist	.000
	Baylor	2007	English as national language, Non-fundamentalist only	Non-South vs. South	.128
	Baylor	2007	English as national language, Fundamentalist only	Non-South vs. South	.000
	Baylor	2007	Punish criminals, Non-South only	Non-fundamentalist vs. Fundamentalist	.000
	Baylor	2007	Punish criminals, South only	Non-fundamentalist vs. Fundamentalist	.000
	Baylor	2007	Punish criminals, Non-fundamentalist only	Non-South vs. South	.041
	Baylor	2007	Punish criminals, Fundamentalist only	Non-South vs. South	.035
	Baylor	2007	Gun control, Non-South only	Non-fundamentalist vs. Fundamentalist	.000
	Baylor	2007	Gun control, South only	Non-fundamentalist vs. Fundamentalist	.090
	Baylor	2007	Gun control, Non-fundamentalist only	Non-South vs. South	.001
	Baylor	2007	Gun control, Fundamentalist only	Non-South vs. South	.140
	Baylor	2007	Government bailout of banks, Non-South only	Non-fundamentalist vs. Fundamentalist	.000
	Baylor	2007	Government bailout of banks, South only	Non-fundamentalist vs. Fundamentalist	.000
	Baylor	2007	Government bailout of banks, Non-fundamentalist only	Non-South vs. South	.308
	Baylor	2007	Government bailout of banks, Fundamentalist only	Non-South vs. South	.000
	Baylor	2007	Dated another race, Non-South only	Non-fundamentalist vs. Fundamentalist	.013
	Baylor	2007	Dated another race, South only	Non-fundamentalist vs. Fundamentalist	.000
	Baylor	2007	Dated another race, Non-fundamentalist only	Non-South vs. South	.266
	Baylor	2007	Dated another race, Fundamentalist only	Non-South vs. South	.010
	Baylor	2007	Trust immigrants, Non-South only	Non-fundamentalist vs. Fundamentalist	.309

	Source	Year	Description	Comparison	p
	Baylor	2007	Trust immigrants, South only	Non-fundamentalist vs. Fundamentalist	.037
	Baylor	2007	Trust immigrants, Non-fundamentalist only	Non-South vs. South	.323
	Baylor	2007	Trust immigrants, Fundamentalist only	Non-South vs. South	.003
	Baylor	2010	Men better suited for politics, Non-South only	Non-fundamentalist vs. Fundamentalist	.000
	Baylor	2010	Men better suited for politics, South only	Non-fundamentalist vs. Fundamentalist	.000
	Baylor	2010	Men better suited for politics, Non-fundamentalist only	Non-South vs. South	.039
	Baylor	2010	Men better suited for politics, Fundamentalist only	Non-South vs. South	.012
Figure 9.2	Blair	2012	Healthcare reform, Non-southern only	Non-fundamentalist vs. Fundamentalist	.000
	Blair	2012	Healthcare reform, Southern only	Non-fundamentalist vs. Fundamentalist	.000
	Blair	2012	Healthcare reform, Non-fundamentalist only	Non-southern vs. Southern	.000
	Blair	2012	Healthcare reform, Fundamentalist only	Non-southern vs. Southern	.006
Figure 9.3	Blair	2012	Christian to be American, Non-southern only	Non-fundamentalist vs. Fundamentalist	.000
	Blair	2012	Christian to be American, Southern only	Non-fundamentalist vs. Fundamentalist	.000
	Blair	2012	Christian to be American, Non-fundamentalist only	Non-southern vs. Southern	.000
	Blair	2012	Christian to be American, Fundamentalist only	Non-southern vs. Southern	.000
Table 9.2	Baylor	2007	Morality of war, Non-South only	Non-fundamentalist vs. Fundamentalist	.000
	Baylor	2007	Morality of war, South only	Non-fundamentalist vs. Fundamentalist	.000
	Baylor	2007	Morality of war, Non-fundamentalist only	Non-South vs. South	.151
	Baylor	2007	Morality of war, Fundamentalist only	Non-South vs. South	.007
	Baylor	2007	Christian values, Non-South only	Non-fundamentalist vs. Fundamentalist	.000
	Baylor	2007	Christian values, South only	Non-fundamentalist vs. Fundamentalist	.000
	Baylor	2007	Christian values, Non-fundamentalist only	Non-South vs. South	.030
	Baylor	2007	Christian values, Fundamentalist only	Non-South vs. South	.039
	Baylor	2007	Christian nation, Non-South only	Non-fundamentalist vs. Fundamentalist	.000
	Baylor	2007	Christian nation, South only	Non-fundamentalist vs. Fundamentalist	.000

Table 9.2 (Cont.)				
Baylor	2007	Christian nation, Non-fundamentalist only	Non-South vs. South	.176
Baylor	2007	Christian nation, Fundamentalist only	Non-South vs. South	.001
Baylor	2007	Terrorism, Non-South only	Non-fundamentalist vs. Fundamentalist	.000
Baylor	2007	Terrorism, South only	Non-fundamentalist vs. Fundamentalist	.000
Baylor	2007	Terrorism, Non-fundamentalist only	Non-South vs. South	.438
Baylor	2007	Terrorism, Fundamentalist only	Non-South vs. South	.001
Baylor	2007	Iraq War, Non-South only	Non-fundamentalist vs. Fundamentalist	.000
Baylor	2007	Iraq War, South only	Non-fundamentalist vs. Fundamentalist	.000
Baylor	2007	Iraq War, Non-fundamentalist only	Non-South vs. South	.002
Baylor	2007	Iraq War, Fundamentalist only	Non-South vs. South	.032
Baylor	2010	Media portrayal of Muslims, Non-South only	Non-fundamentalist vs. Fundamentalist	.002
Baylor	2010	Media portrayal of Muslims, South only	Non-fundamentalist vs. Fundamentalist	.000
Baylor	2010	Media portrayal of Muslims, Non-fundamentalist only	Non-South vs. South	.224
Baylor	2010	Media portrayal of Muslims, Fundamentalist only	Non-South vs. South	.001
Blair	2010	Obama's handling of terrorism, Non-southern only	Non-fundamentalist vs. Fundamentalist	.000
Blair	2010	Obama's handling of terrorism, Southern only	Non-fundamentalist vs. Fundamentalist	.002
Blair	2010	Obama's handling of terrorism, Non-fundamentalist only	Non-southern vs. Southern	.008
Blair	2010	Obama's handling of terrorism, Fundamentalist only	Non-southern vs. Southern	.025
Blair	2010	Obama's handling of Afghanistan, Non-southern only	Non-fundamentalist vs. Fundamentalist	.030
Blair	2010	Obama's handling of Afghanistan, Southern only	Non-fundamentalist vs. Fundamentalist	.025
Blair	2010	Obama's handling of Afghanistan, Non-fundamentalist only	Non-southern vs. Southern	.069
Blair	2010	Obama's handling of Afghanistan, Fundamentalist only	Non-southern vs. Southern	.050
Blair	2010	Obama's handling of Iraq, Non-southern only	Non-fundamentalist vs. Fundamentalist	.000
Blair	2010	Obama's handling of Iraq, Southern only	Non-fundamentalist vs. Fundamentalist	.002
Blair	2010	Obama's handling of Iraq, Non-fundamentalist only	Non-southern vs. Southern	.013

Figure 9.4	Blair	2010	Obama's handling of Iraq, Fundamentalist only	Non-southern vs. Southern	.039
	Blair	2016	Global warming, Non-southern only	Non-fundamentalist vs. Fundamentalist	.000
	Blair	2016	Global warming, Southern only	Non-fundamentalist vs. Fundamentalist	.000
	Blair	2016	Global warming, Non-fundamentalist only	Non-southern vs. Southern	.001
	Blair	2016	Global warming, Fundamentalist only	Non-southern vs. Southern	.214
Figure 9.5	Blair	2016	Mexico wall, Non-southern only	Non-fundamentalist vs. Fundamentalist	.000
	Blair	2016	Mexico wall, Southern only	Non-fundamentalist vs. Fundamentalist	.000
	Blair	2016	Mexico wall, Non-fundamentalist only	Non-southern vs. Southern	.005
	Blair	2016	Mexico wall, Fundamentalist only	Non-southern vs. Southern	.000
Figure 9.6	Blair	2016	Ban semi-automatic weapons, Non-southern only	Non-fundamentalist vs. Fundamentalist	.000
	Blair	2016	Ban semi-automatic weapons, Southern only	Non-fundamentalist vs. Fundamentalist	.005
	Blair	2016	Ban semi-automatic weapons, Non-fundamentalist only	Non-southern vs. Southern	.000
	Blair	2016	Ban semi-automatic weapons, Fundamentalist only	Non-southern vs. Southern	.005
Figure 9.7	Blair	2016	Syria, Non-southern only	Non-fundamentalist vs. Fundamentalist	.000
	Blair	2016	Syria, Southern only	Non-fundamentalist vs. Fundamentalist	.000
	Blair	2016	Syria, Non-fundamentalist only	Non-southern vs. Southern	.257
	Blair	2016	Syria, Fundamentalist only	Non-southern vs. Southern	.014
Figure 9.8	Blair	2016	Trump's religion, Non-southern only	Non-fundamentalist vs. Fundamentalist	.000
	Blair	2016	Trump's religion, Southern	Non-fundamentalist vs. Fundamentalist	.000
	Blair	2016	Trump's religion, Non-fundamentalist only	Non-southern vs. Southern	.186
	Blair	2016	Trump's religion, Fundamentalist only	Non-southern vs. Southern	.013
Figure 9.9	Blair	2012	Christian to be American	See Figure 9.3	
	Blair	2012	General Election vote for Romney	See Figure 8.3B	
	Blair	2016	Christian to be American, Non-southern only	Non-fundamentalist vs. Fundamentalist	.000
	Blair	2016	Christian to be American, Southern only	Non-fundamentalist vs. Fundamentalist	.000

Figure/Table	Source	Year	Variable	Comparison Groups	p <=
	Blair	2016	Christian to be American, Non-fundamentalist only	Non-southern vs. Southern	.000
	Blair	2016	Christian to be American, Fundamentalist only	Non-southern vs. Southern	.000
	Blair	2016	General Election vote for Trump	See Figure 8.5B	

CONCLUSION

Figure/Table	Source	Year	Variable	Comparison Groups	p <=
Figure C.1A & Figure C.1B	Blair	2016	Racial Resentment only	Non-southern vs. Southern	.006
	Blair	2016	Modern Sexism only	Non-southern vs. Southern	.432
	Blair	2016	Christian Fundamentalism only	Non-southern vs. Southern	.001
	Blair	2016	Racial Resentment and Modern Sexism only	Non-southern vs. Southern	.159
	Blair	2016	Modern Sexism and Christian Fundamentalism only	Non-southern vs. Southern	.301
	Blair	2016	Christian Fundamentalism and Racial Resentment only	Non-southern vs. Southern	.111
	Blair	2016	Racial Resentment, Modern Sexism, and Christian Fundamentalism only	Non-southern vs. Southern	.000
Figure C.2	Blair	2016	Party identification	Above vs. Below CF scale	.000
	Blair	2016	Party identification	Above vs. Below RR scale	.000
	Blair	2016	Party identification	Above vs. Below MS scale	.000
	Blair	2016	Party identification	Above vs. Below CF & RR scales	.000
	Blair	2016	Party identification	Above vs. Below CF & MS scales	.000
	Blair	2016	Party identification	Above vs. Below MS & RR scales	.000
	Blair	2016	Party identification	Above vs. Below CF & RR & MS scales	.000
Table C.1	Blair	2016	Combinations of Above, Neutral, and Below the Modern Sexism, Racial Resentment, and Christian Fundamentalism scales		
	Blair	2016	MS (above) RR (above) CF (above)	Non-South vs. South	.000
	Blair	2016	MS (neutral) RR (above) CF (above)	Non-South vs. South	.002
	Blair	2016	MS (above) RR (above) CF (neutral)	Non-South vs. South	.024

Table C.1 (Cont.)					
Blair	2016	MS (above) RR (neutral) CF (above)	Non-South vs. South	.022
Blair	2016	MS (below) RR (above) CF (above)	Non-South vs. South	.059
Blair	2016	MS (neutral) RR (above) CF (neutral)	Non-South vs. South	.176
Blair	2016	MS (neutral) RR (neutral) CF (above)	Non-South vs. South	.148
Blair	2016	MS (above) RR (above) CF (below)	Non-South vs. South	.341
Blair	2016	MS (above) RR (neutral) CF (neutral)****	Non-South vs. South	N/A
Blair	2016	MS (above) RR (below) CF (above)	Non-South vs. South	.017
Blair	2016	MS (below) RR (above) CF (neutral)	Non-South vs. South	.010
Blair	2016	MS (neutral) RR (above) CF (above)	Non-South vs. South	.008
Blair	2016	MS (neutral) RR (above) CF (below)	Non-South vs. South	.366
Blair	2016	MS (neutral) RR (neutral) CF (neutral)****	Non-South vs. South	N/A
Blair	2016	MS (neutral) RR (below) CF (above)	Non-South vs. South	.079
Blair	2016	MS (above) RR (neutral) CF (below)	Non-South vs. South	.271
Blair	2016	MS (above) RR (below) CF (neutral)	Non-South vs. South	.149
Blair	2016	MS (below) RR (above) CF (below)	Non-South vs. South	.021
Blair	2016	MS (below) RR (neutral) CF (neutral)****	Non-South vs. South	N/A
Blair	2016	MS (below) RR (below) CF (above)	Non-South vs. South	.353
Blair	2016	MS (neutral) RR (below) CF (below)	Non-South vs. South	.223
Blair	2016	MS (neutral) RR (below) CF (neutral)****	Non-South vs. South	N/A
Blair	2016	MS (above) RR (below) CF (below)	Non-South vs. South	.289
Blair	2016	MS (below) RR (neutral) CF (below)	Non-South vs. South	.085
Blair	2016	MS (below) RR (below) CF (neutral)	Non-South vs. South	.481
Blair	2016	MS (neutral) RR (below) CF (below)	Non-South vs. South	.040
Blair	2016	MS (below) RR (below) CF (below)	Non-South vs. South	.000

Table C.1 (Cont.)					
	Blair	2016	MS (above) RR (above) CF (above)	Non-southern vs. Southern	.000
	Blair	2016	MS (neutral) RR (above) CF (above)	Non-southern vs. Southern	.000
	Blair	2016	MS (above) RR (above) CF (neutral)	Non-southern vs. Southern	.003
	Blair	2016	MS (above) RR (neutral) CF (above)	Non-southern vs. Southern	.008
	Blair	2016	MS (below) RR (above) CF (above)	Non-southern vs. Southern	.000
	Blair	2016	MS (neutral) RR (above) CF (neutral)	Non-southern vs. Southern	.031
	Blair	2016	MS (neutral) RR (neutral) CF (above)	Non-southern vs. Southern	.131
	Blair	2016	MS (above) RR (above) CF (below)	Non-southern vs. Southern	.270
	Blair	2016	MS (above) RR (neutral) CF (neutral)*****	Non-southern vs. Southern	N/A
	Blair	2016	MS (above) RR (below) CF (above)*****	Non-southern vs. Southern	N/A
	Blair	2016	MS (below) RR (above) CF (neutral)	Non-southern vs. Southern	.163
	Blair	2016	MS (below) RR (neutral) CF (above)	Non-southern vs. Southern	.000
	Blair	2016	MS (neutral) RR (above) CF (below)	Non-southern vs. Southern	.011
	Blair	2016	MS (neutral) RR (neutral) CF (neutral)*****	Non-southern vs. Southern	N/A
	Blair	2016	MS (neutral) RR (below) CF (above)*****	Non-southern vs. Southern	N/A
	Blair	2016	MS (above) RR (neutral) CF (below)	Non-southern vs. Southern	.055
	Blair	2016	MS (above) RR (below) CF (neutral)*****	Non-southern vs. Southern	N/A
	Blair	2016	MS (below) RR (above) CF (below)	Non-southern vs. Southern	.433
	Blair	2016	MS (below) RR (neutral) CF (neutral)*****	Non-southern vs. Southern	N/A
	Blair	2016	MS (below) RR (below) CF (above)	Non-southern vs. Southern	.081
	Blair	2016	MS (neutral) RR (neutral) CF (below)	Non-southern vs. Southern	.018
	Blair	2016	MS (neutral) RR (below) CF (neutral)*****	Non-southern vs. Southern	N/A
	Blair	2016	MS (above) RR (below) CF (below)	Non-southern vs. Southern	.043

	Blair	2016	MS (below) RR (neutral) CF (below)	Non-southern vs. Southern	.000
	Blair	2016	MS (below) RR (below) CF (neutral)	Non-southern vs. Southern	.118
	Blair	2016	MS (neutral) RR (below) CF (below)	Non-southern vs. Southern	.020
	Blair	2016	MS (below) RR (below) CF (below)	Non-southern vs. Southern	.000
Figure C.4	Blair	2016	Long Southern Strategy Scale	Non-South vs. South	.000
	Blair	2016	Long Southern Strategy Scale	Party identification—3 categories	.000
	Blair	2016	Long Southern Strategy Scale	Non-South Republican vs South Republican	.000
	Blair	2016	Long Southern Strategy Scale	Non-southern Republican vs. Southern Republican	.000
	Blair	2016	Long Southern Strategy Scale	Trump voters vs. Non-Trump voters	.000
Table C.2	Blair	2016	Vote for Trump (model)	Significance tests included in table	

* No southern women in this sample voted for Stein in the 2016 General Election.

** No southern, non-married women in this sample voted "other" in the 2016 General Election.

*** All southern fundamentalists who identify as Republican in this sample voted for Romney in the 2012 General Election.

**** No Non-South and/or South respondents fell into this category.

***** Non Non-southern and/or Southern respondents fell into this category.

Notes

INTRODUCTION

1. Glen Feldman, "Introduction: Has the South Become Republican," in *Painting Dixie Red: When, Where, Why, and How the South Became Republican*, ed. Glen Feldman (Gainesville: University Press of Florida, 2011), 5.

2. Lillian Smith, *Killers of the Dream* (New York: W. W. Norton & Company, Inc., 1949), 192.

3. V. O. Key Jr. *Southern Politics in State and Nation* (New York: Alfred A. Knopf, 1949), 11, 5.

4. Barry Goldwater, quoted in: D. Sunshine Hillygus and Todd Shields, *The Persuadable Voter: Wedge Issues in Presidential Campaigns* (Princeton: Princeton University Press, 2009), 117.

5. Rebecca Miller Davis, "Dixiecrats, Dissenting Delegates, and the Dying Democratic Party: Mississippi's Right Turn from Roosevelt to Johnson," in *Nation within a Nation: The American South and the Federal Government*, ed. Glen Feldman (Gainesville: University Press of Florida, 2014), 135.

6. Matthew W. Hughey and Gregory S. Parks, *The Wrongs of the Right: Language, Race, and the Republican Party in the Age of Obama* (New York: New York University Press, 2014), 24.

7. James K. Martin, quoted in: Walter Dean Burnham, "The Alabama Senatorial Election of 1962: Return of Inter-Party Competition," *The Journal of Politics* 26, no. 4 (1964): 810.

8. Burnham, "The Alabama Senatorial Election of 1962," 829.

9. Charles Mohr, "Goldwater Links the Welfare State to Rise in Crime," *New York Times*, September 11, 1964, http://www.nytimes.com/1964/09/11/goldwater-links-the-welfare-state-to-rise-in-crime.html.

10. Jeremy D. Mayer, "LBJ Fights the White Backlash: The Racial Politics of the 1964 Presidential Campaign, Part 2," *Prologue Magazine* 33, no. 1 (2001): https://www.archives.gov/publications/prologue/2001/spring/lbj-and-white-backlash-2.html.

11. Kevin P. Phillips, *The Emerging Republican Majority* (New Rochelle: Arlington House, 1969), 225.

12. Hodding Carter III, quoted in: Davis, "Dixiecrats," 139.

13. Charles Bullock, Ronald Keith Gaddie, and Justin J. Wert. *The Rise and Fall of the VRA* (Norman: University of Oklahoma Press, 2016).

14. Reg Murphy and Hal Gulliver, *The Southern Strategy* (New York: Charles Scribner's Sons, 1971), 2.

15. See: Joseph Crespino, *Strom Thurmond's America* (New York: Macmillan, 2012).

16. Jeffrey Frank, "When Martin Luther King Jr. and Richard Nixon Were Friends," *Daily Beast*, January 21, 2013, https://www.thedailybeast.com/when-martin-luther-king-jr-and-richard-nixon-were-friends.

17. See: Yvonne Ryan, *Roy Wilkins: The Quiet Revolutionary and the NAACP* (Lexington: University Press of Kentucky, 2014).

18. Paul N. McCloskey Jr., "The Republican Conventions of 1968 and 2016," *The Blog: Huffington Post*, March 31, 2017, http://www.huffingtonpost.com/congressman-paul-n-/republican-convention-1968-2016_b_9574256.html.

19. Emily Dufton, "The War on Drugs: How President Nixon Tied Addiction to Crime," *The Atlantic*, March 26, 2012, https://www.theatlantic.com/health/archive/2012/03/the-war-on-drugs-how-president-nixon-tied-addiction-to-crime/254319/.

20. Matthew Lassiter, *Suburban Politics in the Sunbelt South* (Princeton: Princeton University Press, 2006), 237.

21. George Brown Tindall, *The Ethnic Southerners* (Baton Rouge: Louisiana State University Press, 1974), 124; see also: George Brown Tindall, *The Disruption of the Solid South* (New York: W. W. Norton & Company, Inc., 1972).

22. Hilary A. Herbert, Zebulon B. Vance, John J. Hemphill, Henry G. Turner, Samuel Pasco, Ira P. Jones, Robert Stiles, O. S. Long, William L. Wilson, George G. Vest, William M. Fishback, Ethelbert Barksdale, Charles Stewart, and B. J. Sage, *Why the Solid South? Reconstruction and Its Results* (Baltimore: R. H. Woodward & Co., 1890), 24.

23. Tindall, *The Ethnic Southerners*, 132.

24. Murphy and Gulliver, *The Southern Strategy*, 3.

25. Jacqueline Dowd Hall, "The Long Civil Rights Movement and the Political Uses of the Past," *The Journal of American History* 91, no. 4 (2005): 1253.

26. See: Kate Manne, *Down Girl: The Logic of Misogyny* (New York: Oxford University Press, 2018).

27. Earl Black and Merle Black, *The Rise of Southern Republicans* (Cambridge: Harvard University Press, 2002), 4.

28. Murphy and Gulliver, *The Southern Strategy*, 271.

29. Laura Kalman, *Right Start Rising: A New Politics, 1974–1980* (New York: W. W. Norton & Company, Inc., 2010), 179.

30. Murphy and Gulliver, *The Southern Strategy*, 272.

31. Black and Black, *The Rise of Southern Republicans*, 34.

32. Robert H. Swansbrough and David Michael Brodsky, *The South's New Politics: Realignment and Dealignment* (Columbia: University of South Carolina Press, 1988), 272.

33. Smith, *Killers of the Dream*, 16.

34. Daniel Patrick Moynihan, quoted in: Ian Haney López, *Dog Whistle Politics: How Coded Racial Appeals Have Reinvented Racism & Wrecked the Middle Class* (New York: Oxford University Press, 2014), 96.

35. Lawrence Bobo and James R. Kluegel, "Status, Ideology, and Dimensions of Whites' Racial Beliefs and Attitudes: Progress and Stagnation," in *Racial Attitudes in the 1990s: Continuity and Change*, ed. Steven A. Tuch and Jack K. Martin (New York: Praeger, 1997), 95.

36. Melanie E. L. Bush, *Everyday Forms of Whiteness: Understanding Race in a Post Racial World*, 2nd ed. (Lanham: Rowman & Littlefield Publishers, Inc., 2011), 20.

37. Glenda Gilmore, "But She Can't Find Her [V. O.] Key: Writing Gender and Race into Southern Political History," in *Taking Off the White Gloves: Southern Women and Women Historians*, ed. Michele Gillespie and Catherine Clinton (Columbia: University of Missouri Press, 1998), 126.

38. Sue Sturgis, "Institute Index: Southern Legislatures' Woman Problem," *Facing South*, September 18, 2015, http://mail.southernstudies.org/2015/09/institute-index-southern-legislatures-woman-proble.html.

39. See: Marjorie J. Spruill, "Gender and America's Right Turn," in *Rightward Bound: Making America Conservative in the 1970s*, ed. Bruce J. Schulman and Julian E. Zelizer (Cambridge: Harvard University Press, 2008), 82.

40. Marjorie Spruill, *Divided We Stand: Women's Rights, Family Values, and the Polarization of American Politics* (New York: Bloomsbury, 2017), 65.

41. Spruill, *Divided We Stand*, 66.

42. Donald T. Critchlow, *The Conservative Ascendancy: How the Republican Right Rose to Power in Modern America*, 2nd rev. ed. (Lawrence: University Press of Kansas, 2011), 161.

43. Daniel K. Williams, "Voting for God and the GOP: The Role of Evangelical Religion in the Emergence of the Republican South," in *Painting Dixie Red: When, Where, Why, and How the South Became Republican*, ed. Glenn Feldman (Gainesville: University Press of Florida, 2011), 27.

44. See: Karen L. Cox, *Dixie's Daughters: The United Daughters of the Confederacy and the Preservation of Confederate Culture* (Gainesville: University Press of Florida, 2003); Joseph Crespino, "Civil Rights and the Religious Right," in *Rightward Bound: Making America Conservative in the 1970s*, ed. Bruce J. Schulman and Julian E. Zelizer (Cambridge: Harvard University Press, 2008), 90–105.

45. Catherine E. Rymph, *Republican Women: Feminism and Conservatism from Suffrage through the Rise of the New Right* (Chapel Hill: University of North Carolina Press, 2006), 214.

46. Kiera V. Williams, *Gendered Politics in the Modern South: The Susan Smith Case and the Rise of New Sexism* (Baton Rouge: Louisiana State University Press, 2012), 3.

47. Critchlow, *The Conservative Ascendancy*, 164.

48. See: Richard E. Nisbett and Dov Cohen, *Culture of Honor: The Psychology of Violence in the South* (Boulder: Westview Press, 1996).

49. Tanya Melich, *The Republican War Against Women: An Insider's Report from Behind the Lines* (New York: Bantam Books, 1996), 16.

50. Molly Dragiewicz, *Equality with a Vengeance: Men's Rights Groups, Battered Women, and Antifeminist Backlash* (Boston: Northeastern University Press, 2011), 15.

51. Spruill, *Divided We Stand*, 251.

52. Robert Menzies, "Virtual Backlash: Representations of Men's 'Rights' and Feminist 'Wrongs' in Cyberspace," in *Reaction and Resistance: Feminism, Law, and Social Change*, ed. Dorothy E. Chunn, Susan B. Boyd, and Hester Lessard (Vancouver: University of British Columbia Press, 2007), 91.

53. Michael Kimmel, *Manhood in American: A Cultural History*, 2nd ed. (New York: Oxford University Press, 2006), 247.

54. Trent Watts, "Introduction: Telling White Men's Stories," in *White Masculinity in the Recent South*, ed. Trent Watts (Baton Rouge: Louisiana State University Press, 2008), 20.

55. Dan Schill, *Stagecraft and Statecraft: Advance and Media Events in Political Communication* (Lanham: Lexington Books, 2009), 65–66.

56. Hadley Meares, "Ronald Reagan's Other White House," *LA Curbed*, June 7, 2016, https://la.curbed.com/2016/6/7/11843562/ronald-reagan-western-white-house.

57. Ann McFeatters, "Watch Out for 'Coded Sexism' if Hillary Clinton Runs," *The Seattle Times*, April 2, 2015, http://www.seattletimes.com/opinion/editorials/watch-out-for-coded-sexism-if-hillary-clinton-runs/.

58. Phyllis Schlafly, *A Choice, Not an Echo: The Inside Story of How American Presidents Are Made* (Alton: Pere Marquette Press, 1964).

59. Matthew Levendusky, *The Partisan Sort: How Liberals Became Democrats and Conservatives Became Republicans* (Chicago: University of Chicago Press, 2009), 14, 63.

60. Alexander P. Lamis, "The Two-Party South: From the 1960s to the 1990s," in *Southern Politics in the 1990s*, ed. Alexander P. Lamis (Baton Rouge: Louisiana State University Press, 1999), 31.

61. Trent Lott, "'Jefferson Davis's Descendants' . . . Are Becoming Involved with the Republican Party': Southern Partisan Interview with Trent Lott (1984)," in *Debating the American Conservative Movement: 1945–Present*, ed. Donald T. Critchlow and Nancy MacLean (Lanham: Rowman & Littlefield Publishers, Inc., 2009), 201.

62. See: Ruel W. Tyson Jr., James L. Peacock, and Daniel Patterson, ed., *Diversities of Gifts: Field Studies in Southern Religion* (Urbana: University of Illinois Press, 1988).

63. See: Peter L. Berger. *The Sacred Canopy: Elements of a Sociological Theory of Religion* (Garden City: Doubleday & Company, Inc., 1967).

64. Ted Jelen, "Sources of Political Intolerance: The Case of the American South," in *Contemporary Southern Political Attitudes and Behaviors: Studies and Essays*, ed. Laurence W. Moreland, Tod A. Baker, and Robert P. Steed (New York: Praeger, 1982), 86.

65. Jelen, "Sources of Political Intolerance," 81.

66. Ted G. Jelen and Clyde Wilcox, ed., *Religion and Politics in Comparative Perspective: The One, the Few, and the Many* (New York: Cambridge University Press, 2002), 287.

67. See: David T. Morgan, *The New Crusades, The New Holy Land: Conflict in the Southern Baptists Convention 1969–1991* (Tuscaloosa: University of Alabama Press, 1996), 155–157.

68. Steve Bruce, *The Rise and Fall of the New Christian Right: Conservative Protestant Politics in America 1978–1988* (New York: Oxford University Press, 1988), 164.

69. Kevin Kruse, *One Nation Under God: How Corporate America Invented Christian America* (New York: Basic Books, 2015), 73–74.

70. Kruse, *One Nation Under God*, 249.

71. James Davison Hunter, *American Evangelicalism: Conservative Religion and the Quandary of Modernity* (New Brunswick: Rutgers University Press, 1983), 55.

72. Ted G. Jelen, "Culture Wars and the Party System: Religion and Realignment, 1972–1993," in *Culture Wars in American Politics: Critical Reviews of a Popular Myth*, ed. Rhys H. Williams (New York: Aldine de Gruyter, 1997), 151.

73. Bryan F. Le Beau, "The Political Mobilization of the New Christian Right," n.d., http://are.as.wvu.edu/lebeau1.htm.

74. Steve Bruce, "Zealot Politics and Democracy: The Case of the New Christian Right," *Political Studies* 48, no. 2 (2000): 273.

75. Paul A. Djupe and J. Tobin Grant, "Religious Institutions and Political Participation in America," *Journal for the Scientific Study of Religion* 40, no. 2 (2001): 304; Sidney Verba, Kay Lehman Schlozman, and Henry E. Brady, *Voice and Equality: Civic Volunteerism in American Politics* (Cambridge: Harvard University Press, 1995); Sidney Verba, Kay Lehman Schlozman, Henry E. Brady, and Norman H. Nie, "Race, Ethnicity and Political Resources: Participation in the United States," *British Journal of Political Science* 23, no. 4 (1993): 453–497.

76. Charles Reagan Wilson, "Preachin', Prayin', and Singin' on the Public Square," in *Religion and Public Life in the South: In the Evangelical Mode*, ed. Charles Reagan Wilson and Mark Silk (Walnut Creek: Rowman & Littlefield Publishing Group, Inc., 2005), 9–26, 23.

77. Seth Dowland, "'Family Values' and the Formation of a Christian Right Agenda," *Church History* 78, no. 3 (2009): 614.

78. John C. Green, Mark J. Rozell, and Clyde Wilcox, ed., *The Christian Right in American Politics: Marching to the Millennium* (Washington, DC: Georgetown University Press, 2003), 4–5.

79. John C. Green, James L. Guth, Corwin E. Smidt, and Lyman A. Kellstedt, *Religion and the Culture Wars: Dispatches from the Front* (Lanham: Rowman & Littlefield Publishers, Inc., 1996), 8.

80. Numan V. Bartley, quoted in: Black and Black, *The Rise of Southern Republicans*, 212.

81. Ronald Reagan, quoted in: Black and Black, *The Rise of Southern Republicans*, 212.

82. See: Dowland, "'Family Values,'" 606–631.

83. See: Karen M. Kaufmann and John R. Petrocik, "The Changing Politics of American Men: Understanding the Sources of the Gender Gap," *American Journal of Political Science* 43, no. 3 (1999): 864–887.

84. Lassiter, *Suburban Politics*, 4.

85. Smith, *Killers of the Dream*, 34.

86. Angus Campbell, Philip E. Converse, Warren E. Miller, and Donald E. Stokes, *The American Voter* (New York: Wiley, 1960).

87. Norman H. Nie, Sidney Verba, and John R. Petrocik, *The Changing American Voter* (Cambridge: Harvard University Press, 1976).

88. Edward G. Carmines and James A. Stimson, *Issue Evolution: Race and the Transformation of American Politics* (Princeton: Princeton University Press, 1989).

89. Warren E. Miller, "Party Identification, Realignment, and Party Voting: Back to the Basics," *American Political Science Review* 85, no. 2 (1991): 557–568.

90. Morris P. Fiorina with Samuel J. Abrams and Jeremy C. Pope, *Culture War? The Myth of a Polarized America*, 3rd ed. (Boston: Longman, 2011).

91. Jonathan Merritt, "Southern Baptists Call Off the Culture War," *The Atlantic*, June 16, 2018, https://www.theatlantic.com/ideas/archive/2018/06/southern-baptists-call-off-the-culture-war/563000/.

92. Black and Black, *The Rise of Southern Republicans*, 222.

93. See: Seth C. McKee, *Republican Ascendancy in Southern U.S. House Elections* (Boulder: Westview Press, 2010).

94. John A. Clark and Charles L. Prysby, ed., *Southern Political Party Activists: Patterns of Conflict and Change, 1991–2001* (Lexington: University Press of Kentucky, 2004), 2–3.

95. Richard K. Scher, *Politics in the New South: Republicanism, Race, and Leadership in the Twentieth Century*, 2nd ed. (New York: Routledge,1997), 138–140.

96. Byron E. Shafer and Richard Johnston, *The End of Southern Exceptionalism: Class, Race, and Partisan Change in the Postwar South* (Cambridge: Harvard University Press, 2006).

97. Thomas Frank, *What's the Matter with Kansas?: How Conservatives Won the Heart of America* (New York: Metropolitan Books, 2004).

98. Katherine J. Cramer, *The Politics of Resentment: Rural Consciousness in Wisconsin and the Rise of Scott Walker* (Chicago: University of Chicago Press, 2016).

99. John Egerton, *The Americanization of Dixie: The Southernization of America* (New York: Harper's Magazine Press, 1974); Peter Applebome, *Dixie Rising: How the South Is Shaping American Values, Politics, and Culture* (New York: Times Books, 1996); Darren Dochuk, *From Bible Belt to Sunbelt: Plain-Folk Religion, Grassroots Politics, and the Rise of Evangelical Conservatism* (New York: W. W. Norton & Company, Inc., 2010); Jonathan A. Cowden, "Southernization of the Nation and Nationalization of the South: Racial Conservatism, Social Welfare, and White Partisans in the United States, 1956–92," *British Journal of Political Science* 31, no. 2 (2001): 277–301.

100. See: Matthew Yglesias, "Trump Changed the Electoral Map; New Polling Shows It's Changing Back," *Vox*, June 19, 2018, https://www.vox.com/policy-and-politics/2018/6/19/17474984/trump-state-polling.

101. See: Raymond Wolfinger and Robert B. Arseneau, "Partisan Change in the South, 1952–1976," in *Political Parties: Development and Decay*, ed. Sandy Maisel and Joseph Cooper (Beverly Hills: Sage, 1978), 179–210; Paul Allen Beck, "Partisan Dealignment in the Post-War South," *American Political Science Review* 71 (1977): 477–496.

102. See: Lassiter, *Suburban Politics*.

103. For a full summary of southern realignment, see: Ronald Keith Gaddie, "Realignment," in *The Oxford Handbook of Southern Politics*, ed. Charles S. Bullock III and Mark J. Rozell (New York: Oxford University Press, 2012), 289–313.

104. Caroline Matheny Dillman, "The Sparsity of Research and Publications on Southern Women: Definitional Complexities, Methodological Problems, and Other Impediments," *Sociological Spectrum* 6 (1986): 7–29, 15.

105. Warren E. Miller and J. Merrill Shanks, *The New American Voter* (Cambridge: Harvard University Press, 1996), 141.

106. Donald Trump (@realDonaldTrump), "Ed Gillespie will turn the really bad Virginia economy #'s around, and fast. Strong on crime, he might even save our great statues/heritage!" Twitter, October 26, 2017, 8:07 am.

107. Gabriel Pogrund, "Trump Calls on Blacks to 'Honor' Republicans with Votes, Then Praises Confederate General Robert E. Lee," *Washington Post*, October 12, 2018, https://www.washingtonpost.com/politics/trump-calls-on-blacks-to-honor-him-with-votes-then-praises-confederate-general-robert-e-lee/2018/10/12/ab819a9c-ce33-11e8-a360-85875bacob1f_story.html.

108. Joseph A. Aistrup, *The Southern Strategy Revisited: Republican Top-Down Advancement in the South* (Lexington: University Press of Kentucky, 2015), 11–16.

109. See: John H. Aldrich, "Southern Parties in State and Nation," *Journal of Politics* 62, no. 3 (2000): 643–670.

110. López, *Dog Whistle Politics*, 32.

111. See: Thomas Byrne Edsall and Mary D. Edsall, *Chain Reaction: The Impact of Race, Rights, and Taxes on American Politics* (New York: W. W. Norton & Company, Inc., 1991).

112. Frank, *What's the Matter with Kansas?*, 254.

113. López, *Dog Whistle Politics*, 27.

114. Angie Maxwell, "'The Duality of the Southern Thing': A Snapshot of 'Southern' Politics in the Twenty-first Century," *Southern Cultures* (Winter 2014): 85–109; see also: Christopher A. Cooper and H. Gibbs Knotts, *The Resilience of Southern Identity: Why the South Still Matters in the Minds of Its People* (Chapel Hill: University of North Carolina Press, 2017).

115. Feldman, "Introduction: Has the South Become Republican," 3.

116. Susan Middleton-Klein, "Magnolias and Microchips: Regional Subcultural Constructions of Femininity," *Sociological Spectrum* 6 (1986): 83–107, 105.

117. George Wallace, quoted in: *George Wallace: Settin' the Woods on Fire*, directed by Daniel Mccabe and Paul Stekler (Seattle: Big House Productions and Midnight Films Inc., 2000).

118. See: Robert Penn Warren, *The Legacy of the Civil War: Meditations on the Centennial* (New York: Random House, 1961).

119. John Dollard, *Caste and Class in a Southern Town*, 2nd ed. (New York: Harper & Brothers, 1949), 315; the original version of Dollard's book was published in 1937.

120. George Wallace, quoted in: *George Wallace: Settin' the Woods on Fire*.

121. Fiorina, Abrams, and Pope, *Culture War?*, 8–9.

122. López, *Dog Whistle Politics*, 171–172; Frank, *What's the Matter with Kansas?*, 7, 260.

123. Rebecca Solnit, "The American Civil War Didn't End. And Trump Is a Confederate President," *The Guardian*, November 4, 2018, https://www.theguardian.com/commentisfree/2018/nov/04/the-american-civil-war-didnt-end-and-trump-is-a-confederate-president.

124. Christopher Ingraham, "On Confederate Monuments, the Public Stands with Trump," *Washington Post*, August 17, 2017, https://www.washingtonpost.com/news/wonk/wp/2017/08/17/on-confederate-monuments-the-public-stands-with-trump/.

125. See: John Fea, *Believe Me: The Evangelical Road to Donald Trump* (Grand Rapids: William B. Eerdmans Publishing Company, 2018).

PART I

1. George McGovern, quoted in: Ian Haney López, *Dog Whistle Politics: How Coded Racial Appeals Have Reinvented Racism & Wrecked the Middle Class* (New York: Oxford University Press, 2014), 27.

2. Joseph A. Aistrup, *The Southern Strategy Revisited: Republican Top-Down Advancement in the South* (Lexington: University Press of Kentucky, 2015), 19.

3. Earl Black and Merle Black, *The Rise of Southern Republicans* (Cambridge: Harvard University Press, 2002), 218; see also: Dan Carter, *From George Wallace to Newt Gingrich: Race in the Conservative Counterrevolution, 1963–1994* (Baton Rouge: Louisiana State University Press, 1996) and Michael Dawson, *Behind the Mule: Race and Class in African-American Politics* (Princeton: Princeton University Press, 1994).

4. Robert P. Jones, "How Trump Remixed the Republican Southern Strategy," *The Atlantic*, August 14, 2016, https://www.theatlantic.com/politics/archive/2016/08/how-trump-remixed-the-republican-southern-strategy/495719/.

5. Sean Trende, "The Case of the Missing White Voters, Revisited," *Real Clear Politics*, June 21, 2013, https://www.realclearpolitics.com/articles/2013/06/21/the_case_of_the_missing_white_voters_revisited_118893-2.html.

6. Jonathan Chait, "Donald Trump's Race War," *New York Magazine*, April 4, 2017, http://nymag.com/daily/intelligencer/2017/04/trump-is-failing-at-policy-but-winning-his-race-wars.html.

7. "Donald Trump Channels Richard Nixon in Speech about Restoring 'Law and Order,'" *Los Angeles Times*, July 11, 2016, http://www.latimes.com/politics/la-na-trailguide-updates-donald-trump-calls-himself-the-law-and-1468259597-htmlstory.html.

8. Reena Flores, "Donald Trump: Black Lives Matter Calls for Killing Police," *CBS News*, July 19, 2016, https://www.cbsnews.com/news/donald-trump-black-lives-matter-calls-for-killing-police/.

9. Michelle Ye Hee Lee, "Donald Trump's False Comments Connecting Mexican Immigrants and Crime," *Washington Post*, July 8, 2015, https://www.washingtonpost.com/news/fact-checker/wp/2015/07/08/donald-trumps-false-comments-connecting-mexican-immigrants-and-crime/.

10. Julia Jacobo, "Donald Trump Says He Will Get 'Bad Hombres' Out of the US," *ABC News*, October 19, 2016, http://abcnews.go.com/Politics/donald-trump-bad-hombres-us/story?id=42926041.

11. López, *Dog Whistle Politics*, 46.

12. Lillian Smith, *Killers of the Dream* (New York: W. W. Norton & Company, Inc., 1949), 192.

13. See: Bernard Cosman, *Five States for Goldwater: Continuity and Change in Southern Presidential Voting Patterns* (Tuscaloosa: University of Alabama Press, 1996).

14. John Powell, "The New Southern Strategy," *Berkeley Blog*, January 30, 2013, http://blogs. berkeley.edu/2013/01/30/the-new-southern-strategy/.

15. Kevin P. Phillips, *The Emerging Republican Majority* (New Rochelle: Arlington House, 1969), 286.

16. Reg Murphy and Hal Gulliver, *The Southern Strategy* (New York: Charles Scribner's Sons, 1971), 253.

17. Murphy and Gulliver, *The Southern Strategy*, 22.

18. Murphy and Gulliver, *The Southern Strategy*, 254.

19. Tom Jacobs, "How the KKK Helped Create the Solid GOP South," *Pacific Standard*, December 9, 2014, https://psmag.com/social-justice/kkk-helped-create-solid-gop-south-96090.

20. Black and Black, *The Rise of Southern Republicans*, 141.

21. George Brown Tindall, *The Ethnic Southerners* (Baton Rouge: Louisiana State University Press), 141.

22. Noel Ignatiev, *How the Irish Became White* (New York: Routledge, 1995), 214; see also: David R. Roedige, *The Wages of Whiteness: Race and the Making of the American Working Class* (New York: Verso, 1999).

23. Lee Atwater, quoted in: Rick Perlstein, "Exclusive: Lee Atwater's Infamous 1981 Interview on the Southern Strategy," *The Nation*, November 13, 2012, https://www.thenation.com/ article/exclusive-lee-atwaters-infamous-1981-interview-southern-strategy/.

24. Black and Black, *The Rise of Southern Republicans*, 6.

25. Bill O'Reilly, quoted in: Matthew W. Hughey and Gregory S. Parks, *The Wrongs of the Right: Language, Race, and the Republican Party in the Age of Obama* (New York: New York University Press, 2014), 60.

26. Martin Gilens, quoted in: Ray Haberski, "Obama and the Politics of Race in the 21st Century: On Ta-Nehisi Coates's 'Fear of a Black President,' Part I," *US Intellectual History Blog*, 2012, http://s-usih.org/2012/11/obama-and-politics-of-race-in-21st.html.

27. Fred L. Pincus, *Reverse Discrimination: Dismantling the Myth* (Boulder: Lynne Rienner Publishers, 2003), 46.

28. Jonathan Knuckey, "Racial Resentment and the Changing Partisanship of Southern Whites," *Party Politics* 11, no. 1 (2005): 17.

29. Mark Blumenthal and Ariel Edwards-Levy, "HuffPollster: Most Americans Say Race Relations Have Worsened," *Huffington Post*, December 8, 2014, http://www. huffingtonpost.com/2014/12/08/race-relations-poll_n_6287590.html.

30. David Lublin, *The Republican South: Democratization and Partisan Change* (Princeton: Princeton University Press, 2004), 143.

31. Pat Buchanan, quoted in: Oliver Willis, "Pat Buchanan Whitewashing Racist Southern Strategy He Helped Devise," *Media Matters*, July 7, 2014, https://www.mediamatters.org/ blog/2014/07/07/pat-buchanan-whitewashing-racist-southern-strat/200001.

32. Michael Perman, "The Republicans' 'Southern Strategy' Unmasked?," *UNC Press Blog*, April 30, 2010, https://uncpressblog.com/2010/04/30/southern-strategy/.

33. Donald Trump, quoted in: Howard Kurtz, "Trump's Boast: Blacks Will Like Me Better than Obama," *Fox News*, January 24, 2016, http://www.foxnews.com/politics/2016/01/ 24/trumps-boast-blacks-will-like-me-better-than-obama.html.

34. Richard Nixon, quoted in: Matthew D. Lassiter, *The Silent Majority: Suburban Politics in the Sunbelt South* (Princeton: Princeton University Press, 2006), 241.

35. Barry Goldwater, "I Sense Here a Realignment of Southern Conservative Democrats," in *Debating the American Conservative Movement: 1945–Present*, ed. Donald T. Critchlow and Nancy MacLean (Lanham: Rowman & Littlefield Publishers, Inc., 2009), 182; Goldwater's statement first appeared in 1953.

36. Mike Allen, "RNC Chief to Say It Was 'Wrong' to Exploit Racial Conflict for Votes," *Washington Post*, July 14, 2005, http://www.washingtonpost.com/archive/politics/2005/07/14/rnc-chief-to-say-it-was-wrong-to-exploit-racial-conflict-for-votes/66889840-8d59-44e1-8784-5c9b9ae85499.

CHAPTER 1

1. Ian Reifowitz, "The Republicans' Southern Strategy Still Works. Here's How Liberals Can Counter It," *Daily Kos*, May 26, 2014, http://www.dailykos.com/story/2014/05/26/1301173/-The-Republicans-Southern-strategy-still-works-Here-s-how-liberals-can-counter-it.

2. "Did Gore Hatch Horton?," *Slate*, November 1, 1999, http://www.slate.com/articles/news_and_politics/chatterbox/1999/11/did_gore_hatch_horton.html.

3. Roger Simon, "The GOP and Willie Horton: Together Again," *Politico*, May 19, 2015, http://www.politico.com/story/2015/05/jeb-bush-willie-horton-118061.

4. T. J. Raphael, "How One Political Ad Held Back a Generation of American Inmates," *PRI*, May 18, 2015, http://www.pri.org/stories/2015-05-18/what-willie-horton-wrought.

5. Glenn Firebaugh and Kenneth Davis, "Trends in Antiblack Prejudice, 1972–1984: Region and Cohort Effects," *American Journal of Sociology* 94 (1988): 251–272; Howard Schuman and Lawrence Bobo, "Survey-based Experiments on White Racial Attitudes Toward Residential Integration," *American Journal of Sociology* 94 (1988): 273–299; Steven Tuch, "Urbanism, Region, and Tolerance Revisited: The Case for Racial Prejudice," *American Sociological Review* 52 (1987): 504–510; see also: David O. Sears and Tom Jessor, "Whites' Racial Policy Attitudes: The Role of White Racism," *Social Science Quarterly* 77, no. 4 (1996): 751–759.

6. John Shelton Reed, *Surveying the South: Studies in Regional Sociology* (Columbia: University of Missouri Press, 1993).

7. Byron D'Andra Orey, "A New Racial Threat in the New South? (A Conditional) Yes," *American Review of Politics* 22 (2001): 233.

8. See: Thomas F. Pettigrew, "The Nature of Modern Racism in the United States," *Revue Internationale de Psychologie Sociale* 2, no. 3 (1989): 291–293; Donald R. Kinder and David O. Sears, "Prejudice and Politics: Symbolic Racism Versus Racial Threats to the Good Life," *Journal of Personality and Social Psychology* 40, no. 3 (1981): 414–431. Jerry Wilcox and W. Clark Roof, "Percent Black and Black-White Status Inequality: Southern Versus Non-Southern Patterns," *Social Science Quarterly* 59 (1978): 421–434; E. G. Grabb, "Social Class, Authoritarianism, and Race Contact: Recent Trends," *Sociology and Social Research* 64 (1980): 208–220; Mark A. Fossett and K. Jill Keicolt, "The Relative Size of Minority Populations and White Racial Attitudes," *Social Science Quarterly* 70, no. 4 (1989): 820–835.

9. James M. Glaser, "Back to the Black Belt: Racial Environment and White Racial Attitudes in the South," *Journal of Politics* 56, no. 1 (1984): 21–41.

10. Edward G. Carmines and James A. Stimson, *Issue Evolution: Race and the Transformation of American Politics* (Princeton: Princeton University Press, 1989).

11. Doug McAdam and Karina Kloos, "Race and the Modern GOP," *Politico*, September 24, 2014, http://www.politico.com/magazine/story/2014/09/race-and-the-

modern-gop-111218; see also: Doug McAdam and Karina Kloos, *Deeply Divided: Racial Politics and Social Movements in Post-War America* (New York: Oxford University Press, 2014).

12. Laurie Fuller, "Where's My Body and What's on It? Theoretical Twists on Notions of Race and Sexuality," in *Dismantling White Privilege: Pedagogy, Politics, and Whiteness*, ed. Nelson N. Rodriguez and Leila E. Villaverde (New York: Peter Lang, 2000), 81.

13. Ruth Frankenberg, *The Social Construction of Whiteness: White Women, Race Matters* (Minneapolis: University of Minnesota Press, 1993), 1. See also: Nancy Hartstock, "The Feminist Standpoint: Developing the Ground for a Specifically Feminist Historical Materialism," in *Discovering Reality*, ed. Sandra Harding and Merrill B. Hintikka (Dordrecht: D. Riedel, 1983), 283–310.

14. See: Angie Maxwell, *The Indicted South: Public Criticism, Southern Inferiority, and the Politics of Whiteness* (Chapel Hill: University of North Carolina Press, 2014).

15. "Partisan Polarization Surges in Bush, Obama Years: Trends in American Values: 1987–2012," *Pew Research Center: US Politics & Policy*, June 4, 2012, http://www.people-press.org/2012/06/04/partisan-polarization-surges-in-bush-obama-years/.

16. Emily Flitter and Chris Kahn, "Exclusive: Trump Voters More Likely to View Blacks Negatively—Reuters/Ipsos Poll," *Reuters*, June 28, 2016, https://www.reuters.com/article/us-usa-election-race/exclusive-trump-supporters-more-likely-to-view-blacks-negatively-reuters-ipsos-poll-idUSKCN0ZE2SW.

17. Benedict Anderson, *Imagined Communities: Reflections on the Origin and Spread of Nationalism* (New York: Verso, 1998).

18. "Civil War at 150: Still Relevant, Still Divisive," *Pew Research Center: US Politics & Policy*, April 8, 2014, http://www.people-press.org/2011/04/08/civil-war-at-150-still-relevant-still-divisive/.

19. Maxwell, *The Indicted South*, 26.

20. Tony Greenwald, Mahzarin Banaji, and Brian Nosek, "Project Implicit," 1998, https://implicit.harvard.edu/implicit/aboutus.html; Tim Donovan, "White People Are More Racist Than They Realize," *Salon*, January 16, 2015, http://www.salon.com/2015/01/16/white_people_are_more_racist_than_they_realize_partner/.

21. Tessa M. Ditonto, Richard R. Lau, and David O. Sears, "AMPing Racial Attitudes: Comparing the Power of Explicit and Implicit Racism Measures in 2008," *Political Psychology* 34, no. 4 (2013): 487–510.

22. Beth Schwartzapfel and Bill Keller, "Willie Horton Revisited," *The Marshal Project*, May 13, 2015, https://www.themarshallproject.org/2015/05/13/willie-horton-revisited.

23. Michael Tesler, "The Return of Old-Fashioned Racism to White Americans' Partisan Preferences in the Early Obama Era," *Journal of Politics* 75, no. 1 (2013): 110–123.

24. Southern Poverty Law Center, "Active Ku Klux Klan Groups," *SPLC Center*, n.d., http://www.splcenter.org/get-informed/intelligence-files/ideology/ku-klux-klan/active_hate_groups; for a map, see: News One Staff, "How Many KKK Chapters Are in Your Area?," *NewsOne*, June 19, 2014, http://newsone.com/3062375/text-news-to-71007-get-breaking-news-daily/.

25. Frances Lee Ansley, "White Supremacy (And What We Should Do About It)," in *Critical White Studies: Looking Behind the Mirror*, ed. Richard Delgado and Jean Stefancic (Philadelphia: Temple University Press, 1997), 592. The chapter is excerpted from: Frances Lee Ansley, "Stirring the Ashes: Race, Class, and the Future of Civil Rights Scholarship," *Cornell Law Review* 74 (1989).

26. David Gillborn, "Rethinking White Supremacy: Who Counts in 'WhiteWorld?,'" *Ethnicities* 6, no. 3 (2006): 335.

27. "Did Gore Hatch Horton?," *Slate*.

28. Richard Nixon, "Accepting the Republican Nomination," *PBS: American Experience*, August 8, 1968, http://www.pbs.org/wgbh/americanexperience/features/primary-resources/nixon-accept68/.

29. Josh Adams and Vincent J. Roscigno, "White Supremacists, Oppositional Culture, and the World Wide Web," *Social Forces* 84, no. 2 (2005): 759–778.

30. Michael Kimmel, *Angry White Men: American Masculinity at the End of an Era* (New York: Nation Books, 2013).

31. Desmond S. King and Stephen G. N. Tuck, "De-centering the South: America's Nationwide White Supremacist Order After Reconstruction," *Past & Present* 194 (2007): 213–254.

32. Thomas Nelson Page, quoted in: James W. Vander Zanden, "The Ideology of White Supremacy," *Journal of the History of Ideas* 20, no. 3 (1959): 393–394.

33. Sue Sturgis, "NAACP Links Proposed NC Voting Changes to Historical White Supremacist Politics," *Facing South*, July 24, 2013, http://www.southernstudies.org/2013/07/naacp-links-proposed-nc-voting-changes-to-historic.html.

34. Shaun King, "Mississippi Judge Gets Indicted for Assaulting and Calling a Disabled African American a N*gger," *Daily Kos*, February 16, 2015, http://www.dailykos.com/story/2015/02/16/1364750/-A-Mississippi-Judge-gets-indicted-for-assaulting-and-calling-a-disabled-African-American-a-nigger.

35. David Ferguson, "Texas Students Flash 'White Power' Signs During Basketball Game Against Rival High School," *Raw Story*, February 17, 2015, http://www.rawstory.com/2015/02/texas-students-flash-white-power-signs-during-basketball-game-against-mostly-black-high-school/.

36. Chuck Thompson, "What Paula Deen Could Teach John Roberts," *New Republic*, July 1, 2013, http://www.newrepublic.com/article/113708/paula-deen-melts-down-supreme-court-declares-southern-racism-dead.

37. Don Terry, "A Weekend in the Fairytale Kingdom of Post-Racial America," *Southern Poverty Law Center*, March 9, 2015, http://www.splcenter.org/blog/2015/03/09/a-weekend-in-the-fairytale-kingdom-of-post-racial-america/.

38. "Knoxville Police Remove White Supremacy Banners from I-640 Overpass," *WATE.COM*, December 30, 2013), http://www.wate.com/story/24327762/knoxville-police-remove-white-supremacist-banner-from-i-640-overpass.

39. Matt Mershon, "Controversial 'White Pride' Billboards Taken Down in Harrison," *KATV*, September 19, 2017, http://katv.com/news/local/controversial-billboards-taken-down-in-harrison.

40. Bret Schulte, "The Alt-Right of the Ozarks," *Slate*, April 3, 2017, http://www.slate.com/articles/news_and_politics/politics/2017/04/what_harrison_arkansas_fight_with_the_kkk_says_about_the_alt_right.html; see also: Matthew Rowza, "5 Reason 'White Pride' Is Always Racist," *Salon*, January 9, 2015, http://www.salon.com/2015/01/09/5_reasons_white_pride_is_always_racist_partner/.

41. "Mapping Racist Tweets in Response to President Obama's Re-election," *Floating-Sheep*, November 8, 2012, http://www.floatingsheep.org/2012/11/mapping-racist-tweets-in-response-to.html; see also: Josh Wolford, "Alabama & Mississippi Win the Most-Racist-on-Twitter Award Surrounding the Election," *WebProNews*, November 8, 2012, http://www.webpronews.com/alabama-mississippi-win-the-most-racist-on-twitter-award-following-the-election-2012-11.

42. Leonie Huddy, David O. Sears, and Jack Levy, ed., *The Oxford Handbook of Political Psychology* (New York: Oxford University Press, 2013).

43. Frankenberg, *The Social Construction of Whiteness*, 2.

44. W. J. Cash, *The Mind of the South*, rev. ed. (New York: Vintage Books, 1969), 51; Cash's book was originally published in 1941.

45. James Weldon Johnson, quoted in: George Brown Tindall, *The Ethnic Southerners* (Baton Rouge: Louisiana State University Press), 60.

46. "Lynching in America: Confronting the Legacy of Racial Terror," *Equal Justice Initiative*, 2015, http://www.eji.org/reports/lynching-in-america.

47. E. M. Beck and Stewart E. Tolnay, "The Killing Fields of the Deep South: The Market for Cotton and the Lynching of Blacks, 1882–1930," *American Sociological Review* 55, no. 4 (1990): 526; see also: Stewart E. Tolnay and E. M. Beck, *A Festival of Violence: An Analysis of Southern Lynchings, 1882–1930* (Champaign: University of Illinois Press, 1995).

48. Lillian Smith, *Killers of the Dream* (New York: W. W. Norton & Company, Inc., 1949), 176.

49. Bill D. Moyers, *Moyers on America: A Journalist and His Times*, 2nd ed. (New York: Anchor Books, 2005), 194.

50. Smith, *Killers of the Dream*, 176.

51. Ronald Reagan, quoted in: Schwartzapfel and Keller, "Willie Horton Revisited."

52. Schwartzapfel and Keller, "Willie Horton Revisited."

53. Schwartzapfel and Keller, "Willie Horton Revisited."

54. Schwartzapfel and Keller, "Willie Horton Revisited."

55. "Did Gore Hatch Horton?," *Slate*.

56. Derald Wing Sue, "The Invisible Whiteness of Being: Whiteness, White Supremacy, White Privilege, and Racism," in *Addressing Racism: Facilitating Cultural*, ed. Madonna G. Constantine and Derald Wing Sue (Hoboken: John Wiley & Sons, Inc., 2006), 27.

57. John Dollard, *Caste and Class in a Southern Town*, 2nd ed. (New York: Harper & Brothers, 1949), 316; the original version of Dollard's book was published in 1937.

58. Donald R. Kinder and Cindy D. Kam, *Us Against Them: Ethnocentric Foundations of American Opinion* (Chicago: University of Chicago Press, 2009), 1; see also: Cindy D. Kam and Donald R. Kinder, "Ethnocentrism as a Short-Term Force in the 2008 Presidential Election," *American Journal of Political Science* 56 (2012): 326–340.

59. Kinder and Kam, *Us Against Them*, 31.

60. Cheryl R. Kaiser, Benjamin J. Drury, Kerry E. Spalding, Sapna Cheryan, and Laurie T. O'Brien, "The Ironic Consequences of Obama's Election: Decreased Support for Social Justice," *Journal of Experimental Social Psychology* 45 (2009): 556–559.

61. Ward Kay and Jeremy Mayer, "Immigration in the 2008 Virginia Presidential Election: A Cultural Issue Remains Puissant Despite an Economic Crisis," *The Social Science Journal* 47 (2010): 646–658.

62. Kinder and Kam, *Us Against Them*, 327.

63. Kasomo Daniel, "Historical Manifestation of Ethnocentrism and Its Challenges Today," *International Journal of Applied Sociology* 1, no. 1 (2011): 8–14.

64. Brian Bizumic and John Duckitt, "What Is and Is Not Ethnocentrism? A Conceptual Analysis and Political Implications," *Political Psychology* 33, no. 6 (2012): 887–909.

65. Byron E. Shafer and Richard Johnston, *The End of Southern Exceptionalism: Class, Race, and Partisan Change in the Postwar South* (Cambridge: Harvard University Press, 2006), 127.

66. "Workers Called 'Lazy, Stupid Africans' Awarded $15 Million in Discrimination Suit," *NewsOne*, February 22, 2012, http://newsone.com/3093060/colorado-trucking-workers-awarded-15m-in-discrimination-suit/.

67. Nicholas A. Valentino and David O. Sears, "Old Times Are Not Forgotten: Race and Partisan Realignment in the Contemporary South," *American Journal of Political Science* 49, no. 3 (2005): 672–688.

68. Robert Penn Warren, *Segregation: The Inner Conflict of the South* (1956; reiss., Athens: University of Georgia Press, 1994), xiv.

69. Grace Elizabeth Hale, *Making Whiteness: The Culture of Segregation in the South, 1890–1940* (New York: Pantheon Books, 1998), 284.

70. Mary R. Jackman and Marie Crane, "'Some of My Best Friends Are Black . . .': Interracial Friendships and Whites' Racial Attitudes," *Public Opinion Quarterly* 50, no. 4 (1986): 459.

71. Benjamin Schwarz, "The South in Black and White," *The Atlantic*, November 2004, http://www.theatlantic.com/magazine/archive/2004/11/the-south-in-black-and-white/303566/.

72. Melvin Patrick Ely, *Israel on the Appomattox: A Southern Experiment in Black Freedom from the 1790s to the Civil War* (New York: Knopf Doubleday Publishing Group, 2010), 443.

73. See: Peggy Pascoe, *What Comes Naturally: Miscegenation Law and the Making of Race in America* (New York: Oxford University Press, 2009).

74. *Prom Night in Mississippi*, directed by Paul Saltzman (Return to Mississippi Productions, 2009).

75. Robbie Brown, "A Racial Divide Closes as Students Step Up," *New York Times*, April 26, 2013, http://www.nytimes.com/2013/04/27/us/in-rural-georgia-students-step-up-to-offer-integrated-prom.html.

76. Tom Jensen, "MS GOP: Bryant for Gov., Barbour or Huckabee for Pres.," *Public Policy Polling*, April 7, 2011, http://www.publicpolicypolling.com/pdf/2011/PPP_Release_MS_0407915.pdf.

77. Tom Jensen, "Very Close Race in Both Alabama and Mississippi," *Public Policy Polling*, March 12, 2011, http://www.publicpolicypolling.com/pdf/2011/PPP_Release_SouthernSwing_312.pdf.

78. Ann Banks, "Dirty Tricks, South Carolina, and John McCain," *The Nation*, January 14, 2008, https://www.thenation.com/article/dirty-tricks-south-carolina-and-john-mccain/.

79. Jake Tapper and Suzi Parker, "McCain's Ancestor's Owned Slave," *Salon*, February 15, 2000, http://www.salon.com/2000/02/15/mccain_90/.

80. Michelle Alexander, *The New Jim Crow: Mass Incarceration in the Age of Colorblindness* (New York: The New Press, 2010).

81. Schwartzapfel and Keller, "Willie Horton Revisited."

82. T. J. Raphael, "How One Political Ad Held Back a Generation of American Inmates," *PRI*, May 18, 2015, http://www.pri.org/stories/2015-05-18/what-willie-horton-wrought.

83. Michelle Brattain, *The Politics of Whiteness: Race, Workers, and Culture in the Modern South* (Princeton: Princeton University Press, 2001), 243–245.

84. Sarah Carr, "In Southern Towns, 'Segregation Academies' Are Still Going Strong," *The Atlantic*, December 13, 2012, http://www.theatlantic.com/national/archive/2012/12/in-southern-towns-segregation-academies-are-still-going-strong/266207/.

85. Michael F. Higginbotham, *Ghosts of Jim Crow: Ending Racism in Post-Racial America* (New York: New York University Press, 2013), 151.

86. Janet Loehrke and Jolie Lee, "Still Apart: Map Shows States with Most-Segregated Schools," *USA Today*, May 15, 2014, http://www.usatoday.com/story/news/nation-now/2014/05/15/school-segregation-civil-rights-project/9115823/; see also: Jessica Epperly, "UCLA Report Finds Changing U.S. Demographics Transform School Segregation Landscape 60 Years After *Brown v. Board of Education*," *The Civil Rights Project*,

May 15, 2014, http://civilrightsproject.ucla.edu/news/press-releases/2014-press-releases/
ucla-report-finds-changing-u.s.-demographics-transform-school-segregation-landscape-
60-years-after-brown-v-board-of-education.

87. Emma Brown, "Judge Orders Mississippi School District to Desegregate, 62 Years
After *Brown v. Board of Education*," *Washington Post*, May 16, 2016, https://www.
washingtonpost.com/news/education/wp/2016/05/16/judge-orders-mississippi-school-
district-to-desegregate-62-years-after-brown-v-board-of-education/.

88. Lingyu Lu and Sean Nicholson-Crotty, "Reassessing the Impact of Hispanic
Stereotypes on White Americans' Immigration Preferences," *Social Science Quarterly*
91, no. 5 (2010): 1312–1328; Justin Allen Berg, "Opposition to Pro-Immigrant Public
Policy: Symbolic Racism and Group Threat," *Sociological Inquiry* 83, no. 1 (2013): 1–31;
Nicholas A. Valentino, Ted Brader, and Ashley E. Jardina, "Immigration Opposition
Among U.S. Whites: General Ethnocentrism or Media Priming of Attitudes about
Latinos?," *Political Psychology* 34, no. 2 (2013): 149–166.

89. Jessica Brown, "The 'Southwestern Strategy': Immigration and Race in GOP Discourse,"
Working Paper No. 2015-01, Kinder Institute for Urban Research (2015), https://
kinder.rice.edu/uploadedFiles/Kinder_Institute_for_Urban_Research/Publications/
White_Papers/Brown_WP1501.pdf, 3; see also: Jessica Autumn Brown, "Running on
Fear: Immigration, Race, and Crime Framings in Contemporary GOP Presidential
Debate Discourse," *Critical Criminology* 24 (2016): 315–341.

90. Brian Beutler, "Trump's White Supremacy Platform Comes into Focus," *The New
Republic*, September 23, 2016, https://newrepublic.com/article/137064/trumps-white-
supremacy-platform-comes-focus.

91. Ron Paul, quoted in: Brown, "The 'Southwestern Strategy,'" 22.

92. Mitt Romney, quoted in: Brown, "The 'Southwestern Strategy,'" 21.

93. Ta-Nehisi Coates, "The First White President," *The Atlantic*, October, 2017, https://www.
theatlantic.com/magazine/archive/2017/10/the-first-white-president-ta-nehisi-coates/
537909/.

94. See: Ian Haney López, "How the GOP Became the 'White Man's Party,'" *Salon*, December
22, 2013, http://www.salon.com/2013/12/22/how_the_gop_became_the_white_mans_
party/; Paul Rosenberg, "It Is All Still About Race: Obama Hatred, the South, and the
Truth About GOP Wins," *Salon*, November 4, 2014, http://www.salon.com/2014/11/
04/it_is_all_still_about_race_obama_hatred_the_south_and_the_truth_about_gop_
wins/.

95. "President Donald J. Trump Restores Responsibility and the Rule of Law to Immigration,"
TheWhite House.gov, September 5, 2017, https://www.whitehouse.gov/briefings-statements/
president-donald-j-trump-restores-responsibility-rule-law-immigration/.

96. Jeremy Diamond, "Trump: Black Lives Matter Has Helped Instigate Police Killings,"
CNN, July 18, 2016, http://www.cnn.com/2016/07/18/politics/donald-trump-black-
lives-matter/index.html.

97. Sean Sullivan, "Trump Says Judge's Mexican Heritage Presents 'Absolute Conflict' in
Trump University Cases," *Washington Post*, June 2, 2016, https://www.washingtonpost.
com/news/post-politics/wp/2016/06/02/trump-says-judges-mexican-heritage-presents-
absolute-conflict-in-trump-university-cases/.

98. Gerald Ford, quoted in: Earl Ofari Hustchinson, "Gerald Ford: The Conflicted President
on Civil Rights," *AlterNet*, December 28, 2006, http://www.alternet.org/story/46034/
gerald_ford%3A_the_conflicted_president_on_civil_rights.

99. Byron P. White, "Moving On with Race and Rhetoric," *Chicago Tribune*, October 27, 1996, http://articles.chicagotribune.com/1996-10-27/news/9610270400_1_republicans-dole-and-jack-kemp-bob-dole.

100. M. V. Hood III and Seth C. McKee, "True Colors: White Conservatives Support for Minority Republican Candidates," *Public Opinion Quarterly* 79, no. 1 (2015): 28–52.

101. Jeet Heer, "Making It in (Right-Wing) America: Dinesh D'Souza and the Shame of Immigrant Self-Hatred," *New Republic*, February 20, 2015, http://www.newrepublic.com/article/121105/dinesh-dsouzas-anti-black-racism-rooted-national-review.

102. Ian Haney López, *Dog Whistle Politics: How Coded Racial Appeals Have Reinvented Racism & Wrecked the Middle Class* (New York: Oxford University Press, 2014), 137.

103. Schwartzapfel and Keller, "Willie Horton Revisited."

104. Dan Carter, *From George Wallace to Newt Gingrich: Race in the Conservative Counterrevolution, 1963–1994* (Baton Rouge: Louisiana State University Press, 1996), 4.

105. "Legacy of Slavery Still Fuels Anti-Black Attitudes in the Deep South," *University of Rochester*, September 18, 2013, http://www.rochester.edu/news/show.php?id=7202; see also: Sue Sturgis, "How Slavery Continues to Shape Southern Politics," *Facing South*, September 23, 2013, http://www.southernstudies.org/2013/09/how-slavery-continues-to-shape-southern-politics.html.

CHAPTER 2

1. Tim Wise, "Frequently Asked Questions—And Their Answers," *TimWise.org*, December, 2014, http://www.timwise.org/f-a-q-s/.

2. J. William Middendorf II, *A Glorious Disaster: Barry Goldwater's Presidential Campaign and the Origins of the Conservative Movement* (New York: Basic Books, 2006), 212.

3. "Carolina Crowds Hail Goldwater," *New York Times*, November 1, 1964, http://www.nytimes.com/1964/11/01/carolina-crowds-hail-goldwater.html.

4. Middendorf, *A Glorious Disaster*, 212.

5. "Carolina Crowds Hail Goldwater," *New York Times*.

6. George H. W. Bush, *All the Best, George Bush: My Life in Letters and Other Writings* (New York: Simon and Schuster, 2013), 88.

7. Katherine Q. Seelye, "Politics: Bob Dole; In Visit to Arizona, Senator Emphasizes Goldwater Roots," *New York Times*, February 26, 1996, http://www.nytimes.com/1996/02/26/us/politics-bob-dole-in-visit-to-arizona-senator-emphasizes-goldwater-roots.html.

8. Charles Mohr, "Goldwater Links the Welfare State to Rise in Crime," *New York Times*, September 11, 1964, http://www.nytimes.com/1964/09/11/goldwater-links-the-welfare-state-to-rise-in-crime.html.

9. Jeremy D. Mayer, "LBJ Fights the White Backlash: The Racial Politics of the 1964 Presidential Campaign, Part 2," *Prologue Magazine* 33, no. 1 (2001): https://www.archives.gov/publications/prologue/2001/spring/lbj-and-white-backlash-2.html.

10. Richard H. Rovere, "The Campaign: Goldwater," *The New Yorker*, October 3, 1964, http://www.newyorker.com/magazine/1964/10/03/the-campaign-goldwater.

11. Peggy McIntosh, quoted in: Joshua Rothman, "The Origins of 'Privilege,'" *The New Yorker*, May 12, 2014, http://www.newyorker.com/online/blogs/books/2014/05/the-woman-who-coined-the-term-white-privilege.html.

12. Dion the Socialist (admin), "This . . . Is White Privilege," *Tumblr*, n. d. http://thisiswhiteprivilege.tumblr.com/.

13. Rega Jha and Tommy Wesely, "How Privileged Are You?," *BuzzFeed*, April 10, 2014, http://www.buzzfeed.com/regajha/how-privileged-are-you.

14. Tal Fortang, "Checking My Privilege: Character as the Basis of Privilege," *The Princeton Tory*, April 2, 2014, http://theprincetontory.com/main/checking-my-privilege-character-as-the-basis-of-privilege/.

15. Peggy McIntosh, quoted in: Rothman, "The Origins of 'Privilege.'"

16. "The White Privilege Conference," n.d., http://www.whiteprivilegeconference.com/keynotes.html; see also: Pat Schneider, "Controversial National 'White Privilege' Conference Coming to Madison in March," *The Cap Times*, February 11, 2014, http://host.madison.com/news/local/writers/pat_schneider/controversial-national-white-privilege-conference-coming-to-madison-in-march/article_bdc7052c-92b8-11e3-ae53-0019bb2963f4.html.

17. See: Angie Maxwell and T. Wayne Parent, "A 'Subterranean Agenda?': Racial Attitudes, Presidential Evaluations, and Tea Party Membership," *Race and Social Problems* 5, no. 3 (September 2013): 226–237.

18. "Survey: Religion and the Tea Party in the 2010 Elections," *Public Religion Research Institute*, October 5, 2010, http://publicreligion.org/research/2010/10/religion-tea-party-2010/.

19. Susan Brooks Thistlewait, quoted in: Penny Starr, "Tea Partiers 'Comfortable with White Privilege,' Liberal Analyst Claims," *Cnsnews.com*, October 7, 2010, http://www.cnsnews.com/news/article/tea-partiers-comfortable-white-privilege-liberal-analyst-claims.

20. James Webb, "Diversity and the Myth of White Privilege," *The Wall Street Journal*, July 22, 2010, http://online.wsj.com/articles/SB10001424052748703724104575379630952309408.

21. Larry Yates, "A Response to Webb's 'Diversity and the Myth of White Privilege,'" *Virginia Organizing*, 2010, http://www.virginia-organizing.org/content/response-webbs-diversity-and-myth-white-privilege.

22. See: Fred L. Pincus, *Reverse Discrimination: Dismantling the Myth* (Boulder: Lynne Rienner Publishers, 2003).

23. See: David R. Roediger, *Working Toward Whiteness: How America's Immigrants Became White: The Strange Journey from Ellis Island to the Suburbs* (Cambridge: Basic Books, 2005); David R. Roediger, *The Wages of Whiteness: Race and the Making of the American Working Class* (New York: Verso, 1999).

24. David Lublin, *The Republican South: Democratization and Partisan Change* (Princeton: Princeton University Press, 2004), 142.

25. Ronald Reagan, quoted in: Ian Haney López, *Dog Whistle Politics: How Coded Racial Appeals Have Reinvented Racism & Wrecked the Middle Class* (New York: Oxford University Press, 2014), 58.

26. Thomas Byrne Edsall and Mary D. Edsall, *Chain Reaction: The Impact of Race, Rights, and Taxes on American Politics* (New York: W. W. Norton & Company, Inc., 1991), 214.

27. Joseph A. Aistrup, *The Southern Strategy Revisited: Republican Top-Down Advancement in the South* (Lexington: University Press of Kentucky, 2015), 45.

28. See: Kevin M. Kruse, *White Flight: Atlanta and the Making of Modern Conservatism* (Princeton: Princeton University Press, 2005); Matthew D. Lassiter, *The Silent Majority: Suburban Politics in the Sunbelt South* (Princeton: Princeton University Press, 2006).

29. Earl Black and Merle Black, *The Rise of Southern Republicans* (Cambridge: Harvard University Press, 2002), 246.

30. Tim Wise, *White Like Me: Reflections on Race from a Privileged Son* (Berkeley: Soft Skull Press, 2007); Tobin Miller Shearer, *Enter the River: Healing Steps from White Privilege Toward Racial Reconciliation* (Harrisonburg: Herald Press, 1994).

31. Kim A. Case, Jonathan Iuzzini, and Morgan Hopkins, "Systems of Privilege: Intersections, Awareness, and Applications," *Journal of Social Issues* 68, no. 1 (2012): 1–10.

32. Elaine Pinderhughes, *Understanding Race, Ethnicity, and Power: The Key to Efficacy in Clinical Practice* (New York: Free Press, 1989).

33. Derald Wing Sue, *Overcoming Racism: The Journey to Liberation* (San Francisco: Jossey-Bass, 2003).

34. E. Janie Pinterits, V. Paul Poteat, and Lisa B. Spanierman, "The White Privileges Attitudes Scale: Development and Initial Validation," *Journal of Counseling Psychology* 56, no. 3 (2009): 417–429.

35. Shawn O. Utsey, Carol A. Gernat, and Lawrence Hammar, "Examining White Counselor Trainees' Reactions to Racial Issues in Counseling and Supervision Dyads," *The Counseling Psychologist* 33 (2005): 449–478.

36. Barbara J. Flagg, "'Was Blind, but Now I See': White Consciousness and the Requirement of Discriminatory Intent," *Michigan Law Review* 91 (1993): 969n.

37. Peggy McIntosh, "White Privilege and Male Privilege: A Personal Account of Coming to See Correspondences Through Work in Women's Studies," in *Power, Privilege, and Law: A Civil Rights Reader*, ed. Leslie Bender and Daan Braveman (St. Paul: West Publishing, 1995), 23.

38. Maxwell Strachan, "The Definitive History of 'George Bush Doesn't Care About Black People,'" *Huffington Post*, August 28, 2015, http://www.huffingtonpost.com/entry/kanye-west-george-bush-black-people_us_55d67c12e4b020c386de2f5e.

39. Mychal Denzel Smith, "The Rebirth of Black Rage: From Kanye to Obama, and Back Again," *The Nation*, August 13, 2015, https://www.thenation.com/article/the-rebirth-of-black-rage/.

40. Adam A. Powell, Nyla B. Branscombe, and Michael T. Schmitt, "Inequality as Ingroup Privilege or Outgroup Disadvantage: The Impact of Group Focus on Collective Guilt and Interracial Attitudes," *Personality and Social Psychology Bulletin* 31, no. 4 (2005): 508–521.

41. Tracie L. Stewart, Ioana M. Latu, Nyla R. Branscombe, Nia L. Phillips, and H. Ted Denney, "White Privilege Awareness and Efficacy to Reduce Racial Inequality Improve White Americans' Attitudes Toward African Americans," *Journal of Social Issues* 68, no. 1 (2012): 11–27.

42. Brian S. Lowery, Eric D. Knowles, and Miguel M. Unzueta, "Framing Inequity Safely: Whites' Motivated Perceptions of Racial Privilege," *Personality and Social Psychology Bulletin* 33 (2007): 1237–1250.

43. Carole L. Lund and Scipio A. J. Collin III, "Editor's Notes," *New Directions for Adult and Continuing Education* 125 (Spring 2010): 5.

44. "Barry Goldwater Speaks Out for a Stronger America," 1964 Campaign Brochure, http://www.4president.org/brochures/goldwater1964brochure.htm.

45. See: Amanda Moore, "Tracking Down Martin Luther King Jr.'s Word on Health Care," *Huffington Post*, January 18, 2013, http://www.huffingtonpost.com/amanda-moore/martin-luther-king-health-care_b_2506393.html.

46. Mitt Romney, "Mitt Romney's '47 Percent' Comments," *YouTube*, September 18, 2012, https://www.youtube.com/watch?v=M2gvY2wq17M; see also: López, *Dog Whistle Politics*, 162.

47. Michael Tesler, "The Spillover of Racialization into Health Care: How President Obama Polarized Public Opinion by Racial Attitudes and Race," *American Journal of Political Science* 56, no. 3 (2012): 690.

48. Antoine J. Banks, "The Public's Anger: White Racial Attitudes and Opinions Toward Health Care Reform," *Political Behavior* 36, no. 3 (2014): 493.

49. Antoine J. Banks and Nicholas A. Valentino, "Emotional Substrates of White Racial Attitudes," *American Journal of Political Science* 56, no. 2 (2012): 286.

50. Antoine J. Banks and Heather M. Hicks, "Fear and Implicit Racism: Whites' Support for Voter ID Laws," *Political Psychology* 37, no. 5 (2016): 641–658.

51. Aric Jenkins, "Poll: A Third of Americans Don't Know Obamacare and the Affordable Care Act Are the Same Thing," *Fortune*, February 7, 2017, http://fortune.com/2017/02/07/obamacare-affordable-care-act-repeal-poll/.

52. Flagg, "'Was Blind, but Now I See,'" 953.

53. H. Roy Kaplan, *The Myth of Post-Racial America: Searching for Equality in the Age of Materialism* (New York: Rowman & Littlefield Education, 2011), 152.

54. Banks, "The Public's Anger," 494.

55. Fred L. Pincus, *Reverse Discrimination: Dismantling the Myth* (Boulder: Lynne Rienner Publishers, 2003), 81.

56. Ryan Cooper, "How the South's Ugly Racial History Is Haunting Obamacare," *This Week*, October 31, 2014, http://theweek.com/articles/442582/how-souths-ugly-racial-history-haunting-obamacare.

57. Sarah Varney, "Mississippi, Burned: How the Poorest, Sickest State Got Left Behind by Obamacare," *Politico Magazine*, November/December, 2014, http://www.politico.com/magazine/story/2014/10/mississippi-burned-obamacare-112181_full.html.

58. James M. Glaser, *The Hand of the Past in Contemporary Southern Politics* (New Haven: Yale University Press), 180–181; see also: Devin Caughey, *The Unsolid South: Mass Politics and National Representation in a One-Party Enclave* (Princeton: Princeton University Press, 2018).

59. V. O. Key Jr., *Southern Politics in State and Nation* (New York: Alfred A. Knopf, 1949), 655.

60. Kevin P. Phillips, *The Emerging Republican Majority* (New Rochelle: Arlington House, 1969), 238; Cathleen Decker, "Trump's War Against Elites and Expertise," *Los Angeles Times*, July 27, 2017, https://www.latimes.com/politics/la-na-pol-trump-elites-20170725-story.html.

61. Frank Annunziata, "The Revolt Against the Welfare State: Goldwater Conservatism and the Election of 1964," *Presidential Studies Quarterly* 10, no. 2 (1980): 255.

62. Barry Goldwater, *The Conscience of a Conservative* (Shephardsville: Victor, 1960), 66.

63. Michael Levy, "An Angry, Divided, Pessimistic, Older, White Electorate: What the 2010 Exit Polls Tell Us," *Encyclopedia Britannica Blog*, November 3, 2010, http://www.britannica.com/blogs/2010/11/an-angry-divided-pessimistic-older-white-electorate-what-the-2010-exit-polls-tell-us.

64. Jon Cohen and Dan Balz, "Poll: Whites Without College Degrees Especially Pessimistic About Economy," *Washington Post*, February 22, 2011, http://www.washingtonpost.com/wp-dyn/content/story/2011/02/22/ST2011022200019.html.

65. Jim Tankersley, Ron Fournier, and Nancy Cook, "Why Whites Are More Pessimistic About Their Futures Than Minorities," *The Atlantic*, October 7, 2011, http://www.theatlantic.com/business/archive/2011/10/why-whites-are-more-pessimistic-about-their-future-than-minorities/246366/.

66. "The Lost Decade of the Middle Class: Fewer, Poorer, Gloomier," *Pew Research Social & Demographic Trends*, August 22, 2012, http://www.pewsocialtrends.org/2012/08/22/the-lost-decade-of-the-middle-class/.

67. Tankersley, Fournier, and Cook, "Why Whites Are More Pessimistic."

68. Bonnie Kavoussi, "Young Whites More Pessimistic About Future than Minorities: Study," *The Huffington Post*, November 2, 2011, http://www.huffingtonpost.com/2011/11/02/young-whites-pessimistic_n_1071284.html.

69. Trevor Tompson and Jennifer Benz, "The Public Mood: White Malaise but Optimism Among Blacks, Hispanics," *The Associated Press-NORC Center for Public Affairs Research*, 2013, http://www.apnorc.org/projects/Pages/the-public-mood-white-malaise-but-optimism-among-blacks-hispanics.aspx.

70. Richard M. Weaver, "Integration Is Communization," *National Review* 4 (July 13, 1957): 67–68.

71. "Martin Luther King Jr., RIP," *The New Guard* 8, no. 5 (1968): 3–4.

72. Chris Kromm, "The Racist Roots of 'Right to Work' Laws," *Facing South*, December 13, 2012, http://www.southernstudies.org/2012/12/the-racist-roots-of-right-to-work-laws.html.

73. "Republican Party Platform of 1964," *The American Presidency Project*, July 12, 1964, http://www.presidency.ucsb.edu/documents/republican-party-platform-1964.

74. Charles Mohr, "Goldwater Links the Welfare State to Rise in Crime," *New York Times*, September 11, 1964, http://www.nytimes.com/1964/09/11/goldwater-links-the-welfare-state-to-rise-in-crime.html.

75. Edsall and Edsall, *Chain Reaction*, 7.

76. Laura Kalman, *Right Start Rising: A New Politics, 1974–1980* (New York: W. W. Norton & Company, Inc., 2010), 189.

77. John Dollard, *Caste and Class in a Southern Town*, 2nd ed. (New York: Harper & Brothers, 1949), 315; the original version of Dollard's book was published in 1937.

78. Noel Ignatiev, *How the Irish Became White* (New York: Routledge, 1995).

79. WFBMM, "'Honorary' White Privilege, New Southern Strategies, & the GOP," *Daily Kos*, November 20, 2012, http://www.dailykos.com/story/2012/11/20/1163328/--Honorary-White-Privilege-New-Southern-Strategies-The-GOP; Pam Spaulding, "Will We See a New 'Southern Strategy'—Break Up the 2012 Minority Vote Coalition by Doling Out Privilege?," *Pam's House Blend*, November 19, 2012, http://pamshouseblend.firedoglake.com/2012/11/19/will-we-see-a-new-southern-strategy-break-up-the-2012-minority-vote-coalition-by-doling-out-privilege/.

80. David Lublin, *The Republican South: Democratization and Partisan Change* (Princeton: Princeton University Press, 2004), 146.

81. John L. Jackson Jr., *Racial Paranoia: The Unintended Consequences of Political Correctness: The New Reality of Race in America* (New York: Basic Books, 2008), 217.

82. Lanhee Chen, quoted in: Trip Gabriel, "Romney Presses Obama on Work in Welfare Law," *New York Times*, August 7, 2012, http://www.nytimes.com/2012/08/08/us/politics/romney-accuses-obama-of-taking-work-out-of-welfare-law.html.

83. "New Census Bureau Report Analyzes U.S. Population Projections," *United States Census Bureau*, March 3, 2015, https://www.census.gov/newsroom/press-releases/2015/cb15-tps16.html; see also: Catherine Woodiwiss, "The Era of White Anxiety Is Just Beginning," *Sojourners*, March 8, 2016, https://sojo.net/articles/era-white-anxiety-just-beginning.

84. Sean McElwee and Jason McDaniel, "Economic Anxiety Didn't Make People Vote for Trump," *The Nation*, May 8, 2017, https://www.thenation.com/article/economic-anxiety-didnt-make-people-vote-trump-racism-did/; Sean McElwee and Jason McDaniel, "Fear

of Diversity Made People More Likely to Vote Trump," *The Nation*, March 14, 2017, https://www.thenation.com/article/fear-of-diversity-made-people-more-likely-to-vote-trump/.

85. Thomas B. Edsall, "Donald Trump's Identity Politics," *New York Times*, August 24, 2017, https://www.nytimes.com/2017/08/24/opinion/donald-trump-identity-politics.html.

86. Byron E. Shafer and Richard Johnston, *The End of Southern Exceptionalism: Class, Race, and Partisan Change in the Postwar South* (Cambridge: Harvard University Press, 2006); Lassiter, *Suburban Politics*.

87. Edward G. Carmines and James A. Stimson, *Issue Evolution: Race and the Transformation of American Politics* (Princeton: Princeton University Press, 1989); Alan I. Abramowitz, "Issue Evolution Reconsidered: Racial Attitudes and Partisanship in the U.S. Electorate," *American Journal of Political Science* 38 (1994): 1–24.

88. Seth Ackerman, "Tea Party Yankees," *Jacobin*, October 2013, https://www.jacobinmag.com/2013/10/tea-party-yankees/.

89. Nate Cohn, "The GOP Division over the Fiscal Cliff Is Not Going Away," *New Republic*, January 7, 2013, http://www.newrepublic.com/blog/electionate/111621/gop-faultlines-resurface-in-fiscal-cliff-battle.

90. Zach Beauchamp, "Yes, the South Really Is Different—And It's Because of Race," *Think Progress*, October 18, 2013, http://thinkprogress.org/justice/2013/10/18/2786841/yes-south-different-race/.

91. Beauchamp, "Yes, the South Really Is Different."

92. Edsall and Edsall, *Chain Reaction*, 10.

93. Chris Boeskool, "'When You're Accustomed to Privilege, Equality Feels Like Oppression,'" *Huffington Post*, March 3, 2016, https://www.huffingtonpost.com/chris-boeskool/when-youre-accustomed-to-privilege_b_9460662.html.

94. Jack Levin, quoted in: Melanie Bush, *Perspectives on a Multiracial America: Everyday Forms of Whiteness: Understanding Race in a "Post-Racial" World*, 2nd ed. (New York: Rowan & Littlefield Publishers, Inc., 2011).

95. John Blake, "Are Whites Racially Oppressed?," *CNN*, March 4, 2011, http://www.cnn.com/2010/US/12/21/white.persecution/.

96. Michael I. Norton and Samuel R. Sommers, "Whites See Racism as a Zero-Sum Game That They are Now Losing," *Perspectives on Psychological Science* 6, no. 3 (2011): 215–218.

97. Scott Huffman, "Latest Winthrop Poll Surveys Southern States About Racism and the Economy," *Winthrop University*, November 8, 2017, https://www.winthrop.edu/news-events/article.aspx?id=49965.

98. Pincus, *Reverse Discrimination*, 5.

99. "Republican Party Platform of 1964," *The American Presidency Project*.

100. See: Wesley Lowery, "Read the Letter Coretta Scott King Wrote Opposing Jeff Sessions's 1986 Federal Nomination," *Washington Post*, January 10, 2017, https://www.washingtonpost.com/news/powerpost/wp/2017/01/10/read-the-letter-coretta-scott-king-wrote-opposing-sessionss-1986-federal-nomination/.

101. Jack Moore, "The Trump Administration Plans to Sue Colleges for Affirmative Action Policies That 'Discriminate' Against White People," *GQ*, August 2, 2017, https://www.gq.com/story/trump-college-admissions.

102. George Brown Tindall, *The Ethnic Southerners* (Baton Rouge: Louisiana State University Press, 1976).

103. Edsall and Edsall, *Chain Reaction*, 10.

104. Michael Cushman, "Michael Savage on the 'Ethnic Replacement' of Whites," *Southern National Network*, July 15, 2014, http://southernnationalist.com/blog/2014/07/15/michael-savage-on-us-ethnic-replacement-of-whites/.

105. Clyde Wilson, "Southerners as an Ethnic Group," *Know Southern History*, n. d., http://www.knowsouthernhistory.net/Articles/Culture/southerners_as_an_ethnic_group.html.

106. John Shelton Reed, *One South: An Ethnic Approach to Regional Culture* (Baton Rouge: Louisiana State University Press, 1982); see also: "Southern Focus Poll Dataverse," Center of the Study of the American South and the Odum Institute for Research in Social Science, University of North Carolina at Chapel Hill, https://dataverse.unc.edu/dataverse/sfp.

107. Gerald Ford, quoted in: Maarten Zwiers, "From Traitor to Martyr: Robert E. Lee and the Myth of White Victimhood," *The Activist History Review*, October 27, 2017, https://activisthistory.com/2017/10/27/from-traitor-to-martyr-robert-e-lee-and-the-myth-of-white-victimhood/.

108. Max McClure, "White Republicans and Southern Evangelicals Most Likely to Claim Reverse Discrimination, Stanford Research Finds," *Stanford Report*, January 23, 2013, http://news.stanford.edu/news/2013/january/white-reverse-discrimination-012312.html.

109. Damon Mayrl and Aliya Saperstein, "When White People Report Racial Discrimination: The Role of Region, Religion, and Politics," *Social Science Research* 42, no. 3 (2013): 743–754.

110. See: Angie Maxwell, *The Indicted South: Public Criticism, Southern Inferiority, and the Politics of Whiteness* (Chapel Hill: University of North Carolina Press, 2014).

111. Fletcher M. Green, "Resurgent Southern Sectionalism, 1933–1955," *The North Carolina Historical Review* 33, no. 2 (1956): 225.

112. Steve Reilly, "Hundreds Allege Donald Trump Doesn't Pay His Bills," *USA Today*, June 9, 2016, https://www.usatoday.com/story/news/politics/elections/2016/06/09/donald-trump-unpaid-bills-republican-president-laswuits/85297274/.

113. Nell Irwin, "Confidence Boomed After the Election. The Economy Hasn't," *New York Times*, July 4, 2017, https://www.nytimes.com/2017/07/04/upshot/confidence-boomed-after-the-election-the-economy-hasnt.html.

114. Maxwell and Parent, "A 'Subterranean Agenda?'"

115. Michael V. Apple, "Foreword," in *White Reign: Deploying Whiteness in America*, ed. Joe L. Kincheloe, Shirley R. Steinberg, Nelson M. Rodriguez, and Ronald E. Chennault (New York: St. Martin's Press, 1998), ix.

116. Mayer, "LBJ Fights the White Backlash," [Part 2].

117. Jeremy D. Mayer, "LBJ Fights the White Backlash: The Racial Politics of the 1964 Presidential Campaign, Part 1," *Prologue Magazine* 33, no. 1 (2001), https://www.archives.gov/publications/prologue/2001/spring/lbj-and-white-backlash-1.html.

118. George Brown Tindall. *The Ethnic Southerners* (Baton Rouge: Louisiana State University Press, 1976), 68.

119. Phillips, *The Emerging Republican Majority*, 230.

CHAPTER 3

1. Ian Haney López, *Dog Whistle Politics: How Coded Racial Appeals Have Reinvented Racism & Wrecked the Middle Class* (New York: Oxford University Press, 2014), 226.

2. Robert P. Jones, "How Trump Remixed the Republican Southern Strategy," *The Atlantic*, August 14, 2016, https://www.theatlantic.com/politics/archive/2016/08/how-trump-remixed-the-republican-southern-strategy/495719/.

3. Joseph Crespino, "Did David Brooks Tell the Full Story About Reagan's Neshoba County Fair Visit?," *History News Network*, November 11, 2007, http://historynewsnetwork.org/article/44535.

4. David Kopel, "Reagan's Infamous Speech in Philadelphia, Mississippi," *The Volokh Conspiracy*, August 16, 2011, http://volokh.com/2011/08/16/reagans-infamous-speech-in-philadelphia-mississippi/.

5. Ian Haney López, "The Racism at the Heart of the Reagan Presidency," *Salon*, January 11, 2014, http://www.salon.com/2014/01/11/the_racism_at_the_heart_of_the_reagan_presidency/.

6. López, "The Racism at the Heart of the Reagan Presidency."

7. Ian Haney López, "How Conservatives Hijacked 'Colorblindness' and Set Civil Rights Back Decades," *Salon*, January 20, 2014, http://www.salon.com/2014/01/20/how_conservatives_hijacked_colorblindness_and_set_civil_rights_back_decades/.

8. Joshua F. J. Inwood, "Neoliberal Racism: The 'Southern Strategy' and the Expanding Geographies of White Supremacy," *Social and Cultural Geography* 16, no. 4 (2015): 407–423.

9. Barack Obama, "A More Perfect Union," ConstituionCenter.org, March 18, 2008, http://constitutioncenter.org/amoreperfectunion/.

10. Patrick J. Buchanan, "A Brief for Whitey," *Patrick J. Buchanan—Official Website*, March 21, 2008, http://buchanan.org/blog/pjb-a-brief-for-whitey-969.

11. Derald Wing Sue, *Overcoming our Racism: The Journey to Liberation* (San Francisco: Jossey-Bass, 2003), 149.

12. Jamelle Boule. 2014. "Why Do Millennials Not Understand Racism?," *Slate*, May 16, 2014, http://www.slate.com/articles/news_and_politics/politics/2014/05/millennials_racism_and_mtv_poll_young_people_are_confused_about_bias_prejudice.html; see also: Mychal Denzel Smith, "White Millennials Are Products of a Failed Lesson in Colorblindness," *PBS Newshour*, March 26, 2015, http://www.pbs.org/newshour/updates/white-millennials-products-failed-lesson-colorblindness/.

13. Dan Balz and Scott Clement, "On Racial Issues, America Is Divided both Black and White and Red and Blue," *Washington Post*, December 27, 2014, http://www.washingtonpost.com/politics/on-racial-issues-america-is-divided-both-black-and-white-and-red-and-blue/2014/12/26/3d2964c8-8d12-11e4-a085-34e9b9f09a58_story.html; see also: Jonathan Capehart, "The Fallacy of a 'Post-Racial' Society," *Washington Post*, December 29, 2014, http://www.washingtonpost.com/blogs/post-partisan/wp/2014/12/29/the-fallacy-of-a-post-racial-society/.

14. Michael F. Higginbotham, *Ghosts of Jim Crow: Ending Racism in Post-Racial America* (New York: New York University Press, 2013), 145.

15. Touré, "No Such Place as 'Post-Racial' America," *New York Times*, November 8, 2011, http://campaignstops.blogs.nytimes.com/2011/11/08/no-such-place-as-post-racial-america/.

16. Michelle Brattain, *The Politics of Whiteness: Race, Workers, and Culture in the Modern South* (Princeton: Princeton University Press, 2001), 247.

17. Paul M. Sniderman, Richard A. Brody, and James H. Kuklinski, "Policy Reasoning and Political Values: The Problem of Racial Equality," *American Journal of Political Science* 28, no. 1 (1984): 75–94.

18. Steven A. Tuch and Michael Hughes, "Whites' Racial Policy Attitudes in the Twenty-First Century: The Continuing Significance of Racial Resentment," *The ANNALS of the American Academy of Political and Social Science* 634, no. 1 (2011): 134–152.

19. Donald R. Kinder and David O. Sears, "Prejudice and Politics: Symbolic Racism Versus Racial Threats to the Good Life," *Journal of Personality and Social Psychology* 40, no. 3 (1981): 416.

20. Moira Weigel, "Political Correctness: How the Right Invented a Phantom Enemy," *The Guardian*, November 30, 2016, https://www.theguardian.com/us-news/2016/nov/30/political-correctness-how-the-right-invented-phantom-enemy-donald-trump.

21. Matthew Dessem, "In Statement on Orlando Shooting, Trump Says, 'We Can't Afford to Be Politically Correct Anymore,'" *Slate*, June 12, 2016, http://www.slate.com/blogs/the_slatest/2016/06/12/donald_trump_statement_on_orlando_shooting_says_we_can_t_afford_to_be_politically.html.

22. Derald Wing Sue, *Race Talk and the Conspiracy of Silence: Understanding and Facilitating Difficult Dialogues on Race* (Hoboken: John Wiley & Sons, Inc., 2015), 158.

23. Byron D'Andra Orey, Marvin Overby, Pete Hatemi, and Baodong Liu, "White Support for Racial Referenda in the Deep South," *Politics & Policy* 39, no. 4 (2011): 539–558; David Lublin, *The Republican South: Democratization and Partisan Change* (Princeton: Princeton University Press, 2004), 144.

24. Obama, "A More Perfect Union."

25. Michael Perman, *Pursuit of Unity: Political History of the American South* (Chapel Hill: University of North Carolina Press, 2009), 325.

26. Reg Murphy and Hal Gulliver, *The Southern Strategy* (New York: Charles Scribner's Sons, 1971), 23–24.

27. Joseph A. Aistrup, *The Southern Strategy Revisited: Republican Top-Down Advancement in the South* (Lexington: University Press of Kentucky, 2015), 35.

28. Edward Morgan, quoted in: Robert Mason, *Richard Nixon and the Quest for a New Majority* (Chapel Hill: University of North Carolina Press, 2004), 147.

29. Edward Morgan, quoted in: Mason, *Richard Nixon*, 148.

30. Matthew D. Lassiter, *The Silent Majority: Suburban Politics in the Sunbelt South* (Princeton: Princeton University Press, 2006), 225, 247.

31. Perman, *Pursuit of Unity*, 316.

32. Rowland Evans and Robert Novak, "Ford Southern Strategy Considered as Too Weak," *Lawrence Journal-World*, June 4, 1975, https://news.google.com/newspapers?nid=2199&dat=19750604&id=9QAyAAAAIBAJ&sjid=IeUFAAAAIBAJ&pg=4419,399537&hl=en, 4.

33. Fred Arthur Bailey, "M. E. Bradford, the Reagan Rights, and the Resurgence of Confederate Nationalism," in *Painting Dixie Red: When, Where, Why, and How the South Became Republican*, ed. Glenn Feldman (Gainesville: University Press of Florida, 2011), 306.

34. Antonin Scalia, quoted in: Amy Davidson, "In Voting Rights, Scalia Sees a 'Racial Entitlement,'" *The New Yorker*, February 28, 2013, http://www.newyorker.com/news/amy-davidson/in-voting-rights-scalia-sees-a-racial-entitlement.

35. Spencer Overton, "Against a 'Post-Racial' Voting Rights Act," *The American Prospect*, August 21, 2013, http://prospect.org/article/against-post-racial-voting-rights-act.

36. Ari Berman, "The Trump Administration Is Planning an Unprecedented Attack on Voting Rights," *The Nation*, June 20, 2017, https://www.thenation.com/article/the-trump-administration-is-planning-an-unprecedented-attack-on-voting-rights.

37. Earl Black and Merle Black, *The Rise of Southern Republicans* (Cambridge: Harvard University Press, 2002), 28.
38. Ronald Reagan, "Inaugural Address," The American Presidency Project, UC Santa Barbara, January 20, 1981, https://www.presidency.ucsb.edu/documents/inaugural-address-11.
39. Barry Goldwater, "A Conservative Opposed the Civil Rights Act of 1964," in *Debating the American Conservative Movement: 1945–Present*, ed. Donald T. Critchlow and Nancy MacLean (Lanham: Rowman & Littlefield Publishers, Inc., 2009), 85.
40. Bill Blaylock, quoted in: Brattain, *The Politics of* Whiteness, 231.
41. Maria Krysan, "Prejudice, Politics, and Public Opinion: Understanding the Sources of Racial Policy Attitudes," *Annual Review of Sociology* 26 (2000): 146.
42. Jay Barth, "The Continuing Role of Race in Southern Organizations," in *Southern Political Party Activists: Patterns of Conflict and Change, 1991–2001*, ed. John A. Clark and Charles L. Prysby (Lexington: University Press of Kentucky, 2004), 36.
43. Lassiter, *The Silent Majority*, 324.
44. William Bradford, quoted in: Aistrup, *The Southern Strategy Revisited*, 45.
45. Pew Research Center, "Public Backs Affirmative Action, but Not Minority Preferences," *Pew Research Center*, July 9, 2009, http://www.pewresearch.org/2009/06/02/public-backs-affirmative-action-but-not-minority-preferences/.
46. Tom Boggioni, "Spike Lee: Idea that America Is a Post-racial Society under Obama is 'Bullsh∗t,'" *Raw Story*, November 1, 2014, http://www.rawstory.com/2014/11/spike-lee-idea-that-america-is-a-post-racial-society-under-obama-is-bullsht/.
47. Tim Stanley, "Selma and Obama: The Post-racial President's Difficult History with Speaking about Race," *The Telegraph*, March 7, 2015, http://www.telegraph.co.uk/news/worldnews/barackobama/11455949/Selma-and-Obama-the-post-racial-presidents-difficult-history-with-speaking-about-race.html.
48. Paul Rosenberg, "GOP's Post-racial Fantasy: Secession, Delusion, and the Truth about America's Most Hateful Dividers," *Salon*, August 16, 2014, http://www.salon.com/2014/08/16/gops_post_racial_fantasy_secession_delusion_and_the_truth_about_americas_most_hateful_dividers/.
49. Alice Speri, "Half of America Thinks We Live in a Post-racial Society—The Other Half, Not So Much," *Vice News*, December 9, 2014, https://news.vice.com/article/half-of-america-thinks-we-live-in-a-post-racial-society-the-other-half-not-so-much.
50. Thomas Byrne Edsall and Mary D. Edsall, *Chain Reaction: The Impact of Race, Rights, and Taxes on American Politics* (New York: W. W. Norton & Company, Inc., 1991), 36.
51. Don Gonyea, "Bush Again Declines Invite to NAACP Convention," *NPR Morning Edition*, July 15, 2005, http://www.npr.org/templates/story/story.php?storyId=4755349.
52. Scott Jaschik, "McCain Comes Out Against Affirmative Action," *Inside Higher Ed*, July 29, 2008, https://www.insidehighered.com/news/2008/07/29/mccain.
53. Bob Dole, quoted in: Michael A. Fletcher, "Losing Its Preference: Affirmative Action Fades as an Issue," *Washington Post*, September 18, 1996, http://www.washingtonpost.com/wp-srv/politics/special/affirm/stories/aa091896.htm.
54. Felicia Sonmez, "Mitt Romney: 'No One's Ever Asked to See My Birth Certificate,'" *Washington Post*, April 24, 2012, https://www.washingtonpost.com/news/post-politics/wp/2012/08/24/mitt-romney-no-ones-asked-for-my-birth-certificate/.
55. David O. Sears and Donald R. Kinder, "Whites' Opposition to Busing: On Conceptualizing and Operationalizing Group Conflict," *Journal of Personality and Social Psychology* 4, no. 5 (1985): 1141–1147; David O. Sears and Harris M. Allen Jr., "The Trajectory of Local Desegregation Controversies and Whites' Opposition to Busing," in

Groups in Contact: The Psychology of Desegregation, ed. Norman Miller and Marilyn B. Brewer (Orlando: Academic Press, Inc., 1984), 149.

56. Michael G. Hagan, "References to Racial Issues," *Political Behavior* 17, no. 1 (1995): 49–88.

57. Paul M. Sniderman and Thomas Piazza, *The Scar of Race* (Cambridge: Harvard University Press, 1993); Warren E. Miller and J. Merrill Shanks, *The New American Voter* (Cambridge: Harvard University Press, 1996).

58. Alan I. Abramowitz, "Issue Evolution Reconsidered: Racial Attitudes and Partisanship in the U.S. Electorate," *American Journal of Political Science* 38 (1994): 1–24.

59. Brad T. Gomez and J. Matthew Wilson, "Rethinking Symbolic Racism: Evidence of Attribution Bias," *The Journal of Politics* 68, no. 3 (2006): 611–625.

60. Edward G. Carmines, Paul M. Sniderman, and Beth Easter, "On the Meaning, Measurement, and Implications of Racial Resentment," *The ANNALS of the American Academy of Political and Social Science* 634, no. 1 (2011): 98.

61. P. J. Henry and David O. Sears, "The Symbolic Racism 2000 Scale," *Political* Psychology 23, no. 2 (2002): 258.

62. Christopher Tarman and David O. Sears, "The Conceptualization and Measurement of Symbolic Racism," *The Journal of Politics* 67, no. 3 (2005): 733; see also: David O. Sears and P. J. Henry, "The Origins of Symbolic Racism," *Journal of Personality and Social Psychology* 85, no. 2 (2003): 259–75 and David O. Sears and P. J. Henry, "Over Thirty Years Later: A Contemporary Look at Symbolic Racism and Its Critics," *Advances in Experimental Social Psychology* 37, no. 1 (2005): 95–150.

63. Joshua L. Rabinowitz, David O. Sears, Jim Sidanius, and Jon A. Krosnick, "Why Do White Americans Oppose Race-Targeted Policies? Clarifying the Impact of Symbolic Racism," *Political Psychology* 30, no. 5 (2009): 805–828.

64. See: Michael Hughes, "Symbolic Racism, Old Fashioned Racism, and Whites' Opposition to Affirmative Action," in *Racial Attitudes in the 1990s: Continuity and Change*, ed. Steven A. Tuch and Jack K. Martin (Westport: Praeger, 1997), 48.

65. Kerry O'Brien, Walter Forrest, Dermot Lynott, and Michael Daly, "Racism, Gun Ownership, and Gun Control: Biased Attitudes in US Whites May Influence Policy Decisions," *PLOS One* 8, no. 10 (2013): 1–10.

66. Eva G. T. Green, Christian Staerkle, and David O. Sears, "Symbolic Racism and Whites' Attitudes Towards Punitive and Preventive Crime Policies," *Law and Human Behavior* 30, no. 4 (2006): 435–454.

67. Gary M. Segura and Ali A. Valenzuela, "Hopes, Tropes, and Dopes: Hispanic and White Racial Animus in the 2008 Election," *Presidential Studies Quarterly* 40, no. 3 (2010): 497–514.

68. Black and Black, *The Rise of Southern Republicans*, 217.

69. Edsall and Edsall, *Chain Reaction*, 186.

70. Matthew Levendusky, *The Partisan Sort: How Liberals Became Democrats and Conservatives Became Republicans* (Chicago: University of Chicago Press, 2009), 53, 57.

71. James H. Kuklinski, Michael D. Cobb, and Martin Gilens, "Racial Attitudes in the 'New South,'" *Journal of Politics* 59, no. 2 (1997): 330.

72. George Lipsitz, *The Possessive Investment of Whiteness: How White People Profit from Identity Politics*, rev. ed. (Philadelphia: Temple University Press, 2006), 36.

73. *Fisher v. Univ. of TX at Austin* 570 U.S. ___ (2013); *Schuette v. Coal. Defend Affirmative Action, Integration & Immigration Rights* 572 U.S. ___ (2014).

74. Scott Clement, "Discrimination Against Whites Was a Core Concern of Trump's Base," *Washington Post*, August 2, 2017, https://www.washingtonpost.com/news/the-fix/wp/2017/08/02/discrimination-against-whites-was-a-core-concern-of-trumps-base.

75. Max Ehrenfreund, "Americans Now Think It's Okay to Say What They Really Think About Race," *Washington Post*, June 17, 2016, https://www.washingtonpost.com/news/wonk/wp/2016/06/17/americans-now-think-its-okay-to-say-what-they-really-think-about-race/.

76. John D. Foster, *White Race Discourse: Preserving Racial Privilege in a Post-racial Society* (Lanham: Lexington Books, 2013); see also: Bianca Gonzalez-Sobrino and Matthew W. Hughey, "Review of *White Race Discourse: Preserving Racial Privilege in a Post-racial Society*," *Ethnic and Racial Studies* 38, no. 3 (2014): 493–495.

77. "Putting 'Post-Racial' to Rest," *The Crisis*: Centennial Issue, 2010, https://www.thecrisismagazine.com.

78. Lawrence D. Bobo, "Somewhere Between Jim Crow & Post-Racialism: Reflections on the Racial Divide in America Today," *Daedalus* 140, no. 2 (2011): 32.

79. Mark Anthony Neal, quoted in: Rebecca Roberts, "The 'Post-Racial' Conversation, One Year In," *NPR*, January 18, 2010, http://www.npr.org/templates/story/story.php?storyId=122701272.

80. Ta-Nehisi Coates, "Fear of a Black President," *The Atlantic*, September 2012, http://www.theatlantic.com/magazine/archive/2012/09/fear-of-a-black-president/309064/.

81. Touré, "No Such Place."

82. Nikole Hannah-Jones, "The End of the Postracial Myth," *New York Times Magazine*, November 15, 2016, https://www.nytimes.com/interactive/2016/11/20/magazine/donald-trumps-america-iowa-race.html.

83. Hannah-Jones, "The End of the Postracial Myth."

84. Robin Kelley, quoted in: Hannah-Jones, "The End of the Postracial Myth."

85. Tim Wise, *Dear White America: Letter to a New Minority* (San Francisco: City Lights Books, 2012), 27.

86. Tim Wise, *Colorblind: The Rise of Post-Racial Politics and the Retreat from Racial Equity* (San Francisco: City Lights Books, 2010).

87. Sean McElwee, "Five Signs We're Not a 'Post-Racial' Society," *Huff Post Politics*, October 29, 2014, http://www.huffingtonpost.com/sean-mcelwee/five-signs-were-not-a-pos_b_5737794.html.

88. Stephen A. J. Colin III, "White Racist Ideology and the Myth of a Postracial Society," *New Directions for Adult and Continuing Education* 125 (2010): 7.

89. Ian Haney López, "Is the Post in Post-Racial the Blind in Colorblind?," *Cardozo Law Review* 32, no. 3 (2010): 827.

90. Mason, *Richard Nixon*, 160.

91. Lawrence J. McAndrews, "Missing the Bus: Gerald Ford and School Desegregation," *Presidential Studies Quarterly* 27, no. 4 (1997): 793.

92. Steven A. Holmes, "The Nation; When the Subject Is Civil Rights, There Are Two George Bushes," *New York Times*, June 9, 1991, http://www.nytimes.com/1991/06/09/weekinreview/the-nation-when-the-subject-is-civil-rights-there-are-two-george-bushes.html.

93. López, *Dog Whistle* Politics, 92.

94. Ruth Frankenberg, *The Social Construction of Whiteness: White Women, Race Matters* (Minneapolis: University of Minnesota Press, 1993), 15.

95. Sean McElwee, "Millennials Are More Racist than They Think: Just Look at the Numbers," *Politico Magazine*, March 9, 2015, http://www.politico.com/magazine/story/2015/03/millenials-race-115909.html.

PART II

1. Lillian Smith, *Killers of the Dream* (New York: W. W. Norton & Company, Inc., 1949), 118.

2. David Dismore, "Today in Herstory: Republican Party Official Endorses ERA in Party Platform," *Feminist Majority Foundation*, June 26, 2015, https://feminist.org/blog/index.php/2015/06/26/today-in-herstory-republican-party-officially-endorses-era-in-party-platform/.

3. Catherine E. Rymph, *Republican Women: Feminism and Conservatism from Suffrage through the Rise of the New Right* (Chapel Hill: University of North Carolina Press, 2006), 203.

4. Rymph, *Republican Women*, 222.

5. Phyllis Schlafly, quoted in: Michael Martin, "Phyllis Schlafly Still Championing the Anti-Feminist Fight," *NPR*, March 30, 2011, http://www.npr.org/templates/story/story.php?storyId=134981902.

6. Quoted in: James C. Cobb, *The South and America Since World War II* (New York: Oxford University Press, 2012), 229.

7. Kent Anderson Leslie, "A Myth of the Southern Lady: Antebellum Proslavery Rhetoric and the Proper Place of Woman," *Sociological Spectrum* 6, no. 1 (1986): 31.

8. Grace Elizabeth Hale, "'Some Women Have Never Been Reconstructed': Mildred Lewis Rutherford, Lucy M. Stanton, and the Racial Politics of White Southern Womanhood, 1900–1930," in *Georgia in Black and White: Exploration in the Race Relations of a Southern State, 1865–1950*, ed. John C. Inscoe (Athens: University of Georgia Press, 1994), 195.

9. Sara Evans, "Myth Against History: The Case of Southern Womanhood," in *Myth and Southern History: Volume 2, The New South*, 2nd ed., ed. Patrick Gerster and Nicholas Cords (Urbana: University of Illinois Press, 1989), 150.

10. Tanya Melich, *The Republican War Against Women: An Insider's Report from Behind the Lines* (New York: Bantam Books, 1996), 47.

11. See: Wanda Rushing, "'Sin, Sex, and Segregation': Social Control and the Education of Southern Women," *Gender and Education* 14, no. 2 (2002): 167–179.

12. Akiba Solomon, "The New-Old Southern Strategy Mixes Racism and Sexism for Nasty Results," *Colorlines*, February 28, 2012, http://www.colorlines.com/articles/new-old-southern-strategy-mixes-racism-and-sexism-nasty-results.

13. Arthur Remillard, *Southern Civil Religions: Imagining the Good Society in the Post-Reconstruction Era* (Athens: University of Georgia Press, 2011), 80.

14. Karen DeCrow, quoted in: Robert O. Self, *All in the Family: The Realignment of American Democracy Since the 1960s* (New York: Hill and Wang, 2012), 317.

15. Marjorie Spruill, *Divided We Stand: Women's Rights, Family Values, and the Polarization of American Politics* (New York: Bloomsbury, 2017), 12.

16. Spruill, *Divided We Stand*, 304.

17. Rymph, *Republican Women*, 231.

18. Melich, *The Republican War*, 122.

19. Richard E. Nisbett and Dov Cohen, *Culture of Honor: They Psychology of Violence in the South* (Boulder: Westview Press, 1996), 59.

20. Craig Thompson Friend, "From Southern Manhood to Southern Masculinities: An Introduction," in *Southern Masculinity: Perspectives on Manhood in the South Since Reconstruction*, ed. Craig Thompson Friend (Athens: University of Georgia Press, 2009), xxiii.

21. See: Dov Cohen, Richard E. Nisbett, Brian F. Bowdle, and Norbert Schwarz, "Insult, Aggression, and the Southern Culture of Honor: An 'Experimental Ethnography,'" *Journal of Personality and Social Psychology* 70, no. 5 (1996): 945–960.

22. Sam Ervin, quoted in: Donald G. Matthews and Jane Sherron de Hart, *Sex, Gender, and the Politics of the ERA* (New York: Oxford University Press, 1990), 41.

23. Anna Gavanas, *Fatherhood Politics in the United States: Masculinity, Sexuality, Race, and Marriage* (Urbana: University of Illinois Press, 2004), 10.

24. Robert Menzies, "Virtual Backlash: Representations of Men's 'Rights' and Feminist 'Wrongs' in Cyberspace," in *Reaction and Resistance: Feminism, Law, and Social Change*, ed. Dorothy E. Chunn, Susan B. Boyd, and Hester Lessard (Vancouver: University of British Columbia Press, 2007), 67.

25. Carol Mueller, "The Gender Gap and Women's Political Influence," *Annals of the American Academy of Political Science and Social Science* 515 (1991): 25.

26. Bill Peterson, "Reagan Did Understand Women," *Washington Post*, March 3, 1985, https://www.washingtonpost.com/archive/opinions/1985/03/03/reagan-did-understand-women/a710c0a0-38f0-4c04-ad3b-ae791371ccf2/.

27. Norman D. Sandler, "Reagan Still Wrestling Women Woes," *UPI*, September 18, 1983, https://www.upi.com/Archives/1983/09/18/Reagan-still-wrestling-women-woes/7387432705600/.

28. Karen M. Kaufmann and John R. Petrocik, "The Changing Politics of American Men: Understanding the Sources of the Gender Gap," *American Journal of Political Science* 43, no. 3 (1999): 864–887.

29. Louis Bolce, "The Role of Gender in Recent Presidential Elections: Reagan and the Reverse Gender Gap," *Presidential Studies Quarterly* 15, no. 2 (1985): 372.

30. Eric Plutzer and John F. Zipp, "Identity Politics, Partisanship, and Voting for Women Candidates," *Public Opinion Quarterly* 60 (1996): 30–57.

31. Kathleen Dolan, "Gender Differences in Support for Women Candidates," *Women & Politics* 17, no. 2 (1997): 27–41.

32. Glenda Gilmore, "But She Can't Find Her [V. O.] Key: Writing Gender and Race into Southern Political History," in *Southern Women: Taking Off the White Gloves: Southern Women and Women Historians*, ed. Michele Gillespie and Catherine Clinton (Columbia: University of Missouri Press, 1998), 126.

33. Jane J. Mansbridge, *Why We Lost the ERA* (Chicago: University of Chicago Press, 1986), 5–6.

CHAPTER 4

1. Carl Carmer, *Stars Fell over Alabama* (New York: Doubleday, 1934), 14–15.

2. Karrin Vasby Anderson, "From Spouses to Candidates: Hillary Rodham Clinton, Elizabeth Dole, and the Gendered Office of U.S. President," *Rhetoric & Public Affairs* 5, no. 1 (2002): 120.

3. Anderson, "From Spouses to Candidates," 118.

4. Anderson, "From Spouses to Candidates," 119.

5. Maria L. La Ganga, "Dole's 'Southern Strategy' Is Major Political Asset: Wife Elizabeth Raises Money and Never Lowers Her Guard," *St. Louis Post-Dispatch*, August 11, 1996, https://www.questia.com/newspaper/1P2-33019748/dole-s-southern-strategy-is-major-political-asset.

6. La Ganga, "Dole's 'Southern Strategy.'"

7. Susan Baer, "Mrs. Dole Portrays a Kinder, Gentler Bob," *Baltimore Sun*, August 15, 1996, http://articles.baltimoresun.com/1996-08-15/news/1996228057_1_bob-dole-elizabeth-dole-dole-campaign.

8. Frank Clifford, "Elizabeth Dole Becomes Husband's Southern Strategy," *Los Angeles Times*, October 27, 1987, http://articles.latimes.com/1987-10-27/news/mn-16899_1_elizabeth-dole.

9. La Ganga, "Dole's 'Southern Strategy.'"

10. Rachel B. Friedman and Ronald E. Lee, *The Style and Rhetoric of Elizabeth Dole: Public Persona and Political Discourse* (Lanham: Lexington Books, 2013), 12.

11. Elizabeth Fox-Genovese, *Within the Plantation Household: Black and White Women of the Old South* (Chapel Hill: University of North Carolina Press, 1988), 41.

12. Jacqueline Boles and Maxine P. Atkinson, "Ladies: South by Northwest," *Sociological Spectrum* 6, no. 1 (1986): 70.

13. Michael Peckerar, "20 Reasons to Date a Southern Girl," *Rant Lifestyle*, January 18, 2014, http://www.rantlifestyle.com/2014/01/18/20-reasons-date-southern-girl/.

14. Dana Oliver, "21 Beauty Secrets Southern Belles Swear By," *Huffington Post*, December 6, 2017, https://www.huffpost.com/entry/southern-belle-beauty-secrets_n_4098506.

15. Phoebe M. Bronstein, "Televising the South: Race, Gender, and Region in Primetime, 1955–1980" (PhD diss., University of Oregon, 2013).

16. Florence King, *Southern Ladies and Gentlemen* (New York: Stein and Day, 1975), 37.

17. King, *Southern Ladies and Gentlemen*, 47, 55.

18. Robert O. Self, *All in the Family: The Realignment of American Democracy Since the 1960s* (New York: Hill and Wang, 2012), 317.

19. Lillian Smith, *Killers of the Dream* (New York: W. W. Norton & Company, Inc., 1949), 137.

20. Jean M. Twenge, "Attitudes Toward Women, 1970–1995: A Meta-Analysis," *Psychology of Women Quarterly* 21 (1997): 35–51.

21. Smith, *Killers of the Dream*, 35.

22. Tom W. Rice and Diane L. Coates, "Gender Role Attitudes in the Southern United States," *Gender and Society* 9, no. 6 (1995): 744–756.

23. Rebecca S. Powers, J. Jill Suitor, Susana Guerra, Monisa Shackleford, Dorothy Mecom, and Kim Gusman, "Regional Differences in Gender-Role Attitudes: Variations by Gender and Race," *Gender Issues* (Spring 2003): 40–54.

24. Samantha Lachman, "Virginia GOP Rescinds Support for Equal Rights Amendment," *Huffington Post*, February 4, 2015, http://www.huffingtonpost.com/2015/02/04/virginia-equal-rights-amendment-_n_6615180.html.

25. Andrew DeMillo, "Arkansas Senate Panel Rejects Equal Rights Amendment," *Associated Press*, April 3, 2013, http://www.memphisdailynews.com/news/2013/apr/3/ark-senate-panel-rejects-equal-rights-amendment/.

26. Seth A. Dowland, "A New Kind of Patriarchy: Inerrancy and Masculinity in the Southern Baptist Convention, 1979–2000," in *Southern Masculinity: Perspectives on Manhood in the South Since Reconstruction*, ed. Craig Thompson Friend (Athens: University of Georgia Press, 2009), 247.

27. Trent Watts, "Introduction: Telling White Men's Stories," in *White Masculinity in the Recent South*, ed. Trent Watts (Baton Rouge: Louisiana State University Press, 2008), 10.

28. Angela Boswell, "Married Women's Property Rights and the Challenge to the Patriarchal Order: Colorado County, Texas," in *Negotiating Boundaries of Southern Womanhood: Dealing with the Powers That Be*, ed. Janet L. Coryell, Thomas H. Appleton Jr., Anastasia Sims, and Sandra Gioia Treadway (Columbia: University of Missouri Press, 2000), 90.

29. Jacqueline Boles and Maxine P. Atkinson, "Ladies: South by Northwest," *Sociological Spectrum* 6, no. 1 (1986): 74–75.

30. Cherry Good, "The Southern Lady, or the Art of Dissembling," *Journal of American Studies* 23, no. 1 (1989): 75.

31. Rachel B. Friedman and Ronald E. Lee, *The Style and Rhetoric of Elizabeth Dole: Public Persona and Political Discourse* (Lanham: Lexington Books, 2013), 12.

32. Karrin Vasby Anderson, "From Spouses to Candidates: Hillary Rodham Clinton, Elizabeth Dole, and the Gendered Office of U.S. President," *Rhetoric & Public Affairs* 5, no. 1 (2002): 106.

33. Donald G. Matthews and Jane Sherron de Hart, *Sex, Gender, and the Politics of the ERA* (New York: Oxford University Press, 1990), 34.

34. Daniella Diaz, "Trump Calls Clinton a 'Nasty Woman,'" *CNN*, October 20, 2016, http://www.cnn.com/2016/10/19/politics/donald-trump-hillary-clinton-nasty-woman/index.html.

35. Sarah Wilkerson-Freeman, "Stealth in the Political Arsenal of Southern Women: A Retrospective for the Millennium," in *Southern Women at the Millennium: A Historical Perspective*, ed. Melissa Walker, Jeanette R. Dunn, and Joe P. Dunn (Columbia: University of Missouri Press, 2003), 76–77.

36. Nina Baym, *Feminism and American Literary History* (New Brunswick: Rutgers University Press, 1992), 183.

37. Holly Baer, "My Failures as a Southern Woman," *Sex, Religion, Politics and Other Topics to Avoid at the Dinner Table*, April 28, 2015, http://hollybaer.com/2015/04/28/my-failures-as-a-southern-woman/.

38. Margaret Ripley Wolfe, "The Southern Lady: Long-Suffering Counterpart of the Good Ole' Boy," *Journal of Popular Culture* 11, no. 1 (1977), 18.

39. Kent Anderson Leslie, "A Myth of the Southern Lady: Antebellum Proslavery Rhetoric and the Proper Place of Woman," *Sociological Spectrum* 6, no. 1 (1986): 45.

40. Sara Evans, "Myth Against History: The Case of Southern Womanhood," in *Myth and Southern History: Volume 2, The New South*, 2nd ed., ed. Patrick Gerster and Nicholas Cords (Urbana: University of Illinois Press, 1989), 152.

41. Wolfe, "The Southern Lady," 26.

42. Boswell, "Married Women's Property Rights," 108–109.

43. Evans, "Myth Against History," 152.

44. Jane Turner Censer, *The Reconstruction of White Southern Womanhood, 1865–1895* (Baton Rouge: Louisiana State University Press, 2003).

45. Evans, "Myth Against History," 151.

46. Elizabeth Fox-Genovese, *Within the Plantation Household: Black and White Women of the Old South* (Chapel Hill: University of North Carolina Press, 1988), 38.

47. Anna Gavanas, *Fatherhood Politics in the United States: Masculinity, Sexuality, Race, and Marriage* (Urbana: University of Illinois Press, 2004), 7.

48. Fox-Genovese, *Within the Plantation* Household, 61.

49. Richard H. Rovere, "The Campaign: Goldwater," *The New Yorker*, October 3, 1964, http://www.newyorker.com/magazine/1964/10/03/the-campaign-goldwater.

50. Joel Williamson, *The Crucible of Race: Black-White Relations in the American South Since Emancipation* (New York: Oxford University Press, 1984), 497.

51. Baym, *Feminism and American Literary History*, 195.

52. Fox-Genovese, *Within the Plantation Household*, 81.

53. Evans, "Myth Against History," 150.

54. See: Grace Elizabeth Hale, "'Some Women Have Never Been Reconstructed': Mildred Lewis Rutherford, Lucy M. Stanton, and the Racial Politics of White Southern

Womanhood, 1900–1930," in *Georgia in Black and White: Exploration in the Race Relations of a Southern State, 1865–1950*, ed. John C. Inscoe (Athens: University of Georgia Press, 1994), 173–201.

55. Virginia Foster, "The Emancipation of Pure, White, Southern Womanhood," *New South* 26 (1971): 47.

56. Clifford, "Elizabeth Dole."

57. Kristin J. Anderson, *Modern Misogyny: Anti-Feminism in a Post-Feminist Era* (Oxford: Oxford University Press, 2015), 77.

58. Fox-Genovese, *Within the Plantation* Household, 99.

59. Julie E. Press and Eleanor Townsley, "'Wives' and Husbands' Housework Reporting Gender, Class, and Social Desirability," *Gender and Society* 12, no. 2 (1998): 188–216.

60. Michael Lempert and Michael Silverstein, *Creatures of Politics: Media, Message, and the American Presidency* (Bloomington: Indiana University Press, 2012), 220; Miranda Weinberg, "Presidents Evaluating Women's Attractiveness, 1973 and 2013" *The Society Pages*, June 5, 2013, https://thesocietypages.org/socimages/2013/06/05/presidents-evaluating-womens-attractiveness-1973-and-2013/.

61. Linda Hales, "For This Old House and Senate, It's Makeover Time," *Washington Post*, November 13, 2006, http://www.washingtonpost.com/wp-dyn/content/article/2006/11/12/AR2006111201124_2.html.

62. Samantha Henig, "Sarah Palin, Miss Alaska, and the Vice Presidency," *Newsweek*, August 28, 2008, http://www.newsweek.com/sarah-palin-miss-alaska-and-vice-presidency-88227.

63. Leslie Savan, "A Mad Men Cameo for John McCain," *The Guardian*, August 8, 2008, https://www.theguardian.com/commentisfree/2008/aug/08/johnmccain.gender.

64. Angela Moon, "President Trump Says French First Lady Is in 'Such Good Shape,'" *Reuters*, July 13, 2017, https://www.reuters.com/article/us-france-usa-trump-brigitte-macron/president-trump-says-french-first-lady-is-in-such-good-shape-idUSKBN19Y2XT.

65. Diane Roberts, *Faulkner and Southern Womanhood* (Athens: University of Georgia Press, 1994), 111.

66. Lauren A. Stealey, "Lady Bird Johnson, Betty Ford, and Second Wave Feminism" (MA thesis, University of Southern Mississippi, 2014), 49–53.

67. Janet K. Swim, Kathryn J. Aiken, Wayne S. Hall, and Barbara A. Hunter, "Sexism and Racism: Old-Fashioned and Modern Prejudices," *Journal of Personality and Social Psychology* 68, no. 2 (1995): 199–214; see also: Melanie A. Morrison, Todd G. Morrison, Gregory A. Pope, and Bruno D. Zumbo, "An Investigation of Measures of Modern and Old-Fashioned Sexism," *Social Indicators Research* 48, no. 1 (1999): 39–50.

68. Maureen C. McHugh and Irene Hanson Frieze, "The Measurement of Gender-Role Attitudes: A Review and Commentary," *Psychology of Women Quarterly* 21 (1997): 8.

69. Twenge, "Attitudes Toward Women," 35–51.

70. Anderson, "From Spouses to Candidates," 122.

71. Chloe Angyal, "Affirmative Action Is Great for White Women. So Why Do They Hate It?," *Huffington Post*, January 21, 2016, https://www.huffingtonpost.com/entry/affirmative-action-white-women_us_56a0ef6ae4bod8cc1098d3a5.

72. Kenneth Wilson and Patricia Yancey Martin, "Regional Differences in Resolving Family Conflicts: Is There a Legacy of Patriarchy in the South?," *Sociological Spectrum* 8 (1988): 207.

73. Fox-Genovese, *Within the Plantation* Household, 59.

74. Matthews and de Hart, *Sex, Gender, and the Politics of the ERA*, 20.

75. Roy Reed, "In the South, Road to Equality Rights Is Rocky and Full of Detours," *New York Times*, March 20, 1975, http://www.nytimes.com/1975/03/20/archives/in-the-south-road-to-equal-rights-is-rocky-and-full-of-detours.html.

76. Sue Tolleson-Rinehart, "Can the Flower of Southern Womanhood Bloom in the Garden of Southern Politics?," *Southern Cultures* 4, no. 1 (1998): 84.

77. Marjorie Spruill, *Divided We Stand: Women's Rights, Family Values, and the Polarization of American Politics* (New York: Bloomsbury, 2017), 86.

78. Spruill, *Divided We Stand*, 186–187.

79. Spruill, *Divided We Stand*, 81.

80. Phyllis Schlafly, "What's Wrong with 'Equal Rights' for Women?," in *Debating the American Conservative Movement: 1945 to the Present*, ed. Donald T. Critchlow and Nancy MacLean (Lanham: Rowman & Littlefield Publishers, Inc., 2009), 200; Schlafly's statement first appeared in 1972.

81. McKay Coppins, "Ann Romney's 'Childhood Nanny' Dishes on Privileged Upbringing," *Buzzfeed News*, April 13, 2012, https://www.buzzfeed.com/mckaycoppins/ann-romneys-childhood-nanny-dishes-on-privilege.

82. Doug Barry, "Ann Romney Wants to Be America's First Professional Mother First Lady in a Century," *Jezebel*, April 15, 2012, http://jezebel.com/5902095/ann-romney-wants-to-be-americas-first-professional-mother-first-lady-in-a-century.

83. Ann Romney, "Republican National Convention Speech," *NPR*, August 28, 2012, http://www.npr.org/2012/08/28/160216442/transcript-ann-romneys-convention-speech.

84. Dowland, "A New Kind of Patriarchy," 255.

85. Dowland, "A New Kind of Patriarchy," 256.

86. Letha Scanzoni and Nancy Hardesty, quoted in: Dowland, "A New Kind of Patriarchy," 257.

87. Dowland, "A New Kind of Patriarchy," 258.

88. Dowland, "A New Kind of Patriarchy," 258.

89. "Southern Baptists Lead the Way," *The Council on Biblical Manhood and Womanhood*, June 1, 1998, http://cbmw.org/uncategorized/southern-baptists-lead-the-way/.

90. Dowland, "A New Kind of Patriarchy," 253, 259–260.

91. Bob Allen, "Southern Baptist Leaders' Comments Echo 'Biblical Patriarchy' Theology," *EthicsDaily.com*, April 25, 2008, http://www.ethicsdaily.com/southern-baptist-leaders-comments-echo-biblical-patriarchy-theology-cms-12562.

92. Allen, "Southern Baptist Leaders' Comments."

93. Robert Menzies, "Virtual Backlash: Representations of Men's 'Rights' and Feminist 'Wrongs' in Cyberspace," in *Reaction and Resistance: Feminism, Law, and Social Change*, ed. Dorothy E. Chunn, Susan B. Boyd, and Hester Lessard (Vancouver: University of British Columbia Press, 2007), 78.

94. Matthew D. Lassiter, "Inventing Family Values," in *Rightward Bound: Making America Conservative in the 1970s*, ed. Bruce J. Schulman and Julian E. Zelizer (Cambridge: Harvard University Press, 2008), 14.

95. Lassiter, "Inventing Family Values," 17.

96. Laura Kalman, *Right Start Rising: A New Politics, 1974–1980* (New York: W. W. Norton & Company, Inc., 2010), 75.

97. Renee Feinberg, ed., *The Equal Rights Amendment: An Annotated Bibliography of the Issues, 1976–1985* (New York: Greenwood Press, 1986), 47–57.

98. Kalman, *Right Start Rising*, 262.

99. Self, *All in the Family*, 365.

100. Sally K. Gallagher, "Where Are the Antifeminist Evangelicals? Evangelical Identity, Subcultural Location, and Attitudes Towards Feminism," *Gender and Society* 18, no. 4 (2004): 451–472.

101. Daniel K. Williams, "Voting for God and the GOP: The Role of Evangelical Religion in the Emergence of the Republican South," in *Painting Dixie Red: When, Where, Why, and How the South Became Republican*, ed. Glenn Feldman (Gainesville: University Press of Florida, 2011), 28.

102. Dana D. Nelson, *National Manhood: Capitalist Citizenship and the Imagined Fraternity of White Men* (Durham: Duke University Press, 1998), 19.

103. Glenda Gilmore, *Gender and Jim Crow: Women and the Politics of White Supremacy in North Carolina, 1896–1920* (Chapel Hill: University of North Carolina Press, 1996), 37.

104. Anne Frior Scott, *The Southern Lady: From Pedestal to Politics, 1830–1930* (Chicago: University of Chicago Press, 1970); Boles and Atkinson, "Ladies: South by Northwest," 67.

105. "Women's Rights Backlash Troubles Carter Aide," *Gadsden Times*, July 10, 1977, Records of the National Commission on the Observance of International Women's Year, Schlesinger Library on the History of Women in America, Harvard University; see also: Spruill, *Divided We Stand*, 183.

106. Alan Rappeport, "Donald Trump's Uncomplimentary Comments about Carly Fiorina," *New York Times*, September 10, 2015, https://www.nytimes.com/politics/first-draft/2015/09/10/donald-trumps-uncomplimentary-comments-about-carly-fiorina/; Adam Howard, "Donald Trump Resurrects Decade-Old Rosie O'Donnell Feud (Again)," *NBC News*, September 27, 2016, https://www.nbcnews.com/storyline/2016-presidential-debates/donald-trump-resurrects-decade-old-rosie-o-donnell-feud-again-n655306.

107. Amanda Marcotte, "The Mystery of Republican Women Backing Sexist Trump: They're Female Misogynists Who've Grow to Accept Oppression," *Salon*, April 8, 2016, https://www.salon.com/2016/04/08/the_mystery_of_republican_women_backing_sexist_trump_theyre_female_misogynists_whove_grown_to_accept_oppression/.

108. La Ganga, "Dole's 'Southern Strategy.'"

109. Clifford, "Elizabeth Dole."

110. Roberts, *Faulkner and Southern Womanhood*, 103.

111. See: Catherine Fosl, "Anne Braden and the 'Protective Custody' of White Southern Womanhood," in *Throwing Off the Cloak of Privilege: White Southern Women Activists in the Civil Rights Era*, ed. Gail S. Murray (Gainesville: University Press of Florida, 2004), 101–130 and Jacquelyn Dowd Hall, *Revolt Against Chivalry: Jessie Daniel Ames and the Women's Campaign Against Lynching* (New York: Columbia University Press, 1993).

112. Cynthia Roldan, "Sen. Corbin's 'Jokes' Expose Sexism in South Carolina Legislature, Activists Say," *The Post and Courier*, February 21, 2015, http://www.postandcourier.com/article/20150221/PC1603/150229867/1031; Kay Steiger, "Southern Carolina's Only Female State Senator Didn't Find Colleague's Sexist Joke Very Funny," *ThinkProgress*, February 14, 2015, http://thinkprogress.org/politics/2015/02/14/3623294/south-carolinas-female-state-senator-didnt-find-colleagues-sexist-joke-funny/.

113. Sam Kleiner, "The GOP's History of Sexist Hillary-Bashing," *The Daily Beast*, December 26, 2013, http://www.thedailybeast.com/articles/2013/12/26/the-last-time-republicans-fought-hillary-they-used-sexism.html.

114. Grace Drake, "Southern Society and Sexism," *Feministing*, January 2, 2012, http://feministing.com/2012/01/02/southern-society-and-sexism/; Allison Glock, "Southern

Women: A New Generation of Women Who Are Redefining the Southern Belle," *Garden & Gun,* August/September 2011, http://gardenandgun.com/article/southern-women.

CHAPTER 5

1. W. J. Cash, *The Mind of the South* (Garden City: Doubleday, 1941), 62.
2. Mitt Romney, quoted in: Maria Cardona, "Romney's Empty 'Binders Full of Women,'" *CNN,* October 18, 2012, http://www.cnn.com/2012/10/17/opinion/cardona-binders-women/index.html.
3. Tom Meltzer, "'Binders Full of Women': Romney's Four Words That Alienated Women Voters," *The Guardian,* October 17, 2012, https://www.theguardian.com/world/shortcuts/2012/oct/17/binders-full-of-women-romneys-four-words.
4. Amy Sullivan, "Mitt the Jerk: A Woman's View of the Debate," *New Republic,* October 16, 2012, https://newrepublic.com/article/108711/mitt-jerk-womans-view-debate.
5. Alec MacGillis, "Romney and Women," *Washington Post,* October 15, 2007, http://voices.washingtonpost.com/44/2007/10/romney-vs-woman.html.
6. Maureen Dowd, "The 1992 Campaign: Campaign Trail; From Nixon, Predictions on the Presidential Race," *New York Times,* February 6, 1992, http://www.nytimes.com/1992/02/06/us/the-1992-campaign-campaing-trail-from-nixon-predictions-on-the-presidential-race.html.
7. Sally Denton, "A Long History of Sexism in Politics," *Los Angeles Times,* December 22, 2009, http://articles.latimes.com/2009/dec/22/opinion/la-oe-denton22-2009dec22/2.
8. Sullivan, "Mitt the Jerk."
9. Susan Brooks Thistlewait, "Why We Need Feminist Ideology: Romney and 'Binders Full of Women,'" *On Faith,* October 17, 2012, https://www.onfaith.co/onfaith/2012/10/17/why-we-need-feminist-theology-romney-and-binders-full-of-women/10843.
10. Craig Thompson Friend, "From Southern Manhood to Southern Masculinities: An Introduction," in *Southern Masculinity: Perspectives on Manhood in the South Since Reconstruction,* ed. Craig Thompson Friend (Athens: University of Georgia Press, 2009), xi.
11. Trent Watts, "Introduction: Telling White Men's Stories," in *White Masculinity in the Recent South,* ed. Trent Watts (Baton Rouge: Louisiana State University Press, 2008), 20; see also: Steve Estes, "A Question of Honor: Masculinity and Massive Resistance to Integration," in *White Masculinity in the Recent South,* ed. Trent Watts (Baton Rouge: Louisiana State University Press, 2008), 99–120.
12. Kristin J. Anderson, *Modern Misogyny: Anti-Feminism in a Post-Feminist Era* (Oxford: Oxford University Press, 2015), 86.
13. Anderson, *Modern Misogyny,* 95.
14. Betty A. Dobratz and Stephanie L. Shanks-Meile, *"White Power, White Pride!": The White Separatists Movement in the United States* (New York: Twayne Publishers, 1997), 19.
15. Laura Chapin, "A Sexist Smorgasbord," *U.S. News & World Report,* August 7, 2015, http://www.usnews.com/opinion/blogs/laura-chapin/2015/08/07/the-gop-debates-sexist-stand-against-womens-rights.
16. Stephanie Marken, "Trump Favorability Among Women Typical for GOP Candidates," *Gallup,* August 17, 2015, http://www.gallup.com/poll/184634/trump-favorability-among-women-typical-gop-candidates.aspx.
17. "GOP Women Dig 'The Donald,'" *FitsNews,* August 28, 2015, http://www.fitsnews.com/2015/08/28/gop-women-dig-the-donald/.

18. Dana Schwartz, "Why Angry White Men Love Calling People 'Cucks,'" *GQ*, August 16, 2016, https://www.gq.com/story/why-angry-white-men-love-calling-people-cucks.

19. Chauncey DeVega, "The Secret History of 'Cuckservative': The Fetish That Became a Right-Wing Rallying Cry," *Salon*, August 9, 2015, http://www.salon.com/2015/08/09/the_secret_history_of_cuckservative_the_fetish_that_became_a_right_wing_rallying_cry/.

20. Daniel Florien, "Jimmy Carter on Southern Baptist Sexism," *Patheos*, July 21, 2009, http://www.patheos.com/blogs/unreasonablefaith/2009/07/jimmy-carter-on-southern-baptist-sexism/.

21. K. Michael Prince, "Neo-Confederates in the Basement: The League of the South and the Crusade Against Southern Emasculation," in *White Masculinity in the Recent South*, ed. Trent Watts (Baton Rouge: Louisiana State University Press, 2008), 161.

22. Bertram Wyatt-Brown, *Honor and Violence in the Old South*, abridged ed. (New York: Oxford University Press, 1986), vii.

23. Jason T. Eastman and Alana N. Iapalucci, "Satan, Sinners, and Damnation: Religion and Heritage in the Contemporary Rock Music Revival," *Rock Music Studies* 1, no. 3 (2014): 231–250.

24. Dana D. Nelson, *National Manhood: Capitalist Citizenship and the Imagined Fraternity of White Men* (Durham: Duke University Press, 1998), 181.

25. Nelson, *National Manhood*, 204.

26. Joelle C. Ruthig, Andre Kehn, Bradlee W. Gamblin, Karen Vanderzanden, and Kelly Jones, "When Women's Gains Equal Men's Losses: Predicting a Zero-Sum Perspective of Gender Status," *Sex Roles* 76 (2017): 17–26.

27. David Savran, *Taking It Like a Man: White Masculinity, Masochism, and Contemporary American Culture* (Princeton: Princeton University Press, 1998), 51.

28. See: Christina Hoff Sommers, *The War Against Boys: How Misguided Feminism Is Harming our Young Boys* (New York: Simon & Schuster, 2001) and Kathleen Parker, *Save the Males: Why Men Matter, Why Women Should Care* (New York: Random House, 2008).

29. Hannah Rosin, "The End of Men," *The Atlantic*, July/August 2010, http://www.theatlantic.com/magazine/archive/2010/07/the-end-of-men/308135/.

30. Anderson, *Modern Misogyny*, 79.

31. Michael S. Kimmel, *Manhood in America: A Cultural History*, 2nd ed. (New York: Oxford University, 2006), 216.

32. Jonathan Mahler, "Commute to Nowhere," *New York Times Magazine*, April 13, 2003, http://www.nytimes.com/2003/04/13/magazine/commute-to-nowhere.html.

33. Kimmel, *Manhood in America*, 216.

34. Kimmel, *Manhood in America*, 217.

35. Susan J. Tolchin, *The Angry American: How Voter Rage Is Changing the Nation*, 2nd ed. (Boulder: Westview Press, 1999), 33.

36. Tolchin, *The Angry* American, 22.; see also: Robert Jay Lifton, *The Protean Self: Human Resilience in an Age of Fragmentation* (New York: Basic Books, 1993).

37. Tolchin, *The Angry* American, 49.

38. Brenda Major, Dean B. McFarlin, and Diana Gagnon, "Overworked and Underpaid: On the Nature of Gender Differences and Personal Entitlement," *Journal of Personality and Social Psychology* 47 (1984): 1399–1412.

39. Ronnee Schreiber, *Righting Feminism: Conservative Women & American Politics* (New York: Oxford University Press, 2008), 3.

40. Robert Menzies, "Virtual Backlash: Representations of Men's 'Rights' and Feminist 'Wrongs' in Cyberspace," in *Reaction and Resistance: Feminism, Law, and Social Change*, ed. Dorothy E. Chunn, Susan B. Boyd, and Hester Lessard (Vancouver: University of British Columbia Press, 2007), 83.

41. Menzies, "Virtual Backlash," 82.

42. Anna Gavanas, *Fatherhood Politics in the United States: Masculinity, Sexuality, Race, and Marriage* (Urbana: University of Illinois Press, 2004).

43. Kimmel, *Manhood in America*, 186.

44. Kimmel, *Manhood in America*, 200.

45. Michael Kimmel, *Angry White Men: American Masculinity at the End of an Era* (New York: Nation Books, 2013), 111.

46. Gavanas, *Fatherhood Politics*, 11.

47. Claire Landsbaum, "Men's Rights Activists Are Finding a New Home with the Alt-Right," *The Cut*, December 14, 2016, https://www.thecut.com/2016/12/mens-rights-activists-are-flocking-to-the-alt-right.html.

48. David Futrelle, "The Southern Poverty Law Center Takes On the Violent Misogyny So Pervasive in Men's Rights Movement," *We Hunted the Mammoth*, March 8, 2012, http://www.wehuntedthemammoth.com/2012/03/08/the-southern-poverty-law-center-takes-on-the-violent-misogyny-so-pervasive-in-the-mens-rights-movement/.

49. Menzies, "Virtual Backlash," 65.

50. "Misogyny: The Sites," *Southern Poverty Law Center*, March 1, 2012, https://www.splcenter.org/fighting-hate/intelligence-report/2012/misogyny-sites.

51. "Misogyny: The Sites."

52. "Misogyny: The Sites."

53. Kimmel, *Manhood in America*, 221.

54. James E. Cameron, "Social Identity, Modern Sexism, and Perceptions of Personal and Group Discrimination by Women and Men," *Sex Roles* 45, no. 11/12 (2001): 743–766.

55. Lorri Glover, "An Education in Southern Masculinity: The Ball Family of South Carolina in the New Republic," *Journal of Southern History* 69, no. 1 (2003): 45.

56. Bertram Wyatt-Brown, *Honor and Violence in the Old South*, abridged ed. (New York: Oxford University Press, 1986), 88.

57. Watts, "Introduction," 14.

58. Craig Thompson Friend and Lorri Glover, "Rethinking Southern Masculinity: An Introduction," in *Southern Manhood: Perspectives of Masculinity in the Old South*, ed. Craig Thompson Friend and Lorri Glover (Athens: University of Georgia Press, 2004), viii.

59. Wyatt-Brown, *Honor and Violence*, 63.

60. Wyatt-Brown, *Honor and Violence*, xv.

61. Friend and Glover, "Rethinking Southern Masculinity," viii.

62. Kenneth Wilson and Patricia Yancey Martin, "Regional Differences in Resolving Family Conflicts: Is There a Legacy of Patriarchy in the South?," *Sociological Spectrum* 8 (1988):197.

63. Dov Cohen, Richard E. Nisbett, Brian F. Bowdle, and Norbert Schwarz, "Insult, Aggression, and the Southern Culture of Honor: An 'Experimental Ethnography,'" *Journal of Personality and Social Psychology* 70, no. 5 (1996): 945.

64. Jason T. Eastman, "Rebel Manhood: The Hegemonic Masculinity of the Southern Rock Music Revival," *Journal of Contemporary Ethnography* 20, no. 10 (2011): 1.

65. Friend, "From Southern Manhood," vii.

66. Jon D. Bohland, "Look Away, Look Away, Look Away to Lexington: Struggles over Neo-Confederate Nationalism, Memory, and Masculinity in a Small Virginia Town,"

Southeastern Geographer 53, no. 3 (2013): 282; see also: Friend, "From Southern Manhood," xi.

67. Bohland, "Look Away," 282.

68. Nancy MacLean, *Behind the Mask of Chivalry: The Making of the Second Ku Klux Klan* (New York: Oxford University Press, 1994), 11.

69. MacLean, *Behind the Mask of Chivalry*, xii.

70. Richard E. Nisbett and Dov Cohen, *Culture of Honor: They Psychology of Violence in the South* (Boulder: Westview Press, 1996), 3, 5.

71. Wyatt-Brown, *Honor and Violence*, 366.

72. Wyatt-Brown, *Honor and Violence*, 367.

73. Harry M. Caudill, *Night Comes to the Cumberlands* (Boston: Little, Brown and Co., 1962), 45.

74. Wyatt-Brown, *Honor and Violence*, 381; Dov Cohen and Richard E. Nisbett, "Self-Protection and the Culture of Honor: Explaining Southern Violence," *Personality and Social Psychology Bulletin* 20, no. 5 (1994): 551–567.

75. Nisbett and Cohen, *Culture of Honor*, 50.

76. See: Christopher G. Ellison, "An Eye for an Eye? A Note on the Southern Subculture of Violence Thesis," *Social Forces* 69, no. 4 (1991): 1223–1239; Timothy C. Hayes and Matthew R. Lee, "The Southern Culture of Honor and Violent Attitudes," *Sociological Spectrum* 25, no. 5 (2006): 593–617.

77. Nisbett and Cohen, *Culture of Honor*, 83.

78. Frank Gene Jordan Jr., "The Laughter Behind: Curriculum of Place, the Hypermasculine Imperative, and the Critical Education of Southern Cops" (MA thesis, Georgia Southern University, 2013).

79. See: Cohen and Nisbett, "Self-Protection," 551–567; William B. Bankston, Carol Y. Thompson, Quentin A. L. Jenkins, and Craig J. Forsyth, "The Influence of Fear of Crime, Gender, and Southern Culture on Carrying Firearms for Protection," *The Sociological Quarterly* 31, no. 2 (1990): 287–305; Richard B. Felson, Paul-Phillipe Pare, "Firearms and Fisticuffs: Region, Race, and Adversary Effects on Homicide and Assault," *Social Science Research* 39, no. 2 (2010): 272–284; Jo Dixon and Alan J. Lizotte, "Gun Ownership and the 'Southern Subculture of Violence,'" *American Journal of Sociology* 93, no. 2 (1987): 202–405.

80. John Shelton Reed, "To Live—and Die—in Dixie: A Contribution to the Study of Southern Violence," *Political Science Quarterly* 86, no. 3 (1971): 429–443; Sheldon Hackney, "Southern Violence," *American Historical Review* 74, no. 3 (1969): 906–925.

81. Watts, "Introduction," 22.

82. Watts, "Introduction," 22.

83. Wyatt-Brown, *Honor and Violence*, 377.

84. Wyatt-Brown, *Honor and Violence*, 373.

85. Mary R. Rose and Christopher G. Ellison, "Violence as Honorable? Racial and Ethnic Differences in Attitudes Towards Violence," *Crime & Delinquency* 62, no. 6 (2016): 800.

86. Stephen Marche, "How Toxic Masculinity Poisoned the 2016 Election," *Esquire*, March 9, 2016, https://www.esquire.com/news-politics/news/a42802/toxic-masculine-discourse/.

87. "Peace Little Girl (Daisy)," *Museum of the Moving Image: The Living Room Candidate*, 1964, http://www.livingroomcandidate.org/commercials/1964/peace-little-girl-daisy.

88. Rob Okun, "New Brand of Masculinity Wins the Pro-Change Vote," *WE News*, November 3, 2008, http://womensenews.org/2008/11/new-brand-masculinity-wins-the-pro-change-vote/.

89. J. Weston Phippen, "Has Anything Changed with Arizona's Immigration Law?," *The Atlantic*, September 16, 2016, https://www.theatlantic.com/news/archive/2016/09/arizona-law/500426/.

90. Estes, "A Question of Honor," 99.

91. Anderson, *Modern Misogyny*, 75.

92. Peggy McIntosh and Barry Deutsch, "The Male Privilege Checklist: An Unabashed Imitation of an Article," in *The Battle and the Backlash Rage On: Why Feminism Cannot Be Obsolete*, ed. Stacey Elin Rossi (Bloomington: Xlibris Corporation, 2004), 72–75.

93. Friend and Glover, "Rethinking Southern Masculinity," xiii.

94. Seth Dowland, "A New Kind of Patriarchy: Inerrancy and Masculinity in the Southern Baptist Convention, 1979–2000" in *Southern Masculinity: Perspectives on Manhood in the New South*, ed. Craig Thompson Friend (Athens: University of Georgia Press, 2009), 247.

95. Randy Stinson and Dan Dumas, "A Guide to Biblical Manhood," *The Southern Baptist Theological Seminary*, n.d., http://www.sbts.edu/a-guide-to-biblical-manhood/.

96. Hannah Fingerhut, "In Both Parties, Men and Women Differ over Whether Women Still Face Obstacles to Progress," *Pew Research Center*, August 16, 2016, http://www.pewresearch.org/fact-tank/2016/08/16/in-both-parties-men-and-women-differ-over-whether-women-still-face-obstacles-to-progress/.

97. Susan Faludi, *Stiffed: The Betrayal of the American Man* (New York: William Morrow and Company, Inc., 1999), 227–228.

98. Faludi, *Stiffed*, 229.

99. Maureen Dowd, "Other Side of 'Gender Gap:' Reagan Seen as Man's Man," *New York Times*, September 17, 1984, https://www.nytimes.com/1984/09/17/us/other-side-of-gender-gap-reagan-seen-as-man-s-man.html.

100. William Greider, "Women vs. Reagan," *The Rolling Stone*, August 19, 1982, http://www.rollingstone.com/politics/news/women-vs-reagan-19820819.

101. Josh King, "Dukakis and the Tank: The Inside Story of the Worst Campaign Photo Op Ever," *Politico*, November 17, 2013, http://www.politico.com/magazine/story/2013/11/dukakis-and-the-tank-099119.

102. Menzies, "Virtual Backlash," 75.

103. Kevin Coe, David Domke, Meredith M. Bagley, Sheryl Cunningham, and Nancy Van Leuven, "Masculinity as Political Strategy: George W. Bush, the 'War on Terrorism,' and an Echoing Press," *Journal of Women, Politics & Policy* 29, no. 1 (2007): 31–55.

104. Aaron J. Moore and David Dewberry, "The Masculine Image of Presidents as Sporting Figures," *Sage Open* 2, no. 3 (2012), http://sgo.sagepub.com/content/2/3/2158244012457078.

105. Zillah Eisenstein, "Antifeminism in the Politics and Election of 1980," *Feminist Studies* 7, no. 2 (1981): 200.

106. Maureen Dowd, "The 1992 Campaign: Campaign Trail; From Nixon, Predictions on the Presidential Race," *New York Times*, February 6, 1992, http://www.nytimes.com/1992/02/06/us/the-1992-campaign-campaing-trail-from-nixon-predictions-on-the-presidential-race.html.

107. Katharine Q. Seelye, "Dole Says He Has a Plan to Win Votes of Women," *New York Times*, May 8, 1996, http://www.nytimes.com/1996/05/08/us/dole-says-he-has-plan-to-win-votes-of-women.html.

108. Ruth Rosen, "The Tea Party and Angry White Women," *Dissent* (Winter 2012): 61.

109. Julia M. D'Antonio-Del Rio, Jessica M. Doucet, and Chantel D. Chauvin, "Violent and Vindictive Women: A Re-Analysis of the Southern Subculture of Violence," *Sociological Spectrum* 30, no. 5 (2010): 484–503.

110. Nisbett and Cohen, *Culture of Honor*, 87.

111. MacLean, *Behind the Mask of Chivalry*, 123, 120.

112. Phyllis Schlafly, "What's Wrong with 'Equal Rights' for Women?," in *Debating the American Conservative Movement: 1945 to the Present*, ed. Donald T. Critchlow and Nancy MacLean (Lanham: Rowman & Littlefield Publishers, Inc., 2009), 198; Schlafly's statement first appeared in 1972.

113. Robert O. Self, *All in the Family: The Realignment of American Democracy Since the 1960s* (New York: Hill and Wang, 2012), 316.

114. Marjorie J. Spruill, "Gender and America's Right Turn," in *Rightward Bound: Making America Conservative in the 1970s*, ed. Bruce J. Schulman and Julian E. Zelizer (Cambridge: Harvard University Press, 2008), 82.

115. Marjorie Spruill, *Divided We Stand: Women's Rights, Family Values, and the Polarization of American Politics* (New York: Bloomsbury, 2017), 101.

116. Elizabeth Gillespie McCrae, "The Women Behind White Power," *New York Times*, February 2, 2018, https://www.nytimes.com/2018/02/02/opinion/sunday/white-supremacy-forgot-women.html; see also: Elizabeth Gillespie McCrae, *Mothers of Massive Resistance: White Women and the Politics of White Supremacy* (New York: Oxford University Press, 2018); Elizabeth Gillespie McCrae, "How the 'Grassroots Resistance' of White Women Shaped White Supremacy," *Jezebel*, January 31, 2018, https://pictorial.jezebel.com/how-the-grassroots-resistance-of-white-women-shaped-whi-1822340338.

117. Self, *All in the* Family, 317.

118. Christal Hayes, "White Men Feel Stricter Gun Laws Are Attacks on Their Masculinity, Study Says," *Newsweek*, November 27, 2017, http://www.newsweek.com/white-men-find-stricter-gun-laws-attacks-masculinity-study-723586.

119. Felson and Pare, "Gun Cultures or Honor Cultures," 1357–1378.

120. Olga Khazan, "The Precarious Masculinity of 2016 Voters," *The Atlantic*, October 12, 2016, https://www.theatlantic.com/politics/archive/2016/10/male-trump-voters-masculinity/503741/.

121. David D. Gilmore, *Misogyny: The Male Malady* (Philadelphia: University of Pennsylvania Press, 2001), 13.

122. Kimmel, *Angry White* Men, 106.

123. Glenda Gilmore, *Gender and Jim Crow: Women and the Politics of White Supremacy in North Carolina, 1896–1920* (Chapel Hill: University of North Carolina Press, 1996), 44.

124. Marcie Bianco, "What Sisterhood? White Women Voted for Trump in 2016 Because They Still Believe White Men Are Their Saviors," *Quartz*, November 14, 2016, https://qz.com/835567/election-2016-white-women-voted-for-donald-trump-in-2016-because-they-still-believe-white-men-are-their-saviors/.

CHAPTER 6

1. Hadley Freeman, "I've Heard Enough of the White Male Rage Narrative," *The Guardian*, November 10, 2016, https://www.theguardian.com/commentisfree/2016/nov/10/misogyny-us-election-voters.

2. Samantha Henig, "Sarah Palin, Miss Alaska, and the Vice Presidency," *Newsweek*, August 28, 2008, http://www.newsweek.com/sarah-palin-miss-alaska-and-vice-presidency-88227.

3. Nicolle Wallace, "Sarah Palin, Rage Whisperer," *New York Times*, January 25, 2016, http://www.nytimes.com/2016/01/26/opinion/sarah-palin-rage-whisperer.html.

4. Bob Cesca, "Southern Strategist Sarah Palin Denies the Southern Strategy," *Huffington Post*, July 14, 2010, http://www.huffingtonpost.com/bob-cesca/southern-strategist-sarah_b_646554.html.

5. Wallace, "Sarah Palin, Rage Whisperer"; Tim Shipman, "Sarah Palin: Barack Obama 'Palling around with Terrorists,'" *The Telegraph*, October 4, 2008, http://www.telegraph.co.uk/news/worldnews/sarah-palin/3137197/Sarah-Palin-accuses-Barack-Obama-of-terrorist-links.html.

6. Adele M. Stan, "Sarah Palin's Brand of 'Feminism' More Popular with Men than Women," *Alternet*, November 25, 2010, http://www.alternet.org/story/148976/sarah_palin%27s_brand_of_%27feminism%27_more_popular_with_men_than_women.

7. Stan, "Sarah Palin's Brand."

8. Sarah Palin, "Speech at Susan B. Anthony List's 'Celebration of Life' Breakfast," *Democracy in Action*, May 14, 2010, http://www.p2012.org/photos10/palin051410spt.html.

9. Cesca, "Southern Strategist."

10. Stan, "Sarah Palin's Brand."

11. Kathleen Hall Jamieson, *Beyond the Double Bind: Women and Leadership* (New York: Oxford University Press, 1995).

12. Karrin Vasby Anderson, "From Spouses to Candidates: Hillary Rodham Clinton, Elizabeth Dole, and the Gendered Office of U.S. President," *Rhetoric & Public Affairs* 5, no. 1 (2002): 107.

13. "Teaching with Documents: The Civil Rights Act of 1964 and the Equal Employment Opportunity Commission: Background," National Archives, n.d., https://www.archives.gov/education/lessons/civil-rights-act.

14. Mary Frances Berry, *Why ERA Failed: Politics, Women's Rights, and the Amending Process of the Constitution* (Bloomington: Indiana University Press, 1986), 86.

15. Ashlie Quesinberry Stokes, "Constituting Southern Feminists: Women's Liberation Newsletters in the South," *Southern Communication Journal* 70, no. 2 (2009): 96.

16. Marjorie Spruill, *Divided We Stand: Women's Rights, Family Values, and the Polarization of American Politics* (New York: Bloomsbury, 2017), 108.

17. Tanya Melich, *The Republican War Against Women: An Insider's Report from Behind the Lines* (New York: Bantam Books, 1996), 48.

18. Jo Freeman, "The 1976 Republican Convention," *JoFreeman.com*, n.d., http://www.jofreeman.com/photos/repub1976/GOPConvention1976-01.htm.

19. Spruill, *Divided We Stand*, 62.

20. Ronnee Schrieber, *Righting Feminism: Conservative Women and American Politics* (New York: Oxford University Press, 2008), 9.

21. Robert O. Self, *All in the Family: The Realignment of American Democracy Since the 1960s* (New York: Hill and Wang, 2012), 315.

22. Laura Kalman, *Right Start Rising: A New Politics, 1974–1980* (New York: W. W. Norton & Company, Inc., 2010), 70.

23. Kalman, *Right Start Rising*, 71.

24. Richard L. Hughes, "The Civil Rights Movement of the 1990s? The Anti-Abortion Movement and the Struggle for Racial Justice," *The Oral History Review* 33, no. 2 (2006): 1.

25. Zillah Eisenstein, "Antifeminism in the Politics and Election of 1980," *Feminist Studies* 7, no. 2 (1981): 187–205.

26. Melich, *The Republican War*, 15.

27. See: Spruill, *Divided We Stand*, 34, 359n73.

28. Joanna Brooks, "Mitt Romney's Best-Known Mormon Critic Tells It All—One Last Time," *Religion Dispatches: USC Annenberg*, September 11, 2012, http://religiondispatches.org/mitt-romneys-best-known-mormon-critic-tells-it-all-one-last-time/.

29. Matthew Levendusky, *The Partisan Sort: How Liberals Became Democrats and Conservatives Became Republicans* (Chicago: University of Chicago Press, 2009), 67–69.

30. Spruill, *Divided We Stand*, 227–228.

31. Berry, *Why ERA Failed*, 89.

32. Karen M. Kaufmann, "Culture Wars, Secular Realignment, and the Gender Gap in Party Identification," *Political Behavior* 24, no. 3 (2002): 283.

33. Alice H. Eagly and Amanda B. Dickman, "Examining Gender Gaps in Sociopolitical Attitudes: It's Not Mars and Venus," *Feminism Psychology* 16, no. 1 (2006): 26–34.

34. Jeff Manza and Clem Brooks, "The Gender Gap in U.S. Presidential Elections: When? Why? Implications?," *American Journal of Sociology* 103, no. 5 (1998): 1235–1266.

35. Lena Edlund and Rohini Pande, "Why Have Women Become Left-Wing? The Political Gender Gap and the Decline of Marriage," *The Quarterly Journal of Economics* 117, no. 3 (2002): 917–961.

36. Carol Kennedy Chaney, R. Michael Alvarez, and Jonathan Nagler, "Explaining the Gender Gap in U.S. Presidential Elections, 1980–1992," *Political Research Quarterly* 51, no. 2 (1998): 311–339.

37. Michele L. Swers, "Are Women More Likely to Vote for Women's Issue Bills Than Their Male Colleagues?," *Legislative Studies Quarterly* 23, no. 3 (1998): 435–448.

38. David Fite, Marc Genest, and Clyde Wilcox, "Gender Differences in Foreign Policy Attitudes: A Longitudinal Analysis," *American Politics Quarterly* 18, no. 4 (1990): 508.

39. Pamela Johnston Conover, "Feminists and the Gender Gap," *The Journal of Politics* 50, no. 4 (1998): 985–1010; Barbara Norrander, "The Evolution of the Gender Gap," *The Public Opinion Quarterly* 63, no. 4 (1999): 566–576.

40. Terrel L. Rhodes, *Republicans in the South: Voting for the State House, Voting for the White House* (Westport: Praeger, 2000), 117.

41. Daniel Wirls, "Reinterpreting the Gender Gap," *The Public Opinion Quarterly* 50, no. 3 (1986): 329.

42. Conover, "Feminists and the Gender Gap," 998.

43. Conover, "Feminists and the Gender Gap," 1005.

44. Elizabeth Adell Cook and Clyde Wilcox, "Feminism and the Gender Gap—A Second Look," *The Journal of Politics* 53, no. 4 (1991): 1111–1122.

45. Catherine I. Bolzendahl and Daniel J. Myers, "Feminist Attitudes and Support for Gender Equality: Opinion Change in Women and Men, 1974–1998," *Social Forces* 83, no. 2 (2004): 782.

46. Leonie Huddy and Johanna Wilmann, "Partisan Sorting and the Feminist Gap in American Politics" (unpublished manuscript, July 17, 2017), https://www.researchgate.net/project/The-Feminist-Gap-in-American-Politics, 36.

47. Lori Wilson, quoted in: "The Prime Sponsor of the E.R.A. Speaks," *Pensacola NOW Newsletter* 5, no. 4 (April 13, 1977): http://flnowarchive.org/mediawiki/images/Box_23_Folder_2_Document_33.pdf.

48. Sue Tolleson-Rinehart, "Can the Flower of Southern Womanhood Bloom in the Garden of Southern Politics?," *Southern Cultures* 4, no. 1 (1998): 78–87.

49. Angela Boswell, "Married Women's Property Rights and the Challenge to the Patriarchal Order: Colorado County, Texas," in *Negotiating Boundaries of Southern*

Womanhood: Dealing with the Powers That Be, ed. Janet L. Coryell, Thomas H. Appleton Jr., Anastasia Sims, and Sandra Gioia Treadway (Columbia: University of Missouri Press, 2000), 91.

50. Elizabeth Fox-Genovese, *Within the Plantation Household: Black and White Women of the Old South* (Chapel Hill: University of North Carolina Press, 1988), 47.

51. Martha H. Swain, Elizabeth Anne Payne, and Marjorie Julian Spruill, ed., *Mississippi Women: Their Histories, Their Lives* (Athens: University of Georgia Press, 2003), 2.

52. Victoria E. Bynum, *Unruly Women: The Politics of Social and Sexual Control in the Old South* (Chapel Hill: University of North Carolina Press, 1992), 89.

53. Mary Martha Thomas, *The New Women in Alabama: Social Reforms and Suffrage, 1890– 1920* (Tuscaloosa: University of Alabama Press, 1992), 5.

54. Donna Kelleher Darden, "Southern Women Writing About Southern Women: Jill McCorkle, Lisa Alther, Ellen Gilchrist, and Lee Smith," *Sociological Spectrum* 6 (1986): 110.

55. Boswell, "Married Women's Property Rights," 91.

56. Jeane J. Kirkpatrick, *Political Woman* (New York: Basic Books, Inc., 1974), 9.

57. Kirkpatrick, *Political Woman,* 19.

58. Julia Christine James, "The Political Participation of Older Southern Women" (MS thesis, University of Arkansas, 2002), 43.

59. Susan Middleton-Klein, "Magnolias and Microchips: Regional Subcultural Constructions of Femininity," *Sociological Spectrum* 6 (1986): 103, 98.

60. Donald G. Matthews and Jane Sherron de Hart, *Sex, Gender, and the Politics of the ERA* (New York: Oxford University Press, 1990), 20.

61. Melich, *The Republican War,* 94.

62. Françoise Coste, "'Women, Ladies, Girls, Gals . . .': Ronald Reagan and the Evolution of Gender Roles in the United States," *Miranda* 12 (2016): https://miranda.revues.org/ 8602.

63. David C. King and Richard E. Matland, "Sex and the Grand Old Party: An Experimental Investigation of the Effect of Candidate Sex on Support for a Republican Candidate," *American Politics Research* 31, no. 6 (2003): 595–612.

64. Jeffrey M. Jones and David W. Moore, "Generational Differences in Support for a Woman President," *Gallup,* June 17, 2003, http://www.gallup.com/poll/8656/generational-differences-support-woman-president.aspx.

65. Andrew Kohut, "Are Americans Ready to Elect a Female President?," *PewResearchCenter,* May 9, 2007, https://www.pewresearch.org/2007/05/09/are-americans-ready-to-elect-a-female-president/.

66. Matthew J. Streb, Barbara Burrell, Brian Frederick, and Michael A. Genovese, "Social Desirability Effects and Support for a Female American President," *Public Opinion Quarterly* 72, no. 1 (2008): 76–89.

67. Leonie Huddy and Nayda Terkildsen, "The Consequences of Gender Stereotypes for Women Candidates at Different Levels and Types of Offices," *Political Research Quarterly* 46, no. 3 (1993): 503–525; David Lublin and Sarah E. Brewer, "The Continuing Dominance of Traditional Gender Roles in Southern Elections," *Social Science Quarterly* 84, no. 2 (2003): 380–396.

68. Judith S. Trent, "The 1984 Bush-Ferraro Vice Presidential Debate," in *Rhetorical Studies of National Political Debates, 1960–1992,* 2nd ed., ed. Robert V. Friedenberg (Westport: Praeger, 1993), 38, 133.

69. Michaele L. Ferguson, Lori Jo Marso, ed., *W Stands for Women: How the George W. Bush Presidency Shaped a New Politics of Gender* (Durham: Duke University Press, 2007), 1.

70. Jeanne Hurlbert, "The Southern Region: A Test of the Hypothesis of Cultural Distinctiveness," *Sociological Quarterly* 30, no. 2 (1989): 245–266.

71. Mary McThomas and Michael Tesler, "The Growing Influence of Gender Attitudes on Public Support for Hillary Clinton, 2008–2012," *Politics & Gender* 12 (2016): 30; see also: Michael Tesler and David O. Sears, *Obama's Race: The 2008 Election and the Dream of a Post Racial America* (Chicago: University of Chicago Press, 2016).

72. Jarrod Bock., Jennifer Byrd-Craven, and Melissa Burkley, "The Role of Sexism in the 2016 Presidential Election," *Personality and Individual Differences* 119 (2017): 189–193; Angie Maxwell and Todd Shields, "The Impact of Modern Sexism on the 2016 Presidential Election," *Blair Center of Southern Politics and Society*, June 6, 2017, https://blaircenter. uark.edu/the-impact-of-modern-sexism/; see also: Rebecca Onion, "Bad News: We're Sexist: New Data Show How Sexism Played a Role in Donald Trump's Election," *Slate*, June 7, 2017, http://www.slate.com/articles/double_x/doublex/2017/06/new_research_ on_role_of_sexism_in_2016_election.html; Carly Wayne, Marzia Oceno, and Nicholas Valentino, "How Sexism Drives Support for Donald Trump," *Washington Post*, October 23, 2016, https://www.washingtonpost.com/news/monkey-cage/wp/2016/10/23/how-sexism-drives-support-for-donald-trump/; Morris P. Fiorina, "The 2016 Presidential Election—Identities, Class, and Culture," *Hoover Institution* 11, June 22, 2017, https:// www.hoover.org/research/2016-presidential-election-identities-class-and-culture.

73. Hillary Clinton, quoted in: Eugene Scott, "Like It or Not, Studies Suggest That Clinton May Not Be Wrong on White Women Voting Like Their Husbands," *Washington Post*, March 13, 2018, https://www.washingtonpost.com/news/the-fix/wp/2018/03/13/like-it-or-not-studies-suggest-that-clinton-may-not-be-wrong-on-white-women-voting-like-their-husbands/.

74. Louis Bolce, Gerald De Maio, and Douglas Muzzio, "The Equal Rights Amendment, Public Opinion, & American Constitutionalism," *Polity* 19, no. 4 (1987): 551–569.

75. Donald T. Critchlow, *The Conservative Ascendancy: How the Republican Right Rose to Power in Modern America*, 2nd rev. ed. (Lawrence: University Press of Kansas, 2011), 128.

76. Spruill, *Divided We Stand*, 104.

77. Spruill, *Divided We Stand*, 322.

78. Diane Roberts, *Faulkner and Southern Womanhood* (Athens: University of Georgia Press, 1994), 104.

79. Schrieber, *Righting Feminism*, 5.

80. Michelle Rodino-Colocino, "'Feminism' as Ideology: Sarah Palin's Anti-feminist Feminism and Ideology Critique," *Triple C* 10, no. 2 (2012): 469.

81. Jay Newton-Small, "House Republicans Unveil Women's Legislation in Push for Female Voters," *Time*, July 30, 2014, http://time.com/3055190/house-republican-women-unveil-womens-legislation/.

82. Karen Paget, "The Gender Gap Mystique," *The American Prospect*, Fall 1993, http://prospect.org/article/gender-gap-mystique.

PART III

1. Brian D. McLaren, "The 'Alt-Right' Has Created Alt-Christianity," *Time*, August 25, 2017, http://time.com/4915161/charlottesville-alt-right-alt-christianity/.

2. See: John Shelton Reed, *The Enduring South: Subcultural Persistence in Mass Society* (Lexington: D. C. Heath, 1972).

3. Laurence R. Iannaccone and Michael D. Makowsky, "Accidental Atheists? Agent-Based Explanations for the Persistence of Religious Regionalism," *Journal for the Scientific Study of Religion* 46, no. 1 (2007): 1–16.

4. See: Linford D. Fisher, "Evangelicals and Unevangelicals: The Contested History of a Word, 1500–1950," *Religion and American Culture: A Journal of Interpretation* 26, No. 2 (Summer 2016): 184–226.

5. Tod A. Baker, Robert P. Steed, and Laurence W. Moreland, ed., *Religion and Politics in the South: Mass and Elite Perspectives* (New York: Praeger, 1983), 28–29.

6. "What Is an Evangelical?' *National Association of Evangelicals*, n.d., https://www.nae.net/what-is-an-evangelical/; David W. Bebbington, *Evangelicalism in Modern Britain: A History from the 1730s to the 1930s* (London: Unwin Hyman, 1989).

7. James Leo Garrett Jr., E. Glenn Hinson, and James E. Tull, *Are Southern Baptists "Evangelicals"?* (Macon: Mercer University Press, 1983), 87.

8. Kathleen Murphy Beatty and B. Oliver Walter, "Fundamentalists, Evangelicals, and Politics," *American Politics Quarterly* 16, no. 1 (1988): 55.

9. Clyde Wilcox, "Fundamentalists and Politics: An Analysis of the Effects of Differing Operational Definitions," *The Journal of Politics* 48, no. 4 (1986): 1041–1051.

10. Samuel S. Hill, ed., *Varieties of Southern Religious Experience* (Baton Rouge: Louisiana State University Press, 1988), 7.

11. Anthony M. Orum, "Religion and the Rise of the Radical White: The Case of Southern Wallace Support in 1968," *Social Science Quarterly* 51, no. 3 (1970): 677.

12. Joe R. Feagin, "Prejudice and Religious Types: A Focused Study of Southern Fundamentalists," *Journal for the Scientific Study of Religion* 4, no. 1 (1964): 3.

13. Thomas M. Huebner Jr., "A House Divided: Heresy and Orthodoxy in the Southern Baptist Convention," *Journal of Communication & Religion* 14, no. 2 (1991): 34–43.

14. David Edwin Harrell Jr., "The Evolution of Plain-Folk Religion in the South, 1835–1920," in *Varieties of Southern Religious Experience*, ed. Samuel S. Hill (Baton Rouge: Louisiana State University Press, 1988), 28.

15. Paul Harvey, *Freedom's Coming: Religious Culture and the Shaping of the South from the Civil War Through the Civil Rights Era* (Chapel Hill: University of North Carolina Press, 2005), 222.

16. Samuel S. Hill Jr., *Southern Churches in Crisis* (New York: Holt, Rinehart, and Winston, 1964), 26.

17. Barry Hankins, *Uneasy in Babylon: Southern Baptist Conservatives and American Culture* (Tuscaloosa: University of Alabama Press, 2002), 21.

18. Kenneth D. Wald, Dennis E. Owen, and Samuel S. Hill, "Churches as Political Communities," *American Political Science Review* 82, no. 2 (1988): 531–548.

19. Donald G. Matthews, Samuel S. Hill, Beth Barton Schweiger, and John B. Boles, "Forum: Southern Religion," *Religion and American Culture: A Journal of Interpretation* 8, no. 2 (1998): 150.

20. Charles Reagan Wilson, "Preachin', Prayin', and Singin' on the Public Square," in *Religion and Public Life in the South: In the Evangelical Mode*, ed. Charles Reagan Wilson and Mark Silk (Walnut Creek: Rowman & Littlefield Publishers, Inc., 2005), 12.

21. David T. Morgan, *The New Crusades, The New Holy Land: Conflict in the Southern Baptists Convention 1969–1991* (Tuscaloosa: University of Alabama Press, 1996), 5.

22. Nancy Tatom Ammerman, *Bible Believers: Fundamentalists in the Modern World* (New Brunswick: Rutgers University Press, 1988), 189.

23. See: Daniel Vaca, "Believing Within Business: Evangelicalism, Media, and Financial Faith," in *The Business Turn in American Religious History*, ed. Amanda Porterfield, Darren Grem, and John Corrigan (New York: Oxford University Press, 2017), 20–45.

24. Peter L. Berger, *The Precarious Vision: A Sociologist Looks at Social Fictions and Christian Faith* (Garden City: Doubleday & Company, Inc., 1961), 102.

25. Ernest Kurtz, "The Tragedy of Southern Religion," *The Georgia Historical Quarterly* 66, no. 2 (1982): 217.

26. Samuel S. Hill, "Fundamentalism in Recent Southern Culture: Has It Done What the Civil Rights Movement Couldn't Do?," in *Southern Crossroads: Perspectives on Religion and Culture*, ed. Walter H. Conser Jr. and Rodger M. Payne (Lexington: University Press of Kentucky, 2008), 357.

27. Matthew Avery Sutton, *American Apocalypse: A History of Modern Evangelicalism* (Cambridge: The Belknap Press of Harvard University Press, 2014), 179.

28. Ammerman, *Bible Believers*, 202.

29. Ammerman, *Bible Believers*, 202.

30. John B. Boles, *The Great Revival, 1787–1805: The Origins of the Southern Evangelical Mind* (Lexington: University Press of Kentucky, 1996), 125.

31. Clifford A. Grammich Jr., *Local Baptists, Local Politics: Churches and Communities in the Middle and Uplands South* (Knoxville: University of Tennessee Press, 1999), 24.

32. Christopher G. Ellison and Marc A. Musick, "Southern Intolerance: A Fundamentalist Effect?," *Social Forces* 72, no. 2 (1993): 382.

33. Hankins, *Uneasy in Babylon*, 10.

34. Ellen M. Rosenberg, *The Southern Baptists: A Subculture in Transition* (Knoxville: University of Tennessee Press, 1989), 191.

35. Kevin Kruse, *One Nation Under God: How Corporate America Invented Christian America* (New York: Basic Books, 2015), 252.

36. Ted Ownby, *Subduing Satan: Religion, Recreation, and Manhood in the Rural South, 1865–1920* (Chapel Hill: University of North Carolina Press, 1990), 11, 14.

37. W. A. Crisswell, quoted in: Charles Reagan Wilson, "Preachin', Prayin', and Singin' on the Public Square," in *Religion and Public Life in the South: In the Evangelical Mode*, ed. Charles Reagan Wilson and Mark Silk (Walnut Creek: Rowman & Littlefield Publishers, Inc., 2005), 22.

38. Dwight Dorough, *The Bible Belt Mystique* (Philadelphia: Westminster Press, 1974), 199.

39. John C. Green, Lyman A Kellstedt, Corwin E Smidt, and James L. Guth, "The Soul of the South: Religion and the New Electoral Order," in *The New Politics of the Old South: An Introduction to Southern Politics*, ed. Charles S. Bullock III and Mark J. Rozell (Lanham: Rowman & Littlefield Publishers, Inc., 1998): 267.

40. Geoffrey Layman, *The Great Divide: Religious and Cultural Conflict in American Party Politics* (New York: Columbia University Press, 2001), 179.

41. Green, Kellstedt, Smidt, and Guth, "The Soul of the South," 264.

42. Charlotte Gendron and Daniel Cox, "Religious, Cultural, and Political Breakdown of the 2016 Early Primary State," *PRRI*, May 13, 2015, http://www.prri.org/spotlight/23993-2/.

43. Kevin Diaz, "Cruz Campaigns Like a Moral Crusader," *San Antonio Express-News*, July 11, 2015, http://www.expressnews.com/news/local/article/Cruz-campaigns-like-a-moral-crusader-6379705.php.

44. Richard L. Gorsuch and Daniel Aleshire, "Christian Faith and Ethnic Prejudice: A Review and Interpretation of Research," *Journal for the Scientific Study of Religion* 13, no. 3, (1974): 281–307.

45. John Pavlowitz, "Donald Trump Is a Christian Leader, South Carolina and the GOP Just Said So," JohnPavlovitz.com, February 21, 2016, http://johnpavlovitz.com/2016/02/21/donald-trump-is-a-christian-leader-south-carolina-and-the-gop-just-said-so/.

46. Molly Worthen, *Apostles of Reason: The Crisis of Authority in American Evangelicalism* (New York: Oxford University Press, 2014), 3.

47. Charles Reagan Wilson, *Southern Missions: The Religion of the American South in Global Perspective* (Waco: Baylor University Press, 2006), 35; see also: Thomas Tweed, "Our Lady of Guadeloupe Visits the Confederate Monument: Latino and Asian Religions in the South," in *Religion in the Contemporary South: Changes, Continuities, and Contexts*, ed. Corrie E. Norman and Don S. Armentrout (Knoxville: University of Tennessee Press, 2005), 139–158.

48. Charles Reagan Wilson, *Baptized in Blood: The Religion of the Lost Cause, 1865–1920* (Athens: University of Georgia Press, 1980), 3.

49. Daniel W. Stowell, *Rebuilding Zion: The Religious Reconstruction of the South, 1863–1877* (New York: Oxford University Press, 1998), 48.

50. Wilson, *Southern* Missions, 1.

CHAPTER 7

1. Victor Irvine Masters, *The Call of the South*, 2nd ed. (Atlanta: Publicity Department of the Home Mission Board of the Southern Baptist Convention, 1920), 18.

2. Barry Bozeman, "40 Year Anniversary—A Political Education." *Protest & Activism at UT—40 Years On*, June 1, 2010, http://knoxville22.blogspot.com/.

3. Steven P. Miller, "Billy Graham, Civil Rights, and the Changing Postwar South," in *Politics and Religion in the White South*, ed. Glen Feldman (Lexington: University Press of Kentucky, 2005), 175.

4. Bozeman, "40 Year Anniversary—A Political Education."

5. Bozeman, "40 Year Anniversary—A Political Education."

6. Richard M. Nixon, "Remarks at Dr. Billy Graham's East Tennessee Crusade," *The American Presidency Project*, May 28, 1970, http://www.presidency.ucsb.edu/documents/remarks-dr-billy-grahams-east-tennessee-crusade.

7. Nixon, "Remarks at Dr. Billy Graham's East Tennessee Crusade."

8. Jon Elliston, "Newly Released White House Diaries Reveal More About Billy Graham's Alliance with Richard Nixon," *Carolina Public Press*, November 12, 2014, http://carolinapublicpress.org/21103/newly-released-white-house-diaries-reveal-more-about-billy-grahams-alliance-with-richard-nixon/.

9. Miller, "Billy Graham," 174.

10. Miller, "Billy Graham," 179.

11. Miller, "Billy Graham," 177.

12. Donald G. Matthews, Samuel S. Hill, Beth Barton Schweiger, and John B. Boles, "Forum: Southern Religion," *Religion and American Culture: A Journal of Interpretation* 8, no. 2 (1998): 166.

13. John Egerton, *The Americanization of Dixie: The Southernization of America* (New York: Harper's Magazine Press, 1974), 195.

14. Ted Ownby, "Evangelical but Differentiated: Religion by the Numbers," in *Religion and Public Life in the South: In the Evangelical Model*, ed. Charles Reagan Wilson and Mark Silk (Walnut Creek: Rowman & Littlefield Publishers, Inc., 2005), 39.

15. John Shelton Reed, *My Tears Spoiled My Aim, and Other Reflections on Southern Culture* (Columbia: University of Missouri Press, 1993), 141.

16. See: Rosemary M. Magee, "Recent Trends in the Study of Southern Religion," *Religious Studies Review* 6, no. 1 (1980): 35–39.

17. Charles Reagan Wilson, "The Religion of the Lost Cause: Ritual and Organization of the Southern Civil Religion, 1865–1920," *The Journal of Southern History* 46, no. 2 (1980): 219–238.

18. George L. Maddox and Joseph H. Fichter, "Religion and Social Change in the South," *Journal of Social Issues* 22, no. 1 (1966): 44–58.

19. Thomas A. Tweed, "Our Lady of Guadeloupe Visits the Confederate Memorial," *Southern Cultures* 8, no. 2 (2002): 72–93.

20. James Leo Garrett Jr., E. Glenn Hinson, and James E. Tull, *Are Southern Baptists "Evangelicals?"* (Macon: Mercer University Press, 1983), 119; see also: Mary Beth Swetham Matthews, *Rethinking Zion: How the Print Media Place Fundamentalism in the South* (Knoxville: University of Tennessee Press, 2006).

21. Christine Leigh Heyrman, *Southern Cross: The Beginnings of the Bible Belt* (New York: Alfred A. Knopf, 1997), 27; see also: Charles F. Irons, *The Origins of Proslavery Christianity: White and Black Evangelicals in Colonial and Antebellum Virginia* (Chapel Hill: University of North Carolina Press, 2008).

22. Rita Whitlock, "Queerly Fundamental: Christian Fundamentalism, Southern Queerness, and Curriculum Studies," *Journal of Curriculum and Pedagogy* 3, no. 1 (2006): 165–186.

23. 12 Southerners, *I'll Take My Stand: The South and the Agrarian Tradition* (1930; reiss., New York: Harper & Row Publishers, 1962), xxiv.

24. Eugene D. Genovese, *The Southern Tradition: The Achievement and Limitations of an American Conservatism* (Cambridge: Harvard University Press, 1994), xi.

25. See: Angie Maxwell, *The Indicted South: Public Criticism, Southern Inferiority, and the Politics of Whiteness* (Chapel Hill: University of North Carolina Press, 2014).

26. Nancy Tatom Ammerman, *Bible Believers: Fundamentalists in the Modern World* (New Brunswick: Rutgers University Press, 1988), 196.

27. Donald G. Matthews, *Religion in the Old South* (Chicago: University of Chicago Press, 1977), 82.

28. Clifford Geertz, *Interpretations of Cultures: Selected Essays* (New York: Basic Books, 1973), 90.

29. Rick Perlstein, *Nixonland: The Rise of a President and the Fracturing of America* (New York: Simon and Schuster, 2010), 500.

30. Miller, "Billy Graham," 177.

31. John B. Boles, "The Southern Way of Religion," *Virginia Quarterly Review* 75, no. 2 (1999): 226.

32. Charles Reagan Wilson, *Judgment and Grace in Dixie: Southern Faiths from Faulkner to Elvis* (Athens: University of Georgia Press, 1995), 7–11.

33. Charles A. Heatwole, "The Bible Belt: A Problem in Regional Definition," *Journal of Geography* 77, no. 2 (1978): 53.

34. Dean G. Kilpatrick, Louis W. Sutker, and Patricia B. Sutker, "Dogmatism, Religion, and Religiosity, a Review and Re-evaluation," *Psychological Reports* 26, no. 1 (1970): 21.

35. Randy J. Sparks, "Religion in the Pre–Civil War South," in *A Companion to the American South*, ed. John B. Boles (Malden: Blackwell Publishers, 2002), 157.

36. Michael O. Emerson and Christian Smith, *Divided by Faith: Evangelical Religion and the Problem of Race in America* (New York: Oxford University Press, 2000), 25.

37. Rhys Isaac, *The Transformation of Virginia: 1740–1790* (Chapel Hill: University of North Carolina Press, 1982), 68–69.

38. Wilson, *Judgment and Grace in Dixie*, 5.

39. John B. Boles, *The Great Revival, 1787–1805: The Origins of the Southern Evangelical Mind* (Lexington: University Press of Kentucky, 1996), ix.

40. John B. Boles, *The Irony of Southern Religion* (New York: Peter Lang, 1994), 23.

41. Boles, *The Great Revival*, 70.

42. Richard C. Wolf, "1900–1950 Survey: Religious Trends in the United States," *The Living Church* 138 (1959): 9.

43. Matthews, *Religion in the Old South*, 50.

44. Samuel S. Hill Jr., *The South and the North in American Religion* (Athens: University of Georgia Press, 1980), 8.

45. Susan M. Shaw, *God Speaks to Us, Too: Southern Baptist Women on Church, Home, and Society* (Lexington: University Press of Kentucky, 2008), 5.

46. Ted Ownby, *Subduing Satan: Religion, Recreation, and Manhood in the Rural South, 1865–1920* (Chapel Hill: University of North Carolina Press, 1990), 1.

47. Ownby, *Subduing Satan*, 123.

48. John Stratton Hawley, ed. *Fundamentalism and Gender* (New York: Oxford University Press, 1994), 21; Rita Whitlock, "Queerly Fundamental: Christian Fundamentalism, Southern Queerness, and Curriculum Studies," *Journal of Curriculum and Pedagogy* 3, no. 1 (2006): 173.

49. Boles, *The Great Revival*, x.

50. Brent Simpson, "The Poverty of Trust in the Southern United States," *Social Forces* 84, no 3 (2006): 1625–1638.

51. Jacob Weisburg, "The Bush Tragedy," *Slate*, March 13, 2008, http://www.slate.com/articles/news_and_politics/politics/2016/12/the_gop_is_coming_after_medicare_and_the_democrats_can_barely_contain_themselves.html.

52. Charles Reagan Wilson, *Southern Missions: The Religion of the American South in Global Perspective* (Waco: Baylor University Press, 2006), 12.

53. Ammerman, *Bible Believers*, 188.

54. Boles. *The Great Revival*, 114.

55. John Crowe Ransom, *God Without Thunder: An Unorthodox Defense of Orthodoxy* (New York: Harcourt Brace, 1930).

56. William R. Glass, *Strangers in Zion: Fundamentalism in the South, 1900–1950* (Macon: Mercer University Press, 2001), 275–276.

57. Douglas Carl Abrams, *Selling the Old-Time Religion: American Fundamentalists and Mass Culture, 1920–1940* (Athens: University of Georgia Press, 2001), 9.

58. Rob James and Gary Leazer with James Shoopman, *The Fundamentalist Takeover in the Southern Baptist Convention: A Brief History* (Timişoara, Romania: Impact Media, 1999), 23.

59. James and Leazer with Shoopman, *The Fundamentalist Takeover*, 23.

60. Wilson, *Southern Missions*, 15.

61. James and Leazer with Shoopman, *The Fundamentalist Takeover*, 23.

62. Edward J. Larson, *Summer for the Gods: The Scopes Trial and America's Continuing Debate over Science and Religion* (New York: BasicBooks, 1997), 93.

63. Larson, *Summer for the Gods*, 93.

64. Larson, *Summer for the Gods*, 117.

65. See: Maxwell, *The Indicted South*.

66. Glass, *Strangers in Zion*, 276.

67. Michael Lienesch, "Right-wing Religion: Christian Conservatism as a Political Movement," *Political Science Quarterly* 97, no. 3 (1982): 404.

68. Daniel W. Stowell, *Rebuilding Zion: The Religious Reconstruction of the South, 1863–1877* (New York: Oxford University Press, 1998), 13.

69. Elizabeth Fox-Genovese and Eugene D. Genovese, "The Divine Sanction of Social Order: Religious Foundations of the Southern Slaveholders' World View," *Journal of the American Academy of Religion* 55, no. 2 (1987): 211.

70. Genovese, *The Southern Tradition*, 27.

71. Genovese, *The Southern Tradition*, 24.

72. Mitchell Snay, *Gospel of Disunion: Religion and Separatism in the Antebellum South* (New York: Cambridge University Press, 1993), 217.

73. Matthews, *Religion in the Old South*, 1.

74. Randy J. Sparks, "Religion in the Pre–Civil War South," in *A Companion to the American South*, ed. John B. Boles (Malden: Blackwell Publishers, 2002), 159; see also: Rhys Isaac, *The Transformation of Virginia: 1740–1790* (Chapel Hill: University of North Carolina Press, 1982).

75. Julia Kirk Blackwelder, "Southern White Fundamentalists and the Civil Rights Movement," *Phylon* 40, no. 4 (1979): 334–341.

76. Samuel S. Hill Jr., *Southern Churches in Crisis* (New York: Holt, Rinehart, and Winston, 1964), 23.

77. Hill, *Southern Churches in Crisis*, 31, 33.

78. See: Ted G. Jelen, *The Political World of the Clergy* (Westport: Praeger, 1993), 39–63.

79. Peter L. Berger. *The Sacred Canopy: Elements of a Sociological Theory of Religion* (Garden City: Doubleday & Company, Inc., 1967), 25.

80. Ammerman, *Bible Believers*, 194.

81. Clyde Wilcox and Ted G. Jelen, "Religion and Politics in an Open Market: Religious Mobilization in the United States," in *Religion and Politics in Comparative Perspective: The One, the Few, and the Many*, ed. Ted G. Jelen and Clyde Wilcox (New York: Cambridge University Press, 2002), 293.

82. Heyrman, *Southern Cross*, 11.

83. Stowell, *Rebuilding Zion*, 33.

84. Randall M. Miller, Harry S. Stout, and Charles Reagan Wilson, ed., *Religion and the American Civil War* (New York: Oxford University Press, 1998), 16.

85. Miller, Stout, and Wilson, ed., *Religion and the American Civil War*, 10.

86. Stowell, *Rebuilding Zion*, 7.

87. Matthews, *Religion in the Old South*, 249.

88. Angus Campbell, Philip E. Converse, Warren E. Miller, and Donald E. Stokes, *Elections and the Political Order* (New York: John Wiley and Sons, Inc., 1966), 115.

89. Thomas A. Tweed, "Our Lady of Guadeloupe Visits the Confederate Memorial," *Southern Cultures* 8, no. 2 (2002): 72–93.

90. See: Maxwell, *The Indicted South*.

91. David Stricklin, *A Genealogy of Dissent: Southern Baptist Protest in the Twentieth Century* (Lexington: University Press of Kentucky, 1999), 5.

92. Sara Diamond, *Not by Politics Alone: The Enduring Influence of the Christian Right* (New York: The Guilford Press, 1998), 21.

93. Diamond, *Not by Politics Alone*, 60.

94. Abrams, *Selling the Old-Time Religion*, 125.

95. Diamond, *Not by Politics Alone*, 60.

96. Abrams, *Selling the Old-Time Religion*, 125.

97. Ted G. Jelen, *To Serve God and Mammon: Church-State Relations in American Politics* (Boulder: Westview Press, 2000), 86.

98. Chip Berlet, "Who Is Mediating the Storm: Right Wing Alternative Information Networks," in *Media, Culture, and the Religious Right*, ed. Linda Kintz and Julia Lesage (Minneapolis: University of Minnesota Press, 1998), 249.

99. Kintz and Lesage, ed., *Media, Culture, and the Religious Right*, xv.

100. Ted Jelen, "Reflections on Scholarship in Religion and Southern Politics," in *Writing Southern Politics: Contemporary Interpretations and Future Directions*, ed. Robert P. Steed and Laurence W. Moreland (Lexington: University Press of Kentucky, 2006), 143; Elizabeth Noelle-Neumann, *The Spiral of Silence: Public Opinion, Our Social Skin* (Chicago: University of Chicago Press, 1984).

101. Laura M. Moore and Reeve Vanneman, "Context Matters: Effects of the Proportion of Fundamentalists on Gender Attitudes," *Social Forces* 82, no. 1 (2003): 115–139.

102. John Lee Eighmy, *Churches in Cultural Captivity: A History of the Social Attitudes of Southern Baptists* (Knoxville: University of Tennessee Press, 1972), 208.

103. Eighmy, *Churches in Cultural Captivity*, 208.

104. Matthews, *Religion in the Old South*, 5.

105. Gary M. Maranell, "Regional Patterns of Fundamentalistic Attitude Configurations," *Kansas Journal of Sociology* 4, no. 4 (1968): 166.

106. Jon W. Anderson, "An Ethnographic Overview of Cultural Differences of Bible Belt Catholics," in *The Culture of Bible Belt Catholics*, ed. Jon W. Anderson and William B. Friend (New York: Paulist Press, 1995), 15.

107. Samuel S. Hill, "A Survey of Southern Religious History," in *Religion in the Southern States: A Historical Study*, ed. Samuel S. Hill (Macon: Mercer University Press, 1983), 395.

108. Paul Harvey, "Religion in the American South Since the Civil War," in *A Companion to the American South*, ed. John B. Boles (Malden: Blackwell Publishers, 2002), 402.

109. Hill, "A Survey of Southern Religious History," 411.

110. Wilson, "The Religion of the Lost Cause," 238.

111. David Hummel, "Revivalist Nationalism Since World War II: From 'Wake Up, America!' to 'Make America Great Again,'" *Religions* 7, no. 11 (2016): 10.

112. Hummel, "Revivalist Nationalism Since World War II," 13.

113. David Silliman, "How One Purist Tried to Save the Religious Right from the Republicans," *Religion & Politics*, August 8, 2017, http://religionandpolitics.org/2017/08/08/how-one-purist-tried-to-save-the-religious-right-from-the-republicans/.

114. John McCain, quoted in: Barbara Bradley Hagerty, "How McCain Shed Pariah Status Among Evangelicals," *NPR*, October 23, 2008, https://www.npr.org/templates/story/story.php?storyId=96031231.

115. Peter Hamby, "McCain's Christmas Ad Puts Cross Front and Center," *CNN*, December 20, 2007, http://politicalticker.blogs.cnn.com/2007/12/20/mccains-christmas-ad-puts-cross-front-and-center/.

116. George W. Bush, quoted in: Laura Goodstein, "The 2000 Campaign: Matters of Faith; Bush Uses Religion as Personal and Political Guide," *New York Times*, October 22, 2000, http://www.nytimes.com/2000/10/22/us/2000-campaign-matters-faith-bush-uses-religion-personal-political-guide.html.

117. Mitt Romney, quoted in: Ashley Parker, "Romney Tells Evangelicals Their Values Are His Too," *New York Times*, May 12, 2012, http://www.nytimes.com/2012/05/13/us/politics/romney-woos-evangelicals-treading-lightly-on-gay-marriage.html.

118. Richard Weaver, *The Southern Tradition at Bay* (New Rochelle: Arlington House, 1968), 98; Reed, *The Enduring South*, 57.

119. Charles Reagan Wilson and Mark Silk, "Religious Affiliation in the South and the Nation," in *Religion and Public Life in the South: In the Evangelical Mode*, ed. Charles Reagan Wilson and Mark Silk (Walnut Creek: Rowman & Littlefield Publishers, Inc., 2005), 28–29.

120. Susan M. Shaw, *God Speaks to Us, Too: Southern Baptist Women on Church, Home, and Society* (Lexington: University Press of Kentucky, 2008), 3.

121. Kenneth K. Bailey, *Southern White Protestantism in the Twentieth Century* (Gloucester: Peter Smith, 1968), 162.

122. Jerald C. Brauer, "Regionalism and Religion in America," *Church History* 54, no. 3 (1985): 373.

123. George L. Maddox and Joseph H. Fichter, "Religion and Social Change in the South," *Journal of Social Issues* 22, no. 1 (1966): 45.

124. Samuel S. Hill, "Fundamentalism in Recent Southern Culture: Has It Done What the Civil Rights Movement Couldn't Do?," in *Southern Crossroads: Perspectives on Religion and Culture*, ed. Walter H. Conser Jr. and Rodger M. Payne (Lexington: University Press of Kentucky, 2008), 360.

125. Paul Harvey, *Freedom's Coming: Religious Culture and the Shaping of the South from the Civil War Through the Civil Rights Era* (Chapel Hill: University of North Carolina Press, 2005), 220.

126. Harvey, *Freedom's Coming*, 233.

127. Jane Dailey, "Sex, Segregation, and the Sacred After *Brown*," *The Journal of American History* 91, no. 1 (2004): 123.

128. Donald G. Matthews, "Lynching Is Part of the Religion of Our People: Faith in the Christian South," in *Religion in the American South: Protestants and Others in History and Culture*, ed. Beth Barton Schweiger and Donald G. Matthews (Chapel Hill: University of North Carolina Press, 2004): 156.

129. Matthews, "Lynching Is Part of the Religion of Our People," 162.

130. Stricklin, *A Genealogy of Dissent*, 17.

131. Rory McVeigh, *The Rise of the Ku Klux Klan: Right-Wing Movements and National Politics* (Minneapolis: University of Minnesota Press, 2009), 138.

132. Paul Harvey, "Religion, Race, and the Right in the South, 1945–1990," in *Politics and Religion in the South*, ed. Glenn Feldman (Lexington: University Press of Kentucky, 2005), 112–113.

133. Harvey, "Religion, Race, and the Right in the South," 103.

134. Harvey, *Freedom's Coming*, 229.

135. Jane Dailey, "Sex, Segregation, and the Sacred after *Brown*," *The Journal of American History* 91, no. 1 (2004): 122–123.

136. Matthews, "Lynching Is Part of the Religion of Our People," 155.

137. Harvey, "Religion, Race, and the Right in the South," 105.

138. Harvey, "Religion, Race, and the Right in the South," 113; see also: David Chappell, *A Stone of Hope* (Chapel Hill: University of North Carolina Press, 2003). Chappell argues that minister involvement was minimal in defense of segregation as compared to slavery.

139. Nancy T. Ammerman, "The Civil Rights Movement and the Clergy in a Southern Community," *Sociology of Religion* 41, no. 4 (1980): 339–350.

140. Blackwelder, "Southern White Fundamentalists," 334–335.

141. Blackwelder, "Southern White Fundamentalists," 336.

142. David L. Chappell, "Religious Ideas of the Segregationists," *Journal of American Studies* 32, no. 2 (1998): 240–241.

143. Wilcox and Jelen, "Religion and Politics in an Open Market," 305.

144. Emerson and Smith, *Divided by Faith*, 63–67.

145. Russell Moore, "Southern Baptists and the Confederate Flag," *RussellMoore.com*, June 14, 2016, https://www.russellmoore.com/2016/06/14/southern-baptists-confederate-flag/.

146. Emma Green, "A Resolution Condemning White Supremacy Causes Chaos at the Southern Baptist Convention," *The Atlantic*, June 14, 2017, https://www.theatlantic.com/politics/archive/2017/06/the-southern-baptist-convention-alt-right-white-supremacy/530244/.

147. Joe R. Feagin, "Prejudice and Religious Types: A Focused Study of Southern Fundamentalists," *Journal for the Scientific Study of Religion* 4, no. 1 (1964): 3.

148. Richard L. Gorsuch and Daniel Aleshire, "Christian Faith and Ethnic Prejudice: A Review and Interpretation of Research," *Journal for the Scientific Study of Religion* 13, no. 3, (1974): 281.

149. R. Hoge and Jackson W. Carroll, "Religiosity and Prejudice in Northern and Southern Churches," *Journal for the Scientific Study of Religion* 12, no. 2 (1973): 181–197.

150. Ted G. Jelen, "The Effects of Religious Separatism on White Protestants in the 1984 Presidential Election," *Sociology of Religion* 48, no. 1 (1987): 30–45.

151. Deborah L. Hall, David C. Matz, and Wendy Wood, "Why Don't We Practice What We Preach? A Meta-Analytic Review of Religious Racism," *Personality and Social Psychology Review* 14, no. 1 (2010): 126.

152. Kenneth D. Wald, Dennis E. Owen, and Samuel S. Hill, "Churches as Political Communities," *American Political Science Review* 82, no. 2 (1988): 531–548.

153. Harvey, *Freedom's Coming*, 246.

154. Layman, *The Great Divide*, 111, 356.

155. Ted G. Jelen, "Culture Wars and the Party System: Religion and Realignment, 1972–1993," in *Culture Wars in American Politics: Critical Reviews of a Popular Myth*, ed. Rhys H. Williams (New York: Aldine de Gruyter, 1997), 152.

156. Linda Kintz, "Clarity, Mothers, and the Mass-Mediated National Soul: A Defense of Ambiguity," in *Media, Culture, and the Religious Right*, ed. Linda Kintz and Julia Lesage (Minneapolis: University of Minnesota Press, 1998), 130.

157. Kintz, "Clarity, Mothers, and the Mass-Mediated National Soul," 132.

158. Ammerman, *Bible Believers*, 201.

159. Kintz, "Clarity, Mothers, and the Mass-Mediated National Soul," 132.

160. Lienesch, "Right-wing Religion," 408.

161. Peter Waldman, "Holy War: Fundamentalists Fight to Capture the Soul of Southern Baptists," *Wall Street Journal*, March 7, 1988, https://o-search-proquest-om.library.uark.edu/abicomplete/docview/398030887/E75A182B28574027PQ/1?accountid=8361.

162. Harvey, "Religion, Race, and the Right in the South," 101.

163. Daniel K. Williams, *God's Own Party: The Making of the Christian Right* (New York: Oxford University Press, 2010), 143.

164. Michael Lienesch, *Redeeming America: Piety and Politics in the New Christian Right* (Chapel Hill: University of North Carolina Press, 1993), 71.

165. Quoted in: James C. Cobb, *The South and America Since World War II* (New York: Oxford University Press, 2012), 227.

166. James and Leazer with Shoopman, *The Fundamentalist Takeover*, 45.

167. Kathleen Murphy Beatty and B. Oliver Walter, "Fundamentalists, Evangelicals, and Politics," *American Politics Quarterly* 16, no. 1 (1988): 55.

168. Brian T. Kaylor, "Gracious Submission: The Southern Baptist Convention's Press Portrayals of Women," *Journal of Gender Studies* 19, no. 4 (2010): 345.

169. Karen McCarthy Brown, "Fundamentalism and the Control of Women," in *Fundamentalism and Gender*, ed. John Stratton Hawley (New York: Oxford University Press, 1994), 175–201.

170. Harvey, "Religion in the American South," 395; Ted Ownby, *Subduing Satan: Religion, Recreation, and Manhood in the Rural South, 1865–1920* (Chapel Hill: University of North Carolina Press, 1990), 12.

171. Randall M. Miller, Harry S. Stout, and Charles Reagan Wilson, ed., *Religion and the American Civil War* (New York: Oxford University Press, 1998), 9.

172. Harvey, "Religion in the American South," 395.

173. James and Leazer with Shoopman, *The Fundamentalist Takeover*, 44.

174. Eileen Renee Campbell-Reed, "Anatomy of a Schism: How Clergywomen's Narratives Interpret the Fracturing of the Southern Baptist Convention" (PhD diss., Wake Forest University, 2008), 2.

175. See: Susan M. Shaw, *God Speaks to Us, Too: Southern Baptist Women on Church, Home, and Society* (Lexington: University Press of Kentucky, 2008), 223.

176. Lienesch, *Redeeming America*, 64.

177. Carolyn Pevey, Christine L. Williams, and Christopher G. Ellison, "Male God Imagery and Female Submission: Lessons from a Southern Baptist Ladies' Bible Class," *Qualitative Sociology* 19, no. 2 (1996): 173–193.

178. Cynthia Lynn Lyerly, "In Service, Silence, and Strength: Women in Southern Churches," in *Religion and Public Life in the South: In the Evangelical Model*, ed. Charles Reagan Wilson and Mark Silk (Walnut Creek: Rowman & Littlefield Publishers, Inc., 2005), 105.

179. Kate Shellnut, "Paige Patterson Fired by Southwestern, Stripped of Retirement Benefits," *Christianity Today*, May 30, 2018, https://www.christianitytoday.com/news/2018/may/paige-patterson-fired-southwestern-baptist-seminary-sbc.html.

180. Shaw, *God Speaks to Us*, 2.

181. Matthews, *Religion in the Old South*, 135.

182. Lyerly, "In Service, Silence, and Strength," 106–107.

183. Ariela Keysar and Barry A. Kosmin, "The Impact of Religious Identification on Differences in Educational Attainment Among American Women in 1990," *Journal for the Scientific Study of Religion* 34, no. 1 (1995): 49–62.

184. J. Scott Carter and Mamadi Corra, "Changing Attitudes Towards Women, 1972–1998," *Michigan Sociological Review* 19 (2005): 19–44.

185. Sarahbeth Caplin, "Tennessee Baptist Convention Expels Church for Having a Female Pastor," *Patheos*, November 17, 2017, http://www.patheos.com/blogs/friendlyatheist/2017/11/17/tennessee-baptist-convention-expels-church-for-having-a-female-pastor/.

186. Lyerly, "In Service, Silence, and Strength," 104.

187. For reasons for neglect see: John C. Green, Lyman A. Kellstedt, Corwin E. Smidt, and James L. Guth, "The Soul of the South: Religion and the New Electoral Order," in *The New Politics of the Old South: An Introduction to Southern Politics*, ed. Charles S. Bullock III and Mark J. Rozell (Lanham: Rowman & Littlefield Publishers, Inc., 1998), 262.

188. John B. Boles, ed. 2001. *Autobiographical Reflections on Southern Religious History* (Athens: University of Georgia Press, 2001), viii.

189. George L. Maddox and Joseph H. Fichter, "Religion and Social Change in the South," *Journal of Social Issues* 22, no. 1 (1966): 50.

190. See: 12 Southerners, *I'll Take My Stand*; Genovese, *The Southern Tradition*, 1.

191. Abrams, *Selling the Old-Time Religion*, 128.

192. Eileen Renee Campbell-Reed, "Anatomy of a Schism: How Clergywomen's Narratives Interpret the Fracturing of the Southern Baptist Convention" (PhD diss., Wake Forest University, 2008), 13.

193. Beth Barton Schweiger, *The Gospel Working Up: Progress and the Pulpit in Nineteenth-Century Virginia* (New York: Oxford University Press, 2000), 195.

194. Ammerman, *Bible Believers*, 212.

195. Wald, Owen, and Hill, "Churches as Political Communities," 531–548.

196. See: Kenneth D. Wald, Adam L. Silverman, and Kevin S. Fridy, "Making Sense of Religion in Political Life," *Annual Review of Political Science* 8 (2005): 121–143.

197. Ernest Kurtz, "The Tragedy of Southern Religion," *The Georgia Historical Quarterly* 66, no. 2 (1982): 217.

198. Genovese, *The Southern Tradition*, 22.

199. Matthews, *Religion in the Old South*, 37.

200. Matthews, Hill, Schweiger, and Boles, "Forum: Southern Religion," 154.

201. Stricklin, *A Genealogy of Dissent*, 6.

202. Williams, *God's Own Party*, 3.

203. Harvey, *Freedom's Coming*, 219.

204. Williams, *God's Own Party*, 106.

205. Sarah Pulliam Bailey, "'Their Dream President: Trump Just Gave White Evangelicals a Big Boost,'" *Washington Post*, May 4, 2017, https://www.washingtonpost.com/news/acts-of-faith/wp/2017/05/04/their-dream-president-trump-just-gave-white-evangelicals-a-big-boost/.

206. Ted Jelen, "Sources of Political Intolerance: The Case of the American South," in *Contemporary Southern Political Attitudes and Behaviors: Studies and Essays*, ed. Laurence W. Moreland, Tod A. Baker, and Robert P. Steed (New York: Praeger, 1982), 77.

207. Christopher G. Ellison and Marc A. Musick, "Southern Intolerance: A Fundamentalist Effect?," *Social Forces* 72, no. 2 (1993): 380.

208. Lyman A. Kellstedt, "Doctrinal Beliefs and Political Behavior: Views of the Bible," in *Rediscovering the Religious Factor in American Politics*, ed. David C. Leege and Lyman A. Kellstedt (Armonk: M. E. Sharpe, 1993), 185.

209. Williams, *God's Own Party*.

210. Matthews, *Religion in the Old South*, 40.

211. John B. Boles, *The Irony of Southern Religion* (New York: Peter Lang, 1994), 105.

CHAPTER 8

1. Dorothy Patterson, quoted in: Sheri Paris, "Dorothy Patterson: On Submission, Family, Friends, Hats, & the Bible," *Baptist Press*, August 25, 1999, http://www.bpnews.net/445/dorothy-patterson-on-submission-family-friends-hats-and-the-bible.

2. "Resolution on Southern Baptists and the Bicentennial," *Southern Baptist Convention*, 1976, http://www.sbc.net/resolutions/742/resolution-on-southern-baptists-and-the-bicentennial.

3. "Resolution on Public Funds and Non-Public Education," *Southern Baptist Convention*, 1971, http://www.sbc.net/resolutions/946/resolution-on-public-funds-and-nonpublic-education.

4. Andrew P. Hogue, "1980: Reagan, Carter, and the Politics of Religion" (PhD diss, Baylor University, 2009), 157.

5. Gerald Ford, "Remarks at the Southern Baptist Convention in Norfolk, Virginia," *The American Presidency Project*, June 15, 1976, http://www.presidency.ucsb.edu/documents/remarks-the-southern-baptist-convention-norfolk-virginia.

6. Ford, "Remarks at the Southern Baptist Convention."

7. Ford, "Remarks at the Southern Baptist Convention."

8. David Hummel, "Revivalist Nationalism Since World War II: From 'Wake Up, America!' to 'Make America Great Again,'" *Religions* 7, no. 11 (2016): 14.

9. "Ronald Reagan's Ascent to Office Paralleled Rise of Religious Right," *Baptist News Global*, June 7, 2004, https://baptistnews.com/article/ronald-reagans-ascent-to-office-paralleled-rise-of-religious-right/.

10. Todd Starnes, "WRAPUP: Southern Baptists Hear from Bush, Elect New President," *Baptist Press*, June 13, 2002, http://www.bpnews.net/13623/wrapup-southern-baptists-hear-from-bush-elect-new-president.

11. Andrew Preston, "The Politics of Realism and Religion: Christian Responses to Bush's New World Order," *Diplomatic History* 34, no. 1 (2010): 95–118.

12. Reena Flores, "Donald Trump Shows Off Bible in Pitch to Evangelicals," *CBS News*, January 30, 2016, https://www.cbsnews.com/news/donald-trump-bible-last-minute-pitch-to-evangelicals-ahead-of-iowa-caucuses-election-2016/.

13. Hogue, "1980," 161.

14. Ford, "Remarks at the Southern Baptist Convention."

15. Hogue, "1980," 156.

16. Hogue, "1980," 164.

17. Barry Hankins, *Uneasy in Babylon: Southern Baptist Conservatives and American Culture* (Tuscaloosa: University of Alabama Press, 2002), 273.

18. See: Hankins, *Uneasy in Babylon*, 3; David T. Morgan, *The New Crusades, The New Holy Land: Conflict in the Southern Baptists Convention 1969–1991* (Tuscaloosa: University of Alabama Press, 1996), 13.

19. Hogue, "1980," 159.

20. George L. Maddox and Joseph H. Fichter, "Religion and Social Change in the South," *Journal of Social Issues* 22, no. 1 (1966): 49.

21. Rob James and Gary Leazer with James Shoopman, *The Fundamentalist Takeover in the Southern Baptist Convention: A Brief History* (Timișoara, Romania: Impact Media, 1999), 14.

22. Morris P. Fiorina with Samuel J. Abrams and Jeremy C. Pope, *Culture War? The Myth of a Polarized America*, 3rd ed. (Boston: Longman, 2011), 2.

23. Nancy Tatom Ammerman, *Bible Believers: Fundamentalists in the Modern World* (New Brunswick: Rutgers University Press, 1988), 190.

24. Hankins, *Uneasy in Babylon*, 141; see also: Robert Audi and Nicholas Wolterstorff, *Religion in the Public Square: The Place of Religious Convictions in Political Debate* (Lanham: Rowman & Littlefield Publishers, Inc., 1997), 6–8.

25. Ted G. Jelen, "The Effects of Religious Separatism on White Protestants in the 1984 Presidential Election," *Sociology of Religion* 48, no. 1 (1987): 30–45.

26. Samuel S. Hill, "A Survey of Southern Religious History," in *Religion in the Southern States: A Historical Study*, ed. Samuel S. Hill (Macon: Mercer University Press, 1983), 408.

27. John C. Green, James L. Guth, Corwin E. Smidt, and Lyman A. Kellstedt, *Religion and the Culture Wars: Dispatches from the Front* (Lanham: Rowman & Littlefield Publishers, Inc., 1996), 14.

28. Daniel K. Williams, *God's Own Party: The Making of the Christian Right* (New York: Oxford University Press, 2010), 5.

29. Williams, *God's Own Party*, 66–67.

30. Kevin Kruse, *One Nation Under God: How Corporate America Invented Christian America* (New York: Basic Books, 2015), 229.

31. Hankins, *Uneasy in Babylon*, 147.

32. Jelen, "The Effects of Religious Separatism," 35–37.

33. Lyman A. Kellstedt, "Doctrinal Beliefs and Political Behavior: Views of the Bible," in *Rediscovering the Religious Factor in American Politics*, ed. David C. Leege and Lyman A. Kellstedt (Armonk: M. E. Sharpe, 1993), 186.

34. James L. Guth, "Southern Baptist Clergy, the Christian Right, and Political Activism in the South," in *Politics and Religion in the South*, ed. Glenn Feldman (Lexington: University Press of Kentucky, 2005), 192.

35. Kenneth D. Wald, Dennis E. Owen, and Samuel S. Hill, "Churches as Political Communities," *American Political Science Review* 82, no. 2 (1988): 531–548.

36. Ted G. Jelen, *The Political World of the Clergy* (Westport: Praeger, 1993), 39.

37. James Davison Hunter, *American Evangelicalism: Conservative Religion and the Quandary of Modernity* (New Brunswick: Rutgers University Press, 1983), 59; Ted Jelen, "Sources of Political Intolerance: The Case of the American South," in *Contemporary Southern Political Attitudes and Behaviors: Studies and Essays*, ed. Laurence W. Moreland, Tod A. Baker, and Robert P. Steed (New York: Praeger, 1982), 90.

38. Clifford A. Grammich Jr., *Local Baptists, Local Politics: Churches and Communities in the Middle and Uplands South* (Knoxville: University of Tennessee Press, 1999), 4.

39. Corwin Smidt, "Born-Again Politics: The Political Behavior of Evangelical Christians in the South and Non-South," in *Religion and Politics in the South: Mass and Elite Perspectives*, ed. Tod A. Baker, Robert P. Steed, and Laurence W. Moreland (New York: Praeger, 1983), 34.

40. Earl W. Hawkey, "Southern Conservatism 1956–1976," in *Contemporary Southern Political Attitudes and Behaviors: Studies and Essays*, ed. Laurence W. Moreland, Tod A. Baker, and Robert P. Steed (New York: Praeger, 1982), 55.

41. Charles A. Heatwole, "The Bible Belt: A Problem in Regional Definition," *Journal of Geography* 77, no. 2 (1978): 50–55.

42. Kate Shellnut, "Paige Patterson Fired by Southwestern, Stripped of Retirement Benefits," *Christianity Today*, May 30, 2018, https://www.christianitytoday.com/news/2018/may/paige-patterson-fired-southwestern-baptist-seminary-sbc.html.

43. Robert Downen, "More Men Accuse Former Texas Judge, Baptist Leader of Sexual Misconduct," *Houston Chronicle*, April 13, 2018, https://www.houstonchronicle.com/news/houston-texas/houston/article/More-men-accuse-former-Texas-judge-Baptist-12831892.php.

44. Robert Downen, "Lawsuit Against Ex-Judge, Southern Baptist Churches Drawing to a Close," *Houston Chronicle*, February 6, 2019, .

45. James and Leazer with Shoopman, *The Fundamentalist Takeover*, 10, 27–28.

46. Arthur Emery Farnsley II, *Southern Baptist Politics: Authority and Power in the Restructuring of an American Denomination* (University Park: Pennsylvania State University Press, 1994), 21.

47. For a full bibliography on these issues, see: Susan M. Shaw, "Gracious Submission: Southern Baptist Fundamentalists and Women," *NWSA Journal* 20, no. 1 (2008): 52.

48. Paul Harvey, "Religion in the American South Since the Civil War," in *A Companion to the American South*, ed. John B. Boles (Malden: Blackwell Publishers, 2002), 403.

49. Morgan, *The New Crusades*, 2–3.

50. "The Baptist Faith and Message," 1925, http://www.utm.edu/staff/caldwell/bfm/1925/1.html.

51. Morgan, *The New Crusades*, 7.

52. Williams, *God's Own Party*, 15–18.

53. Kruse, *One Nation Under God*, xiv.

54. John Lee Eighmy, *Churches in Cultural Captivity: A History of the Social Attitudes of Southern Baptists* (Knoxville: University of Tennessee Press, 1972), 158.

55. Eighmy, *Churches in Cultural Captivity*, 163, 175.

56. Morgan, *The New Crusades*, 8.

57. Ellen M. Rosenberg, *The Southern Baptists: A Subculture in Transition* (Knoxville: University of Tennessee Press, 1989), 186.

58. W. A. Criswell, *Why I Preach the Bible Is Literally True* (Nashville: Broadman, 1969); for a full text and audio file of his 1980 version, see: http://www.wacriswell.com/sermons/1980/why-i-preach-the-bible-is-literally-true/.

59. Susan M. Shaw, *God Speaks to Us, Too: Southern Baptist Women on Church, Home, and Society* (Lexington: University Press of Kentucky, 2008), 10.

60. James and Leazer with Shoopman, *The Fundamentalist Takeover*, 28.

61. James and Leazer with Shoopman, *The Fundamentalist Takeover*, 28–29.

62. Shaw, "Gracious Submission," 51–77.

63. Hankins, *Uneasy in Babylon*, 2.

64. Farnsley, *Southern Baptist Politics*, xi.

65. Donald G. Matthews, *Religion in the Old South* (Chicago: University of Chicago Press, 1977), 184.

66. See E. Glenn Hinson quotation in: James Leo Garrett Jr., E. Glenn Hinson, and James E. Tull, *Are Southern Baptists "Evangelicals?"* (Macon: Mercer University Press, 1983), 121.

67. Frederick C. Harris, *Something Within: Religion in African-American Political Activism* (New York: Oxford University Press, 1999), 135.

68. Alicia M. Cohn, "Romney Talks 'War on Religion' in Iowa," *The Hill*, December 16, 2011, http://thehill.com/blogs/blog-briefing-room/news/200005-romney-talks-war-on-religion-in-iowa?page=2#comments.

69. Krissah Thompson and Jura Koncious, "Trump Vowed to End the 'War on Christmas.' Here's How the White House Is Decorated this Season," *Washington Post*, November 27, 2017, https://www.washingtonpost.com/lifestyle/style/trump-vowed-to-end-the-war-on-christmas-heres-how-the-white-house-is-decorated-this-season/2017/11/27/8a18aa3e-cfbb-11e7-a1a3-0d1e45a6de3d_story.html.

70. Emma Green, "Most American Christians Believe They're Victims of Discrimination," *The Atlantic*, June 30, 2016, https://www.theatlantic.com/politics/archive/2016/06/the-christians-who-believe-theyre-being-persecuted-in-america/488468/.

71. Louis Bolce and Gerald De Maio, "Religious Outlook, Culture War Politics, and Antipathy Toward Christian Fundamentalists," *Public Opinion Quarterly* 63, no. 1 (1999): 38.

72. Louis Bolce and Gerald De Maio, "Our Secularist Democratic Party," *Public Interest* 149 (2002): 13.

73. Nancy Tatom Ammerman, *Baptist Battles: Social Change and Religious Conflict in the Southern Baptist Convention* (New Brunswick: Rutgers University Press, 1990), 271.

74. Ammerman, *Baptist Battles*, 259.

75. Morgan, *The New Crusades*, 38.

76. Ammerman, *Baptist Battles*, 263.

77. David Stricklin, *A Genealogy of Dissent: Southern Baptist Protest in the Twentieth Century* (Lexington: University Press of Kentucky, 1999), 3.

78. Morgan, *The New Crusades*, 87.

79. Morgan, *The New Crusades*, 86.

80. Morgan, *The New Crusades*, 94.

81. James and Leazer with Shoopman, *The Fundamentalist Takeover*, 14.

82. James and Leazer with Shoopman, *The Fundamentalist Takeover*, 75–76.

83. Morgan, *The New Crusades*, 108.

84. Ammerman, *Baptist Battles*, 253.

85. James and Leazer with Shoopman, *The Fundamentalist Takeover*, 12–13.

86. James and Leazer with Shoopman, *The Fundamentalist Takeover*, 39.

87. Carl L. Kell, ed. *Exiled: Voices of the Southern Baptist Convention Holy War* (Knoxville: University of Tennessee Press, 2006), xxxv.

88. Stricklin, *A Genealogy of Dissent*, 22.

89. W. H. Crouch, "The Hijacking of the Southern Baptist Convention," in *Exiled: Voices of the Southern Baptist Convention Holy War*, ed. Carl L. Kell (Knoxville: University of Tennessee Press, 2006), 122.

90. Paul D. Simmons, "Finding a Voice in Exile," in *Exiled: Voices of the Southern Baptist Convention Holy War*, ed. Carl L. Kell (Knoxville: University of Tennessee Press, 2006), 107.

91. Gregory L. Hancock, "A Lot Like Dying," in *Exiled: Voices of the Southern Baptist Convention Holy War*, ed. Carl L. Kell (Knoxville: University of Tennessee Press, 2006), 77.

92. Charles Reagan Wilson, *Baptized in Blood: The Religion of the Lost Cause, 1865–1920* (Athens: University of Georgia Press, 1980), 3.

93. Williams, *God's Own Party*, 129.

94. Shaw, "Gracious Submission," 56.

95. Fiorina, Abrams, and Pope, *Culture War?*, 85; see also: Nancy T. Ammerman, "Southern Baptists and the New Christian Right," *Review of Religious Research* 32, no. 3 (1991): 213–236.

96. Ted G. Jelen, "Respect for Life, Sexual Morality, and Opposition to Abortion," *Review of Religious Research* 25, no. 3 (1984): 220–231.

97. Michele Dillon, "Religion and Culture in Tension: The Abortion Discourses of the US Catholic Bishops and the Southern Baptist Convention," *Religion and American Culture: A Journal of Interpretation* 5, no. 2 (1995): 161.

98. William Saletan, "The Dark Side of Bob Dole," *Mother Jones*, January/February 1996, http://www.motherjones.com/politics/1996/01/dark-side-what-you-need-know-about-bob-dole; Jerry Gray, "Senate Dooms a Vote for Surgeon General," *New York Times*, June 23, 1995, http://www.nytimes.com/1995/06/23/us/senate-dooms-a-vote-for-surgeon-general.html.

99. David Waters, "McCain's Conversion: Political or Spiritual?," *On Faith*, September 5, 2008, https://www.onfaith.co/onfaith/2008/09/05/john-the-baptist-a-political-o/4055.

100. Jason Horowitz, "Mitt Romney and the Fall of Republican Moderates," *Washington Post*, January 18, 2012, https://www.washingtonpost.com/lifestyle/style/mitt-romney-and-the-fall-of-republican-moderates/2012/01/18/gIQAQ2BC9P_story.html.

101. Ted Jelen, "Sources of Political Intolerance: The Case of the American South," in *Contemporary Southern Political Attitudes and Behaviors: Studies and Essays*, ed. Laurence W. Moreland, Tod A. Baker, and Robert P. Steed (New York: Praeger, 1982), 80.

102. Brian Laythe, Deborah G. Finkel, Robert G. Bringle, and Lee A. Kirkpatrick, "Religious Fundamentalism as a Predictor of Prejudice: A Two-Component Model," *Journal for the Scientific Study of Religion* 41, no. 4 (2002): 623–635.

103. John C. Green, Mark J. Rozell, and Clyde Wilcox, ed., *The Christian Right in American Politics: Marching to the Millennium* (Washington, DC: Georgetown University Press, 2003), 9.

104. Rita Whitlock, "Queerly Fundamental: Christian Fundamentalism, Southern Queerness, and Curriculum Studies," *Journal of Curriculum and Pedagogy* 3, no. 1 (2006): 174.

105. Williams, *God's Own Party*, 146–147.

106. Wilson, *Baptized in Blood*, 130–131.

107. Whitlock, "Queerly Fundamental," 167.

108. Brian T. Kaylor, "Gracious Submission: The Southern Baptist Convention's Press Portrayals of Women," *Journal of Gender Studies* 19, no. 4 (2010): 335–348.

109. Amanda Marcotte, "Americans are Growing More Secular All the Time—Which Is One Reason Why Trump Voters Are so Angry," *Salon*, March 14, 2017, https://www.salon.com/2017/03/14/americans-are-getting-more-secular-all-the-time-which-is-one-reason-why-trump-voters-are-so-angry/.

110. Caryle Murphy, "The Most and Least Educated U.S. Religious Groups," *Pew Research Center*, November 4, 2016, http://www.pewresearch.org/fact-tank/2016/11/04/the-most-and-least-educated-u-s-religious-groups/.

111. Ted Ownby, "Evangelical but Differentiated: Religion by the Numbers," in *Religion and Public Life in the South: In the Evangelical Model*, ed. Charles Reagan Wilson and Mark Silk (Walnut Creek: Rowman & Littlefield Publishers, Inc., 2005), 34.

112. Linda Kintz, "Clarity, Mothers, and the Mass-Mediated National Soul: A Defense of Ambiguity," in *Media, Culture, and the Religious Right*, ed. Linda Kintz and Julia Lesage (Minneapolis: University of Minnesota Press, 1998), 130.

113. Steve Bruce, *The Rise and Fall of the New Christian Right: Conservative Protestant Politics in America 1978–1988* (New York: Oxford University Press, 1988), 171.

114. James and Leazer with Shoopman, *The Fundamentalist Takeover*, 53.

115. Bruce, *The Rise and Fall of the New Christian Right*, 168.

116. Ted G. Jelen, "Culture Wars and the Party System: Religion and Realignment, 1972–1993," in *Culture Wars in American Politics: Critical Reviews of a Popular Myth*, ed. Rhys H. Williams (New York: Aldine de Gruyter, 1997), 151.

117. Fiorina, Abrams, and Pope, *Culture War?*, 85.

118. Seth Dowland, "'Family Values' and the Formation of a Christian Right Agenda," *Church History* 78, no. 3 (2009): 606–631; John A. Clark, "Religion: Culture Wars in the New South," in *Southern Political Party Activists: Patterns of Conflict and Change, 1991–2001*, ed. John A. Clark and Charles L. Prysby (Lexington: University Press of Kentucky, 2004), 19; see also: Sunshine Hillygus and Todd Shields, "Southern Discomfort: Regional Differences in Voter Decision Making in the 2000 Presidential Election," *Presidential Studies Quarterly* 38, no. 3 (2008): 506–520; Sunshine Hillygus and Todd Shields, "Moral Issues and Voter Decision Making in the 2004 Presidential Election," *P.S. Political Science* 38, no. 2 (2005): 201–209.

119. Gustav Niebuhr, "Clinton and Dole, Political Rivals, No Longer Pray Together," *New York Times*, May 11, 1995, http://www.nytimes.com/1995/05/11/us/clinton-and-dole-political-rivals-no-longer-pray-together.html.

120. Barry Goldwater, quoted in: John Dean, *Conservatives without Conscience* (New York: Penguin, 2006), xxxvi.

CHAPTER 9

1. Pat Buchanan, quoted in: Theodore J. Lowi, *The End of the Republican Era* (Norman: University of Oklahoma Press, 1996), 212.

2. Jason D. Berggren and Nicol C. Rae, "Jimmy Carter and George W. Bush: Faith, Foreign Policy, and an Evangelical Presidential Style," *Presidential Studies Quarterly* 36, no. 4 (2006): 614.

3. Berggren and Rae, "Jimmy Carter and George W. Bush," 621.

4. George W. Bush, "Speech on the National Day of Prayer and Remembrance," *TeachingAmericanHistory.org*, September 14, 2001, http://teachingamericanhistory.org/library/document/speech-on-the-national-day-of-prayer-and-remembrance/.

5. Juan Stam, "Bush's Religious Language," *The Nation*, December 4, 2003, https://www.thenation.com/article/bushs-religious-language/.

6. Stam, "Bush's Religious Language."

7. Berggren and Rae, "Jimmy Carter and George W. Bush," 614.

8. Berggren and Rae, "Jimmy Carter and George W. Bush," 622.

9. "Bush's Messiah Complex," *The Progressive*, February 2003, http://www.progressive.org/news/2007/07/5069/bushs-messiah-complex.

10. Matthew G. Bonham and Daniel Heradstveit, "The 'Axis of Evil' Metaphor and the Restructuring of Iranian Views Toward the US," *Vaseteh-Journal of the European Society for Iranian Studies* 1, no. 1 (2006): 89.

11. Bonham and Heradstveit, "The 'Axis of Evil' Metaphor," 91.

12. Corwin Smidt, John C. Green, Lyman Kellstedt, and James Guth, "What Does the Lord Require?: Evangelicals and the 2004 Presidential Vote," in *Religion and the Bush Presidency*, ed. Mark J. Rozell and Gleaves Whitney (New York: Palgrave Macmillan, 2007), 44.

13. Andrew Preston, *Sword of the Spirit, Shield of Faith: Religion in American War and Diplomacy* (New York: Alfred A. Knopf, 2012), 579.

14. David Jeffers, *Understanding Evangelicals: A Guide to Jesusland* (Maitland: Xulon Press, 2006), 101; see also: Paul Froese and F. Carson Mencken, "A U.S. Holy War? The Effects of Religion on Iraq War Policy Attitudes," *Social Science Quarterly* 90, no. 1 (2009): 103–116.

15. Ethan Cole, "Most Evangelical Leaders Still Support Iraq War," *Christian Post*, February 12, 2008, https://www.christianpost.com/news/most-evangelical-leaders-still-support-iraq-war-31154/.

16. Lee Quimby, quoted in: "Bush's Messiah Complex."

17. Clyde Wilcox and Ted G. Jelen, "Religion and Politics in an Open Market: Religious Mobilization in the United States," in *Religion and Politics in Comparative Perspective: The One, the Few, and the Many*, ed. Ted G. Jelen and Clyde Wilcox (New York: Cambridge University Press, 2002), 301.

18. Richard Land, quoted in: Rob James and Gary Leazer with James Shoopman, *The Fundamentalist Takeover in the Southern Baptist Convention: A Brief History* (Timişoara, Romania: Impact Media, 1999), 76.

19. Anthony M. Orum, "Religion and the Rise of the Radical White: The Case of Southern Wallace Support in 1968," *Social Science Quarterly* 51, no. 3 (1970): 674.

20. John C. Green, Lyman A Kellstedt, Corwin E Smidt, and James L. Guth, "The Soul of the South: Religion and the New Electoral Order," in *The New Politics of the Old South: An Introduction to Southern Politics*, ed. Charles S. Bullock III and Mark J. Rozell (Lanham: Rowman & Littlefield Publishers, Inc., 1998), 261; see also: Byron E. Shafer, "The Notion of an Electoral Order: The Structure of Electoral Politics at the Accession of George Bush," in *The End of Realignment?Interpreting American Electoral Eras*, ed. Byron E. Shafer (Madison: University of Wisconsin Press, 1991), 38–43.

21. Clifford A. Grammich Jr., *Local Baptists, Local Politics: Churches and Communities in the Middle and Uplands South* (Knoxville: University of Tennessee Press, 1999), 6.

22. Steve Bruce, *The Rise and Fall of the New Christian Right: Conservative Protestant Politics in America 1978–1988* (New York: Oxford University Press, 1988), 193.

23. Kenneth D. Wald, Dennis E. Owen, and Samuel S. Hill, "Churches as Political Communities," *American Political Science Review* 82, no. 2 (1988): 533.

24. John C. Green, "The Christian Right and the 1998 Elections: An Overview," in *Prayers in the Precincts: The Christian Right in the 1998 Elections*, ed. John C. Green, Mark J. Rozell, and Clyde Wilcox (Washington, DC: Georgetown University Press, 2000): 8.

25. Wilcox and Jelen, "Religion and Politics in an Open Market," 307.

26. Duane M. Oldfield, *The Right and the Righteous: The Christian Right Confronts the Republican Party* (Lanham: Rowman & Littlefield Publishers, Inc., 1996), 99.

27. Eric C. Miller, "The Rise and Fall of 'Family Values': How 'Religious Freedom' Became the Rallying Cry of the Christian Right," *Salon*, February 7, 2016, http://www.salon.com/2016/02/07/how_religious_liberty_replaced_family_values_in_framing_the_conservative_movement_partner/; see also: Seth Dowland, *Family Values and the Rise of the Christian Right* (Philadelphia: University of Pennsylvania Press, 2016).

28. John C. Green, Mark J. Rozell, and Clyde Wilcox, ed., *The Christian Right in American Politics: Marching to the Millennium* (Washington, DC: Georgetown University Press, 2003), 4.

29. Bill Scher, "When Reagan Dared to Say 'God Bless America,'" *Politico*, July 17, 2015, http://www.politico.com/magazine/story/2015/07/reagan-god-bless-america-120286.

30. Kevin Kruse, *One Nation Under God: How Corporate America Invented Christian America* (New York: Basic Books, 2015), 254.

31. Sarah Pulliam Bailey, "Photo Surfaces of Evangelical Pastors Laying Hands on Trump in the Oval Office," *Washington Post*, July 12, 2017, https://www.washingtonpost.com/amphtml/news/acts-of-faith/wp/2017/07/12/photo-surfaces-of-evangelical-pastors-laying-hands-on-trump-in-the-oval-office/.

32. Donald G. Matthews, *Religion in the Old South* (Chicago: University of Chicago Press, 1977), 185.

33. Sarah Posner, "Why Republicans Don't Think Obama Is Christian," *Religion Dispatches*, February 25, 2015, http://religiondispatches.org/why-republicans-dont-think-obama-is-christian/.

34. Daniel K. Williams, *God's Own Party: The Making of the Christian Right* (New York: Oxford University Press, 2010), 56.

35. Orum, "Religion and the Rise of the Radical White," 676.

36. Orum, "Religion and the Rise of the Radical White," 681.

37. Williams, *God's Own Party*, 94.

38. Geoffrey Layman, *The Great Divide: Religious and Cultural Conflict in American Party Politics* (New York: Columbia University Press, 2001), 171.

39. Williams, *God's Own Party*, 185.

40. Williams, *God's Own Party*, 1.

41. Steve Bruce, "Zealot Politics and Democracy: The Case of the New Christian Right," *Political Studies* 48, no. 2 (2000): 264.

42. Daniel K. Williams, "Jerry Falwell's Sunbelt Politics: The Regional Origins of the Moral Majority," *Journal of Policy History* 22, no. 2 (2010): 125.

43. Eugene D. Genovese, *The Southern Tradition: The Achievement and Limitations of an American Conservatism* (Cambridge: Harvard University Press, 1994), 83.

44. Ted G. Jelen, *To Serve God and Mammon: Church-State Relations in American Politics* (Boulder: Westview Press, 2000), 83.

45. Williams, *God's Own Party*, 213.

46. Bruce, "Zealot Politics and Democracy," 264.

47. Green, Rozell, and Wilcox, ed., *The Christian Right in American Politics*, 10.

48. Ted G. Jelen, "Culture Wars and the Party System: Religion and Realignment, 1972–1993," in *Culture Wars in American Politics: Critical Reviews of a Popular Myth*, ed. Rhys H. Williams (New York: Aldine de Gruyter, 1997), 153.

49. Clyde Wilcox, Mark J. Rozell, and Roland Gunn, "Religious Coalitions in the New Christian Right," *Social Science Quarterly* 77, no. 3 (1996): 554.

50. Green, Rozell, and Wilcox, ed., *The Christian Right in American Politics*, 6.

51. Ammerman, *Bible Believers*, 204.

52. Orum, "Religion and the Rise of the Radical White," 687.

53. Williams, *God's Own Party*, 74.

54. Seth McLaughlin, "Top Evangelical: Romney 'Not Mormon Enough' for Social Conservatives," *The Washington Times*, January 13, 2012, http://www.washingtontimes.com/news/2012/jan/13/top-evangelical-romney-not-mormon-enough/.

55. Louis Bolce and Gerald De Maio, "Our Secularist Democratic Party," *Public Interest* 149 (2002): 3–20.

56. Charles Reagan Wilson, *Judgment and Grace in Dixie: Southern Faiths from Faulkner to Elvis* (Athens: University of Georgia Press, 1995), xviii.

57. Morris P. Fiorina with Samuel J. Abrams and Jeremy C. Pope, *Culture War? The Myth of a Polarized America*, 3rd ed. (Boston: Longman, 2011), 1.

58. Pat Buchanan, "Speech to the 1992 Republican National Convention," *Live from the Campaign Trail*, 1992, http://www.livefromthetrail.com/about-the-book/speeches/chapter-19/pat-buchanan.

59. Wilcox and Jelen, "Religion and Politics in an Open Market," 310.

60. Williams, *God's Own Party*, 213.

61. Duane M. Oldfield, *The Right and the Righteous: The Christian Right Confronts the Republican Party* (Lanham: Rowman & Littlefield Publishers, Inc., 1996), 217.

62. Sara Diamond, *Not by Politics Alone: The Enduring Influence of the Christian Right* (New York: The Guilford Press, 1998), 57.

63. Diamond, *Not by Politics Alone*, 236.

64. John A. Clark, "Religion: Culture Wars in the New South," in *Southern Political Party Activists: Patterns of Conflict and Change, 1991–2001*, ed. John A. Clark and Charles L. Prysby (Lexington: University Press of Kentucky, 2004), 15.

65. James Moore and Wayne Slater, *The Architect: Karl Rove and the Master Plan for Absolute Power* (New York: Crown Publishers, 2006), 22–23.

66. Moore and Slater, *The Architect*, 23.

67. Kruse, *One Nation Under God*, 10.

68. James Moore and Wayne Slater, *Bush's Brain: How Karl Rove Made George W. Bush Presidential* (Hoboken: Wiley, 2003), 258.

69. Lou Dubose, Jan Reid, and Carl M. Cannon, *Boy Genius: Karl Rove: The Brains Behind the Remarkable Political Triumph of George W. Bush* (New York: Public Affairs, 2003), 91.

70. Dubose, Reid, and Cannon, *Boy Genius*, 74–75.

71. Dubose, Reid, and Cannon, *Boy Genius*, 89–90.

72. Dubose, Reid, and Cannon, *Boy Genius*, 91.

73. Nancy T. Ammerman, "Southern Baptists and the New Christian Right," *Review of Religious Research* 32, no. 3 (1991): 213–236.

74. Jelen, "Culture Wars and the Party System," 153.

75. David Stricklin, *A Genealogy of Dissent: Southern Baptist Protest in the Twentieth Century* (Lexington: University Press of Kentucky, 1999), 11.

76. Ammerman, *Bible Believers*, 206.

77. Williams, "Jerry Falwell's Sunbelt Politics," 126.

78. Sarah Posner, "God's Profits: Faith, Fraud, and the GOP Crusade for Values Voters," *Alternet*, January 21, 2008, http://www.alternet.org/story/74440/god's_profits%3A_faith,_fraud_and_the_gop_crusade_for_values_voters.

79. Lynne Stuart Parramore, "The Christian Right Is Quite Scary, but the GOP's Economic Agenda Is America's Big Nightmare," *Alternet*, February 15, 2015, http://www.alternet.org/economy/christian-right-quite-scary-gops-economic-agenda-americas-big-nightmare.

80. See: Bethany Moreton, *To Serve God and Walmart: The Making of Christian Free Enterprise* (Cambridge: Harvard University Press, 2009); Alison Greene, *No Depression in Heaven: The Great Depression, the New Deal, and the Transformation of Religion in the Delta* (New York: Oxford University Press, 2015); Darren Grem, *The Blessings of Business: How Corporations Shaped Conservative Christianity* (New York: Oxford University Press, 2016); and Timothy Gloege, *Guaranteed Pure: The Moody Bible Institute and the Making of Modern Evangelicalism* (Chapel Hill: University of North Carolina Press, 2015).

81. Darren Dochuk, *From Bible Belt to Sunbelt: Plain-Folk Religion, Grassroots Politics, and the Rise of Evangelical Conservatism* (New York: W. W. Norton & Company, Inc., 2010).

82. James D. Unnever and Francis T. Cullen, "Christian Fundamentalism and Support for Capital Punishment," *Journal of Research in Crime and Delinquency* 43, no. 2 (2006): 172.

83. Orum, "Religion and the Rise of the Radical White," 688.

84. Gerald R. Webster and Jonathan I. Leib, "Political Culture, Religion, and the Confederate Battle Flag Debate in Alabama," *Journal of Cultural Geography* 20, no. 1 (2002): 1–26.

85. Alex Kaplan, "Following Paris Attacks, Right-Wing Media Echo GOP Call to Accept Only Christian Refugees," *Media Matters*, November 16, 2015, http://mediamatters.org/research/2015/11/16/following-paris-attacks-right-wing-media-echo-g/206881.

86. Ammerman, *Bible Believers*, 189.

87. Ammerman, *Bible Believers*, 199.

88. Ammerman, *Bible Believers*, 201.

89. Mitchell Snay, *Gospel of Disunion: Religion and Separatism in the Antebellum South* (New York: Cambridge University Press, 1993), 25.

90. Michael O. Emerson and Christian Smith, *Divided by Faith: Evangelical Religion and the Problem of Race in America* (New York: Oxford University Press, 2000), 33.

91. H. Shelton Smith, *In His Image, but . . . Racism and Southern Religion, 1780–1910* (Durham: Duke University Press, 1972), 69, 55, 74, 4.

92. Randall M. Miller, "A Church in Cultural Captivity: Some Speculations on Catholic Identity in the Old South," in *Catholics in the Old South: Essays on Church and Culture*, ed. Randall M. Miller and Jon L. Wakelyn (Macon, GA: Mercer University Press, 1983), 11–52, 14–15; Jürgen Link and Linda Schulte-Sasse, "Fanatics, Fundamentalists, Lunatics, and Drug Traffickers: The New Southern Enemy Image," *Cultural Critique* 19 (1991): 33–53.

93. Smith, *In His Image*, 129.

94. Matthews, *Religion in the Old South*, 79.

95. Elizabeth Fox-Genovese and Eugene D. Genovese, "The Divine Sanction of Social Order: Religious Foundations of the Southern Slaveholders' World View," *Journal of the American Academy of Religion* 55, no. 2 (1987): 212.

96. Emerson and Smith, *Divided by Faith*, 35.

97. Matthew Avery Sutton, *American Apocalypse: A History of Modern Evangelicalism* (Cambridge: The Belknap Press of Harvard University Press, 2014), 49.

98. Williams, *God's Own Party*, 4.

99. Williams, *God's Own Party*, 36–37.

100. Linda Kintz, "Clarity, Mothers, and the Mass-Mediated National Soul: A Defense of Ambiguity," in *Media, Culture, and the Religious Right*, ed. Linda Kintz and Julia Lesage (Minneapolis: University of Minnesota Press, 1998), 128.

101. Ralph Lord Roy, quoted in: Orum, "Religion and the Rise of the Radical White," 675.

102. Orum, "Religion and the Rise of the Radical White," 675.

103. Kevin M. Kruse, "A Christian Nation? Since When?," *New York Times*, March 14, 2015, http://www.nytimes.com/2015/03/15/opinion/sunday/a-christian-nation-since-when.html.

104. Jelen, *To Serve God and Mammon*, 43.

105. Charles S. Bullock III and Mark C. Smith, "The Religious Right and Electoral Politics in the South," in *Politics and Religion in the South*, ed. Glenn Feldman (Lexington: University Press of Kentucky, 2005), 222–223.

106. Mark J. Rozell and Clyde Wilcox, "Virginia: Birthplace of the Christian Right," in *The Christian Right in American Politics: Marching to the Millennium*, ed. John C. Green, Mark J. Rozell, and Clyde Wilcox (Washington, DC: Georgetown University Press, 2003), 47.

107. Michael Lienesch, "Right-wing Religion: Christian Conservatism as a Political Movement," *Political Science Quarterly* 97, no. 3 (1982): 404.

108. Jelen, *To Serve God and Mammon*, 79.

109. Bruce, "Zealot Politics and Democracy," 264; see also: John H. Garvey, "Fundamentalism and American Law," in *Fundamentalisms and the State*, ed. Martin E. Marty and R. Scott Appleby (Chicago: University of Chicago Press, 1993), 35–36.

110. Green, Rozell, and Wilcox, ed., *The Christian Right in American Politics*, 4.

111. Gene Zubovich, "What's Behind American's Promotion of Religious Liberty Abroad," *The Conversation*, February 1, 2018, https://theconversation.com/whats-behind-americas-promotion-of-religious-liberty-abroad-90746.

112. Chris Mooney, "W's Christian Nation," *Prospect*, May 15, 2003, http://prospect.org/article/ws-christian-nation.

113. Elizabeth Bruenig, "Making Christianity Our National Religion Would the Terrible for Christianity," *New Republic*, February 26, 2015, https://newrepublic.com/article/121153/poll-republican-majority-wants-christianity-be-national-religion.

114. "Remarks by President Trump at National Prayer Breakfast," *White House.gov*, February 2, 2017, https://www.whitehouse.gov/briefings-statements/remarks-president-trump-national-prayer-breakfast/.

115. "Read President Trump's Liberty University Commencement Speech," *Time*, May 13, 2017, http://time.com/4778240/donald-trump-liberty-university-speech-transcript/.

116. Charles Reagan Wilson, *Southern Missions: The Religion of the American South in Global Perspective* (Waco: Baylor University Press, 2006), 17.

117. Williams, "Jerry Falwell's Sunbelt Politics," 138.

118. Michael Lienesch, *Redeeming America: Piety and Politics in the New Christian Right* (Chapel Hill: University of North Carolina Press, 1993), 206.

119. Lienesch, *Redeeming America*, 202.

120. Christopher G. Ellison, Jeffrey A. Burr, and Patricia L. McCall, "The Enduring Puzzle of Southern Homicide: Is Regional Religious Culture the Missing Piece?," *Homicide Studies* 7, no. 4 (2003): 326–352.

121. Lienesch, *Redeeming America*, 196.

122. Lienesch, *Redeeming America*, 195.

123. David Veenstra, "As God Gives Me to See the Right: Gerald Ford, Religion, and Healing after Vietnam and Watergate," *Pro Rege* 43, no. 3 (2015): 15.

124. Ammerman, *Bible Believers*, 210.

125. Carl L. Kell, ed. *Exiled: Voices of the Southern Baptist Convention Holy War* (Knoxville: University of Tennessee Press, 2006), xxxvii.

126. Bruce, *The Rise and Fall of the New Christian Right*, 175.

127. Lienesch, *Redeeming America*, 211.

128. Zach Beauchamp, "How a Handful of Anti-Muslim Crusaders Hijacked Segments of the GOP," *Vox*, January 30, 2015, http://www.vox.com/2015/1/30/7931905/jindal-islam-2016.

129. Robert Dole, "Statement by Senator Bob Dole Following Meeting with Netanyahu," *The American Presidency Project*, October 2, 1996, http://www.presidency.ucsb.edu/documents/statement-senator-bob-dole-following-meeting-with-netanyahu.

130. Ralph Reed, quoted in: Jeremy D. Mayer, "Christian Fundamentalists and Public Opinion Toward the Middle East: Israel's New Best Friends?," *Social Science Quarterly* 85, no. 3 (2004): 695.

131. "Sarah Palin: War in Iraq Is 'God's Plan,'" *YouTube*, September 2, 2008, https://www.youtube.com/watch?v=9H-btXPfhGs&NR=1; Amad Shaikh, "Sarah Palin and Osama Bin Laden Agree on Holy War," *Muslim Matters*, September 10, 2008, http://muslimmatters.org/2008/09/10/sarah-palin-and-osama-bin-laden-agree-on-holy-war/.

132. Dean Obeidallah, "The Conservative Crusade for Christian Sharia Law," *Daily Beast*, February 18, 2014, http://www.thedailybeast.com/articles/2014/02/18/the-conservative-crusade-for-christian-sharia-law.html.

133. Kaili Joy Gray, "GOP: Give Us Your Tired and Your Poor and Your Jesus-Lovers Only," *Wonkette*, November 16, 2015, http://wonkette.com/596012/gop-give-us-your-tired-and-your-poor-and-your-jesus-lovers-only.

134. Leigh Ann Caldwell, "Kasich Proposes New Government Agency to Promote Judeo-Christian Values," *NBCNews*, November 17, 2015, http://www.nbcnews.com/politics/2016-election/kasich-proposes-new-government-agency-promote-judeo-christian-values-n465101.

135. David R. Brockman, "God and Guns: Courting the Christian Fringe in the Texas GOP Primaries," *Texas Observer*, March 1, 2018, https://www.texasobserver.org/god-guns-courting-christian-fringe-texas-gop-primaries/.

136. Kruse, *One Nation Under God*, 237.

137. Diamond, *Not by Politics Alone*, 240.

138. Bruce, "Zealot Politics and Democracy," 273.

139. Richard Florida, "The Conservative States of America," *The Atlantic*, March 29, 2011, http://www.theatlantic.com/politics/archive/2011/03/the-conservative-states-of-america/71827/.

140. Clark, "Religion: Culture Wars in the New South," 25.

141. Barry Goldwater, "Excerpts from Goldwater's Remarks," *New York Times*, September 15, 1981, http://www.nytimes.com/1981/09/16/us/excerpts-from-goldwater-remarks.html.

CONCLUSION

1. Ralph McGill, "A Church, A School," *Atlanta Journal Constitution*, October 13, 1958; see also: Angie Maxwell, "Introduction: *Let Us Now Praise Famous Men*," in *A Church, A School: Pulitzer Prize–Winning Civil Rights Editorials from the Atlanta Constitution*

by Ralph McGill, ed. Angie Maxwell (Columbia: University of Southern Carolina Press, 2012), ix–xxxii.

2. Phyllis Schlafly, *A Choice, Not an Echo: The Inside Story of How American Presidents Are Made* (Alton: Pere Marquette Press, 1964).

3. Thomas Byrne Edsall and Mary D. Edsall, *Chain Reaction: The Impact of Race, Rights, and Taxes on American Politics* (New York: W. W. Norton & Company, Inc., 1991), 5.

4. Chris Ladd, "Southern Conservatives Are America's Third Party," *Forbes*, March 16, 2017, https://www.forbes.com/sites/chrisladd/2017/03/16/southern-conservatives-are-americas-third-party/#1dbe9cd4406b.

5. Ian Haney López, *Dog Whistle Politics: How Coded Racial Appeals Have Reinvented Racism & Wrecked the Middle Class* (New York: Oxford University Press, 2014), 110.

6. V. O. Key Jr., *Southern Politics in State and Nation* (New York: Alfred A. Knopf, 1949), 655.

7. Reg Murphy and Hal Gulliver, *The Southern Strategy* (New York: Charles Scribner's Sons, 1971), 8.

8. Thomas Frank, *What's the Matter with Kansas?: How Conservatives Won the Heart of America* (New York: Metropolitan Books, 2004), 259.

9. Paul Harvey, "Religion, Race, and the Right in the South, 1945–1990," in *Politics and Religion in the South*, ed. Glenn Feldman (Lexington: University Press of Kentucky, 2005), 101.

10. Nikki Graf, "Sexual Harassment at Work in the Era of #MeToo," *Pew Research Center*, April 4, 2018, http://www.pewsocialtrends.org/2018/04/04/sexual-harassment-at-work-in-the-era-of-metoo/; see also: PerryUndem Ressearch/Communication, "The State of the Union on Gender Equality, Sexism, and Women's Rights," *SCRIBD*, January 17, 2017, https://www.scribd.com/document/336804316/PerryUndem-Gender-Equality-Report.

11. See: Linda Gordon and Allen Hunter, "Sex, Family and the New Right, Anti-Feminism as a Political Force," *Radical America* 12, no. 1 (1978): 9–25; see also: Peter Beinart, "The Growing Partisan Divide over Feminism," *The Atlantic*, December 15, 2017, https://www.theatlantic.com/politics/archive/2017/12/the-partisanship-of-feminism/548423/.

12. Charles Reagan Wilson, *Judgment and Grace in Dixie: Southern Faiths from Faulkner to Elvis* (Athens: University of Georgia Press, 1995), 3–4.

13. Kevin Kruse, *One Nation Under God: How Corporate America Invented Christian America* (New York: Basic Books, 2015), 246.

14. Ewen MacAskill, "George Bush: 'God Told Me to End the Tyranny in Iraq,'" *The Guardian*, October 7, 2005, https://www.theguardian.com/world/2005/oct/07/iraq.usa.

15. Jeet Heer, "How the Southern Strategy Made Donald Trump Possible," *The New Republic*, February 18, 2016, https://newrepublic.com/article/130039/southern-strategy-made-donald-trump-possible.

16. Jonathan Knuckey, "The Myth of the 'Two Souths?': Racial Resentment and White Party Identification in the Deep South and Rim South," *Social Science Quarterly* 98, no. 2 (2017): 728–749.

17. Seth C. McKee and Melanie J. Springer, "A Tale of 'Two Souths': White Voting Behavior in Contemporary Southern Elections," *Social Science Quarterly* 96, no. 2 (2015): 588–607.

18. See: Charles Prysby, "The Newest Southerners: Generational Difference in Electoral Behavior in the Contemporary South," *American Review of Politics* 36, no. 1 (2017): 54–74.

19. Logan Strother, Spencer Piston, and Thomas Ogorzalek, "Pride or Prejudice? Racial Prejudice, Southern Heritage, and White Support for the Confederate Battle Flag," *Du Bois Review* 14, no. 1 (2017): 295–323.

20. Mason Adams, "How the Rebel Flag Rose Again—and Is Helping Trump," *Politico*, June 16, 2016, https://www.politico.com/magazine/story/2016/06/2016-donald-trump-south-confederate-flag-racism-charleston-shooting-213954.

21. Daniel K. Williams, "Jerry Falwell's Sunbelt Politics: The Regional Origins of the Moral Majority," *Journal of Policy History* 22, no. 2 (2010): 141.

22. Julia Azari and Marc J. Hetherington, "Back to the Future? What the Politics of the Late Nineteenth Century Can Tell Us About the 2016 Election," *The ANNALS of the American Academy of Political and Social Science* 667 (2016): 92–109.

23. Joshua N. Zingher, "An Analysis of the Changing Social Bases of America's Political Parties: 1952–2008," *Electoral Studies* 35 (2014): 272–282.

24. Jonathan Knuckey, "The Survival of the Democratic Party Outside of the South: An Update and Reassessment," *Party Politics* 21, no. 4 (2015): 539–552.

25. Peter Beinart, "The Republican Party's White Strategy," *The Atlantic*, July/August 2016, https://www.theatlantic.com/magazine/archive/2016/07/the-white-strategy/485612/.

26. Caleb McDaniel, "The South Only Embraced States' Rights as It Lost Control of the Federal Government," *The Atlantic*, November 1, 2017, https://www.theatlantic.com/politics/archive/2017/11/states-rights/544541/.

27. Casey Michel, "How Russia Became the Leader of the Global Christian Right," *Politico*, February 9, 2017, https://www.politico.com/magazine/story/2017/02/how-russia-became-a-leader-of-the-worldwide-christian-right-214755.

28. Frank, *What's the Matter with Kansas?*, 254.

29. Kat Eschner, "White Southerners Said 'Uncle Tom's Cabin' was Fake News," *Smithsonian*, March 20, 2017, https://www.smithsonianmag.com/smart-news/white-southerners-said-uncle-toms-cabin-was-fake-news-180962518/.

30. Christopher Douglas, "The Religious Origins of Fake News and 'Alternative Facts,'" *Religion Dispatches*, February 23, 2017, http://religiondispatches.org/the-religious-origins-of-fake-news-and-alternative-facts/; Molly Worthen, "The Evangelical Roots of Our Post-Truth Society," *New York Times*, April 13, 2017, https://www.nytimes.com/2017/04/13/opinion/sunday/the-evangelical-roots-of-our-post-truth-society.html.

31. John Avlon, "Trump's Immoral Equivalence Between George Washington and Robert E. Lee," *The Daily Beast*, August 17, 2017, http://www.thedailybeast.com/donald-trump-s-immoral-equivalence-between-george-washington-and-robert-e-lee; Steven Lubert and Alfred Brophy, "Why Trump Is Wrong to Equate George Washington with Robert E. Lee," *Chicago Tribune*, August 20, 2017, http://www.chicagotribune.com/news/opinion/commentary/ct-george-washington-lee-slavery-20170820-story.html.

32. Murphy and Gulliver, *The Southern Strategy*, 14.

33. Donald G. Matthews and Jane Sherron de Hart, *Sex, Gender, and the Politics of the ERA* (New York: Oxford University Press, 1990), 155.

34. Paul Harvey, *Freedom's Coming: Religious Culture and the Shaping of the South from the Civil War Through the Civil Rights Era* (Chapel Hill: University of North Carolina Press, 2005), 222–233.

35. David T. Morgan, *The New Crusades, The New Holy Land: Conflict in the Southern Baptists Convention 1969–1991* (Tuscaloosa: University of Alabama Press, 1996), 162–168.

36. George Wallace, quoted in: Debbie Elliot, "Is Donald Trump a Modern-day George Wallace?," *NPR*, April 22, 2016, https://www.npr.org/2016/04/22/475172438/donald-trump-and-george-wallace-riding-the-rage.

37. Frank, *What's the Matter with Kansas?*, 126.

38. See: Jean Hardisty, *Mobilizing Resentment: Conservative Resurgence from the John Birch Society to the Promise Keepers* (Boston: Beacon Press, 2000).

39. Edsall and Edsall, *Chain Reaction*, 10.

40. Michael Perman, *Pursuit of Unity: Political History of the American South* (Chapel Hill: University of North Carolina Press, 2009), 313, 317.

41. Frank, *What's the Matter with Kansas?*, 3.

42. Zell Miller, quoted in: Jarrett Murphy, "Text of Zell Miller's RNC Speech," *CBS News*, September 1, 2004, https://www.cbsnews.com/news/text-of-zell-millers-rnc-speech/.

43. Lillian Smith, *Killers of the Dream* (New York: W. W. Norton & Company, Inc., 1949), 16.

44. Joseph A. Aistrup, *The Southern Strategy Revisited: Republican Top-Down Advancement in the South* (Lexington: University Press of Kentucky, 2015), 58–59.

45. Matthew N. Lyons, "The Alt-Right Hates Women as Much as It Hates People of Colour," *The Guardian*, May 2, 2017, https://www.theguardian.com/commentisfree/2017/may/02/alt-right-hates-women-non-white-trump-christian-right-abortion.

46. Julie Zauzmer, "Christians Are More than Twice as Likely to Blame a Person's Poverty on Lack of Effort," *Washington Post*, August 3, 2017, https://www.washingtonpost.com/news/acts-of-faith/wp/2017/08/03/christians-are-more-than-twice-as-likely-to-blame-a-persons-poverty-on-lack-of-effort/?utm_term=.e37494ac9c8a.

47. Michael Steele, "Southern GOP 'Super Tuesday' Could Be a 2016 Game-Changer," *MSNBC.com*, May 22, 2015, http://www.msnbc.com/msnbc/southern-gop-super-tuesday-could-be-2016-game-changer.

48. Greg Bluestein, "Inside Donald Trump's Sweeping Georgia Primary Victory," *Atlanta Journal Constitution*, March 5, 2016, http://politics.blog.ajc.com/2016/03/05/inside-donald-trumps-sweeping-georgia-primary-victory/.

49. John Dollard, *Caste and Class in a Southern Town*, 2nd ed. (New York: Harper & Brothers, 1949), xiv.

50. See: Robert Wuthnow, *The Left Behind: Decline and Rage in Rural America* (Princeton: Princeton University Press, 2018).

51. Alan I. Abramowitz, *The Great Alignment: Race, Party Transformation, and the Rise of Donald Trump* (New Haven: Yale University Press, 2018), 5.

52. Alexander Vandermaas-Peeler, Daniel Cox, Maxine Najle, Molly Fisch-Friedman, Rob Griffin, and Robert P. Jones, "Partisanship Trumps Gender: Sexual Harassment, Women Candidates, Access to Contraception, and Key Issues in 2018 Midterms," *PRRI*, October 3, 2018, https://www.prri.org/research/abortion-reproductive-health-midterms-trump-kavanaugh/; see also: Tara Isabella Burton, "White Evangelicals Are the only Religious Group to Support Trump," *Vox*, October 3, 2018, https://www.vox.com/identities/2018/10/3/17929696/white-evangelicals-prri-poll-trump-presidency-support.

53. Sean Illing, "This Is Why Evangelicals Love Trump's Israel Policy," *Vox*, May 14, 2018, https://www.vox.com/2017/12/12/16761540/jerusalem-israel-embassy-palestinians-trump-evangelicals.

54. Casey Michel, "How the Russians Pretended to Be Texans—and Texans Believed Them," *Washington Post*, October 17, 2017, https://www.washingtonpost.com/news/democracy-post/wp/2017/10/17/how-the-russians-pretended-to-be-texans-and-texans-believed-them/.

55. See: Susan Chira, "Women Don't Think Alike. Why Do We Think They Do?," *New York Times*, October 12, 2018, https://www.nytimes.com/2018/10/12/sunday-review/conservative-women-trump-kavanaugh.html.

56. Charlotte Alter, "Republicans and Democrats See Sexism Very Differently," *Time*, January 18, 2017, http://time.com/4637680/republican-women-donald-trump-sexism/.

57. "After a Year of #MeToo, American Opinion Has Shifted Against Victims," *The Economist*, October 15, 2018, https://www.economist.com/graphic-detail/2018/10/15/after-a-year-of-metoo-american-opinion-has-shifted-against-victims.

58. "2018 Election Results: Exit Polls," CNN, November 7, 2018, https://www.cnn.com/election/2018/exit-polls/georgia.

59. See: Leslie McCall and Ann Shola Orloff, "The Multidimensional Politics of Inequality: Taking Stock of Identity Politics in the U.S. Presidential Election of 2016," *The British Journal of Sociology* 68, no. 1S (2017): S34–S56; Erin C. Cassese and Tiffany D. Barnes, "Reconciling Sexism and Women's Support for Republican Candidates: A Look at Gender, Class, and Whiteness in the 2012 and 2016 Presidential Races," *Political Behavior* (2018): 1–24.

60. Abraham Lincoln, quoted in: Heather Digby Parton, "'Sore Winner' Syndrome: Why Are Donald Trump's Supporters Still So Angry? Abraham Lincoln Understood," *Salon*, November 17, 2016, http://www.salon.com/2016/11/17/sore-winner-syndrome-why-are-donald-trumps-supporters-still-so-angry-abraham-lincoln-understood/.

Index

Page numbers followed by *f* and *t* indicate figures and tables, respectively. Numbers followed by n indicate notes.